ELECTRICAL MEASUREMENT ANALYSIS

McGraw-Hill Electrical and Electronic Engineering Series
FREDERICK EMMONS TERMAN, *Consulting Editor*
W. W. HARMAN and J. G. TRUXAL, *Associate Consulting Editors*

SMITH – DC MEASUREMENTS – McGRAW-HILL

MARSHALL – Vol II A.C. MEASUREMENTS

MICHEALS – ELECTRICAL METHODS

PARTRIDGE – PRINCIPLES OF ELECTRONIC
               MEASUREMENTS & APPLICATIONS

Electrical Measurement Analysis

ERNEST FRANK

Professor of Electrical Engineering
Executive Officer, Department of Electrical Engineering
The George Washington University

McGRAW-HILL BOOK COMPANY, INC.

New York   Toronto   London

1959

ELECTRICAL MEASUREMENT ANALYSIS

Library of Congress Catalog Card Number 58-11172

II

THE MAPLE PRESS COMPANY, YORK, PA.

PREFACE

This textbook is an outgrowth of a three-semester-hour classroom course presented to juniors at the Moore School of Electrical Engineering (University of Pennsylvania) by a variety of instructors over the past nine years. The material has been arranged and selected to suit the needs of a modern engineering curriculum. On the whole, it has been met with interest and enthusiasm by the students.

The shift in engineering education from art and design considerations to conceptual and theoretical aspects calls for revamping the traditional treatment of the subject of electrical measurements. There is little room for design and construction details of components, instruments, and other apparatus; even less for detailed procedures and manipulative aspects. These and other features must be curtailed to permit incorporation of broader and more enduring ideas. A rich supply of analytical material, highly appropriate for stimulating creative thinking, is available in the field of electrical measurements. Quantitative significance of engineering approximations, theoretical limitations of electrical and electromechanical systems, fundamental bases for various methods of measurement, and many other ideas may be handled without a clutter of detailed practical considerations.

A technician may be trained to perform measurements, but the engineer must contrive experiments and assess their soundness, preferably in advance, to ensure economical use of laboratory time. Limitations and flaws of measurement systems must be uncovered and understood, and this often demands a high level of analytical ability. Estimates of attainable accuracy must be made, and results interpreted and presented intelligently in accordance with accepted scientific practice. These requirements, and others, demand a strong foundation in concepts and basic principles. With such background, the graduate engineer may quickly learn the characteristics and limitations of specific equipment encountered in practice, even though he may never have studied the device explicitly in school. He is able to discern similarities in methods and techniques, rather than becoming lost in a maze of minutiae. If a penetrating and critical attitude is developed, the mistake of simply "taking readings" without an understanding of the basic phenomena and the interaction of all pertinent factors is less likely to occur.

Emphasis on concepts and analysis fits nicely into a measurements course in the junior or senior year. The student is equipped with some knowledge of calculus, differential equations, physics, and electric circuits and fields. He has also had some laboratory experience. The time is ripe for bringing all this information to bear on a single area. The subject of electrical measurements is particularly well suited to provide this consolidation of ideas. The prime intention has been to give the student an opportunity to strengthen and integrate his knowledge, perhaps relearning what he thought he already understood. It may be a stimulating and rewarding experience for the student to apply his knowledge to problems of obvious importance in engineering. The essential objective of this textbook is to develop in the student the attitudes and comprehension necessary for the analytical solution of engineering problems. At the same time, the student should become acquainted with methods of measurement, with the theory of operation of certain electrical instruments, and with the nature and theory of errors of measurement.

This book is intended for classroom use and stresses methods, concepts, and analysis throughout. It is not a treatise on electrical measurement and does not presume to attain complete coverage of this broad field. The treatment departs markedly from conventional types of the past. A discussion of electrical standards, deemed sufficient to orient the student, is confined to one brief section. Systems of units, ably treated in many books from different points of view, are not discussed explicitly. It is assumed that the reader is acquainted with the mks system of units, which is used throughout. Magnetic measurements, instrument transformers, polyphase measurements, and many other topics are omitted. Principles of analysis rather than topical coverage have been sought. The large quantity of empirical and practical information often found in measurement books has been reduced sharply. Also, discussion of manipulative procedures in practical equipment has been suppressed. It is believed that these items are best learned from direct experience in the laboratory when the engineer is confronted with an actual problem whose solution is important enough to make such detail meaningful. Generally, the descriptive material presented is only that judged necessary to provide the student with an intelligent basis upon which to undertake analyses. Finally, the profusion of photographs of commercial apparatus frequently found in texts on this subject has been greatly curtailed. It is felt that such material is, at best, a poor substitute for examination of actual instruments available at most universities.

Much of the analysis is focused on electric circuits, and for that reason a circuit-review chapter is included. Other analyses, such as those required in force calculations, are developed carefully from first principles. A limited treatment of the application of statistics to measurement errors is presented in more complete form than in other measurement texts. The topic of statistics is too often slighted in engineering curricula, and its inclusion represents at least a partial satisfaction of this need. Such analysis techniques as differential methods, application of network theorems, narrow-band approximations, series expansions, and many others not confined exclusively to the field of measurement by any means, are utilized as required. The compensation theorem is highlighted because it is superior to Thévenin's theorem in bridge analysis. Sources of errors in ohmmeters, potentiometers, bridges, and other circuits and systems are treated analytically. Techniques for treatment of data are suggested throughout the text and a final chapter is devoted to this often neglected subject.

The chapter sequence has evolved from classroom experience. Galvanometers are studied first as an obviously important and absorbing topic. This provides a background of examples used in the study of errors of measurement, which for many students is a difficult subject and not as successfully treated at the start of a course. Methods of measurement are approached in the two categories of deflection and null methods, each of which is subdivided further. Conventional categories of resistance measurements, voltage measurements, power measurements, and so forth, are abandoned. Most of the examples are taken from the d-c and low-frequency areas, including both high- and low-precision methods. Electronic instruments are only touched upon, the one serious electronic analysis being that of the diode peak voltmeter. The sequence of the remaining chapters was followed in most of the courses taught, but they may be taken up in any order after Chap. 9 has been completed.

Problems at the end of each chapter constitute one of the important features of this book. In some cases they call upon the student to supply steps omitted in the text development. In most cases, however, they represent new problems that call for originality and careful thought, without excessive computation and formula substitution. Many topics treated lightly in the text are strengthened by problems that expand upon the framework provided. Most of the problems have been used as examination questions. Answers to the problems are given at the end of the book to enable the student to ascertain the correctness of his work. Because the student cannot be expected to know which problem he is ready to attack at any particular phase of study, each problem includes a section number in parenthesis indicating the section the student should reach before attempting the problem. It is strongly recommended that a course based on this book be primarily a problem-solving course. Only in this way does the student acquire a sound, quantitative understanding of analysis.

No claim is made that a classroom course, or a textbook, is a replacement for laboratory experience.⟨ Certain aspects of measurement can be learned only in the laboratory⟩ However, laboratory experience is frequently of limited value to the student because of his failure or inability to analyze his laboratory problem thoroughly.   Concepts and analysis are vital elements required to accomplish a measurement task satisfactorily, and this is the area to which this text is devoted.   However, laboratory matters are not slighted entirely.   Practical implications of theoretical results are suggested throughout the text.   For instance, the important idea that the quantity being measured may be molested in the very act of measuring it is stressed in quantitative detail by many different examples.

The vast literature in periodicals, textbooks, special bulletins, and manufacturer's pamphlets, all pertaining to electrical measurements, is felt to be too extensive to suit the needs of an introductory treatment in which analytical concepts are dominant.   Therefore, only a list of textbooks considered directly pertinent to the subject is given at the end of the book.   Some older works in electrical measurements are included to encourage the student to review the extraordinary growth in the field of measurements over the past few decades.   It is hoped that this treatment will not appear so antiquated in as many years hence.

The author is indebted to his many colleagues who, over the years, made contributions reflected in this book in the form of problems, methods of approach, and analyses.   In many cases, the identity of the individual responsible for a specific item has been lost.   However, the ideas of Donald F. Hunt have been largely incorporated in the statistical approach used in Chaps. 6 and 7, as well as in several other sections.   It is a pleasure to utilize his suggestions.   Contributions of Edward I. Hawthorne and Howard E. Tompkins are also acknowledged.   Neely F. Matthews was kind enough to read and check the entire manuscript. The influence of Harry Sohon, under whose supervision the author first taught this subject, appears in many forms throughout the entire treatment.   The remarkable cooperation of the author's wife has been of vital help and is most gratefully appreciated.

Ernest Frank

CONTENTS

CHAPTER 1

INTRODUCTION

The engineer is inevitably confronted with measurements, whether he merely uses them as tools to obtain information or becomes involved in fundamental studies of measurement theory. He must be acquainted with apparatus, methods, limitations, techniques, and accuracy capabilities of measurements. Yet it is impossible to keep abreast of all the ramifications of this highly developed subject. An effective approach is to become conversant with basic concepts of measurement and some methods that have been found useful. A strong foundation in principles provides the structure that supports and engenders the comprehension necessary for solution of specific problems.

The important thing is to learn the discipline of analytical thought. Without such discipline, individual progress in any scientific field is likely to become frustrated and opportunities for achievement improbable. With such discipline, the horizons are virtually unlimited.

1-1. Development and Scope of Electrical Measurements. The development of science has been inseparable from the development of measurement. Laws of nature have been uncovered after means were found to detect and measure physical quantities. Scientific theories have not been accepted without reservation until confirmed by measurement. Obviously, the role of measurement is intimately interwoven with all the knowledge that has been acquired and put to use in the physical sciences. Measurement remains indispensable as an intrinsic part of scientific method and knowledge.

The laws of electricity represent a relatively recent historical development in the growth of physical science. Most of these laws were uncovered in the latter part of the eighteenth century and the early part of the nineteenth century, and have been closely related to the development of means for detecting and measuring electrical quantities. Men engaged in early investigations of this period, many of whom were physicists, are not easily forgotten because their names have become accepted terminology in specifying units and dimensions of electrical and other physical quantities. Some of the more outstanding contributors, listed in chronological order, include:

William Gilbert (1540–1603)
Charles Augustin de Coulomb (1736–1806)
James Watt (1736–1819)
Alessandro Volta (1745–1827)
André Marie Ampère (1775–1836)
Hans Christian Oersted (1777–1851)
Karl Friedrich Gauss (1777–1855)
George Simon Ohm (1787–1854)
Michael Faraday (1791–1867)
Joseph Henry (1797–1878)
Wilhelm Eduard Weber (1804–1891)
James Prescott Joule (1818–1889)
William Thomson, 1st Baron Kelvin (1824–1907)
James Clerk Maxwell (1831–1879)

While these men have been largely responsible for fundamental developments, there are countless other workers who have made contributions in the general field of electricity as well as in the specific area of electrical measurements. Many of the instruments used today are essentially the same as those originally devised by these dedicated scientists. Few methods and techniques of measurement are new, in the sense that the same basic ideas were used in early developments. The student is urged to explore the lives and contributions of these men.

Accounts of initial progress are fascinating. In this modern day of sensitive instruments and reliable sources of electrical energy, which are largely taken for granted, it is difficult to appreciate the incredible handicaps of equipment limitations with which these workers contended. Their overwhelming success in probing the mysteries of electricity in the face of such handicaps is indeed a tribute to the human mind. Other engaging aspects of the development of electrical measurements include the interplay between mathematics and physics, the unfolding of relationships between electrical and mechanical quantities, and the fact that classic ideas still form the cornerstone upon which much of current practice is based.

The field of electrical measurements has, in its brief history, shown phenomenal growth. In the latter part of the nineteenth century, many different instruments and methods for their use were devised. The galvanometer, thermocouple and rectifier instruments, moving-iron meters, electrodynamometer movement, and others came into being, at least in crude form. The electrical bridge, the potentiometer, and other null methods of measurement were conceived. By the start of the twentieth century, these instruments became more refined, and their general availability in commercial form enabled measurement methods to come into widespread use. These developments, combined with increased avail-ability of reliable sources of electrical energy, created an environment in which many workers could pursue electrical measurements. Their inventiveness and ingenuity generated a flood of new applications as the scope and use of electricity were expanded. Concurrent with this upsurge of activity, it became increasingly evident that participants throughout the world required a common language with which to disseminate and compare their explorations and findings. Fortunately, there was fruitful international cooperation in connection with the establishment of electrical units and standards.

Measurement of nonelectrical quantities by electrical means began to receive more attention early in this century and marked the beginning of one of the most vigorous areas in the development and application of instruments. These developments were, and continue to be, aided substantially by the introduction of electronic devices. Indication and recording of nonelectrical quantities have expanded greatly and now include a tremendous variety of quantities in many different fields such as *fluids* (conductivity, density, hydrogen-ion concentration, humidity, liquid level, pressure, rate of flow, viscosity); *heat* (radiation, temperature); *light* (luminous flux, radiant energy, spectra); *mechanics* (acceleration, displacement, distance, dynamic balance, force, hardness, velocity, vibration); *sound* (acoustical pressure, intensity); *time* (counting, frequency); and others. Examples of electrical measurement of some of these quantities are presented in this text.

The era of instrumentation has arrived. Not only are indication and recording receiving much attention, but electronic computing combined with automatic control is invading an increasing number of fields. These developments have far-reaching implications with respect to advances in technology. Such systems enable routine measurements and manipulations to be carried out automatically with little attention from a human operator. They may be rapid, safe, and accurate. Developments in the field of electronics, when wedded to the field of measurements, enable the frequency range to be extended and permit the sensitivity of apparatus to be pushed to the limits of "noise." Thus, the entire scope of investigation in the field of electrical measurement is broadened.

The surge of research in electronic instrumentation is based fundamentally on older principles and methods and does not eclipse the traditional aspects of electrical measurements. Where highly precise results are required, there is not yet a substitute for experimental ability and creative endeavor. Moreover, there are countless measurement problems in the low-precision area where there is need for individualized measurement work using methods and instruments that have evolved over the past 100 years. Development of new electrical measuring devices, along the lines set forth by the array of instruments presently available, continues in meeting present-day needs. Application of known principles to new problems, improvement of materials, and other facets of electrical measurements represent a substantial interest in the modern laboratory.

1-2. Nature of Measurements and Electrical Standards. Measurement is the process of determining the magnitude of a quantity in comparison with another similar quantity. For example, if there are two different currents in a circuit, each may be measured with the objective of determining their ratio. Unless a quantitative comparison is sought, the problem does not belong in the realm of measurements. Thus, attempts to determine the intrinsic nature of an electric current belong in the field of physics or philosophy. But the determination of a current in comparison with 1.0 amp of current is an appropriate measurement activity.

In principle, any rational basis for intercomparison of measured quantities may be adopted, and this is sometimes done within the narrow framework of a specific investigation. However, general use of different bases of comparison would result in a chaotic state of affairs and would hinder progress. Communication of results and exchange of ideas would be seriously impaired. Indeed, this difficulty was experienced as the field of measurements developed and led to international agreement on accepted standards with which all electrical measurements might be compared. While the apparatus employed in a given experiment may be many steps removed from the basic standard, the unit in which it is calibrated has come from a basic standard that is maintained and used for calibration purposes.

The *fundamental physical standards* are length, mass, and time. The standard of length is the distance between two marks on a certain metal bar; of mass, the weight of a certain metal cylinder; of time, a specified fraction of a mean solar day. These standards are related to electrical quantities by physical laws, such as the force law presented in Sec. 3-3. *Absolute electrical standards* are those which are measured in terms of the three fundamental quantities. The latest step in the evolution of electrical standards was the world-wide adoption, in 1948, of absolute electrical standards.

Electrical standards existing before 1948 were not based on the fundamental quantities length, mass, and time. They consisted of accurately reproducible arrangements measured in *international units*. The international ohm was the resistance of a specified column of mercury; the international ampere was based on electrolytic deposition in a silver nitrate solution; the international volt was based on the potential difference of a cadmium cell. These standards in themselves represented an outgrowth of others that had been previously developed and found lacking. For example, an earlier standard for the ohm was the resistance of a certain coil of platinum-silver alloy, and an earlier standard of potential difference was based on that of a zinc cell. Thus, the present absolute standards represent the product of a continuing evolutionary process in the search for improved constancy, reproducibility, and accuracy. The absolute standards, recently adopted, differ by only a small amount (ranging from 0.033 to 0.05 per cent) from former international standards. These differences are negligible unless very high accuracy is sought.

Measurement of absolute standards (or of the former international standards) is extremely cumbersome and time-consuming. For instance, determination of absolute current entails measurement of force between two coils by means of a weighing balance in a very elaborate and precisely known system. Therefore, there is a need for *secondary standards* that are more convenient to use in calibrating other apparatus. These secondary standards, which are checked periodically by comparison with absolute measurements, consist of wire resistors for resistance and cadmium cells for potential difference. Intercomparison among multiple secondary standard units maintained at the National Bureau of Standards in this country is better than 1 part per million, while absolute standards are accurate to within a few parts per million. Thus, the quantities with which all electrical measurements are fundamentally compared are preserved within limits that meet accuracy requirements of most present-day measurements.

1-3. Role of Force in Electrical Measurements. Electrical quantities desirable to measure include charge, current, potential difference, resistance, capacitance, inductance, and many others. The common entity almost invariably met in the course of measuring these quantities is mechanical force. Force is the vehicle through which useful information is provided. It may seem anomalous to find that electrical measurements are really mechanically based. However, it is the mechanical force associated with either stationary or moving charges that enables electricity to be detected, measured, and put to use.

It is obvious from the analysis of each meter movement presented in this text that a mechanical force on its movable element is responsible for its deflection. This is true of every deflection-type instrument. When the force is related to an electrical quantity, it is customary to say that the electrical quantity is being measured. But what is meant, more precisely, is that the force is being used as a measure of the electrical quantity. Thus, one may regard most electrical measurements as the process of relating mechanical forces to electrical quantities upon which they depend.

Basically, force serves as a mechanism for transference of electrical information lying outside the range of direct human perception into regions where human sensory powers are keen and reliable.   The pointer indication of an ammeter may be estimated by human visual means to within one-tenth of a scale division, and this might represent a millionth of an ampere, or less.   Using the human ability to sense heat, without the aid of force conversion, a current-carrying wire may be held in one's hand and perhaps a factor of 10 change in current, owing to the change in heating produced in the wire, might be perceptible.   Obviously this is not a satisfactory quantitative arrangement.   A similar situation exists for many physical quantities that are measured, including nonelectrical ones as well.

It is fortunate that electrical activity is manifested in terms of mechanical force.   Were this not so, many electrical phenomena might go undetected.   Of course, some evidence would still be apparent, such as light and heat produced by the filament of an incandescent lamp when current is applied.   But exploration of quantitative aspects of electrical phenomena would be severely hampered without the forces that may be used to convert electrical activity into sensitive regions of human perception.   This suggests that there well may be other physical phenomena yet to be discovered of which the human being is presently unaware.   If there are such phenomena, they lie outside the realm of direct sensation and have yet to be brought into the perceptible domain.   What undetected phenomena await discovery?   This line of thinking displays the profound implications of measurement devices.   They are, in broad terms, more than mechanisms enabling quantitative comparison.   In many cases they are devices that make observation possible at all.

1-4. The Art of Measurement.   There is much more to executing measurements than the following of routine standard procedures.   For instance, two individuals confronted with an identical measurement task might pursue entirely different lines of attack and arrive at different results even though every effort was made to achieve objective answers. It is unavoidable that certain matters rest in the realm of technique and constitute a form of artistry.   The situation is not unlike that in other artistic fields where a large, conglomerate array of items are blended together to create an end product.

One characteristic of measurement that must be appreciated, which accounts in part for the art in measurement, is that all observations are subject to error.   These errors must be evaluated critically.   All conditions that may influence the correctness of results must be explored, understood, and remedied wherever possible.   A thorough knowledge of apparatus and of the method employed is indispensable.   Usually a close theoretical analysis is required.   While this book emphasizes analytical aspects of measurements, it should be realized that there is much more to successful performance of measurements than knowledge of underlying theory. Experience is a significant element for which there is often no substitute. However, of all factors involved in a successful experiment, comprehension of underlying theory probably contributes most to obtaining sound results.

The investigator must choose a method, among those known to him, in terms of such factors as required accuracy, available apparatus, cost of the over-all effort, time available to obtain the results, ease of performing the measurements, and skill of personnel to be used. These items are often conflicting. Having selected the optimum method, the experiment must be planned in detail and all foreseeable defects remedied. The apparatus to be used must be studied critically and understood thoroughly with respect to its manipulative aspects, basic characteristics, accuracy, and range limitations. Sound techniques must be devised, treatment of data should be planned in advance, and theoretical analyses involving all pertinent factors should be performed and interpreted.

Many laboratory practices and "recipes" must be observed in the execution of the measurements to avoid false results. Electrical contacts must be tight, solder connections firm and well made, sliding contacts in good condition. A continuous alertness for defective equipment is mandatory. Constant vigilance and an attitude of distrust toward every detail are typically displayed by the experienced investigator. Difficulties with stray fields and interaction of equipment must be circumvented where encountered. If there is hope of completing the work, certain safety precautions and protection of equipment and personnel from injury are desirable. All these factors, and others, are interwoven in a complex fashion that contributes to the over-all result. They also contribute to the satisfaction derived from a job well done.

In the usual type of electrical measurements, accuracy requirements are of prime importance in determining the amount of care that must be exercised. Accuracy on the order of a few per cent is rather easily obtained with modern equipment without excessive skill and technique. Attainment of accuracy on the order of 1 per cent usually requires the use of corrections and considerable care in methods and procedures. Accuracies on the order of 0.1 per cent demand exceedingly meticulous work in every detail. Special methods are often necessary to avoid use of instrument deflections which, with few exceptions, are incapable of rendering so accurate a result. Beyond the range of 0.1 per cent accuracy, specialized techniques of high-precision methods must be employed. Accurate standards, substitution methods, close control of environment, exhaustive reproducibility tests, statistical analysis of data, and other techniques become indispensable if reliable results are to be attained. Thus, required accuracy is often the first coarse guide to the character of the measurement task. This does not mean that one may relax in making even the crudest of measurements, for there is always ample room for mistakes.

So often the difference between a skillfully executed experiment that yields reliable results and a poorly conceived attempt that gives questionable answers resides in that ineluctable quality called technique. Examples of different techniques of measurement are scattered throughout this text. The student is urged to understand them clearly and to think them over critically. On the whole, these items consist of what might be called clever practices having superiority and purposeful advantages over first approaches that might be devised. They are often subtle and evolve only after a thorough study of methods and procedures, or perhaps after repeated failures of trying various schemes in the laboratory. These items of technique do not necessarily come easily. A helpful but often overlooked guide is that of planning the treatment of data in advance of performing the actual experiment. This has the advantage of requiring theoretical analysis to anticipate the results, with other attendant benefits. In addition, advanced planning helps in the conduct of the experiment by indicating ranges of values to be measured, regions in which to concentrate experimental data, and sensitiveness of contributions of various quantities to over-all accuracy.

Even though technique is an elusive matter, much can be learned by example from practices others have found satisfactory. However, a good portion of technique may be learned only from experience, such as certain maintenance and manipulative aspects of equipment, or just how vigorously one should tap an instrument to jar loose a source of erraticness.

1-5. Creativity and Ideas. When informed of a new idea, have you ever wondered whether you could have thought of it? Have you ever engaged in the intellectual pastime of trying to find a better way to accomplish a desired objective?

The field of electrical measurements is fraught with new problems requiring new solutions and represents an area of considerable challenge. Many examples of old ideas that have been found useful are sprinkled throughout this text. They reflect clear and astute thinking on the part of others in the past. Also, certain ingenious improvements in instruments and methods are discussed, some of which are difficult to better in current practice. Many of these ideas will be applicable to new problems of the future, and it is well to analyze and understand them. Once mastered, it only remains to recognize how they may be incorporated into a novel situation.

Unfortunately, there is no formula for creative thinking, for production of new ideas, or for discovering best solutions for new problems. If such a formula existed, it would be extremely overworked. However, one may develop the habit of analytical thought and of formulating new ideas. A keen, inquisitive, well-trained mind is the requisite. Little is known about the stimulation of creative ideas. It has not even been established that thorough comprehension of the problem is a necessary ingredient.

Yet, the demand for such ideas and the opportunities to apply them are without precedent and deserve cultivation.

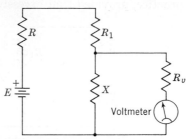

To suggest a line of thought illustrating the evolution of an idea, suppose that a method capable of high accuracy is to be devised for measuring resistance. A voltmeter-ammeter method is ruled out immediately, because the result depends upon calibration and readability errors of *two* instruments.

Fig. 1-1. Resistance measurement by deflection method.

Moreover, certain errors (which are correctable) are inherent in this method, as described in Sec. 5-6. A second attempt might be made using the circuit of Fig. 1-1. The battery of accurately known emf, E, is selected to have an internal resistance, R, that is negligible compared with $R_1 + X$, where R_1 is an accurately known resistance and X is the resistance to be determined. Moreover, the voltmeter is selected to have a resistance, R_v, that is very large compared with X. This is called a deflection method of measurement. The voltmeter reading, V, is obtained from the voltage-divider rule.

$$V = \frac{X}{X + R_1} E \qquad R \ll (R_1 + X),\ R_v \gg X$$

Solve for X.

$$X = \frac{R_1 V}{E - V} \qquad (1\text{-}1)$$

Thus, X may be computed from the reading, V, and the known values E and R_1. For example, if the reading is one-half E, then $X = R_1$.

While this method might be useful for rough measurements of X, its accuracy is severely limited by several factors:

1. Complete reliance is placed on the deflection of the voltmeter, and this entails readability and calibration errors.

2. The voltmeter must draw current to produce a reading. This introduces some error even if the current is very small. In other words, the effect of R_v is never entirely negligible. This error also changes for different values of X, if the same voltmeter is used for all measurements.

3. The internal resistance of an emf is never zero, and it introduces a small error in Eq. (1-1).

4. In practice, the value of an emf from which current is drawn is found

to be an unstable quantity that depends upon time and past history of the emf.

The required knowledge of the resistance, R_1, is not subject to objection. Resistance may be an accurately known and stable entity in practice, provided that excessive current is not used.

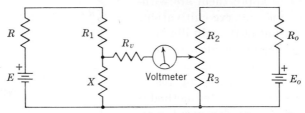

FIG. 1-2. Resistance measurement by null method using two batteries.

After some pondering, one might conceive of the circuit in Fig. 1-2 to overcome both the first and second difficulties simultaneously. Here, a second emf, E_0, with negligible internal resistance, R_0, is used to provide an adjustable voltage that may be "bucked" against the voltage across X. The sliding contact is adjusted until the voltmeter reads *zero*. Then, neither the calibration of the voltmeter nor its resistance enters the determination of X. This is called a null method of measurement. When the slider is adjusted for $V = 0$, the voltage drop across X is equal to that across R_3. Then,

$$\frac{XE}{R_1 + X} = \frac{R_3 E_0}{R_2 + R_3} \qquad R \ll (R_1 + X),\ R_0 \ll (R_2 + R_3)$$

Solve for X.

$$X = \frac{R_1}{\dfrac{E}{E_0}\left(1 + \dfrac{R_2}{R_3}\right) - 1} \tag{1-2}$$

Only the *ratios* E/E_0 and R_2/R_3 need be known accurately, but an accurate value of R_1 is still required. The resistance ratio and R_1 may be known with good accuracy in practice. But the two emf's, both of which supply current, are not stable quantities, nor is their ratio. Moreover, each of their internal resistances must be small. The method still leaves room for improvement, but at least does not rely upon the voltmeter calibration and does not require a high-resistance voltmeter. In fact, any sensitive detector of direct current would serve the purpose in the circuit of Fig. 1-2.

After deep contemplation, one might finally arrive at the remarkable idea of modifying the arrangement in Fig. 1-2 by using the selfsame battery for both E and E_0. Then the ratio E/E_0 in Eq. (1-2) would have to be unity. The circuit in Fig. 1-3 results. When the voltmeter reading is set to zero by adjusting the slider, the voltage across X is the fraction $X/(R_1 + X)$ times the voltage E_a, applied across $R_1 + X$. The potential difference across R_3 is equal to the fraction $R_3/(R_2 + R_3)$ times the *same* applied voltage, E_a. Hence,

$$\frac{XE_a}{R_1 + X} = \frac{R_3E_a}{R_2 + R_3}$$

The applied voltage, E_a, cancels, and the solution for X is

$$X = \frac{R_3}{R_2}\, R_1 \qquad\qquad (1\text{-}3)$$

This agrees with Eq. (1-2) when $E = E_0$. The ratio R_3/R_2 and the value of R_1 may be known with considerable accuracy. The result does not

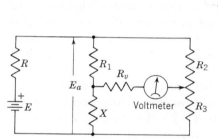

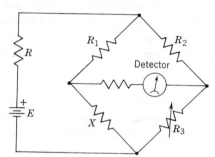

FIG. 1-3. Resistance measurement by null method using one battery.

FIG. 1-4. Wheatstone bridge.

depend upon a knowledge of E, and its internal resistance, R, need not be small, since it does not affect the relationship in Eq. (1-3). Moreover, the result is independent of the voltmeter calibration as well as its resistance. One must admit that this is indeed an unusual arrangement. Its advantages and limitations are analyzed in detail in Chap. 10.

The circuit in Fig. 1-3 is the well-known Wheatstone bridge, drawn in more conventional form in Fig. 1-4. It was first suggested by S. Hunter Christie in 1833, but did not receive attention until Charles Wheatstone applied it to resistance measurements in 1843. It has since become one of the most valuable circuit configurations in the field of measurements and is used widely in many applications. It is not restricted to resistances, and the four arms may consist of a variety of different circuit elements. From one point of view, it consists of a network of circuit elements connected among four nodes in all possible ways. Whether Christie arrived at this idea by the sequence indicated in Figs. 1-1 through 1-3 is a moot question. However, it is a plausible line of thought. Perhaps you can think of another.

1-6. Uncertainties and Theories. A significant feature of measurements is that the "true" value of a measured quantity is never known with absolute certainty. Physical phenomena and the laws describing them are statistical in nature. They always display small fluctuations that ultimately prohibit determination of the true value of a quantity. These matters are discussed in detail in Chaps. 5 to 7.

It may be a disturbing idea to be confronted with an upper limit beyond which invasion is impossible. Fortunately, in most gross (macroscopic) phenomena the uncertainties are entirely negligible, and this is the case in many engineering applications. But in pursuing a quantity more and more closely, the "noise" limit of random fluctuations is inevitably reached. This intrinsic characteristic of physical quantities requires an attitude and state of mind that are appropriate to the situation. Thus, the quantity *zero* is written very glibly in theoretical analysis but is nonexistent experimentally. For instance, the voltmeter reading in the circuit of Fig. 1-3 can never be reduced exactly to zero. This aspect of measured quantities demands increased appreciation as the quest for higher accuracy is intensified. In the last analysis, one must rest content with best estimates of "true" values, and elaborate procedures are often necessary in arriving at the most probable value of a quantity.

The power of measurement as a decisive factor in the development of theory deserves comment. A theory endures only so long as every measurement, without exception, is consistent with that theory. Of course, one must realize that inconsistencies are readily found with an oversimplified theory, but this does not necessarily imply that a theoretical explanation is not known. As in mathematics, so in physics, only a single exception need be found to point up a fallacy. If a result is found to be inexplicable by accepted theories, even though other phenomena are well explained, this becomes a signal for revising the theory or qualifying it further. The principal point is that only one case is required to produce the upset. This represents an extreme demand on theory. The discovery must, of course, be reproducible and confirmed by competent, objective workers. It requires stringent standards, high integrity, and complete objectivity in carrying out measurements.

1-7. Terminology and Notation. Terminology regarding several items in this text is not uniform in electrical literature. Three of these items are particularly prominent and might be bothersome without a brief explanation.

a. Control. The term "control" is used throughout this book to describe a three-terminal resistor in which one terminal is an independently adjustable sliding contact. A control was used in the resistance-measurement examples of Figs. 1-2 and 1-3. This three-terminal device is often referred to incorrectly as a potentiometer. However, potentiometers are more elaborate arrangements of circuit elements and generators (both d-c and a-c) used for precision measurement of potential difference. Alternatively, the three-terminal resistor is sometimes called a voltage divider or a potential divider. This terminology does not distinguish between adjustable and nonadjustable arrangements. Thus, two fixed resistors in series, with a fixed tap at their junction, comprise a potential divider, but this is not a control, as the term is used in this text. A rheostat is a two-terminal variable resistor. When one fixed terminal of a control is unused, it may be called a rheostat.

b. Current. Conduction current is an instantaneous *scalar* quantity defined as the net (average) charge passing a given cross section of a region per unit time. The charge flows through the cross section, and the current is a number describing the rate of flow of charge. It should be clear that the charge flows, not the current. Yet much of the literature refers incorrectly to the "flow" of current. But current *is* the flow, and, in effect, such a statement literally implies that the flow flows. In this text, use of the term current flow is avoided.

c. Voltage. Potential difference between two points is an instantaneous scalar quantity defined as the work done per unit charge in moving the charge from one point to the other. The term voltage, so frequently found in the electrical literature, has a less precise meaning. Indeed, it has become an increasingly vague term because of its varied uses. Despite this difficulty, the term voltage as used here is synonymous with potential difference. This is a matter of economy of words that avoids repetitious reference to the two points between which the potential difference exists. No confusion should result since it is usually clear from context which two points are being considered when the term voltage is used.

An attempt has been made to use accepted notation for all quantities, and to use symbols that are clear and unambiguous. It is impossible, without creating new and strange symbols, or using annoying subscripts, to have each symbol represent a single quantity exclusively. A complete listing of symbols is considered unnecessary, but several over-all guides deserve mention.

In general, all complex quantities (representing steady-state, single-frequency currents, voltages, impedances, admittances, and so forth) have been set in boldface type. Similarly, all three-dimensional vector quantities are set in boldface type. No ambiguity should result from use of boldface type for these distinctly different items, since vectors and complex quantities do not appear together in this text. It is extremely important to distinguish clearly between these quantities and scalars that may be related to them but which are by no means interchangeable with them.

Instantaneous quantities that are functions of time are represented by lower-case letters. Steady quantities such as average and peak values are signified by capital letters. Although the same symbol may be used in different portions of the text for different quantities, the intent should be clear from context. For example, p represents instantaneous power in Chap. 2 but is used for probability in Chap. 6; W designates work in Chap. 2 but signifies the width of a galvanometer coil in Chap. 3. Several symbols are used exclusively to stand for exactly the same quantity throughout the text. These are mostly well-established conventions, including $\epsilon = 2.7183$, $\pi = 3.1416$, $q =$ instantaneous charge, and $\omega =$ angular frequency in radians per second. The symbol θ has been reserved for the angular deflection of a meter movement. In addition, a consistent notation has been used for logarithms: ln = logarithm to the base ϵ; log = logarithm to the base 10.

1-8. Dimensional Checks and Conversion of Units. Dimensional analysis is a general method valuable in exploring limitations and forms of relationships among variables in a physical system. It is sometimes called the principle of similitude. Two relatively minor offshoots of this method are highly useful in routine analysis. These are (1) checking dimensions of equations, and (2) changing from one set of units to another.

Any single functional relationship among physical quantities must possess dimensional homogeneity; that is, each term in the equation must have the same dimensions. It follows that, in addition or subtraction of two terms representing physical quantities, both terms must have the same dimensions. This property of equations provides a rule that often saves analysis time in developing theoretical formulas. Simple mistakes in algebraic or other manipulations may often be immediately detected upon applying a dimensional homogeneity check. Moreover, the particular term in error is usually identifiable and facilitates tracing the error.

For example, suppose in the course of analysis, one portion of an equation that is developed is

$$\frac{R_1}{R_2} + \frac{R_3 R_4}{R_5} + \sqrt{R_6{}^2 + R_7{}^2}$$

where the R symbols represent resistance in ohms. This is obviously in error since the first term is dimensionless while all other terms have the dimension ohms. Probably a resistance term multiplying the R_1/R_2 was dropped inadvertently at an earlier stage. Even so obvious a check as this often saves much labor in the course of working toward a final result. One should continually ask whether expressions are dimensionally homogeneous. It is one of the simplest and most revealing aspects of an equation to check, and it discloses errors in a surprising number of cases.

Another use of dimensional analysis is particularly valuable because it alleviates difficulties with problems involving change of units, which sometimes cause a tangle in thinking. In these applications, the rule for changing from one set of units to another is simply to write out the known dimensional formulas among the quantities involved. To illustrate, take the case of converting angular velocity of 100 radians per min to degrees per second. Since 1 radian contains approximately 57.3 deg, and 1 min contains 60 sec, it follows that

$$100 \ \frac{\text{rad}}{\text{min}} = 100 \ \frac{57.3 \ \text{deg}}{60 \ \text{sec}} = 95.5 \ \frac{\text{deg}}{\text{sec}}$$

In this approach, each unit is replaced by an equivalent number of different units. In effect, the unwanted units are canceled, thus

$$100 \ \frac{\text{rad}}{\text{min}} \times 57.3 \ \frac{\text{deg}}{\text{rad}} \times \frac{1}{60} \ \frac{\text{min}}{\text{sec}} = 95.5 \ \frac{\text{deg}}{\text{sec}}$$

This method is general and straightforward. Note that it is completely unnecessary, and usually undesirable, to express all units first in terms of fundamental units.

The same method may be applied to determine equivalent dimensions of a given quantity. This may be accomplished with a comparatively few elementary physical formulas that contain the units in question. For example, to find the equivalent dimensions of

$$\frac{L}{R} = \frac{\text{henry}}{\text{ohm}}$$

resort to Ohm's law and the relationship for self-inductance:

$$v = Ri \qquad v = L \frac{di}{dt}$$

Clearly, R has the dimensions volt per ampere, and L has dimensions volt-second per ampere. Hence,

$$\frac{\text{henry}}{\text{ohm}} = \frac{\text{volt-sec}}{\text{amp}} \times \frac{1}{\text{volt/amp}} = \text{sec}$$

1-9. Some Omitted Topics. Any book in a field as polymorphic as electrical measurements cannot cover all phases of the subject. However, this text is more confined than most so far as topical coverage is concerned. This results from placing emphasis on concepts and analysis. It should be understood that many topics found in traditional descriptions of the subject are either omitted entirely or merely mentioned in passing. There is ample literature available on these topics, should the student wish to explore them.

Some over-all aspects that are slighted include details and construction of measurement equipment and of components that form a part of this equipment. Thus, design and construction of standard (precision) resistors, shielding in a-c bridges, standard-cell information, and other such matters are excluded. Commercial apparatus and its manipulative features are not presented. Only a few basic types of instruments are analyzed, and little mention is made of many other types that are widely used. While certain applications of instruments and methods are included to make analyses meaningful, no attempt whatever has been made to describe many applications prevalent in this field. In general, electronic equipment and principles are not included, nor are high-frequency aspects of measurements. Stray effects such as lead inductance, contact difference of potential, stray capacitance, and others, sometimes important in practice, are not investigated.

Some specific topics that are omitted which have appeared in many texts of the past are magnetic measurements, instrument transformers, energy measurements, polyphase circuits and measurements. Moreover, such traditional devices as ballistic galvanometers and a-c potentiometers are not analyzed.

It would appear that far more topics have been omitted than included, and this is indeed the case. However, it is hoped that with careful selection of material, the principal concepts and ideas useful in the field of measurement, as well as in related engineering fields, have been retained.

CHAPTER 2

REVIEW OF LINEAR CIRCUIT ANALYSIS

A synopsis of basic circuit concepts utilized in this text is presented for ready reference, and to specify circuit terminology and conventions to be used. It is not intended to be more than a condensed review and brief summary of material to which the student has probably been previously exposed. Ramifications of the highly developed subject of linear circuit analysis are omitted. A knowledge of differential equations, complex algebra, and use of determinants in solving simultaneous equations is assumed.

2-1. Definitions. Length, mass, time, and charge are taken as fundamental (undefinable) quantities. Their units in the mks system are the meter, kilogram, second, and coulomb, respectively. Force and work are mechanical quantities defined in terms of length, mass, and time. Their units in the mks system are newton and joule, respectively. The three primary scalar electrical quantities of circuit theory are defined below.

Conduction current, i, is an instantaneous scalar quantity defined as the net (average) charge, dq, passing a given cross section of a circuit in time dt.

$$i = \frac{dq}{dt} \qquad \text{amp (coulomb per sec)}$$

Potential difference, v, between two points is an instantaneous scalar quantity defined as the work, dW, done on a charge, dq, in moving it from one point to the other.

$$v = \frac{dW}{dq} \qquad \text{volt (joule per coulomb)}$$

The terms *potential difference* and *voltage* are used synonymously in this text.

Electric power, p, is an instantaneous scalar quantity defined as the work, dW, done in a time dt, in carrying a charge through the aforementioned potential difference.

$$p = \frac{dW}{dt} = \frac{dW}{dq}\frac{dq}{dt} = vi \qquad \text{watt (joule per sec)}$$

Power is also equal to the product vi, as indicated, where v is the potential difference between the points that i enters and leaves.

The *average value* of a function of time, $f(t)$, between t_1 and t_2 is defined by

$$F_{\mathrm{av}} = \frac{1}{t_2 - t_1} \int_{t_1}^{t_2} f(t)\, dt \tag{2-1}$$

and may be applied to i, v, or p.

The *root-mean-square (rms) value* of a function of time, $f(t)$, between time t_1 and t_2 is defined by

$$F_{\mathrm{rms}} = \sqrt{\frac{1}{t_2 - t_1} \int_{t_1}^{t_2} [f(t)]^2\, dt} \tag{2-2}$$

and may be applied to i or v, but rms power is not a useful definition.

If $f(t) = f(t + T)$, then $f(t)$ is a periodic function of period T. If the interval $t_2 - t_1$ in the above definitions is not specified, and if $f(t)$ is a periodic function, then the interval is usually implied to be one period.

2-2. Kirchhoff's Laws. The two experimental laws of Kirchhoff are cornerstones of circuit theory. Kirchhoff's current law, tied in with conservation of charge, states that the sum of all currents entering any node (or junction) is equal to zero.

$$\Sigma i_k = 0 \quad \text{at any node, with every } i_k \text{ included}$$

Kirchhoff's voltage law, tied in with conservation of energy (or work), states that the sum of all voltages around any closed mesh (or loop) is zero.

$$\Sigma v_k = 0 \quad \text{around any closed mesh, with every } v_k \text{ included}$$

In both laws, account must be taken of the algebraic signs of the currents and voltages, and a consistent sign convention used in any given instance.

2-3. Two-terminal Circuit Elements. Practical electrical devices may be approximated in varying degree by the idealized linear elements, or combinations of elements, defined below. The currents and voltages referred to in the definitions pertain in all cases to the two terminals of the element, as illustrated in Fig. 2-1.

A *constant resistance* is a two-terminal device in which the ratio of voltage to current is constant.

$$v = Ri$$

The resistance, R, has the dimension ohm = volt per ampere. Since $i = dq/dt$, this may also be written

$$q = \frac{1}{R} \int v\, dt = G \int v\, dt$$

where $G = 1/R$ is the conductance of the resistance R.

A *constant capacitance* is a two-terminal device in which the ratio of charge to voltage is constant.

$$q = Cv$$

The capacitance, C, has the dimension farad = coulomb per volt.   Using $i = dq/dt$, this may also be written

$$i = C \frac{dv}{dt} \qquad \text{or} \qquad v = \frac{1}{C} \int i \, dt$$

A *constant inductance* is a two-terminal device in which the ratio of voltage to time derivative of current is constant.

$$v = L \frac{di}{dt}$$

The self-inductance, L, has the dimension henry = volt-second per ampere.   This also may be written

$$i = \frac{1}{L} \int v \, dt$$

A *constant-voltage source* (or generator) is a two-terminal device in which $v(t) = e(t)$ is independent of the current, $i(t)$, passing through the

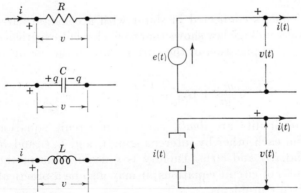

Fig. 2-1. Two-terminal circuit elements.

device.   The arrow alongside the voltage generator in Fig. 2-1 indicates the direction of the voltage rise and is directed from minus to plus.

A *constant-current source* (or generator) is a two-terminal device in which $i(t)$ is independent of the voltage, $v(t)$, across the device.   The arrow alongside the current generator in Fig. 2-1 indicates the direction of flow of positive charge.

2-4. Network Equations and Solutions.   Practical electric circuits may be approximated in varying degree by interconnected two-terminal circuit elements, or combinations thereof. Network equations are differential equations that interrelate instantaneous charge, current, and voltage. The equations are linear with constant coefficients when constant, bilateral, two-terminal elements only appear in the network.

Network equations arise from the application of Kirchhoff's two laws, in combination with the definitions of two-terminal devices. For example, with the three elements of Fig. 2-2a connected in series with a

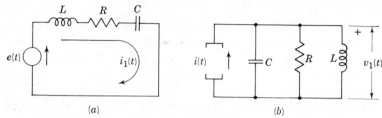

(a)   (b)

Fig. 2-2. Dual circuits.

constant-voltage source, $e(t)$, Kirchhoff's current law reveals that each element must carry the same current, $i_1(t)$. The voltage law yields the equation

$$L \frac{di_1}{dt} + Ri_1 + \frac{1}{C} \int i_1 \, dt = e(t) \qquad (2\text{-}3)$$

For three elements connected in shunt with a constant-current source, $i(t)$, Kirchhoff's voltage law shows that each element experiences the same voltage, $v_1(t)$. Application of the current law to the circuit of Fig. 2-2b results in

$$C \frac{dv_1}{dt} + Gv_1 + \frac{1}{L} \int v_1 \, dt = i(t)$$

These two circuits are *duals*, since their circuit equations may be obtained from each other by interchanging C and L, G and R, L and C, v_1 and i_1, and $i(t)$ and $e(t)$. Duality is a useful concept that helps to unify principles of circuit equations; it may also be a practical timesaver in solving circuit problems.

No matter how complicated the interconnection of any number of two-terminal elements, Kirchhoff's laws may be applied to obtain the network equations. In general, these are simultaneous equations among the voltages and currents in all elements. If all the elements are known and all the boundary conditions are specified (such as initial values of charges and currents for all elements), then these equations may always be solved for the currents and voltages of each element. Because the equations become complicated and numerous for a complex array of interconnected elements, special techniques for writing the equations are used. Mesh equations, or the dual node equations, may be utilized to systematize and organize the equations and their manipulation. These equations stem basically from Kirchhoff's laws.

The solution of network equations for each dependent current or voltage generally consists of a transient term and a steady-state term. For example, in the simple circuit of Fig. 2-3, let Q_0 represent the charge on C before the switch is closed. The constant-voltage generator, E, is not a function of time. If the switch is closed at time $t = 0$, Kirchhoff's current law indicates that the current, $i = dq/dt$, in each element is the same for $t \geqq 0$. The voltage law yields, for $t \geqq 0$, the equation

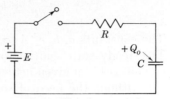

Fig. 2-3. Charging capacitor.

$$R \frac{dq}{dt} + \frac{q}{C} = E \qquad\qquad q = Q_0 \text{ at } t = 0$$

The complete solution for q is

$$q = CE - (CE - Q_0)\epsilon^{-t/RC} \qquad t \geqq 0 \qquad (2\text{-}4)$$

The steady-state term is CE. The remaining portion of the solution is the transient term, which becomes negligible compared with CE as $t \to \infty$.

In more elaborate networks, there may be considerable complexity in determining solutions of simultaneous differential equations, especially if voltage and current generators are not simple functions of time. Techniques such as the Laplace transform may be applied to obtain the solution of such simultaneous equations.

2-5. Solutions in the Steady Sinusoidal State. The steady-state solution (particular integral) of an nth-order linear differential equation with constant coefficients is easily found if the generators are sinusoidal functions of time. Use of complex quantities to represent the steady-state voltages or currents enables the differential equations to be transformed into algebraic equations. Only the steady-state solution is obtained, so that boundary (initial) conditions on the variables do not enter and need not be known.

The basis of the $\epsilon^{j\omega t}$ method, as it is sometimes called, is outlined here for a second-order equation. The same reasoning may be used to extend the results to higher-order equations, to sets of simultaneous equations, and by linear superposition to any number of sinusoidal driving functions. In the latter case, it is especially important to recognize that the complex quantities are functions of frequency; hence, a different set of complex numbers is generally required for each different frequency.

Consider the pair of second-order differential equations

$$a\frac{d^2x}{dt^2} + b\frac{dx}{dt} + cx = A\cos(\omega t + \phi) \qquad (2\text{-}5)$$

$$a\frac{d^2y}{dt^2} + b\frac{dy}{dt} + cy = A\sin(\omega t + \phi) \qquad (2\text{-}6)$$

The constants a, b, c, A, ω, and ϕ are the same in these two equations. The steady-state solution for x or y, which may be instantaneous currents or voltages in a given network, is obtainable from a single complex number without the need of solving the differential equation directly. To demonstrate this, multiply Eq. (2-6) by $j = \sqrt{-1}$ and add the two equations.

$$a\left[\frac{d^2x}{dt^2} + \frac{d^2(jy)}{dt^2}\right] + b\left[\frac{dx}{dt} + \frac{d(jy)}{dt}\right] + c(x + jy)$$
$$= A[\cos(\omega t + \phi) + j\sin(\omega t + \phi)]$$

Define $\mathbf{u} = x + jy$. Then this equation becomes

$$a\frac{d^2\mathbf{u}}{dt^2} + b\frac{d\mathbf{u}}{dt} + c\mathbf{u} = A\epsilon^{j(\omega t + \phi)} \qquad (2\text{-}7)$$

Either x or y may be obtained from the complex number $\mathbf{u}$, appearing in this equation, by the relations

$$x = \mathrm{Re}\,\{\mathbf{u}\} \qquad y = \mathrm{Im}\,\{\mathbf{u}\}$$

where Re signifies the real part, and Im signifies the imaginary part. This is a very practical means for obtaining x or y because it is easy to find the $\mathbf{u}$ that satisfies Eq. (2-7). The complex number $\mathbf{u}$, which is a function of both frequency and time, that will satisfy Eq. (2-7) is known to be in the form

$$\mathbf{u} = \mathbf{U}\epsilon^{j\omega t} \qquad \mathbf{U} = U\epsilon^{j\psi}$$

where the magnitude, U, and the angle, ψ, of $\mathbf{U}$ are not functions of time. Substitute $\mathbf{u}$ into Eq. (2-7) and carry out the time differentiations.

$$[a(j\omega)^2\mathbf{U} + b(j\omega)\mathbf{U} + c\mathbf{U}]\epsilon^{j\omega t} = A\epsilon^{j\phi}\epsilon^{j\omega t}$$

Cancellation of $\epsilon^{j\omega t}$ leads to an algebraic equation from which U and ψ may be determined.

$$\mathbf{U}(c - a\omega^2 + j\omega b) = A\epsilon^{j\phi} = \mathbf{A}$$

The magnitude and angle of $\mathbf{U}$ are

$$U = \frac{A}{\sqrt{(c - a\omega^2)^2 + (\omega b)^2}} \qquad \psi = \phi - \tan^{-1}\frac{\omega b}{c - a\omega^2}$$

The over-all scheme is complete. For example, if Eq. (2-5) is given and the steady-state time function, x, is desired, it is necessary only to find $\mathbf{U}$. This is readily accomplished by replacing the differential equation by its corresponding complex equation. Then the algebraic equation for $\mathbf{U}$ follows. Multiplying the known $\mathbf{U}$ by $\epsilon^{j\omega t}$, and extracting the real part, yields x.

$$x = \text{Re } \{\mathbf{u}\} = \text{Re } \{\mathbf{U}\epsilon^{j\omega t}\}$$

$$= \frac{A}{\sqrt{(c - a\omega^2)^2 + (\omega b)^2}} \cos\left(\omega t + \phi - \tan^{-1}\frac{\omega b}{c - a\omega^2}\right)$$

To illustrate with a first-order electrical example, find the steady-state current in the inductive circuit of Fig. 2-4. The differential equation for the current is

$$L\frac{di}{dt} + Ri = E\cos(\omega t + \phi)$$

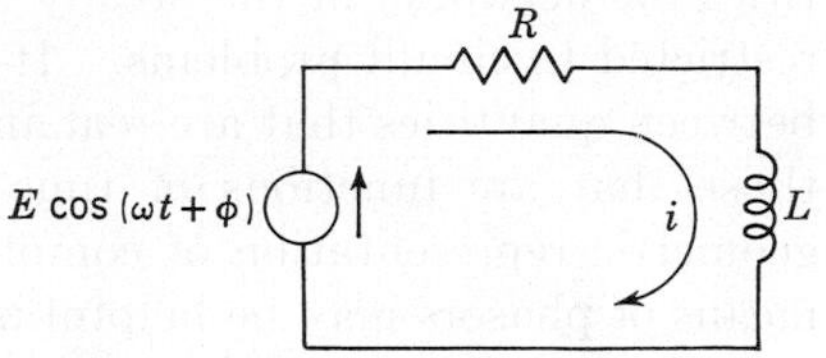

FIG. 2-4. Inductive circuit.

The complex differential equation that replaces, but is not identical to, this equation is

$$L\frac{d\mathbf{i}}{dt} + R\mathbf{i} = E\epsilon^{j(\omega t + \phi)}$$

The complex quantity $\mathbf{i}$, replacing the actual current, i, is known to be in the form

$$\mathbf{i} = \mathbf{I}\epsilon^{j\omega t} = I\epsilon^{j\psi}\epsilon^{j\omega t}$$

The complex current, $\mathbf{I}$, satisfies the algebraic equation in which $\epsilon^{j\omega t}$ has been canceled.

$$L(j\omega)\mathbf{I} + R\mathbf{I} = E\epsilon^{j\phi} = \mathbf{E}$$

Thus, $\mathbf{I}$ is determined.

$$\mathbf{I} = \frac{E\epsilon^{j\phi}}{R + j\omega L} \qquad I = \frac{E}{\sqrt{R^2 + (\omega L)^2}} \qquad \psi = \phi - \tan^{-1}\frac{\omega L}{R}$$

Since the instantaneous voltage applied to the circuit is given by

$$e(t) = \text{Re } \{\mathbf{E}\epsilon^{j\omega t}\} = \text{Re } \{E\epsilon^{j(\omega t + \phi)}\} = E\cos(\omega t + \phi)$$

then the steady-state solution for the instantaneous current must be given by the real part of $\mathbf{i}$.

$$i = \text{Re } \{\mathbf{i}\} = \text{Re } \{\mathbf{I}\epsilon^{j\omega t}\} = \frac{E}{\sqrt{R^2 + (\omega L)^2}} \cos\left(\omega t + \phi - \tan^{-1}\frac{\omega L}{R}\right)$$

There is, of course, nothing unfamiliar about this solution, but the basis upon which it is obtained is important. In actual problems, all these steps are not necessary, once the method is understood. Usually, the algebraic equation of the complex current is written immediately and solved for the unknown complex current, **I**. There is often no interest in returning to the time domain.

If the generator voltage were $E \sin (\omega t + \phi)$ in the foregoing example, there would be no complications. In this case, the instantaneous voltage is given most conveniently by

$$e(t) = \text{Im} \{\mathbf{E}\epsilon^{j\omega t}\} = \text{Im} \{E\epsilon^{j(\omega t+\phi)}\} = E \sin (\omega t + \phi)$$

Therefore, the instantaneous current is given by the imaginary part of $\mathbf{I}\epsilon^{j\omega t}$.

This summary provides a rational basis for the use of complex quantities for networks in the steady alternating state. The method is not restricted to circuit problems. It enables a clear distinction to be made between quantities that are real and those that are complex and between those that are functions of time and those that are not. While the geometric representation of complex quantities in the complex plane by means of phasors may be helpful in visualizing certain relationships, it is sometimes a more cumbersome view. Complex quantities may be handled entirely by rules of algebra, and the geometric representation is not required.

2-6. Impedance and Admittance. If all constant-voltage and constant-current sources in a network consisting of constant two-terminal elements are sinusoidal and have the same frequency, and if all transients have died out to a negligible level, the network is then in the steady sinusoidal state. All voltages, $v(t)$, and all currents, $i(t)$, throughout the network are sinusoidal and of the same frequency. Under these conditions, they may be represented by complex quantities, since the only distinguishing features of a sine wave are its amplitude and phase.

$$v(t) = \text{Re} \{\mathbf{V}\epsilon^{j\omega t}\} = \text{Re} \{V\epsilon^{j\phi_1}\epsilon^{j\omega t}\} = V \cos (\omega t + \phi_1)$$
$$i(t) = \text{Re} \{\mathbf{I}\epsilon^{j\omega t}\} = \text{Re} \{I\epsilon^{j\phi_2}\epsilon^{j\omega t}\} = I \cos (\omega t + \phi_2)$$

The complex voltage **V** and the complex current **I** are not functions of time. They have magnitudes V and I and phase angles ϕ_1 and ϕ_2, respectively. These complex numbers represent peak values of the instantaneous quantities, and this convention will be used throughout (rather than including the factor $\sqrt{2}$ as is done in some treatments). With ϕ_1 and ϕ_2 arbitrary, these are general steady-state representations. However, the instantaneous quantities may also be represented, if desired, in terms of complex quantities by replacing "Re" by "Im" and "cos" by "sin."

Impedance and admittance are single-frequency concepts used to describe passive circuit elements in the steady sinusoidal state. If a two-terminal device displays a constant ratio of complex voltage to complex current, then the complex impedance of the device is defined by $\mathbf{Z}$.

$$\mathbf{Z} = \frac{\mathbf{V}}{\mathbf{I}} \qquad \mathbf{Y} = \frac{1}{\mathbf{Z}} = \frac{\mathbf{I}}{\mathbf{V}}$$

The complex admittance, $\mathbf{Y}$, is the reciprocal of $\mathbf{Z}$. Note that $\mathbf{Z}$ and $\mathbf{Y}$ are, by definition, *independent* of the voltages and currents. However, they are generally functions of frequency.

In the steady sinusoidal state, it may be proved that Kirchhoff's two laws hold for complex currents and voltages (see Prob. 2-5).

$$\begin{aligned} \Sigma \mathbf{I}_k &= 0 \quad \text{at any node, with every } \mathbf{I}_k \text{ included} \\ \Sigma \mathbf{V}_k &= 0 \quad \text{around any closed mesh, with every } \mathbf{V}_k \text{ included} \end{aligned} \tag{2-8}$$

It then follows from the definition of impedance and admittance that, for a constant resistance, R, the impedance is $\mathbf{Z} = R$, and the admittance is $\mathbf{Y} = 1/R$. For a constant capacitance, C, the impedance is $\mathbf{Z} = 1/j\omega C$ and the admittance is $\mathbf{Y} = j\omega C$. For a constant self-inductance, L, the impedance is $\mathbf{Z} = j\omega L$ and the admittance is $\mathbf{Y} = 1/j\omega L$. Moreover, application of Kirchhoff's laws shows that for N series-connected, two-terminal elements, the impedance of the series combination is

$$\mathbf{Z}_s = \sum_{k=1}^{N} \mathbf{Z}_k = \mathbf{Z}_1 + \mathbf{Z}_2 + \cdots + \mathbf{Z}_N \tag{2-9}$$

and the series admittance is given by

$$\frac{1}{\mathbf{Y}_s} = \sum_{k=1}^{N} \frac{1}{\mathbf{Y}_k} = \frac{1}{\mathbf{Y}_1} + \frac{1}{\mathbf{Y}_2} + \cdots + \frac{1}{\mathbf{Y}_N}$$

Similarly, for N parallel-connected two-terminal elements, the impedance of the parallel combination is given by

$$\frac{1}{\mathbf{Z}_p} = \sum_{k=1}^{N} \frac{1}{\mathbf{Z}_k} = \frac{1}{\mathbf{Z}_1} + \frac{1}{\mathbf{Z}_2} + \cdots + \frac{1}{\mathbf{Z}_N}$$

and the parallel admittance is

$$\mathbf{Y}_p = \sum_{k=1}^{N} \mathbf{Y}_k = \mathbf{Y}_1 + \mathbf{Y}_2 + \cdots + \mathbf{Y}_N \tag{2-10}$$

In general, impedance and admittance may consist of both real and imaginary parts. Thus,

$$\mathbf{Z} = Z\epsilon^{j\alpha} = R + jX$$

where the magnitude and angle of $\mathbf{Z}$ in terms of its resistance, R, and its reactance, X, are

$$Z = \sqrt{R^2 + X^2} \qquad \alpha = \tan^{-1} \frac{X}{R}$$

Similarly, for the admittance

$$\mathbf{Y} = Y\epsilon^{j\beta} = G + jB$$

where the magnitude and angle of $\mathbf{Y}$ in terms of its conductance, G, and its susceptance, B, are

$$Y = \sqrt{G^2 + B^2}$$

$$\beta = \tan^{-1} \frac{B}{G}$$

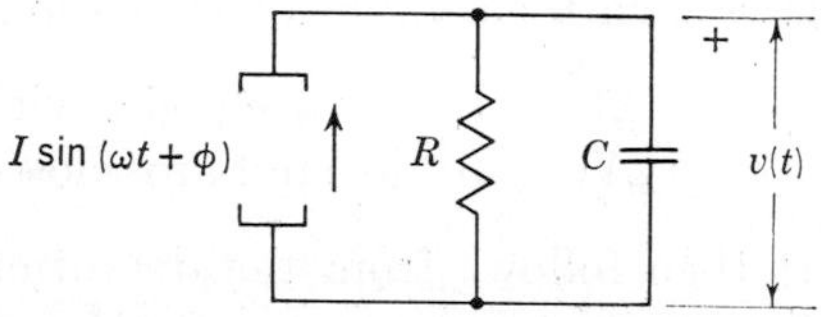

FIG. 2-5. Capacitive circuit.

To illustrate the application of some of these relations, an expression will be found for the steady-state voltage across the current generator of Fig. 2-5. The admittance of the two parallel elements is

$$\mathbf{Y} = \frac{1}{R} + j\omega C = \frac{1 + j\omega RC}{R} = \frac{\sqrt{1 + (\omega RC)^2}}{R} \epsilon^{j\beta}$$

where $\tan \beta = \omega RC$. The complex voltage across the current generator, and across R or C, is

$$\mathbf{V} = \frac{\mathbf{I}}{\mathbf{Y}} = \frac{RI\epsilon^{j\phi}}{\sqrt{1 + (\omega RC)^2}\, \epsilon^{j\beta}} = \frac{RI}{\sqrt{1 + (\omega RC)^2}} \epsilon^{j(\phi - \beta)}$$

The instantaneous current is related to $\mathbf{I}$ by

$$i(t) = \operatorname{Im} \{\mathbf{I}\epsilon^{j\omega t}\} = I \sin (\omega t + \phi)$$

Therefore, the instantaneous voltage is

$$v(t) = \operatorname{Im} \{\mathbf{V}\epsilon^{j\omega t}\} = \frac{RI}{\sqrt{1 + (\omega RC)^2}} \sin (\omega t + \phi - \tan^{-1} \omega RC)$$

2-7. Voltage Dividing and Current Splitting. The occasion arises so frequently to use two special cases, really contained in the preceding section, that separate proofs are given here for emphasis. The voltage-dividing and current-splitting rules, proved below for the steady sinusoidal state, are applied repeatedly throughout the text.

a. Voltage-dividing Rule. The complex voltage across impedance 1 of two series impedances is equal to the voltage across the pair of impedances times a reduction factor. The reduction factor is equal to the ratio of impedance 1 to the sum of the two impedances.

To prove this rule, let a complex voltage, $\mathbf{V}$, be applied to the two series-connected impedances $\mathbf{Z}_1$ and $\mathbf{Z}_2$ of Fig. 2-6.　Suppose $\mathbf{V}_1$, the voltage across $\mathbf{Z}_1$, is the desired voltage.　The complex current through the series combination is

$$\mathbf{I} = \frac{\mathbf{V}}{\mathbf{Z}_s} = \frac{\mathbf{V}}{\mathbf{Z}_1 + \mathbf{Z}_2}$$

The voltage $\mathbf{V}_1$ is $\mathbf{Z}_1$ times this current.

$$\mathbf{V}_1 = \mathbf{Z}_1\mathbf{I} = \frac{\mathbf{Z}_1}{\mathbf{Z}_1 + \mathbf{Z}_2}\mathbf{V} \qquad (2\text{-}11)$$

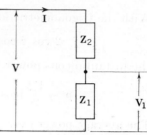

Fig. 2-6. Voltage divider.

This proves the rule.　The reduction factor is $\mathbf{Z}_1/(\mathbf{Z}_1 + \mathbf{Z}_2)$.

　　b. Current-splitting Rule.　The complex current in impedance 1 of two shunt impedances is equal to the current entering their junction times a splitting factor.　The splitting factor is equal to the ratio of the "other" impedance to the sum of the two impedances.

　　To prove this rule, let a complex current, $\mathbf{I}$, enter the junction of two parallel-connected impedances, $\mathbf{Z}_1$ and $\mathbf{Z}_2$, of Fig. 2-7.　Suppose $\mathbf{I}_1$, the current through $\mathbf{Z}_1$, is the desired current.　The complex voltage across the parallel combination is

$$\mathbf{V} = \mathbf{Z}_p\mathbf{I} = \frac{\mathbf{Z}_1\mathbf{Z}_2}{\mathbf{Z}_1 + \mathbf{Z}_2}\mathbf{I}$$

The current $\mathbf{I}_1$ is this voltage divided by $\mathbf{Z}_1$.

$$\mathbf{I}_1 = \frac{\mathbf{V}}{\mathbf{Z}_1} = \frac{\mathbf{Z}_2}{\mathbf{Z}_1 + \mathbf{Z}_2}\mathbf{I} \qquad (2\text{-}12)$$

This proves the rule.　The splitting factor is $\mathbf{Z}_2/(\mathbf{Z}_1 + \mathbf{Z}_2)$.

　　Both of these rules should be memorized.　They are actually duals, but this has been clouded by the use of impedances in both cases.　Replace the impedances of the current-splitting rule by admittances, and the dual nature of the two rules becomes clear.　Then in voltage dividing, the ratio of voltages is equal to the ratio of impedances across which the voltages appear; in current splitting, the ratio of the currents is equal to the ratio of the admittances through which the currents pass.　The impedance form of the current-splitting rule is preferred here because the shunt elements are specified as impedances in most of the measurement circuits encountered.

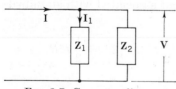

Fig. 2-7. Current splitter.

2-8. Average Power. In the steady sinusoidal state, the instantaneous power is

$$p = vi = V \cos (\omega t + \phi_1) I \cos (\omega t + \phi_2)$$

With the trigonometric identity

$$2 \cos x \cos y = \cos (x - y) + \cos (x + y)$$

the instantaneous power becomes

$$p = \frac{VI}{2} [\cos (\phi_1 - \phi_2) + \cos (2\omega t + \phi_1 + \phi_2)]$$

The average power over the period $T = 2\pi/\omega$ is obtained from Eq. (2-1).

$$P_{\mathrm{av}} = \frac{1}{T} \int_{t_1}^{t_1+T} p \, dt$$

where t_1 is arbitrary and is usually taken as zero. The first term of p is constant, and the integral of the second term of p over the period is zero. Hence,

$$P_{\mathrm{av}} = \frac{VI}{2} \cos (\phi_1 - \phi_2) = V_{\mathrm{rms}} I_{\mathrm{rms}} \cos (\phi_1 - \phi_2) \qquad (2\text{-}13)$$

The cosine of the phase difference between v and i is the *power factor*.

The average power, which is real, may be formulated in terms of complex quantities. Consider the complex voltage and current

$$\mathbf{V} = V \epsilon^{j\phi_1} \qquad \mathbf{I} = I \epsilon^{j\phi_2}$$

The *conjugate* of a complex number, signified by an asterisk, is defined by replacing j by minus j. Therefore,

$$\mathbf{VI^*} = V \epsilon^{j\phi_1} I \epsilon^{-j\phi_2} = VI \epsilon^{j(\phi_1 - \phi_2)}$$

Evidently, this is related to P_{av} by

$$P_{\mathrm{av}} = \frac{1}{2} \operatorname{Re} \{\mathbf{VI^*}\} \qquad (2\text{-}14)$$

If $\mathbf{V}$ and $\mathbf{I}$ are the complex voltage and current associated with an impedance $\mathbf{Z} = \mathbf{V}/\mathbf{I}$, then

$$P_{\mathrm{av}} = \frac{1}{2} \operatorname{Re} \{\mathbf{VI^*}\} = \frac{1}{2} \operatorname{Re} \{\mathbf{ZII^*}\} = \frac{1}{2} I^2 \operatorname{Re} \{\mathbf{Z}\} = \frac{1}{2} I^2 R$$

where R is the real part of $\mathbf{Z}$.

2-9. Mesh Equations. Mesh or node differential equations may be formulated for electric circuits on an instantaneous basis. However, this discussion will be confined to the steady sinusoidal state and to linear, bilateral networks containing constant generators. In this case, the network equations, in terms of complex voltages and currents, become simultaneous algebraic equations that may be solved by use of determinants.　Among the virtues of mesh or node equations are the reduction of the analysis to a systematic routine procedure and the provision of a general framework permitting rapid formulation of the equations while minimizing possibilities for algebraic errors.

An advocated method of selecting mesh currents is to choose all of them positive in the same direction in successive adjacent meshes, including one

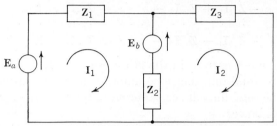

FIG. 2-8. Circuit with two independent mesh currents.

branch previously traversed, until all branches have been covered.　If only one mesh current in a particular branch is desired, the circuit may be redrawn, if necessary, so that this branch becomes an outer branch, rather than assigning mesh currents in haphazard fashion to achieve the same result.

An example of a circuit containing two independent mesh currents will be presented before stating the general formulation.　In the circuit of Fig. 2-8, two clockwise mesh currents, I_1 and I_2, are selected in adjacent meshes.　It is easily verified that Kirchhoff's current law is automatically satisfied by these currents at every node.　Kirchhoff's voltage law yields, for meshes 1 and 2, respectively,

$$I_1Z_1 + (I_1 - I_2)Z_2 = E_a - E_b$$
$$(I_2 - I_1)Z_2 + I_2Z_3 = E_b$$

Group all terms containing the same mesh currents to obtain the standard form of the mesh equations.

$$(Z_1 + Z_2)I_1 - Z_2I_2 = E_a - E_b$$
$$-Z_2I_1 + (Z_2 + Z_3)I_2 = E_b$$

The mesh determinant is

$$\Delta = \begin{vmatrix} Z_1 + Z_2 & -Z_2 \\ -Z_2 & Z_2 + Z_3 \end{vmatrix} = Z_1Z_2 + Z_1Z_3 + Z_2Z_3$$

The mesh currents are given by Cramer's rule.

$$I_1 = \frac{\begin{vmatrix} E_a - E_b & -Z_2 \\ E_b & Z_2 + Z_3 \end{vmatrix}}{\Delta} \qquad I_2 = \frac{\begin{vmatrix} Z_1 + Z_2 & E_a - E_b \\ -Z_2 & E_b \end{vmatrix}}{\Delta}$$

For an n-mesh network, it is intrinsic to the nature of mesh currents that Kirchhoff's current law is always automatically satisfied. With all mesh currents taken positive in the same direction, the following n voltage equations result when Kirchhoff's voltage law is applied and all terms containing the same mesh currents are collected.

$$\mathbf{Z}_{11}\mathbf{I}_1 - \mathbf{Z}_{12}\mathbf{I}_2 - \cdots - \mathbf{Z}_{1n}\mathbf{I}_n = \mathbf{E}_1$$
$$-\mathbf{Z}_{21}\mathbf{I}_1 + \mathbf{Z}_{22}\mathbf{I}_2 - \cdots - \mathbf{Z}_{2n}\mathbf{I}_n = \mathbf{E}_2$$
$$\cdots \quad \cdots \quad \cdots \quad \cdots \quad \cdots \tag{2-15}$$
$$-\mathbf{Z}_{n1}\mathbf{I}_1 - \mathbf{Z}_{n2}\mathbf{I}_2 - \cdots + \mathbf{Z}_{nn}\mathbf{I}_n = \mathbf{E}_n$$

where $\mathbf{I}_r$ is the mesh current in the rth mesh; $r = 1, 2, 3, \ldots, n$

$\mathbf{Z}_{rr}$ is the total impedance common to mesh r (self-impedance)

$\mathbf{Z}_{rk}$ is the total impedance common to both meshes r and k (mutual impedance)

$\mathbf{E}_r$ is the sum of all voltage rises owing to generators in mesh r, taken positive in the same direction as $\mathbf{I}_r$

The mesh determinant is

$$\Delta = \begin{vmatrix} \mathbf{Z}_{11} & -\mathbf{Z}_{12} & \cdots & -\mathbf{Z}_{1n} \\ -\mathbf{Z}_{21} & \mathbf{Z}_{22} & \cdots & -\mathbf{Z}_{2n} \\ \cdots & \cdots & \cdots & \cdots \\ -\mathbf{Z}_{n1} & -\mathbf{Z}_{n2} & \cdots & \mathbf{Z}_{nn} \end{vmatrix}$$

and is symmetrical about the main diagonal of self-impedances, since $\mathbf{Z}_{rk} = \mathbf{Z}_{kr}$ for bilateral impedances. A typical mesh current, say $\mathbf{I}_k$, is obtained by inserting the column of generators, appearing on the right of the mesh equations, into the kth column of Δ and dividing by Δ.

$$\mathbf{I}_k = \frac{\Delta_{1k}\mathbf{E}_1}{\Delta} + \frac{\Delta_{2k}\mathbf{E}_2}{\Delta} + \cdots + \frac{\Delta_{nk}\mathbf{E}_n}{\Delta} \tag{2-16}$$

where Δ_{rk} is the cofactor of the rth row, kth column of Δ; $r = 1, 2, 3, \ldots, n$.

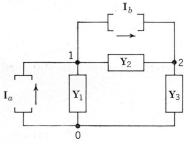

FIG. 2-9. Circuit with two independent node voltages.

2-10. Node Equations. An advocated method of selecting node voltages is to assign all nodes positive with respect to an arbitrary reference node. The potential of the reference node is inconsequential and may for convenience be taken as zero. An example of a circuit with two independent node voltages will be presented before summarizing the general formulation. In the circuit of Fig. 2-9, two node voltages, $\mathbf{V}_1$ and $\mathbf{V}_2$, are assigned as voltage drops from nodes 1 and 2 to reference node 0. It is easily verified that Kirchhoff's voltage law is satisfied by these node voltages around every mesh.   Kirchhoff's current law yields, for nodes 1 and 2, respectively,

$$\mathbf{V}_1\mathbf{Y}_1 + (\mathbf{V}_1 - \mathbf{V}_2)\mathbf{Y}_2 = \mathbf{I}_a - \mathbf{I}_b$$
$$\mathbf{V}_2\mathbf{Y}_3 + (\mathbf{V}_2 - \mathbf{V}_1)\mathbf{Y}_2 = \mathbf{I}_b$$

Group all terms containing the same node voltages to obtain the standard form of the node equations.

$$(\mathbf{Y}_1 + \mathbf{Y}_2)\mathbf{V}_1 - \mathbf{Y}_2\mathbf{V}_2 = \mathbf{I}_a - \mathbf{I}_b$$
$$-\mathbf{Y}_2\mathbf{V}_1 + (\mathbf{Y}_2 + \mathbf{Y}_3)\mathbf{V}_2 = \mathbf{I}_b$$

The node determinant is

$$\mathbf{D} = \begin{vmatrix} \mathbf{Y}_1 + \mathbf{Y}_2 & -\mathbf{Y}_2 \\ -\mathbf{Y}_2 & \mathbf{Y}_2 + \mathbf{Y}_3 \end{vmatrix} = \mathbf{Y}_1\mathbf{Y}_2 + \mathbf{Y}_1\mathbf{Y}_3 + \mathbf{Y}_2\mathbf{Y}_3$$

The node voltages are given by Cramer's rule.

$$\mathbf{V}_1 = \frac{\begin{vmatrix} \mathbf{I}_a - \mathbf{I}_b & -\mathbf{Y}_2 \\ \mathbf{I}_b & \mathbf{Y}_2 + \mathbf{Y}_3 \end{vmatrix}}{\mathbf{D}} \qquad \mathbf{V}_2 = \frac{\begin{vmatrix} \mathbf{Y}_1 + \mathbf{Y}_2 & \mathbf{I}_a - \mathbf{I}_b \\ -\mathbf{Y}_2 & \mathbf{I}_b \end{vmatrix}}{\mathbf{D}}$$

For a network with n independent node voltages, it is intrinsic to the nature of node voltages that Kirchhoff's voltage law is always automatically satisfied.   With all node voltages taken as voltage rises from the reference node, the following n current equations result when Kirchhoff's current law is applied and all terms containing the same node voltages are collected.

$$\mathbf{Y}_{11}\mathbf{V}_1 - \mathbf{Y}_{12}\mathbf{V}_2 - \cdots - \mathbf{Y}_{1n}\mathbf{V}_n = \mathbf{I}_1$$
$$-\mathbf{Y}_{21}\mathbf{V}_1 + \mathbf{Y}_{22}\mathbf{V}_2 - \cdots - \mathbf{Y}_{2n}\mathbf{V}_n = \mathbf{I}_2$$
$$\cdots \quad \cdots \quad \cdots \quad \cdots \quad \cdots$$
$$-\mathbf{Y}_{n1}\mathbf{V}_1 - \mathbf{Y}_{n2}\mathbf{V}_2 - \cdots + \mathbf{Y}_{nn}\mathbf{V}_n = \mathbf{I}_n$$

where $\mathbf{V}_r$ is the voltage drop from node r to the reference node; $r = 1, 2, 3, \ldots, n$

$\mathbf{Y}_{rr}$ is the total admittance attached to node r (self-admittance)

$\mathbf{Y}_{rk}$ is the total admittance between nodes r and k (mutual admittance)

$\mathbf{I}_r$ is the sum of all currents owing to generators attached to node r, taken positive in the direction toward node r

The node determinant is

$$\mathbf{D} = \begin{vmatrix} \mathbf{Y}_{11} & -\mathbf{Y}_{12} & \cdots & -\mathbf{Y}_{1n} \\ -\mathbf{Y}_{21} & \mathbf{Y}_{22} & \cdots & -\mathbf{Y}_{2n} \\ \cdots & \cdots & \cdots & \cdots \\ -\mathbf{Y}_{n1} & -\mathbf{Y}_{n2} & \cdots & \mathbf{Y}_{nn} \end{vmatrix}$$

and is symmetrical about the main diagonal of self-admittances, since $\mathbf{Y}_{rk} = \mathbf{Y}_{kr}$ for bilateral admittances. A typical node voltage, say $\mathbf{V}_k$, is obtained by inserting the column of generators, appearing on the right of the node equations, into the kth column of $\mathbf{D}$, and dividing by $\mathbf{D}$.

$$\mathbf{V}_k = \frac{\mathbf{D}_{1k}\mathbf{I}_1}{\mathbf{D}} + \frac{\mathbf{D}_{2k}\mathbf{I}_2}{\mathbf{D}} + \cdots + \frac{\mathbf{D}_{nk}\mathbf{I}_n}{\mathbf{D}} \qquad (2\text{-}17)$$

where $\mathbf{D}_{rk}$ is the cofactor of the rth row, kth column of $\mathbf{D}$; $r = 1, 2, 3, \ldots, n$.

Either mesh or node equations may be written for a given network, and both sets of equations lead to identical solutions for currents and voltages in every branch. Note that the mesh and node determinants are unequal, $\boldsymbol{\Delta} \neq \mathbf{D}$. The choice between the two methods is a matter of convenience. The method selected is often the one that requires fewer equations.

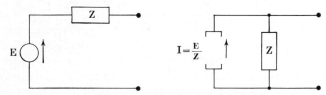

FIG. 2-10. Equivalent generators.

Since mesh equations contain constant-voltage generators and node equations contain constant-current generators, it is necessary to have a means for converting one type of generator to the other. This is accomplished by the equivalence indicated in Fig. 2-10. The output-terminal characteristics of a constant-voltage generator, $\mathbf{E}$, in series with an impedance $\mathbf{Z}$, are indistinguishable from those of a constant-current generator $\mathbf{I} = \mathbf{E}/\mathbf{Z}$ shunted by an impedance $\mathbf{Z}$. The no-load output voltage of each circuit is $\mathbf{E}$, the short-circuit output current is $\mathbf{E}/\mathbf{Z}$ in both cases, and the current drawn from the output terminals by an arbitrary impedance, $\mathbf{Z}_1$, connected across the output terminals is, in both cases, equal to $\mathbf{E}/(\mathbf{Z} + \mathbf{Z}_1)$.

2-11. Driving Point and Transfer Immittance. The ratios of cofactors to network determinants appearing in the mesh-current solutions, $\mathbf{I}_k$, and in the node-voltage solutions, $\mathbf{V}_k$, are important quantities that characterize the network. The reciprocals of these ratios are given special names. Each ratio has a physical network interpretation.

The *driving-point impedance* of mesh k is defined by

$$\mathbf{z}_{kk} = \frac{\boldsymbol{\Delta}}{\boldsymbol{\Delta}_{kk}}$$

If mesh k is the input or output mesh of the network, z_{kk} is often termed the input impedance, and is the driving-point impedance "looking into" the mesh in question.   It will be shown in Sec. 2-15, for the case of a network with an output mesh n, that z_{nn}, the input or driving-point impedance of mesh n, is equal to the Thévenin equivalent impedance. The physical interpretation of z_{kk} resides in Eq. (2-16).   Suppose all generators are zero, and then a *single* generator, E_k, is applied in series with an outer branch of mesh k.   (The stipulation of an outer branch is not restrictive since the network may be redrawn to accomplish this without altering it electrically.)   Then, from Eq. (2-16), z_{kk} is the ratio of the applied generator voltage, E_k, to the current, I_k, drawn from this generator, since all other terms in I_k are zero.

The *transfer impedance* between mesh r and mesh k is defined by

$$z_{kr} = \frac{\Delta}{\Delta_{rk}}$$

The physical significance of z_{kr} is also evident from Eq. (2-16).   Suppose all generators are zero and then a *single* generator, E_r, is inserted into an outer branch of mesh r.   Then z_{kr} is the ratio of the voltage E_r, applied in mesh r, to the current, I_k, that it produces in mesh k.

The transfer impedances z_{kr} and z_{rk} are equal because the mutual impedances Z_{kr} and Z_{rk} are equal for bilateral elements.   This may be demonstrated by interchanging rows and columns of the cofactor, in accordance with rules of manipulation of determinants.   For instance, in the case of $z_{12} = \Delta/\Delta_{21}$, the cofactor Δ_{21} is given by striking out the second row and first column of Δ.

$$\Delta_{21} = - \begin{vmatrix} -Z_{12} & -Z_{13} & \cdots & -Z_{1n} \\ -Z_{32} & Z_{33} & \cdots & -Z_{3n} \\ -Z_{42} & -Z_{43} & \cdots & -Z_{4n} \\ \cdots & \cdots & \cdots & \cdots \\ -Z_{n2} & -Z_{n3} & \cdots & Z_{nn} \end{vmatrix}$$

Replace each mutual impedance Z_{kr} by Z_{rk} and interchange corresponding rows and columns.   These maneuvers do not change the value of Δ_{21}, which then becomes

$$\Delta_{21} = - \begin{vmatrix} -Z_{21} & -Z_{23} & -Z_{24} & \cdots & -Z_{2n} \\ -Z_{31} & Z_{33} & -Z_{34} & \cdots & -Z_{3n} \\ \cdots & \cdots & \cdots & \cdots & \cdots \\ -Z_{n1} & -Z_{n3} & -Z_{n4} & \cdots & Z_{nn} \end{vmatrix}$$

This result is identically the same as Δ_{12}, as may be seen by striking the first row and second column of Δ.   Hence, it has been proved that

$\Delta_{21} = \Delta_{12}$, from which it follows that $z_{12} = z_{21}$. By extension, it may be seen that $z_{kr} = z_{rk}$, $r \neq k$.

Driving-point and transfer admittances are defined in similar fashion.

$$y_{kk} = \frac{D}{D_{kk}} \qquad y_{kr} = \frac{D}{D_{rk}}$$

For bilateral elements, $Y_{rk} = Y_{kr}$. Hence, it follows that $D_{rk} = D_{kr}$, from which $y_{kr} = y_{rk}$, $r \neq k$.

2-12. Equivalent Networks. A definition of equivalence of two networks that serves in both steady-state and transient cases, and is unrestrictive regarding the number of network terminals, follows:

Two networks are equivalent if a set of voltages (or currents) is applied to corresponding terminals of the two networks and the resulting currents (or voltages) at corresponding terminals of the two networks are identical.

Several important special cases may be deduced from this definition for passive, linear, bilateral networks operating in the steady sinusoidal state. For example, networks with only two terminals are equivalent if their input impedances at the two terminals are identical. Thus, a two-terminal network, no matter how complicated internally, may be represented by a single impedance at any given frequency.

An important class of networks is called three-terminal networks, or networks with two pairs of terminals (see Fig. 2-11). These networks

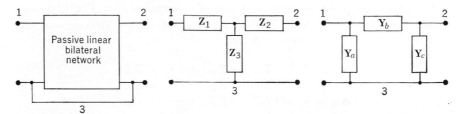

FIG. 2-11. Three-terminal networks.

have a pair of input and output terminals, but are three-terminal networks by virtue of the short circuit joining one of the input and output terminals. Application of the definition of equivalence reveals that, no matter how complicated the three-terminal network, it is characterized by only three independent complex quantities. These are the driving-point impedances at the input and output terminal pairs, and the two transfer impedances between input and output meshes, which are equal. This means that only three independent impedances are required to construct an equivalent network, and the two possible configurations are given in Fig. 2-11. These are the familiar T and Pi networks. It is only necessary that the driving-point and transfer impedances of the T and Pi networks be the same as those of the original network to guarantee equivalence in accordance with the definition.

As an application of the definition of equivalence to instantaneous quantities, consider the case of a three-terminal network containing mutual inductance, shown in Fig. 2-12. *Constant mutual inductance, M,* between two magnetically coupled circuits is defined as the ratio of volt-

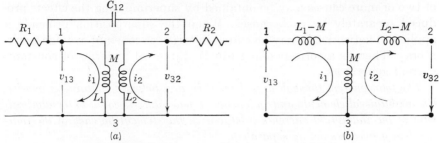

FIG. 2-12. Equivalent circuit for two coupled coils.

age induced in one circuit by the time derivative of the current in the other circuit.

$$e_1 = M_{12} \frac{di_2}{dt} \qquad e_2 = M_{21} \frac{di_1}{dt} \qquad M_{12} = M_{21} = M$$

The algebraic sign of M may be positive or negative, depending upon the directions of magnetic flux and the relative physical orientation of the two coils.

Suppose instantaneous currents, i_1 and i_2, are applied to the input and output terminals as indicated in Fig. 2-12a. The voltages appearing across L_1 and L_2 are given by the instantaneous mesh equations

$$L_1 \frac{di_1}{dt} - M \frac{di_2}{dt} = v_{13}$$

$$-M \frac{di_1}{dt} + L_2 \frac{di_2}{dt} = v_{32}$$

Add and subtract $M \, di_1/dt$ in the first equation, $M \, di_2/dt$ in the second equation, and regroup terms.

$$(L_1 - M) \frac{di_1}{dt} + M \frac{d}{dt} (i_1 - i_2) = v_{13}$$

$$M \frac{d}{dt} (i_2 - i_1) + (L_2 - M) \frac{di_2}{dt} = v_{32}$$

But these are the mesh equations of the circuit in Fig. 2-12b, in which there is no mutual inductance among the three self-inductances. Therefore, if the same currents, i_1 and i_2, are applied to the T network of

Fig. 2-12b, precisely the same instantaneous voltages appear across the input and output terminals of the T network as appeared across the original network.   Therefore, the two networks are equivalent.

2-13. Superposition Theorem.   The principle of superposition is applicable to cause and effect relationships in any *linear* system.   In essence, the principle states that the effect produced by a given cause is independent of all other causes and effects.   In consequence, the total effect of two or more causes may be obtained by superimposing the effects produced separately by each cause.   When the superposition principle is applied to networks, it may be stated in terms of constant-voltage generators.   There is a corresponding (dual) statement in terms of constant-current generators.

The total current through any element in any network containing passive, linear, bilateral elements and independent generators is equal to the algebraic sum of the individual currents produced in the element by each of the independent generators acting separately.

The proof of this theorem has, in effect, already been exposed for the steady sinusoidal state.   Examine the mesh current, I_k, in Eq. (2-16).

$$I_k = \frac{\Delta_{1k}E_1}{\Delta} + \frac{\Delta_{2k}E_2}{\Delta} + \cdots + \frac{\Delta_{nk}E_n}{\Delta}$$

The mesh determinant and all cofactors are constants.   Each voltage represents the sum of voltage rises owing to generators in a given mesh. For a typical mesh r, for example,

$$E_r = E_a + E_b + E_c + \cdots$$

where each term of E_r is an individual generator voltage taken positive in the same direction as I_r.   The form of I_k shows that if every generator except one is zero, the component of I_k produced in mesh k by the remaining generator is a constant times that generator voltage.   This is true whether the generator is in an outer mesh or not.   Hence, the theorem is proved.

2-14. Reciprocity Theorem.   The reciprocity theorem pertains to an interchange of the sites of cause and effect.   In certain restricted systems, the cause and effect relationship is unaffected by such an interchange.   For electric networks, the theorem may be stated in terms of a constant-voltage generator.   There is a corresponding (dual) statement in terms of a constant-current generator.

If a constant-voltage generator in any branch, r, of a passive, linear, bilateral network produces a certain current in any other branch, k, of the network, then this generator, when inserted in branch k of the network, will produce the same current in branch r.

A proof of this theorem for the steady sinusoidal state may be presented compactly in terms of transfer impedances, defined in Sec. 2-11. To simplify the proof with no loss in generality, redraw the network as required, so that the two branches under consideration are outer branches, as in Fig. 2-13a. When E_r is the sole generator applied in series with an outer branch of the rth mesh of an n-mesh network, the current in any other branch, k, is given from Eq. (2-16) by

$$I_k = \frac{\Delta_{rk} E_r}{\Delta} = \frac{E_r}{z_{kr}}$$

When E_r is the sole generator applied in series with an outer branch of the kth mesh, in which the current *was* I_k, it follows that the current in mesh r is given by

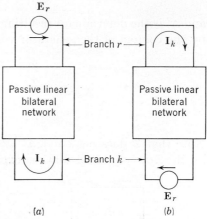

FIG. 2-13. Illustrating the reciprocity theorem.

$$I_r = \frac{\Delta_{kr} E_r}{\Delta} = \frac{E_r}{z_{rk}}$$

Evidently, I_k and I_r are equal, since the transfer impedances z_{kr} and z_{rk} are equal. This proves the theorem.

2-15. Thévenin's Theorem. Thévenin's theorem is a powerful tool for facilitating network calculations and often gives considerable insight into the pertinent factors influencing network behavior. A statement of the theorem follows. There is a corresponding (dual) statement of the theorem in terms of an equivalent current generator, called Norton's theorem.

At any given frequency, any network containing passive, linear, bilateral impedances and constant generators can, when viewed from any two terminals, be replaced by a generator voltage, E_0, in series with an impedance, Z_i, where E_0 is the open-circuit voltage across the two terminals and Z_i is the input impedance at the two terminals.

A proof of this theorem is presented here in terms of mesh determinants. For purposes of the proof, connect an arbitrary impedance, Z, to the two terminals 1-2 of the network to which the theorem is to be applied (see Fig. 2-14a), and let the mesh so formed be designated as the nth mesh of the n-mesh network. The mesh current I_n, which is the current through Z, is given by $I_n = \Delta'/\Delta_z$, where Δ_z is the mesh determinant of the network including the auxiliary element Z,

$$\Delta_z = \begin{vmatrix} Z_{11} & -Z_{12} & \cdots & -Z_{1n} \\ -Z_{21} & Z_{22} & \cdots & -Z_{2n} \\ \cdots & \cdots & \cdots & \cdots \\ -Z_{n1} & -Z_{n2} & \cdots & Z_{nn} + Z \end{vmatrix}$$

and Δ' is the determinant resulting when the nth column of Δ_z is replaced by the column of the generator voltages.

$$\Delta' = \begin{vmatrix} Z_{11} & -Z_{12} & \cdots & E_1 \\ -Z_{21} & Z_{22} & \cdots & E_2 \\ \cdots & \cdots & \cdots & \cdots \\ -Z_{n1} & -Z_{n2} & \cdots & E_n \end{vmatrix}$$

Note that Z does not enter Δ' at all. Moreover, when Δ_z is expanded by the nth column, it may be expressed as $\Delta_z = \Delta + Z\Delta_{nn}$, where Δ is

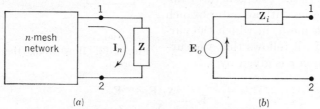

FIG. 2-14. Illustrating Thévenin's theorem.

the mesh determinant of the network with $Z = 0$, and Δ_{nn} is the cofactor of the nth row, nth column of Δ or Δ_z. Neither Δ nor Δ_{nn} contains Z.

The voltage drop from terminal 1 to terminal 2 is given by $I_n Z$. This becomes the open-circuit voltage when Z is allowed to approach infinity. Hence,

$$E_0 = \lim_{Z \to \infty} I_n Z = \lim_{Z \to \infty} \frac{\Delta' Z}{\Delta + Z\Delta_{nn}} = \frac{\Delta'}{\Delta_{nn}}$$

This result enables I_n to be expressed in terms of E_0 as follows

$$I_n = \frac{\Delta'}{\Delta_z} = \frac{E_0 \Delta_{nn}}{\Delta + Z\Delta_{nn}} = \frac{E_0}{\Delta/\Delta_{nn} + Z}$$

But Δ/Δ_{nn} is the input impedance to mesh n, designated by Z_i in the statement of the theorem. It is the impedance looking into terminals 1-2 with all network generators replaced by their internal impedances and, of course, with Z removed. Therefore,

$$I_n = \frac{E_0}{Z_i + Z} \tag{2-18}$$

This proves the theorem.

A circuit representation of Eq. (2-18) is given in Fig. 2-14b, for the

case of $\mathbf{Z} \to \infty$. Note that the short-circuit current in both the actual
and equivalent networks, when terminals 1-2 are joined, is given by
$\mathbf{I}_{sc} = \mathbf{E}_0 / \mathbf{Z}_i$. Hence, there are several ways in which the equivalent circuit may be deduced by analysis of a given network. One method, of
course, is to determine $\mathbf{E}_0$ and $\mathbf{Z}_i$. Another is to calculate $\mathbf{I}_{sc}$ and either
$\mathbf{Z}_i$ or $\mathbf{E}_0$, from which the equivalent circuit may be deduced.

It should be emphasized that the Thévenin equivalent circuit is valid
only in so far as the terminals 1-2 and any external circuit are concerned.
It generally does not give information concerning conditions within the
original network.

2-16. Compensation Theorem. The compensation theorem enables
direct analysis of changes in network currents or voltages resulting from
a change in an impedance in a network. It is especially useful in bridge-
circuit analysis, and many examples are presented in later chapters. A
statement of the theorem follows:

*In a network containing passive, linear, bilateral impedances and con-
stant generators, if any impedance carrying a current* $\mathbf{I}$ *is changed by an
amount* $\mathbf{Z}$, *the changes in currents throughout the network are equal to those
produced by a generator* $\mathbf{IZ}$ *introduced in opposition to* $\mathbf{I}$ *in the branch
containing* $\mathbf{Z}$.

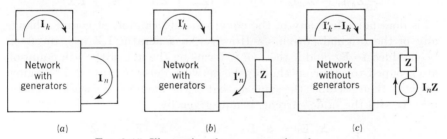

FIG. 2-15. Illustrating the compensation theorem.

A proof of this theorem is presented below in terms of mesh equations.
To simplify the proof with no loss in generality, rearrange the network
so that the impedance to be altered is in an outer branch, as in Fig. 2-15.
Let this outer branch be the nth mesh of an n-mesh network. The mesh
equations, before the impedance is changed, are given by Eq. (2-15).
The impedance to be changed is contained in $\mathbf{Z}_{nn}$, but does not appear
elsewhere in the set of n-mesh equations. The current in a typical mesh
is given by Eq. (2-16). The current $\mathbf{I}_k$ need not traverse an outer branch,
but it is so illustrated for definiteness in Fig. 2-15.

Now let $\mathbf{Z}_{nn}$ change to $\mathbf{Z}_{nn} + \mathbf{Z}$, owing to a change $\mathbf{Z}$ in an outer branch.
(The real part of $\mathbf{Z}$ may be positive or negative.) All the currents in all
the meshes will generally undergo a change as a result. Using primes to

designate the changed currents, the mesh equations become

$$
\begin{aligned}
\mathbf{Z}_{11}\mathbf{I}_1' - \mathbf{Z}_{12}\mathbf{I}_2' - \cdots - \quad \mathbf{Z}_{1n}\mathbf{I}_n' \quad &= \mathbf{E}_1 \\
-\mathbf{Z}_{21}\mathbf{I}_1' + \mathbf{Z}_{22}\mathbf{I}_2' - \cdots - \quad \mathbf{Z}_{2n}\mathbf{I}_n' \quad &= \mathbf{E}_2 \\
\cdots \quad \cdots \quad \cdots \quad \cdots \quad &\cdots \\
-\mathbf{Z}_{n1}\mathbf{I}_1' - \mathbf{Z}_{n2}\mathbf{I}_2' - \cdots + (\mathbf{Z}_{nn} + \mathbf{Z})\mathbf{I}_n' &= \mathbf{E}_n
\end{aligned}
$$

The only place $\mathbf{Z}$ appears is in the nth row, nth column. The current in the typical kth mesh is now given by

$$
\mathbf{I}_k' = \frac{\boldsymbol{\Delta}_{1k}'\mathbf{E}_1}{\boldsymbol{\Delta}'} + \frac{\boldsymbol{\Delta}_{2k}'\mathbf{E}_2}{\boldsymbol{\Delta}'} + \cdots + \frac{\boldsymbol{\Delta}_{nk}\mathbf{E}_n}{\boldsymbol{\Delta}'} \tag{2-19}
$$

where the modified mesh determinant is $\boldsymbol{\Delta}' = \boldsymbol{\Delta} + \mathbf{Z}\boldsymbol{\Delta}_{nn}$. Note that $\boldsymbol{\Delta}_{nk}$ is unaffected by the change.

Now comes the trick. Add the term $\mathbf{I}_n\mathbf{Z}$ to both sides of the nth mesh equation of the original network. The mesh equations are then, from Eq. (2-15),

$$
\begin{aligned}
\mathbf{Z}_{11}\mathbf{I}_1 - \mathbf{Z}_{12}\mathbf{I}_2 - \cdots - \quad \mathbf{Z}_{1n}\mathbf{I}_n \quad &= \quad \mathbf{E}_1 \\
-\mathbf{Z}_{21}\mathbf{I}_1 + \mathbf{Z}_{22}\mathbf{I}_2 - \cdots - \quad \mathbf{Z}_{2n}\mathbf{I}_n \quad &= \quad \mathbf{E}_2 \\
\cdots \quad \cdots \quad \cdots \quad \cdots \quad &\cdots \\
-\mathbf{Z}_{n1}\mathbf{I}_1 - \mathbf{Z}_{n2}\mathbf{I}_2 - \cdots + (\mathbf{Z}_{nn} + \mathbf{Z})\mathbf{I}_n &= \mathbf{E}_n + \mathbf{I}_n\mathbf{Z}
\end{aligned}
$$

This does not affect any of the equations and cannot, of course, change any of the original currents. However, a generator $\mathbf{I}_n\mathbf{Z}$ has, in effect, been added to $\mathbf{E}_n$, and if the two $\mathbf{I}_n$ terms on the left of the nth equation are grouped together, as shown, the network determinant of the original network then becomes the same as that of the modified network. Therefore, $\mathbf{I}_k$, still the same current, is now given by

$$
\mathbf{I}_k = \frac{\boldsymbol{\Delta}_{1k}'\mathbf{E}_1}{\boldsymbol{\Delta}'} + \frac{\boldsymbol{\Delta}_{2k}'\mathbf{E}_2}{\boldsymbol{\Delta}'} + \cdots + \frac{\boldsymbol{\Delta}_{nk}(\mathbf{E}_n + \mathbf{I}_n\mathbf{Z})}{\boldsymbol{\Delta}'}
$$

Comparing with Eq. (2-19), the sum of the first n terms of $\mathbf{I}_k$ is $\mathbf{I}_k'$. Therefore,

$$
\mathbf{I}_k' - \mathbf{I}_k = -\mathbf{I}_n\mathbf{Z}\frac{\boldsymbol{\Delta}_{nk}}{\boldsymbol{\Delta}'} \tag{2-20}
$$

This proves the theorem. The circuit interpretation of Eq. (2-20), shown in Fig. 2-15c, is that a sole generator $\mathbf{I}_n\mathbf{Z}$, in series with mesh n of the *modified* network, acting in opposition to the original direction of $\mathbf{I}_n$, produces a current $\mathbf{I}_k' - \mathbf{I}_k$ in an arbitrary mesh, k. But this is the change in current produced by the change $\mathbf{Z}$ in the original network.

2-17. Approximate Form of Compensation Theorem. The compensation theorem is often most useful when applied in its approximate form, as amply shown by examples later in this text. In the approximate form, the same compensation generator, $\mathbf{IZ}$, is used, but the change in impedance, $\mathbf{Z}$, is omitted from the compensation circuit of Fig. 2-15c. The omission of $\mathbf{Z}$ leads to simplification because the determinant and all the cofactors of the original network are then the same as those of the network to which $\mathbf{IZ}$ is applied. Moreover, in bridge circuits, the unbalance produced by $\mathbf{Z}$ is restored when $\mathbf{Z}$ is omitted, and this leads to considerable simplification of calculations.

The important factor in using the approximate form of the theorem is a knowledge of the error introduced by the approximation. An expression for the error is readily developed from the foregoing analysis of the exact theorem. Let $\mathbf{I}_k'' - \mathbf{I}_k$ be the approximate value of the current change in the kth mesh, resulting from application of a generator $-\mathbf{I}_n\mathbf{Z}$ in the nth mesh with $\mathbf{Z}$ omitted. Because $\mathbf{Z}_{nn}$ is now unaffected, it follows from Eq. (2-20) that

$$\mathbf{I}_k'' - \mathbf{I}_k = -\mathbf{I}_n\mathbf{Z}\frac{\boldsymbol{\Delta}_{nk}}{\boldsymbol{\Delta}} \tag{2-21}$$

Define the fractional error in the two results as

$$\boldsymbol{\delta} = \frac{(\mathbf{I}_k'' - \mathbf{I}_k) - (\mathbf{I}_k' - \mathbf{I}_k)}{\mathbf{I}_k' - \mathbf{I}_k}$$

This is the approximate change in current minus the exact change, expressed as a fraction of the exact change. Substitute from Eqs. (2-20) and (2-21). Then

$$\boldsymbol{\delta} = \frac{-\mathbf{I}_n\mathbf{Z}\boldsymbol{\Delta}_{nk}/\boldsymbol{\Delta} + \mathbf{I}_n\mathbf{Z}\boldsymbol{\Delta}_{nk}/\boldsymbol{\Delta}'}{-\mathbf{I}_n\mathbf{Z}\boldsymbol{\Delta}_{nk}/\boldsymbol{\Delta}'} = \frac{\boldsymbol{\Delta}'}{\boldsymbol{\Delta}} - 1$$

But $\boldsymbol{\Delta}' = \boldsymbol{\Delta} + \mathbf{Z}\boldsymbol{\Delta}_{nn}$. Therefore, the fractional error is

$$\boldsymbol{\delta} = \frac{\boldsymbol{\Delta} + \mathbf{Z}\boldsymbol{\Delta}_{nn}}{\boldsymbol{\Delta}} - 1 = \mathbf{Z}\frac{\boldsymbol{\Delta}_{nn}}{\boldsymbol{\Delta}} = \frac{\mathbf{Z}}{\mathbf{z}_{nn}}$$

The ratio $\boldsymbol{\Delta}/\boldsymbol{\Delta}_{nn}$ is the input impedance to the nth mesh, $\mathbf{z}_{nn}$. Thus, the fractional error entailed in the use of the approximate form of the compensation theorem is equal to the ratio of the change in impedance, $\mathbf{Z}$, to the input impedance of the mesh in which the change is made.

In resistive networks, the input resistance r_{nn} of mesh n is always greater than any resistance R_{no} in a *separate* branch that is a part of the nth mesh. Therefore, if the branch resistance, R_{no}, is changed by an amount $\pm R$, the magnitude of the fractional error in the use of the approximate theorem will be less than R/R_{no}.

$$|\boldsymbol{\delta}| = \frac{R}{r_{nn}} < \frac{R}{R_{no}}$$

Thus, if the approximate current change in some branch of a resistive network is calculated to be 1.0 ma as a result of a 2 per cent change in a resistance, the 1 ma result is in error by less than 20 μa.

PROBLEMS

2-1 (§1). Find the average and rms values of the following functions between the two stated values of the variable:

    a. $f(x) = a + bx^2$ $x_1 = 1, x_2 = 3$

    b. $g(t) = \sin kt$ $t_1 = \pi/2k, t_2 = \pi/k$

    c. $h(y) = \ln ay$ $y_1 = 1/a, y_2 = 3/a$

2-2 (§4). Prove by direct substitution that Eq. (2-4) satisfies the differential equation for the circuit of Fig. 2-3.

2-3 (§5). In the circuit of Fig. 2-3, E is replaced by a generator $E \sin (\omega t + \phi)$. Determine an expression for the steady-state current by use of the $\epsilon^{j\omega t}$ method.

2-4 (§5). Determine the steady-state solution of the following differential equation by the $\epsilon^{j\omega t}$ method.

$$J \frac{d^2y}{dt^2} + D \frac{dy}{dt} + Sy = A \sin \omega t$$

where J, D, S, A, and ω are constants.

2-5 (§6). Prove that Kirchhoff's laws hold for complex voltages and currents [see Eq. (2-8)].

2-6 (§6). Prove Eq. (2-9).

2-7 (§6). Prove Eq. (2-10).

2-8 (§8). If **V** and **I** are the complex voltage and current associated with a passive impedance, prove that the average power dissipated in the impedance is given by

$$P_{\text{av}} = \frac{1}{4} (\mathbf{VI}^* + \mathbf{V}^*\mathbf{I}).$$

2-9 (§10). In the circuit of Fig. 2-9, convert the current generators to voltage generators and determine the current through $\mathbf{Y}_3$ by means of mesh analysis. Prove that the result agrees with that obtained by node analysis.

2-10 (§10). In the circuit of Fig. 2-8, assign the lower terminal of $\mathbf{Z}_2$ as the reference node, convert the voltage generators to current generators, and determine an expression for the node voltage at the junction of $\mathbf{Z}_1$ and $\mathbf{Z}_3$. Prove that the result agrees with that obtained by mesh analysis.

2-11 (§11). In the circuit of Fig. 2-8, determine expressions for (*a*) the driving-point impedance of mesh 1, (*b*) the driving-point impedance of mesh 2, (*c*) the transfer impedance from mesh 1 to mesh 2, and vice versa.

2-12 (§12). What relationships must be satisfied among the three impedances of the T network and the three admittances of the Pi network in Fig. 2-11, such that the two networks are equivalent?

2-13 (§12). A sinusoidal generator (of zero internal impedance) represented by the complex number **E** is connected between the left terminal of R_1 and node 3 in the circuit of Fig. 12-12. A capacitor C is connected from the right terminal of R_2 to node 3. For $L_1 = L_2 = L$ and $\omega = 1/2(L - M)C_{12}$, determine an expression for the complex current through C.

2-14 (§12). In Fig. 2-11, let the input mesh of the passive, linear, bilateral network be signified as mesh 1, and the output mesh as mesh n. Prove that the impedance $\mathbf{Z}_3$ of the equivalent T network is given by

$$\mathbf{Z}_3 = \frac{\Delta \, \Delta_{1n}}{\Delta_{11} \Delta_{nn} - \Delta_{1n}{}^2}$$

where Δ is the mesh determinant and Δ_{11}, Δ_{1n}, and Δ_{nn} are cofactors of the general network.

2-15 (§13). Determine an expression for the current I_2 in the circuit of Fig. 2-8 by application of the superposition theorem; that is, find the current in Z_3 attributable to E_a with $E_b = 0$, and add to this current that attributable to E_b with $E_a = 0$.

2-16 (§14). A sinusoidal generator represented by the complex number E is applied between terminals 1-3 of the Pi network of Fig. 2-11. The generator has an internal impedance Z. A load impedance, Z_L, is connected between terminals 2-3. (a) Determine an expression for the current through Z_L. (b) Prove that the same current is produced in Z when E is connected in series with Z_L.

2-17 (§17). The T network of Fig. 2-11 is purely resistive with $Z_1 = 2$ ohms, $Z_2 = 4$ ohms, and $Z_3 = 6$ ohms. A 6-volt battery with a 1-ohm internal resistance is connected across terminals 1-3, and a 2-ohm resistive load is connected across terminals 2-3. (a) Use the compensation theorem to compute the change in battery current that results from a 1-ohm increase in the load resistance. (b) Since the input impedance at the location of the 1-ohm change is 8 ohms, the approximate compensation theorem should give a result that is high by one-eighth times the answer in part (a). Show that this is so by direct computation.

CHAPTER 3

GALVANOMETERS, SHUNTS, AND D-C METERS

The d'Arsonval meter movement is perhaps the most commonly encountered of all electrical indicating devices. Its operation is based on the interaction between an electric current and a magnetic field. This movement constitutes the heart of many different kinds of deflection instruments. Because of its importance, basic principles of its operation are presented in detail. The static deflection is emphasized in this chapter, and principles of its dynamic behavior are explored in the following chapter.

GALVANOMETERS

A galvanometer is an electromechanical device in which a useful torque is produced as a result of interaction between an electric current, passed through the coil of the instrument, and a steady magnetic field existing in the environment of the coil. There are many different types of galvanometers, such as the tangent galvanometer, the Helmholtz galvanometer, the string galvanometer, the moving-magnet galvanometer, and the moving-coil galvanometer. The d'Arsonval galvanometer is a permanent-magnet moving-coil type, also referred to as a meter movement (especially when portable). It is widely used to provide a direct measure of electric current. D'Arsonval movements are used in portable d-c ammeters and voltmeters as well as in sensitive wall galvanometers. They are also found in many a-c instruments as the final device that produces an observable reading, the alternating current being converted to direct current before application to the movement.

3-1. Advantages of d'Arsonval Movement. It is no accident that this type of indicating instrument has come into such widespread use. Its many advantages make it useful in both portable applications and delicate permanent installations, with appropriate design. Some of the salient advantages of this movement follow: It may be designed to have very low power consumption and yet it inherently possesses a high ratio of torque to weight. A long scale with uniformly spaced scale divisions (uniform scale) may be conveniently achieved. The operation of the instrument is relatively free from effects of stray magnetic fields that

44

often exist in the environment in which such meters may be used. A feature enabling versatility is that resistive shunts may be readily designed and incorporated to give a wide range of sensitivity. Moreover, the movement has desirable dynamic characteristics for many applications, important among which are rapid speed of response to a given change in current and capability of being damped in critical fashion so that objectionable overshoots and undue sluggishness of response may be avoided. The high attainable sensitivity, especially in nonportable version, enables quick measurement of minute currents. This is superior to time-con-

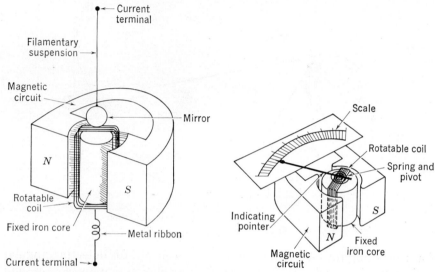

FIG. 3-1. Components of d'Arsonval mirror galvanometer.

FIG. 3-2. Components of d'Arsonval meter movement.

suming chemical deposition methods that may also be employed to measure such small effects. With some sacrifice in sensitivity, it is possible to design very sturdy portable instruments. All these advantages, coupled with low cost, suggest why it is the movement of choice in many applications.

This rather imposing list of advantages should provide an incentive for careful study of the principles of operation. A sound basis may thereby be provided for a good understanding of the many applications of d'Arsonval movements.

3-2. Description of Movement. Two different versions of the d'Arsonval instrument are shown in Figs. 3-1 and 3-2. The mirror galvanometer, usually mounted rigidly on a vibration-free base, is used when high sensitivity combined with a long scale is needed. It is essentially a laboratory instrument, being rather delicate and requiring many precautions in its adjustment and use. In contrast, the portable version, usually housed inside a small case or box, is quite rugged. Ordinarily it may take considerable abuse without injury, but certain reasonable precautions are of course desirable.

Although the two movements pictured are very different in detail, they are basically the same in principle and have the following elements in common: (1) a rotatable coil, (2) a steady magnetic field, (3) provision

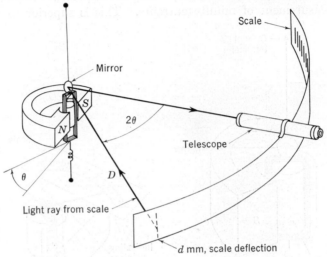

Fig. 3-3. Mirror galvanometer optical system.

for a restoring torque on the coil, and (4) a means for detecting angular deflection of the coil. In both cases the movements employ close-wound coils of multiple turns, and a permanent magnet provides the steady magnetic field, with a core inside the coil (but not attached to it physically) to give a concentrated field of suitable characteristics.

In the case of the mirror galvanometer, the moving coil may hang freely from a fine-wire suspension so that it is capable of rotation about its axis, as shown in Fig. 3-1. (In some designs a double taut suspension is used.) The filamentary suspension also provides a restoring torque, or back twist, to counteract rotation of the coil produced when current is passed through it. A metal ribbon is connected to the bottom of the coil which, to a very slight extent, provides a small portion of the restoring torque. The filamentary suspension and the ribbon are also used as leads via which current is passed through the coil. The angular location of the coil may be determined by optical means as illustrated in Fig. 3-3. A small mirror mounted rigidly to the coil forms a portion of the optical system that also includes a telescope and scale. The scale receives general illumination, and rays of light pass from the scale to the mirror

Fig. 3-4. Mirror galvanometer.   (*Courtesy of Leeds and Northrup Company.*)

and thence into the telescope, in which the observer sees the scale image. Another common optical arrangement consists of a light source whose rays are focused, by means of lenses, onto the mirror and thence to a ground-glass scale.

In the portable version of this galvanometer, the movable coil is pivoted between two low-friction jewel bearings and is free to rotate.   The restoring torque is provided by spiral springs attached to each end of the coil and anchored to the frame of the instrument. Current is delivered to the coil through the restoring springs, and both ends of the circuit are brought out to a pair of terminals. The angular rotation of the coil is indicated directly on a scale by a counterbalanced indicating pointer, rigidly attached to the coil.

While the two movements described are representative, there are many variations in construction details and materials, depending upon the

Fig. 3-5. Pivoted-coil meter movement. (*Courtesy of Weston Electrical Instrument Corporation.*)

application for which the instrument is designed. Photographs of typical instruments are shown in Figs. 3-4 and 3-5. The practical design considerations, many of which are empirical, form the basis of a specialized instrument art. Galvanometers with highly satisfactory performance have been built, and progress continues in response to more exacting demands. It is possible to investigate in some detail the principles on which galvanometer operation is based, making simplifying assumptions as necessary. This leads to a comprehension of its operation and limitations and to an appreciation of several factors influencing its design.

3-3. Basic Force Law. The law of force on an electric charge is perhaps one of the most significant equations in electrical engineering. There are two different origins of electrical forces exerted on an electric charge. These are called the "electrostatic" force and the "magnetic" force. Two vector fields, postulated in electrical theory to be responsible for these forces, are appropriately called the force fields.   They are the electric field intensity, **ε**, and the magnetic flux density, **B**.   In the mks system of units, **ε** has the dimensions volts per meter, and **B** has the dimensions webers per square meter.   The instantaneous force on a point charge q coulombs moving with velocity **v** meters per sec is related to the two fields by the law

$$\mathbf{f} = q(\boldsymbol{\varepsilon} + \mathbf{v} \times \mathbf{B}) \qquad \text{newtons} \qquad (3\text{-}1)$$

This force equation is frequently taken as the defining equation for the two fields in modern approaches to field theory.   If the electric field is negligible, or, more precisely, if $q\boldsymbol{\varepsilon}$ is negligible compared with the cross product $q(\mathbf{v} \times \mathbf{B})$, then a special case of Eq. (3-1) pertains.

$$\mathbf{f} = q(\mathbf{v} \times \mathbf{B}) \qquad\qquad \boldsymbol{\varepsilon} = 0 \qquad (3\text{-}2)$$

For the particular case of electric charges moving within a conductor, as in the galvanometer coil, the force law may be formulated in terms of conduction current rather than charge.   In Fig. 3-6 an infinitesimal vector length $d\mathbf{s}$ of a current-carrying conductor is shown at an angle α with respect to a magnetic field **B**.   The charges in the conductor actually move in very chaotic fashion, but it is usual in ordinary circuits to consider average effects.   A bundle of charge, dq, contained in the length $d\mathbf{s}$ of the thin conductor is thought of as traversing the wire with a certain

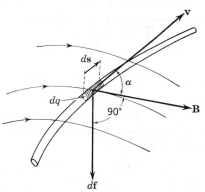

FIG. 3-6. Illustrating force on a current element.

instantaneous velocity $\mathbf{v} = d\mathbf{s}/dt$.   The electric conduction current is, by definition, $i = dq/dt$, where dq is the charge passing a given cross section of the wire in a time dt.   Multiplication of both sides of this defining equation for current by $d\mathbf{s}$ results in

$$i\, d\mathbf{s} = \frac{dq}{dt}\, d\mathbf{s} = dq\, \frac{d\mathbf{s}}{dt} = dq\, \mathbf{v} \qquad (3\text{-}3)$$

The instantaneous force, $d\mathbf{f}$, on this infinitesimal element, assuming $\boldsymbol{\varepsilon} = 0$, is given by Eq. (3-2), where **B** is the magnetic flux density in which dq finds itself.   Combining Eqs. (3-2) and (3-3), there results

$$d\mathbf{f} = i\, d\mathbf{s} \times \mathbf{B} \qquad \text{newtons} \qquad \boldsymbol{\varepsilon} = 0 \qquad (3\text{-}4)$$

This gives the instantaneous vector force, $d\mathbf{f}$, on an infinitesimal current element $i\, d\mathbf{s}$ located in a magnetic field, **B**.   The magnitude of this force is

$iB \sin \alpha \, ds$, its direction is along a line perpendicular to the plane containing ds and **B**, and its sense is given by the direction of advance of a right-hand screw when rotated such that ds swings toward **B** through the

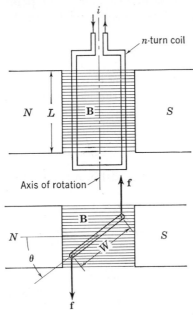

least angle between ds and **B**. The magnitude, direction, and sense are all contained in the compact vector cross-product notation of Eq. (3-4).

3-4. Force on Coil in Uniform Field. An illustration of coil-force calculations for a simple galvanometer configuration may be developed with reference to Fig. 3-7. An n-turn rectangular coil of width W is shown in a uniform **B** field, produced between rectangular pole pieces of a permanent magnet. The precise meaning of a "uniform" field is one that has the same magnitude and direction at every point within the volume of interest.

For an elementary analysis it is necessary to idealize the physical system. Assume that the coil winding consists of such thin wire that the coil cross section is very small (more precisely, the width of the bundle of n

FIG. 3-7. Illustrating force on galvanometer coil.

turns must be negligible compared with W). Furthermore, neglect fringing of the **B** field; that is, assume that the field is confined entirely to the rectangular volume of cross section equal to that of the pole pieces. The coil, carrying a current i, is assumed to have only one degree of freedom, rotation about an axis in the plane of the coil a distance $W/2$ from each of the two coil sides.

The total force on one side of the coil may be determined by application of the basic force law, given in convenient form by Eq. (3-4). Consider an infinitesimal current element $i \, d$s of one of the n turns of the left side of the coil as shown in Fig. 3-8. The infinitesimal vector force on this element is given by $d\mathbf{f}_1 = i \, d$s $\times$ **B**. The direction of $d\mathbf{f}_1$ is mutually perpendicular to ds and **B**, and the sense is given by the right-hand screw rule, as shown pictorially in Fig. 3-8. Since the angle α between ds and **B** is 90° *for any angle of twist*, θ (see Fig. 3-7), the magnitude of this force is $df_1 = iB \, ds$.

To obtain the force on one turn of one coil side, it is necessary to add vectorially all of the infinitesimal forces on each element of which the side is comprised. In many instances this vector integration poses a

formidable problem, but in this case the integration is very simple.   The
formal integral may be set up by defining an s axis along the left coil side,
directed from the top toward the bot-
tom of the coil.   Taking $s = 0$ at the
top edge of the rectangular volume
to which **B** is confined, the force on
one turn of the left coil side is given
by

$$\mathbf{f}_1 = \int_{s=0}^{s=L} d\mathbf{f}_1 = \int_0^L i \, d\mathbf{s} \times \mathbf{B} \quad (3\text{-}5)$$

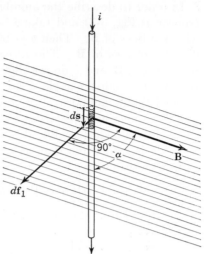

where L is the length of the rectangular volume containing **B**.   For s less
than zero or greater than L, **B** is zero
and hence $d\mathbf{f}_1$ is zero, even though the
coil itself may be longer than L.
Hence, the limits of integration indicated will give the correct result,
within the assumption made concern-
ing no fringing.   Since every $d\mathbf{f}_1$ has
the same magnitude and direction

Fig. 3-8. Force on one element of galvanometer coil.

for every element, α being 90° and i and **B** being fixed, the force $\mathbf{f}_1$
has the same direction as $d\mathbf{f}_1$ and its magnitude is given by the scalar
integral

$$f_1 = \int_0^L iB \, ds = iB \int_0^L ds = BiL \quad (3\text{-}6)$$

This result is a familiar formula for the force on a straight conductor that
is perpendicular to a uniform **B** field.   The restrictions on this result, and
the way in which it evolves from the basic force law, are conceptually
more important that the BiL formula itself.   It is for this reason that it
has been developed from first principles.   The highly specialized nature
of Eq. (3-6) is apparent from the successive restrictions imposed in the
course of developing it.

The same result for $\mathbf{f}_1$ will hold for each of the n-current filaments of
the left coil side.   Therefore, the magnitude of the total force on the left
side of the n-turn coil is

$$f = nf_1 = nBiL \quad (3\text{-}7)$$

and its direction is mutually perpendicular to **B** and to the coil side, as
shown in Fig. 3-7.

3-5. Torque on Coil in Uniform Field.   A similar analysis of the right
side of the n-turn coil leads to the same magnitude of force, but the sense
of **f** is reversed because i is reversed relative to **B**.   Thus, each coil side
experiences the same total force $f = nBiL$, but the net force acting on

the n-turn coil is zero. Hence, there will be no translatory motion.
However, the pair of forces form a *couple* to produce rotation.

In order to describe the angular location of the coil, define an angle θ
(shown in Fig. 3-7) and take $\theta = 0$ when the plane of the coil coincides
with the lines of **B**. Then $\theta = 90°$ when the plane of the coil is perpendicular to lines of **B**. The force on each coil side is independent of θ
because α, i, **B**, and L do not depend on θ. The torque tending to rotate
the coil through an angle θ may be formulated by selecting any axis
parallel to the actual axis of rotation and adding the products f times
the corresponding lever arms. For example, if an axis is taken through
the right coil side (see Fig. 3-7), the lever arm of f acting on the right
coil side is zero while that of f acting on the left coil side is $W \cos \theta$.
Thus, the torque is

$$T = fW \cos \theta = nBiLW \cos \theta = nBiA \cos \theta \qquad (3\text{-}8)$$

where $A = LW$ is the "effective" coil area, and is actually less than the
physical area of the coil when the coil length extends beyond the assumed
confines of the **B** field.

If it is perplexing to determine the torque by means of the convenient
axis selected, this can be dispelled by using the actual physical axis of
rotation, obtaining the same result. For the actual axis of rotation, each
force, f, acts through a lever arm equal to $(W/2) \cos \theta$; hence, each force
contributes equally to the total torque. Consequently, the total torque
is twice the torque produced by one of the forces, and is given by

$$T = 2 \left(f \frac{W}{2} \cos \theta \right) = fW \cos \theta$$

in agreement with Eq. (3-8).

Suppose the coil angle, θ, is zero when $i = 0$. If a constant current, I,
is suddenly applied, a torque, T, will be created and will produce angular
rotation of the coil if it is free to turn. As the coil rotates, the torque
will diminish, despite the fact that **f** remains constant, because the lever
arm becomes smaller as θ approaches $90°$, becoming zero at $\theta = 90°$.
Thus, the coil will experience a variable (angular-dependent) torque.
Though it may initially overshoot $\theta = 90°$, owing to the suddenness of
the disturbance and the inertia of the coil, it will oscillate about $\theta = 90°$
and eventually come to rest in the stable state of zero torque. This will
happen for any direct current, I, large enough to produce a torque over-
coming the friction of the axis on which the coil is pivoted. Thus, it is
seen that this galvanometer is incomplete. It does not produce an angular deflection bearing a unique relationship to the coil current. Inclusion
of a restraining or restoring torque accomplishes the desired result, as
described in the next section.

3-6. Law of Static Deflection and Design.   A restoring torque may be furnished for the rotatable coil by a variety of mechanical spring arrangements.   The usual design provides for a linear restoring torque, one that is proportional to the angular twist of the spring, and given by

$$T_r = S\theta \tag{3-9}$$

where S is a constant (provided the elastic limit of the spring is not exceeded) called the *spring constant*.   Its dimensions are newton-meter (per radian) in the mks system of units.

The equilibrium angle of twist of the coil is determined by the *applied* torque, T, traceable to the interaction of i and $\mathbf{B}$, and the restoring torque, T_r, provided mechanically by the spring, and is defined by $T = T_r$. Expressing this equation of torques in terms of θ, for a direct current $i = I$, results in

$$nBIA \cos\theta = S\theta$$

Solve explicitly for I.

$$I = \frac{S\theta}{nBA \cos\theta} = \frac{K\theta}{\cos\theta} \tag{3-10}$$

where $K = S/nBA$ is called the *instrument constant* and is fixed for a given galvanometer.   The relationship between the direct current I, the independent variable, and the equilibrium angle θ, the dependent variable, is called the law of static deflection.   For the galvanometer that has been analyzed, it is evident that I is a somewhat complicated function of θ.   However, for small currents and corresponding small values of θ, $\cos\theta$ is approximately unity so I is approximately proportional to θ.

Despite the many simplifying assumptions used in the analysis, it is possible to gain insight into some of the factors important in practical galvanometer design, by examining the instrument constant, K.   In designing galvanometers, it is often desired to produce a large θ for a small coil current, that is, to design a sensitive instrument.   This means that a small K is needed.   Since $K = S/nBA$, it follows that K becomes smaller if S is made smaller and if n, B, and A are made larger.   In each case, however, there are conflicting requirements.   This phenomenon is known to the designer as "the law of spite."   For instance, if S is made smaller, the spring (and hence the instrument as a whole) becomes more delicate and fragile.   If n and A are made larger, the weight, size, and inertia of the coil are increased, and this conflicts with a desire for a small, light coil capable of rapid response.   A larger B calls for better permanent-magnet materials, which are more expensive; also, operation above certain levels of B with a given magnet material may impair the "permanence," which would produce instability of galvanometer calibration.   These and other factors not considered here suggest the intri-

cate compromise of all factors that is inevitable in designing a galvanometer for a given application.

3-7. Scale Characteristics. The law of deflection of a galvanometer
bears an intimate relationship to the characteristics of the scale from
which readings related to I are obtained. In the case of a portable
instrument with pointer affixed to the coil, the pointer angle and the

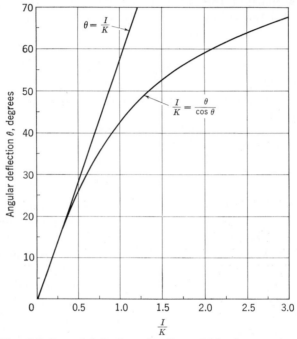

FIG. 3-9. Law of deflection of uniform-field galvanometer.

coil angle are in one-to-one relationship. In the case of the mirror galvanometer described, the scale angle is twice the coil angle for a circular-arc
scale centered on the coil axis (see Fig. 3-3). If a straight scale is used
instead of a circular-arc scale, the scale reading becomes a more complicated function of θ, especially when θ is not small.

In cases where the scale angle is some constant times θ, the law of
deflection discloses complete information. A plot of the law of deflection
for a uniform-field instrument, shown in Fig. 3-9, indicates that for small
values of θ, $I \approx K\theta$, but the departure from a uniform scale increases
progressively as θ approaches 90°. A physical explanation for the nonuniformity may be found by examining the lever arm through which the
force, **f**, exerts a torque, since the cos θ term is responsible for the departure from linearity. For small θ, the lever arm $(W/2) \cos \theta$ remains
sensibly constant, but as θ approaches 90°, the lever arm tends rapidly

toward zero. As the limit is approached, **f**, which is proportional to I, may increase tremendously while a very small angular increase in θ reduces the lever arm by a large percentage.

Another meaningful way of portraying the law of deflection is in terms of an actual scale that might be used in conjunction with a pointer attached directly to the coil, as shown in Fig. 3-10. The uniform por-

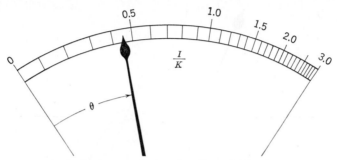

FIG. 3-10. Scale characteristics of uniform-field galvanometer.

tion of the scale is spread out over a considerable arc toward the zero end of the scale. However, the scale readings in terms of coil current become increasingly crowded at larger values of I, so much so that the upper portion of the scale has very limited readability. The value of θ may be calculated from the law of deflection after inserting a designated value of I. For instance, substitution of $I = cK$, where c is any constant, into Eq. (3-10) yields $\theta = c \cos \theta$. The value of θ for any specified numerical value of c may be obtained from this transcendental equation by numerical trial-and-error solution.

The range over which the scale is uniform is often of particular interest. A first-order approximation for departure from uniformity for small deflections may be formulated. In the present case of $I = K\theta/\cos\theta$, the following expansion will converge rapidly for small θ.

$$I = K\theta(\cos\theta)^{-1}$$

$$= K\theta\left(1 - \frac{\theta^2}{2!} + \frac{\theta^4}{4!} + \cdots\right)^{-1} = K\theta\left(1 + \frac{\theta^2}{2!} - \frac{5\theta^4}{4!} + \cdots\right) \quad (3\text{-}11)$$

If $(\theta^2/2) \ll 1$, the law of deflection is given approximately by $I = K\theta$, and the scale is uniform. However, if $\theta^2/2$ is small but not negligible, the difference between the linear law and the actual law is, to a first-order approximation,

$$K\theta - K\theta\left(1 + \frac{\theta^2}{2}\right) = -\frac{K\theta^3}{2} \quad (3\text{-}12)$$

Expressed as a percentage of $K\theta$, this gives $-100\theta^2/2 = -50\theta^2$ per cent. Thus, if the deflection is 0.1 radian = 5.7°, the departure from linearity is approximately $-50(0.1)^2 = -\frac{1}{2}$ per cent. The negative sign indicates that the actual deflection is less than would be obtained if the law of deflection were $I = K\theta$.

3-8. Radial-field Instruments. The uniform-field design is not common because the objectionable $\cos\theta$ term upsets the proportional relation between I and θ. In the most popular version of the d'Arsonval instru-

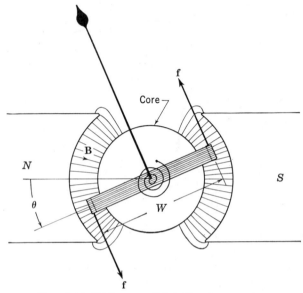

FIG. 3-11. Uniform radial field galvanometer.

ment, a *uniform radial* field is used, as shown in Fig. 3-11, and this yields a uniform scale. Another advantage of this construction is that the **B** field is less susceptible to external stray magnetic effects than in the case of no central core. Shaping of the field is accomplished by use of curved pole pieces and a central core designed so that the field in the air gap is radial. A uniform radial field is constant in magnitude everywhere in the region of the coil, but is not the same as a uniform field because of its variable direction.

Review of the analysis of force on one coil side in the uniform-field case reveals that the *magnitude* of the force is given by the same expression in the case of the uniform radial field. However, in the case of Fig. 3-11, the direction of the force on a coil side depends upon the angle of twist of the coil. **f** remains perpendicular to the plane of the coil for all θ within the working range of the radial field. Therefore, the magnitude of the torque acting on the coil, owing to the forces **f** on the coil sides, is given in this case simply by $T = fW$. This is not a function of θ, as in the uniform-field case, because the lever arm is constant for any θ

as long as the coil side is in a radial-field region. Thus, the essential thing accomplished by the radial field is circumvention of the variable lever arm by maintaining the direction of the force perpendicular to the plane of the coil.

The equation of the torques acting on the coil, using a restoring torque $T_r = S\theta$ as before, now gives $fW = S\theta$. With $fW = nBIA$, the law of deflection for the uniform-radial-field galvanometer becomes

$$I = \frac{S\theta}{nBA} = K\theta \qquad (3\text{-}13)$$

The instrument constant, K, is given by the same expression as in the uniform-field case. Scale readings are now proportional to I, if a circular-

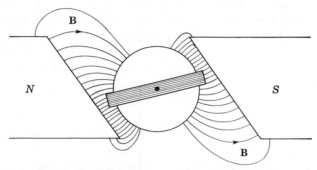

FIG. 3-12. Galvanometer with nonuniform field.

arc scale centered on the mirror is used with a wall galvanometer of this type. Similarly, a circular scale traversed by a pointer attached to the coil, in the case of a portable instrument, is also uniform when calibrated directly in terms of current. In practice, exact uniformity of scale cannot be achieved because of such factors as slight irregularities of the **B** field and variable friction in pivot bearings.

Shaping the **B** field to achieve a prescribed law of deflection is an interesting factor in galvanometer design. The two types of fields described are representative examples, but by no means do they exhaust the possibilities. There are many instances where a prescribed type of nonuniform scale is desirable. For example, a commercial light meter, used in photographic work to determine camera exposure time, might have the pole-piece and core arrangement shown qualitatively in Fig. 3-12. In this case the field is deliberately distorted in a gross manner so as to produce an extremely nonuniform scale. The design is compatible with the sensitivity of photographic film as well as with the characteristics of a photocell that generates the coil current when exposed to illumination.

3-9. Galvanometer Sensitivity. The relation between steady coil current and the steady-state deflection it produces is one of the pertinent

Current Sens   Ball, Sens.
Voltage Sens.   Megohm Sens.

58   ELECTRICAL MEASUREMENT ANALYSIS   [§3-9

static characteristics of a galvanometer. It is useful for specification of galvanometer requirements in certain applications and for describing to other scientific workers the sensitiveness of the instrument used. Galvanometer sensitivity may be a rather treacherous matter because of the multiplicity of definitions extant. This is further compounded by resistive shunts used in conjunction with galvanometers. Fortunately, the matter of sensitivity is somewhat less confusing in the case of packaged instruments.

Before presenting some sensitivity definitions, the meaning of *critical-damping resistance* will be explored in qualitative terms. The transient or dynamic characteristics of the moving coil are controllable by and susceptible to the resistance in the circuit that supplies current to the galvanometer coil. A low-resistance circuit tends to damp the moving coil so that its behavior is sluggish, while a high-resistance circuit may permit prolonged oscillatory motion of the coil. How this interesting effect comes about will be studied in the next chapter. In either case, the time required for the deflection to settle to a steady reading is longer than if some intermediate value of resistance is used. In most applications, a short settling time is desirable and the value of external resistance required to achieve this result is called the critical-damping resistance. It is customary to place a shunt directly across the galvanometer terminals of such value as to produce critical damping. Then a high-resistance circuit is used to supply current to the shunted movement. The portion of the incoming current that is diverted in the shunt obviously does not produce torque on the galvanometer coil. Thus, the resistance of the shunt affects the relationship between current supplied from the external source and instrument deflection produced. The critical-damping resistance is usually counted against the galvanometer sensitivity; that is, it is usually understood that galvanometer sensitivity is specified and measured in terms of a critically damped instrument.

There are at least three different kinds of sensitivity definitions used in mirror galvanometers. These are current sensitivity, voltage sensitivity, and megohm sensitivity. One definition of current sensitivity is the ratio of scale units deflection per unit current. This may be symbolized by $S_I = d/I$, where d represents units of scale deflection produced in steady state as the result of applying a direct current I to the shunted instrument. The scales of mirror galvanometers are usually marked in millimeters, and S_I is often measured with a standard current of 1 μa. Then S_I is specified as d mm where it is understood that $I = 1$ μa. Clearly, the larger the S_I, the more sensitive the instrument. This definition may be deceptive because no provision is made for the distance, D, between mirror and scale. For a given movement, S_I is proportional to D, using a circular-arc scale. Thus, if one investigator uses $D = 50$ cm with the identical movement for which another uses $D = 1$ meter, the first investigator's S_I will be half the second's.

To overcome the difficulty of variable scale distance, another definition of current sensitivity, S_I', may be employed that takes scale distance into account: $S_I' = d/DI$, where D is the scale distance in meters. The standard scale distance is $D = 1$ meter. It is common to specify S_I' in terms of d mm, where it is understood that $D = 1$ meter and $I = 1$ μa. If the galvanometer scale distance is different from 1 meter, the observed deflection in millimeters resulting from application of 1 μa is corrected appropriately.

Even a third kind of current sensitivity definition is used. It is essentially the reciprocal of either S_I or S_I'. It is the current required to produce unit scale deflection, and may or may not be corrected for the standard scale distance of 1 meter. A unit scale deflection of 1 mm is usually employed. Note that the larger the current required to produce 1 mm deflection, the less sensitive the instrument.

Voltage-sensitivity definitions follow a pattern similar to the current sensitivity. The deflection produced by a unit voltage, a standard value of 1 μv, serves as one definition: $S_V = d/V$. If allowance is made for scale distance, $S_V' = d/DV$ is used, again referred to a standard scale distance $D = 1$ meter. Similarly, the voltage required to produce a standard unit scale deflection of 1 mm is also used. Since the voltage source employed in measuring voltage sensitivity usually has very low impedance, it is customary to place the critical-damping resistance in series with the movement.

The megohm sensitivity is defined as the number of megohms required in series with the shunted galvanometer to obtain unit scale deflection with one volt applied to the entire circuit, and referred to a standard scale distance of 1 meter. The equivalent resistance of the shunted galvanometer is negligible compared with the number of megohms, M, required. Hence, the applied current is $1/M$ μa and it produces 1 mm deflection. A little thought indicates that the megohm sensitivity and S_I' are numerically equal, since S_I' is the number of millimeters of deflection produced by 1 μa.

A circuit arrangement useful for measuring galvanometer sensitivity is given in Fig. 3-24 (see Problem 3-10).

GALVANOMETER SHUNTS ⁻ᴷᴸᴾ

In addition to providing critical damping, shunts are also used with galvanometers to deliberately reduce the sensitivity, which is desirable in many applications. For example, when a galvanometer is used as a detector in a bridge circuit, protection of the galvanometer from excessive current is necessary during preliminary balance adjustments.   As bridge balance is approached more and more closely, a corresponding increase in

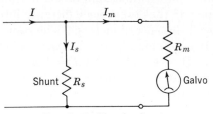

sensitivity is required.   In other applications, the versatility of the galvanometer may be enhanced greatly if there is a rapid means for changing its sensitivity in an accurate prescribed manner, so as to extend the over-all range of the instrument.

FIG. 3-13. Simple shunt.

3-10. Simple Shunts.   A simple shunt consists of a resistor connected directly across the terminals of the galvanometer coil (see Fig. 3-13). The current is often (but not always) supplied from a source whose internal resistance is large compared with the combined parallel resistance of the shunt, R_s, and the resistance of the moving coil, R_m.

The galvanometer current, I_m, is given immediately by the current-splitting rule, $R_s/(R_s + R_m)$ times the incoming current, I.

$$I_m = \frac{R_s}{R_s + R_m} I = FI \tag{3-14}$$

The factor $F = R_s/(R_s + R_m)$, by which I is multiplied, is called the

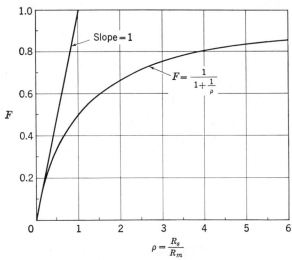

FIG. 3-14. Universal curve for simple shunt.

current-reduction factor.   By suitable choice of R_s, this factor may range from 0 to 1.0 as R_s varies from 0 to infinity (no shunt).   The inverse of the current-reduction factor, $(R_s + R_m)/R_s$, is called the multiplying ratio of the shunt, since it is the quantity by which I_m must be multiplied to deduce the value of I.

A plot of the behavior of the current-reduction factor, F, as a function of the dimensionless independent variable, $\rho = R_s/R_m$, is given in Fig. 3-14. The equation of the curve is obtained by setting $R_s = \rho R_m$ in Eq. (3-14), where $\rho \geqq 0$. Then

$$F = \frac{I_m}{I} = \frac{\rho R_m}{\rho R_m + R_m} = \frac{1}{1 + 1/\rho} \qquad (3\text{-}15)$$

For $\rho \ll 1$ ($R_s \ll R_m$), the 1 may be neglected in the denominator of F in comparison with $1/\rho$, and $F \approx \rho$; hence, the curve is asymptotic to the straight line of slope 1 passing through the origin. The asymptote for $\rho \gg 1$ is $F = 1$ since in this case $1/\rho$ may be neglected in comparison with 1 in the denominator of F. The

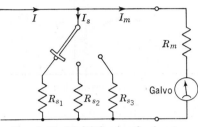

FIG. 3-15. Multiple simple shunts.

two asymptotes intersect at the ordinate $\rho = 1$, where $F = 0.5$.

An arrangement of several different shunt resistors may be constructed, as in Fig. 3-15, so that different fixed values of R_s are provided at the turn of the shorting-type switch.

3-11. Ayrton Shunt. The principal disadvantage of the simple shunt in galvanometer applications is that the value of R_s required to achieve the necessary current reduction is usually not compatible with the value of R_s required for critical damping. However, it is possible to devise a shunt arrangement using two external resistors so that a wide range of current-reduction factors may be obtained while still presenting critical-damping resistance across the galvanometer terminals.

Inclusion of a resistor R_1 in series with the galvanometer, as shown in Fig. 3-16, provides the extra degree of freedom. For simplicity, assume the source of the incoming current has an internal impedance much larger than the parallel resistance of R_s and $R_1 + R_m$. If R_c is the crit-

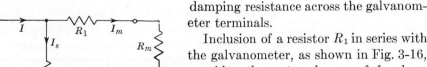

FIG. 3-16. Illustrating principle of Ayrton shunt.

ical-damping resistance required across the galvanometer terminals, then one condition on the shunt arrangement is $R_c = R_1 + R_s$. This means that R_s must be restricted to values equal to or less than R_c. On the other hand, the current-reduction factor for this shunt is

$$F = \frac{R_s}{R_m + R_1 + R_s}$$

which is obtained directly from the current-splitting rule. Hence the
value $R_c = R_1 + R_s$ may be achieved for any $R_s \leqq R_c$ by suitable choice

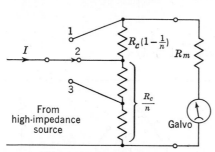

of R_1. At the same time, F may
range over values from $F = 0$
(with $R_s = 0$ and $R_1 = R_c$) to
$F = R_c/(R_m + R_c)$ (with $R_s = R_c$
and $R_1 = 0$). This example illustrates the principle of the Ayrton
shunt.

The usual arrangement, shown in
Fig. 3-17, provides for selection of
several current-reduction factors
while maintaining constant the re-

FIG. 3-17. Ayrton shunt.

sistance seen by the galvanometer. For any given setting, the circuit configuration is the same as in Fig. 3-16. [R_s corresponds to R_c/n and R_1
corresponds to $R_c(1 - 1/n)$.] For a high-impedance source, the resistance seen by the galvanometer is constant and equal to R_c for any switch
position. The current-reduction factor, given directly by the current-
splitting rule, is $F = (R_c/n)/(R_m + R_c)$, where n is any constant equal
to or greater than 1.0, and $1/n$ signifies the fraction of R_c through which
the shunted current passes. With this value of F, the input current, I,
is related to the current through the movement, I_m, by

$$I_m = FI = \frac{R_c}{n(R_m + R_c)} I \tag{3-16}$$

The case $n = 1$ (tap 1 in Fig. 3-17) corresponds to the simple-shunt case
analyzed in the preceding section. The multiplying ratio, $1/F$, of the
Ayrton shunt is $n(R_m + R_c)/R_c$, which is n times the multiplying ratio
of a simple shunt. Hence, n is called the relative multiplying power.
In commercial form, the switch taps are often arranged to give successive
changes in sensitivity in 10:1 ratios.

3-12. Special Shunts. If the source impedance of the current, I,
entering the Ayrton shunt is not large compared with R_c and R_m in
parallel, the ratio relationships in the various switch positions are disrupted, and also the damping does not remain constant. In such cases
an external resistor large compared with $R_c R_m/(R_c + R_m)$ may be inserted
in series with the source to avoid errors, but this might be undesirable
because higher impedance levels tend to be more susceptible to stray
pickup, and also the available current would be reduced.

To illustrate that the source impedance may disrupt the ratio, consider the two-position Ayrton shunt in Fig. 3-18. Application of the current-splitting rule in the case of a constant-current source, I, yields the galvanometer current I_{m1} when the switch is on tap 1.

$$I_{m1} = \frac{(R_1 + R_2)I}{R_1 + R_2 + R_m}$$

When the switch is on tap 2, the galvanometer current is given by

$$I_{m2} = \frac{R_2 I}{R_1 + R_2 + R_m}$$

where the same input current is assumed in the two cases. This will be applicable if the source impedance of I is very large compared with $R_m(R_1 + R_2)/(R_1 + R_2 + R_m)$. Clearly, the ratio of the two galvanometer currents is

$$\frac{I_{m1}}{I_{m2}} = \frac{R_1 + R_2}{R_2} = 1 + \frac{R_1}{R_2} \tag{3-17}$$

Now, instead of a current source, I, suppose a zero-impedance voltage source (an extreme example) of emf E is applied to the shunted galvanometer. Then, with the switch on tap 1, the galvanometer current is given by $I'_{m1} = E/R_m$. When switched to tap 2 the galvanometer current is $I'_{m2} = E/(R_1 + R_m)$. In this case the ratio of the galvanometer currents is

$$\frac{I'_{m1}}{I'_{m2}} = \frac{R_1 + R_m}{R_m} = 1 + \frac{R_1}{R_m} \tag{3-18}$$

This is an entirely different result from the current-source case.

Special shunts may be designed for specific applications in which the source impedance is not large enough to satisfy the conditions assumed in the Ayrton shunt. Moreover, when the source has a resistance smaller than R_c, special shunts may be devised to obtain critical damping accompanied by a specified current-reduction ratio. Suppose the source of incoming current, I, is represented by a direct emf, E, in series with

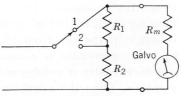

FIG. 3-18. Two-position Ayrton shunt.

an internal resistance, R. If R is less than R_c, a resistor R_1 may be added in series with E as shown in Fig. 3-19a, and a shunt resistance R_2 may be utilized to provide the current reduction. At the same time the resistance seen by the galvanometer, $R_2(R + R_1)/(R + R_1 + R_2)$, is made equal to R_c. Alternatively, the circuit shown in Fig. 3-19b might also be designed to accomplish similar ends.

In cases where R is greater than R_c but not large enough to be ignored, a simple shunt such as in Fig. 3-13 could be used and designed such that the resistance seen by the galvanometer, $RR_s/(R + R_s)$, is made equal to R_c, but the current reduction would be fixed once R and R_c were specified. The arrangement shown in Fig. 3-19b with $RR_3/(R + R_3) \leqq R_c$ might also be employed when $R > R_c$. Thus, a variety of possibilities in

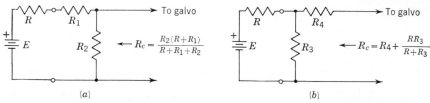

$$(a) \qquad\qquad\qquad (b)$$

FIG. 3-19. Special shunts.

special cases may be deduced from elementary circuit analysis in combination with some ingenuity.

3-13. Attenuators. The special shunts of the preceding section are members of a much broader class of circuits called attenuators which, in turn, belong to the family of networks called filters. A wide variety of resistive circuit configurations are used as attenuators such as T-section, L-section, H-section, and lattice arrangements. These attenuators may consist of cascaded identical sections that enable the ratio of output to input current (or voltage) to be changed by equal decibel increments, at the turn of a switch. While the special attenuators of Sec. 3-12 are usually adequate to meet most galvanometer needs, cascaded switchable attenuator sections are used in many measurement applications. For example, the attenuator may be substituted for an unknown network and adjusted to give the same ratio of input to output current (or voltage) as did the unknown network. Then the unknown network attenuation must be equal to that of the attenuator. Another commonly used application is in the measurement of the voltage gain of amplifiers. In this case the attenuator is placed in series with the amplifier and adjusted so that the output voltage of the series combination is equal to the input voltage. Then the amplifier voltage gain is equal in magnitude to the known attenuation provided by the attenuator. The advantages of these methods of measurement are that the results are independent of the calibration of the indicating devices used and depend primarily upon the accuracy of the attenuator.

An analysis of a symmetrical T-section attenuator serves to illustrate the principles. A single symmetrical T section is shown in Fig. 3-20, terminated in a resistance R. The total series resistance of the T section is R_1. It is divided into two symmetrical parts, each of resistance $R_1/2$, by the shunt resistance R_2. The ratio of the load current, I_1, to the input current, I, is obtained immediately from the current-splitting rule. The current-reduction factor is called the *attenuation*, A, in this case, and is given by

$$A = \frac{I_1}{I} = \frac{R_2}{R_2 + R + R_1/2} \tag{3-19}$$

For a given load resistance, R, the attenuation may be controlled by suitable choice of R_1 and R_2. However, an infinite number of different pairs of R_1 and R_2 produce the same A. Hence, a second condition may be imposed on R_1 and R_2 without restricting A.

The second condition is that the input resistance to the loaded T section shall be equal to the load resistance, R. This input resistance is called the *iterative* impedance in general filter theory. The name is appropriate because the load resistance is "repeated," in effect, at the input of each section. This is an interesting state of affairs because it means that the input resistance to any number of cascaded identical sections will be equal to R, since each section presents the same load resistance to each succeeding section (see Fig. 3-21). Hence, the attenuation of one section will be the same whether it is used alone or in cascade with many other identical sections. The iterative resistance condition is

$$R = \frac{R_1}{2} + \frac{R_2(R + R_1/2)}{R_2 + R + R_1/2} \tag{3-20}$$

Cross-multiply and solve for R^2.

$$R^2 = \frac{R_1{}^2}{4} + R_1 R_2 \tag{3-21}$$

When R and A are specified, the T section (or T pad) may be designed, since R_1 and R_2 are uniquely established. Convenient equations for design purposes may be derived by solving Eqs. (3-19) and (3-21) simultaneously for R_1 and R_2 in terms of R and A.

$$R_1 = \frac{2R(1 - A)}{1 + A} \qquad R_2 = \frac{2RA}{(1 + A)(1 - A)} \tag{3-22}$$

It is interesting that the ratio R_1/R_2 depends only upon A. The pair of relations in Eq. (3-22) may be used to design a T section for any specified R and A. For example, if $R = 150$ ohms and $A = \frac{1}{2}$, which is -6 db, then $R_1 = 100$ ohms and $R_2 = 200$ ohms are obtained from Eq. (3-22). If two such identical sections are cascaded and terminated in $R = 150$ ohms, the attenuation per section remains $\frac{1}{2}$, and the over-all attenuation is $A^2 = \frac{1}{4}$, or -12 db. In general, an n-section attenuator will display an over-all attenuation A^n which, in decibels, is n times the decibel attenuation of each section. The input resistance to each of the n-cascaded sections remains equal to the terminating resistance.

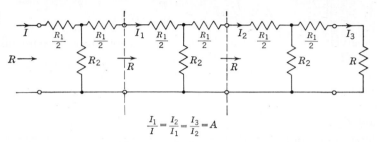

$$\frac{I_1}{I} = \frac{I_2}{I_1} = \frac{I_3}{I_2} = A$$

FIG. 3-21. Cascaded attenuators.

It is obvious from this analysis that there is a unique value of R, given by Eq. (3-21), required for a given attenuator. If the attenuator is not matched to the resistance R, its dial reading in decibels will be in error. Failure to use the attenuator with the load resistance for which it was designed is one of the common errors committed in the laboratory.

DIRECT-CURRENT METERS

When the scale of a d'Arsonval meter is calibrated directly in amperes, the instrument is called a d-c ammeter; when calibrated directly in volts, it is called a d-c voltmeter. A wide range of current and voltage coverage is possible by the use of simple external resistance arrangements, and multirange meters may be designed easily and inexpensively. Thus, this movement becomes a versatile and highly useful measurement tool.

3-14. Ammeters and Shunts. When the portable version of the d'Arsonval movement with direct reading pointer and scale is used as an ammeter, it usually employs a simple shunt (see Fig. 3-13). The shunt may be contained inside the case of the instrument or connected directly across its external terminals. Ammeter sensitivity may be specified in various ways. One common and obvious designation is in terms of the current required for full-scale deflection. This is used widely for ammeters with fixed internal shunts and scales marked directly in amperes, milliamperes, or microamperes. Alternatively, the voltage drop (usually in millivolts) across the movement required to produce full-scale deflection is sometimes specified. If the meter resistance is known, the current required for full-scale deflection may be computed from the voltage rating. Shunts used with ammeters may also be described in terms of the drop across the shunt in millivolts for a specified full-scale deflection. Sometimes the resistance of the shunt is also given. For example, consider a

100-mv 50-amp shunt designed for use with a 200-ma d'Arsonval movement. The interpretation of these specifications is that when the incoming current (or line current) is 50 amp, the drop across the shunt will be 100 mv and the current through the meter movement will be 200 ma while the current through the shunt is 49.8 amp. Note that the 50-amp rating of the shunt does not mean that it carries exactly 50 amp at rated full-scale deflection. From Ohm's law, the movement resistance may be seen to be $0.1/0.2 = 0.5$ ohm while the shunt resistance is $0.1/49.8 = 0.00201$ ohm.

Multirange ammeters may be constructed by providing a group of shunts that give specified current-reduction factors for different switch positions or different terminal connections (see Fig. 3-22). They are usually designed with the assumption that the line into which the ammeter is inserted has an impedance much larger than the largest input resistance of the ammeter. Thus, as low an input resistance as possible is desired in ammeter design and use.

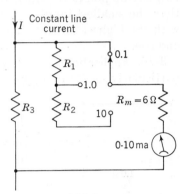

FIG. 3-22. Multirange ammeter.

3-15. Voltmeters. When a large series resistor is placed in series with a d'Arsonval movement, the combination is commonly called a voltmeter. The series resistance is usually located inside the case of the instrument. The distinction between an ammeter and a voltmeter is thus seen to be rather fine. The principal difference is found in the input resistance to the instrument, but both essentially measure current. The input resistance of an ammeter is made as small as possible while the input resistance of a voltmeter is made as large as possible.

Voltmeters may be rated in several ways. The voltage required across the instrument terminals for full-scale deflection is a common designation. Single-range voltmeters show this figure directly on the upper end of the scale in volts, millivolts, or microvolts. Another frequently used specification is in terms of ohms per volt. This is an indirect way of specifying the fixed internal series resistance, whose value is given by the product of volts required for full-scale deflection times the ohms per volt rating. It should be emphasized that the internal series resistance is fixed for a given range and *does not vary with the voltmeter reading* on that range. The reciprocal of the ohms per volt rating is equal to the current in amperes required to produce full-scale deflection. The total resistance of the voltmeter is also sometimes specified. This resistance, in combination with the full-scale current rating of the movement, gives the voltage required for full-scale deflection.

Multirange voltmeters may be constructed by providing a group of different series resistors each of which provides a different voltage requirement for full-scale deflection. In some designs, a single resistor with multiple taps is used. The range of the voltmeter may be changed by a switch or by use of separate terminals for each range. Such voltmeters are designed with the assumption that the impedance looking into the two circuit points to which the voltmeter is connected is much smaller than the smallest input resistance to the voltmeter. Thus, a voltmeter with the highest possible input resistance is desired in voltmeter design and use.

3-16. Applications of Thévenin's Theorem. Thévenin's theorem is particularly useful in analysis of circuits when the current or voltage of a given circuit branch is sought, or when the effect on the circuit of insertion or withdrawal of a circuit element (such as a meter) is desired. In taking inventory of the various methods of approach to circuit problems, Thévenin's theorem should always be considered. It is frequently a timesaver. However, certain techniques and facility with this method are necessary to exploit the theorem fully.

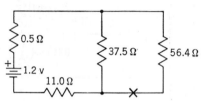

Fig. 3-23. Illustrating an application of Thévenin's theorem.

Two examples of the application of Thévenin's theorem are presented here. Additional problems at the end of the chapter should be solved to obtain practice with the method, and to obtain a good working knowledge of the theorem.

Example 1. In the circuit shown in Fig. 3-23, what change in current will occur in the 56.4-ohm resistor when a milliammeter with a resistance of 7.8 ohms is inserted at point ✕? What will be the reading on the milliammeter, assuming no error in its calibration?

Solution: Remove the 56.4-ohm resistor from the circuit and designate the broken connections as terminals 1-2 of the Thévenin equivalent circuit to be found. Analysis of the circuit to the left of terminals 1-2 discloses, by the voltage-divider rule, that the open-circuit voltage is

$$E_0 = \frac{37.5(1.2)}{11.0 + 0.5 + 37.5} = 0.92 \text{ volt}$$

The input resistance, R_i, is obtained as the parallel combination of 37.5 ohms and (11.0 + 0.5) ohms, replacing the 1.2-volt emf by a short circuit.

$$R_i = \frac{37.5(11.5)}{37.5 + 11.5} = 8.8 \text{ ohms}$$

When the 56.4-ohm resistor is reconnected to terminals 1-2, the current in it will be $I = E_0/(R_i + 56.4) = 14.1$ ma. When the meter of 7.8 ohms resistance is added, the current will be $I' = E_0/(R_i + 56.4 + 7.8) = 12.6$ ma. Thus, the decrease in current resulting from insertion of the milliammeter is $14.1 - 12.6 = 1.5$ ma, and the meter will read 12.6 ma.

Example 2. The voltage between output terminals 1-2 of a certain d-c circuit is precisely 120 volts with no external connections. When two accurate 0 to 100-volt voltmeters, A and B, are connected in series across terminals 1-2, voltmeter A indicates 60 volts and voltmeter B indicates 48 volts. Voltmeter A is a 500-ohm-per-volt instrument but the resistance of voltmeter B is not specified. What will voltmeter B indicate when it is connected alone across terminals 1-2?

Solution: Represent the network behind the two terminals by a d-c emf, E, in series with a resistance, R. Evidently, $E_0 = E = 120$ volts. The resistance of voltmeter A is $R_A = 500$ ohms per volt $\times$ 100 volts full scale $= 50,000$ ohms. The ratio of resistances of voltmeters A and B must be the same as the ratio of voltages across them when they are series-connected; hence, $R_A/R_B = {}^{60}\!/_{48}$, whence $R_B = 40,000$ ohms. Thus, the total resistance of the two voltmeters in series is 90,000 ohms with a total drop of $60 + 48 = 108$ volts. By the voltage-divider rule, it follows for the series-connected case that $108 = 120(90)/(90 + R)$, whence $R = 10$ kilohms. With E and R known, the fraction of the 120 volts that will appear across voltmeter B (of $R_B = 40,000$ ohms) when it is connected alone is easily found to be $40,000/50,000$. Hence, voltmeter B will read $(\frac{4}{5})(120) = 96$ volts.

PROBLEMS

3-1 (§3). A long straight conductor carrying a current $i = 10$ ma is located in a uniform magnetic field $B = 0.1$ weber per sq meter. The angle between a current element $i\,d\mathbf{s}$ of the conductor and the vector $\mathbf{B}$ is 20°. What are the magnitude and direction of the force per unit length exerted on the conductor?

3-2 (§5). An n-turn circular coil of radius R is located in a uniform $\mathbf{B}$ field and oriented so that the component of $\mathbf{B}$ normal to the plane of the coil is zero. If a current, i, is passed through the coil, determine an expression for the torque acting about a coil axis that is perpendicular to $\mathbf{B}$ and in the plane of the coil.

3-3 (§6). If a current, I, of K amp (where K is the instrument constant) is passed through a galvanometer whose law of deflection is $I = K\theta/\cos\theta$, what will be the angle of rotation, θ, of the movement?

3-4 (§7). A mirror galvanometer employing a telescope and scale has a *uniform* field throughout the region occupied by the coil. It is used with either of two zero-center scales, a straight scale or a curved scale with radius of curvature 1 meter; both scales are used with their centers a distance 1 meter from the mirror, in a direction perpendicular to the uniform field. Express the galvanometer current, I, in terms of the deflection in millimeters, d, for each case, and show that for small deflections the departure from a linear relationship $I = Ad$ (where A is a constant) when using the straight scale is $-\frac{5}{3}$ times the departure from linearity when using a curved scale. Hint:

$$\tan^{-1} x = \sum_{r=0}^{\infty} (-1)^r \frac{x^{2r+1}}{2r+1}$$

3-5 (§8). A d'Arsonval mirror galvanometer employing a telescope and scale has a *uniform radial* field throughout the region occupied by the coil. It is used with either of two zero-center scales, a straight scale or a curved scale with radius of curvature D. Both scales are used with their centers a distance D from the mirror, and both scales show a reading of zero for zero coil current. If each scale is graduated with the same divisions, find the angle of rotation, θ, of the movement that gives a reading on the straight scale which is 1.2 times that on the circular-arc scale.

3-6 (§8). A d'Arsonval mirror-type wall galvanometer is to be designed for use with a straight scale such that the deflection on the scale is some constant times the coil current (a uniform scale). This is to be accomplished by suitable design of the permanent magnet such that the magnetic field in which the coil is located is radial but deliberately nonuniform in a manner that produces the desired result. Specify the equation for the magnitude of **B** as a function of the angle of twist, θ, of the coil. Would it be practical to produce such a field in an actual instrument?

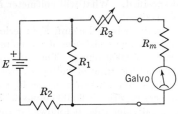

Fig. 3-24. Circuit for measuring galvanometer sensitivity.

3-7 (§9). A mirror galvanometer employing a scale distance $D = 50$ cm has a coil resistance of 50 ohms and requires an external shunt of 100 ohms for critical damping. When a current of 10 μa is applied to the critically damped instrument, a deflection of 3 mm is produced. Compute the current sensitivities S_I and S'_I, the voltage sensitivities S_V and S'_V, and the megohm sensitivity.

3-8 (§9). Will the following changes in a d'Arsonval mirror galvanometer with a uniform radial field increase, decrease, or not affect its *megohm sensitivity?* (a) An increase in the distance between scale and mirror. (b) An increase in the flux density produced by the permanent magnet. (c) An increase in the stiffness of the suspension wire. (d) An increase in the number of turns on the coil. (e) An increase in the moment of inertia of the moving system.

3-9 (§9). A mirror galvanometer is connected in a series circuit of 100 ohms resistance (including galvanometer resistance), and yields a deflection of 10 cm on a scale (one division = 1 mm) located 50 cm from the mirror, when 50 μv is applied to the circuit. (a) Calculate the megohm sensitivity of the galvanometer. (b) Through what angle does the mirror rotate when 0.03 μa is passed through this galvanometer?

3-10 (§9). A galvanometer is tested in the circuit shown in Fig. 3-24. When $R_3 = 450$ ohms, the deflection is 150 mm. When $R_3 = 950$ ohms, the deflection is 75 mm. Find the resistance and current sensitivity of the galvanometer. $E = 1.5$ volts, $R_1 = 1.0$ ohm, $R_2 = 2,500$ ohms.

3-11 (§9). The megohm sensitivity of galvanometer A is 20 megohms and the current sensitivity of galvanometer B is 0.1×10^{-6} amp/div. Readings on A can be estimated accurately to $\pm \frac{1}{2}$ division and readings on B can be estimated accurately to ± 0.2 division. Which galvanometer allows the more precise measurements?

3-12 (§10). Design a switchable set of three simple shunts for a galvanometer of resistance $R_m = 100$ ohms and current sensitivity 10 mm, so that current sensitivities of 5 mm, 1 mm, and 0.1 mm are available. Assume that the current will always be supplied from a circuit of internal resistance far in excess of 50 ohms.

3-13 (§10). Why is a shorting-type switch desirable to use in the shunt arrangement of Fig. 3-15?

3-14 (§10). The current sensitivity of a shunted galvanometer (considering the shunt an integral part of the instrument) is given by

$$S = \frac{2 + 0.02R_s}{R_s}.$$

where S is the sensitivity of the instrument in microamperes per scale division, and

R_s is the resistance in ohms of the shunt connected directly across the galvanometer terminals. The source impedance is assumed to be very much larger than R_s. (a) What is the current sensitivity of the galvanometer when no external shunt is employed? (b) What is the current sensitivity of the instrument when a 200-ohm shunt is employed? (c) What is the resistance of the galvanometer itself?

3-15 (§11). The galvanometer in Fig. 3-17 has a resistance of 100 ohms and an undamped current sensitivity of 0.06 mm. It is to be critically damped with the Ayrton shunt shown. The required value of critical-damping resistance is $R_c = 500$ ohms. Specify the resistance between switch taps such that the galvanometer circuit has three sensitivities in the ratio 1:10:100. What is the maximum current sensitivity of the shunted instrument?

3-16 (§11). The current, I, is delivered to the Ayrton shunt of Fig. 3-17 from an emf, E, in series with a resistance $R = 500$ ohms, rather than from a high-impedance source. Using the numerical values provided in Prob. 3-15, including resistance values given in the answers, determine the ratios of the galvanometer currents for the three switch positions.

3-17 (§12). The output current of a d-c generator of internal resistance 10 ohms is to be measured with a d'Arsonval galvanometer of coil resistance 90 ohms, which requires a 280-ohm shunt for critical damping. What values and arrangement of two resistors may be inserted between the generator and the galvanometer to yield critical damping as well as a galvanometer current that is exactly one-tenth the current drawn from the generator?

3-18 (§13). Verify Eq. (3-22).

3-19 (§13). Plot the pair of design curves R_1/R and R_2/R vs. A for a symmetrical T-pad attenuator. At what value of A is $R_1 = R_2$?

3-20 (§13). A symmetrical T-pad attenuator is designed to produce 3-db attenuation when used with a load resistance $R = 1,000$ ohms. What is the actual attenuation when this T pad is mistakenly used with a 2,000-ohm load?

3-21 (§13). Design a two-section, symmetrical T-pad attenuator for use with a 500-ohm load so that attenuations of 1.5 and 3.0 db are available. What is the over-all attenuation of the two sections when erroneously used with a 600-ohm load?

3-22 (§14). A 0.1-amp 50-mv shunt is designed for use with a 50-mv, 1-ma movement. (a) What per cent error in the current reading will result if this shunt is used with a 50-mv 10-ma movement? (b) What should be the resistance of a 0.1-amp 50-mv shunt for a 50-mv 10-ma movement?

3-23 (§14). A shunt of unknown resistance and two ammeters are used to measure a constant current. Ammeter A has a range 0 to 10 amp, and a resistance of 0.0025 ohm; ammeter B has a range 0 to 5 amp, and a resistance of 0.005 ohm. When meter A is connected in parallel with the shunt it reads 7.54 amp. When meter B is connected in parallel with the shunt (A having been removed), its reading is 4.16 amp. What is the constant current?

3-24 (§14). A 0 to 10-ma d-c meter has an internal resistance of 6 ohms. It is converted into a multirange ammeter by means of the shunt arrangement shown in Fig. 3-22. (a) What values of R_1, R_2, and R_3 are required to obtain full-scale meter deflections for line currents of 0.1, 1.0, and 10 amp at the switch settings shown? (b) What is the maximum power dissipation that each of these three resistors is required to sustain under normal meter-reading conditions?

3-25 (§14). A set of 50-mv shunts designed for use with a 40-ma movement includes the following sized shunts: 100-amp, 5-amp, 1-amp, and 0.5-amp. (a) What is the per cent error on each range in the readings of a 10-ma 50-mv movement used with these shunts? (b) What resistance may be connected directly in series with the 10-ma movement if it is to read correctly with the 1-amp shunt? (The shunt is to be connected across the series combination of resistor and movement.) (c) What resistance must be shunted across the 10-ma movement and 1-amp shunt if the meter is to read correctly?

3-26 (§14). Two ammeters, designated by A and B in Fig. 3-25, are used in parallel to measure a current of 26 amp. The resistance of the wires used to make the parallel connection is not negligible, however, and it is found that the division of current between the two meters is therefore different for the two connections shown.   Meter

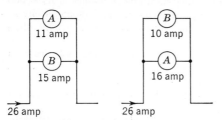

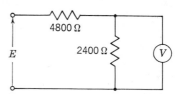

Fig. 3-25. Parallel connection of ammeters.   Fig. 3-26. Voltmeter measurement.

readings are given on the diagram.   The resistance of meter A is known to be 0.01 ohm.   Find the resistance of meter B.

3-27 (§15). The 1,200-ohm voltmeter, V, shown in Fig. 3-26, registers 19 volts. Find E.

3-28 (§15). Three d-c voltmeters are connected in series across a 120-volt d-c supply.   The voltmeters are specified as follows: voltmeter A: 100 volt, 5 ma; voltmeter B: 100 volt, 250 ohms per volt; voltmeter C: 15,000 ohm, 10 ma.   (a) What is the ohms-per-volt rating of voltmeter A?   (b) What is the full-scale current rating of voltmeter B?   (c) What is the voltage rating of voltmeter C?   (d) What voltage does each meter read?

3-29 (§15). Two voltmeters are connected in series. Voltmeter A is rated at 100 volts full-scale deflection and has a sensitivity of 1,000 ohms per volt.   Voltmeter B has a 1-ma movement and a full-scale rating of 150 volts.   Voltmeter B reads 57 volts, but the pointer on voltmeter A is badly bent so its reading cannot be trusted. What is the total voltage across the two voltmeters?

3-30 (§15). The Simpson Model 260 volt-ohm-milliammeter has d-c voltage ranges of 2.5, 10, 50, 250, 1,000, and 5,000 volts full scale.   The meter is rated at 20,000 ohms per volt.   (a) What is the input resistance of the voltmeter on each of the above ranges?   (b) If the least sensitive movement consistent with the above specifications were used in this instrument, what would be its current sensitivity in microamperes for full-scale deflection?

3-31 (§16). When the volt-ohm-milliammeter of Prob. 3-30 is attached to a linear circuit, it reads 5 volts on the 10-volt range, and 15 volts on the 50-volt range.   What would be the reading on the 250-volt range, and what is the no-load voltage of the circuit?

3-32 (§16). Two accurate 0 to 25-volt voltmeters are connected in parallel across points 1 and 2 of a linear d-c circuit.   Voltmeter A reads 20 volts.   Voltmeter A is a 1,000-ohm-per-volt meter and voltmeter B is a 2,000-ohm-per-volt meter.   When voltmeter A is removed, voltmeter B reads 22 volts.   What will be the short-circuit current in a wire connected from point 1 to point 2?

3-33 (§16). A 25,000-ohm resistor is one of the elements in a certain linear d-c circuit.   When a 0 to 100-volt voltmeter of 500-ohm-per-volt rating is connected in series with this resistor, it reads 50 volts. When the same voltmeter is connected across the 25,000-ohm resistor it reads 32.5 volts. Compute the power dissipated in the 25,000-ohm resistor when the voltmeter is removed from the circuit.

3-34 (§16). A 60,000-ohm resistor is connected between points 1 and 2 in a certain d-c circuit. Two accurate voltmeters are available. Voltmeter A is a 0 to 75-volt meter and requires 5 ma to produce full-scale deflection. It reads 60 volts when connected across the resistor. When voltmeter A is replaced by a different voltmeter B, the reading on B is 90 volts. When *both* voltmeters are connected simultaneously, voltmeter B reads 45 volts. (*a*) What is the voltage across the 60,000-ohm resistor when neither voltmeter is connected? (*b*) What will be the voltage across points 1 and 2 when the 60,000-ohm resistor is removed from the circuit (neither voltmeter connected)?

CHAPTER 4

GALVANOMETER DYNAMICS

Knowledge of the laws and circuits governing static deflection of galvanometers and d-c meters is useful but by no means represents a balanced understanding of this remarkable movement. It is frequently necessary to comprehend the more difficult problem of motion of the suspended coil, thus obtaining a fuller appreciation of uses and limitations of galvanometers. Fundamental principles on which dynamic behavior of galvanometers is based are presented in this chapter along with representative solutions.

The study of galvanometer dynamics is highly instructive and valuable to the engineer since it involves the behavior of an electromechanical system. The value of the analysis resides perhaps more in the concepts and methods of formulating and interpreting equations of a moderately complicated system, than in specific solutions and information concerning galvanometers. As such, it is hoped that the student will join in the challenge with vigor; the thinking and methods employed here are too often encountered in engineering problems to be passed over casually.

4-1. Transient Response. The transient response of d'Arsonval movements is a matter of considerable practical interest. To illustrate, suppose a battery of emf, E, in series with a resistance, R, is used to energize a uniform-radial-field movement as shown in Fig. 4-1. If the coil is initially at rest at an angular deflection $\theta = 0$ with the switch open, and then the switch is closed at time $t = 0$, the resulting angular motion of the coil may follow several patterns. The coil may turn very slowly and sluggishly, creeping gradually up to the final (steady-state) angular deflection, θ_s, corresponding to the steady current $I = E/(R + R_m)$. Or it may twist rather briskly and settle quickly at θ_s, without ever going

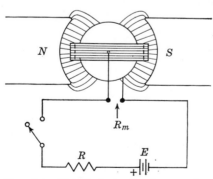

Fig. 4-1. Circuit for actuating a galvanometer.

74

beyond θ_s. Or it might undergo rather violent motion, swinging well beyond θ_s initially and oscillating back and forth over a prolonged period of time but with diminished amplitude about the value θ_s. These possibilities, portrayed graphically in Fig. 4-2, are readily demonstrated in the laboratory. They show the significance of the problem and give some suggestion of its complexity.

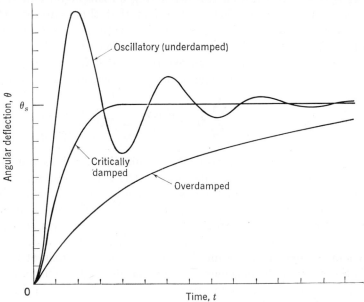

FIG. 4-2. Modes of galvanometer behavior.

The mode of behavior is determined by a number of factors inherent in the d'Arsonval movement such as the instrument constant, K, the moment of inertia, J, of the suspended system, and the air damping of the moving coil. But, interestingly enough, the value of the *external* resistance, R, also has a pronounced effect on dynamic behavior, as will be shown. Thus, the transient performance is, to some extent, within control of the user of the instrument.

In some applications, the desired behavior is similar to that shown in the critically damped curve of Fig. 4-2, which represents attainment of steady deflection in least time without overshoot. This mode of operation usually can be produced by suitable choice of R. Critical damping is desirable to achieve in sensitive galvanometers because undue sluggishness or prolonged oscillation may waste many seconds of time while waiting for the deflection to settle at θ_s.

4-2. Differential Equation of Torques. A mathematical description of the angular motion of the galvanometer coil may be found by recourse

to the classical-mechanics subject called "dynamics of rigid bodies."
The basic equation applying to such motion is

$$\sum_{k=1}^{N} \mathbf{T}_k = \frac{d\mathbf{H}}{dt} \qquad (4\text{-}1)$$

where $\mathbf{T}_k$ is one of N external torques acting on the body, and $\mathbf{H}$ is the
angular momentum of the body.   The fact that the resultant external
torque about any point is equal to the time rate of change of angular
momentum about that point follows from Newton's laws of motion.   It
will be recalled that the sum of all external forces, $\mathbf{f}_k$, acting on a body
is equal to the time rate of change of linear momentum of the body,

$$\sum_{k=1}^{N} \mathbf{f}_k = \frac{d(m\mathbf{v})}{dt}$$

The angular-momentum vector, $\mathbf{H}$, is quite involved in the general
case, but collapses to a very simple form for the galvanometer coil.   The
coil is assumed to be a rigid body so constrained that it has only one
degree of freedom, pure rotation, and an axis of rotation coincident with
the axis of symmetry of the coil.   In this case, $\mathbf{H}$ has only a single component, directed along the axis of rotation, given by $H = J\,d\theta/dt$. J is
the moment of inertia of the moving system about its axis of rotation,
and θ is the angular displacement of the coil, defined in Chap. 3.   The
time derivative of θ is, of course, the angular velocity of the coil.

For the galvanometer, each contribution, $\mathbf{T}_k$, to the resultant external
torque has a component only along the axis of rotation.   There are at
least three separate constituents of the resultant external torque.

$$\sum_{k=1}^{3} T_k = T - T_r - T_a \qquad (4\text{-}2)$$

The applied torque, T, results from the interaction of the galvanometer
current with the magnetic field, $\mathbf{B}$, in the air gap.   The restoring torque,
T_r, is provided by the suspension.   The restraining torque, T_a, results
from air resistance to coil motion.   The last two torques act in opposition
to the applied torque; hence, the negative signs.   The restoring torque
was specified in Chap. 3, $T_r = S\theta$, where S is the spring constant.   For a
uniform-radial-field instrument, the applied torque was also seen to be
$T = nBiA$, for any θ within the working range.   Note that in T the
steady current, I, of Chap. 3 has been replaced by the instantaneous
current, i, which varies with time during the transient.   Restraining
torque owing to friction has been neglected in Eq. (4-2), an acceptable

omission in the case of mirror galvanometers employing filamentary suspensions. However, in instruments employing pivoted coils, the bearing-friction torque is often a significant factor.

Thus, the equation of torques that must be satisfied in this case is

$$T - T_r - T_a = \frac{d}{dt}\left(J\frac{d\theta}{dt}\right) = J\frac{d^2\theta}{dt^2} \tag{4-3}$$

It is assumed in Eq. (4-3) that J is constant, which is well justified for filamentary suspensions, but subject to some small error in the case of spiral-restoring springs. Changes in spring shape under rotation contribute small variations in J. But the spring mass is usually small compared with the mass of the coil, so even this effect may be negligible. Incorporate the expressions for T and T_r into Eq. (4-3), recalling that the instrument constant, previously defined, is $K = S/nBA$, and the torque equation becomes

$$J\frac{d^2\theta}{dt^2} + T_a + S\theta = \frac{S}{K}i \tag{4-4}$$

The expression generally used for the torque owing to air damping, T_a, is based on the somewhat questionable assumption of *viscous damping*, which by definition means that T_a is proportional to the angular velocity of the coil. Hence, $D_a\,d\theta/dt$ may be used as an approximation for T_a, where D_a is a constant of proportionality called the *air-damping coefficient*. The degree to which this approximation is applicable to the system is usually not critical. Air damping frequently represents a small portion of the total damping of the moving coil, the bulk of which is often traceable to a magnetic braking effect that will be analyzed in the next section. Damping is accomplished in many instruments by a metallic frame on which the coil is wound. Eddy currents, set up in this frame when the coil moves, produce a damping torque. Frame damping is neglected in this entire chapter.

Substitution for T_a yields the following differential equation of torques:

$$J\frac{d^2\theta}{dt^2} + D_a\frac{d\theta}{dt} + S\theta = \frac{S}{K}i \tag{4-5}$$

This equation cannot be solved immediately since the current, i, is some function of θ, yet to be determined. Only a portion of the total instantaneous current appearing in Eq. (4-5) is an independent driving function. This is because the motional emf, induced in the coil as a result of its movement through the magnetic field, depends upon θ and, of course, influences i.

4-3. Differential Equation for Current. The equation for instantaneous current in the galvanometer coil may be determined by analyzing the circuit of Fig. 4-3, which shows the electrical portion of Fig. 4-1. It should be recognized that there is no loss in generality in considering a voltage, E, in series with a resistance, R, applied to the galvanometer. Thévenin's theorem shows that any linear d-c network may be placed in this form. In the circuit of Fig. 4-3, R_m represents the resistance of the coil, L_m its self-inductance, and e_m the *motional* emf induced in the coil when it moves through the magnetic field. When the switch is closed, Kirchhoff's voltage law yields

$$E - e_m = i(R + R_m) + L_m \frac{di}{dt} \qquad (4\text{-}6)$$

The algebraic sign associated with e_m follows from Lenz's law, which states that the induced emf must have a polarity such as to oppose the

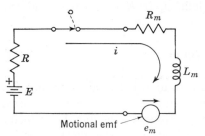

FIG. 4-3. Galvanometer circuit.

cause that produced it. Hence, as i increases from zero, e_m must act in opposition and tends to reduce the net emf acting on the circuit. With the sign established, only the magnitude of e_m need be found.

In many practical galvanometers, the self-inductance of the coil is so small that it is a good approximation to neglect the term $L_m \, di/dt$. It will be shown subsequently that i cannot change instantaneously, even with L_m neglected, because of the motional emf, e_m. Neglecting L_m leads to a considerable simplification by eliminating the derivative of the current from Eq. (4-6). Accordingly, it is assumed that $L_m = 0$.

The effect of the motional emf may be quite pronounced, despite neglect of the $L_m \, di/dt$ drop. As an extreme example, suppose the galvanometer coil is swinging from some sizable deflection back toward zero, and a short circuit is suddenly placed across the coil terminals. The coil will suffer a sudden deceleration (especially if R_m is small) which may be so abrupt that the coil becomes virtually frozen in angle. This magnetic braking may be understood qualitatively by observing that the short-circuit current produced by the motional emf yields a torque opposing the coil motion. The smaller the R_m, the larger the current and the associated torque. When the coil tends to move, it "cuts its own throat" by generating an e_m that counteracts the motion. This damping effect is useful in practice. By appropriate manual manipulation of a shorting switch, a galvanometer oscillating about zero may be "clamped" by closing the switch just before the coil angle passes through zero. The net effect of this technique is to reduce the time required for the instrument to stabilize at a zero reading. It is also standard practice to short-circuit the galvanometer terminals when moving the instrument to prevent excessive coil motion and possible damage.

The magnitude of the motional emf may be determined from the basic force law using the definition of emf

$$e = \oint \frac{\mathbf{f}}{q} \cdot d\mathbf{s} \qquad (4\text{-}7)$$

The emf, e, is the line integral around a closed path of the force per unit charge. The vector $d\mathbf{s}$ represents an element of path length. Because $\mathbf{f} \cdot d\mathbf{s}$ represents work, e may also be regarded as the line integral of the work per unit charge around the closed path.

Divide the basic force law, given in Eq. (3-1), by q and insert the result into Eq. (4-7).

$$e = \oint (\boldsymbol{\varepsilon} + \mathbf{v} \times \mathbf{B}) \cdot d\mathbf{s}$$

This may be broken into the sum of two separate line integrals

$$e = \oint \boldsymbol{\varepsilon} \cdot d\mathbf{s} + \oint \mathbf{v} \times \mathbf{B} \cdot d\mathbf{s}$$

the first of which is zero, since the line integral of any electrostatic field around any closed path is zero. The remaining line integral is the motional emf.

$$e_m = \oint \mathbf{v} \times \mathbf{B} \cdot d\mathbf{s} \qquad (4\text{-}8)$$

The line integral in Eq. (4-8) may be evaluated for the n-turn galvanometer coil moving with radial velocity $\mathbf{v}$ in the uniform radial field, $\mathbf{B}$, shown in Fig. 4-4. For every element $d\mathbf{s}$ of those portions of the coil that lie in $\mathbf{B}$, it may be seen that $\mathbf{v}$ and $\mathbf{B}$ are mutually perpendicular and constant at a given instant of time. Hence, $\mathbf{v} \times \mathbf{B}$ has a magnitude vB and an upward direction along the left side of the coil in Fig. 4-4, and downward along the right side. This means that forces owing to motion of the coil act *along* the wire on charges inside the wire, and in the same sense in going completely around all n turns. The line integral path around one turn includes the distance $2L$ plus some remaining path length along which $\mathbf{B}$ is zero, if fringing is neglected. Since $\mathbf{v} \times \mathbf{B}$ has the same direction as every $d\mathbf{s}$ along this effective path length $2L$, the dot product in Eq. (4-8) does not yield a trigonometric term. However, the algebraic

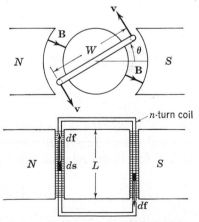

Fig. 4-4. Illustrating motional emf.

sign of the product depends upon whether $d\mathbf{s}$ and $\mathbf{v} \times \mathbf{B}$ have the same or opposite sense, and depends on the direction of line integration. But the sign of e_m has already been established in Eq. (4-6). The magnitude of the motional emf for one turn is seen to be $vB(2L)$. Therefore, for n turns

$$e_m = 2nBLv \qquad (4\text{-}9)$$

The result in Eq. (4-9) may be deduced, perhaps in a less satisfying manner, by a suitable interpretation of Faraday's law:

$$\text{induced emf} = -\frac{d\Phi}{dt}$$

where Φ is the magnetic flux in webers. One filament, of effective length L, of one coil side moving with radial velocity $v = dx/dt$ sweeps out an area $da = L\,dx$ in a time dt. Hence, $da/dt = L\,dx/dt = Lv$. With $\mathbf{B}$ constant and normal to da, the flux cut in time dt is $d\Phi = B\,da$. Therefore, the magnitude of the induced emf in one filament is

$$\frac{d\Phi}{dt} = B\frac{da}{dt} = BLv$$

But there are $2n$ such filaments, each of effective length L and each with aiding induced-emf polarity. Therefore, the magnitude of the total induced emf is $2nBLv$, in agreement with Eq. (4-9).

The motional emf may be expressed in terms of θ by noting that $dx = (W/2)\,d\theta$, where W is the total width of the coil. Hence,

$$\frac{dx}{dt} = v = \frac{W}{2}\frac{d\theta}{dt}$$

and using this velocity in Eq. (4-9),

$$e_m = 2nBL\frac{W}{2}\frac{d\theta}{dt} = nBA\frac{d\theta}{dt} = \frac{S}{K}\frac{d\theta}{dt} \qquad (4\text{-}10)$$

where $K = S/nBA$ is the instrument constant, and $A = LW$ is the effective coil area. Insert this result into Eq. (4-6), with $L_m = 0$, and the desired functional relationship between i and θ is obtained.

$$i(R + R_m) = E - \frac{S}{K}\frac{d\theta}{dt} \qquad (4\text{-}11)$$

Substitute this expression for i into Eq. (4-5).

$$J\frac{d^2\theta}{dt^2} + D_a\frac{d\theta}{dt} + S\theta = \frac{S}{K}\frac{E}{R + R_m} - \frac{S^2}{K^2(R + R_m)}\frac{d\theta}{dt}$$

For a more manageable result, collect the two $d\theta/dt$ terms and define the *damping coefficient*

$$D = D_a + \frac{S^2}{K^2(R + R_m)} \qquad (4\text{-}12)$$

which consists of air damping plus circuit damping owing to e_m. When θ has reached a steady value, $d\theta/dt = 0$ and $e_m = 0$. Then, the direct current in the coil is, from Eq. (4-11),

$$I = \frac{E}{R + R_m} \qquad (4\text{-}13)$$

Finally, using D and I, the torque equation to be solved for θ becomes

$$J\frac{d^2\theta}{dt^2} + D\frac{d\theta}{dt} + S\theta = \frac{S}{K}I \qquad (4\text{-}14)$$

4-4. General Solution of Torque Equation.   Second-order linear differential equations with constant coefficients, such as Eq. (4-14), occur profusely in engineering analysis.   An example familiar to the reader is Eq. (2-3) for the mesh current in the series RLC circuit shown in Fig. 2-2a.

$$L\frac{di}{dt} + Ri + \frac{1}{C}\int i\,dt = e(t) = E$$

With $i = dq/dt$, this becomes

$$L\frac{d^2q}{dt^2} + R\frac{dq}{dt} + \frac{q}{C} = E$$

This has exactly the same form as Eq. (4-14).   Evidently, the analogy between the electric circuit quantities and the electromechanical galvanometer quantities is

Galvanometer............	θ	J	D	S	SI/K	$d\theta/dt$
Series RLC circuit........	q	L	R	$1/C$	E	i

This analogy helps to anticipate and understand the galvanometer results in terms of the familiar.   For example, the effect of D in the galvanometer is analogous to that of R in the series circuit; θ and q are analogues; and it may be expected that there will be a counterpart to the series-circuit resonance frequency $\omega_0 = 1/\sqrt{LC}$ in the form of $\sqrt{S/J}$, replacing L by J and C by $1/S$ in ω_0.   The student is urged to pursue this analogy, but it will not be referred to specifically in the transient development that follows.

The general solution of any linear differential equation with constant coefficients consists of the sum of a steady-state term (particular integral) and a transient term (complementary function).   It must contain arbitrary constants equal in number to the order of the differential equation. The arbitrary constants may be evaluated from the boundary (initial) conditions in any particular case. For a constant right member, as in Eq. (4-14), the steady-state term is obtained simply by imposing that the independent variable be constant. The transient term is the solution of the *homogeneous* equation, defined as the equation resulting from setting the right member equal to zero.

Accordingly, the general solution of Eq. (4-14) must be in the form

$$\theta = \theta_s + \theta_t$$

where θ_t is the transient term that eventually goes to zero as t approaches infinity, and θ_s is the steady-state term, the final value of θ attained as θ_t approaches zero. The steady-state term is obtained by imposing $\theta = \theta_s = $ constant, whence $d\theta/dt = 0$ and $d^2\theta/dt^2 = 0$. Then Eq. (4-14) becomes $S\theta_s = SI/K$ or

$$\theta_s = \frac{I}{K} = \frac{E}{K(R + R_m)} \tag{4-15}$$

This is the static law of deflection deduced previously in Eq. (3-13), a comforting consistency.

The transient term is a solution of the homogeneous equation

$$J\frac{d^2\theta_t}{dt^2} + D\frac{d\theta_t}{dt} + S\theta_t = 0 \tag{4-16}$$

and is known to be expressible in exponential form. Hence, a solution $\theta_t = A\epsilon^{pt}$, where $A = $ constant, will apply provided p is chosen properly. To find acceptable values of p, insert $\theta_t = A\epsilon^{pt}$ into Eq. (4-16) with the result

$$A\epsilon^{pt}(Jp^2 + Dp + S) = 0$$

This equation must be satisfied for all t. The solution $A = 0$ is trivial since $\theta_t = 0$ obviously satisfies Eq. (4-16), but is of no interest. Similarly for the solution $p \to -\infty$. Hence, suitable values of p are given by the solution of the so-called characteristic equation, $Jp^2 + Dp + S = 0$. The quadratic formula yields two roots

$$p_1 = -\alpha + \sqrt{\alpha^2 - \frac{S}{J}} \qquad p_2 = -\alpha - \sqrt{\alpha^2 - \frac{S}{J}} \tag{4-17}$$

where $\alpha = D/2J$. When p_1 and p_2 are not equal, it is evident that either $\theta_t = A\epsilon^{p_1 t}$ or $\theta_t = B\epsilon^{p_2 t}$, where B is a constant different from A, will satisfy Eq. (4-16). The sum of these two solutions must also satisfy Eq. (4-16) because of its linearity. Therefore, $\theta_t = A\epsilon^{p_1 t} + B\epsilon^{p_2 t}$ is the transient solution containing the requisite number of arbitrary constants for a second-order equation. Thus, the general solution of Eq. (4-14) is

$$\theta = \theta_s + A\epsilon^{p_1 t} + B\epsilon^{p_2 t} \qquad p_1 \neq p_2 \qquad (4\text{-}18)$$

where θ_s is given by Eq. (4-15).

On the other hand, if $p_1 = p_2 = -\alpha$, which occurs when $D^2/4J^2 = S/J$, θ_t has essentially one arbitrary constant because $\theta_t = (A + B)\epsilon^{-\alpha t}$. Hence, θ_t is not complete in this singular case. The complete transient term may be squeezed out of the form used for $p_1 \neq p_2$ by setting $p_2 = p_1 + \Delta$, and allowing Δ to approach zero.

$$\theta_t = \lim_{p_2 \to p_1} (A\epsilon^{p_1 t} + B\epsilon^{p_2 t}) = \lim_{\Delta \to 0} [\epsilon^{p_1 t}(A + B\epsilon^{\Delta t})]$$

Use the series expansion for $\epsilon^{\Delta t}$ and remove the factor $\epsilon^{p_1 t}$.

$$\theta_t = \epsilon^{p_1 t} \lim_{\Delta \to 0} \left\{ A + B\left[1 + \Delta t + \frac{(\Delta t)^2}{2!} + \cdots \right] \right\}$$

Discard all terms in $(\Delta t)^2$ and higher order in passing to the limit.

$$\theta_t = \epsilon^{p_1 t}(C + Gt)$$

where the constants $C = A + B$ and $G = B\Delta$ are chosen to be finite as $\Delta \to 0$. Hence, the general solution of Eq. (4-14) for the case of equal roots is

$$\theta = \theta_s + C\epsilon^{-\alpha t} + Gt\epsilon^{-\alpha t} \qquad p_1 = p_2 = -\alpha \qquad (4\text{-}19)$$

4-5. Boundary Conditions. The constants appearing in the general solutions of Eq. (4-14) are arbitrary in the sense that they may have any finite values without invalidating the solution. However, they are not arbitrary in any given system where unique and unambiguous conditions of operation are specified. These conditions pertain to relations between θ and t and are called boundary conditions. If they are specified at the onset of the transient they are sometimes called *initial conditions*. Two examples of the application of different initial conditions to the general solution will be developed to illustrate the procedure for evaluating arbitrary constants. Two independent conditions are required to evaluate the pair of arbitrary constants. The two conditions must be independent, for if one can be derived from the other via the relationship between θ and t, then only one of the arbitrary constants may be evaluated.

Example 1. Zeroed Inert Coil. Suppose the two initial conditions specified at $t = 0$ are $\theta = 0$ and $d\theta/dt = 0$. This is the case of a zeroed galvanometer whose coil is stationary prior to closing the switch in Fig. 4-1. It may be seen intuitively that these two conditions are independent, for the initial reading of the galvanometer may be made independent of the initial angular velocity of the coil. For instance, suppose that the coil is swinging freely under open-circuited conditions and that the switch is closed at the instant θ is passing through zero. Then $\theta = 0$ at $t = 0$, but $d\theta/dt$ is not zero. Contrariwise, the coil might be at rest at $t = 0$, but adjusted to have some fixed angular displacement different from zero. Then, $d\theta/dt = 0$ at $t = 0$, but θ is not zero.

An analytical test for independence of the two conditions is the demonstration that the pair of arbitrary constants become established unambiguously upon application of the conditions. Consider the case of unequal roots. Imposing $\theta = 0$ at $t = 0$ on Eq. (4-18) yields $0 = \theta_s + A + B$. Imposing $d\theta/dt = 0$ at $t = 0$ yields $0 = Ap_1 + Bp_2$. Thus, two independent equations in A and B are obtained. When solved for A and B and inserted into Eq. (4-18), the result is

$$\theta = \theta_s \left(1 + \frac{p_2\epsilon^{p_1t}}{p_1 - p_2} + \frac{p_1\epsilon^{p_2t}}{p_2 - p_1} \right) \qquad p_1 \neq p_2 \qquad (4\text{-}20)$$

In the case of equal roots, imposing $\theta = 0$ at $t = 0$ on Eq. (4-19) yields $0 = \theta_s + C$. Imposing $d\theta/dt = 0$ at $t = 0$ gives $0 = -\alpha C + G$. Hence, the arbitrary constants are determined: $C = -\theta_s$, $G = -\alpha\theta_s$. Equation (4-19) becomes

$$\theta = \theta_s(1 - \epsilon^{-\alpha t} - \alpha t\epsilon^{-\alpha t}) \qquad p_1 = p_2 = -\alpha \qquad (4\text{-}21)$$

There is nothing arbitrary about the results for θ in Eqs. (4-20) and (4-21) which are now specified completely in terms of the parameters of the system J, D, S, K, E, R, and R_m.

Example 2. Return to Rest from Steady Deflection. Suppose the switch of Fig. 4-1 has been closed for a long time so that θ has attained the steady value θ_s, and the coil velocity is zero. Then a resistance, R_1, is suddenly placed across the galvanometer terminals at $t = 0$. The initial conditions are $\theta = \theta_s$ and $d\theta/dt = 0$ at $t = 0$. It would be incorrect to insert these initial conditions into the solutions that have been developed, because Eq. (4-14) contains the term $I = E/(R + R_m)$, which pertains to the circuit arrangement of Fig. 4-1. In the present case, the final steady-state current drawn from E is $I_1 = E/(R + R_p)$ where $R_p = R_1R_m/(R_1 + R_m)$, and the steady-state current through the galvanometer after it finally comes to rest at its new deflection will be $I' = R_1I_1/(R_1 + R_m)$ (using the current-splitting rule) rather than I. Evidently, Eq. (4-14) may be used if I is replaced by I', and if θ is interpreted as the instantaneous value of θ starting at the instant R_1 is introduced. Then, for the case of $p_1 \neq p_2$, imposing $\theta = \theta_s$ at $t = 0$ on Eq. (4-18), with I replaced by I', yields $\theta_s = I'/K + A + B$. Imposing $d\theta/dt = 0$ at $t = 0$ yields $0 = Ap_1 + Bp_2$. Solve for A and B and insert into Eq. (4-18).

$$\theta = \left(\theta_s - \frac{I'}{K} \right) \left(\frac{p_2\epsilon^{p_1t}}{p_2 - p_1} + \frac{p_1\epsilon^{p_2t}}{p_1 - p_2} \right) + \frac{I'}{K} \qquad p_1 \neq p_2 \qquad (4\text{-}22)$$

It may be readily verified that, for $\alpha \neq 0$, this result yields $\theta = \theta_s$ at $t = 0$, and $\theta = I'/K$ as $t \to \infty$. If the added shunt resistor, R_1, is zero, or if $R \to \infty$ (switch of Fig. 4-1 opened), then $I' = 0$. Therefore, the coil returns from $\theta = \theta_s$ to a zero deflection, because p_1 and p_2 each have negative real parts.

4-6. Nonoscillatory Solutions.

There are three possible forms for the roots p_1 and p_2, depending upon the size of D^2 relative to $4SJ$.

1. If $\alpha^2 > S/J$ $(D^2 > 4SJ)$ then p_1 and p_2 are unequal, real, and negative since $\sqrt{\alpha^2 - (S/J)}$ is not zero and is smaller in magnitude than α. In this case, $p_1 = -\alpha + \beta$ and $p_2 = -\alpha - \beta$, where $\beta = \sqrt{\alpha^2 - (S/J)}$.

2. If $\alpha^2 = S/J$ $(D^2 = 4SJ)$ then p_1 and p_2 are equal, real, and negative; $p_1 = p_2 = -\alpha$.

3. If $\alpha^2 < S/J$ $(D^2 < 4SJ)$ then p_1 and p_2 are conjugate complex

numbers. In this case, $p_1 = -\alpha + j\omega$ and $p_2 = -\alpha - j\omega$, where $\omega = \sqrt{(S/J) - \alpha^2} = j\beta$.

The first two possibilities correspond to the overdamped and critically damped cases, respectively. In the overdamped case, the deflection, θ, is given as a function of time by Eq. (4-18) with $p_1 = -\alpha + \beta$ and $p_2 = -\alpha - \beta$. These are both real numbers calculable from D/J and S/J using Eq. (4-17). Expressing Eq. (4-18) in terms of α and β,

$$\theta = \theta_s + \epsilon^{-\alpha t}(A\epsilon^{\beta t} + B\epsilon^{-\beta t}) \qquad (4\text{-}23)$$

The result for θ in the case of an overdamped galvanometer with an initially inert and zeroed coil is given in Eq. (4-20), which becomes, in terms of α and β,

$$\frac{\theta}{\theta_s} = 1 - \frac{\epsilon^{-\alpha t}}{2\beta}\left[(\alpha + \beta)\epsilon^{\beta t} + (\beta - \alpha)\epsilon^{-\beta t}\right] \qquad (4\text{-}24)$$

This may also be expressed in terms of the hyperbolic functions

$$\sinh \beta t = \frac{\epsilon^{\beta t} - \epsilon^{-\beta t}}{2} \qquad \cosh \beta t = \frac{\epsilon^{\beta t} + \epsilon^{-\beta t}}{2}$$

as follows:

$$\frac{\theta}{\theta_s} = 1 - \epsilon^{-\alpha t}\left(\frac{\alpha}{\beta} \sinh \beta t + \cosh \beta t\right) \qquad (4\text{-}25)$$

The result for the case of an overdamped galvanometer returning to rest from an initial steady reading is given by Eq. (4-22). Expressed in terms of α and β, this becomes

$$\theta = \left(\theta_s - \frac{I'}{K}\right)\frac{\epsilon^{-\alpha t}}{2\beta}\left[(\alpha + \beta)\epsilon^{\beta t} + (\beta - \alpha)\epsilon^{-\beta t}\right] + \frac{I'}{K} \qquad (4\text{-}26)$$

This result also may be expressed in hyperbolic form.

$$\theta = \left(\theta_s - \frac{I'}{K}\right)\epsilon^{-\alpha t}\left(\frac{\alpha}{\beta} \sinh \beta t + \cosh \beta t\right) + \frac{I'}{K} \qquad (4\text{-}27)$$

In the critically damped case, θ is given by Eq. (4-19). If the coil is initially at $\theta = 0$ and motionless, θ attains the final deflection θ_s in accordance with Eq. (4-21).

Several examples of nonoscillatory behavior of θ as a function of time in the case of a zeroed, initially inert galvanometer are given in Fig. 4-5. Because the degree of damping depends upon the size of α relative to $\sqrt{S/J}$, it is desirable to define a dimensionless *damping coefficient*, k, by

$$k = \frac{\alpha}{\sqrt{S/J}} = \alpha\sqrt{\frac{J}{S}} \qquad (4\text{-}28)$$

For critical damping, $k = 1$, and for overdamped cases $k > 1$. The curves in Fig. 4-5 indicate that θ approaches θ_s more rapidly for critical damping than for overdamping. Using the definition of relative damping coefficient in Eq. (4-28), it follows that

$$\beta = \sqrt{\alpha^2 - \frac{S}{J}} = \sqrt{\frac{S}{J}} \sqrt{k^2 - 1} \tag{4-29}$$

If $k^2 \gg 1$, then β and α are approximately equal, but β is always less than α. The relative damping coefficient, k, may also be expressed in terms of α and β, eliminating $\sqrt{S/J}$ from Eqs. (4-28) and (4-29).

$$k = \alpha \sqrt{\frac{J}{S}} = \frac{1}{\sqrt{1 - (\beta/\alpha)^2}} \tag{4-30}$$

4-7. Oscillatory Solution. The third possibility for the roots p_1 and p_2 occurs when $\alpha^2 < S/J$ ($D^2 < 4SJ$). Then p_1 and p_2 are conjugate complex roots, $p_1 = -\alpha + j\omega$ and $p_2 = -\alpha - j\omega$. This is the underdamped or oscillatory case, and is of most interest from a practical standpoint because a slightly underdamped galvanometer displays a faster speed of response than in the critically damped case. Also, operation with a barely visible overshoot in applications where actual scale readings are being taken (rather than null detection) gives the observer a clue that there is no impairment of coil movement, such as erratic frictional interference.

In the oscillatory case it is revealing to express Eq. (4-18) in trigonometric form. Insert $p_1 = -\alpha + j\omega$ and $p_2 = -\alpha - j\omega$ into the transient part of Eq. (4-18).

$$\theta_t = \epsilon^{-\alpha t}(\mathbf{A}\epsilon^{j\omega t} + \mathbf{B}\epsilon^{-j\omega t})$$

Since $\epsilon^{\pm j\omega t}$ is complex and θ_t *must* be real, because it represents a physical quantity, it follows that $\mathbf{A}$ and $\mathbf{B}$ must be complex. Let $\mathbf{A} = a + jb$ and $\mathbf{B} = c + jd$. Then use $\epsilon^{\pm j\omega t} = \cos \omega t \pm j \sin \omega t$.

$$\theta_t = \epsilon^{-\alpha t}[(a + jb)(\cos \omega t + j \sin \omega t) + (c + jd)(\cos \omega t - j \sin \omega t)]$$

The imaginary part *must* be zero for all t.

$$(b + d) \cos \omega t + (a - c) \sin \omega t = 0$$

Therefore, $a = c$ and $b = -d$. In other words, $\mathbf{A}$ and $\mathbf{B}$ are complex conjugates, $\mathbf{A} = \mathbf{B}^*$.

The real part of θ_t, which is all that remains, is

$$\theta_t = 2\epsilon^{-\alpha t}(c \cos \omega t + d \sin \omega t)$$

Express this in terms of a single trigonometric function, and add θ_s.

$$\theta = \theta_s + M\epsilon^{-\alpha t} \sin (\omega t + \gamma) \tag{4-31}$$

where $M = 2 \sqrt{c^2 + d^2}$ and $\gamma = \tan^{-1} c/d$. This trigonometric equivalent of Eq. (4-18), containing two arbitrary constants, M and γ, shows clearly that the transient term is a damped sinusoid.

The angular frequency of oscillation is $\omega = \sqrt{(S/J) - \alpha^2}$ where $\alpha = D/2J$. Hence, the period is

$$T = \frac{2\pi}{\omega} = \frac{2\pi}{\sqrt{(S/J) - \alpha^2}} \tag{4-32}$$

The *free period* is defined as the value of T with no damping ($\alpha = 0$ or $D = 0$), and is smaller than T. It is a useful theoretical quantity, but not exactly attainable in practice because of small air damping.

$$T_0 = \frac{2\pi}{\omega_0} = \frac{2\pi}{\sqrt{S/J}} = 2\pi \sqrt{\frac{J}{S}} \tag{4-33}$$

The ratio of these periods is useful.

$$\frac{T}{T_0} = \frac{\sqrt{S/J}}{\sqrt{(S/J) - \alpha^2}} = \frac{1}{\sqrt{1 - \alpha^2 J/S}} = \frac{1}{\sqrt{1 - k^2}} \tag{4-34}$$

where k is the relative damping coefficient defined in Eq. (4-28) and is less than 1 in the oscillatory case.

Other useful relations among the various parameters may be developed. For example,

$$\frac{\omega}{\alpha} = \frac{2\pi}{\alpha T} = \frac{T_0}{\alpha T} \sqrt{\frac{S}{J}} = \frac{T_0}{kT} = \frac{\sqrt{1 - k^2}}{k} \tag{4-35}$$

and also

$$\sqrt{\alpha^2 + \omega^2} = \sqrt{\frac{S}{J}} = \frac{2\pi}{T_0} = \frac{\alpha}{k} \tag{4-36}$$

For the specific case of an initially zeroed, motionless galvanometer energized at $t = 0$, the initial conditions may be applied to Eq. (4-31). [The result may also be obtained from Eq. (4-24) with $\beta = j\omega$.] Imposing $\theta = 0$ at $t = 0$ on Eq. (4-31) yields $0 = \theta_s + M \sin \gamma$. The time derivative of Eq. (4-31) is

$$\frac{d\theta}{dt} = M\epsilon^{-\alpha t}[\omega \cos (\omega t + \gamma) - \alpha \sin (\omega t + \gamma)]$$

Imposing $d\theta/dt = 0$ at $t = 0$ yields

$$0 = \omega \cos \gamma - \alpha \sin \gamma \qquad \text{or} \qquad \tan \gamma = \frac{\omega}{\alpha}$$

Consequently,

$$\sin \gamma = \frac{\omega}{\sqrt{\alpha^2 + \omega^2}} = \frac{T_0}{T} \qquad \text{and} \qquad M = \frac{-\theta_s}{\sin \gamma} = \frac{-\theta_s T}{T_0}$$

Thus, the result for θ with arbitrary constants evaluated in terms of these initial conditions is

$$\theta = \theta_s \left[1 - \frac{T}{T_0} \epsilon^{-\alpha t} \sin \left(\omega t + \tan^{-1} \frac{\omega}{\alpha} \right) \right] \qquad (4\text{-}37)$$

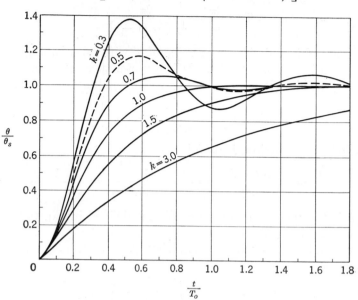

FIG. 4-5. Modes of galvanometer behavior.

Several examples of oscillatory behavior of θ as a function of time in the case of a zeroed, initially inert galvanometer are given in Fig. 4-5, in terms of the dimensionless quantities θ/θ_s, t/T_0, and relative damping coefficient, k. These are universal curves that may be used regardless of the specific values of the galvanometer parameters. The oscillations are seen to become more prolonged, the smaller the k. For k approaching 1 (critical damping), θ settles to θ_s more rapidly.

4-8. Speed of Response. The approach of θ to θ_s may be studied more closely and compared analytically with the critically damped case, by first defining the quantity

$$\Delta = 1 - \frac{\theta}{\theta_s} \qquad (4\text{-}38)$$

This is the fractional deviation of θ from its final value θ_s. The expression for Δ in the oscillatory case follows from Eq. (4-37).

$$\Delta = \frac{T}{T_0} \epsilon^{-\alpha t} \sin (\omega t + \gamma) \qquad (4\text{-}39)$$

The fractional deviation for critical damping is obtained from Eq. (4-21).

$$\Delta_c = \epsilon^{-\alpha_c t}(1 + \alpha_c t) \qquad \alpha_c > \alpha \qquad (4\text{-}40)$$

where the value of α_c in the critically damped case is greater than α in the underdamped case.   It may be shown that $\Delta = \Delta_c$ at $t = 0$, with $\sin \gamma = T_0/T$, and this must be so because all curves of Fig. 4-5 start at $\theta = 0$, $t = 0$.

The *initial* approach of θ to θ_s is more rapid in the oscillatory case than in the critically damped case, as indicated in the curves of Fig. 4-5.   But as time progresses, θ crosses and oscillates about θ_s and the real question is: Does θ get to and *stay within* a specified fraction of θ_s at a time earlier or later than for the same specified fraction in the critically damped case?

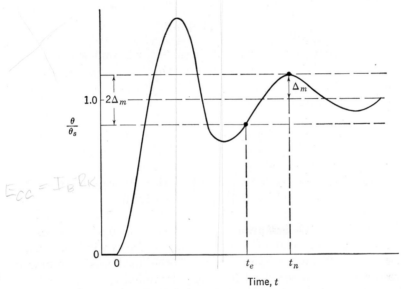

$E_{CC} = I_B^R K$

FIG. 4-6. Illustrating speed of response.

The answer to this question is complicated by the fact that Δ is an oscillating quantity.   The deflection θ may pass through a fixed zone about θ_s many times before staying within it (see Fig. 4-5).   The times, t_n, at which Δ is a maximum or a minimum may be found by setting the time derivative of Eq. (4-39) to zero.

$$\frac{d\Delta}{dt} = 0 = \frac{T}{T_0} \epsilon^{-\alpha t_n}[\omega \cos (\omega t_n + \gamma) - \alpha \sin (\omega t_n + \gamma)]$$

Therefore, t_n must satisfy

$$\tan (\omega t_n + \gamma) = \frac{\omega}{\alpha} = \tan \gamma \qquad \text{or} \qquad t_n = \frac{n\pi}{\omega} = \frac{nT}{2} \qquad n = 0, 1, 2, \ldots$$

Consequently, at $t = t_n$, $\sin(\omega t_n + \gamma) = \pm T_0/T$ and the maximum magnitude of Δ is obtained from Eq. (4-39).

$$|\Delta_m| = \epsilon^{-\alpha t_n} = \epsilon^{-\alpha n T/2} \qquad (4-41)$$

Now consider a prescribed zone $\pm \Delta_m$ about $\theta/\theta_s = 1$, as shown in Fig. 4-6. In the oscillatory case, θ will enter this zone at a time $t_e < t_n$ and stay within this zone for all t thereafter. The question is whether Δ_c is equal to or greater than the magnitude of Δ_m at $t = t_e$. As a very conservative approach, the value of Δ_c at $t = t_n$ may be compared with the magnitude of Δ_m. This is given by Eq. (4-40) with $t = t_n$.

$$\Delta_c = \epsilon^{-\alpha_c t_n}(1 + \alpha_c t_n) \qquad \alpha_c > \alpha \qquad (4-42)$$

The ratio of Eq. (4-42) to (4-41) is

$$\frac{\Delta_c}{|\Delta_m|} = \epsilon^{-(\alpha_c - \alpha)t_n}(1 + \alpha_c t_n)$$

and this shows that $\Delta_c > |\Delta_m|$ at $t = t_n$ if $(\alpha_c - \alpha)$ is sufficiently small. It follows that at time t_e, Δ_c is even greater than the magnitude of Δ_m for the same difference between α_c and α. Thus, it is seen that the speed of response in the oscillatory case may be faster than in the critically damped case.

Detailed numerical calculations based on the transcendental equations that have been presented show that in the critically damped case, θ deviates from θ_s by 10 per cent of θ_s ($\Delta = 0.1$) at a time equal to approximately $0.6T_0$. The shortest time to achieve this 10 per cent result in the oscillatory case is less; about $0.4T_0$, with relative damping coefficient $k = 0.6$. For θ to enter and stay within a ± 1 per cent zone about θ_s, a relative damping coefficient approximately equal to 0.8 yields fastest response, a time about equal to two-thirds of the free period, T_0, being required. A longer time, very nearly equal to the free period, is required to achieve the 1 per cent result with critical damping.

4-9. Logarithmic Decrement. The logarithmic decrement, λ, is a quantity used to describe the rate at which galvanometer oscillations die out. It is defined by

$$\lambda = \ln \frac{\theta_n}{\theta_{n+1}} \qquad (4-43)$$

and is the natural logarithm of the ratio of two successive elongations, the nth and the $(n + 1)$th. An elongation is the *magnitude* of the maximum deviation between the instantaneous value of θ and the steady-state value about which θ oscillates, for any given half cycle of oscillation. Thus, an elongation is by definition a positive quantity. The definition of λ implies that the ratio of *any* two successive elongations is constant, and this will be demonstrated subsequently.

A graphical representation of the elongations, θ_n and θ_{n+1}, in the case of a galvanometer initially at rest, is given in Fig. 4-7. It may be seen qualitatively that if θ_{n+1} is only slightly less than θ_n, the oscillations are rather prolonged and λ is small numerically. However, if θ_{n+1} is substantially smaller than θ_n, the oscillations damp out quickly and λ is large numerically. Thus, λ is an inverse measure of the oscillations and a direct measure of the damping. Smaller λ means larger and more prolonged oscillations (less damping), while a larger λ means smaller oscillations of shorter duration (more damping).

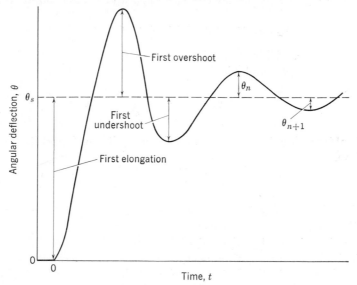

FIG. 4-7. Illustrating elongations.

It is possible to develop a formula for λ in terms of the galvanometer parameters. This is worthwhile because λ is conveniently measurable, and may then be related to the galvanometer parameters whose determination is more evasive. Equation (4-31) describes the behavior of θ with time in the oscillatory case, before insertion of boundary conditions. The times, t_n, at which maximum and minimum values of θ occur may be found by setting the time derivative of Eq. (4-31) to zero.

$$\frac{d\theta}{dt} = 0 = M\epsilon^{-\alpha t_n}[\omega \cos(\omega t_n + \gamma) - \alpha \sin(\omega t_n + \gamma)]$$

Hence, t_n must satisfy

$$\tan(\omega t_n + \gamma) = \frac{\omega}{\alpha} = \tan\gamma \quad \text{and} \quad t_n = \frac{n\pi}{\omega} = \frac{nT}{2} \quad n = 0, 1, 2, \ldots$$

These times are, of course, the same as those for which maximum and minimum fractional deviations were found to occur. The maxima and minima are spaced equally in time and are separated by $T/2$, where T is the period.

The instantaneous value of θ_n at t_n, the time of the nth elongation, is given from Eq. (4-31) by

$$\theta_n = |\theta - \theta_s| = M\epsilon^{-\alpha t_n}|\sin (\omega t_n + \gamma)|$$

which could be either a maximum or a minimum. The bars signify absolute value, which is implicit in the meaning of the term elongation. The next elongation occurs at $t = t_n + T/2$ and is also found from Eq. (4-31).

$$\theta_{n+1} = M\epsilon^{-\alpha t_n}\epsilon^{-\alpha T/2}|\sin (\omega t_n + \pi + \gamma)|$$

where $\omega T/2 = \pi$. This elongation occurs at a minimum of θ, if θ was a maximum at $t = t_n$, and vice versa. The ratio of the two successive elongations is

$$\frac{\theta_n}{\theta_{n+1}} = \epsilon^{\alpha T/2} = \epsilon^{\lambda}$$

since the two sine terms are equal in magnitude (opposite in sign). Therefore,

$$\lambda = \frac{\alpha T}{2} = \frac{DT}{4J} \tag{4-44}$$

and this holds for any two successive elongations because an arbitrary elongation at $t = t_n$ was used in the development.

The first instant at which $d\theta/dt$ is zero, which represents the first instant at which an elongation occurs, is at $t = 0$. However, the literature usually refers to the first elongation as the first overshoot, shown in Fig. 4-7. But the first elongation at $t = 0$ is perfectly legitimate and may be used to determine λ. For an initially inert galvanometer, the first elongation at $t = 0$ is equal to θ_s. The second elongation is $\theta_m - \theta_s$, where θ_m signifies the maximum value of θ, and it occurs at $t = T/2$. Hence,

$$\lambda = \ln \frac{\theta_s}{\theta_m - \theta_s} \tag{4-45}$$

This states that λ is the natural logarithm of the final deflection over the first overshoot. Similarly, if the current is suddenly removed at $t = 0$ from a galvanometer which has an initial steady reading, λ is given by the natural logarithm of the ratio of the initial steady deflection to the first undershoot. It also follows from Eq. (4-45) that the maximum fractional overshoot, occurring at $t = T/2$, is

$$\frac{\theta_m - \theta_s}{\theta_s} = \epsilon^{-\lambda} = \epsilon^{-\alpha T/2}$$

This result is consistent with Eq. (4-41) with $n = 1$.

Another formulation for λ is based on the property demonstrated in Eq. (4-44) that ratios of successive elongations are constant.

$$\frac{\theta_n}{\theta_{n+1}} = \frac{\theta_{n+1}}{\theta_{n+2}} = \cdots = \frac{\theta_{n+r-1}}{\theta_{n+r}}$$

If these r equal ratios are all multiplied together, the result is evidently

$$\left(\frac{\theta_n}{\theta_{n+1}}\right)^r = \frac{\theta_n}{\theta_{n+r}}$$

Therefore,
$$\lambda = \ln \frac{\theta_n}{\theta_{n+1}} = \frac{1}{r} \ln \frac{\theta_n}{\theta_{n+r}} \tag{4-46}$$

The expression in Eq. (4-44) for λ in terms of the galvanometer parameters enables other relations to be developed. A particularly useful one is the relation between λ and the period. From Eq. (4-36),

$$\alpha^2 + \omega^2 = \left(\frac{2\pi}{T_0}\right)^2 = \omega_0{}^2$$

Hence,
$$\left(\frac{T}{T_0}\right)^2 = \left(\frac{\omega_0}{\omega}\right)^2 = 1 + \left(\frac{\alpha}{\omega}\right)^2 = 1 + \left(\frac{\alpha T}{2\pi}\right)^2 = 1 + \left(\frac{\lambda}{\pi}\right)^2$$

Therefore,
$$\frac{T}{T_0} = \sqrt{1 + \left(\frac{\lambda}{\pi}\right)^2} \tag{4-47}$$

This shows that the size of λ relative to π is important. For example, if $\lambda = \pi$, the ratio of the actual period, T, to the theoretical undamped period, T_0, is $T/T_0 = \sqrt{2}$.

The relationship between λ and the relative damping coefficient, k, is easily developed by combining Eqs. (4-47) and (4-34).

$$\left(\frac{\lambda}{\pi}\right)^2 = \left(\frac{T}{T_0}\right)^2 - 1 = \frac{1}{1 - k^2} - 1 = \frac{k^2}{1 - k^2}$$

Hence,
$$\lambda = \frac{\pi k}{\sqrt{1 - k^2}} \tag{4-48}$$

For example, if $k = 1/\sqrt{2}$, then $\lambda = \pi$. In similar fashion it is possible to develop many other relations in which λ appears.

4-10. Determination of Parameters. The parameters of the galvanometer J, D, S, and K appearing in Eq. (4-14) may be determined by various indirect methods. They are very difficult to obtain directly. The general idea is to determine enough conveniently measurable quantities to enable calculation of the four parameters by use of the relationships that have been developed in the oscillatory and critically damped cases.   (The overdamped case is of no interest here.)   In practice, the actual methods employed depend to some extent on the type of galvanometer.   In order to illustrate the principle, it will simply be shown here that it is possible to determine J, D, S, and K by indirect methods in terms of readily measured quantities.

The determination of K may be carried out independently from the other parameters.   In steady-state deflection it has been shown that

$$I = \frac{E}{R + R_m} = K\theta_s$$

All four quantities, E, R, R_m, and θ_s, are easily measured; hence, K may be computed.   For instance, E may be measured accurately with a potentiometer.   A decade-resistance box may be used in the laboratory for R.   The galvanometer resistance, R_m, may be determined easily by the half-deflection method (see Prob. 3-10).   And θ_s may be related directly to the scale reading; for instance, in a mirror galvanometer with a circular-arc scale the scale reading is given by $d = 2D\theta_s$, where D is the distance between scale and mirror.

The remaining three parameters are intimately interrelated, and a group of measurements is required to untangle them.   An example follows.   The galvanometer may be energized from an initially zeroed state and made to oscillate about θ_s.   Then the logarithmic decrement, λ, and period, T, may be measured—the former by observing elongations and the latter by using a stop watch to measure the time duration of a counted number of complete cycles of oscillation.   The deflected galvanometer may be open-circuited and it will then oscillate about its zero rest position with damping determined only by air, since $R \rightarrow \infty$.   The logarithmic decrement, λ_a, may be measured in this instance.   Finally, the external resistance, R, may be adjusted until critical damping is achieved.   This is accomplished by repeatedly energizing the galvanometer from an initial resting state, using different values of R until the first overshoot barely disappears.   The measured quantities λ, T, λ_a, and R_c, the total resistance required for critical damping, permit calculation of the galvanometer parameters J, D, and S, as well as the air-damping coefficient, D_a, as shown below.

With λ and T determined, S/J may be calculated from the relations

$$\frac{T}{T_0} = \sqrt{1 + \left(\frac{\lambda}{\pi}\right)^2} \qquad T_0 = 2\pi \sqrt{\frac{J}{S}}$$

The ratio D/J may also be calculated since

$$\lambda = \frac{\alpha T}{2} = \frac{D}{J} \frac{T}{4}$$

In the case of air damping only, λ_a may be used in conjunction with the determined value of S/J to find D_a/J because

$$\lambda_a = \frac{D_a}{J}\frac{T_a}{4} = \frac{D_a}{2J}\pi\sqrt{\frac{J}{S}}\sqrt{1 + \left(\frac{\lambda_a}{\pi}\right)^2}$$

Hence, S/J, D/J, and D_a/J are calculable from the measured quantities λ, T, and λ_a.

The damping coefficient, D, is given by

$$D = D_a + \frac{S^2}{K^2(R + R_m)}$$

For the special case of critical damping, $R_c = R + R_m$ is known from direct measurement.   Therefore,

$$D_c = D_a + \frac{S^2}{K^2 R_c}$$

where D_c signifies the value of D for critical damping.   Now divide by J.

$$\frac{D_c}{J} = \frac{D_a}{J} + \frac{S}{J}\frac{S}{K^2 R_c}$$

For critical damping, the relative damping coefficient, k, is unity so $\alpha = \sqrt{S/J} = D_c/2J$.   Thus, $D_c/J = 2\sqrt{S/J}$ is known because S/J is known.   Therefore, S may be computed because D_a/J, K, and R_c have all been previously determined.   Then J, D, and D_a follow immediately. An explicit relationship for S in terms of the quantities determined in this example is

$$S = \frac{K^2 T R_c}{\sqrt{\pi^2 + \lambda^2}}\left(1 - \frac{\lambda_a}{\sqrt{\pi^2 + \lambda_a^2}}\right) \tag{4-49}$$

4-11. Operation in Steady Sinusoidal State.   There are many applications of d'Arsonval movements where the galvanometer is energized from sources displaying irregular time variations.   It is often used to measure nonperiodic voltages and currents in a variety of circuits and electrical machines.   Many other applications are found in connection with transducers, devices that convert physical quantities such as pressure, temperature, humidity, and others into electrical outputs providing a measure of the physical quantity.   Galvanometers are also used widely in biological measurements on animals and human beings whose hearts, brains, and nerves produce measurable but irregular time-varying electrical signals.   In many of these applications, it is desirable to record the deflections automatically, thus obtaining a permanent record of the result that may be analyzed at leisure.   This is usually accomplished in mirror galvanometers by directing a focused beam of light on the mirror which reflects it onto a moving strip of photographic paper. As θ varies, the beam on the paper moves proportionately and in a direction perpendicular to the travel of the paper. A record, or graph, of θ vs. time is thereby obtained. In pivoted-coil instruments it is common to use a stylus or pen (rather than an indicating pointer) that writes directly on a chart moving in a direction perpendicular to the swing of the stylus.

The important characteristics of a galvanometer used to record irregular, varying inputs may be found from knowledge of the transient response to a sudden disturbance. The behavior of the coil in going from a given static state to a different static condition, though hardly the same as the galvanometer motion in the irregular-signal case, may be properly interpreted. Quantities such as speed of response and period (or frequency) of oscillation enable the user to judge the faithfulness with which the galvanometer will follow an irregular input. For example, if the fastest change in the signal to be recorded requires a time interval that is long compared with the rise time of the galvanometer, a faithful record may be expected. The rise time is sometimes defined as the time for θ to change from 10 per cent to 90 per cent of θ_s, starting from $\theta = 0$.

On the other hand, an entirely different point of view may be used: the steady-state response characteristics. These are the characteristics displayed by the galvanometer when a sinusoidal signal is applied. Such quantities as bandwidth and phase shift are then considered as measures of galvanometer performance, when confronted with irregular signals. These steady-state quantities do not really provide any more fundamental information than the transient quantities. Indeed, the steady-state response and the transient response are intimately related, and one may be predicted from the other. However, steady-state quantities are frequently used. Accordingly, a brief treatment of galvanometer operation in the steady alternating state will be presented. Steady-state and transient characteristics will also be compared.

The basic starting point of the analysis must be the differential equation for θ. If a voltage $E_p \sin \omega t$, rather than a direct emf, E, is applied to the galvanometer in series with a resistance R, Eq. (4-14) becomes

$$J \frac{d^2\theta}{dt^2} + D \frac{d\theta}{dt} + S\theta = \frac{SE_p \sin \omega t}{K(R + R_m)} = \frac{SI_p}{K} \sin \omega t \qquad (4\text{-}50)$$

This is obtained simply by replacing E in Eq. (4-14) by $E_p \sin \omega t$. The correctness of this procedure may be verified by reviewing each step in the development of Eq. (4-14) and noting that nothing except E has been changed. Even the motional emf, e_m, has the same form, $(S/K) \, d\theta/dt$, for any applied signal. It should also be noted that the self-inductance of the galvanometer coil, L_m, has been neglected once again. The symbol ω represents the angular frequency of the sinusoidal voltage source and is completely independent of the galvanometer characteristics. It is not the same ω that was used in the transient analysis.

The general solution of Eq. (4-50) consists of the sum of a steady-state term and a transient term. However, only the steady-state response is of interest, so the transient term will be ignored. When the voltage $E_p \sin \omega t$ is applied to the galvanometer, θ will undergo rather irregular forced-oscillatory motion but will eventually settle down to a steady sinusoidal vibration of frequency the same as the source. This is expected because damping is present and the differential equation is linear with constant coefficients. It is this periodic motion that constitutes the steady-state response and does not include the intermediate transient.

4-12. Steady-state Solution. The steady-state solution of Eq. (4-50) may be determined by utilizing the $\epsilon^{j\omega t}$ method outlined in Sec. 2-5. Consider the complex equation

$$J \frac{d^2\mathbf{u}}{dt^2} + D \frac{d\mathbf{u}}{dt} + S\mathbf{u} = \frac{SI_p}{K} \epsilon^{j\omega t}$$

The two reasons for introducing this equation are that θ is simply related to $\mathbf{u}$ by

$$\theta = \mathrm{Im}\ \{\mathbf{u}\} = \mathrm{Im}\ \{\mathbf{U}\epsilon^{j\omega t}\}$$

and also the complex angular deflection, $\mathbf{U}$, is easily obtained. Substitute $\mathbf{U}\epsilon^{j\omega t}$ into the complex differential equation, cancel $\epsilon^{j\omega t}$, and the following algebraic equation in $\mathbf{U}$ results.

$$(j\omega)^2 J\mathbf{U} + j\omega D\mathbf{U} + S\mathbf{U} = \frac{SI_p}{K}$$

Solve for $\mathbf{U}$.

$$\mathbf{U} = \frac{SI_p}{K[S - \omega^2 J + j\omega D]} = U\epsilon^{-j\psi}$$

Thus, the desired steady-state solution for θ is obtained.

$$\theta = \mathrm{Im}\ \{\mathbf{U}\epsilon^{j\omega t}\} = \frac{SI_p}{K\ \sqrt{(S - \omega^2 J)^2 + (\omega D)^2}} \sin\left(\omega t - \tan^{-1} \frac{\omega D}{S - \omega^2 J}\right)$$
$$(4\text{-}51)$$

Another procedure for developing θ that is rather tedious, but less sophisticated than the $\epsilon^{j\omega t}$ solution, is based on the recognition that Eq. (4-50) is linear and has constant coefficients. Therefore, the steady-state solution for θ must be expressible in the form $\theta = \theta_p \sin(\omega t + \phi)$. Direct substitution of this form of θ and its first and second derivatives, as appropriate, into Eq. (4-50) enables the peak value and phase angle of θ to be determined. The result agrees with Eq. (4-51).

Even a third procedure may be utilized, based on the analogy with the series RLC circuit, mentioned in Sec. 4-4. The concepts of complex impedance and complex current may be used fruitfully, and the basic method is the same as that employed to develop Eq. (4-51). In carrying out this method, it must be recognized that θ is analogous to the charge, q, on the capacitor, C.

Equation (4-51) may be cast into a highly useful form by introducing the quantities

$$\omega_0 = \sqrt{\frac{S}{J}} \qquad Q = \frac{\omega_0 J}{D} = \frac{S}{\omega_0 D} = \frac{\sqrt{SJ}}{D} \qquad (4\text{-}52)$$

which, in the analogous RLC circuit, correspond to the resonance frequency $\omega_0 = 1/\sqrt{LC}$ and the circuit $Q = \omega_0 L/R$. Note that the period

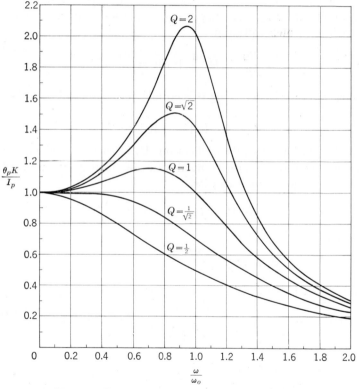

FIG. 4-8. Steady-state amplitude characteristics.

of ω_0 is exactly the same as the free period, T_0, defined in the transient analysis. Moreover, $1/Q$ is equal to twice the relative damping coefficient, k, used in the transient analysis.

Introduction of ω_0 and Q into Eq. (4-51) gives, after some manipulation, the following expressions for θ_p, the peak value of θ, and ψ, the phase angle of θ.

$$\theta_p = \frac{I_p Q}{K \dfrac{\omega}{\omega_0} \sqrt{1 + Q^2 \left(\dfrac{\omega}{\omega_0} - \dfrac{\omega_0}{\omega}\right)^2}} \qquad (4\text{-}53)$$

$$\tan \psi = \frac{1}{Q\left(\dfrac{\omega_0}{\omega} - \dfrac{\omega}{\omega_0}\right)} \qquad (4\text{-}54)$$

These results, while appearing to be a bit more cumbersome than Eq. (4-51), are really easier to interpret. For one thing, they express θ in terms of the pertinent quantities, ω_0 and Q. Furthermore, ω always appears in combination with ω_0, that is, as ω/ω_0, which is a normalized frequency variable. Finally, for any given static sensitivity, I_p/K, both θ_p and ψ are clearly seen to be functions of only two quantities, Q and ω/ω_0.

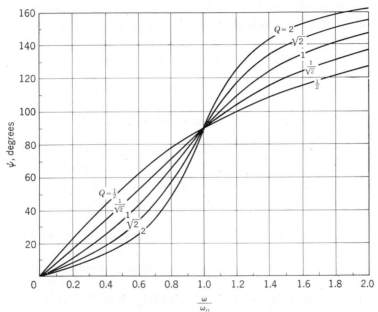

Fig. 4-9. Steady-state phase characteristics.

Curves showing the behavior of θ_p, the peak value of θ, and ψ, the phase angle of θ, as a function of ω/ω_0 are given in Figs. 4-8 and 4-9 for several values of Q. The normalized quantities $\theta_p K/I_p$ and ω/ω_0 permit these curves to be used regardless of the particular values of the galvanometer parameters. It may be seen that for low Q (large relative damping, k) the peak amplitude, θ_p, drops off steadily with frequency. For high Q (small relative damping, k) resonance phenomena occur in the vicinity of ω_0. The higher the Q, the closer the maximum response is to ω_0 and the higher the resonant peak. The angle ψ is positive for all values of Q, which means that θ always lags the applied voltage. It is interesting that $\psi = 90°$ at $\omega = \omega_0$ for any value of Q.

4-13. Galvanometer Resonance and Low-pass Bandwidth. The voltage source $E_p \sin \omega t$ causes a forced steady-state vibration of the galvanometer. If the galvanometer is underdamped, it will tend to oscillate rather vigorously when the forcing frequency is near the natural frequency of oscillation of the galvanometer. This resonance effect may be very pronounced.

The frequency at which the forced vibrations display maximum amplitude may be obtained in principle by setting the derivative of θ_p with respect to ω equal to zero. As a matter of mathematical technique, the normalized frequency variable $x = \omega/\omega_0$ may be used. Furthermore, only the denominator of θ_p need be differentiated, since θ_p is a maximum when the denominator is a minimum. Also, the *square* of the denominator of θ_p will be a minimum at the same value of x for which the denominator itself is a minimum. Therefore, the roots of x in the following equation will give the desired results.

$$\frac{d}{dx}(x^2 + Q^2x^4 - 2Q^2x^2 + Q^2) = 0 = 2x + 4Q^2x^3 - 4Q^2x$$

With ω_m defined as the value of ω at which θ_p is a maximum, there results

$$x_m = \frac{\omega_m}{\omega_0} = \sqrt{1 - \frac{1}{2Q^2}} \qquad \text{and} \qquad x_{m1} = \frac{\omega_{m1}}{\omega_0} = 0 \qquad (4\text{-}55)$$

The root $\omega_{m1} = 0$ gives the value of θ_p at zero frequency. It represents a minimum when ω_m is real and represents a maximum when ω_m is imaginary. For $Q^2 \gg \frac{1}{2}$, ω_m is very nearly equal to ω_0. For smaller Q, ω_m is less than ω_0. The peak of the response curve tends to shift from ω_0 toward $\omega = 0$ as Q is lowered. The peak disappears entirely for $Q^2 \leqq \frac{1}{2}$, and then θ_p is a maximum at $\omega_{m1} = 0$. These trends may be seen in Fig. 4-8.

The maximum value of θ_p is obtained by inserting ω_m/ω_0 into Eq. (4-53). After manipulation, the result becomes

$$\theta_{pm} = \frac{I_p}{K}\frac{2Q^2}{\sqrt{4Q^2 - 1}} \qquad (4\text{-}56)$$

The maximum peak value of θ, θ_{pm}, is thus seen to become larger, the larger the Q. For $Q^2 \gg \frac{1}{4}$, it is approximately

$$\theta_{pm} = \frac{I_pQ}{K} \qquad Q^2 \gg \frac{1}{4} \qquad (4\text{-}57)$$

and this is Q times the static response. For smaller Q, θ_{pm} tends to get smaller, and this is borne out in Fig. 4-8. It is interesting to note that for $Q^2 = \frac{1}{2}$, $\theta_{pm} = I_p/K$. This agrees with the value of θ_p at $\omega = 0$, as it should, because the location of the resonance peak shifts toward $\omega_m = 0$ as $Q^2 \to \frac{1}{2}$.

The curves in Fig. 4-8 indicate that the galvanometer may be regarded as a low-pass filter. The low-pass bandwidth, BW, of the galvanometer may be defined as the range of frequencies over which θ_p is equal to or greater than a prescribed fraction of the peak value of θ at $\omega = 0$. The $100/N$ per cent bandwidth is equal to the frequency at which the response has dropped to $1/N$ times the response at $\omega = 0$ ($N \geq 1$). An expression for the $100/N$ per cent bandwidth may be obtained by setting θ_p equal to I_p/NK in Eq. (4-53), and solving for $x = \omega/\omega_0$. The following quadratic form for x results:

$$x^4 + x^2 \left(-2 + \frac{1}{Q^2} \right) + 1 - N^2 = 0$$

Solve using the quadratic formula and discard extraneous roots.

$$x = \frac{BW}{\omega_0} = \left[1 - \frac{1}{2Q^2} + \sqrt{\left(1 - \frac{1}{2Q^2} \right)^2 + N^2 - 1} \right]^{\frac{1}{2}} \quad (4\text{-}58)$$

The fact that there is only one physically realizable root for $N \geq 1$ proves that the response never dips below I_p/K except at the high-frequency ends of the curves. For a numerical example, take $N = 2$ and $Q = 1$. Equation (4-58) yields $x = 1.5$. This means that the 50 per cent bandwidth is 50 per cent greater than ω_0 for $Q = 1$. In other words, the response drops to one-half its zero-frequency value at $\omega = 1.5\,\omega_0$. This may be checked on the curve in Fig. 4-8. If $2Q^2 \gg 1$, $1/2Q^2$ may be ignored in comparison with 1, and the bandwidth expression simplifies to

$$BW = \omega_0 \sqrt{1 + N} \qquad Q^2 \gg \frac{1}{2}, N \geq 1 \quad (4\text{-}59)$$

The phase angle of ψ at the frequency ω_m is given by substituting ω_m into Eq. (4-54).

$$\tan \psi_m = \sqrt{2(2Q^2 - 1)} \qquad \omega = \omega_m$$

For $Q^2 \gg \frac{1}{2}$, $\tan \psi_m$ is equal to $2Q$, so ψ_m is only slightly less than $90°$ at the resonant peak. For $Q^2 = \frac{1}{2}$, the phase angle is zero, since this corresponds to $\omega_m = 0$.

When $\omega \ll \omega_0$, ω/ω_0 may be ignored compared with ω_0/ω in the denominator of Eq. (4-54), with the result

$$\tan \psi \approx \psi = \frac{\omega}{Q\omega_0} \qquad \omega \ll \omega_0$$

Thus, ψ is proportional to ω over a limited range of frequencies close to zero. The slope of the phase characteristic at small values of ω/ω_0

depends inversely on Q. The curves of Fig. 4-9 indicate that even if ω is too large to permit the above approximation, the phase characteristic may still be maintained fairly close to a constant times ω, provided Q has a value of about $1/\sqrt{2}$.

4-14. Vibration Galvanometer. The sharp resonance peak displayed by the galvanometer when the Q is high has two distinctive features. First, the galvanometer response at the frequency ω_0 may be many times greater than that at $\omega = 0$. Second, the galvanometer behaves essentially as a highly selective bandpass filter. The vibration galvanometer is one that takes advantage of both these desirable characteristics. The most widely used type is a modification of the d'Arsonval galvanometer in which an adjustable taut suspension is used to vary S so that ω_0 may be tuned to the angular frequency of the source, ω. Also, the moment of inertia, J, is designed to be small so that values of ω_0 in the range up to about 1,800 radians per sec (300 cps) are available. Vibration galvanometers of this type are capable of displaying a Q as high as 150 or more, and this yields very high

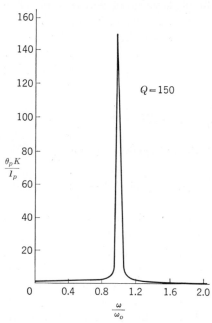

FIG. 4-10. Amplitude characteristic of vibration galvanometer.

sensitivity in combination with excellent discrimination against harmonics of the signal source. This galvanometer is used principally as a sensitive a-c detector in low-frequency bridge circuits. It is usually equipped with a reflecting mirror and light source. When the galvanometer is at rest, a fine bright line of light is seen on its scale. Application of signal causes the line to widen out into a band as the galvanometer coil vibrates. An intense light source is desirable, since the brightness of the band diminishes rapidly as the deflection increases.

The response curve for a vibration galvanometer with $Q = 150$ is given in Fig. 4-10. The sharp resonance peak may be analyzed from relations that have been developed in the preceding section. From Eq. (4-55), it is seen that the maximum response occurs at $\omega = \omega_0$ in this high-Q case. Also, Eq. (4-57) shows that the maximum deflection is I_pQ/K, which is 150 times the static deflection in the case of Fig. 4-10.

The manner in which the response drops off with frequency may be investigated by use of Eq. (4-53). Because θ_p diminishes so markedly when ω deviates from ω_0 by only a small percentage of ω_0, it is justifiable to employ a narrow-band approximation. Define

$$\delta = \frac{\omega}{\omega_0} - 1 \tag{4-60}$$

which is the fractional deviation of ω from the resonance value, ω_0. When $\omega = \omega_0$, $\delta = 0$; and when $\omega = \omega_0 + \Delta\omega$, $\delta = \Delta\omega/\omega_0$. Expressing ω/ω_0 in terms of δ in Eq. (4-53) leads to a considerable simplification for small δ. The term ω_0/ω may be expanded

$$\frac{\omega_0}{\omega} = \frac{1}{1 + \delta} = (1 + \delta)^{-1} = 1 - \delta + \delta^2 + \cdots$$

and terms in δ^2 and higher order may be neglected with small error if $\delta \ll 1$. Then the difference between the two nearly equal frequency ratios becomes

$$\frac{\omega}{\omega_0} - \frac{\omega_0}{\omega} \approx 1 + \delta - (1 - \delta) = 2\delta$$

Meanwhile, the factor ω/ω_0 multiplying K in Eq. (4-53) may be replaced by unity if $\delta \ll 1$. Thus, Eq. (4-53) becomes

$$\theta_p = \frac{I_p Q}{K \sqrt{1 + 4Q^2\delta^2}} \qquad \delta \ll 1 \tag{4-61}$$

This equation contains the information that θ_p is at its maximum value, $I_p Q/K$, at $\delta = 0$. Also, for $\delta = \pm 1/2Q$ (which is only a $\pm \frac{1}{3}$ per cent change in frequency for $Q = 150$), θ_p decreases to $1/\sqrt{2} = 0.707$ times its maximum value (see Fig. 4-11). In other words, the response is 3 db down from its maximum value at $\omega_1/\omega_0 = 1 - 1/2Q$ and at $\omega_2/\omega_0 = 1 + 1/2Q$. Therefore, the 3-db bandwidth is the difference between ω_2 and ω_1.

$$\omega_2 - \omega_1 = \omega_0 \left(1 + \frac{1}{2Q}\right) - \omega_0 \left(1 - \frac{1}{2Q}\right) = \frac{\omega_0}{Q} \tag{4-62}$$

The fact that Q is equal to the resonance frequency divided by the 3-db bandwidth is not surprising, since this is one of the definitions of Q. The 3-db bandwidth definition employed here is, of course, different from the low-pass bandwidth of the preceding section.

A quantitative idea of the excellent discrimination provided by the vibration galvanometer against harmonics of the signal source may be found by determining the response at $\omega = 2\omega_0$. Since Eq. (4-61) is restricted to small values of δ, it must not be used for this calculation.

Instead, return to Eq. (4-53) and replace ω by $2\omega_0$ with the result

$$\theta_p = \frac{I_p Q}{2K \sqrt{1 + 9Q^2/4}} \qquad \omega = 2\omega_0 \qquad (4\text{-}63)$$

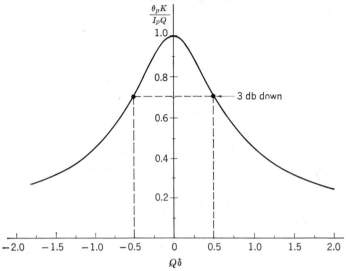

Fig. 4-11. Universal curve for narrow-band approximation.

For the high-Q case, this shows that θ_p has decreased to $I_p/3K$ at $\omega = 2\omega_0$. The maximum response at $\omega = \omega_0$ is $3Q$ times this value, or 450 for the curve in Fig. 4-10. The second harmonic rejection for $Q = 150$ is thus seen to be very substantial, 53 db.

4-15. Relations between Transient and Steady-state Response. To illustrate the relationship between the steady-state and transient response, resonance in the steady state and critical damping in the transient state may be examined. It has been shown that the resonance peak disappears at $Q^2 = \frac{1}{2}$. The corresponding damping, to have no forced-vibration resonance peak, found from Eq. (4-52), is $D = \sqrt{2SJ}$. However, in the transient analysis critical damping exists when $D = D_c = \sqrt{4SJ}$. This damping is larger by a factor of $\sqrt{2}$ than the largest permissible value of D to avoid a resonance peak in the steady-state response. In other words, the maximum permissible value of Q for no resonance peak in steady state is $1/\sqrt{2} = 0.707$, but the value of Q that corresponds to critical damping in the transient state is $\frac{1}{2}$. Thus, even though the frequency response curve displays no resonance peak in steady-state operation, the transient response may display a slight overshoot. The damping for $Q = 1/\sqrt{2}$ represents an underdamped system of relative damping coefficient $k = 1/\sqrt{2} = 0.707$.

A number of other relationships between steady-state and transient operation may be deduced. Perhaps a similarity has been noticed between the frequency of maximum steady-state response, ω_m, and the frequency of oscillation in the transient response of an underdamped galvanometer. To explore this, note that ω_m is given by

$$\omega_m = \omega_0 \sqrt{1 - \frac{1}{2Q^2}} = \sqrt{\frac{S}{J} - 2\alpha^2}$$

The frequency of oscillation in the underdamped transient case is $\omega = \sqrt{(S/J) - \alpha^2}$. It is interesting that these two results are not quite the same.

As a final example, the relationship between Q and logarithmic decrement may be derived. The relation between relative damping coefficient, k, and logarithmic decrement, λ, developed in the transient analysis is given in Eq. (4-48). Since $1/Q = 2k$, it follows that

$$\lambda = \frac{\pi}{\sqrt{4Q^2 - 1}}$$

Thus, when the maximum permissible value of Q for no resonance peak is employed, $Q^2 = \frac{1}{2}$, this corresponds to a logarithmic decrement in transient operation of $\lambda = \pi$. For $Q < \frac{1}{2}$, λ becomes imaginary, which is reasonable since $Q = \frac{1}{2}$ corresponds to critical damping.

These and other relationships between transient and steady-state characteristics show the intimate connection between them. Fundamentally, characteristics of either type may be used to obtain information concerning dynamic behavior of galvanometers.

PROBLEMS

4-1 (§3). Develop the differential equation of the torques for a uniform-radial-field galvanometer when the self-inductance, L_m, of the coil is not neglected. Verify that the result reduces to Eq. (4-14) as $L_m \to 0$. Hint: Differentiate Eq. (4-5).

4-2 (§5). It is entirely conceivable that an initially deflected galvanometer with zero initial coil velocity will not return to zero reading when the source of current is removed. Yet, Example 2 of Sec. 4-5 yields $\theta = 0$ for this case. At what point in the development of the equations for θ was this possibility ruled out, and how may Eq. (4-14) be modified so as to include this possibility?

4-3 (§5). Starting with Eq. (4-18), impose the boundary conditions $d\theta/dt = A_0$ and $\theta = \theta_0$ at $t = 0$. Determine the equation for θ in terms of the constants A_0 and θ_0 with the arbitrary constants A and B eliminated. Compare this result with Eq. (4-20).

4-4 (§6). The coil of the galvanometer of Fig. 4-1 is at rest, and $\theta = 0$ before the switch is closed. When the switch is closed at $t = 0$, the coil motion is critically damped. Show that at time $t = \sqrt{J/S}$ the departure of the instantaneous deflection from its ultimate steady-state value, θ_s, is the fraction $2/\epsilon$ of the steady-state deflection, where $\epsilon = 2.7183$.

4-5 (§7). Derive Eq. (4-37) by substituting $\beta = j\omega$ in Eq. (4-24).

4-6 (§7). The galvanometer in Fig. 4-1 has a free period $T_0 = 2$ sec, and negligible air damping ($D_a = 0$). When $R + R_m = 100$ ohms, the same galvanometer has a period $T = 4$ sec. What total resistance $R + R_m$ is required to critically damp this galvanometer? $50\sqrt{3}$ OHMS

4-7 (§7). A certain galvanometer has negligible air damping ($D_a = 0$) and requires an external circuit resistance $R = 300$ ohms for critical damping (see Fig. 4-1). When used with an external circuit resistance $R = 600$ ohms, the period of the galvanometer is $T = 7$ sec. The galvanometer resistance is $R_m = 100$ ohms. What is the free period, T_0, of the galvanometer?

4-8 (§7). When the switch is closed in the galvanometer circuit shown in Fig. 4-1, where $R_m = 50$ ohms and $R = 100$ ohms, the coil angle vs. time follows the equation

$$\theta = 0.4 - 0.8\epsilon^{-\sqrt{3}\,t} \cos\left(t - \frac{\pi}{3}\right)$$

(a) What is the maximum value of θ?   (b) What value of R is required for critical damping? Assume $D_a = 0$.

4-9 (§7). Repeat Prob. 4-8 for

$$\theta = 0.100 - 0.128\epsilon^{-4t} \cos(5t - 38.67°)$$

4-10 (§7). In the circuit of Fig. 4-1, $E = 10^{-3}$ volt and $R + R_m = 100$ ohms. After the switch is closed at $t = 0$ on an initially inert galvanometer, the deflection reaches a maximum value $\theta_m = 0.604$ radian at $t = \pi/2$ sec. It settles to a final deflection $\theta_s = 0.500$ radian. Assume a uniform radial field and constant galvanometer parameters.   (a) Develop the equation for the deflection, θ, as a function of t with *all* constants evaluated numerically.   (b) If the moment of inertia, J, of the moving coil is 2.4×10^{-9} newton-meter-sec^2 per radian, what is the numerical value of the coefficient of air damping, D_a? (State units of D_a.)   Assume that no damping exists other than air damping and circuit damping.

4-11 (§8). A critically damped galvanometer is initially at rest and its deflection is zero. It is energized from the circuit of Fig. 4-1 at $t = 0$. Calculate the time, in terms of T_0, required for the deflection to reach 99 per cent of the steady-state deflection.

4-12 (§8). The switch in Fig. 4-1 is closed on an underdamped d'Arsonval galvanometer with a uniform radial field and negligible coil inductance. Derive a general expression for the difference in time between the instant that θ goes *through* its steady-state value and the instant at which the following maximum (or minimum) occurs.

4-13 (§9). The period of a galvanometer is measured to be $T = 18.6$ sec, and the ratio of two successive elongations is 1.62. What is the free period, T_0, of the galvanometer?

4-14 (§9). A d'Arsonval mirror galvanometer with a uniform radial magnetic field has a circular-arc scale at a distance 1 meter from the mirror. This galvanometer is zeroed (zero scale reading with zero current through the galvanometer) and then the circuit shown in Fig. 4-12 is connected. With the switch closed, the steady deflection on the scale is 100 mm. At time $t = 0$, the switch is suddenly opened and the system oscillates as shown, just reaching zero on the first undershoot at $t = 1$ sec. (a) Compute the current sensitivity, S_I, of the galvanometer.   (b) Compute d_s, the final scale deflection in millimeters, as $t \to \infty$.   (c) Neglect air damping, D_a, and compute the numerical value of S, the spring constant of the suspension.

4-15 (§9). The deflection of a d'Arsonval galvanometer with a uniform radial field is given as a function of time by

$$\theta = 0.218 - 0.244\epsilon^{-0.50t} \sin (t + 63.5°)$$

Find the maximum value of θ and the logarithmic decrement, λ.

4-16 (§9). The switch in Fig. 4-1 is closed at $t = 0$ on a zeroed initially inert galvanometer whose sensitivity is 0.1 μa per mm. The oscillatory deflection swings up to

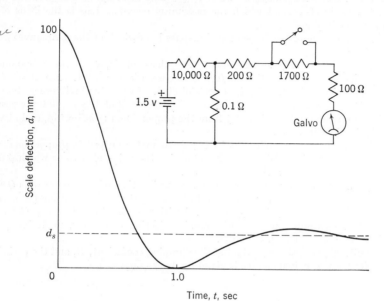

FIG. 4-12. Transient behavior of galvanometer.

a maximum of 80 mm, and next swings back to a minimum point 40 mm from zero. (a) Calculate $I = E/(R + R_m)$. (b) Find the logarithmic decrement.

4-17 (§9). The switch in Fig. 4-1 is closed on an underdamped galvanometer, and the maximum deflection at the first *over*shoot is 20 mm. The total deflection on the fourth *over*shoot is 15 mm and occurs 20 sec after the first overshoot. The final steady deflection is 10 mm. Find the logarithmic decrement, λ, and the period, T, of the underdamped galvanometer.

4-18 (§9). An experimenter energized a highly underdamped galvanometer and was interested in observing the magnitude of the total deflection, d_1, at the first *over*shoot. However, he was too late to take the reading; instead, he read the total deflection $d_2 = 50$ mm at the first *under*shoot, and the total deflection $d_3 = 70$ mm at the second *over*shoot (see Fig. 4-7). Then he calculated the reading, d_1, that he missed. You calculate it.

4-19 (§10). Verify Eq. (4-49).

4-20 (§12). Demonstrate that the solution for θ obtained by direct substitution of $\theta = \theta_p \sin (\omega t + \phi)$ into Eq. (4-50) is the same as that obtained by the $\epsilon^{i\omega t}$ method in Eq. (4-51).

4-21 (§12). Show that Eq. (4-51) may be placed in the form of Eqs. (4-53) and (4-54) by use of the relations in Eq. (4-52).

4-22 (§12). Show that Eq. (4-53) may be written in the form

$$\theta_p = \frac{I_p Q \omega_0}{K \omega} \sin \psi$$

4-23 (§12). Show that $\theta_p = I_p Q / K$ when $\omega / \omega_0 = 1$, and check these five points on the curves of Fig. 4-8.

4-24 (§13). For values of Q between $1/\sqrt{2}$ and 5, compute and plot the curve θ_{pm} vs. the value of ω / ω_0 at which the maximum occurs. This is the locus of the resonant peaks in Fig. 4-8.

4-25 (§13). Compute the 90 per cent low-pass bandwidth of the d'Arsonval galvanometer for $Q = \sqrt{2}$.

4-26 (§13). To avoid phase distortion, the phase angle, ψ, of the galvanometer response must be a constant times ω / ω_0, as discussed in Sec. 11-4. For $Q = 1/\sqrt{2}$, Fig. 4-9 shows that this condition is almost fulfilled. Compute the difference between ψ and $\pi \omega / 2 \omega_0$ for a range of values of ω / ω_0 between 0 and 1, and plot the results. What is the maximum deviation of ψ from the proportional relationship, and at what value of ω / ω_0 does it occur?

4-27 (§13). The phase angle, ψ, of the galvanometer output is proportional to ω for small values of ω / ω_0. With $Q = 2$, determine the value of ω / ω_0 at which ψ deviates by 5° from the proportional relationship.

4-28 (§14). The angular frequency applied to a vibration galvanometer with $Q = 50$ is $\omega = 1.1 \omega_0$. What is the per cent error in the computed response using the narrow-band approximation in Eq. (4-61), compared with that obtained from Eq. (4-53)?

4-29 (§14). Compute the second-harmonic rejection capability, in decibels, of a vibration galvanometer with $Q = 100$.

4-30 (§15). Show that the product of the damping coefficient, D, and the period, T, of an underdamped galvanometer is given by $4\pi J / \sqrt{4Q^2 - 1}$.

CHAPTER 5

ERRORS OF MEASUREMENT

A genuine feeling for the subject "errors of measurement" usually requires at least one thoroughly penetrating laboratory experience in which the experimenter comes to grips with a difficult, high-precision measurement problem. There really is no substitute for this experience. It may be tremendously enlightening and satisfying. In the last analysis, performing an accurate measurement represents a grapple with the unknown, but there are many layers to be unpeeled before this final stage may be reached. No pretense is made that printed words can replace this experience, nor can a classroom treatment of the subject. Moreover, it requires more than the casual type of measurement performed in low-accuracy work to get to the heart of the matter.

Producing an accurate result is not merely a matter of collecting and interconnecting some apparatus and taking readings. An almost incredible effort is involved for highly accurate work. The experimenter must comprehend the theory of his method thoroughly and must intimately know all pertinent characteristics of his equipment. He might have to develop theories and equipment he needs but has been unable to find, despite intensive search of the literature. He must minimize and correct for factors known to influence his results. When the larger factors have been taken into account, smaller ones emerge and must be circumvented. He must employ skill and care and often use ingenious and subtle techniques to achieve his ends. Sometimes subsidiary experiments are necessary to locate and evaluate sources of error. He must *think* about what he has done, or is about to do, questioning every step with an attitude of doubt and distrust, not proceeding until convinced that all is well. He must live with his problem.

When he is through—an arbitrary point because there is no real end to this work—he usually has acquired such complete knowledge of the entire matter that the satisfaction of accomplishment is gratifying indeed. If he has not done his work well, he may find himself in an embarrassing position, as was the case of the following gentleman who presented his findings at a professional meeting.

There was a young man from Purdue
Who had much to report that was new and true.
But that which was true was not new,
And that which was new was not true.

A deep penetration into this complex subject, which in many ways is an art, is difficult at the introductory level. The subject of errors of measurement is ordinarily attacked seriously for the first time in advanced (graduate) laboratories or in the professional experience of the engineer. Accordingly, the aims here are modest. The kinds of errors that may arise will be suggested, with examples taken primarily from the preceding chapters. An introduction to methods of statistics which may be applied to unavoidable errors is presented in Chap. 6. Finally, some methods for estimating errors of results computed from measured quantities will be introduced in Chap. 7.

There are two over-all objectives for studying errors of measurement: (1) to find out how errors may be reduced and (2) to learn how estimates of the reliability of results may be made.

5-1. Some Definitions. Every measurement is in error. If the precision of the equipment is adequate, no matter what its accuracy, a discrepancy will always be observed between two measured results.

These sound like rather provocative statements, but what do they mean? To be understood correctly, the key words *error, precision, accuracy,* and *discrepancy* must be understood clearly in the context usually intended when used with respect to measurements.

> Error: estimated uncertainty
> Precision: sharp definition
> Accuracy: closeness to truth
> Discrepancy: difference between two results

In ordinary usage, the word "error" may have certain unpleasant connotations. It may imply a mistake, a moral offense, or possibly a belief in something untrue. In the extreme sense of a blunder, it commonly implies ignorance, stupidity, and sometimes blame. None of these is implied when the word error is used in connection with electrical measurements. There is nothing shameful about a measurement error; in fact, omission of a statement of the error is poor practice, especially since no measurement is entirely free of error. The concern in measurements is the possibility of overlooking contributions to the estimated uncertainty of the result and the reporting of too small an error. The error of measurement is usually stated in quantitative terms using an accepted measure of the uncertainty which is defined mathematically. The most common of such measures in scientific work is the standard deviation, but others are sometimes used, as will be discussed in Chap. 6.

In ordinary usage, the distinction between the words "precision" and "accuracy" is usually vague. Indeed, the dictionary inevitably links one of these terms with the definition of the other. This state of affairs is in sore need of clarification in the field of measurements, where the two words have sharply different meanings. An instrument may possess high precision by virtue of a clearly legible, finely divided, distinct scale from which readings are taken. At the same time its accuracy may be poor; for example, because of an internal defect or misadjustment. A specific illustration is provided by a mirror galvanometer whose air-gap field has been altered by the presence of iron filings which have inadvertently been collected. Precise scale readings to a fraction of a millimeter might be possible in such a galvanometer, but the corresponding value of coil current, deduced by use of the current sensitivity of the uncontaminated instrument, might be very different from the actual current in the coil.

Precision is also used in measurements to describe the consistency or reproducibility of results. A quantity called the precision index, defined in Chap. 6, describes the spread, or dispersion, of repeated results about some central value. High precision means a tight cluster of the repeated results while low precision indicates a broad scattering of values. Again, there is not necessarily any relationship between precision used in this sense and the accuracy of the result. All the repetitious measurements could be biased in the same way by some systematic effect that produces a deviation of the measured result from the truth. For example, an ammeter used with a shunt designed for a different meter movement could be used repeatedly to measure the same current. Precise scale readings might be possible, and all measurements might display exceptional agreement among themselves, but they all would be inaccurate indications of the value of the current since use of an incorrect shunt introduces a systematic shift of all readings.

Finally, the term "discrepancy" deserves comment, despite its clearly defined meaning in common usage. The difficulty usually encountered is failure to distinguish clearly between discrepancies and errors. For instance, the discrepancy between a measured value of the resistance per unit length of a piece of standard copper wire and the value listed in the standard-wire tables is not necessarily an error of measurement. The characteristics of the copper used in the experiment might be different from that used to establish the "handbook" value. As another example, the distinction between discrepancy and error is important because discrepancies that arise when repeated measurements of the same quantity are performed might constitute only a small portion of the error of the measurements. Finally, if two different experimenters obtained two different results for the same quantity, it is correct to say there was a discrepancy between the two results. But the error reported by either investigator well could be larger than this discrepancy.

While there are other words that must be understood clearly, the four mentioned should serve to alert the student that precise terminology is essential to obtain an accurate understanding of errors.

5-2. Classification of Errors. Because errors may arise from every source imaginable, there are many different ways in which they may be classified. Two broad categories often used are called "systematic" and "residual." Systematic errors are those which, in principle, may be avoided or corrected. They arise from such sources as outright mistakes, defects of instruments, influence of physical environment, poor experimental design, and habits of the observer. Residual errors are those which would inevitably remain if all systematic errors were eliminated.

Both these terms may be confusing. Residual errors are not necessarily those which reside in the final results. Even in the best of experiments, final results generally contain both types of errors. Systematic errors are not necessarily constant or systematic in that they may vary with the conditions of the experiment and may sometimes behave in irregular fashion, fluctuating over a period of time. Because systematic errors may, in principle, be reduced or corrected, perhaps better terms might be "correctable" or "determinate" errors.

It is helpful to consider four categories of systematic errors:

a. Gross Errors. These are mistakes or blunders including misreading of instruments, incorrect adjustment of apparatus, improper application of instruments, computational mistakes, and others.

b. Instrument Errors. These are defects or shortcomings of instruments, such as errors in calibration, damaged internals, unstable internal elements, worn or defective parts, and others.

c. Environmental Errors. These are physical influences on the experimenter, on the equipment he uses, or on the quantity being measured. Such errors are attributable to temperature, pressure, humidity, stray disturbances, and so forth.

d. Observational Errors. These pertain to habits of the observer such as imperfect technique, poor judgment, peculiarities in making observations, and others.

Residual errors cannot be subdivided into convenient categories because they arise from such a wide variety of sources. Some of them may be completely unknown in a given experiment. These uncontrollable errors are unavoidable in any measurement, and they often display random fluctuations that do not follow a regular pattern. They are frequently caused by the erratic combination of a large number of small effects, some of which have known sources and others of which do not. In many cases the experimenter cannot suppress these effects without at the same time altering the quantity he is attempting to measure.

5-3. The Pursuit of Systematic Errors. The many ways in which systematic errors may arise represent an exacting test of the experimenter's alertness, imagination, and inquisitiveness. A competent and reliable experimenter assumes an air of vigilance and an attitude of distrust toward every item that could possibly influence his result. One slip, and his painstaking labor may be nullified.

An organized procedure for handling systematic errors may be envisioned, but more likely than not, it is carried out by the experienced individual in an intuitive and seemingly haphazard manner. For the beginner, it is well to indicate at least some stages of the process. First and foremost, it is necessary to discover that a systematic error exists, or may be expected to exist. This is strongly dependent upon the ability and experience of the investigator. A number of approaches are suggested in Sec. 5-14. Second, a quantitative estimate of the influence of the systematic error on the quantity being measured is desirable. This may be obtained by means of an auxiliary or pilot experiment, or may sometimes be deduced by theoretical analysis. Third, the magnitude of the error is usually appraised in terms of desired over-all accuracy, and the cost and difficulty of possible alternatives to circumvent the error. Finally, if indicated, a means is devised to eliminate or correct for the error. This may be a simple matter of replacing defective equipment; it may require the introduction of additional controls on the conditions of the experiment; or it may even take the form of devising an entirely different method of measurement.

Each and every one of these four steps may represent a highly challenging problem. In some instances, some of the steps may be obvious and trivial, but the greater the desired accuracy, the greater the required effort. The point at which the *hunt-measure-appraise-correct* process really becomes difficult depends largely on desired accuracy and on the nature of the quantity being measured. In the case of low-frequency electrical measurements, accuracy on the order of 1 per cent usually calls for corrections and considerable pains, while accuracies on the order of 0.1 per cent or better represent a formidable challenge.

The ability to detect the presence of a systematic error is of the greatest importance. For that reason, it is well to expand upon the kinds of systematic errors that may be encountered in each of the four categories. Sometimes a general knowledge of the kinds of errors that may occur leads the experimenter to uncover them.

5-4. Gross Errors. Gross errors are usually considered to be so obvious and trivial as to be unworthy of elaboration. However, so long as human beings are involved, it is inevitable that some gross errors will be

committed.   The problem is perhaps not so much to eliminate them completely, which is desirable but probably impossible, but to expect and
correct them wherever they occur.   While many gross errors are readily
detected, some are surprisingly elusive.   Moreover, it is occasionally so
difficult to correct for them that it is easier to repeat the work.

One of the most frequently committed gross errors is treacherous
because it may occur in a multitude of subtle ways that escape the
attention of the experimenter.   This is the error of altering or molesting
the quantity being measured by the very act of measuring it.   Because
the beginner is especially vulnerable to this type of error and because it
occurs so commonly, it is discussed more fully in Sec. 5-5.

Another common gross error, sometimes very evasive, may be called a
theoretical error.   This type of error is committed when an equation used
to calculate a quantity from measured values is based on assumptions
that are not fulfilled in the experiment.   An example is given in Sec. 5-6.
Another form of this type of error occurs when theoretical processing of
results is carried out for data obtained under conditions that violate the
assumptions implicit in the theory used.   For example, the use of normal-
distribution statistics, presented in the next chapter, may be applied
erroneously to data that are not distributed normally.

A variety of gross errors are attributable to outright carelessness or
sloppy habits such as improper reading of an indicating instrument,
recording a result differently from the actual reading taken, or adjusting
instruments incorrectly.   Consider the case of a multirange voltmeter
that employs different numerical designations for each setting of the
range switch on the same set of scale graduations.   A reading is sometimes made that does not correspond to the actual range employed.   Or
a reading of 74.3 volts, called out by one member of a group, might be
recorded by another as 73.4 volts, especially if done in a hurried manner.
The adjustment screw on a meter, usually provided to set the indication
to zero when the instrument is not energized, is another potential source
of gross error.   If it is not set accurately, all readings are thrown off.
Mistakes of this kind, and there are many more, may seem too obvious
to mention.   Yet what experimenter has not committed them at one
time or another?

Another category of gross errors pertains to the use of an instrument
in applications for which it was not intended or in which its operational
limits are exceeded.   For example, a d-c ammeter can hardly be expected
to give a sensible reading of a 60-cps alternating current.   In this case
the error would be readily discerned when zero indication, or needle
vibration about zero, was observed.   However, there are many other
instances where false results may ambush the unwary observer.   For
instance, a signal generator (oscillator) might be used with the intent of

providing a sinusoidal source, and the accuracy of all meter indications might depend upon the purity of the waveform. Yet, the oscillator might be so heavily overloaded, beyond its designed capability, that the signal resembles a square wave.

Errors committed in computation of results are not uncommon. This possibility is present whether the calculations are done by hand, by slide rule, by desk calculator, or by any other means. There are literally an infinite number of ways in which they may occur, and the bothersome thing is that the same individual may make exactly the same errors when he repeats the calculations. There are many mathematical techniques for providing independent checks on computed results. Repeated calculations by more than one individual are sometimes helpful.

5-5. Molesting the Measured Quantity. There are two general approaches to measuring a quantity, whether the methods be direct or indirect. They are:

1. Measure the quantity in such a manner that it is not altered by the method employed.

2. Accept the idea that the quantity will be altered by the measurement process, measure the molested quantity, and then correct for the disturbance.

The first approach can never be strictly accomplished. There is always some effect, no matter how small, produced on the quantity when the environment is changed to measure it. However, this method is useful in many practical cases where the disturbances are so slight as to be undetectable, or in cases where they are less than the allowable errors. The second method is perhaps the more frequent approach when viewing the over-all field of measurements.

It is essential to appreciate that the measured quantity is inevitably altered in the process of measuring it. There are many instances in the development of science and engineering where this effect was overlooked or ignored, and it happens repeatedly today in both student and professional laboratories. It is sometimes a tricky matter to know to what extent the quantity being measured has been changed. An interesting example, far afield from electrical measurements but pertinent nonetheless, arose in attempting to obtain a measure of the efficiency of a group of factory workers. A selected group was studied over a period of time with some rather disconcerting results. The efficiency of the group was found to increase steadily during the test, as the group put forth more and more intensive efforts under the atmosphere of having so much attention paid to them by so many important personages. Needless to say, a good deal was learned about human behavior, but not much about their normal efficiency.

In electrical measurements there are many ways to determine the degree to which the molested quantity has been changed. For example, if it is suspected that a resistor being measured is affected by the current passed through it during the measurement, its resistance may be determined for several different values of current and compared. Use of two independent methods is sometimes helpful, especially when it is known that the quantity is subject to different conditions in the two different tests. Some other techniques are suggested in Sec. 5-14. Several examples in which voltages and currents in electric circuits are altered by insertion of an ammeter or connection of a voltmeter are presented in Chap. 8. These are typical examples in electrical measurements of molesting the quantity which is to be measured. Common as they are, they are often overlooked.

5-6. Voltmeter–ammeter Method. A simple example of a theoretical error is presented by the voltmeter–ammeter method of measuring d-c resistance. This is a popular type of resistance measurement method if high accuracy is not necessary, since the apparatus required is usually conveniently available. If the voltage, V, across the resistance and the current, I, through the resistance are measured, then the unknown resistance, X, is given by

$$X = \frac{V}{I} \tag{5-1}$$

provided the ammeter and voltmeter are ideal. This implies that the ammeter resistance, R_a, and the voltmeter resistance, R_v, must strictly be zero and infinity, respectively. A theoretical error is committed if Eq. (5-1) is applied when the assumptions regarding meter resistances are not satisfied. (All other possible sources of error are ignored, such as incorrect instrument calibration, heating of the resistance, X, and stray field effects.)

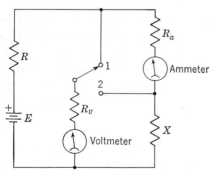

Figure 5-1 shows two possible ways in which the voltmeter and the ammeter may be connected for simultaneous readings. [Simultaneous readings represent a desirable technique to circumvent fluctuations in the d-c supply, of emf E, and internal resistance, R.

FIG. 5-1. Voltmeter–ammeter method for resistance measurement.

Methods may be devised in which the meters are connected sequentially, but these are also subject to theoretical errors if X is calculated from meter readings inserted into Eq. (5-1). See Prob. 5-4.] If the ammeter resistance is zero and the voltmeter resistance is infinite, the readings will be identical for both switch positions, and Eq. (5-1) may be properly used in either case. For nonideal instruments, an analysis of the circuit leads to a quantitative expression for the errors that would result from the mistake of applying Eq. (5-1).

a. *Switch in Position* 1. The ammeter indicates the current through X, but the voltmeter reading is high by an amount equal to the drop across the ammeter. Let the ammeter reading be I_1 and the voltmeter reading be V_1. Erroneous application of Eq. (5-1) leads to the false result $X_1 = V_1/I_1$, where X_1 is the "apparent" resistance and is known to be incorrect. Let I_x be the current through X. Then, $I_1 = I_x$, $V_1 = I_x(X + R_a)$, and X_1 is seen to be

$$X_1 = \frac{V_1}{I_1} = \frac{I_x(X + R_a)}{I_x} = X + R_a$$

Therefore, the per cent error δ_1 in X_1 is

$$\delta_1 = \frac{(X_1 - X)100}{X} = 100\,\frac{R_a}{X} \qquad (5\text{-}2)$$

This is a positive error since the apparent resistance calculated from Eq. (5-1) is larger than the actual resistance because the voltmeter reading is high. The magnitude of the error may be calculated if R_a is known. For example, if $R_a = 0.01X$, the error is 1 per cent. The value of R_v is inconsequential.

b. *Switch in Position* 2. The voltmeter indicates the voltage across X but the ammeter reading is high by an amount equal to the current through the voltmeter. Let the ammeter reading be I_2 and the voltmeter reading be V_2. Erroneous application of Eq. (5-1) leads to the false result $X_2 = V_2/I_2$. Let $I_v = V_2/R_v$ be the current through the voltmeter. Then $I_2 = I_x + V_2/R_v$, $V_2 = V_x$, and X_2 is seen to be

$$X_2 = \frac{V_2}{I_2} = \frac{V_x}{I_x + V_x/R_v} = \frac{1}{1/X + 1/R_v} = \frac{X}{1 + X/R_v}$$

Therefore, the per cent error δ_2 in X_2 is

$$\delta_2 = \frac{(X_2 - X)100}{X} = \left(\frac{1}{1 + X/R_v} - 1\right)100 = -\frac{100}{1 + R_v/X} \quad (5\text{-}3)$$

This is a negative error since the apparent resistance calculated from Eq. (5-1) is, in this case, smaller than the actual resistance because the ammeter current is larger than the current through X. The magnitude of the error may be calculated if R_v is known. For example, if $R_v = 100X$, the error is about -1 per cent. The value of R_a is inconsequential.

In many cases, instruments may be found that yield voltage and current readings whose ratio gives an acceptably accurate result from Eq.

(5-1). However, there is always some error for either arrangement. The arrangement that leads to the smaller error for a given pair of instruments and a given X, assuming Eq. (5-1) is used, may be stated succinctly: If $X/R_a > (1 + R_v/X)$, use switch position 1; otherwise use switch position 2.

5-7. Instrument Errors. A large class of methods of measurement is that in which the actual deflection of the instrument provides a numerical result. These deflection methods are all highly vulnerable to instrument errors, as contrasted with methods in which a null indication is used as a basis for comparing an unknown quantity with an accurately known standard. Systematic errors owing to shortcomings or defects of the instrument employed in making a measurement are normally to be expected. Therefore, deflection methods are usually avoided when seeking extremely high accuracy. Despite the tremendous improvement achieved over the last few decades, instrument errors are still inevitable, and the experimenter must decide whether these errors are small enough to be tolerated in any given instance.

Many instrument errors are covered under the umbrella of the term "off calibration," which refers to the discrepancy between scale readings and the magnitudes of the quantity that produced the readings. Errors in calibration may be an inherent shortcoming of a new instrument, they may be produced by wear and deterioration of internal elements of the instrument, or they may be induced by abuse in which components of the instrument suffer damage.

For each type of instrument there are an enormous number of items that may produce errors, the details depending upon the particular kind of device. The proficient experimenter will always take precautions to ensure that the instrument he uses is operating normally and that it does not contribute excessive errors. Critical tests of instruments to check their performance and accuracy may be made in many different ways. Faults in instruments may sometimes be detected by simple tests in which the behavior is scrutinized for erraticness, instability, and lack of reproducibility. An easily applied method is to compare the instrument with a similar or better one that is known to be reliable. A recommended method for correcting defects in the case of commercial apparatus is to return it to the manufacturer for calibration and repair.

To illustrate some instrument ills that may plague the experimenter, several items that cause errors in pivoted-coil d'Arsonval instruments, which have been studied in preceding chapters, may be cited. Errors may arise from erratic pivot friction resulting from worn bearings. Even if the pivot and bearings are in new condition, errors may arise from this source in some instruments if they are used in a physical orientation for which they were not designed. The springs that provide the restoring torque may undergo change with age and use. The shunt of an ammeter or the series resistance of a voltmeter might shift from its correct value because of abuse, such as extreme overload. The magnetic field in the air gap could become permanently altered as a result of having exposed the meter to an intense external magnetic field at some time in its past. Or, other magnetic effects may cause error, such as use of an unmounted instrument designed for steel-panel installations. Corrosion may cause ill effects on delicate metal parts such as coil wire and springs. Finally, a somewhat subtle example of a source of error in a high-quality meter (usually employing a mirror mounted in the plane of the scale to avoid parallax error) may be mentioned. This type of meter usually has slightly irregular scale graduations owing, for example, to small irregularities in the magnetic field. The scale is tailor-made during factory calibration. If the needle on such an instrument becomes bent, it still might be capable of being zeroed with the screw adjustment provided, but then the scale is no longer accurate and recalibration is required.

It is virtually impossible for the experimenter to be acquainted with all the possible difficulties his apparatus may experience. But the competent man should have a general knowledge of the characteristics, capabilities, and limitations of the instrument and should be able to discern when its errors become excessive for the purpose at hand.

5-8. Calibration of D-C Meters. Direct-current voltmeters and ammeters may be calibrated in a variety of ways so that corrections may be applied to their readings. Sound methods capable of excellent accuracy employ a potentiometer as the basic measuring device. The principle of the potentiometer is presented in Sec. 9-5. For present purposes it may be regarded as a device capable of accurate measurement of small voltages (on the order of a volt) without drawing appreciable current at its input terminals. This valuable precision instrument approaches very closely the infinite resistance requirement of the ideal voltmeter.

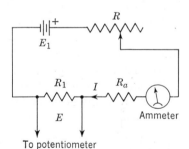

FIG. 5-2. Calibration of ammeter with potentiometer.

Circuit arrangements for calibrating an ammeter and a voltmeter are given in Figs. 5-2 and 5-3. In the case of the ammeter, R_1 is an accurately known standard resistor capable of handling currents over the entire range of the ammeter without overload. The voltage, E, across R_1 is measured by means of a potentiometer, without drawing current. The ammeter current, I, is given simply by

$$I = \frac{E}{R_1} \tag{5-4}$$

where both E and R_1 may be known very accurately.   The rheostat, R, may be set to obtain currents covering the entire range of the ammeter. For each setting of R, the ammeter current may be established by use of Eq. (5-4) and compared with the reading observed on the ammeter scale.

In the case of voltmeter calibration, resistors R_1 and R_2 may be used to divide down the voltage across the voltmeter by a known fraction so that it falls within the range of the potentiometer.   The voltage, V, across

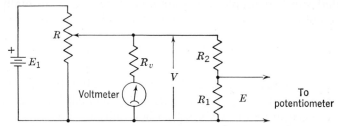

Fig. 5-3. Calibration of voltmeter with potentiometer.

the voltmeter is related to the voltage E, measured by the potentiometer (which does not draw current), by

$$V = \frac{(R_1 + R_2)E}{R_1} = \left(1 + \frac{R_2}{R_1}\right) E \qquad (5\text{-}5)$$

Thus, it is only the ratio of R_2 to R_1 that is important in relating E to V, and this ratio may be known very accurately.   The control, R, may be varied so that V covers the entire range of the voltmeter. V may be determined from Eq. (5-5) for each setting of R, and this result may be compared with the reading observed on the voltmeter under test.

In both of these methods a variety of practical matters contribute to the achievement of satisfactory results.   For example, the supply voltage, E_1, must be stable so that conditions do not fluctuate during the measurements, and R might actually consist of two variable elements so that both coarse and fine adjustments are possible.

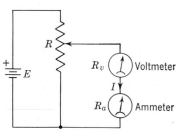

Fig. 5-4. Voltmeter-ammeter calibration.

Other methods for calibration may be devised, depending upon the available equipment and required accuracy.   For instance, suppose it is desired to calibrate a voltmeter whose resistance is known.

If an accurate ammeter is available which, by happy circumstance, covers the current range of the voltmeter movement, the simple method shown in Fig. 5-4 may be used.   It essentially compares the voltmeter with the ammeter.   The voltage, V, across the voltmeter is given by $V = IR_v$, where I is the current read on the ammeter and R_v is the voltmeter resistance, both quantities presumably known with good accuracy.   Alternatively, an accurate voltmeter may be used to calibrate an ammeter in this fashion.

If the voltmeter current required for full-scale deflection exceeds the current rating of the ammeter, then an accurate decade resistance, R_1, may be used in conjunction with the ammeter as shown in Fig. 5-5.   The voltage, V, across the voltmeter is then given by $V = I(R_1 + R_a)$, so the ammeter resistance, R_a, must also be known (it might be negligible compared with R_1 in some cases).   Hence, the control, R, may be varied to

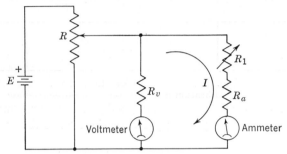

FIG. 5-5. Voltmeter-ammeter calibration.

produce deflections over the entire range of the voltmeter and, with R_1 and R_a fixed and known, the voltage, V, may be computed from the accurate ammeter readings.   Alternatively, this method may also be used to calibrate an ammeter by means of a voltmeter.

Another technique might be employed with the arrangement in Fig. 5-5 by conducting all measurements with a fixed value of ammeter current, thus relying upon its calibration at only one point on its scale.   For different fixed values of R_1, the control, R, may be adjusted to produce a prescribed reading on the ammeter.   Then V may be computed as before, but in this case I is constant and R_1 is variable, but known.   Indeed, it might be well to apply both techniques to see if there is consistent agreement between them.

In the latter method, corrections for the voltmeter would not necessarily be obtained at cardinal points on its scale because R_1 is variable only in discrete steps.   While calibration at cardinal points is conventional, there is really no necessity for this.   Interpolation for actual readings obtained in practice is required in either case.   A correction "curve" that might be found is given in Fig. 5-6.   The correction at each of the points indicated is equal to the difference between the computed value of V and the observed reading on the voltmeter.   The choppy pattern followed by this correction curve is typical.   It is also typical to find that the actual correction in volts is the same order of magnitude over

the entire scale.   This means that the error expressed in per cent of the
actual reading becomes smaller, the larger the reading.   The accuracy
of most instruments is specified in per cent error for *full-scale deflection*.
It follows that the instrument may well have larger per cent errors for

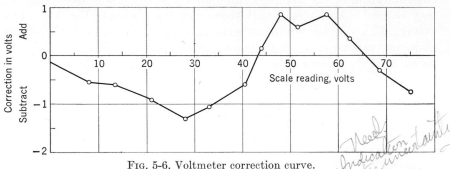

FIG. 5-6. Voltmeter correction curve.

smaller readings.   Therefore, it is not good practice to use meter readings
that are too close to zero; the upper three-fourths of the scale is usually
considered acceptable.

5-9. Environmental Errors.   The physical environment in which an
experiment is performed may have considerable influence upon the results
obtained.   The possibilities cover an extremely wide range.   On a hot,
humid day the observer may be less patient; the quantity being measured
may change its characteristics with time—in the biological field it might
grow; the instruments used may be disturbed by mechanical building
vibrations.   A listing of some environmental influences includes temperature, pressure, humidity, mechanical vibrations, line-voltage fluctuations,
and a host of other disturbances.   If the equipment is light-sensitive,
results might vary from day to night, and a darkroom is indicated.   A
soundproofed room is called for if the equipment is sensitive to acoustic
noise.   These and many other factors must be taken into account when
effects of environment impede attainment of required accuracy.

These few comments are indicative of the large area included in environmental errors.   Every experimenter has his tales to tell about how he
could detect remote trolley cars on his delicate instruments, or how his
meter could be used to deduce the floor at which the elevator in the same
building stopped.   Sunspots, too, are mentioned.

While environmental errors are called systematic, it is obvious that
they are not necessarily constant.   Indeed, they often, but not always,
are very capricious in their behavior, and getting rid of them may not
be simple.   Elaborate means of controlling the environment are used.
Constant-temperature baths, pressurized housings, humidity controls,
line-voltage stabilizers, shock mountings, and shielded rooms are but a

few of the many control methods. Countermeasures in electrical measurements include such techniques as using twisted lead pairs to reduce pickup in them from stray fields, instruments designed with temperature-compensated elements, resistance standards cooled with circulating oil, and metallic cans for shielding of parts. Experience and luck play no insignificant role when it comes to winning the battle of the environment.

5-10. Temperature Effects on D-C Meters. The influence of temperature produces an environmental error that has received considerable attention in the design of d-c meters of the type that have been described in the preceding chapters. It is found that a d'Arsonval movement is subject to at least three kinds of temperature effects. These occur in the restoring spring, the magnetic field in the air gap, and the coil resistance. As the temperature is increased, the restoring torque produced by the spring is reduced for a given deflection, while the magnetic field is weakened by a small amount. These two changes have opposite effects on the sensitivity, as may be seen from the instrument constant, $K = S/nBA$. The spring effect is about twice the field effect, and a typical net result is about 0.02 per cent per degree centigrade decrease in K; that is, there is an increase in the deflection for a given current when the temperature increases. The coil resistance, if made of copper wire, for example, increases nearly linearly with temperature by approximately 0.4 per cent per degree centigrade. These and other effects are taken into account in designing expensive instruments, and attempts are usually made to use shunt arrangements and materials that give an over-all zero temperature coefficient in terms of the external terminal characteristics of the instrument. In some designs this goal is approached very closely.

Without attempting to go into fine detail, it is possible to pursue some elementary illustrations of the effects mentioned. For example, suppose a voltmeter contains a series resistance that has a temperature coefficient of 0.05 per cent per degree centigrade. If the resistance is large, it will "swamp" the coil resistance as well as the electrical resistance of the restoring springs through which the coil current is passed. Hence, these latter resistances may be ignored in rough calculations. At a given temperature, the law of deflection of the radial-field instrument is given by $I = K\theta$. If R is the value of the series resistance, the voltage across the voltmeter will be given by

$$V = RI = RK\theta \tag{5-6}$$

If the temperature is increased by, say, 20°C, then R increases by 1 per cent while K decreases by 0.4 per cent. Hence, for the same deflection, θ, the voltage is now given by

$$V' = 1.01R(0.996K\theta) = 1.006RK\theta \tag{5-7}$$

Thus, the voltages across the instrument for the same deflection differ by 0.6 per cent, and the hot meter will read low.   This oversimplified example suggests that by suitable choice of temperature coefficient for R, complete temperature compensation may be achieved, but additional factors must be taken into account.

If this same movement is used as an ammeter, without a shunt, then for a 20°C temperature rise, the reading will be high by 0.4 per cent for the same current, and the meter resistance will increase by approximately 8 per cent.   If a simple shunt of resistance R_s, having the same temperature coefficient as the series resistor used in the voltmeter example, is placed across the movement, the change in coil resistance may be seen to override the change in instrument constant.   Hence, for rough calculations, the instrument constant may be assumed to be independent of temperature.   The meter current, I_m, for a given temperature is given by

$$I_m = \frac{R_s}{R_s + R_m} I = \frac{I}{1 + R_m/R_s} \tag{5-8}$$

If the temperature increases by 20°C, then the coil resistance, R_m, increases by 8 per cent while the shunt resistance increases by only 1 per cent.   Hence, for the same line current the meter current will be given by

$$I'_m = \frac{I}{1 + 1.08 R_m/1.01 R_s} = \frac{I}{1 + 1.07 R_m/R_s} \tag{5-9}$$

Thus, I'_m is less than in the cold case; the reading will be low.   The per cent difference depends upon the ratio R_m/R_s.   For example, if $R_m/R_s = 10$, the difference is 6 per cent.   Because of oversimplification, this example may suggest that it might be rather easy to achieve complete temperature compensation by using a shunt having the same temperature coefficient as the meter resistance.   In practice, other factors not taken into account here do not permit so simple a solution to the problem.

5-11. Observational Errors.   The experimenter himself, ingenious as he may be in devising his methods, may unknowingly be responsible for contributing errors to his results because of his habits or his inherent limitations of observation.   Human judgment is also involved, as in estimating fractions of a division in the reading of an instrument.   Judgment is also required when, in a series of repeated measurements of the same quantity, an isolated result is obtained that seems substantially different from the others.   A decision must be made either to include or to discard such a result.   The observer may introduce a systematic error because of a peculiarity in his sense of timing, making a reading too early or too late.   Or he may introduce parallax error by reading an instrument along a line of sight different from that used in its calibration. His experimental technique may suffer because of temperamental traits,

For instance, in adjusting a control for a prescribed meter reading he may become impatient and give up when the adjustment is close, rather than being persistently painstaking in getting it just right. If the indication of a quantity being monitored has remained stable for a long period of time, he may fail to note that it has drifted outside acceptable limits.

The reader will undoubtedly envision a variety of other examples of observational errors. They are minimized by adhering to a rigid discipline, by alertness, and by an insistence that the job be done correctly and well. They may be reduced further by having more than one observer participate. The experimenter is bound to have certain habits that are part of his equipment as a human being and cannot be avoided. An example is found in studies of human estimates made of pointer indications on meter scales. Observers usually can *estimate* to a tenth of a scale division. Errors of the estimates depend upon a number of factors such as pointer width, scale-line width, illumination level, contrast, and distance between scale lines. An interesting finding is that the observer tends to display a characteristic pattern of error in his estimates, and the pattern is different for different individuals.

A matter often overlooked is the relationship between observational errors and statistical treatment of results. Repeated measurements of the same quantity may be given useful statistical interpretations with the restriction that each result is obtained with *equal skill and care*. The demand is not only for skill and care but for uniformly high quality throughout.

The whole subject of observational errors can be a fascinating one for those whose curiosity is aroused by the interesting limitations displayed by the human senses. The modern engineering approach to the problem is to introduce automatic controls and automatic recording equipment to eliminate the human element, with many attendant advantages. However, it is far in the future before the need for appreciation of observational errors may be dismissed so neatly.

5-12. Parallax and Reading Meters. An observer who cocks his head to one side while reading the scale of a meter may introduce a parallax error, if the line of sight he uses differs from a direction perpendicular to the plane of the scale. The perpendicular direction is universally used for calibration of meters. High-quality meters are provided with a mirror in the plane of the scale so that the pointer may be lined up with its reflection in the mirror, prior to reading the scale.

An example will be given in analytical terms for the nonuniform scale shown in Fig. 3-10. The law of deflection of this instrument was found to be

$$I = \frac{K\theta}{\cos \theta} \tag{5-10}$$

Suppose a small error, $d\theta$, in the value of θ is introduced. The size of $d\theta$ depends upon the angle between the observer's line of sight and the normal to the scale, and upon the distance between pointer and scale. Since the scale is nonuniform, the error in the current for a given angular error of observation will depend upon the magnitude of the deflection. In this particular case, the larger the deflection, the larger will be the error in current for a given $d\theta$. Thus, a parallax error need not represent a constant error in the quantity being measured.

The differential of Eq. (5-10) shows the way in which $d\theta$ and the corresponding error in the current reading, dI, are interrelated.

$$dI = \frac{K}{\cos\theta} (1 + \theta \tan\theta)\, d\theta \qquad (5\text{-}11)$$

For meter deflections that are near zero, $\tan\theta \approx \theta$ and $\cos\theta \approx 1$, so this becomes approximately

$$dI = K(1 + \theta^2)\, d\theta \qquad\qquad \theta \ll 1 \qquad (5\text{-}12)$$

This shows that the error in the current owing to a fixed angle error, $d\theta$, becomes larger (parabolically) as the deflection, θ, increases from zero.

Equation (5-11) may be expressed in the convenient fractional, or per unit, form by dividing both sides by I.

$$\frac{dI}{I} = (1 + \theta \tan\theta)\frac{d\theta}{\theta} \qquad (5\text{-}13)$$

A little thought shows that the fractional error in current, dI/I, increases for a fixed $d\theta$ as θ approaches zero *and* as θ approaches 90°. This means there is some value of θ for which the fractional error in current will be a minimum, assuming that the same error, $d\theta$, is committed for all readings. Calculation of this minimum is left to the student in Prob. 5-10.

It might become important in accurate work to ascertain the magnitude of errors introduced by reading meters. Perhaps it might be desirable to screen out those individuals who do not display accurate and consistent results. An auxiliary experiment may be performed, as a side pursuit, to evaluate this source of error. For example, the circuit shown in Fig. 5-7 may be used to test the operator's ability to reproduce settings of a voltmeter to a prescribed reading. It is a convenient circuit, because the *differences* among various attempts to set the reading to the same point on the scale may be quickly and sensitively determined. The voltage E supplies current for the voltmeter deflection, which is adjusted by the subject under test using the control, R. The battery E_1 and the pair of known resistors, R_0 and R_2, serve as a stable reference against which the subject's performance is compared. Therefore, E_1 should be a fresh battery of low internal resistance, R_1, and should be checked periodically for drift.

The subject is first requested to set the voltmeter to any desired reading by means of R. The operator of the test then closes the switch and adjusts R_2 until a zero indication is obtained on the sensitive ammeter. This establishes the voltage drop across R_0 equal to that across the voltmeter. He then opens the switch and alters the setting of R. The subject is now requested to readjust R to the same prescribed reading as

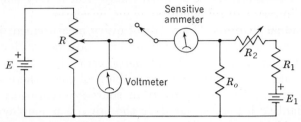

Fig. 5-7. Circuit for measuring reproducibility of meter settings.

before. After he has finished setting R, the operator closes the switch again. If the sensitive ammeter does not read zero, the subject has not reproduced the initial reading, assuming E_1, R_1, R_0, and R_2 have not drifted. The operator adjusts R_2 by a known amount, ΔR_2, until a zero ammeter reading is obtained. Then the voltage across R_0 is once again equal to that across the voltmeter.

The fractional error in the subject's setting may be determined from circuit analysis. The initial voltage across the voltmeter was $E_1R_0/(R_0 + R_1 + R_2)$, while the second voltage is $E_1R_0/(R_0 + R_1 + R_2 + \Delta R_2)$. The fractional error, δ, is given by the difference between the second voltage and the initial voltage, divided by the initial voltage.

$$\delta = \frac{\dfrac{E_1R_0}{R_0 + R_1 + R_2 + \Delta R_2} - \dfrac{E_1R_0}{R_0 + R_1 + R_2}}{\dfrac{E_1R_0}{R_0 + R_1 + R_2}} = \frac{-\Delta R_2}{R_0 + R_1 + R_2 + \Delta R_2}$$

$$(5\text{-}14)$$

The negative sign indicates that, if R_2 is increased (ΔR_2 positive), the second setting was lower than the initial setting. If $\Delta R_2 + R_1$ is very small compared with $R_0 + R_2$, it may be ignored in the denominator. The test may be repeated numerous times in order to study the scatter of the subject's results and to obtain a more reliable measure of his consistency.

A more convenient technique may be used to obtain essentially direct readings of the difference in voltage between the two settings. A large series resistor of known value is placed in series with the sensitive ammeter. Then R_2 is adjusted after the subject's initial setting, as before.

The ammeter current produced by the second setting is then multiplied by the large series resistance to obtain the voltage difference. Further adjustment of R_2 is unnecessary. The result is approximate unless the series resistance is very large compared with the sum of the input resistance looking rightward toward R_0 and the input resistance looking leftward toward the voltmeter. This is called, appropriately, a differential method of measurement. A detailed analysis of a very similar circuit is presented in Sec. 8-16.

5-13. Residual Errors. The result of every measurement is bound to contain systematic errors, despite most elaborate precautions. If it is assumed hypothetically that all systematic errors have been eliminated entirely, or that they are so small as to be negligible, there still remain certain unavoidable errors arising from sources intrinsically associated with the quantity being measured or the apparatus employed. These are called residual errors, and are sometimes referred to as accidental errors, random errors, or uncertainties. The term "accidental" suggests that these errors arise from a haphazard combination of a large number of small events, such as molecular collisions. The term "random" implies an erratic nature and irregular behavior, completely free of any pattern whatever. The term "uncertainty" denotes the effect residual errors produce in the determination of the quantity being measured.

When the sources of these residual errors are known, it may be possible in some cases to reduce their effects. For example, a source of random error in d'Arsonval galvanometers is known to be the chaotic bombardment of the movable coil by air molecules. The resulting Brownian motion of the coil, observable in extremely delicate high-sensitivity systems, is exceedingly small and usually not bothersome. However, one could conceive of placing the galvanometer in an evacuated chamber to reduce this effect. (For this reason, one might argue that the Brownian motion is, after all, an environmental error but it is not normally classified as such.) Even when sources of the residual error are not known, it is sometimes possible by empirical methods to partially suppress the random effects without affecting, at the same time, the quantity being measured.

The contributions of residual errors in electrical measurements are usually very small in a well-designed experiment. (This is not true of all fields in which measurements are made.) For this reason they are not usually considered in low-accuracy work. However, they become increasingly important as the quest for accuracy is intensified. For example, vacuum tubes may be used in electronic instruments for low-accuracy measurements with considerable success, but such devices may become completely unsatisfactory for high-accuracy work. Random effects inherent in the tubes, traceable to irregularities in emission of electrons from the cathode, may become intolerable. Similarly, the emf resulting from thermal agitation of electrons inside a resistor, commonly called the "noise" voltage, may be a significant source of uncertainty in many types of electrical measurements and is inevitably associated with every resistor. The square of the noise voltage is given by

$$e^2 = 4RkT \, \Delta f \qquad \text{volts}^2 \qquad\qquad (5\text{-}15)$$

where R is the resistance in ohms, k is Boltzmann's constant (1.38 $\times$ 10^{-23} joule per °K), T is the temperature in degrees Kelvin, and Δf is the bandwidth in cycles per second. If other conditions permit, the thermal noise voltage may be reduced by decreasing the temperature, the value of the resistance, or the bandwidth. Of course these maneuvers are acceptable only if they do not influence the quantity being measured. Apart from the uncertainties created in high-accuracy work, random fluctuations are also important in placing an upper practical limit on performance that may be obtained in electrical devices. For instance, the upper usable limit of amplification in electronic voltage amplifiers (devices that produce an output voltage larger than the input voltage) is fundamentally determined by the "noise" associated with the amplifier input.

Uncertainties introduced by residual errors that defy the experimenter to the last may be treated by application of statistical methods. Having reduced all systematic errors to an acceptable minimum, the usual procedure is to carry out numerous repeated measurements of the same quantity, each with equal skill and care. A statistical study of the scatter, or dispersion, of the results leads to an estimate of the quantity that may be inferred to be more accurate than any single measurement. Statistical techniques may be employed whether the results are scattered symmetrically or unsymmetrically about some central value. A frequently found type of symmetrical dispersion is called a normal distribution. However, a theoretical error is committed by using statistical methods applicable to normal distributions for results that are not normally distributed.

5-14. Avoiding Errors. A summary of some items that may lead to improved accuracy is presented below. The extent to which these are important depends upon the necessary accuracy and what the measurement problem deserves in terms of time and expense.

a. Comprehension. There is no substitute for a thorough understanding of the characteristics, limitations, and normal performance of every piece of apparatus used, nor for a basic theoretical understanding of all features of the over-all measurement problem itself. The experimenter should be capable of evaluating the soundness of various methods in quantitative mathematical terms and should be capable of devising alternative methods. Theoretical estimates of anticipated results should be compared with actual findings.

b. Techniques. A few of the many techniques that may be employed include replacement of a suspected instrument by another similar one, interchange of two similar instruments, deliberate change of a single parameter to observe its separate contribution to the over-all result, use of two different independent methods to measure the same quantity, use of multiple observers, monitoring and control of conditions to maintain them within required limits, and repeated measurements of the same quantity.

c. Disciplines. Use planned procedures, work carefully and unhurriedly, record measured values directly and in orderly fashion, record all pertinent details of experimental arrangement and conditions.

PROBLEMS

5-1 (§4). The uniform-field instrument with a nonuniform scale, shown in Fig. 3-7, has an instrument constant $K = 1.0$ amp per radian. The "zero" of the meter has not been adjusted correctly; for zero meter current the meter falsely indicates $I = 0.1$ amp. When this meter is energized, it indicates a current $I = 1.50$ amp. Compute the actual value of the current.

5-2 (§5). In order to measure the direct current in a wire, a 5-amp meter is connected in series with it and indicates 4.0 amp. When the 5-amp meter is replaced by a 10-amp meter, the reading is 4.2 amp. Both meters are known to be accurate, and each produces full-scale deflection for a 50-mv instrument drop. What is the value of the current in the wire when neither meter is in the circuit?

5-3 (§5). The voltage existing across two terminals of a linear d-c network is first measured with voltmeter A, rated 10 volts full scale, 500 ohms per volt, and then (after disconnecting A) with voltmeter B, rated 20 volts full scale, 500 ohms per volt. Meter A indicates 10 volts and meter B indicates 10.9 volts. What is the open-circuit voltage across the two terminals?

5-4 (§6). With the switch in position 2 of Fig. 5-1, the voltmeter (of resistance R_v) indicates a reading V_1, when the ammeter is short-circuited. When the voltmeter is removed from the circuit entirely, the ammeter (of resistance R_a) indicates a current I_1, when its short circuit is removed. Assume E and R are constant. (a) Determine the relationship between the ratio V_1/I_1 and the resistance X. (b) If $R = 0$, does V_1/I_1 yield a correct result?

5-5 (§6). In the voltmeter-ammeter method (see Fig. 5-1), demonstrate that if $\sqrt{R_a} \ll 2\sqrt{R_v}$, which is usually satisfied, then the value of X required for the same magnitude of error in either switch position is the geometric mean of R_a and R_v.

5-6 (§6). If the average of the two resistance values computed from Eq. (5-1) for the two switch positions of Fig. 5-1 is used, what will be the per cent error of the result? For what value of X, in terms of R_a and R_v, will the average be exactly equal to X?

5-7 (§8). A 0 to 50-volt voltmeter is calibrated using the circuit of Fig. 5-5. R_1 is set to each value listed on page 131 and then control R is adjusted, for each R_1, to produce a reading of 1.0 ma on the accurate ammeter, whose resistance is $R_a = 8.0$ ohms. Voltmeter readings corresponding to each value of R_1 are also given.

R_1, kilohms	Voltmeter reading, volts
10.00	9.7
20.00	19.5
30.00	29.9
40.00	40.2
50.00	49.8

Plot a correction curve of the type shown in Fig. 5-6.

5-8 (§8). For the correction curve in Fig. 5-6, compute the voltmeter correction as a percentage of the scale reading for each of the experimental points indicated.

5-9 (§10). In the ammeter example of Sec. 5-10, include the change in instrument constant of 0.02 per cent per degree centigrade, and assume $R_m/R_s = 2$. (a) Determine the ratio of line currents such that the same instrument deflection is obtained at the two temperatures which differ by 20°C. (b) Compare this result with that obtained by ignoring the change in K.

5-10 (§12). If the small parallax angle error, $d\theta$, is constant for all readings of the uniform-field meter discussed in Sec. 5-12, for what angular deflection, θ, of the instrument is the corresponding per cent error in the current a minimum? *42°21'*

5-11 (§12). Determine an expression for the fractional error in the meter-setting reproducibility test described in Sec. 5-12 if R_0 is changed to $R_0 + \Delta R_0$, rather than changing R_2. Which adjustment, R_0 or R_2, is more sensitive for a given error in resetting the meter reading?

5-12 (§14). Give an example of an electrical measurement error, and its classification, that might be avoided by use of each item listed under "techniques" for avoiding errors in Sec. 5-14.

$$5\text{-}11 \quad \frac{\Delta R_0}{R_0 \left[1 + (R_0 + \Delta R_0)/(R_1 + R_2) \right]}$$

CHAPTER 6

STATISTICS AND ERRORS

The application of statistical methods to the data of measurements is a widespread procedure. It permits the best value of a quantity to be estimated from repeated, independent determinations and provides analytical measures of the uncertainty of final results. The combined effect of errors in various independent quantities from which results are calculated may also be estimated quantitatively. Beyond these direct applications, statistics also has value in prediction. The ability to estimate, on the basis of sample data, what to expect in situations that have not been explicitly studied in detail is indeed a powerful technique. Moreover, the statistical nature of the physical world may often be understood only in statistical terms; thus, statistics is a fundamental subject in its own right.

Many experiments require a large number of measurements before statistical methods and interpretations become meaningful. Also, it is essential that all systematic errors be small compared with residual errors, especially because statistical treatment of data cannot remove a fixed bias contained in all measurements.

6-1. The Mean of Raw Data. Let v_1, v_2, . . . , v_n be a group of n independent determinations of a quantity. The symbol v_i (where $i = 1$, 2, . . . , n) is used because each of the v_i members of the set is called a *variate* in statistical work. The group of n variates constitutes the *raw data*. The v_i may differ from each other because of either systematic or residual errors.

These data may be described in a number of ways. One method is to tabulate all n of them and pass them on to your supervisor. This will test his patience no end, especially since he wants to know *the* result in a nutshell. Another plan is to give a few salient features of the data. While less complete than the full tabulation, this achieves brevity and utility, if done properly, and usually there is no loss in *significant* information about the data.

The *mean* of a set of variates, v_i, is defined as

$$\bar{v} = \frac{1}{n} (v_1 + v_2 + \cdots + v_n) = \frac{1}{n} \sum_{i=1}^{n} v_i \qquad (6\text{-}1)$$

This is the sum of all the individual variates divided by the total number of variates. The mean is synonymous with the terms "arithmetic mean" and "arithmetic average." The single number $\bar{v}$ conveys one of the most important features of the data, and in some cases might be all that is necessary. But the detailed information contained in the raw data has been lost when $\bar{v}$ alone is presented.

The mean does not necessarily represent the "best value" of the quantity measured. For example, if the raw data were unreliable to begin with and highly influenced by systematic errors, the mean could still be computed from the defining Eq. (6-1), but it would be of limited significance. On the other hand, if the differences among the v_i are believed to be entirely attributable to residual errors, the mean is usually assumed to be the "most probable value," or "best value," of the quantity. To deserve this interpretation, it is necessary to ensure that all gross errors, instrument errors, and environmental errors have been reduced to acceptable levels and that each v_i has been determined with equal skill and care using unbiased human techniques.

Single quantities other than the mean are sometimes used to describe the entire set of n variates. The *median* of a set of variates is equal to that variate for which there are equal numbers of variates greater than and less than that variate. Thus, if the variates are listed in ascending or descending order, the median is located at the middle of the list. (If n is even, the median is specified as lying between two variates, if these two variates are not the same.) The *mode* of a set of variates are those variates that occur more frequently than their neighbors. A set of variates may have more than one mode, but if one mode is dominantly more popular than the others, the smaller modes are sometimes ignored, especially if attributable to residual variations. When the variates display a single mode, they are called unimodal.

The mean, median, and mode of a given set of variates are not necessarily equal numerically. The mean is the usual quantity dealt with in electrical measurements.

6-2. Deviations. The mean has more significance from a statistical point of view than appears on the surface of the grammar-school idea of arithmetic average. The basis of the use of the term "best value" or "most probable value" is found in terms of quantities called deviations. Study of the deviations gives insight into the role played by the mean.

Let v be an arbitrary number subtracted from each of the n variates. The *deviation* of a variate, v_i, from this arbitrary number, v, is defined as $y_i = v_i - v$. It is simply the difference between the variate and some other number, and may be a positive or negative quantity. The deviations for the n variates may be listed.

$$y_1 = v_1 - v, \quad y_2 = v_2 - v, \quad \ldots, \quad y_n = v_n - v$$

The sum of the n deviations is

$$y_1 + y_2 + \cdots + y_n = \sum_{i=1}^{n} y_i = (v_1 + v_2 + \cdots + v_n) - nv$$

Now if the number v has the property that the sum of the deviations is zero, then

$$0 = (v_1 + v_2 + \cdots + v_n) - nv$$

and the resulting v is

$$v = \frac{1}{n}(v_1 + v_2 + \cdots + v_n) = \bar{v}$$

Thus, it is seen that the mean is that number for which the sum of the deviations is zero. As such it may be thought of as the "best value" of the quantity around which positive and negative deviations are equally likely to occur and to balance out to zero.

The *deviation from the mean* of the variate v_i will be designated by

$$x_i = v_i - \bar{v} \tag{6-2}$$

The preceding development constitutes a proof that the sum of the deviations about the mean must be zero, for any set of n variates.

$$\sum_{i=1}^{n} x_i = 0 \tag{6-3}$$

In other words, the sum of the deviations of variates less than the mean is always precisely equal in magnitude to the sum of the deviations of variates greater than the mean.

Another viewpoint, based on the squares of the deviations, also leads to a satisfying rationale for "most probable value." It is commonplace in statistics to develop mathematical relations by methods in which a minimum is imposed on the sum of the squares of the deviations. For example, in the method of least squares used for fitting a curve to a given set of points, a "best" fit is established by demanding that the sum of the squares of the deviations between the curve and the given points be a minimum.

By application of the principle of least squares, it may be shown that the mean is that number with respect to which the sum of the squares of the deviations is a minimum. This may be proved by taking the deviations from any number, v, and then investigating which value of v leads to a minimum of the sum of the squares of the deviations.

Designate the deviation of a variate, v_i, from an arbitrary v by $y_i = v_i - v$, as before. The square of the deviation is

$$y_i{}^2 = (v_i - v)^2 = v_i{}^2 - 2v_iv + v^2$$

The sum, S, of the squares of all n deviations is

$$S = \sum_{i=1}^{n} y_i{}^2 = \sum_{i=1}^{n} v_i{}^2 - 2v \sum_{i=1}^{n} v_i + nv^2$$

Now let v be variable and find that value of v which makes S a minimum, by imposing $dS/dv = 0$. Since all the v_i are constant,

$$\frac{dS}{dv} = -2 \sum_{i=1}^{n} v_i + 2nv = 0$$

Thus, for minimum sum of the squares of the deviations,

$$v = \frac{1}{n} \sum_{i=1}^{n} v_i = \bar{v}$$

It is because of this property of the mean that it may be called the "most probable value."

It should be emphasized that these properties of the mean based on relationships to the deviations *do not ensure* that the mean is the best estimate of the quantity being measured. These same properties hold rigorously for any given set of n variates, whether the variates are trustworthy or not and regardless of how the variates are distributed. Indeed, these properties hold for any arbitrary group of n numbers.

6-3. The Spread of Raw Data. All the detail of the n variates is lost when a single number (such as the mean) is used to summarize the raw data. It is customary to express results in the form

$$\bar{v} \pm \delta \tag{6-4}$$

as the next simplest manner of providing further information. The quantity δ conveys information about the extent by which the variates differ from their mean. There are at least four quantities commonly used for δ, and they each give information concerning the spread or dispersion of the data about the mean. These measures are particularly revealing when the data are unimodal.

The *limit of error*, L, is defined as the value of $\delta = L$ such that all variates of the set of data lie between $\bar{v} - L$ and $\bar{v} + L$. There is no reason to expect the upper and lower limits of error to be the same for a given set of variates. Sometimes the larger limit is used for both. Since

$\bar{v} \pm L$ encompasses all the variates, limit of error obviously represents a very conservative statement of the spread of the data.

Unequal limits of error may be used, if desired. In fact, in such cases as tolerance of machine parts, it is customary to specify unequal limits on a dimension. For example, the specification $2.500 \, {}^{+0.002}_{-0.010}$ signifies that parts meeting these specifications will lie between 2.490 and 2.502. Once the parts are made and measured, the mean is not necessarily equal to 2.500. In this case, 2.500 is called the *nominal* value.

The *probable error, P*, is defined as the value of $\delta = P$ such that half the variates lie between $\bar{v} - P$ and $\bar{v} + P$. Thus, the variates included between $\bar{v} \pm P$ represent that half of all the variates which cluster about the mean. There need not be an equal number of variates above and below the mean within this group, as in the case of variates not distributed symmetrically about the mean. Obviously, P can never exceed the limit of error, L.

Two other quantities used for δ are defined in terms of the deviations from the mean, x_i. The *average deviation*, A, is the value of $\delta = A$ defined in terms of the magnitudes of the deviations by

$$A = \frac{1}{n} (|x_1| + |x_2| + \cdots + |x_n|) = \frac{1}{n} \sum_{i=1}^{n} |x_i| \qquad (6\text{-}5)$$

The bars around x_i signify the absolute value of x_i, which is the value of x_i with its minus sign, if any, deleted. Obviously, this deletion of sign is important; otherwise a zero result would be obtained as shown by Eq. (6-3). Thus, A is the arithmetic average of all the n deviations taken without regard to sign. While the average deviation never exceeds the limit of error, L, it may be equal to, greater than, or less than the probable error, P, depending upon how the variates are distributed.

A fourth quantity used for δ is called the *standard deviation, σ, and is the usual choice in most scientific work.* It is discussed more fully in Sec. 6-4.

The four possibilities for δ are generally unequal numerically for any given set of variates. Therefore, it is important to know which definition of δ was used when a result is given in the form of Eq. (6-4). In the absence of a definition, it may be assumed that δ is the standard deviation, although P is often used by engineers. Despite the differences among these various δ, they all possess the following properties:

1. If all the deviations, x_i, are zero, $\delta = 0$.
2. All n of the variates, and their corresponding deviations, are included.
3. The dimensions of δ are the same as those of $\bar{v}$.

The third property suggests that the result of the n determinations may be expressed in terms of fractional dimensionless quantities, thus:

$$\bar{v} \pm \delta = \bar{v} \left(1 \pm \frac{\delta}{\bar{v}}\right) \tag{6-6}$$

The quantity $\delta/\bar{v}$ is a dimensionless fractional measure of the extent by which the variates differ from their mean. *Per cent errors*, used frequently, are 100 times these fractional errors.

6-4. Standard Deviation. The *standard deviation*, σ, is the value of $\delta = \sigma$ defined in terms of the squares of the deviations from the mean by

$$\sigma = \sqrt{\frac{1}{n-1}(x_1{}^2 + x_2{}^2 + \cdots + x_n{}^2)} = \sqrt{\frac{1}{n-1}\sum_{i=1}^{n} x_i{}^2} \tag{6-7}$$

The square of the standard deviation is called the *variance*, σ^2. Since the squares of the deviations are used in the definition of σ, the signs of the negative deviations are automatically eliminated. Moreover, larger deviations are thereby emphasized more than smaller ones. For this reason, the standard deviation is usually larger than the average deviation, A, and the probable error, P. Therefore, it represents a more conservative measure of the spread of the data but is not as pessimistic as L.

The standard deviation is essentially a root-mean-square quantity, so familiar to the electrical engineer in connection with alternating currents and voltages. Indeed, if $n \gg 1$, the standard deviation is numerically equal to the root-mean-square deviation, defined by replacing $n - 1$ by n in σ. Even with n as small as 25, the rms deviation is only about 2 per cent less than the standard deviation. For this reason, the rms deviation is frequently called the standard deviation. This is not unreasonable because σ is usually small compared with $\bar{v}$, and the distinction becomes a second-order matter of an error in the error. However, it is considered good scientific practice to use the more conservative measure, σ, especially for small n.

It is natural to inquire why the simpler rms deviation is not generally acceptable. The reason for the $n - 1$ factor, rather than n, is based on the fact that $\bar{v}$ is not an independent quantity, but one derived from the variates. For example, with $n = 2$, the mean and two deviations may be computed, but the deviations are equal in magnitude. Thus, there is only one independent deviation for $n = 2$. By extension, there are $n - 1$ independent deviations for n variates. This suggests why the factor $n - 1$ is employed, rather than n, which is also indicated by other statistical considerations not presented here.

Finally, it is desirable to point out that, contrary to statements found in many engineering treatments of the subject of errors, the standard deviation and not the probable error is today the widely accepted quantity used for δ. While the probable error did at one time enjoy limited popularity in the United States, its use has been condemned by many workers in a variety of fields where statistical treatment of data is employed. Substantially all scientific results are now stated in terms of standard deviation, but engineering texts have lagged behind this practice.

6-5. Grouped Data. When variates are gathered together into subcategories, the data are said to be grouped. Grouped data are often used for two very sound reasons: (1) the amount of computation required to determine $\bar{v}$ and σ may be reduced greatly, especially when n is large, and (2) the data may be presented in a pictorial form from which their salient features may be easily grasped. Grouped data are also worth investigating for conceptual reasons. A logical path is opened toward ideas in probability and distribution functions, which are highly useful concepts.

Grouped data are formed from raw data by the following procedure. The total interval over which the variates lie is subdivided into smaller intervals called *ranges*. The ranges are usually chosen to be equal in length and are specified by their *midpoints*. All variates within a given range are then lumped together and assigned the same value as the range midpoint. This is the key move that simplifies calculations without serious loss in accuracy. If the selected ranges are small compared with the total interval, the accuracy is excellent, but more ranges are required to cover the total interval and, hence, more calculations. Larger ranges demand less calculation but there may be some loss in accuracy. Therefore, choice of range is a matter of judgment in which a compromise between desired accuracy and computational effort is sought. To avoid question about the range in which a variate lies, it is desirable to have no variates coincide with the end points of the ranges. If some variates do coincide with the range end points, half of them may be assigned to the higher range and the other half to the lower range.

Let v_r designate the midpoint of the rth range of width Δv_r. The number of variates, n_r, lying within the range Δv_r is called the *frequency* of the variate and is designated by $f(v_r) = n_r$. Functional notation is used because n_r is a function of v_r which changes by discrete amounts as r ranges over its integral values. Since $f(v_r)$ is simply the number of occurrences of v_i within the range Δv_r, it is always a whole number. For a total of R ranges that span the complete interval over which the variates lie,

$$\sum_{r=1}^{R} n_r = \sum_{r=1}^{R} f(v_r) = n \qquad (6-8)$$

This expresses the fact that the sum of the number of variates in each of the ranges must be equal to the total number of variates, n.

The variates in any range, Δv_r, are generally scattered above and below the range midpoint, v_r. Therefore, these variates may each be assigned the value v_r, usually without serious error, if the ranges have been chosen wisely. The sum of all the variates is then given approximately by

$$\sum_{i=1}^{n} v_i = \sum_{r=1}^{R} v_r n_r = \sum_{r=1}^{R} v_r f(v_r) \qquad (6\text{-}9)$$

Insertion of this result into Eq. (6-1) shows that the mean is given approximately in terms of the range midpoints and the frequency of the variate by

$$\bar{v} = \frac{1}{n} \sum_{r=1}^{R} v_r f(v_r) \qquad (6\text{-}10)$$

The deviation from the mean of a range midpoint, v_r, is $x_r = v_r - \bar{v}$, and there are n_r such deviations associated with variates that have been assigned the value v_r within the range Δv_r. Consequently, the sum of the magnitudes of all the deviations is given approximately by

$$\sum_{i=1}^{n} |x_i| = \sum_{r=1}^{R} |v_r - \bar{v}| n_r = \sum_{r=1}^{R} |x_r| f(v_r) \qquad (6\text{-}11)$$

and the sum of the squares of the deviations in terms of grouped data is approximately

$$\sum_{i=1}^{n} x_i^2 = \sum_{r=1}^{R} (v_r - \bar{v})^2 n_r = \sum_{r=1}^{R} x_r^2 f(v_r) \qquad (6\text{-}12)$$

Thus, the average deviation, Eq. (6-5), is given approximately by

$$A = \frac{1}{n} \sum_{r=1}^{R} |x_r| f(v_r) \qquad (6\text{-}13)$$

and the variance [the square of Eq. (6-7)] in terms of grouped data is given approximately by

$$\sigma^2 = \frac{1}{n-1} \sum_{r=1}^{R} x_r^2 f(v_r) \qquad (6\text{-}14)$$

A detailed summary of calculations for both raw data and grouped data is given in Table 6-1 for a hypothetical set of 20 variates. The variates have been listed in ascending order. The range midpoints are

TABLE 6-1. EXAMPLE OF GROUPED DATA

	Raw data*				Grouped data†					
i	v_i	x_i	$x_i{}^2$	r	v_r	$f(v_r)$	$v_r f(v_r)$	x_r	$x_r f(v_r)$	$x_r{}^2 f(v_r)$
1	100.4	−4.0	16.0	1	100	1	100	−4.3	−4.3	18.5
				2	101	0	0	−3.3	0	0
2	101.9	−2.5	6.3	3	102	2	204	−2.3	−4.6	10.6
3	102.2	−2.2	4.8							
4	102.8	−1.6	2.6	4	103	4	412	−1.3	−5.2	6.8
5	103.0	−1.4	2.0							
6	103.3	−1.1	1.2							
7	103.3	−1.1	1.2							
8	103.9	−0.5	0.3	5	104	3	312	−0.3	−0.9	0.3
9	104.3	−0.1	0							
10	104.4	0	0							
11	104.9	0.5	0.3	6	105	5	525	0.7	3.5	2.5
12	104.9	0.5	0.3							
13	105.2	0.8	0.6							
14	105.3	0.9	0.8							
15	105.4	1.0	1.0							
16	105.7	1.3	1.7	7	106	3	318	1.7	5.1	8.7
17	106.1	1.7	2.9							
18	106.4	2.0	4.0							
19	107.0	2.6	6.8	8	107	1	107	2.7	2.7	7.3
20	107.6	3.2	10.2	9	108	1	108	3.7	3.7	13.7
Sums	2,088.0	14.5 −14.5	63.0	...	...	20	2,086	....	15 −15	68.4

* Raw data: $\bar{v} = \dfrac{2,088.0}{20} = 104.40$

$$A = \frac{2(14.5)}{20} = 1.5$$

$$\sigma = \sqrt{\frac{63}{19}} = 1.8$$

$$P = 1.1, L = \begin{cases} -4.0 \\ +3.2 \end{cases}$$

† Grouped data: $\bar{v} = \dfrac{2,086}{20} = 104.3$

$$A = \frac{2(15)}{20} = 1.5$$

$$\sigma = \sqrt{\frac{68.4}{19}} = 1.9$$

whole numbers varying from 100 to 108, and equal ranges, $\Delta v_r = 1.0$, are employed. Thus, for example, the three variates in the interval 104 ± 0.5 lie within range $r = 5$, and are assigned the range midpoint value $v_r = 104$ and the frequency $f(v_r) = 3$. Even with a small $n = 20$, the economy in calculation resulting from grouping the data is evident from Table 6-1. For larger n, it is even greater. Moreover, the results of calculations of the mean, $\bar{v}$, the average deviation, A, and the standard deviation, σ, from both raw and grouped data using the equations that have been presented, may be seen to be in close agreement in this example.

A pictorial display of the grouped data is given in Fig. 6-1. This is a bar graph with bar heights equal to the frequencies, $f(v_r)$, and bar widths coinciding with the ranges Δv_r. This graphical representation is called a *histogram* or a frequency-distribution graph. It conveys a readily grasped picture of the distribution of the variates. This has been accomplished by suppressing the identity of the individual variates within a given range. A graphical representation of each individual variate by a line segment erected at each value of v_i is shown below the bar graph. The latter method of portraying data is sometimes used, but it can be seen that this is less satisfactory in terms of the over-all picture conveyed.

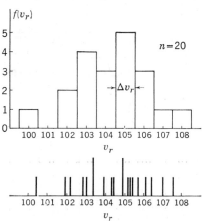

Fig. 6-1. Histogram of grouped data of Table 6-1.

6-6. Normalization of Histogram Ordinates. Since the bar heights of the histogram are equal to the number of occurrences of v_i within a given range, it is to be expected that if n is increased, the bar heights will generally increase. For example, if n is doubled to $n = 40$, the histogram might be similar to that shown in Fig. 6-2, which is hypothetical but represents what might actually be found in practice. The variation from bar to bar has been smoothed out to some extent, and the total interval over which the variates now lie is slightly larger than in the case of $n = 20$. Hence, the number of occurrences of v_i in each range has not exactly doubled.

Comparison of these two histograms is somewhat hampered by having bar heights in one which are generally larger than bar heights in the other. An improvement results from the application of a rather logical normalization procedure. If each bar height for a given histogram is divided by its n, then the two histograms will have identical bar-height scales, and the comparison is clarified. The normalized bar height for

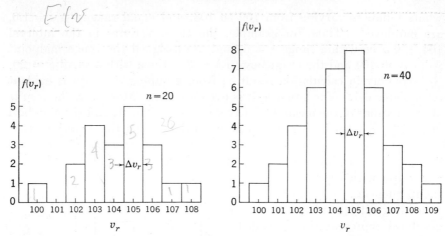

Fig. 6-2. Illustrating effects on histogram of increasing n.

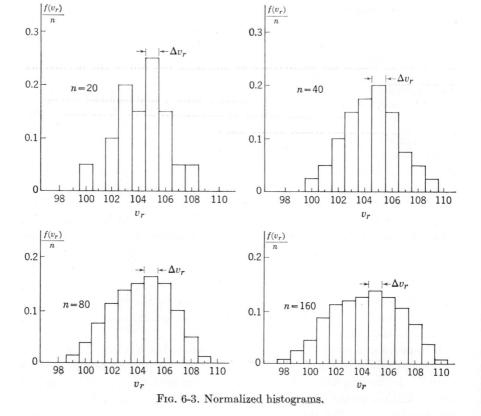

Fig. 6-3. Normalized histograms.

each histogram is equal to the *fraction of the total number* of variates that lie in a given range. Normalized histograms showing $f(v_r)/n$ are given in Fig. 6-3. It is apparent that if n is increased further, the histogram bar heights of Fig. 6-2 will increase, but those of the normalized histogram will have heights comparable to the cases shown in Fig. 6-3, assuming that Δv_r is held constant. The quantity $f(v_r)/n$ is a highly significant one in statistics. It is equal to the probability of occurrence of a variate in the range Δv_r, as discussed in the next section. For this reason, the normalized histogram is called the *probability histogram,* and the term *probability distribution* is used for $f(v_r)/n$, which might be expected from use of the term frequency distribution for $f(v_r)$.

6-7. Probability. It is customary to define probability in terms of "events." Events may be a wide variety of things. Simple examples are the numbers on a pair of dice or the colors of black and white balls. Events may also be variates, which means that probability may be applied to almost any measurable entity. Probability is defined in terms of events with the important provisions that the events are equally likely and independent. Equally likely events are those in which there is no way to tell exactly which one of all possible events, in the class of events under consideration, will occur in a given instance. Independent events are those in which the occurrence of one does not affect the occurrence of any others.

Suppose that of a total of E equally likely, independent events, a certain number, E_i, of these events is considered to be favorable. The probability that a favorable event will occur is defined as

$$p(E_i) = \frac{E_i}{E} \tag{6-15}$$

where $p(E_i)$ is read "probability of occurrence of E_i" or, more briefly, "probability of E_i." If E consists of k separate portions that cover all possible events, then

$$E = E_1 + E_2 + \cdots + E_k = \sum_{i=1}^{k} E_i \tag{6-16}$$

Thus, it is seen that E_i can at most be equal to E, and it follows that $p(E_i)$ can never exceed unity. Moreover,

$$\sum_{i=1}^{k} p(E_i) = \sum_{i=1}^{k} \frac{E_i}{E} = 1.0 \tag{6-17}$$

which states that the sum of the probabilities of all possible events must be equal to unity. Thus, in the case of a finite number of events, a probability of unity implies "certainty," and a probability of zero implies "impossibility."

The definition of probability may be applied to the grouped data to show that $f(v_r)/n$ is the probability that a variate will lie in the range Δv_r. Suppose that each of the 20 variates of Table 6-1 is written down on a separate slip of paper and that all 20 slips are placed in a hat. What is the probability of drawing a slip that designates a variate in a given range Δv_r? In this case, the events are the variates, and the favorable events are those variates which lie in the range Δv_r.

From the definition of probability,

$$p(v_r) = \frac{n_r}{n} = \frac{f(v_r)}{n} \tag{6-18}$$

where $n_r = f(v_r)$ is the number of slips of paper in the hat marked with variates in the range Δv_r, and n is the total number of slips of paper in the hat. Thus, it is seen that the bar heights of the histogram are, when divided by n, equal to the probability. Moreover, it follows from Eq. (6-17) that

$$\sum_{r=1}^{R} p(v_r) = \sum_{r=1}^{R} \frac{f(v_r)}{n} = \frac{n}{n} = 1.0 \tag{6-19}$$

This states that the 20 variates must lie somewhere in the total interval spanned by all R ranges.

It is evident from Fig. 6-3 that $p(v_r)$ depends to some extent on n, especially for small n. As n increases, the ratio $f(v_r)/n$, which is the probability, tends to decrease because the total interval over which the variates lie tends to increase. But $f(v_r)/n$ tends to become more stable the higher the n. For any finite n, no matter how large, $f(v_r)/n$ still depends to a slight extent on n.

6-8. Continuous Curves Representing Distributions. The dependence of the frequency distribution $f(v_r)$ on the number of variates is largely overcome by dividing $f(v_r)$ by n. However, the resulting probability distribution, $p(v_r)$, is still open to an objection. While the bar heights have been made relatively insensitive to n, they are still strongly dependent on the range, Δv_r. For example, if in a given probability histogram the ranges, Δv_r, are all doubled, the height of all bars will approximately double. This is so because the frequency, $f(v_r)$, for a doubled range will be approximately doubled, while n remains the same. Similarly, if the ranges are all halved, the heights of the bars will be approximately halved. An illustration of this effect is given in Fig. 6-4.

For a finite number of variates, the bar heights are not exactly proportional to Δv_r, because of the scatter of the individual v_i within the ranges.　For example, consider two adjacent bars of unequal height spanning a range $2\,\Delta v_r$.　If a new range $(2\,\Delta v_r)$ spanning these same bars is used, the bar covering $(2\,\Delta v_r)$ will have a height equal to the sum of the heights of the two unequal adjacent bars.　For large n, the ratio of bar height to Δv_r tends to be constant, provided Δv_r is not too small.

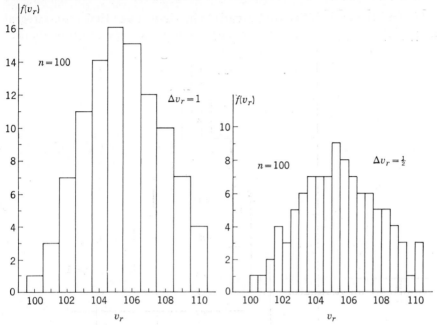

FIG. 6-4. Illustrating effects on histogram of changing Δv_r.

A function may be defined that is approximately invariant with respect to both n and Δv_r by dividing $p(v_r)$ by Δv_r.

$$y(v_r) = \frac{p(v_r)}{\Delta v_r} = \frac{f(v_r)}{n\,\Delta v_r} \tag{6-20}$$

It is called a *probability-distribution function.*　A bar graph of $y(v_r)$ vs. v_r may be constructed as before.　An example is shown in Fig. 6-5.　The over-all contour of the resulting bar graph will be relatively insensitive to both n and Δv_r.　For large n and small Δv_r, the bar widths will be very narrow and will display very small steps between adjacent bars. Thus, $y(v_r)$ approaches a smooth curve as n is increased and Δv_r is decreased, provided that Δv_r is not too small.

The probability-distribution function, $y(v_r)$, or the corresponding continuous curve, $y(v)$, is commonly encountered in statistics.　Consequently, it is important to understand how it is related to probability. In the case of a probability-distribution histogram, the probability that a variate lies in the range Δv_r is given by the *height* of the bar located on the range Δv_r. But in the case of the probability-distribution function, the probability that a variate lies in the range Δv_r is given by the *area* of the bar located on the range Δv_r. This is clear from Eq. (6-20).

$$p(v_r) = y(v_r)\,\Delta v_r = \text{area of bar of height } y(v_r) \text{ and base } \Delta v_r \quad (6\text{-}21)$$

To find the probability that a variate lies in a range that is an integral multiple of Δv_r, it is merely necessary to add the separate probabilities

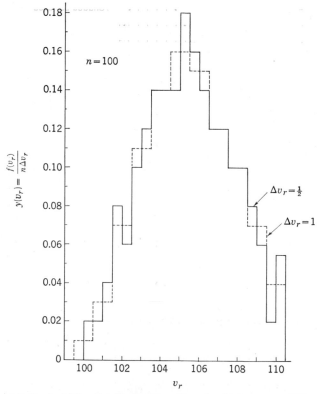

Fig. 6-5. Probability-distribution functions for histograms of Fig. 6-4.

associated with each bar. This follows from Eq. (6-15), where it can be seen that with $p(E_1) = E_1/E$ and $p(E_2) = E_2/E$, the probability that both E_1 and E_2 occur is

$$\frac{E_1 + E_2}{E} = \frac{E_1}{E} + \frac{E_2}{E} = p(E_1) + p(E_2) \quad (6\text{-}22)$$

This may be extended to any number of ranges. Therefore, the problem of finding the probability that a variate lies in an interval that is large compared with Δv_r may be formulated as the sum of many small

bar areas.   To illustrate, suppose the probability of occurrence of variates between the two range midpoints v_1 and v_k, shown in Fig. 6-6, is
desired.   For simplicity, assume that the interval between v_1 and v_k is
subdivided into k equal intervals, Δv.   This is justified if n is large because
the probability-distribution function, $y(v_r)$, has been deliberately defined
in such a manner as to be relatively insensitive to the range width.   Thus,
there is no restriction on the difference between the range midpoints v_1

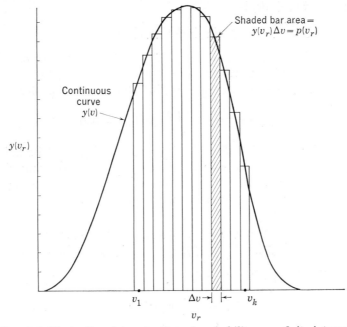

Fig. 6-6. Illustrating determination of probability over finite interval.

and v_k.   Denote $p(v_1,v_k)$ as the probability of finding a variate in the
range lying between v_1 and v_k.   Then,

$$p(v_1,v_k) = p(v_1) + p(v_2) + \cdots + p(v_k)$$
$$= y(v_1)\,\Delta v + y(v_2)\,\Delta v + \cdots + y(v_k)\,\Delta v$$
$$= \sum_{r=1}^{k} y(v_r)\,\Delta v \tag{6-23}$$

6-9. Integral Forms.   The summation in Eq. (6-23) may be expressed
in terms of an integral, by allowing Δv to approach zero.   The definition
from integral calculus may be used:

$$\lim_{\Delta v \to 0} \sum_{r=1}^{k} y(v_r)\,\Delta v = \int_{v_1}^{v_k} y(v)\,dv \tag{6-24}$$

where $y(v)$ is the continuous function approximated by the bar heights. Therefore, the probability that a variate lies between v_1 and v_k is given in integral form by

$$p(v_1,v_k) = \int_{v_1}^{v_k} y(v)\, dv \tag{6-25}$$

Two special cases of this important result are worth noting. If $v_k = v_1 + dv$, then the probability of finding a variate in the range dv, between v_1 and $v_1 + dv$, is

$$p(v_1, v_1 + dv) = y(v)\, dv \tag{6-26}$$

This is the differential form of Eq. (6-25). The probability of finding a variate somewhere in the range $-\infty < v < \infty$ must be 1.0. Since this corresponds to $v_1 \to -\infty$ and $v_k \to \infty$, it follows from Eq. (6-25) that

$$p(-\infty, \infty) = \int_{-\infty}^{\infty} y(v)\, dv = 1.0 \tag{6-27}$$

The area under the probability-distribution function must be unity.

Other integral relations may be developed by considering the limit of the sum, replacing $y(v_r)$ by the function $y(v)$. The mean may be expressed as an integral by starting with Eq. (6-10).

$$\bar{v} = \frac{1}{n} \sum_{\text{all } r} v_r f(v_r) = \sum_{\text{all } r} v_r p(v_r) = \sum_{\text{all } r} v_r y(v_r)\, \Delta v$$

Passing to the limit, with $\Delta v \to 0$,

$$\bar{v} = \int_{-\infty}^{\infty} v\, y(v)\, dv \tag{6-28}$$

Similarly, the average deviation may be expressed in integral form, starting with Eq. (6-13).

$$A = \frac{1}{n} \sum_{\text{all } r} |x_r| f(v_r) = \sum_{\text{all } r} |v_r - \bar{v}| y(v_r)\, \Delta v$$

Let $\Delta v \to 0$.

$$A = \int_{-\infty}^{\infty} |v - \bar{v}| y(v)\, dv \tag{6-29}$$

For the integral form of the variance, start with Eq. (6-14),

$$\sigma^2 = \frac{1}{n-1} \sum_{\text{all } r} x_r^2 f(v_r) = \sum_{\text{all } r} (v_r - \bar{v})^2 y(v_r)\, \Delta v$$

and let $\Delta v \to 0$.

$$\sigma^2 = \int_{-\infty}^{\infty} (v - \bar{v})^2 y(v)\, dv \tag{6-30}$$

An integral expression for the probable error, P, is obtained by specifying two limits, v_1 and v_k, that are symmetrical about the mean and between which half the variates lie. The probability of finding a variate between such limits is one-half, since half the events are favorable. With $v_1 = \bar{v} - P$, $v_k = \bar{v} + P$, and $p(v_1, v_k) = \frac{1}{2}$ in Eq. (6-25), the integral expression for probable error is

$$\frac{1}{2} = \int_{\bar{v}-P}^{\bar{v}+P} y(v)\ dv \qquad (6\text{-}31)$$

The integral forms that have been developed are applicable to a variety of probability-distribution functions, $y(v)$, the only restriction being Eq. (6-27). These relations have been developed by assuming n to be large enough, and Δv_r to be small enough, so that an essentially continuous probability-distribution function is obtained. Then the limit of the sum could be expressed in integral form. An alternative point of view is to *define* the various quantities $\bar{v}$, A, σ, and P in terms of continuous probability-distribution functions to begin with, using the integral relations that have been derived here. The case of finite n is then regarded as an estimate of the theoretically continuous case.

6-10. The Gaussian Error Curve. The entire development in this chapter so far is applicable to various shapes of the probability-distribution function, $y(v)$. The definitions and relations obtained are useful for multimodal data, for skewed distributions (which are unsymmetrical about $\bar{v}$), and many others.

There are numerous functions, $y(v)$, that have been found useful in practice. These include Chi-squared distributions, t distributions, F distributions, Poisson distributions, and Bernoulli distributions. One probability-distribution function known by a variety of names such as the Gaussian distribution, Gaussian law of error, and the normal error curve, will be examined in detail. It frequently gives a good description of many results found in nature that are affected by random errors. Carefully performed repeated measurements follow this particular distribution in many cases. The equation of this probability-distribution function is

$$y(v) = \frac{h}{\sqrt{\pi}}\ \epsilon^{-h^2(v-\bar{v})^2} \qquad h > 0 \qquad (6\text{-}32)$$

The factor h is called the *precision index* and will be discussed subsequently. This probability-distribution function may be derived from theoretical considerations by several different methods. The student is urged to consult one of the many textbooks in which such a development may be found.

A graph of $y(v)$ vs. v is given in Fig. 6-7. The Gaussian distribution is seen to be a bell-shaped curve centered on $\bar{v}$. Let $x = v - \bar{v}$ be the deviation from the mean. This change of variable represents a shift in the abscissa origin to zero at $v = \bar{v}$, as shown in Fig. 6-7. Because this shift does not change the shape of the function, it is commonly expressed in terms of x as

$$y(x) = \frac{h}{\sqrt{\pi}} \epsilon^{-h^2 x^2} \qquad h > 0 \qquad (6\text{-}33)$$

Four important characteristics of $y(x)$ or $y(v)$ are worthy of emphasis since they are helpful in probability applications.

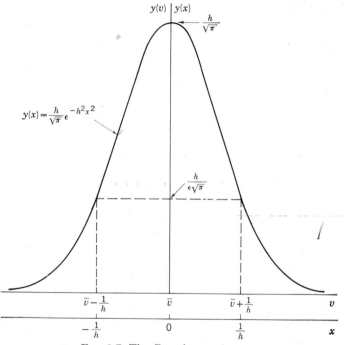

FIG. 6-7. The Gaussian error curve.

a. *Maximum Value.* It may be seen, by inspection, that the maximum value of $y(x)$ is $h/\sqrt{\pi}$ and occurs at $x = 0$ (or $v = \bar{v}$).

b. *Symmetry.* If x is replaced by $-x$ in $y(x)$, the value of $y(x)$ is unchanged. Hence, $y(x)$ is an even function, symmetrical about $x = 0$ (or $v = \bar{v}$).

c. *Area under Curve.* The total area under the Gaussian curve is given by

$$\text{Total area} = \int_{-\infty}^{\infty} y(x)\, dx = \int_{-\infty}^{\infty} \frac{h}{\sqrt{\pi}} \epsilon^{-h^2 x^2}\, dx = \frac{2h}{\sqrt{\pi}} \int_{0}^{\infty} \epsilon^{-h^2 x^2}\, dx$$

From a table of integrals, one finds

$$\int_0^\infty \epsilon^{-a^2x^2}\, dx = \frac{\sqrt{\pi}}{2a} \qquad\qquad a > 0 \qquad (6\text{-}34)$$

Therefore, $$\text{Total area} = \frac{2h}{\sqrt{\pi}}\left(\frac{\sqrt{\pi}}{2h}\right) = 1.0$$

The result of unit area under the Gaussian error curve may have been expected because Eq. (6-27) holds for many different distribution curves. Indeed, in the theoretical development of the Gaussian error curve, the multiplying factor $h/\sqrt{\pi}$ is derived by insisting that Eq. (6-27) be satisfied.

   d. Width.   If the convenient values of $x = \pm 1/h$ are selected, then the function $y(x)$ is seen to fall to $1/\epsilon$ of its maximum value, $h/\sqrt{\pi}$, when $x = \pm 1/h$. Hence, for large h the curve is narrow and the peak is high; for small h the curve is broad and the peak is low. Under all circumstances the area remains constant and equal to 1.0.

   Each of these four characteristics has a corresponding probability interpretation when $y(v)$ represents the probability-distribution function of a set of variates. Recall from Eq. (6-25) that the probability that a variate lies in the range between v_1 and v_k is given by

$$p(v_1,v_k) = \int_{v_1}^{v_k} y(v)\, dv \qquad (6\text{-}35)$$

and represents the area under the probability-distribution function between ordinates at v_1 and v_k. The same probability may be expressed in terms of deviations, with $x_1 = v_1 - \bar{v}$, $x_k = v_k - \bar{v}$, and $dv = dx$.

$$p(v_1,v_k) = p(x_1,x_k) = \int_{x_1}^{x_k} y(x)\, dx \qquad (6\text{-}36)$$

   a. Maximum Value.   The probability that a variate lies in a range centered on the mean is greater than the probability that a variate lies in any other range of equal size.

   b. Symmetry.   The probability that a variate lies within a given range about any deviation x is identical with the probability that a variate lies in an equal range with a deviation $-x$.

   c. Area under Curve.   The probability of finding a variate somewhere in the range $-\infty < x < \infty$ is unity. [This is not peculiar to the Gaussian curve; see Eq. (6-27).]

   d. Width.   The probability that a variate lies in a given range becomes less as the deviation of the range becomes greater. For a given deviation, x, the probability is less the greater the h, and vice versa. Thus, the name *precision index* is reasonable. A large h represents high precision of the data because the probability of occurrence of variates in a given range falls off rapidly as the deviation increases; the variates cluster into a narrow zone. A small h represents low precision of the data because the probability of occurrence of variates in a given range falls off gradually as the deviation increases; the variates are spread out over a wide zone.

Additional properties of the Gaussian error curve may be found by evaluating the integral forms for the specified function, $y(v)$. The following definite integrals, found in a table of integrals, are useful in addition to the one presented in Eq. (6-34):

$$\int_0^\infty x\epsilon^{-x^2}\,dx = \tfrac{1}{2} \qquad \int_0^\infty x^2\epsilon^{-x^2}\,dx = \frac{\sqrt{\pi}}{4} \qquad (6\text{-}37)$$

These in combination with change of variable, as necessary, lead to the establishment of definite numerical relations among A, σ, and h. The detailed integrations are left as problems at the end of the chapter.

From Eq. (6-28),

$$\bar{v} = \int_{-\infty}^\infty v\,y(v)\,dv = \int_{-\infty}^\infty v\,\frac{h}{\sqrt{\pi}}\,\epsilon^{-h^2(v-\bar{v})^2}\,dv \qquad (6\text{-}38)$$

one finds consistency; $\bar{v} = \bar{v}$. That is, the mean of $y(v)$ *is* $\bar{v}$.

From Eq. (6-29),

$$A = \int_{-\infty}^\infty |v - \bar{v}|y(v)\,dv = 2\int_0^\infty x\,\frac{h}{\sqrt{\pi}}\,\epsilon^{-h^2x^2}\,dx \qquad (6\text{-}39)$$

one finds $A = 1/h\sqrt{\pi}$.

From Eq. (6-30),

$$\sigma^2 = \int_{-\infty}^\infty (v - \bar{v})^2\,y(v)\,dv = 2\int_0^\infty x^2\,\frac{h}{\sqrt{\pi}}\,\epsilon^{-h^2x^2}\,dx \qquad (6\text{-}40)$$

one finds $\sigma^2 = 1/2h^2$.

The probable error is determined from the integral form given in Eq. (6-31) by use of the probability table, as shown in the next section, where the result is found to be $P = 0.4769/h$.

Thus, it is seen that A, σ, and P have specific values in terms of h and are uniquely related to each other. For the Gaussian error curve, the standard deviation is larger than the average deviation which is larger than the probable error. The following ratios, of the many which may be formed from the results, are frequently useful:

$$\frac{P}{\sigma} = 0.6744 \qquad \frac{\sigma}{A} = 1.253 \qquad (6\text{-}41)$$

The precision index, h, is related to quantities calculable directly from the raw data, and it may be determined for any normally distributed set of variates. A plot of the Gaussian error curve superimposed upon the histogram of the grouped data is sometimes used to give a pictorial idea of the degree to which the variates fit the normal-probability function.

6-11. Probability Tables. The probability that a variate lies between v_1 and v_k is given from Eqs. (6-25) and (6-32) by

$$p(v_1,v_k) = \int_{v_1}^{v_k} \frac{h}{\sqrt{\pi}} \epsilon^{-h^2(v-\bar{v})^2} \, dv \qquad h > 0 \qquad (6\text{-}42)$$

provided the Gaussian error curve is a reasonable approximation to the probability-distribution function of the variates. The parameters $h = 1/\sqrt{2}\,\sigma$ and $\bar{v}$ may be calculated from the raw data.

Evaluating this integral is a formidable task. However, widespread use of the Gaussian error curve has justified the preparation of tables by skilled computers. These tables may be used to evaluate any integral once the limits have been specified, and a knowledge of $\bar{v}$ and h is not required. For greater utility, the variable v is changed to a different variable and normalized so as to be useful for any particular h and $\bar{v}$.

The probability given in Eq. (6-42) depends upon four parameters, v_1, v_k, h, and $\bar{v}$. This number may be reduced by the following substitutions: let $x = v - \bar{v}$, and let $t = \sqrt{2}\,h(v - \bar{v}) = \sqrt{2}\,hx = x/\sigma$. These substitutions shift the origin of the curve so that its peak coincides with $x = 0 = t$, and introduce an abscissa that is measured in units of σ. This follows because the deviation, x, is equal to σt; viz., $x = \sigma$, $t = 1$; $x = 2\sigma$, $t = 2$. With these substitutions, the probability becomes

$$p(v_1,v_k) = p(t_1,t_k) = \frac{1}{\sqrt{2\pi}} \int_{t_1}^{t_k} \epsilon^{-t^2/2} \, dt \qquad (6\text{-}43)$$

where $t_1 = \sqrt{2}\,h(v_1 - \bar{v})$ and $t_k = \sqrt{2}\,h(v_k - \bar{v})$. This may also be written

$$p(t_1,t_k) = \frac{1}{\sqrt{2\pi}} \int_0^{t_k} \epsilon^{-t^2/2} \, dt - \frac{1}{\sqrt{2\pi}} \int_0^{t_1} \epsilon^{-t^2/2} \, dt \qquad (6\text{-}44)$$

Each of the integrals in Eq. (6-44) is a function of a single parameter, t_k or t_1. Consequently, values of the integral

$$p = \frac{1}{\sqrt{2\pi}} \int_0^t \epsilon^{-t^2/2} \, dt \qquad (6\text{-}45)$$

may be tabulated, as in Table 6-2, and used to compute the probability for any specified limits, t_1 or t_k. Tabulated values of the integral represent the area under the normalized Gaussian error curve between $t = 0$ and $t = t$, as shown in Fig. 6-8. Since the curve is symmetrical, the same table may be used for negative deviations; replacing t by $-t$ in Eq. (6-45) does not affect p.

TABLE 6-2. AREAS OF THE GAUSSIAN ERROR CURVE
Table gives values of the area under the curve between the ordinates
at $t = 0$ and t. Example: Area $= 0.1331$ for $t = 0.34$.

t	0	.01	.02	.03	.04	.05	.06	.07	.08	.09
.0	.0000	.0040	.0080	.0120	.0160	.0199	.0239	.0279	.0319	.0359
.1	.0398	.0438	.0478	.0517	.0557	.0596	.0636	.0675	.0714	.0754
.2	.0793	.0832	.0871	.0910	.0948	.0987	.1026	.1064	.1103	.1141
.3	.1179	.1217	.1255	.1293	.1331	.1368	.1406	.1443	.1480	.1517
.4	.1554	.1591	.1628	.1664	.1700	.1736	.1772	.1808	.1844	.1879
.5	.1915	.1950	.1985	.2019	.2054	.2088	.2123	.2157	.2190	.2224
.6	.2258	.2291	.2324	.2357	.2389	.2422	.2454	.2486	.2518	.2549
.7	.2580	.2612	.2642	.2673	.2704	.2734	.2764	.2794	.2823	.2852
.8	.2881	.2910	.2939	.2967	.2996	.3023	.3051	.3079	.3106	.3133
.9	.3159	.3186	.3212	.3238	.3264	.3289	.3315	.3340	.3365	.3389
1.0	.3413	.3438	.3461	.3485	.3508	.3531	.3554	.3577	.3599	.3621
1.1	.3643	.3665	.3686	.3708	.3729	.3749	.3770	.3790	.3810	.3830
1.2	.3849	.3869	.3888	.3907	.3925	.3944	.3962	.3980	.3997	.4015
1.3	.4032	.4049	.4066	.4082	.4099	.4115	.4131	.4147	.4162	.4177
1.4	.4192	.4207	.4222	.4236	.4251	.4265	.4279	.4292	.4306	.4319
1.5	.4332	.4345	.4357	.4370	.4382	.4394	.4406	.4418	.4430	.4441
1.6	.4452	.4463	.4474	.4485	.4495	.4505	.4515	.4525	.4535	.4545
1.7	.4554	.4564	.4573	.4582	.4591	.4599	.4608	.4616	.4625	.4633
1.8	.4641	.4649	.4656	.4664	.4671	.4678	.4686	.4693	.4700	.4706
1.9	.4713	.4719	.4726	.4732	.4738	.4744	.4750	.4756	.4762	.4767
2.0	.4773	.4778	.4783	.4788	.4793	.4798	.4803	.4808	.4812	.4817
2.1	.4821	.4826	.4830	.4834	.4838	.4842	.4846	.4850	.4854	.4857
2.2	.4861	.4865	.4868	.4871	.4875	.4878	.4881	.4884	.4887	.4890
2.3	.4893	.4896	.4898	.4901	.4904	.4906	.4909	.4911	.4913	.4916
2.4	.4918	.4920	.4922	.4925	.4927	.4929	.4931	.4932	.4934	.4936
2.5	.4938	.4940	.4941	.4943	.4945	.4946	.4948	.4949	.4951	.4952
2.6	.4953	.4955	.4956	.4957	.4959	.4960	.4961	.4962	.4963	.4964
2.7	.4965	.4966	.4967	.4968	.4969	.4970	.4971	.4972	.4973	.4974
2.8	.4974	.4975	.4976	.4977	.4977	.4978	.4979	.4980	.4980	.4981
2.9	.4981	.4982	.4983	.4983	.4984	.4984	.4985	.4985	.4986	.4986
3.0	.4987	.4987	.4987	.4988	.4988	.4989	.4989	.4989	.4990	.4990
3.1	.4990	.4991	.4991	.4991	.4992	.4992	.4992	.4992	.4993	.4993
3.2	.4993	.4993	.4994	.4994	.4994	.4994	.4994	.4995	.4995	.4995
3.3	.4995	.4995	.4996	.4996	.4996	.4996	.4996	.4996	.4996	.4997
3.4	.4997	.4997	.4997	.4997	.4997	.4997	.4997	.4997	.4998	.4998
3.5	.4998	.4998	.4998	.4998	.4998	.4998	.4998	.4998	.4998	.4998
3.6	.4998	.4999	.4999	.4999	.4999	.4999	.4999	.4999	.4999	.4999
3.7	.4999	.4999	.4999	.4999	.4999	.4999	.4999	.4999	.4999	.4999
3.8	.4999	.4999	.4999	.4999	.4999	.4999	.4999	.5000	.5000	.5000

The student should be cautioned that probability tables of the Gaussian error curve are not all the same. Some tabulate twice the area represented by Eq. (6-45) and are, therefore, the probability of occurrence between symmetrical deviations about the mean. In other cases, a different abscissa normalization factor is employed; for example, the variable $u = t/\sqrt{2}$ is used instead of t. In this case the abscissa is measured in units of $1/h$, since $x = u/h$. A further variation is found in tables that give the area between $t = -\infty$ and t.

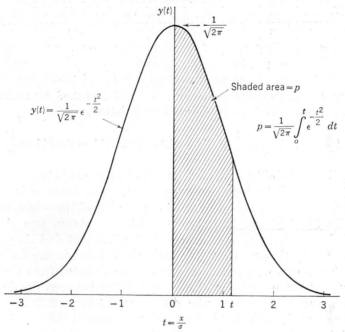

FIG. 6-8. Graphical representation of probability.

Several examples of the use of Table 6-2 are presented below. It is assumed that the probability-distribution function of the variates is the Gaussian error function. Suppose it is desired to find the probability that a variate lies between $\bar{v}$ and $\bar{v} + \sigma$. The deviations corresponding to these limits are $x_1 = 0$ and $x_k = \sigma$, respectively. Hence, $t_1 = 0$ and $t_k = x_k/\sigma = 1$. Thus, the probability is given by the integral

$$p = \frac{1}{\sqrt{2\pi}} \int_0^1 \epsilon^{-t^2/2} \, dt \qquad (6\text{-}46)$$

The table indicates the result $p = 0.3413$, listed for $t = 1.0$. Because of the symmetry of the Gaussian error curve, it follows that an equal probability exists for a variate between the limits $\bar{v} - \sigma$ and $\bar{v}$. Hence, the probability that a variate lies between $\bar{v} + \sigma$ and $\bar{v} - \sigma$ is the sum of these two equal probabilities, 0.6826. Since the area under the entire curve is 1.0, it follows that about 68 per cent of all variates lie within plus or minus one standard deviation from the mean. An exactly similar use of the table for $x = \pm 3\sigma$ leads to the conclusion that $p = 0.9974$. Hence, there are only 3.6 chances in a thousand that v_i will lie more than three standard deviations from the mean.

Another way in which the table may be used is illustrated by determining the expression for the probable error in terms of σ (or h). This is the inverse of the case above, for it is known that the area between symmetrical limits about the mean must be one-half, and it is necessary to find the corresponding value of t. Half of this symmetrical area lies to the right of the origin; hence, the desired t is given in the table for an area of 0.2500. Referring to the table, it is found that interpolation is necessary, the two closest values of t are 0.67 and 0.68 for areas 0.2486 and 0.2518, respectively. By linear interpolation,

$$t = 0.67 + \frac{0.0014}{0.0032}(0.01) = 0.67 + 0.0044 = 0.6744 = \frac{P}{\sigma} \quad (6\text{-}47)$$

Next, the probability that a variate lies in a range between $\bar{v} - 0.85\sigma$ and $\bar{v} + 1.76\sigma$ will be found as an exercise. The areas of interest are shown in Fig. 6-9. To obtain area A_1 to the left of the origin, enter the table with $t = 0.85$ and find $A_1 = 0.3023$. To obtain area A_2 to the right of the origin, enter the table with $t = 1.76$ and find $A_2 = 0.4608$. The probability that a variate lies somewhere between the limits is the sum of the two areas, 0.7631. It can also be deduced from these same numbers that the probability that a variate lies between the deviations $x = 0.85\sigma$ and 1.76σ will be the difference $0.4608 - 0.3023 = 0.0585$. The same result will hold for variates lying between deviations $x = -0.85\sigma$ and -1.76σ. It can further be seen that the probability that a variate lies in the range between $x = 1.76\sigma$ and $x = \infty$ is given by the area $A_3 = 0.5000 - A_2$, which is 0.0392.

As a final example, consider a criterion due to Chauvenet for discarding an isolated variate which seems to have fallen outside reasonable limits for no apparent reason. The criterion is that the variate may be rejected if its probability of occurrence is less than $1/2n$, where n is the total number of variates. How many standard deviations away from the mean must the variate be, to be rejected as a maverick? For the case of $n = 100$, the corresponding value of $1/2n$ is 0.005. Thus, to find the deviation that a suspect variate must exceed, it is necessary to find that value of t which represents symmetrical limits for which the area under the entire curve is 0.995. Or, a half area of 0.4975. The value of t found in the table is $t = 2.81$. Thus, if a suspicious variate lies more than 2.8 standard deviations away from the mean in a sample of 100 variates, it may be rejected.   The criterion for rejection demands a larger deviation for a larger n.   Chauvenet's criterion, or any other, for

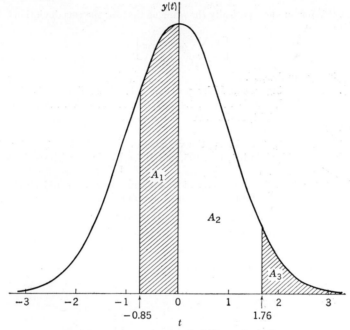

FIG. 6-9. Illustrating probability calculations.

rejection of data must be used with extreme caution.   There is always a danger of rejecting a valid piece of data which might be the only one of real interest in the group.

PROBLEMS

6-1 (§1). Computing the mean, $\bar{v}$, is often facilitated by selecting any convenient number, K, and then calculating the mean using the formula

$$\bar{v} = \frac{1}{n} \sum_{i=1}^{n} (v_i - K) + K$$

Prove that $\bar{v}$ in this formula is identically the same as in defining Eq. (6-1) for any arbitrary number, K.

6-2 (§2). Consider the first nine integers, from 1 to 9, to be a set of variates.   (a) Compute the mean.   (b) Demonstrate that the sum of the deviations from the mean is zero.   (c) Compute the sum of the squares of the deviations from the mean.   (d) Demonstrate that the sum of the squares of the deviations from the number 4 exceeds the result in part (c).

6-3 (§4). Computing the rms deviation is often facilitated by selecting any convenient number, K, and then using the formula

$$\left[\frac{1}{n}\sum_{i=1}^{n}(v_i - K)^2 - (K - \bar{v})^2\right]^{1/2}$$

Prove that this formula is identically the same as that for the rms deviation

$$\left[\frac{1}{n}\sum_{i=1}^{n}(v_i - \bar{v})^2\right]^{1/2}$$

for any arbitrary number, K.

6-4 (§4). In measuring an emf with a potentiometer, the following five independent readings were obtained, in volts: 1.485, 1.478, 1.480, 1.482, 1.483. Assuming that all readings are of equal weight, find the best value to take for the emf, and the per cent standard deviation.

6-5 (§5). Compute $\bar{v}$, A, and σ for the variates given in Table 6-1 by forming four groups with range midpoints 101, 103, 105, and 107. Compare with results at bottom of Table 6-1.

6-6 (§5). A resistor rated nominally at 1,000 ohms was measured 60 times under identical conditions. The data were grouped as follows:

Resistance value, ohms	Number of times obtained
993 and below	0
994	1
995	2
996	4
997	7
998	10
999	13
1,000	10
1,001	7
1,002	3
1,003	2
1,004	0
1,005	1
1,006 and above	0

(a) Find the median, mode, and mean. (b) Compute the standard deviation. (c) What percentage of the readings were within two standard deviations of the mean?

6-7 (§9). A probability-distribution function is given by

$$y = \frac{k}{2}\,\epsilon^{-k|x|}$$

where $|x|$ signifies the magnitude of x, and $k > 0$ is a constant. (a) Prove that the area under the entire curve is unity. (b) Determine the relationship between the probable error and k. (c) Is this a useful distribution function?

6-8 (§10). Show that the integral of Eq. (6-38) works out to be $\bar{v}$.

6-9 (§10). Evaluate the integral of Eq. (6-39) and thus prove that $A = 1/\sqrt{\pi}\,h$ for a normal curve.

6-10 (§10). Evaluate the integral of Eq. (6-40) and thus prove that $\sigma = 1/\sqrt{2}\,h$ for a normal curve.

6-11 (§10). Prove that the points of inflection of the Gaussian error curve lie at $x = \pm \sigma$.

6-12 (§11). The value $R = 92.2 \pm 0.1$ ohm is specified for a batch of 1,000 resistors. How many of them would you estimate have values in the range $R = 92.2 \pm 0.15$ ohm? Assume normal distribution.

6-13 (§11). An underdamped d'Arsonval galvanometer was energized 100 different times under the same carefully controlled experimental conditions, and the maximum deflection was read in each case. The readings were normally distributed about a mean value of 26.3 mm and had a *probable error* of 2.5 mm. How many of the 100 readings would you estimate exceeded 30 mm?

6-14 (§11). A machine shop manufactured 25,000 steel rods of nominal length 0.400 in. which were not to exceed 0.401 in. and not be shorter than 0.398 in.; i.e., the limit of error specification was

$$0.400^{+0.001\,\text{in.}}_{-0.002\,\text{in.}}$$

It was found that 2,000 of the rods were too long to fit into a gage set to 0.401 in. Predict the number of the remaining 23,000 rods which will conform to the specifications, assuming normal distribution.

6-15 (§11). In a scholastic aptitude test the following results were obtained for a sample of 100 students:

Number of students......	0	5	25	40	24	6	0
Grades received were between..............	0–50	50–70	70–90	90–110	110–130	130–150	150 and higher

Assuming the above sample is a random selection from a group of 2,000 students who took the test, how many of the 2,000 students would you estimate received grades greater than 150?

6-16 (§11). A resistor manufacturer received a customer's order for 50,000 precision resistors of nominal resistance 10,000 ohms, which were not to exceed 10,025 ohms and not to be less than 9,950 ohms. The manufacturer made a sample batch of 1,000 resistors, and it was found that 80 resistors of this batch exceeded 10,025 ohms. Assuming normal distribution, (a) predict the number of the remaining 920 resistors which will conform to the specifications, (b) predict the total number of resistors the manufacturer would have to make to obtain 50,000 which meet customer requirements, assuming the sample batch of 1,000 resistors is representative. (Assume that the sample batch of 1,000 resistors is thrown away after test.)

6-17 (§11). A manufacturing company made 10,000 ball bearings in connection with a certain customer's order. The customer had specified the ball-bearing diameter as $0.1000^{+0.001\,\text{in.}}_{-0.0005\,\text{in.}}$ where the tolerances stated are limits of error. The 10,000 ball bearings were passed through a "go–no-go" gage which was set to pass diameters of 0.101 in. or less. 200 failed to pass. How many of the remaining 9,800 ball bearings will meet the customer's requirements? (Assume normal distribution.)

6-18 (§11). Using Chauvenet's criterion for rejection of an isolated variate displaying a large deviation, determine enough points to plot a curve of $|v_m - \bar{v}|/\sigma$ vs. n, for different values of n between 20 and 200. The magnitude of the deviation the variate must exceed to be considered for discarding is $|v_m - \bar{v}|$.

6-19 (§11). A current, I, used for electrolysis was measured 1,000 times with the same equipment and under identical conditions. No reading was greater than 255 amp and none was less than 245 amp. The arithmetic mean of all the readings was 250 amp. It was found that the following normal distribution curve could most closely approximate the histogram of the grouped data:

$$y(I) = \sqrt{\frac{0.2826}{\pi}} \, \epsilon^{-0.2826(I-250)^2}$$

(a) Find the standard deviation.   (b) If the actual distribution of the current readings was described *exactly* by the above theoretical equation, how many readings were less than one standard deviation from the mean, and how many were less than three standard deviations from the mean?   (c) What is the probability that the 1,001st reading will lie less than two-thirds of a standard deviation away from the mean?

6-20 (§11). The following data were taken for the demand for electric power in a region where it is desired to build a new generating station.   The data were taken for 10 working days chosen at random.

Day	Megawatts, maximum demand	Day	Megawatts, maximum demand
1	2.0	6	2.9
2	1.2	7	1.8
3	2.1	8	1.6
4	2.3	9	2.0
5	3.1	10	2.6

(a) Plot a histogram of these data.   (b) Determine the mean and standard deviation. (c) What capacity generating station (in megawatts) must be built if it is to be able to supply the full regional demand for power on 84 per cent of the working days, requiring the transmission of some power from outside sources on only 16 per cent of the working days?   Assume that the future demand may be predicted by a normal distribution curve based on the above sample.

CHAPTER 7

COMBINATIONS OF ERRORS

The mean and standard deviation may be computed for a given set of variates as indicated in the preceding chapter. The set of variates may be described compactly in the form $\bar{v} \pm \sigma$. The mean is inferred to be the best estimate of the quantity and, for a normally distributed set, approximately 68 per cent of all variates lie within $\pm\sigma$ of the mean.

Further study of statistical treatment of data is necessary to explore the estimated uncertainty of the mean itself, and the estimated uncertainty to be expected in a quantity computed from others which have specified errors. These two matters are closely related, and both require investigation of combinations of sets of variates.

7-1. Mean of the Sum of Two Sets. As a preliminary step, the intuitively acceptable result will be established that the sum of two independent sets of variates has a mean equal to the sum of the means of each set. The proof consists of writing out the sum and then dividing by the total number. The compact summation notation is very useful, but the student may wish to write out the summations in detail, since they are complicated by the fact that two sets of variates are involved.

Let $v_1, v_2, \ldots, v_n$ be a set of n variates, and let $w_1, w_2, \ldots, w_k$ be an independent set of k variates, where k and n are not necessarily equal. The mean of the first set is

$$\bar{v} = \frac{1}{n} \sum_{i=1}^{n} v_i \qquad\qquad i = 1, 2, \ldots, n$$

and the mean of the second set is

$$\bar{w} = \frac{1}{k} \sum_{j=1}^{k} w_j \qquad\qquad j = 1, 2, \ldots, k$$

Denote the sum of two variates, one chosen from v_i and the other from w_j, by

$$s_{ij} = v_i + w_j \tag{7-1}$$

This is called a sum set. There is a total of nk different variates in the sum set for all possible combinations of i and j. Consequently, the mean

161

of the sum set is

$$\bar{s} = \frac{1}{nk} \sum_{i,j} (v_i + w_j) = \frac{1}{nk} \sum_{i,j} v_i + \frac{1}{nk} \sum_{i,j} w_j \qquad (7\text{-}2)$$

where $\sum_{i,j}$ indicates summation over all i and j. However,

$$\sum_{i,j} v_i = k \sum_{i=1}^{n} v_i = kn\bar{v}$$

Similarly,

$$\sum_{i,j} w_j = n \sum_{j=1}^{k} w_j = nk\bar{w}$$

Therefore, it has been proved that the mean of the sum of two sets of variates is equal to the sum of the means of each set.

$$\bar{s} = \bar{v} + \bar{w} \qquad (7\text{-}3)$$

7-2. Variance of the Sum of Two Sets. The preceding result is utilized in proving that the variance of the sum set, $s_{ij} = v_i + w_j$, is approximately equal to the sum of the variances of v_i and w_j. The variance of the v_i set is

$$\sigma_v{}^2 = \frac{1}{n-1} \sum_{i=1}^{n} (v_i - \bar{v})^2$$

and the variance of the w_j set is

$$\sigma_w{}^2 = \frac{1}{k-1} \sum_{j=1}^{k} (w_j - \bar{w})^2$$

The variance of the sum set is very nearly

$$\sigma_s{}^2 = \frac{1}{nk} \sum_{i,j} (s_{ij} - \bar{s})^2 = \frac{1}{nk} \sum_{i,j} (v_i + w_j - \bar{v} - \bar{w})^2 \qquad (7\text{-}4)$$

using the result of Sec. 7-1. Recall from the previous discussion of the $n - 1$ factor in the standard deviation that the deviations in a set, $v_i - \bar{v}$, have one less degree of freedom than the number of variates in the set. Hence, there are actually less than nk degrees of freedom in the deviations $s_{ij} - \bar{s}$. In this development, however, it is assumed that both n and k are much larger than 1, in which case the error introduced in Eq. (7-4) is negligible.

The student may wish to write out the squares of the deviations of the sum set in detail. The compact summation notation will be employed here. Expand

$$\sum_{i,j} (v_i - \bar{v} + w_j - \bar{w})^2 = \sum_{i,j} (v_i - \bar{v})^2 + 2\sum_{i,j} (v_i - \bar{v})(w_j - \bar{w}) + \sum_{i,j} (w_j - \bar{w})^2$$

However, $\quad \displaystyle\sum_{i,j} (v_i - \bar{v})^2 = k \sum_{i=1}^{n} (v_i - \bar{v})^2 = k(n-1)\sigma_v^2 \approx kn\sigma_v^2$

Similarly, $\quad \displaystyle\sum_{i,j} (w_j - \bar{w})^2 = n \sum_{j=1}^{k} (w_j - \bar{w})^2 = n(k-1)\sigma_w^2 \approx nk\sigma_w^2$

Also, $\quad \displaystyle\sum_{i,j} (v_i - \bar{v})(w_j - \bar{w}) = \sum_{i=1}^{n} (v_i - \bar{v}) \sum_{j=1}^{k} (w_j - \bar{w}) = 0$

since the sum of the deviations from the mean is zero. Therefore, the variance of the sum is very nearly

$$\sigma_s^2 = \sigma_v^2 + \sigma_w^2 \qquad (7\text{-}5)$$

Thus, it has been proved that the variance of the sum of two sets is approximately equal to the sum of the variances of each set.

The significance of σ_s is basically the same as that of σ_v or σ_w. For example, with a normal distribution, approximately 68 per cent of the nk variates in the sum set lie within $\pm\sigma_s$ of the mean of the sum. Alternatively, if one variate is picked at random from v_i and another is picked at random from w_j, their sum has 68 chances in 100 of lying within $\pm\sigma_s$ of the mean of the sum, provided that the distribution is normal.

7-3. Extensions and Interpretations. The result for the variance of the sum of two sets is the cornerstone on which the remaining discussion is based. For that reason it is well to examine its extensions and to interpret the extended results from a probability viewpoint.

Relations for the *difference* between two sets follow directly from the preceding developments and may be established directly by replacing w_j by $-w_j$. Then the difference set is $d_{ij} = v_i - w_j$. It follows immediately that the mean of the differences of two sets is equal to the difference of the means of each set:

$$\bar{d} = \bar{v} - \bar{w} \qquad (7\text{-}6)$$

Moreover, examination of the steps in the variance development reveals that the variance of the difference of two sets is approximately equal to the *sum* of the variances of each set, as before:

$$\sigma_d^2 = \sigma_v^2 + \sigma_w^2 \qquad (7\text{-}7)$$

All these results are immediately extensible to more than two sets of independent variates. It follows, therefore, that for p independent sets of standard deviation $\sigma_1, \sigma_2, \ldots, \sigma_p$, the variance of the sum set, formed by adding one member from each set, is given approximately by

$$\sigma_s{}^2 = \sigma_1{}^2 + \sigma_2{}^2 + \cdot \cdot \cdot + \sigma_p{}^2 \qquad (7\text{-}8)$$

An interpretation of this result is that if one variate is selected at random from each of p sets, then the probability that the random sum lies within $\pm \sigma_s$ of the mean of the combined set is about 0.68, provided that the distribution is normal. Thus, there is available a measure of the likelihood that the randomly selected variates lie within a given range from the mean of all possible combinations of selectees.

This result may be extended one step further by recognizing that the standard deviation of a set of variates c times as large as some original set, where c is a constant, is c times the standard deviation of the original set. The proof is simple. The standard deviation of the original set is

$$\sigma_v = \sqrt{\frac{1}{n-1} \sum_{i=1}^{n} (v_i - \bar{v})^2}$$

If each of the v_i of this set is multiplied by c, then the mean of the new set is $c\bar{v}$ and the standard deviation of the new set is

$$\sqrt{\frac{1}{n-1} \sum_{i=1}^{n} (cv_i - c\bar{v})^2} = c\sigma_v \qquad (7\text{-}9)$$

which is c times the standard deviation of the original set.

In using this to extend Eq. (7-8), consider p independent sets, as before. Form a sum set consisting of one variate from each of the p sets and, further, multiply each of the variates by a different constant in defining the sum set (c_1 for the first set, c_2 for the second set, . . . , c_p for the pth set). Then it follows from Eqs. (7-8) and (7-9) that the variance of this sum set is approximately

$$\sigma_s{}^2 = (c_1\sigma_1)^2 + (c_2\sigma_2)^2 + \cdot \cdot \cdot + (c_p\sigma_p)^2 \qquad (7\text{-}10)$$

This final result will be used to establish the standard deviation of the mean, and in the discussion of combinations of errors arising in calculated quantities.

7-4. Standard Deviation of the Mean. It is reasonable to expect that the mean of a set of variates should provide a more reliable estimate of the quantity than does a single variate. To illustrate this qualitatively, suppose n repeated determinations of the same quantity are carried out. Then the set of n variates has a unique and calculable mean. If a second group of additional determinations of the same quantity is obtained, the second set of variates will usually have a mean that differs somewhat from the mean of the first set. However, the discrepancy between the two means may be expected to be less than the differences among the variates of either set, assuming that equal skill and care have been exercised throughout. Extending this reasoning to a large number of such sets, the corresponding large number of means will, in themselves, constitute a set. The dispersion of these means around their average will be less than the dispersion displayed by the individual variates of a given set about their average. In other words, the standard deviation of the mean will be less than the standard deviation of an individual variate.

A quantitative expression for the standard deviation of the mean may be obtained by using a somewhat different approach. From a statistical viewpoint, each of the n variates of a given set may be thought of as having been selected at random from a large group of standard deviation σ. (This large group is called the "population" in statistics.) Accordingly, the mean of a set of n variates

$$\bar{v} = \frac{1}{n} \sum_{i=1}^{n} v_i = \frac{v_1}{n} + \frac{v_2}{n} + \cdots + \frac{v_n}{n} \tag{7-11}$$

may be looked upon as one of many possible sums consisting of n variates selected at random from n sets, each with the same standard deviation, σ. Each of the selected variates is multiplied by the same constant, $c = 1/n$, before forming the sum, $\bar{v}$. The variance of the sum set, of which $\bar{v}$ is a typical member, is equal to the sum of the variances of each of the n sets and is given by Eq. (7-10) with each of the constants set equal to $1/n$ and each of the variances set equal to σ^2.

$$\sigma_s{}^2 = \left(\frac{\sigma}{n}\right)^2 + \left(\frac{\sigma}{n}\right)^2 + \cdots + \left(\frac{\sigma}{n}\right)^2 = n\left(\frac{\sigma}{n}\right)^2 \tag{7-12}$$

But this is the variance of $\bar{v}$. Therefore, the standard deviation of the mean is

$$\sigma_{\bar{v}} = \frac{\sigma}{\sqrt{n}} \tag{7-13}$$

Thus, by use of statistical reasoning, it has been possible to deduce an expression for the standard deviation of the mean without actually obtaining and analyzing a large group of different means. By doing some thinking, labor has been conserved.

The alert reader will detect a potential difficulty involved in applying Eq. (7-13) to a set of n variates. The standard deviation appearing in Eq. (7-13) is the standard deviation of the entire group of all possible variates and is not necessarily equal to the standard deviation of a set of n variates selected at random from the entire group. However, if the sample is large, $n \gg 1$, it is plausible to expect that the standard deviation of the set is reasonably close to that of the entire group. Hence, the standard deviation of the set of n variates may be used in Eq. (7-13) for purposes of estimating the standard deviation of the mean.

An important practical principle may be gleaned from Eq. (7-13) by observing that the standard deviation of the mean diminishes rather slowly as n is increased. For example, a hundredfold increase in n will give only a tenfold improvement in the estimated uncertainty of the mean. Therefore, there is usually some n arrived at in practice which is not worth exceeding for a relatively small improvement in accuracy.

The results may be interpreted in terms of a simple illustration. If the standard deviation of a *normal* set of 100 variates is 1.0 and the mean is 8.0, then 68 per cent of the variates lie between 7.0 and 9.0, and the standard deviation of the mean is $1.0/\sqrt{100} = 0.1$. The probability is 0.68 that a single variate chosen at random from the 100 variates will lie in the range 7.0 to 9.0. Moreover, the probability is 0.68 that a group of 100 new variates from the same population will have a mean lying between 7.9 and 8.1.

Another more intricate interpretation is sometimes useful. If a *normal* set of variates has a mean $\bar{v} \pm \sigma_{\bar{v}}$, then the probability is 0.68 that another set with a mean $\bar{w}$ lying between $\bar{v} + \sigma_{\bar{v}}$ and $\bar{v} - \sigma_{\bar{v}}$ comes from a population with the same mean. For example, suppose on one day an experiment yields a mean of 100 ± 2 ohms, where 2 ohms is the standard deviation of the mean. Then, a week later a mean of 96 ohms is obtained. Since the second mean differs from the first by two standard deviations, the probability is only about 0.05 that the experimental setup has remained unchanged during the week.

7-5. Errors of Computed Results. A problem frequently encountered is the estimation of the error in a quantity computed from some known function of several variables each of whose errors is specified. For example, the value of the average power, P, dissipated in a resistor, R, may be computed from measurements of the current, I, through the resistance, R, using the known function $P = I^2 R$. But what is the error in P if the errors in I and R are given?

In general, each of the measured quantities used in the calculation of a result is subject to error. If the errors of these quantities are specified, it is then possible to estimate the error in the computed result. This is true for any functional relationship and for any number of independent variables. Except in very simple cases, however, it is expedient to make an approximate determination of the error in the computed result.

As a simple example, suppose $I_1 = 100 \pm 2$ amp and $I_2 = 200 \pm 5$ amp, and it is desired to determine the error in the sum $I = I_1 + I_2$.

If the stated errors are limits of error, L, the maximum and minimum values of I may be determined by inspection.

$$I_{max} = 102 + 205 = 307 \text{ amp}$$
$$I_{min} = 98 + 195 = 293 \text{ amp}$$

Consequently, $I = 300 \pm 7$ amp. Limits of error of 2 per cent in I_1 and 2.5 per cent in I_2 combine, in this case, to give a limit of error of 2.3 per cent in I. If the given errors are standard deviations, σ, then Eq. (7-5) may be used to estimate the standard deviation of the sum, I.

$$\sigma_I = \sqrt{2^2 + 5^2} = 5.4 \text{ amp}$$

Hence, $I = 300 \pm 5.4$ amp. Standard deviations of 2 per cent in I_1 and 2.5 per cent in I_2 combine, in this case, to give a standard deviation of 1.8 per cent in I. The use of σ, rather than L, gives a more optimistic result. This is reasonable since the probability that *both I_1 and I_2* are far from their respective means is small.

For another example, suppose $V = 100 \pm 12$ volts and $I = 10 \pm 2$ amp, and it is desired to determine the error in the resistance $R = V/I$. If the stated errors are limits of error, L, the maximum and minimum values are again determinable by inspection.

$$R_{max} = \frac{112}{8} = 14.0 \text{ ohms}$$

$$R_{min} = \frac{88}{12} = 7.3 \text{ ohms}$$

Hence, $R = 10.0^{+4.0}_{-2.7}$ ohms. The limits of error are unequal in this case.

If the stated errors are standard deviations, σ, it is relatively difficult, even in this simple case, to determine the standard deviation of R unless an approximate method is used. The sensitiveness of R to changes in V and I is not the same and, moreover, account must be taken of the different probabilities of various combinations of V and I. An approximate method for solving this problem, as well as those involving other functional forms, is given in the following section.

7-6. Approximate Standard Deviation of Computed Results. It is possible to develop an approximate formula that enables the standard deviation of a computed result to be estimated for a given functional relationship involving any number of variables of specified standard deviation.

Let w be a known function of the two independent variables u and v.

$$w = f(u,v) \tag{7-14}$$

If $u = u_0$ and $v = v_0$ are measured values of the variables, then the computed result is $w = w_0 = f(u_0,v_0)$. The change in w resulting from infinitesimal changes $du = u - u_0$ and $dv = v - v_0$ is given by the total differential of w.

$$dw = \left(\frac{\partial w}{\partial u}\right)_{u_0, v_0} du + \left(\frac{\partial w}{\partial v}\right)_{u_0, v_0} dv \qquad (7\text{-}15)$$

where the partial derivatives are evaluated at $u = u_0$ and $v = v_0$. Now du and dv are deviations from the constants u_0 and v_0. Therefore, if u_0 and v_0 represent the means of the measured variables, then du and dv are deviations from these means. While Eq. (7-15) holds only for infinitesimal changes, it is approximately true for small deviations. It is assumed that the function may be expressed in this linear form without the need of higher-order terms in the Taylor series expansion.

The deviations du and dv may be regarded as two independent sets of variates, each of which is multiplied by a different constant in Eq. (7-15) and added to form the sum, dw. Consequently, Eq. (7-10) may be used to express the variance of dw in terms of the variance of the deviations.

$$\sigma_{dw}{}^2 \approx \left[\left(\frac{\partial w}{\partial u}\right)_{u_0, v_0}\sigma_{du}\right]^2 + \left[\left(\frac{\partial w}{\partial v}\right)_{u_0, v_0}\sigma_{dv}\right]^2 \qquad (7\text{-}16)$$

It may be shown that the variances of the deviations dw, du, and dv are equal to the variances of w, u, and v, respectively. For example, $u = u_0 + du$ may be regarded as the sum of two sets of variates, the first of which is constant, and therefore has zero variance, and the second of which has a variance $\sigma_{du}{}^2$. It follows from Eq. (7-5) that

$$\sigma_u{}^2 = \sigma_{u_0}{}^2 + \sigma_{du}{}^2 = \sigma_{du}{}^2$$

In similar fashion, it follows for $v = v_0 + dv$, that

$$\sigma_v{}^2 = \sigma_{v_0}{}^2 + \sigma_{dv}{}^2 = \sigma_{dv}{}^2$$

and for $w = w_0 + dw$, that

$$\sigma_w{}^2 = \sigma_{w_0}{}^2 + \sigma_{dw}{}^2 = \sigma_{dw}{}^2$$

Therefore, the interrelationship among the variances of u, v, and w is

$$\sigma_w{}^2 \approx \left[\left(\frac{\partial w}{\partial u}\right)_{u_0, v_0}\sigma_u\right]^2 + \left[\left(\frac{\partial w}{\partial v}\right)_{u_0, v_0}\sigma_v\right]^2 \qquad (7\text{-}17)$$

This approximate result may be extended immediately to more variables. It is approximate because Eq. (7-15) holds only for infinitesimal deviations, and because Eq. (7-5) is approximate for small numbers of variates.

In the final working result, Eq. (7-17), the partial derivatives serve the role of weighting factors determined by the functional dependence of w on u and v, and the constants u_0 and v_0. The square root of the sum of the squares of the weighted variances yields a standard deviation that takes into account the improbability that *both u and v* are far from their values u_0 and v_0. The student is cautioned to observe the requirement that u and v must be *independent* variables.

An approximate solution for the last example in Sec. 7-5 may now be readily obtained. First, translate the notation of Eq. (7-17) to the problem involving $R = V/I$.

$$\sigma_R{}^2 \approx \left[\left(\frac{\partial R}{\partial V}\right)_{V_0,I_0} \sigma_V\right]^2 + \left[\left(\frac{\partial R}{\partial I}\right)_{V_0,I_0} \sigma_I\right]^2 \tag{7-18}$$

where $V_0 = 100$ volts, $\sigma_V = 12$ volts, $I_0 = 10$ amp, $\sigma_I = 2$ amp, $R_0 = V_0/I_0 = 10$ ohms. The standard deviation of R may be computed after determining and evaluating the partial derivatives appearing in Eq. (7-18).

$$\frac{\partial R}{\partial V} = \frac{1}{I} \qquad \left(\frac{\partial R}{\partial V}\right)_{V_0,I_0} = \frac{1}{10} = 0.1$$

$$\frac{\partial R}{\partial I} = -\frac{V}{I^2} \qquad \left(\frac{\partial R}{\partial I}\right)_{V_0,I_0} = -\frac{100}{100} = -1.0$$

Therefore, $\qquad \sigma_R{}^2 \approx [0.1(12)]^2 + [-1.0(2)]^2 = 5.44$

Hence, $R = 10 \pm 2.3$ ohms. A standard deviation of 12 per cent in V and 20 per cent in I combine, in this case, to give a standard deviation of 23 per cent in R. As expected, the result is less pessimistic than in the limit-of-error case, where per cent limits of error were found to be $+40$ per cent and -27 per cent.

Notice in this example that the partial-derivative weighting factors differ in magnitude by 10 to 1 but that the weighted contributions of σ_V and σ_I to σ_R are comparable in magnitude, 1.2 and 2.0, respectively. This shows that Eq. (7-17) is capable of indicating which of the several variables of a function contributes most to the over-all error, and hence serves as a guide toward improving the accuracy of the final result. In this example, an improvement in accuracy in I, rather than in V, is indicated for the greatest reduction in σ_R.

7-7. Approximate Limit of Error of Computed Results. In many cases the limits of error in the computed quantity may be determined by inspecting the known function and inserting appropriate maximum and minimum values of the variables to give two extreme results. This was done in the two previous examples. However, in complicated functions it may not always be obvious from inspection how to proceed, and extended computations may be encountered. The differential approach used for standard deviation in Sec. 7-6 is also applicable to limit of error. One result of the differential approximation is that the two limits of error always turn out to be equal in magnitude.

The infinitesimal deviations, du and dv, in Eq. (7-15) may be regarded as limits of error of the variables u and v, reckoned from u_0 and v_0, respectively. Use of Eq. (7-15) in this manner is again approximate, since the limits of error may be small but not infinitesimal. It may be seen by inspection of Eq. (7-15) that dw has its maximum value when both terms are maximum in magnitude and numerically positive, and its minimum value when both terms are maximum in magnitude and numerically negative. Therefore, the limit of error of w is

$$L_w \approx \left| \left(\frac{\partial w}{\partial u} \right)_{u_0, v_0} L_u \right| + \left| \left(\frac{\partial w}{\partial v} \right)_{u_0, v_0} L_v \right| \qquad (7\text{-}19)$$

where the bars indicate absolute value. This result may be extended immediately to more variables. Equation (7-19) is similar to Eq. (7-17) in possessing partial-derivative weighting factors for each limit of error, but it does not embody the square root of the sum of the squares feature of Eq. (7-17). Hence, it is more pessimistic.

It is informative to illustrate the use of this approximate formula for the $R = V/I$ example previously worked out in accurate detail. First transform Eq. (7-19) to the notation of the example.

$$L_R \approx \left| \left(\frac{\partial R}{\partial V} \right)_{V_0, I_0} L_V \right| + \left| \left(\frac{\partial R}{\partial I} \right)_{V_0, I_0} L_I \right|$$

Using the numerical values of the example, with $L_V = 12$ volts and $L_I = 2$ amp, it is found that

$$L_R \approx |0.1(12)| + |-1.0(2)| = 3.2$$

Thus, $R = 10.0 \pm 3.2$ ohms. The result is more pessimistic than in the case of standard deviations where ± 2.3 ohms was found. Moreover, it is in approximate agreement with the accurately computed results and is almost precisely equal to the average magnitudes of the accurate limits of error.

7-8. Special Functional Forms. Functional forms that occur frequently are worth analyzing once and for all to avoid duplication of work. Investigation of some special cases also serves to illustrate further the application of Eq. (7-17) which may be applied to any function that is representable by a linear approximation over a small interval.

a. Sum and Difference. Let $w = u \pm v$. Then $\partial w / \partial u = 1$ and $\partial w / \partial v = \pm 1$. Substitute into Eq. (7-17).

$$\sigma_w \approx \sqrt{\sigma_u^2 + \sigma_v^2} \qquad (7\text{-}20)$$

The standard deviation of the sum or difference of two variables is equal to the square root of the sum of the squares of the standard deviations of the variables.   The result may be extended immediately to more than two variables.

b. *Simple Product.*   Let $w = uv$.   Then $\partial w / \partial u = v$, and $\partial w / \partial v = u$. Substitute into Eq. (7-17).

$$\sigma_w{}^2 \approx v^2\sigma_u{}^2 + u^2\sigma_v{}^2 = u^2v^2\left(\frac{\sigma_u{}^2}{u^2} + \frac{\sigma_v{}^2}{v^2}\right)$$

Hence, $\qquad \dfrac{\sigma_w}{w} \approx \sqrt{\left(\dfrac{\sigma_u}{u}\right)^2 + \left(\dfrac{\sigma_v}{v}\right)^2}$ $\hspace{3cm}$ (7-21)

The fractional standard deviation of the product of two variables is equal to the square root of the sum of the squares of the fractional standard deviations of the variables.   The result may be extended immediately to more than two variables.

c. *Simple Quotient.*   Let $w = u/v$.   Then

$$\frac{\partial w}{\partial u} = \frac{1}{v} \qquad \text{and} \qquad \frac{\partial w}{\partial v} = -\frac{u}{v^2}$$

Substitute into Eq. (7-17).

$$\sigma_w{}^2 \approx \frac{1}{v^2}\sigma_u{}^2 + \frac{u^2}{v^4}\sigma_v{}^2 = \frac{u^2}{v^2}\left(\frac{\sigma_u{}^2}{u^2} + \frac{\sigma_v{}^2}{v^2}\right)$$

Hence, $\qquad \dfrac{\sigma_w}{w} \approx \sqrt{\left(\dfrac{\sigma_u}{u}\right)^2 + \left(\dfrac{\sigma_v}{v}\right)^2}$ $\hspace{3cm}$ (7-22)

This result is identical to the case of the simple product.

d. *Simple Power.*   Let $w = u^a$, where a is a constant.   Then

$$\frac{\partial w}{\partial u} = au^{a-1} \qquad \text{and} \qquad \frac{\partial w}{\partial v} = 0$$

Substitute into Eq. (7-17).

$$\sigma_w{}^2 \approx a^2u^{2a-2}\sigma_u{}^2 = u^{2a}a^2\frac{\sigma_u{}^2}{u^2}$$

Hence, $\qquad \dfrac{\sigma_w}{w} \approx a\left(\dfrac{\sigma_u}{u}\right)$ $\hspace{3cm}$ (7-23)

The fractional standard deviation of a quantity raised to a power, a, is a times the fractional deviation of the quantity so raised.

The foregoing three results may be generalized into a single form

$$w = \frac{u^a v^b}{x^c}$$ $\hspace{3cm}$ (7-24)

where a, b, and c are constants. Equation (7-24) may be differentiated directly, but it is simpler to first take the logarithm of both sides.

$$\ln w = a\ln u + b\ln v - c\ln x$$

Now differentiate.

$$\frac{1}{w}\frac{\partial w}{\partial u} = \frac{a}{u} \qquad \frac{1}{w}\frac{\partial w}{\partial v} = \frac{b}{v} \qquad \frac{1}{w}\frac{\partial w}{\partial x} = -\frac{c}{x}$$

Substitute into Eq. (7-17).

$$\sigma_w{}^2 \approx \left(\frac{wa}{u}\right)^2 \sigma_u{}^2 + \left(\frac{wb}{v}\right)^2 \sigma_v{}^2 + \left(-\frac{wc}{x}\right)^2 \sigma_x{}^2$$

Hence,
$$\frac{\sigma_w}{w} \approx \sqrt{a^2\left(\frac{\sigma_u}{u}\right)^2 + b^2\left(\frac{\sigma_v}{v}\right)^2 + c^2\left(\frac{\sigma_x}{x}\right)^2} \qquad (7\text{-}25)$$

For the simple product, $c = 0$, $a = 1$, $b = 1$; for the simple quotient, $b = 0$, $a = 1$, $c = 1$; for the simple power, $c = 0$, $b = 0$.

Special cases of the limit of error formula may be developed by similar means.

7-9. Examples of Combinations of Standard Deviations. Several examples of combinations of errors for specified standard deviations are given here to further illustrate the application of the results that have been presented.

a. Resistors in Series. Two resistors are connected in series.

$$R_1 = 200 \pm 3 \text{ ohms} \qquad \text{and} \qquad R_2 = 300 \pm 6 \text{ ohms}$$

where the errors are standard deviations of the given mean values. Find the (approximate) standard deviation of the equivalent series resistance, $R_s = R_1 + R_2$. This is special case a of Sec. 7-8. Hence, applying Eq. (7-20),

$$\sigma_{R_s} \approx \sqrt{3^2 + 6^2} = 6.7 \text{ ohms}$$

Therefore, $R_s = 500 \pm 6.7$ ohms. A standard deviation of 1.5 per cent in R_1 and 2 per cent in R_2 combine, in this case, to give a 1.3 per cent standard deviation in R_s.

b. Resistors in Parallel. If the same two resistors are connected in parallel, find the (approximate) standard deviation of the equivalent parallel resistance.

The equivalent parallel resistance is

$$R_p = \frac{R_1 R_2}{R_1 + R_2}$$

This is *not* in the form of special case c in Sec. 7-8 because the numerator and the denominator of R_p are *not* independent.   Resort to Eq. (7-17), and first determine the partial derivatives.

$$\frac{\partial R_p}{\partial R_1} = \left(\frac{R_2}{R_1 + R_2}\right)^2 \qquad \left(\frac{\partial R_p}{\partial R_1}\right)_{\text{at mean}} = \left(\frac{300}{500}\right)^2 = 0.36$$

$$\frac{\partial R_p}{\partial R_2} = \left(\frac{R_1}{R_1 + R_2}\right)^2 \qquad \left(\frac{\partial R_p}{\partial R_2}\right)_{\text{at mean}} = \left(\frac{200}{500}\right)^2 = 0.16$$

Insert these results into Eq. (7-17).

$$\sigma_{R_p}^2 \approx [0.36(3)]^2 + [0.16(6)]^2 = 2.09$$

Therefore, $R_p = 120 \pm 1.4$ ohms.   A standard deviation of 1.5 per cent in R_1 and 2 per cent in R_2 combine, in this case, to give a standard deviation of 1.2 per cent in R_p.   It is interesting that while R_1 is the more accurate resistor, its contribution to the error in R_p exceeds that of R_2. This is because R_1, being smaller than R_2, has a stronger influence on R_p.

As an exercise, the student may wish to rework this example in terms of conductances $G_1 = 1/R_1$ and $G_2 = 1/R_2$.

c. Charge on Capacitor.   A capacitor $C = 1.0 \pm 0.1$ μf is charged to a voltage $V = 20 \pm 1$ volt, where the errors are standard deviations.   Find the charge on the capacitor and its (approximate) standard deviation.

Since $Q = CV$, this is special case *b* of Sec. 7-8, in which the fractional deviations are used.   The standard deviation of C is 10 per cent and that of V is 5 per cent.   Consequently, the fractional standard deviation of Q is given by Eq. (7-21).

$$\frac{\sigma_Q}{Q} \approx \sqrt{(0.1)^2 + (0.05)^2} = 0.11$$

or 11 per cent.   Since $Q = 20 \times 10^{-6}$ coulomb, then $\sigma_Q = 2.2 \times 10^{-6}$ coulomb.

d. Temperature Influence on Resistance.   The resistance, R, of a copper wire is given by

$$R = r_0[1 + \alpha(t - 20)]$$

where $r_0 = 4$ ohms ± 0.2 per cent is the resistance of the wire at 20°C, $\alpha = 0.004$ per degree centigrade ± 1 per cent is the temperature coefficient of the copper, and $t = 25 \pm 1$°C is the actual temperature of the wire.   The stated errors refer to standard deviations.   Find the resistance, R, and its (approximate) standard deviation.

The equation may be written as the sum of three terms,

$$R = r_0 + r_0\alpha t - 20r_0\alpha$$

However, special case *a* of Sec. 7-8 is *not* applicable because the three terms are *not* independent.   Resort to Eq. (7-17) and first establish the partial derivatives.

$$\frac{\partial R}{\partial r_0} = 1 + \alpha(t - 20) \qquad \left(\frac{\partial R}{\partial r_0}\right)_{\substack{at \\ mean}} = 1 + 0.004(25 - 20) = 1.02$$

$$\frac{\partial R}{\partial \alpha} = r_0(t - 20) \qquad \left(\frac{\partial R}{\partial \alpha}\right)_{\substack{at \\ mean}} = 4(25 - 20) = 20$$

$$\frac{\partial R}{\partial t} = r_0\alpha \qquad \left(\frac{\partial R}{\partial t}\right)_{\substack{at \\ mean}} = 4(0.004) = 0.016$$

Extending Eq. (7-17) to the case of three variables, one obtains

$$\sigma_R{}^2 \approx (1.02\sigma_{r_0})^2 + (20\sigma_\alpha)^2 + (0.016\sigma_t)^2$$

where $\sigma_{r_0} = 8 \times 10^{-3}$ ohm (converting 0.2 per cent), $\sigma_\alpha = 4 \times 10^{-5}$ per °C (converting 1 per cent), and $\sigma_t = 1$°C.   With these values

$$\sigma_R{}^2 \approx (67 + 64 + 3) \times 10^{-8} = 134 \times 10^{-8}$$

The mean value of R is

$$R = 4[1 + 0.004(25 - 20)] = 4.08 \text{ ohms}$$

Therefore, $R = 4.08 \pm 0.3$ per cent.

7-10. Limit of Error in Control Setting.   A final example illustrating approximate limit of error calculations in a case requiring circuit analysis

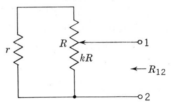

Fig. 7-1. Shunted control.

is presented here.   In the circuit of Fig. 7-1, a control resistance, R, is shunted by a fixed resistor, r, to produce different types of resistance variations between points 1 and 2.   The fraction of the control resistance appearing directly between points 1 and 2 is designated by k, where $0 \leqq k \leqq 1.0$.   The problem is to find the limit of error of the input resistance, R_{12}, that results from specified limits of error in R, r, and the setting of the sliding contact, k.   The results depend in an interesting manner on the size of r relative to R.   Since this is a useful arrangement which, effectively, changes the taper of the control, it will be investigated in general terms prior to solving a specific numerical example.

The resistance R_{12} is given by the rule for combining two parallel resistors, one of which is kR, in the circuit of Fig. 7-1, and the other is $r + (1 - k)R$.   Hence,

$$R_{12} = \frac{kR[r + (1 - k)R]}{r + R}$$

Define $\rho = r/R$. Then

$$R_{12} = \frac{kR[\rho R + (1-k)R]}{\rho R + R} = \frac{Rk(1 + \rho - k)}{1 + \rho} \qquad (7\text{-}26)$$

A plot of the dimensionless quantities R_{12}/R vs. k for various values of ρ is given in Fig. 7-2. It is apparent that a variety of resistance characteristics is possible. The slope of the curves is revealing and is given by

$$\frac{\partial}{\partial k}\left(\frac{R_{12}}{R}\right) = \frac{\partial}{\partial k}\left[\frac{k(1 + \rho - k)}{1 + \rho}\right] = 1 - \frac{2k}{1 + \rho} \qquad (7\text{-}27)$$

Thus, for $\rho \to \infty$ (r removed), the slope is constant and equal to 1.0. For $\rho = 0$ (r a short circuit), the slope is $1 - 2k$ and is, therefore, zero at

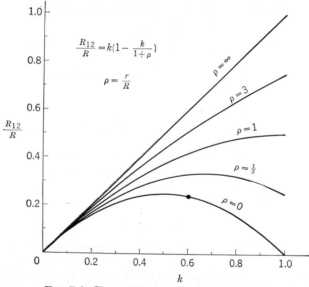

FIG. 7-2. Characteristics of shunted control.

$k = \frac{1}{2}$, which is a point of maximum R_{12}/R. The maximum value, $R_{12}/R = \frac{1}{4}$, may be calculated from Eq. (7-26) with $\rho = 0$ and $k = \frac{1}{2}$. For $\rho = 1$ ($r = R$), the slope is $1 - k$ and is, therefore, zero at $k = 1$. For $\rho > 1$, the slope is always positive since k cannot exceed unity. The curves of Fig. 7-2 suggest the complicated manner in which deviations of ρ and k may affect R_{12}/R, depending upon the actual values of ρ and k.

As a specific example, suppose $R = 10,000 \pm 100$ ohms, $r = 0$, and $k = 0.6 \pm 0.03$, where the given deviations are limits of error. (This is the point marked on the $\rho = 0$ curve of Fig. 7-2.) There are two procedures available for finding the limit of error in R_{12}, which, in the case of

$r = 0$, is given by

$$R_{12} = Rk(1 - k) = R(k - k^2) \qquad (7\text{-}28)$$

An accurate computation may be made after careful study of Eq. (7-28) to determine by inspection the most unfavorable combinations of R and k. The slope of the $\rho = 0$ curve in Fig. 7-2 at $k = 0.6$ is negative. Hence, the most unfavorable combinations for R and k occur when R is high and k is low, and vice versa. Therefore,

$$R_{12_{\max}} = 10,100(0.57)(1 - 0.57) = 2,475 \text{ ohms}$$
$$R_{12_{\min}} = 9,900(0.63)(1 - 0.63) = 2,307 \text{ ohms}$$

Thus, $R_{12} = 2,400^{+75}_{-93}$ ohms, and the limits of error are unequal.

An approximate computation may be carried out by applying Eq. (7-19), thereby avoiding the inspection problem above, but with some sacrifice in accuracy. The required partial derivatives are

$$\frac{\partial R_{12}}{\partial R} = k(1 - k) \qquad \left(\frac{\partial R_{12}}{\partial R}\right)_{\substack{at \\ mean}} = 0.6(1 - 0.6) = 0.24$$

$$\frac{\partial R_{12}}{\partial k} = R(1 - 2k) \qquad \left(\frac{\partial R_{12}}{\partial k}\right)_{\substack{at \\ mean}} = 10^4(1 - 1.2) = -0.2 \times 10^4$$

Inserting these values into Eq. (7-19), one obtains

$$L_{R_{12}} \approx |0.24(100)| + |-0.2 \times 10^4(0.03)| = 84$$

Therefore, $R_{12} = 2,400 \pm 84$ ohms. The limits are reasonably close to the previous calculation, and equal to the average magnitude of the two unequal limits of error.

PROBLEMS

7-1 (§2). Show that the result in Eq. (7-5) for the variances holds equally well for the squares of probable errors, or for the squares of average deviations.

7-2 (§4). A large set of normally distributed variates of standard deviation σ is divided randomly into two equal parts. (a) What is the standard deviation of each of the smaller sets? (b) What is the ratio of the standard deviation of the mean of one-half the set to the standard deviation of the mean of the original set? (c) What is the standard deviation of a sum set, a typical member of which is the sum of one variate picked at random from one-half the variates, and the other picked from the other half?

7-3 (§4). The mean value of a standard resistance was determined by elaborate precision methods to be 1.0000 ohms $\pm$ 0.03 per cent (standard deviation of the mean). Six months later, the resistance was measured again with equal skill and care with the mean result 0.9998 ohm. What is the probability that the standard resistance has not changed?

7-4 (§4). A box contains 49 nominally identical "little fuses." The resistance of each fuse is measured independently with equal skill and care. Analysis of the data shows a normal distribution with mean value of resistance equal to 200 ohms and a standard deviation of 7 ohms. If the above box is one of a large set of boxes, each containing 49 fuses of the same nominal resistance and selected at random from the same production run, what is the probability of finding, among this set, a box for which the mean value of fuse resistance is less than 197 ohms?

7-5 (§6). Two resistors, $R_1 = 400 \pm 40$ ohms and $R_2 = 600 \pm 80$ ohms, are connected in parallel. The stated errors are standard deviations. What are the resistance and standard deviation of the parallel combination?

7-6 (§6). The voltage drop across a resistor, of specified standard deviation 0.1 per cent, must be maintained within ± 0.2 per cent of its mean value. What must be the accuracy of an ammeter used in series with the resistor to monitor the current?

7-7 (§8). The voltage, V, across a resistance and the current, I, through the resistance are determined with the same per cent accuracy. The error in the resistance, calculated from $R = V/I$, is 1.0 per cent. With what accuracy were V and I determined?

7-8 (§8). Determine an expression for σ_w in terms of σ_u if $w = k\ln u$, where k is a constant.

7-9 (§8). Determine an expression for L_w in terms of L_u, L_v, and L_x for the function in Eq. (7-24), and show that it reduces to the correct results for the last three special cases of Sec. 7-8.

7-10 (§9). The current, I, through a resistor of value 50 ± 5 ohms (standard deviation) is measured with the result $I = 10.0$ amp ± 5 per cent standard deviation. (a) Compute the power dissipated in the resistance and its standard deviation. (b) Which contributes more to the uncertainty in the power, the uncertainty in the current or in the resistance?

7-11 (§9). Five resistors are available, one of 20 ohms and four of 10 ohms each. The standard deviation of the 20-ohm resistor is 5 per cent, and the standard deviation of each 10-ohm resistor is 10 per cent. Three possible connections using these resistors are shown in Fig. 7-3. Which connection would you use to obtain a resistance of 30 ohms with the least error? What is the standard deviation of the best connection?

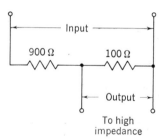

FIG. 7-3. Connections for 30-ohm resistance. FIG. 7-4. Voltage divider.

7-12 (§9). The voltage divider shown in Fig. 7-4 is to produce an output equal to one-tenth of its input. The standard deviation of the ratio of output to input must be 0.1 per cent or less. A 100-ohm precision resistor of standard deviation 0.02 per cent is available. What is the maximum allowable standard deviation of the 900-ohm resistor?

7-13 (§9). The law of deflection of a uniform-field d'Arsonval galvanometer was shown to be $I = K\theta/\cos\theta$. If the angle of deflection, θ, is known to be within $\pm 0.1°$ (standard deviation) of $15°$, what is the per cent standard deviation of the current, I?

7-14 (§9). An experiment was performed in order to accurately determine the period, T, and the ratio of total damping to the moment of inertia, D/J, for an underdamped d'Arsonval galvanometer with a uniform radial field and negligible coil inductance. Starting at rest with zero scale deflection, d, the switch in Fig. 4-1 was closed at $t = 0$. The maximum deflection, d_m, and the time, t_m, at which it occurred were measured. The final steady-state deflection, d_s, was measured after the galvanometer had stopped oscillating. The entire procedure was repeated 20 times with the results shown below. In each case, $d_s = 20.0$ mm was the final observed deflection.

Trial No.	d_m, mm	t_m, sec	Trial No.	d_m, mm	t_m, sec
1	27.6	2.8	11	30.1	3.1
2	23.7	3.1	12	26.4	2.8
3	26.0	2.9	13	27.8	2.9
4	28.3	3.0	14	25.2	3.2
5	27.1	2.9	15	27.4	3.0
6	29.2	3.0	16	24.6	3.1
7	24.8	3.0	17	28.7	3.0
8	28.0	3.1	18	29.0	2.8
9	27.2	2.9	19	26.2	3.2
10	25.9	3.2	20	26.8	3.0

Calculate the mean and standard deviation of T and D/J.

7-15 (§10). Compute the accurate and approximate limits of error of the input resistance, R_{12}, in Fig. 7-1, for $R = 10,000 \pm 100$ ohms (limit of error), $k = 0.3 \pm 0.03$ (limit of error), and $r = 0$.

7-16 (§10). Repeat Prob. 7-15 using $k = 0.5 \pm 0.03$ (limit of error).

CHAPTER 8

DEFLECTION METHODS OF MEASUREMENT

A vast number of different methods of measurement have been devised and found useful. They encompass a wide range of techniques and approaches and utilize every conceivable type of apparatus. In any given instance, the choice among this large assortment is usually determined by balancing all pertinent factors, including such items as required accuracy, cost, time, convenience, and availability of equipment.

To provide a framework for an over-all discussion, two types of measurement, direct and indirect, are described. While the distinction between these two types is not fundamental, it permits an initial view of a broad subject. Measurement methods are classified into the two major categories of deflection and null methods. An attempt is made to subdivide these further into a number of basic types. Several common deflection methods of measurement in popular use, as well as a few special methods, are described. Examples are presented primarily from the d-c and low-frequency electrical areas. However, the student should realize that similar concepts and methods are used in high-frequency electrical measurements and in other experimental fields.

This chapter provides perspective on a number of possibilities that exist for performing deflection-type measurements. It is hoped that the variety is sufficient to stimulate the student's imagination and creative thoughts. The examples represent the collective product of individual minds driven by curiosity and the will to do something better. There is ample room for further ingenuity. At the same time, close thought and analysis, required for a firm grasp of the principles, should be interwoven so that some depth is provided along with the over-all view of a gangling subject.

8-1. Direct and Indirect Measurements. Direct measurements are those in which the desired result is obtained immediately in the form of raw data. For example, if the objective is to determine the current in a circuit, it may be measured directly with an ammeter. Indirect measurements are those in which the desired result is computed from the raw data, as a separate operation, using a formula or physical law that relates the measured quantities to the quantity of interest. For instance, if the objective is to determine the voltage across a resistor, its resistance and the current through it may be measured, and the voltage computed from their product.

Direct measurements are usually more convenient and rapid than indirect ones. Consequently, they are appealing if they meet other requirements of the measurement task. To illustrate, a wattmeter, yielding direct readings of power, is preferable from a convenience standpoint to calculating the power from voltage and current readings. However, the attainable accuracy in direct measurements may be less than in the indirect case. This may seem curious because of the separate steps necessary in indirect measurements, each of which invites error, but it may be clarified by taking a closer look at direct measurements.

The distinction between direct and indirect measurements is an important practical matter. But there is really very little fundamental difference between the two. The direct measurement in many instances turns out to employ an instrument that responds to the same quantities as those obtainable indirectly, but carries out the computation automatically. Consider a voltmeter equipped with a scale that already takes into account the current times resistance calculation. It provides a direct voltage reading, but is essentially an ammeter in series with a known resistance. Similarly, a wattmeter may be constructed using a meter movement in which the deflection depends upon the product of two different currents in two separate coils. If the current in one coil is the load current, and the current in the other coil is proportional to load voltage (a known series resistor may be used), then the scale may be calibrated directly in watts. But, fundamentally, this direct-reading instrument does not really measure power directly at all. In direct methods of this type, reliance is placed on the instrument to carry out a calculation that otherwise would be necessary had indirect measurements been employed. Since the instrument "computation" always contains some error, it becomes clear why indirect measurements, entailing no subsequent computational error, might be capable of greater accuracy. Moreover, some direct-reading instruments are designed primarily for convenience and do not purport to be highly accurate.

It is an interesting mental exercise to review various direct measurements and to discover that each one involves a built-in computation that otherwise would have to be performed separately if indirect measurements were used. This principle applies even in such simple direct measurements as length (with a ruler), or time interval (with a stop watch), although the simplicity of the computation might cause it to be overlooked in these cases.

8-2. Methods of Measurement. Direct or indirect measurements may be undertaken by use of two general methods:

1. Deflection methods, in which the deflection of an instrument provides a basis for determining the quantity.

2. Null methods, in which a zero or null indication of an instrument leads to a determination of the quantity from other known conditions. Deflection methods that provide a direct reading of the quantity rely on the calibration of the instrument. However, some deflection methods do not utilize the instrument calibration but merely require that the reading of the instrument be the same under two different sets of conditions. The prime distinction between deflection and null methods is that in the former the instrument actually displays a deflection, while in the latter the indication is as close to zero as attainable.

Deflection methods are usually intuitively acceptable on superficial exposure, while some null methods tend to be more obscure and subtle. Null methods are often capable of greater precision than deflection methods and are usually preferred in accurate work. Deflection methods are vulnerable to instrument errors, especially when reliance is placed upon the calibration of the instrument. Null methods sometimes require multiple manipulations to obtain a satisfactory zero indication, while deflection methods may be very rapid. However, some null methods are actually easier and faster to execute than deflection methods. Moreover, there are commercially available automatic-control instruments that maintain a continuous null under varying conditions, and they eliminate the need for manipulative operations.

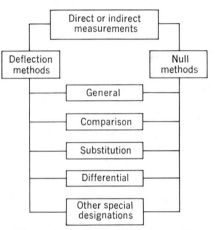

FIG. 8-1. Methods of measurement.

An attempt is made to classify deflection and null methods into the subdivisions indicated in Fig. 8-1. The first "general" category includes a variety of methods that do not appropriately fit elsewhere. General deflection methods will be discussed first in this chapter. Basic methods in common use include the comparison method, substitution method, and the differential method. These will be described further in this and the following chapter. A multitude of other methods having special designations, indicated at the bottom of Fig. 8-1, deserve comment here.

A method will frequently be designated by the name of the individual associated with its development. This is particularly true in bridge circuits where such names as Wheatstone, Kelvin, Schering, Campbell, Wien, and *many* others are used to describe the circuit. But bridge

methods are basically comparison methods and would be so classified in
Fig. 8-1.   Personal designations, however well deserved, are often misleading from the standpoint of the principles involved.

On the other hand, there are additional methods, not specifically shown
in Fig. 8-1, that do merit special designation on the basis of principle.
For example, the ballistic method is a basic one in which a sudden
mechanical or electrical impulse produces a measurable result.   The ballistic method is used to determine magnetic flux by inducing a short-lived
emf in a galvanometer circuit.   The charge that flows in the circuit is
proportional to the change in flux linkages and may be determined from
the deflection of a ballistic galvanometer.

Many methods are difficult to classify on the basis of their customary
designations.   For instance, there are resonance methods, heterodyne
methods, feedback methods, transmission-line methods, attenuator methods, and many others.   Careful study of the principles upon which these
methods rest might reveal that they properly belong in some category
already designated in Fig. 8-1.   Or, they might represent the combination
of two separate methods, as in the case of a resonance bridge that will be
analyzed later.   The truth of the matter is that the field of measurement
has developed in so many different directions that it is nearly impossible
to organize it into neat packages.   Understanding the method itself is,
of course, far more important than deciding upon its classification.   However, the classification may be worthwhile to organize one's thinking and
to highlight similarities that exist among methods of the same basic type.

8-3. Direct General Deflection Methods.   Direct measurements employing general deflection methods will be discussed first.   Two illustrations have already been presented in Chap. 3: the ammeter (calibrated
to read current) and the voltmeter (calibrated to read voltage).   Other
examples include ohmmeters (calibrated to read resistance) and wattmeters (calibrated to read power).   The ohmmeter is discussed in the
following sections while the electrodynamometer wattmeter is presented
in Chap. 12.   Direct measurements may also be carried out with such
instruments as frequency meters, phase-angle meters, watthour meters,
power-factor meters, capacitance meters, Z-angle meters, and a host of
others.

The ohmmeter is a popular device used for rapidly measuring d-c
resistance of passive electrical elements or networks by the direct deflection method.   Of the many different types, only series and shunt ohmmeters employing d'Arsonval movements are analyzed here.   The principles upon which ohmmeters are based, their nonuniform scales, and errors
arising from changes in their batteries are items that will be emphasized.

8-4. Series Ohmmeter.   The principle of a series ohmmeter is disclosed from a study of Fig. 8-2.   A d'Arsonval uniform-radial-field movement in series with a battery and an external resistance, R_1, constitutes

the basic arrangement.   (Use of a resistive shunt across the meter movement will be discussed subsequently.)   A resistor whose resistance, X,
is to be determined completes the circuit when connected across the ohmmeter input leads.   There is a definite relationship between the meter
current and the value of X.   This relationship also involves the parameters E (the battery emf), R (the internal resistance of the battery),
R_m (the resistance of the meter movement), and R_1.   If these parameters
are fixed, the scale of the instrument may be calibrated directly in ohms.

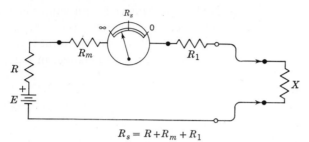

$$R_s = R + R_m + R_1$$

Fig. 8-2. Series ohmmeter.

For $X = 0$ (input leads shorted together), the values of E, R, R_1, and
R_m are selected such that the meter indicates full-scale deflection.   For
$X \to \infty$ (X removed), the meter current is zero.   Hence, the scale in
ohms is "backward," being marked " ∞ " at the left and "0" at the
right.   Moreover, the scale is nonuniform, despite the fact that the
angular deflection is proportional to the meter current.

For any value of X, the meter current, I_x, is given by

$$I_x = \frac{E}{R + R_m + R_1 + X} = \frac{E}{R_s + X} \tag{8-1}$$

where R_s is the equivalent input resistance of the ohmmeter.   Equation
(8-1) shows that for $X \to \infty$, $I_\infty = 0$, and for $X = 0$, $I_0 = E/R_s$, which
is the current required for full-scale deflection in the correctly adjusted
instrument.   Now I_x may be expressed in terms of the full-scale current,
I_0, which is a constant.

$$I_x = \frac{E/R_s}{1 + X/R_s} = \frac{I_0}{1 + \rho} \qquad \rho = \frac{X}{R_s} \tag{8-2}$$

where ρ is the fractional value of X compared with the input resistance
of the ohmmeter.   This equation shows that when $\rho = 1$, $I_x = I_0/2$;
that is, the deflection is at mid-scale when $X = R_s$.

The ohms scale may be studied in terms of the dimensionless quantities
$F = I_x/I_0$, which is the fractional scale deflection, and $\rho = X/R_s$, which
is proportional to the variable X.

$$F = \frac{1}{1 + \rho} \tag{8-3}$$

Note that judicious definitions of terms have stripped this equation to its bare essentials. Moreover, it is a universal equation since it holds regardless of specific values of parameters in the circuit of Fig. 8-2.

Figure 8-3 portrays the way in which F varies inversely and nonuniformly with ρ. The slope of the curve is given by

$$\frac{dF}{d\rho} = \frac{-1}{(1 + \rho)^2} \tag{8-4}$$

This shows that the slope is always negative for all values of $\rho > 0$. The slope at $\rho = 0$ is -1. Therefore, the tangent to the curve at $\rho = 0$ also passes through the point $\rho = 1$, $F = 0$, where the actual fractional scale deflection is $\frac{1}{2}$. The change in F for a given change in ρ depends upon

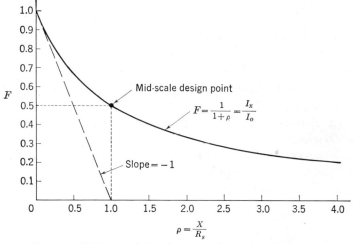

FIG. 8-3. Universal deflection curve for series ohmmeter.

ρ—the greater the ρ, the less the change in F. This is because the magnitude of the slope steadily decreases as ρ becomes larger.

The curve of Fig. 8-3 may be converted to angular deflection, θ, and plotted as shown in Fig. 8-4. This represents the actual appearance of the ohmmeter scale, but one element of generality has been lost by the need for specifying the total angular excursion of the pointer, which is taken as $100°$. The law of deflection of the movement is $I_x = K\theta_x$, where K is the instrument constant. It follows that F and θ_x are proportional, $\theta_x = (I_0/K)F$. Because of the cramped nature of the scale, its readability becomes increasingly inaccurate for values of X that are much greater than the mid-scale value, R_s, where $\rho = 1$. However, R_s is within control of the designer, since it depends upon the accessible external resistance, R_1. But for each value of R_1, the meter must be designed to produce full-scale deflection for $X = 0$. This may be accomplished in a number of ways in multirange ohmmeters by use of different batteries for each different R_1, or by employing shunts directly across the movement that are changed for each value of R_1.

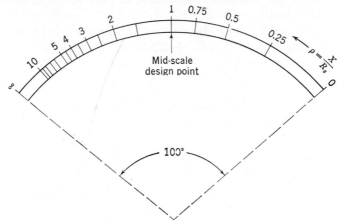

FIG. 8-4. Meter scale for series ohmmeter.

8-5. Shunt Ohmmeter. The minimum mid-scale design value of a series ohmmeter is established by the minimum attainable value of its equivalent input resistance, $R_s = R + R_m + R_1$. With $R_1 = 0$ there may still be too high a value of R_s to permit accurate determination of very small resistances. An alternative arrangement, given in Fig. 8-5,

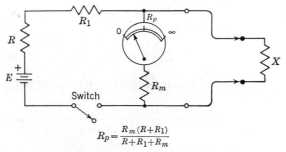

$$R_p = \frac{R_m(R+R_1)}{R+R_1+R_m}$$

FIG. 8-5. Shunt ohmmeter.

is well suited to the measurement of low resistance. It is called a shunt ohmmeter because the unknown resistance, X, is placed in shunt with the movement. The circuit remains closed when X is removed, so a switch is provided to prevent battery drain when the instrument is not in use. The parameters E, R, R_m, and R_1 are selected such that the movement indicates full-scale deflection when X is removed. For $X = 0$, the meter current is zero because its resistance, R_m, is shunted by a short circuit. Therefore, the scale of this instrument is the reverse of the series ohmmeter, and this provides an obvious external clue for distinguishing between the two instruments. The shunt-ohmmeter scale is also non-uniform, despite use of a uniform-radial-field movement, as disclosed by analysis of the circuit.

For any value of X, the meter current, I_x, may be deduced by use of the current-splitting rule: $X/(R_m + X)$ times the battery current. The battery current for any X is

$$I_b = \frac{E}{R + R_1 + R_m X/(R_m + X)} \tag{8-5}$$

Hence, the meter current is

$$I_x = \frac{X}{R_m + X} I_b = \frac{EX}{(R_m + X)(R + R_1) + R_m X} \tag{8-6}$$

It may be seen from this equation that for $X = 0$, $I_0 = 0$, and for $X \to \infty$,

$$I_\infty = \frac{E}{R + R_1 + R_m} \tag{8-7}$$

which represents full-scale deflection in the correctly adjusted instrument. As in the series-ohmmeter case, it is desirable to define appropriate dimensionless quantities to obtain uncumbersome and universal results. Define $F = I_x/I_\infty$, the fractional scale deflection, and form the ratio of Eq. (8-6) to Eq. (8-7).

$$F = \frac{I_x}{I_\infty} = \frac{(R + R_1 + R_m)X}{(R_m + X)(R + R_1) + R_m X}$$
$$= \frac{(R + R_1 + R_m)X}{R_m(R + R_1) + (R + R_1 + R_m)X} \tag{8-8}$$

The following definition of an equivalent resistance is indicated.

$$R_p = \frac{R_m(R + R_1)}{R + R_1 + R_m}$$

Again this is the equivalent input resistance of the ohmmeter. Finally, with $\rho = X/R_p$, which is the fractional value of X as compared with R_p, Eq. (8-8) becomes

$$F = \frac{X}{R_p + X} = \frac{1}{1 + 1/\rho} \tag{8-9}$$

This universal equation holds for any values of parameters in the circuit of Fig. 8-5. It contains information from which the ohmmeter may be understood and designed. It shows, for instance, that at $\rho = 0$, $F = 0$; for $\rho \rightarrow \infty$, $F = 1$ (full-scale deflection); and the value of ρ required for half-scale deflection, $F = \frac{1}{2}$, is clearly $\rho = 1$. This means that mid-scale deflection occurs when X is equal to the input resistance of the ohmmeter.

A plot of this universal equation is given in Fig. 8-6. The curve is essentially upside down from that of the series ohmmeter in Fig. 8-3. Indeed, the slope of the shunt-ohmmeter curve is the same as that for the series-ohmmeter, except for sign.

$$\frac{dF}{d\rho} = \frac{1/\rho^2}{(1 + 1/\rho)^2} = \frac{1}{(1 + \rho)^2} \tag{8-10}$$

It follows that the scale characteristics of the shunt ohmmeter have the same nonuniform characteristics as that of the series ohmmeter, but in

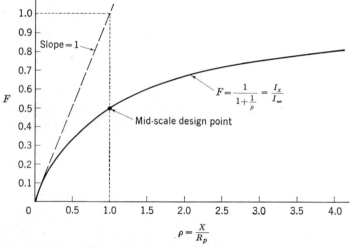

FIG. 8-6. Universal deflection curve for shunt ohmmeter.

reverse. Equation (8-10) shows that the slope of the curve in Fig. 8-6 is always positive for all values of $\rho > 0$. The slope at $\rho = 0$ is $+1$. The tangent to the curve at the point $F = 0$, $\rho = 0$ intersects the asymptote to the curve for $\rho \gg 1$ at the ordinate $\rho = 1$, where the actual fractional scale deflection is $\frac{1}{2}$.

The universal curve of Fig. 8-6 may be converted to angular deflection, θ, as shown in Fig. 8-7, using $\theta_x = (I_\infty/K)F$. Cramping of the scale for values of X greater than R_p is evident; the readability becomes progressively impaired as ρ increases. However, as in the series-ohmmeter case, the mid-scale design value may be established by suitable choice of circuit parameters that also maintain I_∞ at the value required for full-scale deflection. Multirange shunt ohmmeters may be designed in various ways, using different batteries for each range or by employing switchable resistors in series with the movement for different ranges. The principles are the same as those in the series-ohmmeter case.

Series and shunt ohmmeters are seen to be complementary instruments, the former being useful for measurement of large resistances and the latter for small values. Resistances ranging from microohms to megohms are encompassed by this pair of instruments, with moderate accuracy on the order of a few per cent. One of the major reasons for limited accuracy, in addition to inherent shortcomings of deflection-type instruments that depend upon scale calibration, is presented in the section following. It is traceable to deterioration of the ohmmeter battery with age and use.

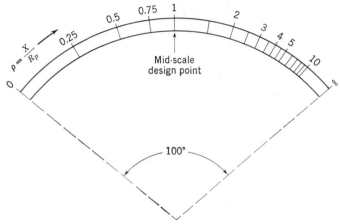

FIG. 8-7. Meter scale for shunt ohmmeter.

8-6. Ohmmeter Battery-aging Errors. It is evident from the foregoing analyses that ohmmeters require an initial adjustment prior to their use. Specifically, I_0 in the series case, or I_∞ in the shunt case, must produce full-scale deflection if the ohmmeter scale calibration is to be directly useful. An adjustment is provided in the instrument for meeting this requirement and to permit use of a given battery over a reasonable range of E and R before it has to be discarded. When E and R change, owing to battery aging, I_0 or I_∞ may be set to their full-scale values by adjusting one of the circuit elements. However, this introduces error in the fixed scale calibration which depends upon all the circuit elements. Examples of analysis of this error are presented here for two types of adjustments in series ohmmeters.

The full-scale current adjustment of the series ohmmeter of Fig. 8-8a is provided by the rheostat, R_1. Prior to measuring a resistance, X, the input leads are shorted together ($X = 0$), and R_1 is adjusted to produce full-scale deflection.   The full-scale current, I_0, is given by

$$I_0 = \frac{E}{R + R_1 + R_m} = \frac{E}{R_s} \qquad (8\text{-}11)$$

Subsequent connection of any unknown resistance, X, produces a meter current

$$I_x = \frac{E}{R_s + X} = \frac{I_0 R_s}{R_s + X} \qquad (8\text{-}12)$$

Assume that the ohmmeter has been calibrated correctly over its entire scale for the values E, R, R_1, and R_m.   Suppose, then, that owing to

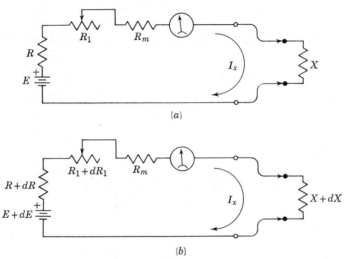

(a)

(b)

FIG. 8-8. Series adjustment of series ohmmeter.

aging of the battery, its emf changes to $E + dE$, and its internal resistance changes to $R + dR$.   In normal use, R_1 is then adjusted to $R_1 + dR_1$ so that the same full-scale deflection is obtained with the input leads shorted.   This current is given by

$$I_0 = \frac{E + dE}{R + dR + R_1 + dR_1 + R_m} \qquad (8\text{-}13)$$

and is the same I_0 as that in Eq. (8-11).   However, the current I_x', for any given X, will now be

$$I_x' = \frac{E + dE}{R + dR + R_1 + dR_1 + R_m + X} \qquad (8\text{-}14)$$

This current is not the same as that in Eq. (8-12) for the same value of X. Hence, the calibration will be in error.

It appears difficult to obtain an expression for the error in the *observed resistance indication* because the scale is not uniform. The change in the resistance reading for a given change in I_x will depend importantly on the portion of the scale from which the deflection is read. This obstacle may be overcome by a clever analysis device. Introduce a change in X that forces I'_x to agree with the value in Eq. (8-12), as indicated diagrammatically in Fig. 8-8b. Then, the error in X will be obtained directly from dX without the need of coping with the nonuniformity of the scale! By this devious technique it is possible to find the change, dX, in X that corresponds to the battery changes dE and dR, and the concomitant change dR_1.

It is justifiable to work with differentials when only small changes are involved. The change in I_x resulting from changes dE, dR, and dR_1 is deliberately offset by introducing a change dX in X. Therefore, the differential of Eq. (8-12) is zero.

$$dI_x = 0 = I_0 \left[\frac{\partial}{\partial R_s} \left(\frac{R_s}{R_s + X} \right) dR_s + \frac{\partial}{\partial X} \left(\frac{R_s}{R_s + X} \right) dX \right] \quad (8\text{-}15)$$

where I_0 is constant because of the adjustment of R_1. Since the meter resistance is constant, $dR_m = 0$, and $dR_s = dR + dR_1$. Work out the partial derivatives and Eq. (8-15) becomes

$$\frac{X \, dR_s}{(R_s + X)^2} - \frac{R_s \, dX}{(R_s + X)^2} = 0$$

Therefore,
$$\frac{dX}{X} = \frac{dR_s}{R_s} = \frac{d(R + R_1)}{R + R_1 + R_m} \quad (8\text{-}16)$$

This result may also be expressed in terms of dE. From Eq. (8-11), $I_0 \, dR_s = dE$. Hence,

$$\frac{dX}{X} = \frac{dR_s}{R_s} = \frac{dE}{E} \quad (8\text{-}17)$$

The fractional error in X is equal to the fractional change in the battery emf. Thus, the error in X may be quite sizable when R_1 is used for the full-scale current adjustment. For this reason, the adjustment control, S, shown in the series-ohmmeter circuit of Fig. 8-9, is usually preferred because the errors it introduces are smaller than in the case analyzed. This might be expected because the equivalent series resistance of the ohmmeter is quite insensitive to S, since R_m is usually much smaller than R_1. At the same time, the meter current is highly susceptible to the value of S.

The meter current for any X in the circuit of Fig. 8-9 is given by the current-splitting rule: $S/(R_m + S)$ times the battery current, I_b.

$$I_b = \frac{E}{R + R_1 + R_m S/(R_m + S) + X} = \frac{E}{M + X} \tag{8-18}$$

where M is the equivalent input resistance of the ohmmeter.   Then,

$$I_x = \frac{S}{R_m + S} \frac{E}{M + X} \tag{8-19}$$

The current for full-scale deflection, I_0, obtained by adjusting S, is found by imposing $X = 0$ in Eq. (8-19).

$$I_0 = \frac{SE}{(R_m + S)M} \tag{8-20}$$

Therefore, I_x expressed in terms of I_0 is

$$I_x = \frac{I_0 M}{M + X} \tag{8-21}$$

This form is exactly the same as in the preceding example, Eq. (8-12).

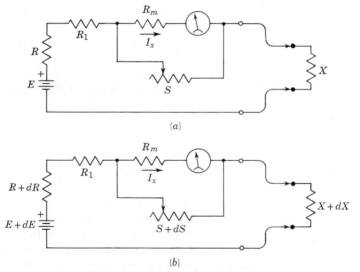

(a)

(b)

FIG. 8-9. Shunt adjustment of series ohmmeter.

The error in X, resulting from battery aging, may be obtained by the same differential technique employed previously.   Assume the ohmmeter is calibrated correctly over its entire scale for the values E, R, R_1, R_m, and S.   If the battery emf changes to $E + dE$, and its internal resistance changes to $R + dR$, then S is adjusted to $S + dS$ so that the same I_0 is maintained.   The change in I_x resulting from the changes dE, dR, and dS is offset by introducing a change dX in X.   Then, the differential of Eq. (8-21) is zero.   Since Eqs. (8-21) and (8-12) are in the same form, it follows immediately that the fractional error in X is in the same form as Eq. (8-16).

$$\frac{dX}{X} = \frac{dM}{M} \tag{8-22}$$

This result may be expressed in terms of dR and dS by evaluating dM/M.

$$M = R + R_1 + \frac{R_m S}{R_m + S}$$

where R_1 and R_m are constant.   Consequently,

$$dM = dR + \left(\frac{R_m}{R_m + S}\right)^2 dS \tag{8-23}$$

The reader is invited in Prob. 8-12 to show that Eq. (8-22), expressed in terms of dR and dE, is

$$\frac{dX}{X} = \frac{1}{R + R_1}\left[dR - \left(\frac{R_m S}{R_m + S}\right)\frac{dE}{E}\right] \tag{8-24}$$

Because R_1 is usually large compared with R_m, it is seen from this analysis that calibration errors owing to battery aging may be reduced substantially by use of the circuit of Fig. 8-9.   Another method that may be susceptible to even less error utilizes a special meter movement.   An adjustable soft iron shunt across the pole pieces of the movement may be designed to control the meter sensitivity by changing the magnitude of the **B** field in the air gap.   As the battery ages, the meter is zeroed by altering its instrument constant, $K = S/nBA$, without the need of changing any circuit elements.   Then, if dR is small compared with $R_1 + R_m$, a negligible error is introduced by battery aging.

8-7. Indirect General Deflection Methods.   Indirect measurements employing general deflection methods are used widely.   The voltmeter-ammeter method of determining resistance is one illustration, described in Sec. 5-6.   Another simple example, also mentioned previously, is the measurement of voltage across a known resistor to determine the current through the resistor.   Several additional examples in the realm of d-c measurements are presented here.

However, general deflection methods are by no means restricted to d-c applications.   An elementary example in the a-c case is the determination of mutual inductance, M, between two coils by an a-c voltmeter-ammeter method.   The ammeter is connected to measure the rms current applied to one coil, while the voltmeter, connected across the second coil, responds to the induced emf (with small error if the voltmeter impedance is large compared with the input impedance to the second coil).   If the angular frequency, $\omega = 2\pi f$, is known, M may be calculated from the ratio of the voltmeter reading to the ammeter reading, which is equal to ωM.

Another classical method, not discussed in detail here, is the loss of charge method of determining leakage resistance across a capacitor of known capacitance, by use of a ballistic galvanometer. It is based on the theoretical expression for the decay of charge, q, across a capacitor, C, shunted by its leakage resistance, R.

$$q = Q_0 \epsilon^{-t/RC} \tag{8-25}$$

where Q_0 is the charge on the capacitor at time $t = 0$ [see Eq. (2-4) with $E = 0$]. The capacitor is first charged to Q_0 and then immediately discharged through the ballistic galvanometer, whose deflection is proportional to Q_0. The capacitor is charged to Q_0 again, allowed to discharge through its leakage resistance for a measured interval of time, t, and then discharged through the ballistic galvanometer again. The second deflection is proportional to $Q_0 \epsilon^{-t/RC}$. The unknown resistance, R, may be computed from the ratio of the first to the second deflection, $\epsilon^{t/RC}$, since both t and C are known. A detailed example of this method, using an electrostatic voltmeter, is presented in Sec. 14-7.

These two illustrations suggest the diversity of general deflection methods, and there are many more not mentioned.

8-8. Circumvention of Ammeter Resistance. It has been emphasized that insertion of an ammeter into a circuit to measure current may give

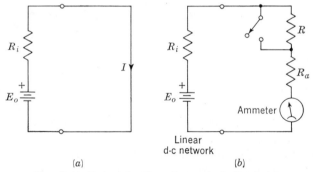

FIG. 8-10. Determination of unmolested current.

a false result if the meter resistance is not negligible. For instance, suppose the current in the circuit of Fig. 8-10a is to be measured by an ammeter of equivalent resistance, R_a, including its shunt. Let E_0 and R_i represent the network responsible for the branch current I. If the meter is inserted into this branch, it will indicate a current that is smaller than I, assuming perfect instrument calibration. The desired current is E_0/R_i, while the meter current is $E_0/(R_i + R_a)$. If R_i and R_a are known, the meter reading may be multiplied by $(1 + R_a/R_i)$ to correct for this systematic error. Also, if $R_a \ll R_i$, the correction is negligible.

In many instances, R_i is not known. When the ammeter is inserted into such a circuit there should always be uneasiness concerning how close its reading may be to the unmolested value that is sought, especially because there may be no outward clue to guide the experimenter. A simple indirect method may be employed to determine the current, I, without a knowledge of R_i or E_0. An auxiliary resistor, R, shunted by a switch, is placed in series with the ammeter as illustrated in Fig. 8-10b. The ammeter is read with the switch open and closed, and these two readings enable the current I to be computed. Although E_0 and R_i need not be known, it is assumed they are constant.

When the switch of Fig. 8-10b is open, the meter responds to a current

$$I_1 = \frac{E_0}{R_i + R + R_a} \tag{8-26}$$

When R is shorted out, the meter current becomes, with $R = 0$,

$$I_2 = \frac{E_0}{R_i + R_a} \tag{8-27}$$

and is greater than I_1. By straightforward algebraic manipulation, using $I = E_0/R_i$, E_0 and R_i may be eliminated from these equations with the result

$$I = \frac{I_1 I_2}{\dfrac{R_a}{R}(I_1 - I_2) + I_1} \tag{8-28}$$

The current, I, may be computed from the readings, I_1 and I_2, and only the *ratio* R_a/R need be known. However, in some cases the computation may not be necessary. If both readings are substantially the same, then Eq. (8-28) shows that $I = I_1 = I_2$. This situation occurs when $(R + R_a) \ll R_i$ and gives assurance that the current is not molested by insertion of the ammeter.

If an auxiliary resistance equal to the meter resistance is available, a simplification results. With $R = R_a$, Eq. (8-28) becomes

$$I = \frac{I_1 I_2}{2I_1 - I_2} \qquad R = R_a \tag{8-29}$$

A similar method may also be devised using a resistor in shunt with the meter, as is evident from Prob. 8-17.

8-9. Multirange Voltmeter Loading. Concern about molesting the measured quantity should be ever present in voltage measurements. If the input resistance across the two terminals to which the voltmeter is connected is known, a correction may be applied to the voltmeter reading, provided that its resistance is known. To illustrate, suppose the voltage across terminals 1-2 in Fig. 8-11 is measured for the purpose of determining E_0, the open-circuit voltage. If the network has an input resistance R_i, and the voltmeter resistance is R_v, the voltmeter will read $E_0 R_v/(R_i + R_v)$, assuming perfect calibration. This reading is less than E_0. But E_0 may be obtained, if both R_i and R_v are known, by multiplying the reading by $(1 + R_i/R_v)$. If $R_v \gg R_i$, the correction is negligible.

In the treacherous case of an unknown R_i, it is not readily apparent from the voltage measurement whether or not the current drawn by the voltmeter has caused an appreciable drop across the input resistance of the network. However, an indirect determination of E_0 may be made without a knowledge of R_i by using a principle similar to that described for the ammeter in the preceding section. This method is easily implemented with a multirange voltmeter, although an external series resistor may also be used as in the case of the ammeter.

A two-range voltmeter connected across terminals 1-2 is shown in Fig. 8-11. On range 1, the voltmeter resistance is R_v; on range n, it is nR_v. Hence, the voltmeter ranges are in the ratio $n:1$. The voltmeter reading on range 1 is given by the voltage-divider rule.

$$V_1 = \frac{R_v E_0}{R_i + R_v} \qquad (8\text{-}30)$$

On range n, the voltmeter reading is

$$V_2 = \frac{nR_v E_0}{R_i + nR_v} \qquad (8\text{-}31)$$

and will generally be larger than V_1, since $n > 1$. The ratio of these two readings is

$$\frac{V_1}{V_2} = \frac{R_i + nR_v}{n(R_i + R_v)} \qquad (8\text{-}32)$$

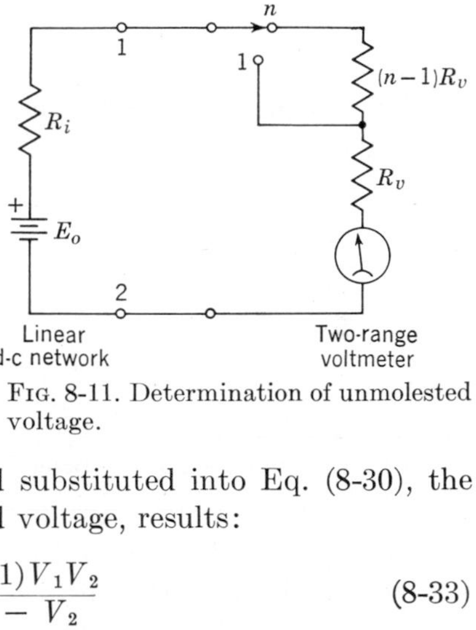

FIG. 8-11. Determination of unmolested voltage.

When Eq. (8-32) is solved for R_i and substituted into Eq. (8-30), the following expression for E_0, the desired voltage, results:

$$E_0 = \frac{(n-1)V_1 V_2}{nV_1 - V_2} \qquad (8\text{-}33)$$

Therefore, E_0 may be computed from the readings, V_1 and V_2, and a knowledge of the range ratio, n. If $R_v \gg R_i$, then nR_v does not load the network either, so both readings will be the same under these conditions. Indeed, if $V_1 = V_2$, Eq. (8-33) yields $E_0 = V_1 = V_2$. This provides a useful loading check, even though it is a negative result. If a voltmeter with a $2:1$ range ratio is available, calculation of E_0 is particularly simple, for then E_0 is given by

$$E_0 = \frac{V_1 V_2}{2V_1 - V_2} \qquad n = 2 \qquad (8\text{-}34)$$

A similar method may also be devised using an external resistance in shunt with the voltmeter, as indicated in Prob. 8-19.

8-10. Half-deflection Method. A useful method for determining the resistance of d-c meters is suggested by the foregoing examples. An indirect determination of meter resistance may be carried out in terms of the deflection of the instrument itself and an auxiliary known resistor. This method may be applied to any d-c instrument. The general procedure is to energize the instrument so that a sizable deflection is produced. Then the deflection is reduced by inserting a known resistor in series with the meter. The meter resistance is computed from the readings of the two deflections and the series resistance. If the series resistance is adjusted so that its insertion produces half the initial deflection, the computation may be very simple; namely, the series resistance is equal to the meter resistance. However, this simple result relies upon the assumption that the input resistance of the source of current is very small compared with the meter resistance, as will be shown by analysis.

The resistance, R_v, of a voltmeter, shown in Fig. 8-12, may be determined by use of the auxiliary series resistor, R_1. An emf, E, of internal resistance R provides the voltmeter current. With the switch open, the voltmeter reading is obtained from the voltage-divider rule.

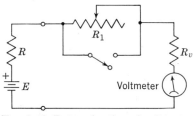

$$V_1 = \frac{R_v E}{R_v + R_1 + R} \qquad (8\text{-}35)$$

With the switch closed, the reading is larger and may be obtained by setting $R_1 = 0$ in Eq. (8-35).

$$V_2 = \frac{R_v E}{R_v + R} \qquad (8\text{-}36)$$

Fig. 8-12. Determination of voltmeter resistance.

where it is assumed that both E and R are constant. The ratio V_1/V_2 may be formed and solved for the voltmeter resistance, R_v, with the following result:

$$R_v = \frac{R_1 V_1}{V_2 - V_1} - R \qquad (8\text{-}37)$$

If $R_v \gg R$, this simplifies to

$$R_v = \frac{R_1}{V_2/V_1 - 1} \qquad R_v \gg R \qquad (8\text{-}38)$$

Consequently, R_v may be computed from the *ratio* of the two readings and the known value of R_1. Furthermore, if $V_2/V_1 = 2$, then $R_v = R_1$, and this is then called the *half-deflection* method because the introduction of R_1 has halved the deflection. However, it may be seen from Eq. (8-37) that the result determined by the half-deflection method is larger than the actual voltmeter resistance by an amount equal to R. This is also clear from direct inspection of the original circuit. With the switch closed, the total circuit resistance is $R_v + R$. Obviously, the total resistance must be doubled to halve the current; hence, $R_1 = R_v + R$ for half deflection.

A similar analysis applies for an ammeter of resistance R_a. Since the voltmeter of Fig. 8-12 is basically a current-measuring device, the voltage readings, V_1 and V_2, may be divided by R_v to obtain the meter current. Therefore, the ammeter result follows immediately from Eq. (8-37), replacing R_v by R_a, and voltage readings by corresponding current readings.

$$R_a = \frac{R_1 I_1}{I_2 - I_1} - R \qquad (8\text{-}39)$$

I_1 is the current with the switch open, and $I_2 > I_1$ is the current with the switch closed. Again, if $R_a \gg R$, and R_1 has been selected to produce $I_1 = I_2/2$, then $R_a = R_1$, and this becomes the half-deflection method. Because ammeter resistance is much less than voltmeter resistance, the requirement on R is more stringent in this case. This is an elusive source of error, because the two current readings may be obtained in practice, and R_a may be computed from the formula with R omitted. There is no surface clue indicating that R must be taken into account. For accurate results, it is desirable to use a source of known low resistance.

A similar method may be devised using a resistor in shunt with the meter, as suggested in Prob. 8-20.

8-11. Determination of Battery Internal Resistance. The interesting problem of determining the internal resistance of a battery serves as a final example of indirect measurements employing general deflection methods. The chief difficulty associated with this determination is the danger of overloading and damaging the battery. This is because sufficient current must be drawn from the battery to produce an appreciable voltage drop across its internal resistance. It is possible to obtain satisfactory results with the method outlined below, provided good technique is employed to avoid damage to the battery. However, the differential method described in Sec. 8-16 might be preferable.

The battery of emf E whose internal resistance, R, is to be determined is shown in Fig. 8-13. The terminal voltage of the battery may be measured with a voltmeter for various settings of a low-resistance loading rheostat, R_L, both connected directly across the battery terminals. The switch permits R_L to be connected momentarily, whenever a voltage reading is desired, thus avoiding excessive current drain over a prolonged period of time.

The terminal voltage of the battery, under load, is given by the voltmeter reading, V, when the switch is closed. Application of the voltage-divider rule yields

$$V = \frac{ER_L R_v/(R_L + R_v)}{R + R_L R_v/(R_L + R_v)} = \frac{ER_L}{R(1 + R_L/R_v) + R_L} \qquad (8\text{-}40)$$

If $R_v \gg R_L$, which will almost invariably be true, then Eq. (8-40) becomes

$$V = \frac{ER_L}{R + R_L} \qquad\qquad R_v \gg R_L \qquad (8\text{-}41)$$

A plot of V as a function of R_L, assuming E and R are constant, is given in Fig. 8-14. If $R_L \gg R$, V approaches E. When $R_L = R$, $V = E/2$. When $R_L \ll R$, $V \approx ER_L/R$, and the curve approaches the origin asymptotically to a line of slope E/R. This curve, based on Eq. (8-41), shows

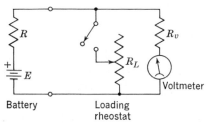

R
R_v
R_L
+
E
Voltmeter

Battery   Loading
                 rheostat

FIG. 8-13. Determination of battery resistance.

that the terminal voltage of the battery does not decrease substantially with load resistance until R_L becomes comparable to R. This is reasonable since V differs from E only because of the drop across R. The typical battery has a very small internal resistance, so $R_L = R$ represents an extremely heavy current drain. It is probably not advisable to load a battery this heavily. Hence, one is confined to the upper portions of the curve. This is a relatively insensitive region in which to take measurements, so several voltage readings for different values of R_L are desirable to enable an average determination.

A good experimental procedure and analysis technique is uncovered by rewriting Eq. (8-41) in linear form in terms of $1/V$ and $1/R_L$.

$$\frac{1}{V} = \frac{R + R_L}{ER_L} = \left(\frac{R}{E}\right)\frac{1}{R_L} + \frac{1}{E} \qquad (8\text{-}42)$$

If $1/V$ is plotted against $1/R_L$, this equation indicates that the result will be a straight line of slope R/E and intercept $1/E$, as shown in Fig. 8-15. Several points, such as A, B, C, D, may be determined experimentally. The best straight line drawn through them will lead to the value of R. For example, E may first be measured with R_L removed. This gives the point $1/E$ at $1/R_L = 0$, provided $R_v \gg R$. Then, several values of R_L may be connected momentarily, just long enough to read

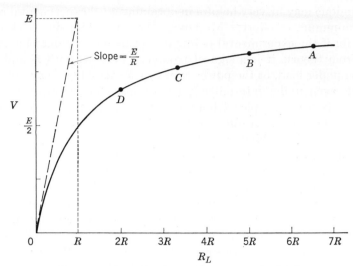

FIG. 8-14. Battery terminal voltage under load.

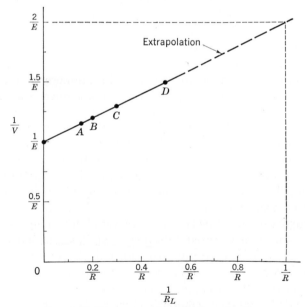

FIG. 8-15. Linear graph for battery loading.

the meter in each case.   The best straight line joining these points may be
extended to $2/E$, and the corresponding ordinate yields $1/R$ by extrapolation.   This gives a weighted determination of R in which all experimental points are blended by rapid graphical analysis.

Though quite an uncomplicated example, it illustrates how thought and technique may be very helpful in obtaining good experimental results, with a minimum of effort. Moreover, there is a built-in check on the results, for if the experimental points do not lie on a straight line as predicted from theory, it is a sign of trouble. Perhaps both E and R are changing under load, or the power rating of R_L may be too low to handle the load, even under intermittent conditions. The student would do well to study this example with a view in mind of applying similar techniques to other cases. Additional examples are presented in Chap. 14.

8-12. Comparison Method. A rather obvious method of measurement is the direct comparison of two like quantities. The two quantities compared may be any like electrical quantities, elements, or devices. Since the very process of measurement is basically one of comparison, one might argue that all measurements are essentially comparison methods. While it is true that all measurements are comparative in nature, the term "comparison method" is appropriate only when two like quantities being compared are both immediately available. Thus, if a current is measured with an ammeter, the measured current is being compared, in principle, with the absolute standard of current at the National Bureau of Standards. However, the absolute standard is not actually employed in the measurement so this is not considered to be a comparison method. The essential point is that the two quantities being compared must coexist in the experiment.

Calibration of a voltmeter by means of an ammeter was described in Sec. 5-8 and provides one example of the comparison method. The like quantities compared were the voltmeter current and the ammeter current. Other examples include comparison of readings of two ammeters connected in series, both carrying the same current. Similarly, two voltmeters may be connected directly in parallel for comparison purposes. Most comparison methods follow this unsophisticated pattern. Yet the method is highly useful because there are many instances when a direct comparison is most revealing.

Some comparison methods that appear sound in principle entail practical difficulties when attempted on a deflection basis, as illustrated in the following section. The departure from ideal of the instruments used may disturb the comparison. For that reason, most comparison methods are carried out using null techniques, as will be described in Chap. 9. However, certain deflection-type comparison methods are sound, as is the case in the meter comparisons mentioned above.

8-13. Comparison of Two Resistors. A comparison method of determining resistance is illustrated in Fig. 8-16. A voltmeter of resistance R_v is used to compare the voltage across R_1 with that across R_2. Since R_1 and R_2 carry the same current, voltage drops across the resistors are proportional to their resistances. However, unless the voltmeter resistance is large enough, it will upset this proportionality. In switch position 1, the voltmeter reading is given by the voltage-divider rule.

$$V_1 = \frac{ER_1R_v/(R_1 + R_v)}{R + R_2 + R_1R_v/(R_1 + R_v)} \tag{8-43}$$

Similarly, in switch position 2,

$$V_2 = \frac{ER_2R_v/(R_2 + R_v)}{R + R_1 + R_2R_v/(R_2 + R_v)} \tag{8-44}$$

The ratio of these two readings becomes, after a little manipulation,

$$\frac{V_1}{V_2} = \frac{R_1}{R_2}\left[\frac{R_v + R_2(R_1 + R)/(R_2 + R_1 + R)}{R_v + R_1(R_2 + R)/(R_2 + R_1 + R)}\right] \tag{8-45}$$

Clearly, this ratio is not generally equal to the ratio of the resistances, even though both resistors carry the same current with the voltmeter removed entirely from the circuit. However, if R_v is large compared with the parallel combination of $(R_1 + R)$ and R_2, as well as with the parallel combination of $(R_2 + R)$ and R_1, then the ratio is given approximately by

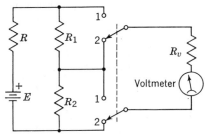

$$\frac{V_1}{V_2} \approx \frac{R_1}{R_2} \qquad R_v \text{ large} \qquad (8-46)$$

Fig. 8-16. Comparison of voltages across two resistors.

Hence, the resistors may be compared by comparing the voltage readings, provided R_v is sufficiently large. It is interesting to note that if both R_1 and R_2 are very large compared with R, the bracketed ratio in Eq. (8-45) becomes essentially unity for any R_v. Then, Eq. (8-46) is very nearly exact, even though V_1 and V_2 themselves are not equal to the unmolested voltages across R_1 and R_2. In another special case, $R_1 = R_2$, Eq. (8-45) reveals that V_1 and V_2 will be equal for any R and R_v, because of the symmetry of the circuit. Again, Eq. (8-46) yields an accurate result in this case, even though V_1 and V_2 are individually less than the unmolested voltages across R_1 and R_2.

8-14. Substitution Method. The substitution method is capable of providing a highly accurate measure of an unknown quantity in terms of an equal known standard with which it is compared directly. The method is very simple in principle, and yet powerful. It is capable of avoiding errors owing to the calibration of instruments as well as the loading effects they introduce. Moreover, errors traceable to lead resistance, to thermal emf's at electrical contacts, and to other sources are also avoided. The price paid for these many attractive features may be considerable. A known standard of the same value as the unknown quantity being measured must be available. (In certain null methods, the standard need not be precisely equal to the unknown. See Sec. 9-14.)

The essential idea of the substitution method is to bodily replace the unknown by a standard, adjusted in such a manner that the effects it produces upon insertion are indistinguishable from those produced by the unknown. Hence, the substitution method may be looked upon as

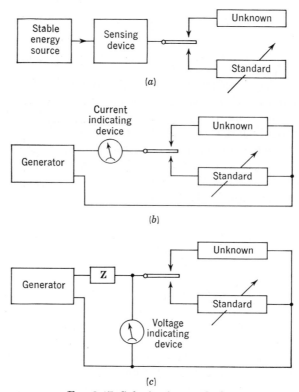

FIG. 8-17. Substitution methods.

a special case of the comparison method. In the substitution method, the unknown is literally replaced by the standard with which it is compared. The unknown and standard are not energized or measured simultaneously, as is often true in the comparison method.

A block diagram showing the essential features of the substitution method in broad terms is given in Fig. 8-17a. The source of energy may be a battery, a d-c or a-c generator, or virtually any signal source. The main requirement is that this source be steady over the period of time necessary to carry out the measurements. This is not a severe requirement because the two measurements may be carried out in rapid sequence, and the load on the source during the two measurements of unknown and standard is practically identical. Any device providing a *sensitive* measure of the transfer of energy from the source to the load (unknown or standard) may be used to indicate a difference between the unknown and the standard. This device need not be calibrated, because the *difference* it indicates is reduced to zero in the final adjustment of the standard. The procedure is to adjust the standard, by successive steps, as necessary, until the sensing device displays the same indication regardless of which load is connected. It is then deduced that the unknown and standard are equal.

Two general arrangements for the substitution method in which current- and voltage-sensing devices are used are also given in Fig. 8-17. The current-indicating device may be an ammeter, voltmeter, galvanometer, a-c meter, or any other instrument that responds to current. The unknown and standard may be any pair of like elements such as resistors, capacitors, or inductors. As a specific illustration, the generator may be a battery, connected through a galvanometer to measure an unknown resistance in terms of a standard, such as a decade-resistance box. When the decade box is adjusted so that the same galvanometer deflection is produced in either switch position, the unknown resistance is then equal to that of the decade box. The determination is independent of the calibration of the galvanometer, as well as of voltage drops in the leads and other parasitic effects, since both the unknown and the standard are measured under identical circuit conditions.

While this method approaches the ideal for accurate work, it is also sometimes handy for rough measurements. For example, an ohmmeter that does not have a trustworthy calibration may be used to determine an unknown resistance in a very satisfactory manner. The ohmmeter is convenient because it contains both the generator and the sensing device. The unknown resistance may be connected first, and then replaced by a known resistor that produces the same deflection. The unknown is thereby determined, even though the ohmmeter may be off calibration, may be incapable of being zeroed properly, may contain defective shunts, and may suffer from any number of ills. So long as it produces a deflection that is sensitive to the resistance connected to its input leads, it may be used to determine resistance by the substitution method.

The switching arrangement is not an intrinsic part of this method, but is a matter of technique. The unknown may be removed from the circuit by disconnecting it and then reconnecting a standard in its place. However, the load on the energy source is changed for an appreciable period of time during the replacement, and also a longer total interval of time between the two measurements invites drift. Substitution of unknown and standard may be accomplished very rapidly by use of a switch, with only a momentary change of load on the energy source. This is a preferred technique. It is customary to use a switch capable of extremely quick action so that, after final adjustment of the standard, the unknown and standard may be interchanged repeatedly with no discernible change resulting in the reading of the sensing device.

8-15. Differential Method. In many measurements, the *change* of a quantity from some initial value is of primary concern. Moreover, the change might constitute only a small percentage of the value of the quantity itself. The differential method is well suited for such applications. The general idea of this method is to first provide an arrangement capable of balancing out the initial value of the quantity, so the device indicating the change is initially set for a zero reading. Thereafter, any change in the quantity is reflected in the reading of the indicator. It is essential that the system used to balance out the initial value of the quantity be stable; otherwise, subsequent changes indicated by the sensing device are contaminated by drift of the reference.

Again, this method is fundamentally one of comparison. A slightly variable quantity is compared with a fixed-reference quantity. It is distinguished from the comparison method by its capability of producing a direct measure of the difference between two nearly equal quantities.

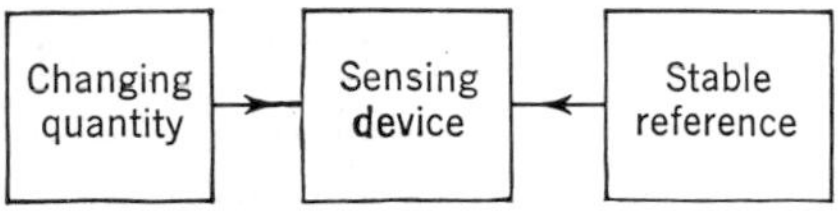

A functional diagram of the differential method is given in Fig. 8-18. The changing quantity may be a voltage, a resistance, or some other electrical entity. It may vary above and below the value provided by the stable reference. The sensing device responds accordingly, giving a measure of positive or negative differences between the changing quantity and the reference value.

FIG. 8-18. Differential method.

The differential method is most useful when the sensing device gives a direct reading of the difference, without further correction or computation. This is sometimes difficult to achieve because of the loading effect produced by the indicating device when it draws current from the system. In most cases, the impedance of the sensing device should be large compared with the input impedance to the changing quantity as well as to the stable reference. Whether or not the disparity in impedance levels permits the loading effects to be neglected depends upon the particular case.

8-16. Differential Voltmeter. The differential method is well adapted to measurement of regulation characteristics of a d-c power supply. If the change in voltage from no load to full load is only a small percentage of the no-load value, an ordinary voltmeter connected across the output terminals does not provide an adequate indication of the change. A differential voltmeter may be devised as shown in Fig. 8-19. The stable reference is provided by a battery, and the control, R_2, may be used to set the voltmeter reading to zero when the power-supply load, R_L, is removed. Under these conditions, the voltage across terminals 3-4 is equal to the open-circuit voltage, E, of the power supply. Subsequent loading of the supply with different values of R_L changes its terminal voltage. If R_v is sufficiently large, the voltmeter will indicate directly the change in voltage from the open-circuit value, provided that the reference remains stable. This circuit is essentially the same as that mentioned in connection with meter-setting errors in Sec. 5-12.

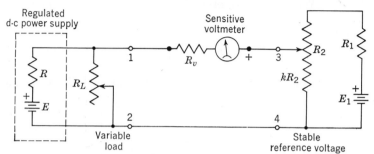

FIG. 8-19. Differential voltmeter.

If $R_v \to \infty$, the reference system and the power supply are isolated from each other, and the voltmeter provides the desired voltage difference directly with no loading error. However, any practical voltmeter has a finite resistance, so it is desirable to obtain a quantitative criterion to assess the loading effects of R_v. Thévenin's theorem is useful to expedite the analysis. The equivalent circuit of the power supply is shown in Fig. 8-20, including R_L as part of the voltage source whose change is being measured. The open-circuit voltage looking into terminals 1-2 is

$$E_0 = \frac{R_L E}{R + R_L} \qquad (8\text{-}47)$$

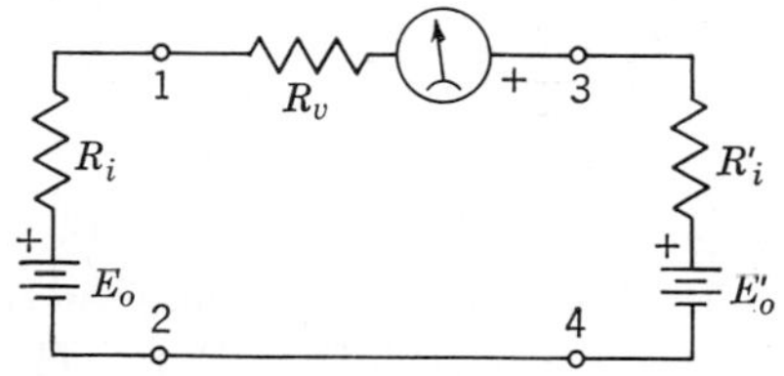

FIG. 8-20. Thévenin equivalent circuit of Fig. 8-19.

where E is the no-load power-supply voltage ($R_L \to \infty$), and R is the input resistance of the unloaded supply. The input resistance of the loaded supply is clearly

$$R_i = \frac{R R_L}{R + R_L} \qquad (8\text{-}48)$$

The equivalent circuit of the reference supply is obtained similarly and is shown in Fig. 8-20. The open-circuit voltage at terminals 3-4 is

$$E_0' = \frac{k R_2 E_1}{R_2 + R_1} \qquad (8\text{-}49)$$

and the input resistance looking into terminals 3-4 is

$$R'_i = \frac{kR_2[R_2(1 - k) + R_1]}{R_2 + R_1} \qquad (8\text{-}50)$$

In these equations, E_1 is the reference battery emf, R_1 is its internal resistance, and k is the fraction of the control resistance, R_2, directly between terminals 3 and 4.

The usefulness of Thévenin's theorem is apparent because an expression for the voltmeter reading is now immediately obtained by the voltage-divider rule. With the voltmeter polarity as indicated in Figs. 8-19 and 8-20, the voltmeter reading is given by

$$V = \frac{(E'_0 - E_0)R_v}{R_i + R_v + R'_i} \qquad (8\text{-}51)$$

Now suppose k is adjusted for zero voltmeter reading when R_L is removed. Equation (8-51) becomes, with $R_L \to \infty$, $E_0 = E$, and $R_i = R$,

$$0 = \frac{(E'_0 - E)R_v}{R + R_v + R'_i} \qquad (8\text{-}52)$$

Therefore, $E'_0 = E$, and the corresponding value of k may be obtained from Eq. (8-49). Since R'_i is also fixed by this adjustment, it too may be obtained from Eq. (8-50). Call this fixed value R_0.

$$R_0 = \frac{E}{E_1}\left(1 - \frac{E}{E_1}\right)(R_2 + R_1) \qquad (8\text{-}53)$$

Then V is given for any value of R_L in terms of this fixed initial adjustment by

$$V = \frac{[E - R_L E/(R + R_L)]R_v}{R_i + R_v + R_0} = \frac{ER}{R + R_L}\left[\frac{1}{1 + (R_i + R_0)/R_v}\right] \qquad (8\text{-}54)$$

where R_i is given by Eq. (8-48).

In this final result, it may be seen that if $R_v \to \infty$, the voltmeter reading is $V = ER/(R + R_L)$. This is the actual difference between the no-load power-supply voltage and its loaded value. Hence, the voltmeter reading is always proportional to this actual difference, even though R_v is not infinite. Equation (8-54) indicates that the following inequality must be well satisfied if R_v is to have a negligible effect on the reading, V.

$$R_v \gg \frac{RR_L}{R + R_L} + \frac{E}{E_1}\left(1 - \frac{E}{E_1}\right)(R_2 + R_1) \qquad (8\text{-}55)$$

This states that the voltmeter resistance must be large compared with the *sum* of the input resistances to the loaded supply and to the reference system.   Then the voltmeter reading will yield the actual voltage change.

If R_v is large but not negligible, a first-order correction term may be obtained by expanding the error term in Eq. (8-54) by the binomial expansion.

$$\left(1 + \frac{R_i + R_0}{R_v}\right)^{-1} = 1 - \frac{R_i + R_0}{R_v} + \cdots$$

Then, the fractional error, δ, in the voltmeter reading is

$$\delta = \frac{ER/(R + R_L) - V}{ER/(R + R_L)} \approx \frac{R_i + R_0}{R_v} \tag{8-56}$$

Since this error is positive, the reading V is less than would be obtained with an ideal voltmeter.

8-17. Differential Ammeter.   A similar arrangement may be used to devise a differential ammeter that yields direct indications of small variations in the current, I, shown in Fig. 8-21.   For simplicity, assume the

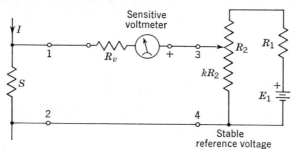

FIG. 8-21. Differential ammeter.

fixed resistance, S, is much smaller than the source impedance of the current I.   Then the preceding analysis may be applied directly with E_0 replaced by IS, and R_i replaced by S.   The voltmeter reading is obtained from Eq. (8-51).

$$V = \frac{(E_0' - IS)R_v}{S + R_v + R_i'} \tag{8-57}$$

Now if k is adjusted to yield $V = 0$ for a current I, then $E_0' = IS$ and $R_i' = R_0$ are fixed.   The value of R_0 is obtained from Eq. (8-53) with $E = IS$.

$$R_0 = \frac{IS}{E_1}\left(1 - \frac{IS}{E_1}\right)(R_2 + R_1) \tag{8-58}$$

Thereafter, a change in I to $I + \Delta I$, where ΔI is not necessarily small, will produce a change in the voltmeter reading

$$\Delta V = \frac{-S\,\Delta I}{1 + (S + R_0)/R_v} \tag{8-59}$$

The change in voltage is seen to be proportional to the change in current. Moreover, if $R_v \gg (S + R_0)$, the actual change in current from its value I (where $V = 0$) may be computed by dividing the voltmeter reading by S.

One application of this differential ammeter is in monitoring a current that must be maintained within very narrow limits of some fixed value, I. The reference supply must, of course, display a much smaller per cent variation than that permissible for the current being monitored.

8-18. Differential Galvanometer. A special type of galvanometer may be designed for use in differential measurements. Its operating principles are the same as an ordinary d'Arsonval type, but it is equipped with two separate coils insulated from each other and wound in an intertwined manner on the same coil form. The two coils are made as nearly identical as possible. An auxiliary "zero adjust" coil is usually provided to eliminate the small residual unbalance between the two coils inevitably encountered in practice.

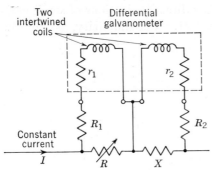

FIG. 8-22. Application of differential galvanometer.

The differential galvanometer may be used to measure small changes in resistance that result from heating effects of current. In Fig. 8-22, one coil of resistance r_1 is connected through a resistor R_1 to an adjustable temperature-compensated resistor, R. This resistor is capable of carrying large currents without appreciable effects on its resistance. Resistor X, under test, is connected through R_2 to the other coil of resistance r_2. The portion of the constant incoming current I that passes through the coil across R is given by the current-splitting rule.

$$I_1 = \frac{RI}{R + R_1 + r_1} \tag{8-60}$$

The current in the other coil is, similarly,

$$I_2 = \frac{XI}{X + R_2 + r_2} \tag{8-61}$$

When $I_1 = I_2$, the correctly adjusted galvanometer will indicate zero deflection, in which case Eq. (8-60) and Eq. (8-61) may be equated and solved for X.

$$X = R \frac{R_2 + r_2}{R_1 + r_1} \tag{8-62}$$

For a given initial value of X, R may be adjusted to satisfy this equation so that zero reading is produced. Thereafter, as X changes owing to the heating effect of the current through it, the current I_2 will change, but I_1 will remain constant.

The change in I_2 resulting from a small change dX in X is given by the differential of Eq. (8-61).

$$dI_2 = \frac{(R_2 + r_2)I\ dX}{(X + R_2 + r_2)^2} \qquad (8\text{-}63)$$

Since the galvanometer responds to dI_2, its deflection may be used as a measure of dX. If $(R_2 + r_2) \gg X$, Eq. (8-63) reduces to

$$dI_2 = \frac{I\ dX}{R_2 + r_2} \qquad (R_2 + r_2) \gg X \qquad (8\text{-}64)$$

With I known and constant, the readings may be related to dX very simply in this case. This inequality is usually easily satisfied in practice. It is desirable to do so because I_2 is then negligible compared with I, and the current through X remains substantially constant despite changes in X.

Other applications of the differential galvanometer may be readily envisioned. For instance, the circuit of Fig. 8-22 may be used to determine X in terms of the known resistance R. Indeed, if in Eq. (8-62), $R_1 + r_1 = R_2 + r_2$, then R and X are equal when the galvanometer indicates zero deflection. This is really a null method for determining resistance. Such methods are discussed in more detail in the following chapter.

PROBLEMS

8-1 (§4). In the series ohmmeter of Fig. 8-2, $E = 1.5$ volts, $R = 1.0$ ohm, $R_m = 10$ ohms, and the meter has a 10-ma movement. (a) What value of R_1 is required to produce full-scale deflection when X is zero? (b) What value of X will produce half-scale deflection? (c) Show that the meter deflection (as a fraction of full-scale deflection) vs. the logarithm of X/R_s is a symmetrical curve.

(a.) 139 Ω.

(b.) 150 Ω

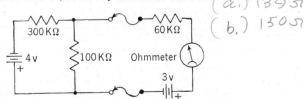

FIG. 8-23. Ohmmeter connected to "live" circuit.

8-2 (§4). A series ohmmeter consists of a 3-volt battery in series with a 60,000-ohm resistor and the meter movement. It is accidentally connected into a "live" circuit as shown in Fig. 8-23. What *resistance* does the ohmmeter indicate? Assume meter and battery resistances are negligible compared with 60,000 ohms.

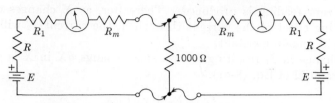

FIG. 8-24. Comparison of identical ohmmeters.

8-3 (§4). An engineer wanted to compare two identical series ohmmeters. He connected them simultaneously to a 1,000-ohm resistor as shown in Fig. 8-24. What are the readings of the ohmmeters?

8-4 (§4). A series ohmmeter with mid-scale design of 5,000 ohms has a worn battery, but you are too lazy to replace it. Instead, you decide to use it "as is," even though it reads 500 ohms rather than zero with the ohmmeter leads shorted. When the resistor whose resistance you seek is connected to the ohmmeter, the scale reading is 30,000 ohms. What is the actual value of the resistance?

8-5 (§4). The uncertainty in readability of the angular deflection of the pointer in a series ohmmeter employing a linear d'Arsonval movement is $\frac{1}{100}$ of the total angle between zero and full-scale deflection. Over what range of values of X, placed across the ohmmeter terminals, will this readability uncertainty amount to less than a 10 per cent error in the determination of X? Express answer as a multiple of R_s, the mid-scale design value of the ohmmeter.

8-6 (§5). An ohmmeter of unconventional type is shown in Fig. 8-25. The fractional full-scale deflection of the meter is defined as $F = I_x/I_0$, where I_x is the meter

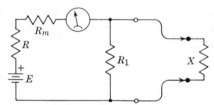

FIG. 8-25. Unconventional ohmmeter circuit.

current for any X, and I_0 is the full-scale meter current occurring when $X = 0$. (a) Sketch the F vs. X curve and specify the values of F for $X = 0$ and $X \rightarrow \infty$, in terms of R_1, R_m, and R. (b) For what value of X (in terms of R_1, R_m, and R) is $F = \frac{1}{2}$? (c) For the F vs. X curve, prove that the ratio of the slope at $X = 0$ to the slope at any X is given by $(1 + GX)^2$, where G is the input conductance of the ohmmeter.

8-7 (§5). Design a 20-ohm mid-scale shunt-ohmmeter circuit using a 1.5-volt battery and a 50-mv 500-μa meter movement. Include a means for adjusting the circuit to compensate for aging of the battery.

8-8 (§6). A series ohmmeter consists of a 4.5-volt battery, a 4,000-ohm fixed resistance, a 1,000-ohm variable resistance, and a 1-ma instrument of 50-ohm resistance. (a) What is the mid-scale design value of this ohmmeter? (b) If the same 1,000-ohm variable resistance is connected in shunt (instead of in series) with the movement, thus producing a shunt-adjusted series ohmmeter, what unknown resistance will now produce half-scale deflection?

8-9 (§6). A dual-range ohmmeter has been designed in accordance with Fig. 8-26. There is a switch, not shown, on the ohmmeter which reads "high-low." When the switch is on "high" position, the unknown resistance connects to A-B with C-D left open. When the switch is on "low" position, the unknown connects to C-D, and A-B are shorted together. The meter has a 1-ma 50-mv movement. If the 50- and 1,000-ohm resistors are unchanged by the switching operation, what are the exact mid-scale readings in the two cases?

8-10 (§6). A series ohmmeter of the type shown in Fig. 8-9 employs a 100-μa meter movement that has a 5-mv full-scale drop across the movement. Assume the battery resistance is negligible compared with $R_1 = 7,500$ ohms. (a) Specify the maximum and minimum values of the shunt, S, required to enable the ohmmeter to be "zeroed" for a battery that has a "new" voltage $E = 1.5$ volts and an "aged" voltage of 1.1 volts. (b) Assuming perfect ohmmeter calibration for $E = 1.5$ volts, calculate the *reading* on the ohmmeter scale when an 8,000-ohm resistor is measured under minimum battery-voltage conditions ($E = 1.1$ volts).

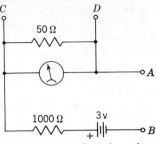

FIG. 8-26. Portion of an ohm-meter circuit.

$50.3 \quad 108.7 \quad 7990$

8-11 (§6). For the series ohmmeter shown in Fig. 8-9, determine an expression for the change, dS, in the shunt resistance, S, required to reestablish rated full-scale meter current if the battery emf changes by a small amount, dE, and the battery resistance changes by a small amount, dR.

8-12 (§6). Derive Eq. (8-24).

8-13 (§6). A two-range ohmmeter is to be designed using a 20-μa d'Arsonval movement of resistance 12 ohms; a dry battery of initial emf $E = 6$ volts and initial resistance $R = 1$ ohm; and the circuit shown in Fig. 8-27. With the double-pole switch in position 1, the mid-scale reading is to be 1,000 ohms. With the switch in position 2, the mid-scale reading is to be 100,000 ohms. The battery is to be used until E has dropped to approximately 5 volts, at which point R will have risen to about 20 ohms.

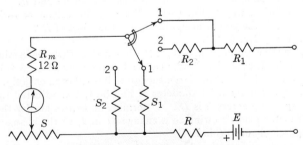

FIG. 8-27. Two-range ohmmeter design.

The user of the ohmmeter should be forced to change the battery under these conditions, by being unable to obtain "zero" during the initial adjustment of the ohmmeter. Specify the values of resistances R_1, R_2, S_1, S_2, and S required to realize this design.

8-14 (§7). Refer to the voltmeter-ammeter analysis presented in Sec. 5-6. Derive a quantitative algebraic rule in terms of meter readings for determining which of the two switch positions yields the better approximation, if the unknown resistance, X, is calculated from the ratio of the voltmeter to ammeter readings. The rule should be expressed in terms of the four observed meter readings only: V_1, I_1, V_2, I_2. Assume zero battery resistance, $R = 0$.

8-15 (§7). In the loss of charge method of determining leakage resistance, the ratio of the first to the second ballistic galvanometer deflection is measured to be 6.0 ± 1 per cent, when a discharge time interval $t = 100$ sec ± 1 per cent is employed. The capacitance, C, is 1.0 μf ± 1 per cent. All stated errors are standard deviations. Compute the leakage resistance, R, and its standard deviation.

8-16 (§8). Verify Eq. (8-28).

8-17 (§8). An auxiliary resistor, R, is used in *shunt* with an ammeter of resistance R_a to enable correction for the reduction in current owing to insertion of the ammeter. Ammeter readings I_1 and I_2 are observed with the shunt resistor, R, disconnected and connected, respectively. Derive a formula from which the short-circuit current that existed before the ammeter was inserted may be computed from the known quantities I_1, I_2, R, and R_a.

8-18 (§9). Verify Eq. (8-33).

8-19 (§9). An auxiliary resistor, R, is used in *shunt* with a voltmeter of resistance R_v to enable correction for the reduction in voltage owing to connection of the voltmeter. Voltmeter readings V_1 and V_2 are observed with the shunt resistor, R, disconnected and connected, respectively. Derive a formula from which the open-circuit voltage that existed before the voltmeter was connected may be computed from the known quantities V_1, V_2, R, and R_v.

8-20 (§10). An auxiliary resistor, R_1, is used in *shunt* with an ammeter for the purpose of determining its resistance, R_a. Ammeter readings I_1 and I_2 are observed with the shunt disconnected and connected, respectively. (a) Derive a formula that expresses R_a in terms of I_1, I_2, R_1, and the source resistance, R. (b) Under what conditions is a half-deflection method most conveniently carried out?

8-21 (§11). The internal resistance, R, of a battery is determined indirectly using the circuit of Fig. 8-13. Five voltmeter readings, in volts, with corresponding values of R_L in ohms in parentheses, are obtained as follows: 5.00(∞), 4.45(1.00), 4.00(0.50), 3.77(0.40), 3.50(0.30). Make a weighted determination of R using the graphical technique of Fig. 8-15 and compare this result with the mean of the four individually computed results. Assume that R_v is much greater than R_L and R.

8-22 (§11). In what way is Eq. (8-42) altered if the voltmeter resistance is not neglected? What is the graphical significance of the effect of R_v?

8-23 (§13). Verify Eq. (8-45).

8-24 (§13). In the circuit of Fig. 8-16, $R \gg R_1$ and $R \gg R_2$. Determine an approximate expression for the fractional error entailed in the use of Eq. (8-46) if R_v is large compared with R_1 and R_2, but not large enough to be neglected entirely.

8-25 (§17). In the differential ammeter of Fig. 8-21, k is adjusted to yield $V = 0$ when the voltage drop across S is IS. Determine an expression for the ratio of the change in voltmeter reading owing to a change dI in I, to the change in voltmeter reading owing to a change dS in S.

8-26 (§18). In the differential galvanometer circuit of Fig. 8-22, R is adjusted for zero galvanometer deflection for a constant current I. What will be the change in galvanometer reading if I changes subsequently to $I + \Delta I$, all other parameters remaining constant? ΔI is not necessarily small compared with I.

8-27 (§18). In the differential galvanometer circuit of Fig. 8-22, $I = 20$ ma and is constant, $R_2 + r_2 = 10X$, and R is adjusted for zero galvanometer deflection. Then X is increased by 10 per cent to $1.1X$. The galvanometer sensitivity is 0.1 mm per μa. Compute the exact galvanometer deflection and compare with approximate results obtained from Eqs. (8-63) and (8-64).

CHAPTER 9

NULL METHODS OF MEASUREMENT

While deflection methods of measurement may have advantages of speed and convenience, they are incapable of providing the accuracy required in many instances. It is often necessary to resort to null methods for an improvement in accuracy. Some null methods even have operational advantages over deflection methods. Various d-c and low-frequency applications of null methods are presented in this chapter. These should serve to indicate the basic principles and attributes of null measurements.

9-1. The Null Method. The null method is one in which a zero or null indication of an instrument leads to a determination of the quantity from other known conditions. It demands that the sensitivity of the null indicator be adequate, but does not rely upon its calibration. Therefore, it is free of errors traceable to instrument calibration.

Results obtained with the null method depend upon other conditions in the system. For example, circuit elements, or their ratios, are presumed to be known from some other evidence. Currents, voltages, or frequency are presumed to be stable in many instances. Such conditions must inevitably enter, and the result is no more trustworthy than are these "known" conditions. A pitfall exists in employing null methods because departures from conditions that are presumed to be known are not always self-evident. The null method might be carried out with no apparent sign of difficulty, leaving the experimenter unaware of an erroneous result. The difference between sound and unsound results in all measurements is often attributable to the technique and astuteness of the experimenter. But particularly so in the null method.

The conditions under which a null is obtained are usually approached by successive experimental adjustments. In the final adjustment stages, the sensitivity of the null detector must be adequate to detect the smallest significant change in any quantity upon which the null depends. This sometimes demands extremely high sensitivity. Yet, if this same sensitivity were used in the initial stages, the null indicator might be permanently damaged by excessive overload. Consequently, the usual procedure is to adjust the sensitivity of the detector in accordance with the degree to which the null is approached. This is easily accomplished with shunts. All the manipulative operations may be mastered with a little practice and need not be prohibitively cumbersome or lengthy, if done with thought and skill.

It should be understood clearly that a null or zero *indication* does not mean that a true mathematically zero result has been obtained. There is always a departure from zero, even though it may not be observable with the null detector employed. An increase in sensitivity will reveal this departure experimentally. The departure from zero might be traceable to drift of current, or instability of circuit elements. Even if such effects are overcome, there still remain such residual effects as thermal noise in resistors, minute emf's produced at junctions of dissimilar metals, or random effects inherent in the apparatus. The residuals place an upper useful limit on sensitivity. In a given situation, the sensitivity employed should be no greater than is necessary to detect the smallest changes of interest. The greater the sensitivity, the more awkward and time-consuming becomes the attainment of a null. It is usually possible by appropriate experimental design to control conditions so that adequate sensitivity is available without serious disturbance from residual effects.

9-2. General Null Methods. Most null methods are classified in the comparison or substitution categories (see Fig. 8-1). However, there are some special types, and even some combined null and deflection methods. There are also a number that do not fall into any particular category, and these may be given a general designation.

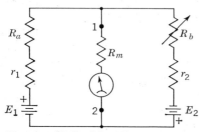

FIG. 9-1. Null with aiding batteries.

The simple d-c circuit of Fig. 9-1 is capable of producing a null across terminals 1-2 and may be used for measurement of the battery emf's and internal resistances under variable load. The current through the indicating device, of resistance R_m, may be obtained by mesh or node analysis, or by application of Thévenin's theorem. Using Thévenin's theorem, the meter may be removed, and the clockwise circulating current is

$$I = \frac{E_1 + E_2}{R_1 + R_2}$$

where $R_1 = r_1 + R_a$ and $R_2 = r_2 + R_b$. Therefore, the open-circuit voltage rise from terminal 2 to terminal 1 is

$$E_0 = E_1 - IR_1 = \frac{E_1R_2 - E_2R_1}{R_1 + R_2} \tag{9-1}$$

The input resistance, R_i, to terminals 1-2 is obtained by replacing the batteries by their internal resistances, r_1 and r_2. Then R_1 is in parallel with R_2 and

$$R_i = \frac{R_1 R_2}{R_1 + R_2} \tag{9-2}$$

With the Thévenin equivalent circuit established, the current through the meter is given immediately by

$$I_m = \frac{E_0}{R_i + R_m} \tag{9-3}$$

Zero meter current results when $E_0 = 0$. This occurs when R_b is adjusted to satisfy the relation

$$\frac{E_1}{E_2} = \frac{r_1 + R_a}{r_2 + R_b} = \frac{R_1}{R_2} \tag{9-4}$$

as may be seen from Eq. (9-1). Equation (9-4) is called the null condition. The external resistances, R_a and R_b, may easily be made much larger than r_1 and r_2, respectively. Then the null condition becomes approximately

$$\frac{E_1}{E_2} = \frac{R_a}{R_b} \qquad R_a \gg r_1,\ R_b \gg r_2 \tag{9-5}$$

Several applications of this circuit are evident. For example, if the ratio of R_a to R_b required to produce a null is known in Eq. (9-5), the ratio of the two emf's is established. This ratio is determined under conditions of equal current, I, through each battery. Once the emf ratio is determined, additional nulls may be obtained with small known values of R_a and R_b, from which the battery resistances may be deduced, using Eq. (9-4). Moreover, different values of R_a and R_b, all much greater than r_1 and r_2, may be used to investigate the emf ratio for various battery currents.

It is unnecessary to perform a complete circuit analysis if only the null condition is sought. The null requirement may be inserted at the outset, and the null condition obtained directly. For instance, zero current through R_m in the circuit of Fig. 9-1 implies zero voltage between terminals 1-2. Therefore, with a clockwise circulating current, I, as before,

$$E_1 - I R_1 = 0 \qquad \text{and} \qquad E_2 - I R_2 = 0$$

Transpose the emf terms, and I cancels in the ratio of the two equations, giving Eq. (9-4) immediately. This technique will be used when only the null condition is sought, since it leads simply and directly to the result.

To illustrate this technique further, the null condition for the circuit of Fig. 9-2 may be obtained directly by the following reasoning. A null exists when the meter current, I_m, is zero. Then the voltage across the lower portion, kR, of control R, is simply given by $E_1kR/(R + r_1)$, and this must be equal to E_2. Hence, the null condition is

$$E_2 = \frac{E_1kR}{R + r_1} \tag{9-6}$$

This would have been more difficult to deduce had the general expression for I_m been obtained first, and then set equal to zero. If $R \gg r_1$, the

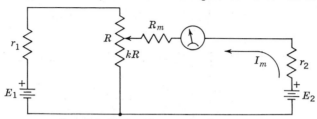

FIG. 9-2. Null with opposing batteries.

null condition becomes simply $E_2 = kE_1$. Therefore, with E_1 and k known, the emf E_2 is determined independently of its internal resistance, r_2, since no current is drawn from E_2 when $I_m = 0$.

This circuit is virtually the same as that used in the differential methods of the preceding chapter, but here it is used exclusively under null conditions. The strong similarity between null and differential methods will be discussed more fully in Sec. 9-15. Moreover, the circuit of Fig. 9-2 is very closely related to the potentiometer, to be discussed subsequently.

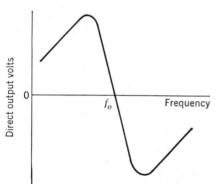

FIG. 9-3. Discriminator characteristic.

Side-stepping the off-null solutions should not create the impression that such solutions are unimportant. On the contrary, they contain valuable information regarding sensitivity, accuracy, and stability of the null arrangement. Frequently, the off-null circuit behavior is rather complex, and special methods of analysis are called into play. The compensation theorem, in particular, is a very suitable tool, as will be shown.

Many other general null methods are used in practice, in both precision and rough measurements. To give a glimpse of the possibilities, one more illustration will be presented in qualitative form. A device called a discriminator, employed in detection of frequency-modulated signals, may be used as the heart of a null method for determining frequency. The basic elements of a discriminator are resonant circuits and rectifiers, designed to produce a d-c output voltage characteristic of the kind shown in Fig. 9-3, as a function of the input frequency applied to the discriminator. The frequency f_0, of zero d-c output voltage, called the crossover frequency, is determined by tuning adjustments inside the discriminator. This device may be used to adjust an oscillator to the frequency f_0 by obtaining a zero reading of a voltmeter connected across the discriminator output. While not necessarily a precision method, it might be highly useful in a rapid production-line adjustment procedure where large numbers of oscillators must be set to the same frequency with a minimum of complication. When the oscillator output is fed into the discriminator, a simple screwdriver adjustment of the oscillator may be made until the voltmeter indication is zero.

9-3. Slide-back Voltmeter. In most null methods, the null indicator produces an output that always deviates from zero unless the null condition is satisfied. In such cases, a unidirectional adjustment of one of the parameters causes the indicator to pass *through* zero, thus defining the null sharply and unambiguously. However, some null methods display a "one-sided" zero, as exemplified by the highly useful slide-back voltmeter. In this instance, a unidirectional adjustment decreases the indication as the null is approached from one side, but the zero indication reached at the null condition persists after the actual null has been passed. This is less desirable than the sharply defined null in more conventional cases. But the capability of the slide-back voltmeter to measure the peak value of a signal, regardless of its waveform, offsets this disadvantage.

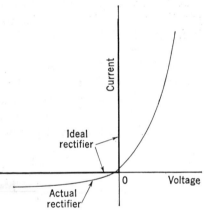

Fig. 9-4. Rectifier characteristics.

The slide-back voltmeter employs a device called a rectifier. Rectifiers are useful in several types of instruments and will be referred to again in later chapters. An *ideal rectifier* is a nonlinear, two-terminal element displaying zero resistance for one polarity of applied voltage, called the forward voltage, and infinite resistance for the opposite polarity, called the reverse voltage. The voltage-current characteristic of an ideal rectifier is given in Fig. 9-4. The slope of the voltage vs. current curve is equal to the reciprocal of the rectifier resistance. Practical rectifiers depart from the ideal, as suggested by the representative characteristic displayed in Fig. 9-4. Typical ratios of reverse resistance to forward resistance are 50:1 to 100:1, rather than infinity in the ideal case. Neither the forward nor the reverse resistances are constant, but vary with applied voltage. Indeed, if too large a forward voltage or too large a reverse voltage is applied, the rectifier undergoes breakdown and permanent damage. In some rectifiers, a small current exists even when the applied voltage is zero, if the rectifier is in a closed circuit. This is called the "dark current."

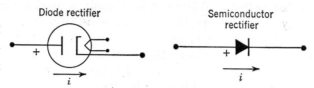

FIG. 9-5. Rectifier symbols.

A diode vacuum tube, shown schematically in Fig. 9-5, is one type of practical rectifier in which electrons pass from cathode to plate, opposite to i, under the influence of an electric force field produced within the tube by the forward voltage. Filament power is required to produce thermionic emission at the cathode, and this is the diode's prime disadvantage. Other forms of rectifiers may be obtained by use of a metal in contact with a semiconductor. This type has no filament. The symbol designating this type of rectifier is also given in Fig. 9-5. The tip of a fine metallic wire resting on a germanium or silicon crystal forms the "cat

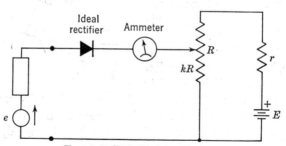

FIG. 9-6. Slide-back voltmeter.

whisker" type of crystal rectifier. Another form, a copper disk with a layer of copper oxide, is often used in instruments because multiple rectifier units may be stacked compactly.

A slide-back voltmeter circuit employing a single ideal rectifier is shown in Fig. 9-6. A signal voltage, e, of any waveshape, is applied in series with the rectifier for the purpose of measuring its peak value. The box in series with e contains any arbitrary internal circuit elements that may be associated with e. A controllable reverse voltage in series with the rectifier is introduced by the battery across the portion kR of the control, R. The rectifier will conduct whenever e is a voltage rise in the direction of the arrow alongside e, provided that the magnitude of e exceeds the voltage across kR. The resulting unidirectional rectifier current may be detected by the sensitive d-c ammeter. The reverse voltage may be increased by increasing k until the ammeter deflection is reduced to zero. At this setting, the voltage across kR is equal to the peak voltage rise of e. The ammeter reading remains at zero as k is increased further, since e cannot overcome the reverse voltage across kR. Because of the one-sided nature of this null, a desirable technique is deliberately to increase k beyond the first point at which a zero reading is observed and then to slide k back until the ammeter barely deflects. Hence, the name "slide back" is well deserved.

This circuit permits determination of the peak value of e regardless of its waveform, and independent of its internal circuit elements. In practice, a voltmeter may be connected across kR to provide a direct indication of the peak value of e. If e is an alternating signal, the last trace of the signal across kR is lost when k is adjusted for zero rectifier current. Therefore, a calibrated oscilloscope may be used across kR, and the ammeter and voltmeter become unnecessary. This is an especially useful technique when e is a short pulse, for then the average ammeter current is small even before k approaches the cutoff point. A high-gain oscilloscope permits observation of the last vestiges of the pulse across kR as k is increased. More sensitive circuits combining rectification and amplification are used in practice, but the principles of operation are the same as those described.

9-4. Comparison Methods. When a comparison method is used on a null basis, it may overcome the loading effects often encountered when the same method is attempted on a deflection basis. Moreover, reliance is not placed on instrument calibration. Thus, the comparison null method is generally capable of high accuracy and requires few, if any, corrections. Because all methods are fundamentally comparative, the distinction applied to the comparison method must be borne in mind carefully. The comparison method is one in which two like quantities that coexist in the experiment are compared directly. While the slide-back voltmeter of the preceding section compares two voltages, it is not classified here as a comparison method. A fine distinction is made between the steady voltage across kR and the peak value of the time-varying voltage, e. Again, the classification is far less important than the comprehension of any given method.

The comparison method is simple yet powerful. It is perhaps the most widely used precision method of measurement. When combined with null techniques, some circuits become elaborate, but others are quite elementary, as illustrated in Fig. 9-7. Here, a comparison method employing a null is utilized to measure an unknown mutual inductance, M, in terms of a standard mutual inductance, M_1, capable of being adjusted through the value M. A sinusoidal source delivers the same current to the series-connected primaries of the unknown and standard coils. The induced voltages in the secondaries, connected in series opposition, will be equal and opposite when M_1 is adjusted for a null indication of the detector, D. Hence, the null condition is $M = M_1$, because the primary currents are equal and, of course, must have the same frequency. Neither the impedance of the detector nor that of the source molests this conclusion.

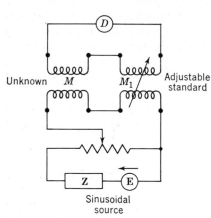

FIG. 9-7. Mutual inductance measurement.

9-5. Potentiometer Principles. The potentiometer is one of the important direct-voltage-measuring devices. It compares, on a null basis, an unknown emf with that of a standard cell. The measurement is independent of the internal resistance of either emf and is carried out through the intermediary of an accurately known resistance ratio. There are a multitude of different types of general-purpose and special-purpose potentiometers. Some of these include the Leeds and Northrup Type K, the Rubicon Type B, the Brown, the Brooks, the Diesselhorst, the Wenner, and the White potentiometers. Alternating-current potentiometers have also been devised by Drysdale, Gall, Larsen, Pedersen, and others, but they will not be discussed.

Most general-purpose d-c potentiometers operate on the same basic principles. These may be described in terms of the slide-wire potentiometer circuit given in Fig. 9-8. The battery of emf E, called the working battery, supplies a working current I, controllable by R, to a length of resistance wire, called the slide-wire. With the galvanometer key thrown to standard-cell position, s, a null galvanometer indication may be obtained by adjusting the sliding contact to location 1, provided the polarities of E and E_s are compatible. Then the voltage drop across the slide-wire between points 0 and 1, of resistance R_{01}, is equal to the standard-cell emf, E_s.

$$E_s = IR_{01} \qquad (9\text{-}7)$$

No current is drawn from the standard cell under this null condition. When the galvanometer key is thrown to the unknown emf position, x, a different setting of the sliding contact, at location 2, for example, will generally be required to produce a null galvanometer indication.   Then, the voltage drop across the slide-wire between points 0 and 2, of resistance R_{02}, is equal to the unknown emf, E_x.

$$E_x = IR_{02} \qquad (9\text{-}8)$$

Again, no current is drawn from E_x when the galvanometer current is zero.   The current, I, will cancel in the ratio of Eq. (9-7) to Eq. (9-8), provided that it has not changed in the time intervening between the attainment of these two nulls.   Then,

$$\frac{E_s}{E_x} = \frac{R_{01}}{R_{02}}$$

and the unknown and standard emf may be compared in terms of the slide-wire resistance ratio.

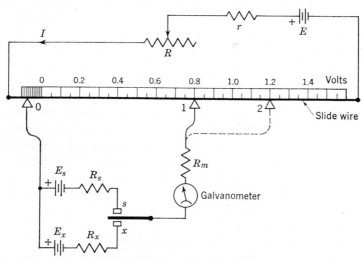

Fig. 9-8. Slide-wire potentiometer.

Potentiometers normally yield a direct reading of the unknown emf, E_x, in volts.   A direct-reading slide-wire potentiometer may be constructed by use of a uniform resistance wire with a uniform voltage scale placed directly adjacent to the wire, as shown in Fig. 9-8.   The procedure for calibration of the scale is, first, to set the slider to a position opposite the scale value corresponding to the known standard-cell voltage.   This value may range from 1.0174 to 1.0205 volts for commonly used standard cells.   Then, with the galvanometer key in position s, the current, I, is set for a null indication by adjusting R.   The potentiometer is then said to be standardized; that is, the current, I, is established at the unique value required to coordinate scale readings with voltage drop across the slide-wire. Thereafter, any other slider position may be read directly in volts. Obviously, any drift in the working current, I, from its standardized value will produce a systematic error in all scale readings. Periodic standardization is desirable, since it may not be obvious when measuring E_x that I has drifted. It must always be recognized that the potentiometer is a ratio instrument, even though it may be calibrated to read volts directly.

9-6. Potentiometer Applications. The potentiometer is capable of accuracy to five significant figures (0.01 per cent accuracy). Moreover, standard cells are highly satisfactory working standards of voltage, as mentioned in Sec. 1-2. The combination of these two facts suggests that the potentiometer is one of the fundamental precision instruments of d-c measurements. It is used widely as a precision voltmeter, especially when current drain from the source being measured cannot be tolerated.

The potentiometer may replace the voltmeter in several examples that have been presented previously. For instance, it may replace the voltmeter of Fig. 8-11 to measure the open-circuit voltage, E_0, without drawing appreciable current. It may be used in the circuit of Fig. 8-16 to determine the ratio of two resistances without disrupting the equality of current through the two resistors. Or it may be used for precision measurement of current, by determining the voltage drop across an accurate standard resistor. Finally, it is frequently used in the calibration of voltmeters and ammeters, as described in Sec. 5-8. It was indicated there how a voltage divider, or volt box, may be used to effectively extend the voltage range of the potentiometer, which is inherently low because of low standard-cell voltage. The volt box draws current from the source under measurement, but this does not introduce error in calibrating a voltmeter. When current drain must be minimized, high resistance values may be used in the volt box.

Another application for which the potentiometer is well suited is the measurement of temperature by means of a thermocouple. The emf produced by a thermocouple is on the order of 1 mv and is dependent on the temperature difference between its hot and cold junctions. If a sensitive voltmeter is used to measure this small emf, the voltage drop in the thermocouple wires, produced by the voltmeter current, may result in gross errors. This is especially so if the wires are long, which is often the case in remote installations. On the other hand, the low voltage range of the potentiometer, combined with its ability to measure emf accurately without drawing appreciable current, makes it a natural choice for this application. Indeed, special portable potentiometers designed specifically for such measurements are commercially available. They have a maximum voltage range of about 100 mv.

There are many other useful applications in a variety of fields. For instance, the potentiometer is used in the field of chemistry to measure hydrogen-ion concentration (pH). In any application where a small d-c emf is related to a quantity of interest, the potentiometer may be used. Moreover, the usefulness of the potentiometer has been extended further by the introduction of direct-recording self-balancing instruments. These motor-driven electrically controlled potentiometers have many applications where continuous and automatic records are desired in permanent chart form.

9-7. Potentiometer Analysis. The null condition was obtained easily for the slide-wire potentiometer without the need of solving for the galvanometer current. But the null condition itself does not provide answers to such relevant questions as:

1. To what extent will a small change in the working current change the reading of the potentiometer?

2. What galvanometer sensitivity is required to detect a small change in the setting of the sliding contact?

3. For a given galvanometer sensitivity, what error will there be in the null setting in terms of the smallest observable galvanometer deflection?

Answers to these questions provide valuable information that contributes to a quantitative appreciation of the requirements and limitations of potentiometers. The potentiometer must be analyzed under conditions that are close to null, where the galvanometer current is small but not zero. There are several possible approaches. A complete solution for the galvanometer current may be obtained by mesh or node analysis, or by application of Thévenin's theorem. However, when only small departures from the null condition are sought, network theorems such as superposition, reciprocity, and especially the compensation theorem are expedient analysis tools, as will be demonstrated. Actually, most of the end results may be found by inspection without elaborate analysis. However, the analysis techniques are worth developing here for the comparatively simple potentiometer circuit because they are invaluable in more complicated circuits to be studied later.

The basic circuit of the slide-wire potentiometer is given in Fig. 9-9 for the case of the galvanometer key in position x of Fig. 9-8. Symbols convenient to work with analytically have been introduced to represent the resistors in Fig. 9-8 as follows: $B = R + r$ and $G = R_m + R_x$. The resistance M represents that portion of the slide-wire resistance directly in the galvanometer circuit, while N represents the remainder of the slide-wire resistance.

The galvanometer current, I_g, may be obtained for any values of the circuit elements shown in Fig. 9-9 by routine mesh analysis. The mesh equations for the mesh currents assumed in Fig. 9-9 are

$$I(B + M + N) - I_g M = E$$
$$-IM + I_g(M + G) = -E_x$$

The mesh determinant is

$$\Delta = \begin{vmatrix} B + M + N & -M \\ -M & M + G \end{vmatrix} = M(B + N) + G(B + M + N)$$

and I_g is given by

$$I_g = \frac{\begin{vmatrix} B + M + N & E \\ -M & -E_x \end{vmatrix}}{\Delta}$$

The complete expression for I_g is

$$I_g = \frac{EM - E_x(B + M + N)}{M(B + N) + G(B + M + N)} \tag{9-9}$$

The null condition is a special case of this result and is given by imposing $I_g = 0$. The null condition is clearly

$$EM = E_x(B + M + N) \tag{9-10}$$

The result in Eq. (9-9) contains all the information of interest concerning the influence of any of the circuit parameters on I_g. A small

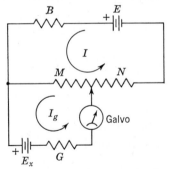

FIG. 9-9. Potentiometer circuit.

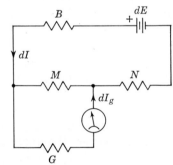

FIG. 9-10. Superposition theorem applied to potentiometer circuit.

change in I_g resulting from a small change in any of the circuit elements may be obtained by examining the differential of Eq. (9-9). For example, the change in I_g resulting from a change in the working-battery emf from E to $E + dE$ is given by

$$dI_g = \frac{\partial I_g}{\partial E} dE \tag{9-11}$$

If the partial derivative is evaluated at the null point, dI_g is then the total galvanometer current since I_g itself is zero before the change, dE.

Differentiation of Eq. (9-9) leads to the result

$$dI_g = \frac{M\ dE}{\Delta} \qquad (9\text{-}12)$$

This same result may be obtained directly from the original circuit without using the general solution for I_g by application of the superposition theorem. If E changes to $E + dE$, the changes in all currents will be those produced by dE, acting as the sole emf in the circuit shown in Fig. 9-10. This circuit may be solved directly for dI_g with little complication. The current, dI, through dE is

$$dI = \frac{dE}{B + N + MG/(M + G)}$$

The current-splitting rule then gives dI_g.

$$dI_g = \frac{M}{M + G}\ dI = \frac{M\ dE}{(M + G)(B + N) + MG} \qquad (9\text{-}13)$$

Since the denominator is Δ, this is the same result that was deduced from the complete solution for I_g in Eq. (9-12).

As another example, find the change in galvanometer current that results if the null condition is first satisfied, and then B is changed to $B + dB$. The solution may be obtained from the appropriate differential of Eq. (9-9).

$$dI_g = \left(\frac{\partial I_g}{\partial B}\right)_0 dB \qquad (9\text{-}14)$$

where the zero subscript on the partial derivative indicates that it is evaluated at the null point. The partial derivative is somewhat involved in this case.

$$\frac{\partial I_g}{\partial B} = \frac{-E_x\Delta + [E_x(B + M + N) - EM](M + G)}{\Delta^2}$$

However, under null conditions, the entire second term in the numerator is zero. Therefore, the change in galvanometer current from its zero condition owing to a change dB is

$$dI_g = \frac{-E_x\ dB}{\Delta} = \frac{-EM\ dB}{\Delta(B + M + N)} \qquad (9\text{-}15)$$

Again this same result may be obtained directly from the circuit without the need of solving for I_g. In this case, the compensation theorem is employed. If B changes to $B + dB$, the change in currents throughout the network may be computed by inserting an emf, $I\ dB$, as shown in Fig. 9-11. I is the original battery current under null conditions and is given simply by

$$I = \frac{E}{B + M + N} \qquad (9\text{-}16)$$

Since dB is infinitesimal, it may be ignored in comparison with B.   Then the circuits in Figs. 9-10 and 9-11 are basically the same, and the current dI_g may be obtained immediately from Eq. (9-13) by replacing dE by $-I\,dB$.

$$dI_g = \frac{-MI\,dB}{\Delta} = \frac{-ME\,dB}{\Delta(B + M + N)}$$

This result is seen to be in exact agreement with Eq. (9-15), despite use

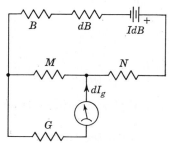

FIG. 9-11. Compensation theorem applied to potentiometer circuit.

of the approximate form of the compensation theorem in which the value B rather than $B + dB$ is used.   This is because the error of the approximation, given in Chap. 2, vanishes for the infinitesimal changes that have been considered here.

A more difficult problem is finding the change in galvanometer current from its null value, owing to a small change in location of the slide-wire contact.   If M is increased owing to movement of the slider, N must decrease by exactly the same amount. Therefore, the change in galvanometer current from its null value may be formulated as follows:

$$dI_g = \left(\frac{\partial I_g}{\partial M}\right)_0 dM + \left(\frac{\partial I_g}{\partial N}\right)_0 dN = \left[\left(\frac{\partial I_g}{\partial M}\right)_0 - \left(\frac{\partial I_g}{\partial N}\right)_0\right] dM \quad (9\text{-}17)$$

Here, M has changed to $M + dM$ with the concomitant change in N to $N + dN = N - dM$.   The partial derivatives of I_g with respect to M and N are quite complicated, as was true in the case of Eq. (9-14). However, insertion of the null condition leads to a similar simplification. These derivatives become, evaluated at the null,

$$\left(\frac{\partial I_g}{\partial M}\right)_0 = \frac{E - E_x}{\Delta} \qquad \left(\frac{\partial I_g}{\partial N}\right)_0 = -\frac{E_x}{\Delta}$$

Therefore, the change in galvanometer current from zero is

$$dI_g = \frac{E\,dM}{\Delta} \qquad (9\text{-}18)$$

Application of the compensation theorem to the original circuit leads to this same conclusion.   The changes in all currents resulting from a change in the slider location will be given by the circuit of Fig. 9-12a, where changes in the resistances dM and dN may be ignored. Also, $I\,dM = -I\,dN$. Convert the voltage generators to current generators, as shown in Fig. 9-12b. Then the change in galvanometer current may be written directly using the current-splitting rule.

$$dI_g = \left[\frac{M(B+N)/(M+B+N)}{G + M(B+N)/(M+B+N)} \right] I\,dM \left(\frac{1}{M} + \frac{1}{B+N} \right)$$

This result, when simplified by straightforward algebra, using the value of I given in Eq. (9-16), may be shown to agree exactly with Eq. (9-18).

The analysis techniques displayed in these examples are also useful in bridge circuits. The techniques are well worth mastering and are particularly suited to determine small changes in any linear circuits. While the actual method used is a matter of choice, it should be clear from these

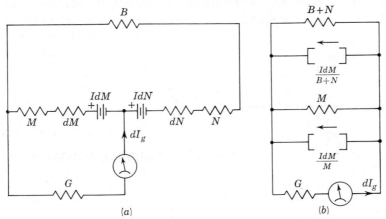

FIG. 9-12. Potentiometer analysis for small slider movement.

examples that use of theorems may involve less work than applying the differential method of analysis to the complete solution. This is especially so when a specific problem arises where it is only desired to obtain the change in current resulting from the change in a particular element.

9-8. Analysis of Potentiometer Errors. The results and methods of the preceding section may be used to assess some of the errors that arise in potentiometer use. The errors are expressed in most meaningful form in terms of the error in the quantity being determined, E_x. Errors arising from changes in the circuit are particularly pertinent because of the assumption implicit in the use of the potentiometer that the working current, I, has not changed from its standardized value at the time E_x is measured. Because standardization is not carried out simultaneously with the determination of E_x, there is always the possibility that the working current will drift from its correct value.

The same analysis device used for ohmmeters may be applied here to translate a change in galvanometer current, dI_g, to an equivalent change, dE_x, in the unknown emf. The general idea is to offset the change dI_g, produced by changes in E, B, M, and N, by deliberately introducing a fictitious change in E_x.

In carrying out this procedure, it is necessary to know the change in I_g owing to a change in E_x to $E_x + dE_x$. The differential of the complete solution for I_g may be used as before.

$$dI_g = \left(\frac{\partial I_g}{\partial E_x}\right)_0 dE_x = -\frac{(B + M + N)\,dE_x}{\Delta} \qquad (9\text{-}19)$$

The same result may also be obtained, without the need of solving for I_g first, by applying the superposition theorem to the original circuit. If E_x changes to $E_x + dE_x$ in the circuit of Fig. 9-9, the change in all currents will be those produced by dE_x acting as the sole emf in the circuit of Fig. 9-13. The change in the galvanometer current is seen immediately to be

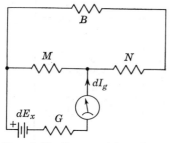

FIG. 9-13. Superposition theorem applied to potentiometer circuit.

$$dI_g = \frac{-dE_x}{G + M(N + B)/(M + N + B)}$$
$$= \frac{-(M + N + B)\,dE_x}{G(M + N + B) + M(N + B)}$$

in agreement with Eq. (9-19).

To illustrate the error-analysis technique, suppose the galvanometer is initially at null and then the working battery, E, changes to $E + dE$. The resulting change in galvanometer current may be offset by allowing E_x to change to $E_x + dE_x$ such that the *resultant* change in galvanometer current is zero. The corresponding mathematical statement is

$$dI_g = 0 = \left(\frac{\partial I_g}{\partial E}\right)_0 dE + \left(\frac{\partial I_g}{\partial E_x}\right)_0 dE_x$$

This really represents the superposition of the two circuits of Figs. 9-10 and 9-13. Using Eqs. (9-12) and (9-19), this becomes

$$0 = \frac{M\,dE}{\Delta} - \frac{(B + M + N)\,dE_x}{\Delta}$$

Therefore,
$$dE_x = \frac{M}{M + B + N}\,dE = \frac{E_x}{E}\,dE$$

where the null condition, Eq. (9-10), has been applied. This means that the fractional error in E_x is equal to the fractional change in E, which is also equal to the fractional change in I.

$$\frac{dE_x}{E_x} = \frac{dE}{E} = \frac{dI}{I} \qquad (9\text{-}20)$$

Thus, if the emf of the working battery changes by c per cent from the value it had when the potentiometer was standardized, the working current will change by c per cent, and the determination of E_x will be in error by c per cent.

While the analysis techniques have been valuable in themselves, this result may be deduced by direct inspection of the original circuit in Fig. 9-9. If E changes to $E + dE$, and the small change in galvanometer current is ignored, then the current through B, M, and N changes by the same per cent as the per cent change in E. Therefore, the per cent change in the voltage drop across M will be the same as the per cent change in E. Since E_x is equal to the drop across M, the per cent error in E_x must also be equal to the per cent change in E.

For a second example, suppose a null exists and then B changes to $B + dB$. The change in galvanometer current is given by Eq. (9-15). But let E_x change to $E_x + dE_x$ such that an equal and opposite change, given by Eq. (9-19), occurs in the galvanometer current. Then

$$dI_g = 0 = -\frac{E_x\, dB}{\Delta} - \frac{(B + M + N)\, dE_x}{\Delta}$$

and this may be regarded as the superposition of the two compensation circuits of Figs. 9-11 and 9-13. Therefore, the fractional error in E_x is

$$\frac{dE_x}{E_x} = \frac{-dB}{B + M + N} = \frac{dI}{I} \qquad (9\text{-}21)$$

and is equal in magnitude to the change dB expressed as a fraction of the total resistance of the working-battery circuit. The negative sign indicates that an increase in B will produce a result for the unknown emf that is less than its actual value. This is reasonable since an increase in B causes a decrease in the working current, I. Thus, the effects on the determination of E_x of small variations in internal resistance, r, of the working battery (see Fig. 9-8) may be reduced by use of a stable rheostat resistance, R, that is large compared with r. Again, Eq. (9-21) may be deduced by reasoning directly from the circuit of Fig. 9-9, without elaborate analysis.

Finally, the error in the determination of E_x resulting from a small error in slider location may be obtained by the same technique, using previous results. If the slider is moved slightly from its null location to the point $M + dM$ (N *must* change to $N - dM$), then dI_g is given by Eq. (9-18). Offset dI_g by a change dE_x, as before. In other words, superimpose the circuits of Figs. 9-12 and 9-13.

$$dI_g = 0 = \frac{E\,dM}{\Delta} - \frac{(B + M + N)\,dE_x}{\Delta}$$

Eliminate E by use of the null condition, Eq. (9-10), and this becomes

$$\frac{dE_x}{E_x} = \frac{dM}{M} \qquad\qquad (9\text{-}22)$$

Because M is proportional to the physical length of the uniform slide-wire, it is seen from this result that a long wire is desirable. If the slider deviates from its correct null location by a fixed distance, the resulting fractional error in E_x becomes more vulnerable to a given deviation in setting, dM, because M must inevitably become smaller as E_x becomes smaller.

Actually, all the results of this section could have been obtained by reasoning directly from the circuit without elaborate analysis. The analysis techniques themselves are valuable, however, and the potentiometer has served as a vehicle for their introduction. Although an elephant gun has been used where a peashooter would suffice, someday the elephant will be encountered.

There are many other sources of error in the use of potentiometers, which become important in highly accurate work. These include difficulties with small emf's resulting from contact difference of potential, thermal drift owing to change in resistance with temperature, and other minute effects not discussed here.

9-9. Galvanometer Sensitivity Limitations. An insensitive galvanometer will indicate zero deflection over a wide range of locations of the sliding contact, because the small off-null current is insufficient to actuate its coil. This introduces an uncertainty in the determination of E_x. If the galvanometer sensitivity is increased, the slider locations for a null indication are confined to a smaller range. However, there is always a slight uncertainty in slider location, depending upon the judgment of the operator in detecting the least discernible galvanometer deflection. This is so even though the galvanometer is keyed intermittently in the final null adjustment so that its deflections are compared when it is in and out of the circuit.

The sensitivity of the galvanometer may be expressed in terms of the smallest current that produces an observable deviation from a zero reading. This current is called the least discernible current, and the corresponding deflection is known as the *least discernible deflection*. The change in galvanometer current from zero arising from a small change in slider location was found in Eq. (9-18). If dI_g in this equation is the least discernible current, then dM is the slider range, in ohms, over which no detectable deviation from null is observed. This range is easily measured in practice simply by displacing the slider from null. If the range is found to be too large, a more sensitive galvanometer should be installed.

It is useful to express the least discernible current in terms of E_x. This may be done by the use of Eq. (9-22) which relates a change of M to a change in E_x. Inserting Eq. (9-22) into Eq. (9-18), and also incorporating the null condition to eliminate E, there results

$$dI_g = \frac{EM}{\Delta} \frac{dE_x}{E_x} = \frac{(B + M + N)\, dE_x}{\Delta} \tag{9-23}$$

This shows explicitly the way in which the least discernible current shows up as an error in the determination of E_x. Since $(B + M + N)$ is always less than Δ, the factor multiplying dE_x is always less than 1 mho. For a numerical example, suppose in a particular case this factor is 0.1 mho. Then, if E_x is to be determined to one part in 10^4, dE_x is 10^{-4} volt, and the least discernible galvanometer current must be at least 10 μa to avoid an error traceable to limited galvanometer sensitivity.

9-10. The Bridge Configuration. Bridges are one of the most widely used circuit arrangements in the field of measurements. Furthermore, the applications of bridge circuits have ramifications over a tremendous area. The bridge configuration is not only used for the measurement of circuit parameters, but is also employed in such applications as sensitive pickup devices, as control devices, and as wave filters. Moreover, in many electrical arrangements not ordinarily regarded as bridge circuits, it is found on close analysis that a bridge circuit does exist.

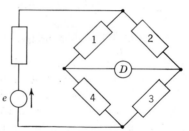

FIG. 9-14. Four-arm bridge network.

The four-arm bridge circuit enables the intercomparison, on a null basis, of the elements in its four arms. The bridge method of determining resistance, inductance, capacitance, or mutual inductance is basically a comparison method. The bridge configuration, shown in Fig. 9-14, consists of four arms interconnected in a closed series loop, numbered 1, 2, 3, 4 in clockwise order. A source of energy is applied across two diagonally opposite junctions of the four arms, and a detector, D, is connected between the remaining two junctions. The many advantages of this ingenious arrangement will gradually unfold.

When the bridge is used for comparison measurements, one or more of the parameters are varied until the detector displays a null indication. The bridge is then said to be balanced. The parameters varied may be circuit elements contained in the arms or parameters associated with the energy source, such as its frequency. The unknown quantity of interest is established by known conditions under which the null is obtained.

The simplest form of a bridge is called the Wheatstone bridge. The source of energy is a d-c supply (battery), the four arms are resistors, and the detector is a device sensitive to voltage or current. In Fig. 9-15, the supply battery of emf E is in series with the resistance, B; the detector resistance is designated by G (for galvanometer), and one of the four resistive bridge arms is signified by X, to be determined by use of the bridge. The null condition may be found easily, without obtaining a general solution for the galvanometer current, by imposing the null requirement of zero galvanometer current at the outset. Then the relations that the parameters must satisfy may be deduced directly. If $I_g = 0$, the voltage across the galvanometer branch must be zero. This

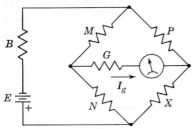

means that the voltage drop across N must be equal to that across X. Also, the voltage drop across M must be equal to that across P. Formulating either of these conditions (which are not independent because the sum of all voltages in traversing all four arms must be zero) leads to the null condition. For instance, the voltage across N is equal to the fraction $N/(N + M)$ times the

FIG. 9-15. Wheatstone bridge.

voltage between the diagonal points of the bridge to which the generator is connected. The voltage across X is equal to the fraction $X/(X + P)$ times this *same voltage*. By similar reasoning it may be deduced that $M/(M + N)$ must be equal to $P/(P + X)$. Hence, the null condition may be expressed in either of the forms

$$\frac{N}{N + M} = \frac{X}{X + P} \qquad \frac{M}{M + N} = \frac{P}{P + X}$$

Cross multiplication and cancellation, as required, leads to a single null condition in either case.

$$MX = NP \qquad\qquad (9\text{-}24)$$

How simple! The products of resistances in opposite arms are equal under balanced conditions for arbitrary values of E, B, and G. If M, N, and P are known at balance, then X is calculable. Suppose M and N are fixed, and P is varied until $I_g = 0$. Then N/M is the ratio by which P is multiplied to obtain X, and these fixed arms are called the ratio arms; X is compared with P via this ratio. Similarly, if M and P are fixed, and N is adjusted for balance, then P/M is the ratio by which N is multiplied to obtain X. Direct-reading Wheatstone bridges in which decade settings of the adjustable arm are marked to give values of X directly, are commercially available.

Two more interesting properties of the bridge circuit deserve emphasis. One is obvious from the development of the null condition [Eq. (9-24)]. The null condition is satisfied for any voltage applied to the bridge. It follows, in principle, that bridge balance is independent of the current through the bridge arms. In practice, heating effects, current-dependent contact difference of potential, and other such effects contradict this

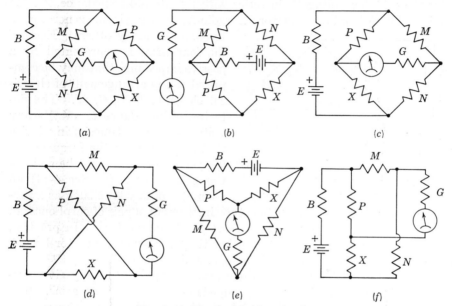

Fig. 9-16. Identical bridge circuits.

theoretical generalization. But the bridge principle is free of the standardization difficulty of the potentiometer. The other property is that interchange of the detector and generator circuits does not change the null condition (though it might change the bridge sensitivity, as will be shown in Chap. 10). To demonstrate this property, perform the interchange, impose $I_g = 0$, and deduce by reasoning similar to that used before that $M/(M + P) = N/(N + X)$ and $P/(M + P) = X/(N + X)$. These ratios are all different from those previously set up, and yet both of these dependent equations lead to the same null condition in Eq. (9-24).

A final point may be seen from Fig. 9-16, which shows a sample of some of the many different ways in which electrically identical bridge circuits may be drawn. Note that the so-called lattice circuit (Fig. 9-16d) is really a bridge circuit. Flexibility in redrawing circuits is, of course, not confined to the resistive d-c case, nor in fact to bridge circuits alone. A puzzling problem often encountered is that of unscrambling a draftsman's circuit diagram to find out what the engineer had in mind.

9-11. Alternating-current Bridges. The Wheatstone bridge, though widely used for resistance measurement, is a highly restricted form of the general case shown in Fig. 9-14. A general a-c bridge of the same form as that in Fig. 9-14 is given in Fig. 9-17. It is used in the sinusoidal alternating state, so complex numbers may be used to describe the behavior. The source of energy is a sinusoidal generator represented by the complex voltage $\mathbf{E}$ in series with its internal impedance, $\mathbf{Z}_g$. It might be an audio oscillator, a radio-frequency signal generator, a dynamo, or many others. Each of the four arms is represented by a passive impedance that may be comprised of any arrangement of electrical elements R, L, C, M. The detector, of impedance $\mathbf{Z}_d$, may be any voltage- or current-measuring device that is sensitive at the frequency of the generator. It might be a vibration galvanometer (see Sec. 4-14), an a-c meter of any type such as a vacuum-tube voltmeter or a rectifier-type instrument, a pair of earphones, an oscilloscope, a communications receiver, and many others. In practice, a transformer is usually used in either the detector or generator branch to permit proper grounding of line-operated equipment.

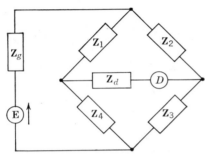

Fig. 9-17. Four-arm a-c bridge.

The null condition for this bridge may be expressed at any given frequency in terms of the complex impedances of the bridge arms. The null requirement is zero detector indication, which means zero voltage across the detector branch. Then, reasoning as before, the voltage drop across $\mathbf{Z}_4$ must be equal to that across $\mathbf{Z}_3$ (or, alternatively, that across $\mathbf{Z}_1$ must be equal to that across $\mathbf{Z}_2$). The drop across $\mathbf{Z}_4$ is the fraction $\mathbf{Z}_4/(\mathbf{Z}_1 + \mathbf{Z}_4)$ of the a-c voltage between the diagonal junctions of the bridge to which the generator is connected. The drop across $\mathbf{Z}_3$ is the factor $\mathbf{Z}_3/(\mathbf{Z}_2 + \mathbf{Z}_3)$ times the *same voltage*. Therefore,

$$\frac{\mathbf{Z}_4}{\mathbf{Z}_1 + \mathbf{Z}_4} = \frac{\mathbf{Z}_3}{\mathbf{Z}_2 + \mathbf{Z}_3} \quad \left(\text{or} \frac{\mathbf{Z}_1}{\mathbf{Z}_1 + \mathbf{Z}_4} = \frac{\mathbf{Z}_2}{\mathbf{Z}_2 + \mathbf{Z}_3}\right)$$

Cross-multiply and cancel as appropriate in either of these dependent equations, and the following null condition results:

$$\mathbf{Z}_1\mathbf{Z}_3 = \mathbf{Z}_2\mathbf{Z}_4 \tag{9-25}$$

The products of impedances in opposite arms are equal under balanced conditions for arbitrary values of $\mathbf{E}$, $\mathbf{Z}_g$, and $\mathbf{Z}_d$. This conclusion is similar to that for the Wheatstone bridge which, from a theoretical point of view, is a special case of the a-c bridge. Moreover, the conclusions that Eq. (9-25) is independent of the applied voltage and applicable for an interchange of generator and detector are also valid, in principle, for the a-c bridge. However, practical matters not considered here, such as heating effects of elements in the arms and stray capacitance effects, make these statements only approximately true in the laboratory.

The similarities between the Wheatstone bridge and the a-c bridge may be deceptive because the a-c null condition is quite different in that it involves complex quantities. Any complex equation is satisfied only if the real and imaginary parts of each side of the equation are *separately* equal. Thus, there are really two *independent* balance conditions contained in Eq. (9-25). *Both* of them must be satisfied to obtain a null.

The two balance conditions may be stated explicitly in many different ways. For example, symbolically,

$$\text{Re } \{\mathbf{Z}_1\mathbf{Z}_3\} = \text{Re } \{\mathbf{Z}_2\mathbf{Z}_4\} \qquad \text{and} \qquad \text{Im } \{\mathbf{Z}_1\mathbf{Z}_3\} = \text{Im } \{\mathbf{Z}_2\mathbf{Z}_4\}$$

If the impedances are expressed in rectangular form, $\mathbf{Z}_k = R_k + jX_k$, where $k = 1, 2, 3, 4$, then Eq. (9-25) becomes

$$(R_1 + jX_1)(R_3 + jX_3) = (R_2 + jX_2)(R_4 + jX_4)$$

Then the two balance conditions may be stated by equating the real and imaginary parts of this equation.

Reals: $R_1R_3 - X_1X_3 = R_2R_4 - X_2X_4$
Imaginaries: $X_1R_3 + X_3R_1 = X_2R_4 + X_4R_2$

It is interesting to note that, if all the reactances are zero, this reduces to the special case of a resistive bridge. The equation of the reals becomes the Wheatstone-bridge balance equation, $R_1R_3 = R_2R_4$, and the equation of the imaginaries is satisfied identically.

If the impedances are expressed in exponential form, $\mathbf{Z}_k = Z_k\epsilon^{j\alpha_k}$, where $k = 1, 2, 3, 4$, then the balance equation becomes

$$Z_1Z_3\epsilon^{j(\alpha_1+\alpha_3)} = Z_2Z_4\epsilon^{j(\alpha_2+\alpha_4)}$$

The two balance equations may then be stated either as

$$Z_1Z_3 = Z_2Z_4 \qquad \text{and} \qquad \alpha_1 + \alpha_3 = \alpha_2 + \alpha_4$$

or in the consistent form

Reals: $Z_1Z_3 \cos (\alpha_1 + \alpha_3) = Z_2Z_4 \cos (\alpha_2 + \alpha_4)$
Imaginaries: $Z_1Z_3 \sin (\alpha_1 + \alpha_3) = Z_2Z_4 \sin (\alpha_2 + \alpha_4)$

These formulations may be restated in terms of admittances of the bridge arms: $\mathbf{Y}_k = 1/\mathbf{Z}_k$, where $k = 1, 2, 3, 4$. Then the balance equation becomes

$$\frac{1}{\mathbf{Y}_1}\frac{1}{\mathbf{Y}_3} = \frac{1}{\mathbf{Y}_2}\frac{1}{\mathbf{Y}_4} \qquad \text{or} \qquad \mathbf{Y}_1\mathbf{Y}_3 = \mathbf{Y}_2\mathbf{Y}_4$$

The products of admittances in opposite arms are equal at balance. It is evident that exactly the same pattern of balance equations exists for admittances as for impedances. It is also possible, and very desirable in some cases, to use impedance for some arms and admittance for others.

No matter what the form of the balance conditions, the important point is that two independent conditions must be satisfied, rather than one as in the resistive case. This means that two adjustable elements are generally required to balance the bridge in practice. It should also be evident from the use of complex quantities, each of which has a real and imaginary part, that there are fundamentally eight quantities involved in the null condition. Six of these must be known so that the remaining two may be determined from the bridge balance; one from each of the independent null conditions. Some of these six elements might be practically negligible, of course. For instance, if one arm contains an essentially pure capacitance, then the real part of the immitance of that arm is zero. Nevertheless, there must still be six known quantities, even if some of these are known to be essentially zero. In addition, the frequency must be known in some cases.

9-12. Classification of A-C Bridge Circuits. There are limitless combinations of bridge-arm impedances capable of satisfying the balance equation, some of which are of theoretical interest only, but a tremendous variety of useful bridge circuits has been developed. Each has particular merits with respect to such factors as ease of adjustment, convenience, cost, accuracy with which certain types of elements may be measured, and susceptibility and correctability for stray effects. Some of these circuits may be placed into two categories called *ratio-arm* and *product-arm* bridges. These are circuits in which only two adjustable elements are required to achieve balance, and in which each adjustment may be used independently to satisfy one of the two balance conditions. However, these two types do not by any means exhaust the possibilities, and many practical and useful bridge circuits belong to neither category.

The ratio-arm bridge circuit is one in which two series-connected, adjustable circuit elements are located in a single arm adjacent to the unknown arm, and the *ratio* of impedances in the other two known arms is either purely real or purely imaginary. If $\mathbf{Z}_3$ is considered to be the impedance of the unknown arm, arms 2 or 4 are adjacent arms. Select, arbitrarily, arm 4 as the doubly adjustable arm containing $\mathbf{Z}_4 = R_4 + jX_4$. Then, in Eq. (9-25), solve for $\mathbf{Z}_3$.

$$\mathbf{Z}_3 = \frac{\mathbf{Z}_2}{\mathbf{Z}_1}(R_4 + jX_4) \qquad\qquad (9\text{-}26)$$

where Z_2/Z_1 is a known, fixed, real or imaginary *ratio*, and R_4 and X_4 are independently adjusted to separately satisfy the real and imaginary parts of the balance equation.

The product-arm bridge circuit contains two shunt-connected adjustable elements both located in the arm opposite the unknown arm, and the *product* of impedances in the remaining known arms is either purely real or purely imaginary. With Z_3 the unknown impedance, as before, the adjustable elements in arm 1 may be expressed in admittance form, $Y_1 = G_1 + jB_1$. Then,

$$Z_3 = Z_2 Z_4 (G_1 + jB_1) \tag{9-27}$$

where $Z_2 Z_4$ is a known, fixed, real or imaginary *product*, and G_1 and B_1 are adjusted independently to separately satisfy the real and imaginary parts of the balance equation.

An example of a ratio-arm bridge is given in Fig. 9-18. This is an Owen bridge often used for measurement of inductance (and its associated resistance). Neither the generator nor the detector is shown

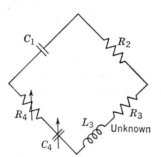

FIG. 9-18. Owen bridge (ratio-arm type).

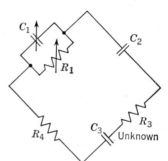

FIG. 9-19. Schering bridge (product-arm type).

since the balance condition is the same when the generator and detector are interchanged. The unknown impedance, Z_3, is given from Eq. (9-26) by

$$Z_3 = R_3 + j\omega L_3 = j\omega C_1 R_2 \left(R_4 + \frac{1}{j\omega C_4} \right) \tag{9-28}$$

which is clearly in ratio-arm form; Z_2/Z_1 is purely imaginary. Equate real and imaginary terms to obtain the two balance conditions.

$$R_3 = \frac{C_1 R_2}{C_4} \qquad L_3 = C_1 R_2 R_4 \tag{9-29}$$

Bridge balance is independent of frequency, in this case, and R_3 and L_3 are given in terms of the independently adjustable elements C_4 and R_4, respectively. The product $C_1 R_2$ is presumably known.

An illustration of the product-arm type of bridge is given in Fig. 9-19.

This is a Schering bridge, used for the measurement of capacitance (and its associated loss resistance). The unknown impedance, $\mathbf{Z}_3$, is given from Eq. (9-27) by

$$\mathbf{Z}_3 = R_3 + \frac{1}{j\omega C_3} = \frac{R_4}{j\omega C_2}\left(\frac{1}{R_1} + j\omega C_1\right) \tag{9-30}$$

Equate real and imaginary terms.

$$R_3 = \frac{R_4 C_1}{C_2} \qquad C_3 = \frac{C_2 R_1}{R_4}$$

Again, frequency drops out of the balance equation, and R_3 and C_3 are given in terms of the independently adjustable elements C_1 and R_1, respectively. The ratio C_2/R_4 is presumably known.

There are many other bridge circuits that do not fall into these classifications and, moreover, the balance of some bridges depends upon frequency. The Hay bridge, useful for measurement of high-Q coils, illustrates both of these points. The product of impedances of opposite arms for this bridge, shown in Fig. 9-20, is

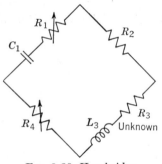

$$(R_3 + j\omega L_3)\left(R_1 + \frac{1}{j\omega C_1}\right) = R_2 R_4 \tag{9-31}$$

Equate real and imaginary terms.

$$R_1 R_3 + \frac{L_3}{C_1} = R_2 R_4 \qquad \omega L_3 R_1 - \frac{R_3}{\omega C_1} = 0$$

FIG. 9-20. Hay bridge.

Solve simultaneously for the unknown R_3 and L_3.

$$R_3 = \frac{\omega^2 C_1{}^2 R_1 R_2 R_4}{1 + (\omega R_1 C_1)^2} \qquad L_3 = \frac{C_1 R_2 R_4}{1 + (\omega R_1 C_1)^2}$$

The balance depends upon frequency, and the adjustable elements, R_1 and R_4, appear in both equations. If the coil Q is high, L_3 is very nearly independent of frequency. This may be seen from the imaginary part of the balance equation where $\omega L_3/R_3 = 1/\omega R_1 C_1$ is very much greater than unity for a high-Q coil. Then, $L_3 \approx C_1 R_2 R_4$, and this is essentially independent of frequency so long as $(\omega R_1 C_1)^2 \ll 1$, and R_4, alone, may be adjusted to satisfy this equation.

Several other bridge circuits are given in Fig. 9-21 to indicate further the wide variety of possibilities. In each case, elements with subscripts x may be considered to be the unknowns for purposes of analysis. The two lower circuits in Fig. 9-21 may not appear to be in the four-arm category, but they actually are. Transforming the delta to a wye in the Anderson bridge reveals its four-arm nature.   In the case of the modified Carey-Foster bridge, use of the T-equivalent circuit for two coupled coils (see Fig. 2-12) shows that the mutual inductance, M_x, appears as a single element in arm 3.

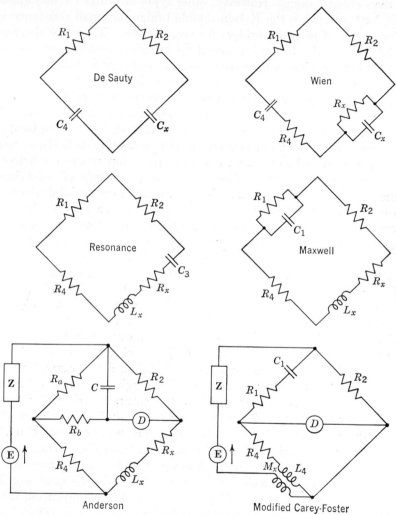

FIG. 9-21. Assorted a-c bridges.

9-13. Bridge Applications.

The Wheatstone bridge is the most commonly used method for accurate measurement of d-c resistance, in terms of a known resistance ratio and a standard resistance.   The bridge is convenient and rapid to use, the result is free of errors traceable to battery or galvanometer resistance and does not depend upon galvanometer calibration. The accuracy is fundamentally limited only by the accuracy with which the ratio and the standard are known. Because of limited galvanometer sensitivity and resistance of leads, the attainable accuracy becomes impaired for resistance values in excess of about 1 megohm and less than about 1 ohm. However, other types of bridge circuits are useful at both extremes, the Kelvin double bridge for small resistance and various types of megohm bridges for large values. There are also many special types of d-c bridges designed for specific purposes, such as comparison of two nearly equal resistances. Direct-current bridges also find use in measurements of physical quantities that affect resistance. For instance, d-c bridges are widely used to measure temperature (resistance thermometer) and are based on the known relationship between the resistance of a metal, such as platinum, and its temperature. The temperature rise of a dynamo may be determined by measuring its field-coil resistance when cold and hot, and then using the temperature coefficient of resistance of copper. Strain gages based on the change of resistance of a wire filament under mechanical stress are also very useful devices.

Alternating-current bridges are more versatile than d-c bridges and, accordingly, have wider application. Their use for accurate measurement of a-c resistance, inductance, capacitance, and mutual inductance in terms of known standards and ratios of known elements is obvious from the examples that have been presented. The availability of very stable and pure-waveform generators over a broad frequency range, accompanied by sensitive detection equipment, has led to a thorough exploitation of the sound bridge principle in a-c measurements of all kinds. The self-inductance of coils may be measured independently of their resistance; similarly, the dielectric losses of capacitors may be separated from the capacitance itself. In addition, direct current may be superimposed on the alternating current through a coil in a bridge circuit, and in this way the permeability and saturation characteristics of iron cores on which the coils are wound may be studied. Bridges afford one of the most suitable means for precision measurement of mutual inductance and coefficient of coupling between two coils. When the balance is dependent on frequency, the bridge may be used to measure frequency in terms of known circuit elements. The bridge is even useful for the measurement of such circuit parameters as the amplification factor, dynamic plate resistance, and transconductance of vacuum tubes. It is also used to measure the conductivity of liquids by immersing a special cell in the liquid.

Apart from the area of parameter measurements, bridge circuits are useful in many different applications. The detector output for slightly unbalanced conditions may be a very large signal for a very small change in one of the bridge arms. This property leads to the use of bridge circuits as delicate sensing devices. For example, it is not uncommon in servomechanism design to use a bridge circuit to provide the error signal to which the system responds. The detector output produced by a small change in capacitance of one of the bridge arms may be used as the basis of a thickness gage, a burglar-alarm system, or a mechanical-pressure-measuring device. This scarcely suggests the profusion of ideas that imaginative designers have developed.

Further, bridge circuits are useful as sharp-cutoff filters that pass a signal from one pair of diagonals to the opposite pair in a selective manner depending upon the bridge design. In this case, the transfer characteristic of the bridge is its pertinent characteristic. As was noted in Fig. 9-16, lattice filters are fundamentally bridge circuits. Bridge circuits are used as selective filters in feedback loops of amplifiers and oscillators, the Wien oscillator being a classic example. In such applications, the phase relationship between input and output signals across the two diagonals of the bridge is of critical importance.

In addition to the uses mentioned, there are a number of circuits which are really governed by bridge-circuit principles, although they are not ordinarily called bridges. For example, field-mapping circuits, employing an electrolytic trough and a search probe located for a null reading in mapping out an equipotential line, are basically bridge circuits. The two arms of the bridge, in this case, consist of the equivalent resistance of the electrolyte, but that does not change the principle. Another example is the push-pull power amplifier which really employs a bridge-type circuit, though there are a pair of balanced generators in two adjacent arms. The freedom of such circuits from power-supply hum, for example, stems from the fact that the bridge circuit involved is balanced, and therefore the hum signal does not produce an appreciable signal across the output terminals of the circuit. A very similar condition exists in balanced vacuum-tube voltmeter circuits.

These applications, in total, represent an important segment of electrical engineering and demand careful study. Detailed analyses of bridge characteristics pertinent to many of the applications that have been mentioned are presented in subsequent chapters and accompanying problems.

9-14. Substitution Method. The substitution method, carried out on a null basis, enables results to be obtained that are essentially as accurate as any available standard. Negligible errors owing to uncertainties in other circuit elements are encountered, and difficulties with stray effects are minimized. The general principle of the substitution method has been discussed in Sec. 8-14 in connection with deflection methods. The main difference, when carried out on a null basis, is that a more sensitive comparison of unknown and standard is possible. This leads to the practical difficulty, often not met in deflection methods, of obtaining a standard that is so nearly identical to the unknown as to be virtually unattainable. A small difference between standard and unknown may be below the threshold of observation in a deflection method, but this same difference might be so highly magnified in a sensitive null circuit that no setting of the standard could be found to produce a null. Of course, this means that the attainable accuracy on a null basis is better than on a deflection basis.

The substitution method, with a minor modification to overcome the above difficulty, is still a practical and extremely useful null method. Indeed, it represents the ultimate in attainable accuracy. An illustration in terms of a bridge, used as the null arrangement, will reveal the underlying principles. In the simple DeSauty bridge of Fig. 9-21, a capacitance, C_x, is measured in terms of the resistance ratio and the known capacitance, C_4. Suppose balance is attained by employing an adjustable value of R_1, with C_4 and R_2 fixed. Then, when the bridge is balanced by varying R_1, C_x may be computed from

$$C_x = \frac{R_1 C_4}{R_2} \tag{9-32}$$

The error in the determination of C_x will be at least equal to the combined errors in the three bridge elements. If ample detector sensitivity is assumed, there still might be additional errors resulting from such effects as stray capacitance and lead inductance.

If, instead, C_x is determined by a substitution method with this bridge, the arrangement in Fig. 9-22 might be used. The standard capacitor, C_s, may be substituted for C_x using the switching arrangement shown. It is assumed that the standard capacitor is capable of certain fixed-step adjustments, but is *not continuously variable.* This is the usual case with highly accurate standards. The bridge is first balanced with C_x in arm 3 by adjustment of R_1, and Eq. (9-32) applies. Next, C_x is replaced by C_s which is then adjusted in steps for minimum detector output. For the typical case in which a highly sensitive detector is used, an exact null will not be achieved, since C_s is incapable of continuous adjustment. However, R_1 may then be changed slightly by a known amount, ΔR_1, to achieve a null. Then

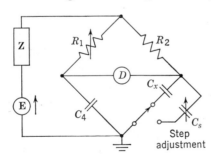

Fig. 9-22. Substitution bridge.

$$C_s = \frac{(R_1 + \Delta R_1)C_4}{R_2} = C_x + \frac{\Delta R_1 C_4}{R_2} \tag{9-33}$$

Therefore, the ratio of C_s to C_x is

$$\frac{C_s}{C_x} = 1 + \frac{\Delta R_1}{R_1} \tag{9-34}$$

The uncertainty in this ratio is far less than in the case of C_x in Eq. (9-32). Suppose, for example, that ΔR_1 is about 2 per cent of R_1 and that R_1 is known to 0.1 per cent. Then the ratio of C_s to C_x is known to 0.002 per cent, and the values of C_4 and R_2 do not enter at all. Think this over. The ratio is known to 20 parts per million in this example.

While there are other techniques that may be used, this example illustrates the way in which the error of the substitution method may be reduced to a very low level, usually sufficient to take full advantage of the accuracy of any standard with which the unknown is compared. The substitution method may be pushed to comparative accuracy levels of one or two parts per million with good techniques, if a standard close enough to the unknown is available.

9-15. Differential Method. A discussion of differential methods using indicators whose deflection yields the difference between two quantities has been presented in Chap. 8. These methods are very useful but may entail errors attributable to loading effects of the indicator. Inherent errors of the deflection instrument also constitute important limitations. Even though it is the difference between two quantities that is indicated in the differential method, greater accuracy than is afforded by deflection methods may still be desired in certain cases. Incorporation of a null technique has the disadvantage of requiring null adjustment for each differential result obtained, but may yield increased sensitivity and accuracy.

An initial null is intrinsic to any differential method, as was shown in Chap. 8. Hence, any null arrangement is capable of being used as a differential deflection method, by using the detector output as an indication of the changed quantity. Moreover, if the circuit is readjusted for null to compensate for the change in the quantity, there is virtually no distinction, in principle, from a comparison null method. There is only a difference in detail. Generally, comparison null methods that have restricted ranges designed to encompass only small differences between two quantities fall into this differential classification. The devices used incorporate specially designed elements to enable accurate control and direct dial reading of small differences. Examples of such devices include several types of difference potentiometers and special d-c bridges used for comparison of two nearly equal resistors, such as ratio sets, slide-wire bridges, and limit bridges. The example of the substitution method presented in the preceding section may be regarded as a differential null method, in which the change $\Delta R_1/R_1$ may be read directly as the fractional difference between C_s and C_x.

A simple example of a differential null method applied to temperature measurements using a thermocouple is shown in Fig. 9-23.   The circuit is essentially the same as that of the differential voltmeter of Fig. 8-19 and is really a portion of a potentiometer circuit.   The control resistance, R, is much less than resistances R_1 and R_2, so the total drop across R is very small compared with the emf E.   The angular location of the control shaft may be read directly on the associated dial.   When control R

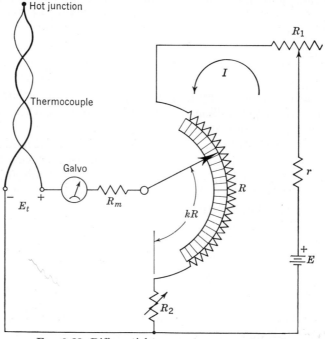

FIG. 9-23. Differential temperature measurement.

is adjusted for a null (zero galvanometer current) the thermocouple emf is given by

$$E_t = I(R_2 + kR)$$

where k is the fraction of R in the lower portion of the control.   When E_t changes to $E_t + \Delta E_t$, owing to a change in temperature of the thermocouple junction, then k is readjusted to $k + \Delta k$ so that the null is reestablished.   Then,

$$E_t + \Delta E_t = I(R_2 + kR + \Delta kR)$$

Clearly, the change in thermocouple emf is directly proportional to the change in k.

$$\Delta E_t = I R \, \Delta k$$

If I is standardized in terms of a standard cell (as in the conventional potentiometer) and remains constant, the dial may be calibrated directly in degrees. This would be a very special purpose calibration restricted to only one type of thermocouple. Greater flexibility could be achieved by calibrating the dial directly in microvolts, and the temperature could then be found by referring to the temperature-emf characteristic of whatever type of thermocouple is used.

The same circuit may be used on a deflection basis, by relying on the calibration of the galvanometer and using a fixed setting k. If the galvanometer is sufficiently sensitive, the voltage drop produced in the thermocouple wires might not seriously affect E_t.

9-16. Combined Null-deflection Methods. It is sometimes necessary or desirable to use null and deflection methods in combination. Two illustrations of such combinations are described here.

Iron-core coils used as chokes or filter elements often carry substantial direct current in normal operation. This direct current increases the

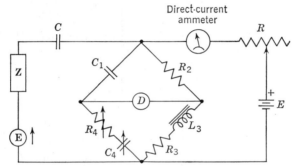

FIG. 9-24. Inductance measurement with d-c superimposed.

flux density in the core and alters the magnetic permeability and hence the inductance. Accordingly, it is desirable to study the way in which the inductance of such coils is affected by direct current. A bridge may be used to measure the inductance, while an ammeter simultaneously indicates the direct current through the inductance. A modified Hay bridge is usually used in practice, but a simpler example in terms of an Owen bridge is given in Fig. 9-24. The balance equations for this bridge are given by Eq. (9-29). Direct current, passed through the coil from the d-c source, E, is controllable by R. Capacitor C blocks the direct current from the signal generator, **E**. For each setting of R, the bridge may be balanced, and L_3 determined from $L_3 = C_1 R_2 R_4$. The corresponding direct current through L_3 is indicated by the ammeter. This gives the general idea, but many practical factors, not mentioned here, are important in actually carrying out the measurements.

A more intimate combination of deflection and null methods is illustrated in Fig. 9-25. This circuit may be used to measure the galvanometer resistance and sensitivity, without the need of a null instrument. Although the galvanometer is in one arm of the Wheatstone bridge, it may be used indirectly to indicate bridge balance. The galvanometer current generally depends upon whether the switch in the detector branch is open or closed. When the bridge is balanced, however, the voltage across the switch is zero, and the galvanometer current will then be the same whether the switch is open or closed.

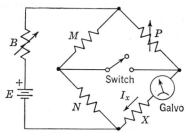

Fig. 9-25. Combined null-deflection bridge.

Rheostat B may be adjusted to produce the desired galvanometer deflection, while the adjustable resistance, P, may be used to attain balance. The galvanometer resistance, X, is given by $X = NP/M$ at balance. The fraction of the battery current passing through the galvanometer at balance is

$$\frac{M + N}{M + N + P + X} = \frac{M}{M + P} \tag{9-35}$$

since $MX = NP$. Therefore, the galvanometer current, I_x, at balance is

$$I_x = \frac{M}{M + P}\left(\frac{E}{B + R}\right) \tag{9-36}$$

where R is the equivalent parallel resistance of $(M + N)$ and $(P + X)$. The galvanometer resistance, X, is given by a knowledge of M, N, and P, required for balance, and I_x may be calculated if, in addition, E and B are known. Then the galvanometer sensitivity may be computed from the observed deflection of the galvanometer.

PROBLEMS

9-1 (§2). Determine a general expression for the current, I_m, in the circuit of Fig. 9-2. Show that this expression is zero when Eq. (9-6) is satisfied.

9-2 (§5). A slide-wire potentiometer is used to measure the voltage between two points of a certain d-c circuit. The potentiometer reading is 1.5 volts. A 20,000-ohm-per-volt voltmeter indicates 0.25 volt on its 2.5-volt range when it is connected across the same two points in the circuit. What is the input resistance of the circuit between the two points?

9-3 (§6). A potentiometer that is accurate to ± 0.0001 volt (standard deviation) is used to measure the current through a standard resistance of 0.1000 ohm $\pm$ 0.1 per cent (standard deviation). The voltage across the resistance is measured to be 0.2514 volt. What is the current, and with what accuracy has it been determined?

9-4 (§7). The slide-wire potentiometer of Fig. 9-8 is used to measure an emf, E_x, of internal resistance R_x. The galvanometer has a sensitivity of 0.1 μa per mm and a resistance $R_m = 50$ ohms. The potentiometer is first standardized, by means of a standard cell, to establish $I = 0.02$ amp. It is then switched to position x and adjusted for zero galvanometer deflection. A reading of 1.0200 volts is obtained. The slide-wire is then moved to a setting of 1.0201 volts, and a galvanometer deflection of 8.0 mm is observed. What are the values of E_x and R_x?

9-5 (§8). Prove that $dE/E = dI/I$ with M, N, and B constant; and also that $dI/I = -dB/(B + M + N)$ with E, M, and N constant, as indicated in Eqs. (9-20) and (9-21), respectively.

9-6 (§8). A slide-wire potentiometer is standardized and then used to measure an unknown emf, E_x. By the time the null is obtained, the working current has decreased from its standardized value owing to heating of the slide-wire. $M + N$ has suffered a total increase in resistance, dR, that is uniformly distributed throughout the wire. Assume that B and E in Fig. 9-9 have not changed. Determine an expression for the fractional error in E_x, in terms of dR.

9-7 (§8). A null is obtained in the circuit of Fig. 9-1. For simplicity, assume that $R_a \gg r_1$ and $R_b \gg r_2$. (a) If R_b is changed to $R_b + dR$, determine an expression for dI_m, the resulting change in current through R_m. (b) Starting with a null, E_1 changes to $E_1 + dE$. Determine an expression for the corresponding change in R_b required to restore the null.

9-8 (§9). In the potentiometer circuit of Fig. 9-9, $E = 3.2$ volts, $I = 1.0$ ma when $I_g = 0$, $(M + N) = 3,000$ ohms, $G = 2,000$ ohms, and the galvanometer sensitivity is 10 μa per mm. The potentiometer is balanced when $M = 200$ ohms. (a) Determine E_x. (b) What are the limits of error in the measurement of E_x attributable to the smallest discernible galvanometer deflection of 0.1 mm?

9-9 (§9). It is desired to measure an unknown emf that has an internal resistance of 1,000 ohms to an accuracy of 1 per cent or better. A slide-wire potentiometer with a 12-volt working battery and a standardized working current of $I = 0.02$ amp is used in conjunction with a galvanometer of sensitivity 50 μa per mm and least discernible deflection of 0.1 mm. The measured result for the unknown emf is 0.220 volt. (a) Assuming that the potentiometer itself is perfect, determine whether or not the desired 1 per cent accuracy has been achieved. (b) How could you determine this answer quickly if you were making the measurement in the laboratory?

9-10 (§9). In the potentiometer circuit of Fig. 9-9, it is known from standardization that with $I_g = 0$, $I = 20$ ma ± 0.1 per cent. Also, $(B + M + N) = 100$ ohms. Settings of the slide-wire are known to within ± 0.05 ohm. The galvanometer has a resistance of 200 $\pm$ 2 ohms, a sensitivity of 100 μa per scale division, and a minimum perceptible deflection of 0.1 division. All inaccuracies are stated as standard deviations. (a) When the potentiometer is used to measure E_x, which is approximately 1 volt, what is the expression for the standard deviation of the measurement? (b) What value of R_x, the internal resistance of E_x, will make the standard deviation in the measurement of E_x equal to 0.01 volt?

9-11 (§10). A nonlinear resistance, X, is known to follow the law $X = A + CI$, where A is the zero-current value of X, I is the current through X, and C is a constant. The Wheatstone bridge of Fig. 9-15, with $M = 200$ ohms, $E = 10$ volts, and $B = 0$, is used to determine A and C. With $N = 100$ ohms, a value $P = 110$ ohms is required for balance. With $N = 200$ ohms, the value of P required for balance is 60 ohms. Compute A and C.

9-12 (§10). The Wheatstone bridge of Fig. 9-26 is used normally to measure an unknown resistance connected to terminals A-B. However, in this problem a voltage controlled by the setting k (where $0 \leq k \leq 1$) is applied to A-B instead of the usual

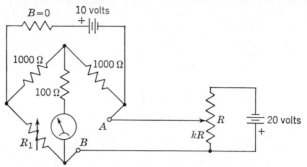

FIG. 9-26. Active circuit in arm of Wheatstone bridge.

passive resistance. Specify the complete range of settings, in terms of k, for which bridge balance is impossible even though R_1 is variable from zero to infinity.

9-13 (§11). The a-c bridge shown in Fig. 9-27 is used to measure an unknown inductance, L_x, that has inherent resistance, R_x. The bridge parameters are $R_1 = 20,000$ ohms, $R_2 = 50,000$ ohms, $C_2 = 0.003$ μf, $\omega = 10^5$ radians per sec. C_1 is adjustable from 10 μμf to 150 μμf, and R_4 is adjustable from 0 to 10,000 ohms. (a) Show that the equations for resistive and reactive balance are independent of each other. Derive expressions for R_x and L_x in terms of ω, R_1, R_2, R_4, C_1, and C_2. (b) Determine the largest values of R_x and L_x that are measurable with the given parameters.

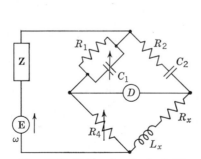

FIG. 9-27. Bridge for Prob. 9-13.

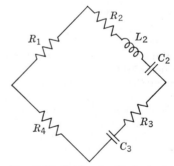

FIG. 9-28. Bridge for Prob. 9-17.

9-14 (§12). For the DeSauty bridge of Fig. 9-21, (a) Derive the balance equations. (b) How many adjustments are necessary to achieve balance for any value of C_x?

9-15 (§12). Derive the balance equations for the resonance bridge of Fig. 9-21.

9-16 (§12). Show that the balance equations of the Maxwell bridge of Fig. 9-21 are independent of frequency.

9-17 (§12). (a) Determine the balance equations for the bridge in Fig. 9-28. (b) For what range of frequencies is it impossible to balance this bridge by varying R_1, R_3, R_4, or C_3? (c) For $C_2R_1 > C_3R_4$, can the bridge be balanced?

9-18 (§12). The Wien bridge shown in Fig. 9-21 is balanced at an angular frequency ω_0. (a) Derive an expression for ω_0 in terms of the bridge parameters. (b) If a stray capacitance, C_2, exists in parallel with R_2, the bridge is not balanced at ω_0, but is balanced at a new frequency ω_1. Determine an expression for ω_0/ω_1. (c) If all resistors except R_x are each 1,000 ohms, and $C_x = C_4 = 500 \ \mu\mu f$, by what percentage does the ratio ω_0/ω_1 differ from unity when $C_2 = 10 \ \mu\mu f$, and what is the value of R_x?

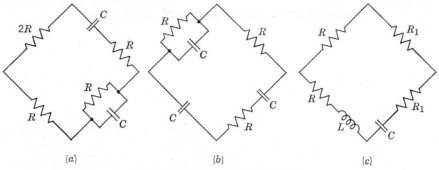

FIG. 9-29. Bridges for Prob. 9-19.

9-19. (§12). At what frequencies will the three bridge circuits of Fig. 9-29 be balanced?

9-20 (§12). Derive the balance equations for the modified Carey-Foster bridge shown in Fig. 9-21.

9-21 (§12). For the Anderson bridge of Fig. 9-21, (a) Derive the balance equations and solve explicitly for R_x and L_x. (b) Is it possible to find two independent resistance adjustments that permit attainment of bridge balance? (c) If generator and detector are interchanged, do the same balance equations apply?

9-22 (§16). Verify Eq. (9-35).

9-23 (§16). The resistance and sensitivity of a galvanometer are measured in the circuit of Fig. 9-25. Resistance P is adjusted until the galvanometer indicates the same current whether the switch is open or closed, and B is adjusted to 48,200 ohms to produce a galvanometer deflection of 80 mm. The adjusted value of P is 3,000 ohms. The ratio arms are fixed at $M = 2,000$ ohms and $N = 1,000$ ohms. $E = 1.0$ volt. (a) Compute the galvanometer resistance, X. (b) Compute the galvanometer sensitivity in microamperes per millimeter.

CHAPTER 10

DIRECT-CURRENT BRIDGE ANALYSIS

The bridge configuration consists of three meshes, and its analysis is somewhat complicated for general values of bridge parameters, even in the purely resistive case. The complexity may be reduced somewhat by ignoring the resistance, B, of the battery circuit, and this is done in many treatments of the subject. Yet, this resistance may be important in affecting bridge performance. Accordingly, B is included throughout this chapter. Several different Wheatstone-bridge analyses are presented, including the complete mesh solution as well as the compensation-theorem approach, which is found to be highly valuable for the slightly unbalanced bridge. Thévenin's theorem is also applied, but it is a less facile tool than the compensation theorem.

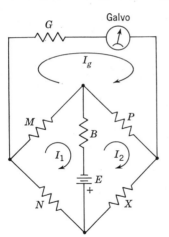

FIG. 10-1. Mesh currents in Wheatstone bridge.

The influence of galvanometer sensitivity and limited bridge-arm current is explored, as well as the dependence of bridge accuracy on the size of the unknown being measured. Effects on bridge sensitivity of interchanging the galvanometer and battery circuits are investigated. The slide-wire bridge, limit bridge, and Kelvin double bridge are also analyzed.

This chapter provides an excellent opportunity for the exercise of some highly useful circuit-analysis techniques that are germane to bridge design and application. Moreover, there is opportunity to correlate mathematical results with their physical significance. While some of the algebra is of necessity laborious, it is expected that the student will discern the difference between complexity and perplexity.

10-1. Unbalanced Wheatstone Bridge: Exact Solution. A complete solution for the galvanometer current in a Wheatstone bridge may be obtained for any values of the bridge parameters by use of routine circuit analysis. The Wheatstone bridge circuit of Fig. 9-15 is redrawn in Fig.

10-1 with the galvanometer in an outer branch for convenience in mesh analysis. With the assumed clockwise mesh currents I_1, I_2, and $I_3 = I_g$, the mesh equations are

$$(M + B + N)I_1 - BI_2 - MI_g = E$$
$$-BI_1 + (B + P + X)I_2 - PI_g = -E$$
$$-MI_1 - PI_2 + (M + P + G)I_g = 0$$

The mesh determinant is

$$\Delta = \begin{vmatrix} M + B + N & -B & -M \\ -B & B + P + X & -P \\ -M & -P & M + P + G \end{vmatrix}$$

The galvanometer current is given by

$$I_g = \frac{\Delta'}{\Delta} = \frac{\begin{vmatrix} M + B + N & -B & E \\ -B & B + P + X & -E \\ -M & -P & 0 \end{vmatrix}}{\Delta}$$

This represents the complete and exact solution for I_g, valid for any values of E, B, M, N, P, X, and G. It only remains to manipulate the result into a more usable form.

10-2. Expansion of Determinants. The determinants Δ and Δ' may be expanded by several techniques. However, the algebra is extremely cumbersome unless the determinants are handled with considerable care before writing out their expansions. To illustrate, the value of Δ' is unchanged if rows 2 and 3 are added to row 1. Then

$$\Delta' = \begin{vmatrix} N & X & 0 \\ -B & B + P + X & -E \\ -M & -P & 0 \end{vmatrix} = E \begin{vmatrix} N & X \\ -M & -P \end{vmatrix}$$

Having achieved two zeros in column 3, the result is obtained simply by expanding Δ' by the third column. Thus,

$$\Delta' = E(MX - NP) \tag{10-1}$$

Bridge balance is defined by $I_g = 0$, and X will be considered to be the variable for analysis purposes. Let $X = X_0$ represent the value of X required for balance. Since Δ is not infinite for finite values of the parameters, then Δ' must be zero at balance. Hence, from Eq. (10-1)

$$MX_0 = NP \tag{10-2}$$

The products of resistances in opposite arms are equal at balance, a familiar result. This balance condition is independent of E, B, and G, and also holds for an interchange of battery and detector branches. If

X is not equal to X_0, it may be represented by

$$X = X_0 + R$$

where R represents the deviation, large or small, of X from the value required to satisfy Eq. (10-2). Equation (10-1) is then expressible in terms of the variable R.

$$\Delta' = E(MX_0 + MR - NP) = EMR \qquad (10\text{-}3)$$

using Eq. (10-2).

The network determinant, Δ, may be expressed in terms of R with a minimum of effort by first breaking it into the sum of two determinants. $\Delta = \Delta_1 + \Delta_2$.

$$\Delta_1 = \begin{vmatrix} M + B + N & -B & -M \\ -B & B + P + X_0 & -P \\ -M & -P & M + P + G \end{vmatrix}$$

which is independent of R, and

$$\Delta_2 = \begin{vmatrix} M + B + N & 0 & -M \\ -B & R & -P \\ -M & 0 & M + P + G \end{vmatrix}$$

which is proportional to R. With two zeros in column 2, Δ_2 may be expanded immediately by the second column.

$$\Delta_2 = R \begin{vmatrix} M + B + N & -M \\ -M & M + P + G \end{vmatrix}$$
$$= R[M(P + G) + (B + N)(M + P + G)] \qquad (10\text{-}4)$$

The determinant Δ_1 may be manipulated to produce a row containing two zeros by the steps to be outlined. Attempts to expand it directly lead to exceedingly cumbersome results, so it is worthwhile to put some thought into these laborsaving moves. Add columns 1 and 2 to column 3, add column 2 to column 1, and leave column 2 unchanged. Then multiply row 1 of the resulting determinant by P/M and multiply outside by M/P to maintain Δ_1 unchanged. At this stage, the intermediate result is

$$\Delta_1 = \frac{M}{P} \begin{vmatrix} (M + N)P/M & -BP/M & NP/M \\ P + X_0 & B + P + X_0 & X_0 \\ -M - P & -P & G \end{vmatrix}$$

Now subtract row 2 from row 1. This produces two zeros in row 1, when Eq. (10-2) is incorporated. Hence, Δ_1 may be expanded by the second column with the result, using Eq. (10-2) to simplify,

$$\Delta_1 = M \left(B + P + X_0 + \frac{BP}{M} \right) \left(G + N + X_0 + \frac{GN}{M} \right) \qquad (10\text{-}5)$$

The solution for I_g may now be written in algebraic form in terms of the bridge parameters, using Eqs. (10-3) to (10-5). A revealing form of the complete final result is

$$I_g = \frac{E}{(B + P + X_0 + BP/M)(G + N + X_0 + GN/M)}\left[\frac{R}{1 + kR}\right] \quad (10\text{-}6)$$

$$\text{where} \quad k = \frac{M(P + G) + (B + N)(M + P + G)}{M(B + P + X_0 + BP/M)(G + N + X_0 + GN/M)}$$

10-3. Some Interpretations of the Exact Solution. Several aspects of the general solution for I_g are helpful to recognize immediately with a view toward future applications. The factor k is always positive since $M, P, N, X_0, G,$ and B are always greater than zero. Moreover, in many bridges the order of magnitude of k is $1/X_0$. Two gross examples demonstrate this property. For instance, if *all* resistances are equal to X_0,

$$k = \frac{8X_0{}^2}{X_0(4X_0)(4X_0)} = \frac{1}{2X_0}$$

Similarly, if G and B are negligible compared with all other resistances, and if $M, P, N,$ and X_0 are equal,

$$k = \frac{MP + N(M + P)}{M(P + X_0)(N + X_0)} = \frac{3}{4X_0}$$

While it cannot be relied upon invariably, k usually does not differ too much from $1/X_0$.

If the bridge is only slightly unbalanced, then $kR \ll 1$, and the factor $1 + kR$ in Eq. (10-6) is nearly unity. This simplifies the current expression considerably. In addition, I_g is then directly proportional to R. The fact that k is often on the order of $1/X_0$ means that when R differs from X_0 by a small percentage, the galvanometer current is proportional to R. Therefore, the ratio of a small change in I_g from its balance value, ΔI_g, to a small change in X_0 from balance, $\Delta X = R$, is a constant given by

$$\frac{\Delta I_g}{\Delta X} = \frac{E}{[B(1 + P/M) + P + X_0][G(1 + N/M) + N + X_0]} \quad kR \ll 1$$

$$(10\text{-}7)$$

It will be shown later that this same result is obtained by use of the compensation theorem without the need of knowing the solution for I_g.

The slope of the curve of I_g vs. X at the point $I_g = 0$, where $X = X_0$, is dI_g/dX, and is given exactly by Eq. (10-7). This slope is referred to as the *current sensitivity* of the bridge. Equation (10-7) shows that the current sensitivity is always increased by a decrease in the galvanometer resistance, G, by a decrease in the battery-circuit resistance, B, and by an increase in the battery emf, E. The *voltage sensitivity* of the bridge is

G times the current sensitivity and is the change in voltage across the galvanometer resulting from a small change in X from its balance value. The voltage sensitivity is seen to increase with an *increase* in G, a decrease in B and an increase in E. For a given battery emf, E, the maximum current sensitivity is given by Eq. (10-7) with $G = 0 = B$.

$$\left(\frac{dI_g}{dX}\right)_0 = \frac{E}{(P + X_0)(N + X_0)} = \frac{E}{X_0 S}$$

where S is defined as the sum of the four bridge-arm resistances at balance.

$$S = M + N + P + X_0 \tag{10-8}$$

The maximum voltage sensitivity occurs when $B = 0$ and $G \to \infty$ and is also obtainable from Eq. (10-7).

$$G\left(\frac{dI_g}{dX}\right)_0 = \frac{EM}{(P + X_0)(M + N)} = \frac{EP}{(P + X_0)^2}$$

Other conclusions that may be drawn from the general solution will be developed later in this chapter. The fact that most of the pertinent results are obtained when $kR \ll 1$, which means that part of the general solution is thrown away, suggests that there may be a more direct approach to the solution of the slightly unbalanced bridge. This is, indeed, the case as shown in the following section.

10-4. Unbalanced Wheatstone Bridge: Approximate Solution. The solution for the change in galvanometer current, from its balance value of zero, resulting from a small change in X from X_0, may be obtained without the general solution for I_g. The compensation theorem, in combination with the reciprocity theorem, leads to an elegant solution. This direct approach to the problem of the slightly unbalanced bridge utilizes approximate circuit-analysis techniques that are useful in solving a variety of problems. In many cases this approach provides the most expedient tool when the general solution is unavailable or unduly cumbersome.

When the bridge of Fig. 10-1 is balanced ($I_g = 0$), the current through X_0 is obtained easily by multiplying the battery current by the factor $(M + N)/S$, where S is defined in Eq. (10-8). Let I_x be the branch current through X_0 in a direction *opposite* to I_2 of Fig. 10-1. Then, at balance,

$$I_x = \frac{E}{B + (M + N)(P + X_0)/S}\left[\frac{M + N}{S}\right] = \frac{E(M + N)}{BS + (M + N)(P + X_0)} \tag{10-9}$$

If X_0 is changed to $X_0 + R$, the change in all the currents throughout the network may be obtained by applying the compensation theorem.

Introduce the "compensation" emf, $I_x R$, shown in Fig. 10-2, where I_x is given by Eq. (10-9) and is the current that existed in X_0 before it was changed. The solution for the change in galvanometer current may be obtained exactly from the circuit of Fig. 10-2. This circuit is almost as complicated as the original circuit so it would appear as if little has been accomplished. However, if R is small compared with X_0, the case of most interest, then a simplification results. With $R = \Delta X$, the resistance ΔX may be ignored compared with X_0, but, of course, the compensation emf, $I_x \Delta X$, is retained.

The simplification may not be immediately apparent from Fig. 10-2, but look at the circuit in Fig. 10-3 in which the reciprocity theorem has been applied by "interchanging" the emf $I_x \Delta X$ and the current ΔI_g.

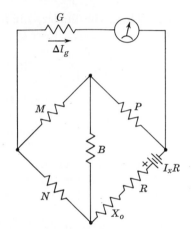

FIG. 10-2. Compensation theorem applied to Wheatstone bridge.

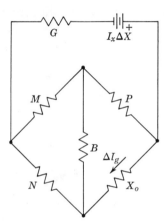

FIG. 10-3. Reciprocity theorem applied to circuit of Fig. 10-2.

It is known from the reciprocity theorem that if, in Fig. 10-2, the emf $I_x R$ in branch X produces a current ΔI_g in branch G, then this emf when placed in branch G, will produce the same current, ΔI_g, in branch X. The value of this theorem is now evident, for with ΔX neglected compared with X_0, the emf $I_x \Delta X$ in Fig. 10-3 is applied to a balanced bridge! Hence, the current through B is zero (within the approximation of this method), and any convenient value of B may be assigned for analysis purposes. To illustrate, let $B \to \infty$ in the circuit of Fig. 10-3, and ΔI_g may be immediately obtained by use of the current-splitting rule.

$$\Delta I_g = \frac{I_x \Delta X}{G + (M + P)(N + X_0)/S} \left[\frac{M + P}{S} \right] = \frac{I_x \Delta X (M + P)}{GS + (M + P)(N + X_0)}$$

$$(10\text{-}10)$$

The same result is found in the circuit of Fig. 10-3 with $B = 0$, or, indeed, with *any* value of B.   Moreover, Eq. (10-10) may also be obtained from Fig. 10-2 with $R = \Delta X$ neglected compared with X_0, for any value of B.

The approximate solution for ΔI_g is thus complete.   All that remains is to insert I_x from Eq. (10-9) into Eq. (10-10) and to manipulate it into best form.   Inserting I_x from Eq. (10-9) there results

$$\Delta I_g = \frac{E(M + N)(M + P)\,\Delta X}{[BS + (M + N)(P + X_0)][GS + (M + P)(N + X_0)]} \quad (10\text{-}11)$$

Divide numerator and denominator by $(M + N)(M + P)$ and use the relations

$$\frac{S}{M + N} = 1 + \frac{P}{M} \qquad \frac{S}{M + P} = 1 + \frac{N}{M} \qquad (10\text{-}12)$$

which are proved readily from $MX_0 = NP$.   Then, the final result for ΔI_g is

$$\Delta I_g = \frac{E\,\Delta X}{[B(1 + P/M) + P + X_0][G(1 + N/M) + N + X_0]} \quad (10\text{-}13)$$

This result agrees with Eq. (10-7), obtained from the general solution for I_g.   The term that has been lost by the approximate use of the compensation theorem may be seen in Eq. (10-6) and is the denominator factor $1 + kR = 1 + k\,\Delta X$.   The error of the approximate result in Eq. (10-13), from the proof in Chap. 2, is at most equal to $\Delta I_g\,(\Delta X/X_0)$. For example, if ΔX is a 1 per cent change in X_0, then the galvanometer current given in Eq. (10-13) cannot differ by more than 1 per cent, and usually less, from the exact current.

In applying the compensation theorem to bridge-circuit arms, it is unnecessary to go through the reasoning concerning the handling of B, having done so once.   Henceforth, B may be omitted in the compensation circuit, and the circuit solved directly for the small change in current produced by the compensation emf.

The compensation theorem is, of course, not restricted to X, but may be applied to any changed resistance.   Two trivial applications are interesting because they show that balance is not upset by a change in B or G, which must be so because the balance equation $MX_0 = NP$ is independent of B and G.   In the case of a change in B to $B + \Delta B$, the compensation emf in series with $B + \Delta B$ is $I_b\,\Delta B$, where I_b is the battery current at bridge balance.   This emf is applied to a balanced bridge (without approximation) and therefore produces zero ΔI_g.   In the case of a change in G to $G + \Delta G$, the compensation emf in series with $G + \Delta G$ is $I_g\,\Delta G$, where I_g is the galvanometer current at bridge balance, which is zero. Hence, the compensation emf is zero, and there is no change in any of the bridge currents.

10-5. Compensation Theorem Example. A Wheatstone bridge in which $B = 100$ ohms, $N = 100$ ohms, $M = 200$ ohms, $P = 300$ ohms, $G = 200$ ohms, and $E = 28$ volts is balanced. Then X_0 is changed by 4 per cent. Compute the galvanometer current.

The solution will be obtained directly by use of the approximate form of the compensation theorem, and then checked against the exact solution. Products of resistances in opposite arms must be equal at balance, so $X_0 = 150$ ohms. The battery current at balance (see Fig. 10-4a) is determined by the 100-ohm battery resistance in series with 300 ohms and 450 ohms in shunt, a total equivalent series resistance of 280 ohms. Hence, $I_b = 28/280 = 0.1$ amp. Using a current-splitting factor of $300/750 = 0.4$, the current through X_0 at balance is $I_x = 40$ ma.

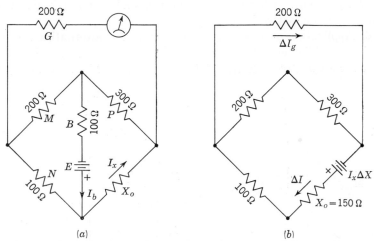

(a)   (b)

FIG. 10-4. Compensation theorem applied to unbalanced bridge.

If X_0 is changed by 4 per cent, $\Delta X = 0.04(150) = 6$ ohms. Therefore, the compensation emf shown in Fig. 10-4b is $0.04(6) = 0.24$ volt. The equivalent resistance across the compensation emf consists of two series-connected resistors of 100 ohms and 150 ohms each, and an equivalent resistance of 143 ohms (500 ohms in shunt with $G = 200$ ohms). The total series resistance is thus 393 ohms. Note that the battery resistance, B, has been omitted. Hence, the current drawn from the 0.24-volt emf is $\Delta I = 0.24/393 = 0.61$ ma. Five-sevenths of this current passes through G. Hence, $\Delta I_g = 0.436$ ma.

Application of the compensation theorem reduces the problem to a series of minor calculations, when numerical results are sought. The solution $\Delta I_g = 0.436$ ma is approximate, but cannot be in error by more than 4 per cent, i.e., by more than 0.0174 ma. This may be checked numerically by substitution of all given numbers into the exact formula,

Eq. (10-6). The value of k is

$$k = \frac{200(500) + 200(700)}{200(700)(550)} = \frac{240}{200(385)} = 0.00312$$

Since $R = \Delta X = 6$ ohms, then $kR = 0.0187$ and is small compared with 1 so the approximation is seen to be good. Using this value of kR in Eq. (10-6), the exact change in current is given by

$$\Delta I_g = \frac{28}{385 \times 10^3} \left[\frac{6}{1.0187} \right] = \frac{0.436}{1.0187} = 0.429 \text{ ma}$$

The approximate solution is seen to be 0.007 ma (1.6 per cent) higher than the exact solution, and this error is less than half the maximum possible error of 4 per cent. (Note that the approximate answer is given in the numerator of the last ratio for ΔI_g.)

10-6. Application of Thévenin's Theorem. An alternative method of analysis using Thévenin's theorem may be used to find the galvanometer current for an unbalanced Wheatstone bridge. While an exact solution

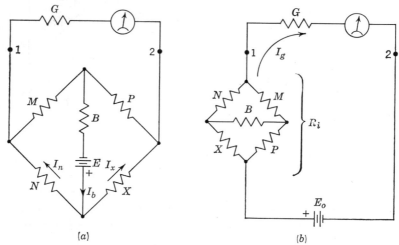

FIG. 10-5. Application of Thévenin's theorem.

may be obtained by use of this theorem, as is also true in the case of the compensation theorem if R is not neglected in the circuit of Fig. 10-2, an approximate solution is simpler. The approximate result using Thévenin's theorem agrees with that obtained by use of the compensation theorem.

Remove the galvanometer of resistance G from the two terminals 1-2 of Fig. 10-5a, for which the Thévenin equivalent circuit will be found. The open-circuit voltage, E_0, considered a voltage rise from terminal 2 to terminal 1, is given by $XI_x - NI_n$, where I_x and I_n are the branch currents through X and N, respectively, with G removed. The current I_x is given by Eq. (10-9) with X_0 replaced by X, and I_n may be obtained in exactly similar fashion.

$$I_n = \frac{E(P + X)}{B(M + N + P + X) + (M + N)(P + X)}$$

This has the same denominator as I_x. The difference in the numerator of E_0 will, therefore, be

$$E[X(M + N) - N(P + X)] = E(MX - NP)$$

Hence, $\quad E_0 = \dfrac{E(MX - NP)}{B(M + N + P + X) + (M + N)(P + X)} \qquad (10\text{-}14)$

The open-circuit voltage is clearly zero at bridge balance ($MX_0 = NP$).

The Thévenin equivalent resistance, R_i, is the input resistance at terminals 1-2 with $E = 0$. It may be represented as shown in Fig. 10-5b. An expression for R_i may be obtained by using a T-to-Pi transformation. The galvanometer current is given by

$$I_g = \frac{E_0}{R_i + G} \qquad (10\text{-}15)$$

where E_0 is given in Eq. (10-14). This is an exact solution, but the expression for R_i is required.

If the bridge is only slightly unbalanced, then $X = X_0 + \Delta X$, and Eq. (10-14) becomes approximately

$$E_0 = \frac{EM \,\Delta X}{BS + (M + N)(P + X_0)} \qquad (10\text{-}16)$$

where X_0 has been used rather than $X + \Delta X$ in the insensitive denominator, but in the numerator the ΔX portion of X has been retained. This is justified because the denominator of Eq. (10-14) is affected very little by a small change in X, but in the range where MX and NP are nearly equal, the numerator is very sensitive to a small change in X.

The input resistance, R_i, may be readily found for the slightly unbalanced bridge. If the bridge in Fig. 10-5b that comprises R_i is nearly balanced, the voltage across B will be very nearly zero. The value of B will, accordingly, have little influence on R_i. With ΔX neglected compared with X_0, this approximation is the same as that employed when using the reciprocity theorem in Fig. 10-3. Thus, any convenient value of B may be used to evaluate R_i. Either $B = 0$ or $B \to \infty$ is a satisfactory choice, and both give the same result for R_i. With $B \to \infty$,

$$R_i = \frac{(M + P)(N + X_0)}{S} \qquad (10\text{-}17)$$

The change in galvanometer current from its balance value of zero will now be small. Call it ΔI_g. Then, insert E_0 from Eq. (10-16) and R_i from Eq. (10-17) into Eq. (10-15).

$$\Delta I_g = \frac{EM \, \Delta X}{BS + (M + N)(P + X_0)} \left[\frac{1}{G + (M + P)(N + X_0)/S} \right]$$
$$= \frac{EMS \, \Delta X}{[BS + (M + N)(P + X_0)][GS + (M + P)(N + X_0)]} \quad (10\text{-}18)$$

This agrees exactly with the result obtained by the compensation theorem in Eq. (10-11), since $MS = (M + N)(M + P)$ as indicated in Eq. (10-12).

Thévenin's theorem may be applied directly to bridge circuits without regard to formulas that have been developed, as was done in the compensation theorem example of Sec. 10-5. However, computational difficulties may be encountered in determining E_0 for the slightly unbalanced bridge, unless careful techniques are employed. To appreciate fully the importance of this factor, attempt to solve the example of Sec. 10-5 by use of Thévenin's theorem. If $B = 0$, the complications are alleviated somewhat, but E_0 is still a small difference between two nearly equal large numbers. When using Thévenin's theorem to find ΔI_g, one could resort to the formula, Eq. (10-16), to obtain E_0. This has the considerable disadvantage of requiring a correlation between symbols used here and those of the given bridge and may result in a severe notation tangle. Because of the computational difficulty with E_0, use of the compensation theorem, dealing directly with the changes of interest, is advocated. However, Thévenin's theorem might be useful in cases where the resistance, R_i, presented by the bridge to the galvanometer is of primary interest.

10-7. Galvanometer Sensitivity Limitations. The sensitivity of the galvanometer may be expressed in terms of the smallest current that produces an observable deviation from a zero reading, as discussed in Sec. 9-9. The least discernible deflection associated with this current is typically about one-tenth of a scale division. The unobservable deviation from zero of the galvanometer current contributes an error in the determination of the unknown resistance, X. This error is combined with those traceable to uncertainties in the three known arms of the bridge.

If two arms of the Wheatstone bridge are fixed, the third arm may be adjusted to attain bridge balance for a given value of X. Small changes in the adjustment, above and below the value required for $I_g = 0$, may not produce observable deflections. This uncertainty in the adjustment of one of the arms may be expressed directly in terms of the corresponding uncertainty in X_0 by the same analysis device used previously. For purposes of analysis, let all three arms be fixed and consider X to be variable.   When X_0 is changed by a small amount, to $X_0 + dX$, such that the least discernible current, dI_g, is produced, then dI_g may be related directly to dX.

The least discernible galvanometer deflection is usually produced by a very small percentage change in the bridge arm.   This is deliberately arranged by the user of the bridge to avoid excessive errors from this source.   Consequently, the error in the approximate result obtained by use of the compensation theorem, Eq. (10-13), is negligible under these conditions, and it may be used to express dI_g in terms of dX.   Similarly, the exact result, Eq. (10-6), may be used with $R = dX$ and with the factor $1 + k\,dX$ replaced by 1.   Therefore, the error, dX, in X_0 attributable to the least discernible galvanometer current, dI_g, is given by

$$dX = \frac{dI_g}{E}\left[B\left(1 + \frac{P}{M}\right) + P + X_0 \right]\left[G\left(1 + \frac{N}{M}\right) + N + X_0 \right] \quad (10\text{-}19)$$

solving either Eqs. (10-13), (10-6), or (10-7) explicitly for dX.   This expression may be divided by X_0 to obtain the fractional error in X_0. Equation (10-19) is, of course, subject to $MX_0 = NP$ which may be used to eliminate X_0 wherever desired.

As a simple illustration, suppose all resistances are equal to $X_0 = 1,000$ ohms, and $E = 16$ volts.   Then

$$dX = 16X_0{}^2\frac{dI_g}{E} = 10^6\,dI_g$$

If the least discernible galvanometer current is 1 μa, it will result in an error of 0.1 per cent in the determination of X_0 in this case.   A more sensitive galvanometer will result in a smaller error from this source.

10-8. Bridge Current Limitations.   The error in the determination of X_0 resulting from limited galvanometer sensitivity is inversely proportional to the battery emf, E, as shown in Eq. (10-19).   Hence, the error in X_0 may be reduced by increasing E.   Theoretically, allowing E to approach infinity will reduce the error traceable to galvanometer sensitivity to zero.   There is, however, an upper practical limit beyond which dX may not be reduced by this means.

The practical limitation often arises from the maximum allowable current in the bridge arms.   This may be a severe limitation because accurately known resistors cannot tolerate excessive current without overheating and becoming unstable.   Therefore, the value of E must be restricted accordingly.   Currents through the bridge arms $M + N$ and $P + X$ are generally unequal at balance.   The resistor with the smallest current-handling capability places an upper limit on the maximum allowable current delivered to the entire bridge from E.   Hence, the maximum battery current, I_{bm}, rather than the maximum battery emf is the pertinent quantity. This same current may be provided by an infinite number of different combinations of E and B.

Examination of Eq. (10-19) shows that as B is reduced and E increased, without exceeding I_{bm}, the error dX is reduced. With $B = 0$ the most favorable conditions exist, and with E at the maximum permissible value, the minimum error in X_0 becomes

$$dX_{\min} = \frac{dI_g}{E_{\max}} (P + X_0) \left[G\left(1 + \frac{N}{M}\right) + N + X_0 \right] \qquad B = 0 \qquad (10\text{-}20)$$

This error is reduced even further, the smaller the resistance, G, of the galvanometer. Equation (10-20) may be expressed directly in terms of I_{bm}. If $B = 0$, and E is at its maximum permissible value, then the current supplied to the bridge is at its maximum permissible value. It consists of two components, one through $M + N$ and one through $P + X_0$.

$$I_{bm} = \frac{E_{\max}}{M + N} + \frac{E_{\max}}{P + X_0} = \frac{SE_{\max}}{(M + N)(P + X_0)} = \frac{(M + P)E_{\max}}{M(P + X_0)}$$

Insert this value of $E_{\max}$ into Eq. (10-20).

$$dX_{\min} = \frac{dI_g(1 + P/M)[G(1 + N/M) + N + X_0]}{I_{bm}} \qquad (10\text{-}21)$$

This result, expressed in terms of the fixed value I_{bm}, does not contain E or B. It shows clearly that an increase in E with the corresponding increase in B required to avoid exceeding the maximum permissible current, I_{bm}, cannot affect $dX_{\min}$.

10-9. Accurate Range of Fixed Bridge. For a given Wheatstone bridge, the error in the determination of the value of an unknown resistance, X_0, depends upon the value of X_0. For instance, in the special case given in Sec. 10-7, dX depended upon $X_0{}^2$. In general, there is a considerable range of high attainable accuracy, but the uncertainty in the determination of X_0 becomes excessive if X_0 is too small or too large in a given bridge.

Consider a specific Wheatstone bridge with fixed ratio arms M and P, with a given galvanometer of least discernible current dI_g and resistance G, and a fixed battery circuit of resistance B and emf E. This bridge may be used to measure different values of X_0 by adjusting N to satisfy the balance equation, $MX_0 = NP$. The error, ΔX, for any X_0 may be expressed in terms of all the fixed parameters and X_0. If ΔX is reasonably small compared with X_0, it is given by Eq. (10-19).

$$\Delta X = \frac{dI_g}{E} \left[B\left(1 + \frac{P}{M}\right) + P + X_0 \right] \left[G\left(1 + \frac{N}{M}\right) + N + X_0 \right]$$

Since N is a dependent variable, it may be replaced by $X_0 M / P$. Then, after algebraic manipulation and collecting like terms in X_0, there results

$$\Delta X = \frac{dI_g}{EMP} (BM + BP + MP + MX_0)[GP + X_0(G + M + P)]$$

All quantities in this relationship are fixed by the bridge, except X_0. Define

$$K = BM + BP + MP \qquad C = G + M + P$$

Expand the compound product, divide both sides of the equation by X_0, and obtain

$$\delta = \frac{\Delta X}{X_0} = \frac{dI_g}{EMP} \left(CMX_0 + KC + MGP + \frac{KGP}{X_0} \right) \qquad (10\text{-}22)$$

This final result shows the way in which δ, the fractional error in X_0, depends upon the value of X_0 for a given bridge in which the battery circuit is connected to the junction of the adjustable and unknown arms. (If P had been taken as the adjustable arm, a different result would have been obtained. With P adjustable, then for small values of X_0, P would also have to be small and the battery current through X_0 would be limited only by B as $X_0 \to 0$. With N adjustable, the fixed arms, M and P, limit the battery current even when $X_0 = 0$.)

Inspection of Eq. (10-22) reveals a very interesting behavior. For very large values of X_0, the fractional error, δ, will soar owing to the CMX_0 term. On the other hand, for very small values of X_0, δ again will increase owing to the KGP/X_0 term. Therefore, there must be some value of X_0 between these extremes where δ is a minimum. This value of X_0 may be found by setting the derivative of δ with respect to X_0 equal to zero. Thus,

$$\frac{d\delta}{dX_0} = CM - \frac{KGP}{X_0{}^2} = 0$$

Hence, the fractional error in X_0 is a minimum when

$$X_0 = \sqrt{\frac{KGP}{CM}} \qquad (10\text{-}23)$$

The minimum error, obtained by inserting this value of X_0 into Eq. (10-22), is

$$\delta_{\min} = \frac{dI_g}{EMP} (\sqrt{KC} + \sqrt{MGP})^2 \qquad (10\text{-}24)$$

For a numerical illustration, suppose the fixed resistance values are $P = M = G = R$, and $B = R/2$. Then $K = 2R^2$, $C = 3R$, the value of X_0 for minimum error is $0.815R$, and the minimum fractional error is

These two sensitivities may be compared with $V_a = V_b$ by forming the ratio of s_1 to s_2. Then

$$\frac{s_1}{s_2} = \frac{(M + P)(N + X_0)[GS + (P + X_0)(M + N)]}{(M + N)(P + X_0)[GS + (N + X_0)(M + P)]}$$

This rather awkward result may be simplified by dividing numerator and denominator by the common product of four factors, and then using the relations in Eq. (10-12).

$$\frac{s_1}{s_2} = \frac{1 + G(M + P)/M(P + X_0)}{1 + G(M + N)/M(N + X_0)} \qquad (10\text{-}27)$$

This result shows that if $G = 0$, $s_1 = s_2$. Also, if $N = P$, then $s_1 = s_2$

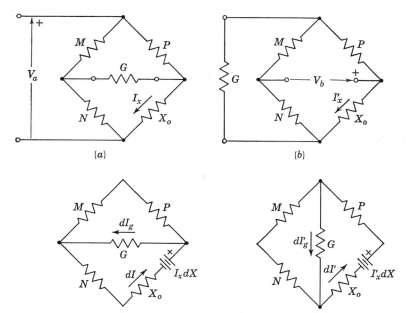

Fig. 10-7. Comparison of interchanged generator and detector.

for any G whether $M > X_0$ or $M < X_0$. Moreover, if

$$\frac{M + P}{P + X_0} > \frac{M + N}{N + X_0}$$

then $s_1 > s_2$ for any $G \neq 0$. This requires both $N > P$, $M > X_0$, or both $N < P$, $M < X_0$. Therefore, in a bridge with two high-resistance arms connected to one junction, and two low-resistance arms connected to the opposite junction, greater sensitivity is obtained with the galvanometer connected from the high-resistance junction to the low-resistance junction. The conclusions based on Eq. (10-27) are, of course, valid only for equal voltage, $V_a = V_b$, applied to the bridge in both cases with all other parameters constant.

If, instead, the current I_x is maintained constant for the two arrangements, other conclusions are found. In case (a), $I_x = V_a/(P + X_0)$ so s_1 is given by Eq. (10-25) with $V_a/(P + X_0)$ replaced by I_x.

$$s_1 = \frac{I_x(M + P)}{GS + (N + X_0)(M + P)} = \frac{I_x}{GS/(M + P) + N + X_0}$$

In case (b), $I_x = V_b/(N + X_0)$, where V_b is selected to maintain the same I_x. So, s_2 is given by Eq. (10-26) with $V_b/(N + X_0)$ replaced by the same I_x as in case (a).

$$s_2 = \frac{I_x(M + N)}{GS + (P + X_0)(M + N)} = \frac{I_x}{GS/(M + N) + P + X_0}$$

The ratio of these two sensitivities, in which I_x cancels, becomes, with the use of Eq. (10-12),

$$\frac{s_1}{s_2} = \frac{G(M + P) + M(P + X_0)}{G(M + N) + M(N + X_0)} \tag{10-28}$$

This result shows that for $N = P$, $s_1 = s_2$ for all G whether $M > X_0$ or $M < X_0$. This is the same conclusion as in the case of constant voltage. However, if $N > P$, $s_1 < s_2$ for all G, including $G = 0$, and this is far different from the constant-voltage case.

It should be no surprise to find that results depend upon conditions imposed. Yet, conditions are frequently overlooked in the zeal of applying results. A similar situation exists in the simple case of maximum power transfer from an emf, E, of internal resistance r to a load resistance, R. The result $R = r$ for maximum power transfer to R is often stated with little regard for the conditions under which the result holds; namely, E and r fixed, and R variable. If the conditions are changed, so is the result. For instance, if E and R are fixed and r is varied, maximum power transfer to R occurs not when $r = R$ but when $r = 0$.

10-11. Decade-box Techniques. Accurate adjustable resistors usually consist of switched or plug-in arrangements of resistance coils, to provide definite resistance settings. Switch-type decade-resistance boxes are used widely. The input resistance to the two terminals of the box may be varied in small equal steps over the entire range of the box. A circuit of one type of box, employing series coils, is shown in Fig. 10-8.

With two fixed ratio arms, M and N, the decade box may be used for P to balance the Wheatstone bridge of Fig. 10-8. Rheostat B is used to maintain the current in the bridge arms within the allowable ratings of M, N, P, and X. Usually a null cannot be observed in the circuit of Fig. 10-8 if there is ample galvanometer sensitivity. This is not a serious limitation in using the bridge, as will be shown, and the inability to obtain a null suggests several interesting experimental possibilities.

To illustrate, suppose P is adjusted to a value P_1, and the galvanometer displays a small deflection of $+d_1$ divisions. Then, with P increased by the smallest available step to $P_1 + r$, the observed deflection is on the other side of zero, $-d_2$ divisions. Clearly, the bridge would balance at some value of P between these two settings, but the requisite value of P is unattainable with this box. However, the balance value of P may be calculated by linear interpolation. This is justified for small bridge

Decade resistance box

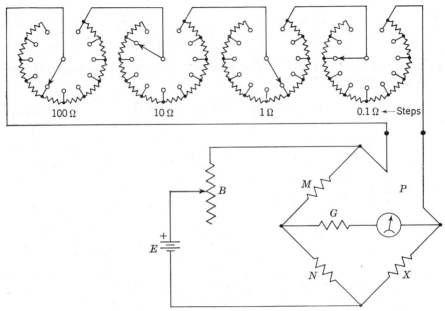

FIG. 10-8. Decade box in Wheatstone bridge.

unbalance because ΔI_g is directly proportional to a change in X when the change is only a small percentage of X, and the same applies for P. The two galvanometer deflections differ by a total of $d_1 + d_2$ divisions. Hence, the value of P required for balance, obtained by linear interpolation as shown in Fig. 10-9, is

$$P = P_1 + \frac{rd_1}{d_1 + d_2} \qquad (10\text{-}29)$$

The unknown X is given by N/M times this interpolated value of P. Interpolation is used frequently in bridge work and is not subject to serious instrument error because most galvanometers are very nearly linear in the range close to zero reading. Moreover, the interpolation is meaningful only within the limits of uncertainty of the decade box itself. With ample galvanometer sensitivity, the instrument errors become negligible compared with the decade-box uncertainty.

These same data may be used to determine the fractional error in the determination of X owing to limited galvanometer sensitivity. Suppose the least discernible deflection is 0.1 scale division. Then, in the preceding example, where $d_1 + d_2$ corresponds to a change r, the calculable resistance change in P corresponding to the least discernible deflection is $0.1r/(d_1 + d_2)$ ohms. For example, let $d_1 + d_2 = 5$ divisions and $r = 0.1$ ohm. Then if P could be changed by 0.02 ohm it would produce a total change of 1 division, and a change in P of 0.002 ohm would produce a barely discernible change in deflection of 0.1 division. The corresponding change in X may be found by multiplying this minimum discernible change in P by N/M since $M \Delta X = N \Delta P$.

Finally, if all resistances in the entire bridge circuit are known, and if E is known, the galvanometer current ΔI_g may be computed for the change, r, in P_1. The compensation theorem would lead quickly to the value of ΔI_g. The current

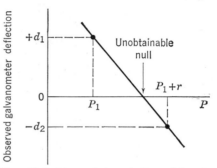

FIG. 10-9. Linear interpolation of decade settings.

sensitivity of the galvanometer is then obtained by dividing the known deflection change, $d_1 + d_2$, by the corresponding calculated value of ΔI_g.

10-12. Slide-wire Bridge. A slide-wire resistance may be incorporated in a Wheatstone bridge as shown in Fig. 10-10. The slide-wire of resistance $r = m + n$ may be wound on a circular drum, as suggested schematically in Fig. 10-10, or may take the rectilinear form shown in the slide-wire potentiometer of Fig. 9-8. The balance equation of this bridge is obtained by equating products of resistances in opposite arms.

$$X(M + m) = P(N + n) \qquad (10\text{-}30)$$

The fixed resistors, M and N, called *extensions*, may be used to control the total effective range of the slide-wire. If $M = 0 = N$, the unknown resistance, X, of the *simple* slide-wire bridge is, from Eq. (10-30),

$$X = \frac{n}{m} P = \frac{n}{r - n} P \qquad (10\text{-}31)$$

The ratio $n/(r - n)$ may be determined from the scale associated with a uniform slide-wire.

An interesting technique for improving the accuracy of the determination of X is to interchange X and P and to rebalance the bridge. Then X may be computed from the *change* in slider location required to balance the bridge in the two cases. Let d be the increase in m required to rebalance the bridge when X and P are interchanged. Then, n must change to $n - d$. The second balance condition is

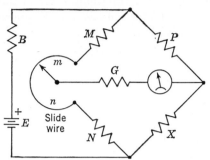

FIG. 10-10. Slide-wire bridge.

$$P(M + m + d) = X(N + n - d)$$

The total resistance of the slide-wire with extensions is

$$R = M + N + r$$

and this remains constant. The ratio X/P for the initial balance, given by Eq. (10-30), must be the same as for the second balance. Hence,

$$\frac{X}{P} = \frac{N + n}{R - (N + n)} = \frac{R - (N + n) + d}{(N + n) - d} \qquad (10\text{-}32)$$

It may be shown from this equation that

$$N + n = \frac{1}{2}(R + d)$$

Therefore,
$$\frac{X}{P} = \frac{R + d}{R - d} = \frac{1 + d/R}{1 - d/R} \qquad (10\text{-}33)$$

The technique of interchanging X and P is especially valuable when X and P are nearly equal. Then the resistance d, which is equal to the resistance of the slide-wire between the two balance settings, is very small compared with R.

When the slide-wire bridge is unbalanced by changing the slide-wire adjustment, an interesting analysis problem is posed, because a double unbalance is created in the bridge. A similar effect was found in the case of the potentiometer. If the slider is changed from balance so as to increase m to $m + \Delta m$, then n *must* change to $n - \Delta m$. A little thought shows that both of these changes act in concert to produce galvanometer current in the same direction. It follows that this is a more sensitive adjustment than when only one arm of the bridge is varied. For this reason, the slide-wire bridge is sometimes used in servomechanism error-measuring devices, in which case the slider is geared to the shaft of a positioning motor.

The compensation theorem may be applied to find the galvanometer current that results from a change in slider position from balance. A general analysis in terms of symbols is too unwieldy to present here. Instead, consider the numerical case of $E = 24$ volts, $P = 1,000$ ohms, $X = 1,500$ ohms, $M = 950$ ohms, $N = 1,450$ ohms, $r = 100$ ohms, $B = 750$ ohms, and $G = 300$ ohms. These values are all given in Fig. 10-11a. Clearly, $m = n = 50$ ohms for the initial balance. The total current drawn from the battery is determined by B in series with the parallel combination of $P + X$ and $M + N + r$, a total resistance of 2,000 ohms. Hence, with $E = 24$ volts, the battery current is 12 ma. By use of the current-splitting rule, it is seen that one-half of this current passes through r. Thus, the current through M, N, and r at balance is $I_r = 6$ ma. Now let m change by Δm; then n must change by $-\Delta m$. The resulting change in galvanometer current, ΔI_g, will be produced by the compensation emf's shown in Fig. 10-11b, where $\Delta m = -\Delta n$

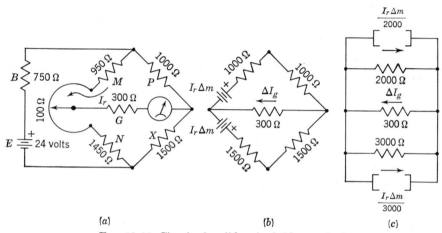

(a)   (b)   (c)

FIG. 10-11. Circuits for slide-wire bridge analysis.

have been neglected compared with M and N, respectively, and B has been removed. None of these steps introduces an appreciable error if Δm is a small percentage change of $M + m$ and $N + n$. Convert the voltage generators to current generators as indicated in Fig. 10-11c. The current generator associated with m produces a current 3 Δm μa (with Δm in ohms), since $I_r = 6$ ma. The current generator associated with n produces a current 2 Δm μa. Since the galvanometer is shunted by an equivalent resistance of 1,200 ohms, the fraction $1,200/1,500 = 0.8$ of the total current entering the galvanometer node passes through the galvanometer, the rest being bypassed in the shunt resistors. Thus

$$\Delta I_g = 0.8(2 \Delta m + 3 \Delta m) = 4 \Delta m \ \mu a$$

For example, if Δm is a 0.1 per cent change in r, then $\Delta m = 0.1$ ohm, and $\Delta I_g = 0.4$ μa.

This is more galvanometer current than would be produced if only one arm, say N, were changed by $\Delta N = 0.1$ ohm, for then the current generator associated with m would become zero while the compensation emf in series with N would become $I_r \, \Delta N$. Evidently, the galvanometer current that would be produced (starting with a balanced bridge) by a 0.1-ohm change in N will be only 0.16 μa.

From another point of view, an increase in N to $N + \Delta N$ may be determined to offset the change in galvanometer current produced by Δm. The change ΔN is greater than Δm. The magnitude of this change may be found by superimposing a current generator of 5 Δm μa directed oppositely to those shown in Fig. 10-11c, in order to nullify the galvanometer current. This current generator must also be equal to 2 ΔN μa. Therefore, $\Delta N = 2.5 \, \Delta m$. The versatility of the compensation theorem and the insight it provides are well demonstrated by these examples.

10-13. Limit Bridge. Another application of the slide-wire bridge may be seen by examining Eq. (10-30) under conditions of extreme settings of the slider. When the slider is moved from one extreme position ($n = r$, $m = 0$) to the other extreme position ($n = 0$, $m = r$), the corresponding balance values of X are, respectively,

$$X_1 = \frac{N + r}{M} P \qquad X_2 = \frac{N}{M + r} P \tag{10-34}$$

The difference between the two values of X for which bridge balance is attainable using slider adjustment is then

$$X_1 - X_2 = \left(\frac{N + r}{M} - \frac{N}{M + r} \right) P = \frac{r(N + M + r)P}{M(M + r)} \tag{10-35}$$

The range $X_1 - X_2$ may be established for a given slide-wire by suitable choice of N, M, and P. Thus, the slide-wire bridge may be used as a *limit bridge*. A large group of resistors to be selected within the tolerance $X_1 - X_2$ may be installed consecutively in the X arm. If bridge balance is unattainable with complete traverse of the slider, the resistor being tested falls outside the prescribed limits. If balance is achieved, the value of X is read directly from a resistance scale provided alongside the slide-wire.

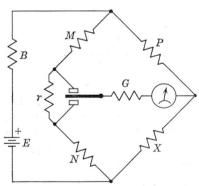

FIG. 10-12. Limit bridge.

A more rapid sorting procedure is possible if the actual value of X is not desired. The slide-wire may be replaced by the two-position key and resistor r, shown in Fig. 10-12. If the galvanometer deflection reverses upon flipping the key from one position to the other, then X falls within the range $X_1 - X_2$. Design equations will be developed for the special case of $M = N$. Let $r = kM$, where k is any constant. Then Eq. (10-35) becomes

$$X_1 - X_2 = \frac{k(2 + k)P}{1 + k}$$

Also, the value of X that is halfway between X_1 and X_2 is obtained from Eq. (10-34).

$$\bar{X} = \frac{X_1 + X_2}{2} = \frac{P}{2}\left(1 + k + \frac{1}{1 + k}\right) = \frac{P(2 + 2k + k^2)}{2(1 + k)} \quad (10\text{-}36)$$

Consequently, the symmetrical fractional limits of error, $\pm\delta$, of $\bar{X}$ are given by

$$\delta = \frac{X_1 - X_2}{X_1 + X_2} = \frac{k(2 + k)}{2 + 2k + k^2} \quad (10\text{-}37)$$

In solving this explicitly for k, the following quadratic equation appears:

$$k^2 + 2k - \frac{2\delta}{1 - \delta} = 0$$

The physically significant positive root is

$$k = -1 + \sqrt{1 + \frac{2\delta}{1 - \delta}} = -1 + \left(1 + \frac{\delta}{1 - \delta} + \cdots\right) = \frac{\delta}{1 - \delta} + \cdots$$

Clearly, if $\delta \ll 1$, then $k \approx \delta$. Thus, if tolerance limits of ± 1 per cent are desired, then $\delta = 0.01$ (which is much less than 1), $k = 0.01$, and $r = 0.01\,M$. Also, if δ and k are small, then $\bar{X}$ and P are essentially equal and $P = \bar{X}$ may be installed in the bridge arm. However, it should be noted that if δ is not negligible compared with 1, then k is larger than δ. Also, $\bar{X}$ is larger than P if k^2 is not negligible compared with $2(1 + k)$. In this case, a value of P that is smaller than $\bar{X}$ must be installed in the bridge arm if the total tolerance, $X_1 - X_2$, is to be centered on $\bar{X}$.

10-14. Kelvin Double Bridge. The precision measurement of resistances less than about 1 ohm presents several problems not encountered with high resistances. One of the difficulties is caused by the contacts between the resistor and its connecting wires. The resistance of the contacts may be on the order of 0.0001 ohm, which might be neglected for a 100-ohm resistor, but constitutes a significant portion of a very low resistance. For instance, it would be intolerable in a 50-mv 50-amp shunt that has a resistance of approximately 0.001 ohm. Moreover, contact resistance is a highly variable entity, depending upon such factors as mechanical pressure of the contact and physical condition of the contacting surfaces. Another difficulty is presented by the resistance of the connecting wires themselves, which cannot be neglected when dealing with low resistance. Such factors as these have led to the development of the four-terminal resistor, indicated in Fig. 10-13. This construction is used for such devices as ammeter shunts and for low-resistance precision standards. The outer pair of terminals provide the current connection, and the inner pair are the terminals across which the useful resistance is presented. The resistance between the voltage terminals does not include the lead resistance of the current-carrying circuit and is unaffected by the contact resistance at the current terminals. Furthermore, the resistance of the circuit connected to the voltage terminals is relatively high and does not draw appreciable current, so the contact resistance of the voltage terminals is negligible.

The Wheatstone bridge is not satisfactory for the measurement of low values of two-terminal resistors because of the lead and contact resistance

Voltage terminals

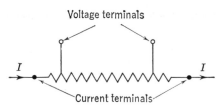

FIG. 10-13. Four-terminal resistor.

effects, mentioned above. If four-terminal resistors are used, as in Fig. 10-14, difficulties still remain. The high-resistance ratio arms, M and N, of this bridge circuit are fixed, P is an adjustable four-terminal resistance standard, and X is an unknown four-terminal resistance. Practically all the battery current, which is usually on the order of 10 amp to achieve adequate sensitivity, passes through X and P; hence, the connection J must be capable of carrying large currents. While the contact and lead resistances of the current terminals of X and P do not enter the bridge arms directly, there is a problem in deciding which galvanometer connection to use at the junction of X and P. The connection between voltage terminals A and B, no matter how short, contributes lead resistance that enters the bridge arms. Further, the resistances behind terminals A and B, leading into the taps on X and P, respectively, are not necessarily equal. Let $r = r_1 + r_2$ represent the total resistance of the "short circuit" joining X and P, and suppose that the galvanometer connection may be varied over r. The balance condition for the bridge is obtained by imposing $I_g = 0$, which means zero voltage across G. Hence, the currents through M and N must be equal at balance. Call this current I_1.

Then

$$I_1N = IX + I_r r_1$$

where I is the current through X and I_r is the current through r (see Fig. 10-14). Similarly, for the other loop

$$I_1M = IP + I_r r_2$$

The ratio of these two equations is

$$\frac{N}{M} = \frac{IX + I_r r_1}{IP + I_r r_2}$$

Solve for X.

$$X = \frac{N}{M} P + \frac{r_2 I_r}{I}\left(\frac{N}{M} - \frac{r_1}{r_2}\right) \tag{10-38}$$

Although r_1 and r_2 are small and N and M are large, the difference in their ratios is not necessarily negligible compared with NP/M because

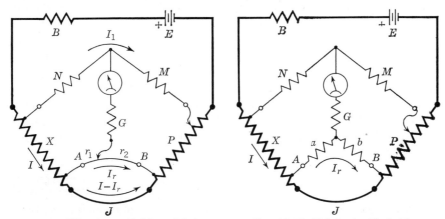

FIG. 10-14. Wheatstone bridge with four-terminal resistors.

FIG. 10-15. Kelvin double bridge.

P is very small. Also, there is no assurance that $r_2 I_r/I$ is small. Thus, it would appear that a precise value of X cannot be found entirely from N, M, and P. If some means could be devised to make $r_1/r_2 = N/M$, then X would be given by the Wheatstone-bridge balance equation, $X = NP/M$. However, this is not possible with the arrangement in Fig. 10-14, because r_1/r_2 is not known.

The Kelvin double bridge is a modification of the Wheatstone bridge that, in effect, reduces the second term of Eq. (10-38) to zero. Two resistances, a and b, very large compared with r, are connected between terminals A and B, and the galvanometer is connected to their junction as shown in Fig. 10-15. Then, the foregoing analysis applies for the balanced Kelvin bridge with r_1 replaced by a and r_2 replaced by b. Moreover, the current I_r is now much smaller than before and is given by the fraction $J/(J + a + b)$ times the current through X.

$$I_r = \frac{J}{a + b + J} I$$

Therefore, Eq. (10-38) becomes the balance equation for the Kelvin double bridge.

$$X = \frac{N}{M} P + \frac{Jb}{a + b + J} \left(\frac{N}{M} - \frac{a}{b} \right) \qquad (10\text{-}39)$$

Two important things have been accomplished. For one, the second term is under control and may be eliminated, in principle, by selecting a/b equal to N/M. Secondly, even if the equality of these ratios is not exactly satisfied, the multiplying factor $Jb/(a + b + J)$ may be made so small, by keeping J small and $a + b$ large, that X is still given very nearly by the simple Wheatstone-bridge balance equation, $X = NP/M$.

The term "double bridge" stems from the existence of essentially two bridges in the circuit of Fig. 10-15. One of them has been analyzed. The other may be seen by opening connection J. This reduces the current through X very markedly because $a + b$ is many orders of magnitude larger than $X + P$. (Opening J may produce severe arcing when interrupting a current that may be 10 amp or more, so it is good practice to reduce the current first by increasing B.) With J open, the balance condition is given simply by equating products of opposite bridge arms, since this is now a Wheatstone-bridge configuration.

$$N(b + P) = M(X + a) \qquad (10\text{-}40)$$

In practice, $a \gg X$ and $b \gg P$, so this balance equation is essentially $Nb = Ma$, which requires that N/M be equal to a/b. This is the same as the requirement on Eq. (10-39), if X is to be given in terms of N, M, and P only. It is interesting to note that if X and P are not neglected, Eq. (10-40) becomes, when solved for X,

$$X = \frac{N}{M} P + b \left(\frac{N}{M} - \frac{a}{b} \right)$$

So, again, if $N/M = a/b$, X is given by the same expression whether J is open or closed.

These equations indicate that if the bridge remains balanced with J either open or closed, then this gives direct experimental assurance that $N/M = a/b$. A ready check on the equality of the double ratio arms is thereby provided. If they are not equal, an adjustment of one of the ratios may be made with J open. In any event, it is desirable to provide as small a J as possible so as to ensure that the second term in Eq. (10-39) is negligible. Hence, the sliding contact of P is placed so that its unused portion is in series with B, rather than contributing to J.

10-15. Unbalanced Kelvin Bridge. The additional complexity of the "bridge within a bridge" would appear to pose a much more difficult analysis task in seeking the unbalanced galvanometer current. However, for small unbalance (which reveals pertinent information on bridge sensitivity and galvanometer errors) the compensation theorem remains an effective tool. The change in galvanometer current from zero resulting from a change in one of the bridge arms may be found without great difficulty, if full advantage is taken of the tremendous differences in order of magnitude of the resistances in the circuit.

An example in terms of a small change, ΔP, in the value of P required for balance will serve to illustrate the technique. The current, I, through P at balance is very nearly equal to

$$I = \frac{E}{B + P + J + X} \tag{10-41}$$

because N, M, a, and b are all very much larger than X, P, and J. In this equation, J includes the resistances of the end portions of X and P as well as the resistance of the connecting wire that joins them. Also, B includes the resistances of the end portions of X and P on the battery side, as well as any additional resistance used in series with E to control the current. In many cases B is also very large compared with P, J, and X. For instance, if $X = 0.001$ ohm and J is a short connection of heavy wire, then P is comparable in magnitude to X for M/N ratios usually used. Then if E is, say, 110 volts and the desired I is 20 amp, then B is about 5.5 ohms and is much greater than P, J, or X.

When P is changed from its balance value by a small amount, ΔP, the change ΔI_g in galvanometer current is produced by a compensation emf $I \Delta P$ acting in series with $P + \Delta P$, as shown in Fig. 10-16a. If ΔP is ignored compared with P, the resulting per cent error in ΔI_g will be less than the per cent change in P. The reciprocity theorem may be applied, as before, by "interchanging" $I \Delta P$ and ΔI_g, as shown in the circuit of Fig. 10-16b. Therefore, within the limits of approximation of neglecting ΔP compared with P, it is seen that B is connected across the diagonals of a balanced bridge, and therefore draws no current. Hence, B may be removed. Also note that resistors a and b are essentially in parallel because J is much less than a or b. Moreover, X and P may be ignored compared with N and M, respectively. With these approximations,

which are usually excellent, the circuit in Fig. 10-16c results.   This has
all been worthwhile because the solution for ΔI_g may now be written
immediately by use of the current-splitting rule.

$$\Delta I_g = \frac{I\ \Delta P}{G + ab/(a+b) + NM/(N+M)}\left[\frac{N}{N+M}\right] \qquad (10\text{-}42)$$

where I is known from Eq. (10-41).   The same result may be obtained,
if desired, by removing B from the circuit of Fig. 10-16a, neglecting ΔP
compared with P and using the other inequalities.

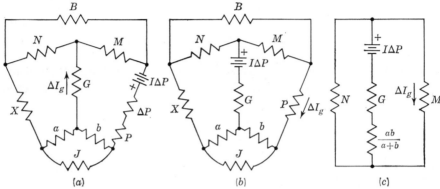

(a)   (b)   (c)

FIG. 10-16. Circuits for unbalanced Kelvin bridge analysis.

A much greater galvanometer sensitivity is required in the Kelvin
bridge than in the Wheatstone bridge for the same per cent accuracy in
the determination of the unknown X.   This is because X itself is so small.
A numerical example is revealing.   Suppose $M = N = a = b = 1{,}000$ ohms,
and $G = 500$ ohms.   Then, from Eq. (10-42)

$$\Delta I_g = \frac{I\ \Delta P}{3{,}000}$$

Now if $X = P = 0.0001$ ohm, which is by no means the smallest size
resistance that may be measured by the Kelvin bridge, and 0.3 per cent
accuracy is desired, then the galvanometer should be able to detect with
ease a current $\Delta I_g = I \times 10^{-10}$ amp.   Even with I as large as 50 amp,
this is a galvanometer current of only 0.005 μa, and this is not the most
severe case encountered with the Kelvin bridge.

Fortunately, the required galvanometer sensitivity is attainable.
There are commercially available galvanometers with sensitivities on the
order of 10^{-5} μa per scale division.   Such a galvanometer would receive
a considerable jolt from the above 0.3 per cent unbalance in P, since it
would deflect hundreds of scale divisions.

PROBLEMS

10-1 (§1). The circuit in Fig. 10-17 (which is basically a Wheatstone bridge) is used to find the location of a ground fault on an underground communications line A-B. The length of the line is 5.2 miles. A second line, C-D, having identical characteristics with the faulted line (except for the fault) is used to complete the circuit. Settings $R_a = 100$ ohms and $R_b = 41.2$ ohms produce zero galvanometer deflection. (a) How far from end A is the fault located? (b) R_a and R_b are decade boxes with limits of error ± 0.5 per cent of the dial reading. The galvanometer has ample sensitivity and the resistance per unit length of line is constant. What is the limit of error in the result of part (a) owing to the errors in R_a and R_b?

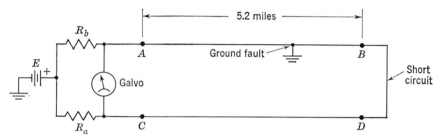

Fig. 10-17. Ground fault location.

10-2 (§4). Verify Eq. (10-12).

10-3 (§4). The Wheatstone bridge of Fig. 10-1 is initially balanced, and then M is changed to $M + dM$. Determine an algebraic expression for the resulting change in galvanometer current, by use of the compensation theorem.

10-4 (§5). Three arms of a Wheatstone bridge have resistances 100.0 ohms, and the resistance of the fourth arm is 100.1 ohms. A galvanometer of 50 ohms resistance and 0.09 μa per mm sensitivity is connected across one diagonal of the bridge. A battery of 3-volt emf is connected in series with a resistance of 200 ohms across the other diagonal. Find the deflection of the galvanometer.

10-5 (§5). In Prob. 9-23, assume all of the stated resistances are known exactly. Compute the maximum error in the measured value of galvanometer resistance if the minimum perceptible change in galvanometer deflection is 0.1 mm.

10-6 (§5). In Fig. 10-1, $E = 3$ volts, $B = 10$ ohms, and $G = 100$ ohms. The bridge is balanced when $M = N = 50$ ohms, and $P = 500$ ohms. (a) What is the value of X? (b) If the galvanometer sensitivity is 10 μa per mm, what per cent change in N will produce a deflection of 1 mm? (c) If galvanometer and battery branches are interchanged, what per cent change in N will produce a deflection of 1 mm? (d) What power is dissipated in N and M in each arrangement?

10-7 (§7). In the Wheatstone bridge of Fig. 10-1, $E = 1$ volt, and $B = 500$ ohms. The galvanometer has a resistance $G = 1,000$ ohms, a sensitivity 4 μa per mm, and a minimum discernible deflection of 0.2 mm. Resistors $M = 4,000$ ohms, $N = 2,000$ ohms, and $P = 1,000$ ohms are each known to within ± 10 ohms. (a) Which source of inaccuracy contributes most to the error in the determination of X (galvanometer sensitivity, M, N, or P)? (b) What is the error caused by the predominant source of inaccuracy?

10-8 (§9). All parameters in the bridge of Fig. 10-1 are fixed except P and X_0. This bridge is used to measure various values of X_0 by adjusting P. (a) Determine an expression for the fractional error in X_0 as a function of X_0 for $0 < X_0 < \infty$, in terms of the fixed bridge parameters. (b) Determine an expression for X_0 that results in minimum fractional error in X_0. (c) With $B = 0$, why doesn't $\Delta X/X_0$ increase as $X_0 \to 0$, as would be the case with N adjustable, and M and P fixed?

10-9 (§10). Prove rigorously that $s_1 > s_2$ in Eq. (10-27) provided that either $N > P$, $M > X_0$ or $N < P$, $M < X_0$.

10-10 (§10). In Fig. 10-1, $B = 2$ ohms, $M = N = 200$ ohms, $P = X = 1,000$ ohms, and $G = 600$ ohms. If battery and galvanometer branches are interchanged, will the bridge be more sensitive to a small change in X? What is the ratio of the sensitivities?

10-11 (§10). The bridge in Fig. 10-1 is used to measure an unknown resistance, X, of approximately 200 ohms. $M = P = 1,000$ ohms, and $G = 100$ ohms. (a) If galvanometer and battery branches are interchanged, determine the value of B required such that the same change in galvanometer current results from a small change in X for both arrangements. (b) If B is greater than the value in part (a), which arrangement is more sensitive?

10-12 (§11). An experienced experimenter uses the Wheatstone bridge of Fig. 10-8, with $M = N = 100$ ohms, to measure an unknown resistance, X. $G = 100$ ohms. He observes a galvanometer deflection of $+9.6$ mm when the decade box is set to 50.0 ohms. After other observations, and assuming that the ratio arms and decade box have no error whatever, he concludes that $X = 50.48 \pm 0.01$ ohm. (a) Compute the smallest galvanometer deflection he is able to observe in the laboratory. (b) What is his estimate of the least discernible galvanometer deflection? (c) Compute the ratio of the current through X to the galvanometer current when the decade box is set to 50.0 ohms.

10-13 (§11). The Wheatstone bridge of Fig. 10-8 is used to make a precise measurement of a resistor X. Rheostat B is 5,000 ohms, maximum, and $E = 150$ volts. The rheostat is set at the value allowing maximum bridge sensitivity while still not exceeding any current and power ratings of the bridge-arm resistors. The maximum permissible decade-box current is 100 ma, the maximum allowable power dissipation in X is 2 watts, and in $M = N = 1,000$ ohms is 5 watts each. The galvanometer resistance is $G = 50$ ohms.

The bridge is balanced with the resistance box set at 312.5 ohms. The resistance-box dial setting indicates the true box resistance with a standard deviation of 0.01 ohm. When the resistance box is set to 312.6 and 312.4 ohms, there are barely discernible galvanometer deflections (± 0.1 scale division); that is, deflections are observable two-thirds of the time. Hence, 0.1 ohm is the standard deviation in the *dial setting* of the resistance box. The 1,000-ohm fixed resistors in the bridge have standard deviations of 0.01 ohm.

1. (a) What is the per cent standard deviation in the measurement of X? (b) How many ohms of the 5,000-ohm rheostat are in the circuit, under the conditions stated? (c) What is the current sensitivity of the galvanometer? (d) What is the power dissipated in each of the 1,000-ohm fixed bridge arms? (e) If the rheostat were set to its full resistance of 5,000 ohms, what would be the per cent standard deviation of the measurement of X?

2. The galvanometer is replaced by a more sensitive one whose resistance is also 50 ohms. The rheostat is again set for least error of the measurement of X, consistent with the power ratings of the bridge. For a setting of 312.6 ohms there is a deflection of 2.0 divisions to the right. For a setting of 312.5 ohms there is a deflection of 0.5 divisions to the left. "Barely discernible" deflection is defined as before. (a) What is the best estimate of the value of X? (b) What is the per cent standard deviation of this estimate? (c) What is the current sensitivity of the new galvanometer?

3. What is the least per cent standard deviation possible in the measurement of X with this bridge, no matter how sensitive a galvanometer is used?

10-14 (§12). In the slide-wire bridge of Fig. 10-10, the unknown resistance, X, is approximately 50 ohms, and the uniform slide-wire is 1 meter long. $M = 0 = N$. The galvanometer has ample sensitivity. The principal error is introduced by inability to read the position of the slider to better than ±0.2 mm. What limit does this set on the per cent error in the unknown when $P = 50$ ohms?

10-15 (§12). Repeat Prob. 10-14 with $P = 200$ ohms.

10-16 (§12). In the slide-wire bridge of Fig. 10-10, $E = 1$ volt, and $B = 0$. When $X = 200$ ohms and $P = 300$ ohms, balance is attained with $n = 0.1$ ohm. Interchanging X and P gives a balance when $n = 9.5$ ohms. What is the total current through the slide-wire?

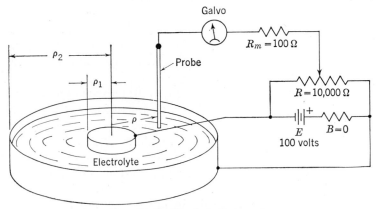

FIG. 10-18. Electrolytic trough.

10-17 (§12). Circular equipotentials in a concentric cylindrical system are to be determined in the electrolytic trough sketched in Fig. 10-18. The cylinders are good metallic conductors of radii $\rho_1 = 2$ cm and $\rho_2 = 20$ cm. The probe diameter is very small. Neglect polarization effects. (a) Determine the smallest difference in settings of the control, R, required to balance the system for two equipotentials that are spaced 1 cm apart. (b) With the probe set at $\rho = 10$ cm, and R adjusted for zero galvanometer deflection, determine the galvanometer current that results from displacing the probe radially outward by 0.1 cm. (Assume that the resistivity of the electrolyte is negligible.)

10-18 (§15). In the Kelvin bridge of Fig. 10-15, $M = N = a = b = 1,000$ ohms, $E = 100$ volts, $B = 5$ ohms, and $G = 500$ ohms. The bridge is balanced when $P = 0.001$ ohm. The end portions of X and P, and the resistance J, are all much less than B. (a) What is the approximate current through the unknown, X, at balance? (b) Determine the approximate value of the galvanometer current when P is changed by 1 per cent from its value at balance.

CHAPTER 11

WAVEFORMS AND A-C METERS

Many aspects of electrical measurements demand a basic understanding of nonsinusoidal steady-state waveforms. Fundamental properties of such waveforms become significant factors in the design and analysis of instruments and systems of measurement. Reliance is frequently placed on the shape of waveforms in carrying out measurements, and a common source of error is the neglect of waveform influence on the electrical system or meter readings.

In this chapter, a number of concepts and methods of analysis applying to the study and measurement of nonsinusoidal waveforms are presented. Average and rms values are defined, and techniques for their determination are described with examples. The Fourier series, so important in relating single-frequency analysis to nonsinusoidal signals, is reviewed and applied to the steady-state response of recording galvanometers to irregularly shaped inputs. The connection between frequency and time-domain analysis is illustrated for the square-wave response of galvanometers. Several rectifier-type instruments are described, and waveform errors are stressed. An approximate analysis of the diode voltmeter, useful for measurement of peak values of nonsinusoidal signals, is presented. The chapter concludes with a brief discussion of the thermocouple-type instrument which responds to the rms value of the input waveform.

These are representative applications of nonsinusoidal concepts and methods of analysis in the field of low-frequency electrical measurements. While complete coverage of the subject is by no means achieved, the principles outlined may be applied to many different problems where periodic, irregularly shaped waveforms are encountered.

11-1. Average Value of Periodic Waveforms. The average value of a function of time over an interval $t_2 - t_1$ was defined in Sec. 2-1. It follows that the average value of a periodic function of time $f(t) = f(t + T)$ over an interval equal to the period, T, is

$$\textbf{DEF.} \qquad F_{av} = \frac{1}{T} \int_0^T f(t) \, dt \qquad (11\text{-}1)$$

For a periodic function, the average value is independent of the choice of $t_1 = 0$, which is arbitrary. Average value is synonymous with d-c value.

282

The integral in Eq. (11-1) may be interpreted geometrically as the area under the curve of $f(t)$ vs. t over any interval T, as illustrated in Fig. 11-1. Areas above the t axis have positive algebraic signs, while shaded areas below the t axis have negative algebraic signs. Dividing the sum of all such areas over the interval T by the period, T, taking due account of algebraic signs, yields the value of F_{av}. Thus, F_{av} may be interpreted as the height of a rectangle of base T which has the same area as that under $f(t)$ over the interval T.

The area interpretation of Eq. (11-1) is often helpful in evaluating F_{av} by short-cut procedures. For example, if positive and negative areas over the interval T are equal in magnitude, their algebraic sum is zero, and $F_{av} = 0$. This is true in the case of a sine wave. Another technique is to subdivide the total interval, T, into two or more smaller intervals.

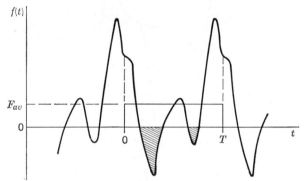

FIG. 11-1. Illustrating average value.

The area under $f(t)$ for each subinterval may be determined. Then, F_{av} is equal to the algebraic sum of all of the subareas divided by the total interval. For example, if T is broken up into two intervals, then, from Eq. (11-1),

$$F_{av} = \frac{1}{T}\left[\int_0^{T_1} f(t)\, dt + \int_{T_1}^{T} f(t)\, dt \right] \qquad (11\text{-}2)$$

The first and second integrals represent the areas A_1 and A_2 under $f(t)$ indicated in Fig. 11-2. The algebraic sum of these two areas divided by T yields F_{av}. This result is especially useful for symmetrical functions for which the two subareas are equal when $T_1 = T/2$. In this special case, the expression in Eq. (11-2) becomes

$$F_{av} = \frac{2}{T} \int_0^{T_1} f(t)\, dt = \frac{1}{T/2} \int_0^{T/2} f(t)\, dt \qquad (11\text{-}3)$$

This shows, for this symmetrical case, that half the total area divided by half the period yields F_{av} for the *entire* wave.

An illustrative example is provided by the equilateral-triangle wave-form of peak value I_p given in Fig. 11-3. The average value may be obtained in several ways. Using the area interpretation, the value of I_{av} is immediately given by the area of the triangle of base T and height I_p, divided by T. Since the triangle area is $\frac{1}{2}TI_p$, then

$$I_{av} = I_{dc} = \frac{1}{T}\left(\frac{1}{2}TI_p\right) = \frac{I_p}{2}$$

Alternatively, application of Eq. (11-3) leads to the same result. The area under $i(t)$ between 0 and $T/2$ is the same as that for the interval

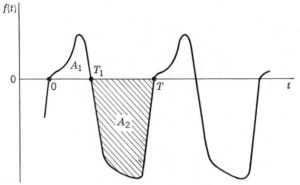

FIG. 11-2. Illustrating technique for determining average value.

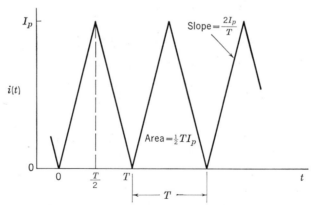

FIG. 11-3. Equilateral-triangle periodic waveform.

$T/2$ to T. This area is equal to $\frac{1}{2}(T/2)I_p$. When it is divided by one-half the period, the average value of the entire waveform, $I_p/2$, is obtained.

The average value may also be determined by carrying out the integration in the defining equation. It is first necessary to express $i(t)$ as a function of t. If an expression for $i(t)$ cannot be determined, graphical methods may be used to find the area under the curve. In the case of Fig. 11-3, $i(t)$ is a constant times t in the interval $0 < t < T/2$.

$$i(t) = bt \qquad\qquad 0 < t < \frac{T}{2} \qquad\qquad (11\text{-}4)$$

The constant, b, is the slope of the $i(t)$ vs. t curve over the specified interval and is equal to I_p divided by $T/2$. Applying Eq. (11-2), I_{av} is given by

$$I_{av} = I_{dc} = \frac{1}{T} \int_0^{T/2} \frac{2I_p}{T} t \, dt + \frac{1}{T} \int_{T/2}^{T} i(t) \, dt$$

The second integral must be equal to the first in this symmetrical case, so it is unnecessary to develop an expression for $i(t)$ in the interval $T/2$ to T. Therefore, I_{av} is given by twice the first term.

$$I_{av} = I_{dc} = \frac{2}{T} \int_0^{T/2} \frac{2I_p}{T} t \, dt = \frac{4I_p}{T^2} \left[\frac{t^2}{2} \right]_0^{T/2} = \frac{I_p}{2}$$

This example demonstrates some techniques for obtaining the average value of a periodic function of time. It should be emphasized that the average value depends entirely on the function. The average value of a sine wave is zero, but this does not mean that the average value of every waveform is zero.

11-2. RMS Value of Periodic Waveforms. The rms value of a function of time over an interval $t_2 - t_1$ was defined in Sec. 2-1. It follows that the rms value of a periodic function of time $f(t) = f(t + T)$ over an interval equal to the period, T, is

$$\textbf{DEF.} \qquad F_{rms} = \sqrt{\frac{1}{T} \int_0^{T} [f(t)]^2 \, dt} \qquad\qquad (11\text{-}5)$$

For a periodic function, the rms value is independent of the choice of $t_1 = 0$, which is arbitrary.

The square of F_{rms} may be interpreted geometrically as the area under the curve of $[f(t)]^2$ vs. t over an interval T, as indicated in Fig. 11-4. Note that $f(t)$ and $[f(t)]^2$ are *different* functions. Since $[f(t)]^2$ is always positive, negative areas are not encountered, and F_{rms} is always greater than zero. The square of F_{rms} may be interpreted geometrically as the height of a rectangle of base T which has the same area as that under the $[f(t)]^2$ curve over the interval T. These geometric interpretations are not ordinarily as helpful in calculations as in the case of F_{av}. It is usually necessary to obtain F_{rms} by integration, when the functional form of $f(t)$ is known. If $f(t)$ is only specified as a curve, ordinates may be squared to develop $[f(t)]^2$ graphically. Then the area under the squared curve may be determined by a planimeter or other graphical means.

There are certain techniques that may be helpful in symmetrical cases. For instance, if areas under the $[f(t)]^2$ curve are equal for two equal intervals 0 to $T/2$ and $T/2$ to T, then the square of Eq. (11-5) becomes

$$F_{\text{rms}}^2 = \frac{1}{T} \int_0^{T/2} [f(t)]^2 \, dt + \frac{1}{T} \int_{T/2}^T [f(t)]^2 \, dt = \frac{1}{T/2} \int_0^{T/2} [f(t)]^2 \, dt \quad (11\text{-}6)$$

Thus, for this symmetrical case, half the area under the squared function

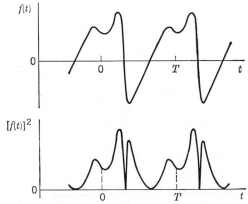

FIG. 11-4. Illustrating square of a time function.

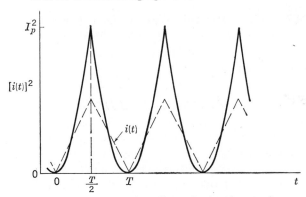

FIG. 11-5. The square of equilateral-triangle waveform.

may be divided by half the period to obtain the square of the rms value of the *entire* wave.

The rms value of the equilateral-triangle current waveform of Fig. 11-3 will be determined as an illustration. The function $[i(t)]^2$ is shown in Fig. 11-5. Note that the area under the squared function is *not* equal to the square of the area under $i(t)$. In general,

$$\int [f(t)]^2 \, dt \neq \left[\int f(t) \, dt \right]^2$$

The area under the equilateral triangle was seen to be $TI_p/2$, and it will be shown that the area under $[i(t)]^2$ over the interval T is $I_p{}^2T/3$, which is far different from $(TI_p/2)^2$.

The instantaneous current during the interval 0 to $T/2$ is given by Eq. (11-4), with $b = 2I_p/T$. Hence, from Eq. (11-6),

$$I_{\text{rms}}^2 = \frac{1}{T} \int_0^{T/2} \frac{4I_p{}^2}{T^2} t^2 \, dt + \frac{1}{T} \int_{T/2}^T [i(t)]^2 \, dt$$

The second integral is equal to the first, in this symmetrical case, so it is unnecessary to develop an expression for $i(t)$ in the interval $T/2$ to T. Then, I_{rms}^2 is given by twice the first term.

$$I_{\text{rms}}^2 = \frac{2}{T} \int_0^{T/2} \frac{4I_p{}^2}{T^2} t^2 \, dt = \frac{8I_p{}^2}{T^3} \left[\frac{t^3}{3} \right]_0^{T/2} = \frac{I_p{}^2}{3}$$

Therefore, $I_{\text{rms}} = I_p/\sqrt{3}$.

As another example, consider the sinusoidal voltage $v(t) = V_p \sin \omega t$, where V_p is the peak value of $v(t)$. The area under $[v(t)]^2$ from $t = 0$ to $t = T/2$ is equal to that from $T/2$ to T. Hence, from Eq. (11-6),

$$V_{\text{rms}}^2 = \frac{1}{T/2} \int_0^{T/2} V_p{}^2 \sin^2 \omega t \, dt = \frac{2V_p{}^2}{T} \int_0^{T/2} \left(\frac{1}{2} - \frac{1}{2} \cos 2\omega t \right) dt$$

$$= \frac{2V_p{}^2}{T} \left[\frac{t}{2} \right]_0^{T/2} + 0 = \frac{V_p{}^2}{2}$$

Therefore, $V_{\text{rms}} = V_p/\sqrt{2}$. The integral of the double-frequency term is zero because the cosine function is integrated over its complete period, and the net area represented by this integral is zero.

It should be emphasized that the rms value depends upon the function. The rms value of a sine wave is $1/\sqrt{2}$ times its peak value, but this does not mean that the rms value of every waveform is 0.707 times the peak value of the waveform. Indeed, in the case of the triangular wave it was found that the rms value is $1/\sqrt{3}$ times the peak value.

The *form factor* of a periodic function of time is defined as the ratio of the rms value to the average value.

$$\text{Form factor} = \frac{F_{\text{rms}}}{F_{\text{av}}}$$

When $f(t)$ is a constant, the form factor is unity, since both the rms and average values are equal to the d-c value. For other waveforms, the form factor exceeds unity. For instance, the form factor of the equilateral triangle wave in Fig. 11-3 is $2/\sqrt{3} = 1.15$.

The form factor of a sine wave is infinite, since $F_{\text{av}} = 0$ and F_{rms} is finite. However, the form factor of the rectified sine wave shown in Fig.

11-6 is finite. The rms value of this wave is the same as that of a sine wave, since inverting negative half cycles does not affect $[f(t)]^2$. The average value may be obtained from Eq. (11-3) with $f(t) = F_p \sin \omega t$ because the area from $t = 0$ to $t = T/2$ is equal to that from $T/2$ to T.

$$F_{av} = \frac{1}{T/2} \int_0^{T/2} F_p \sin \omega t \, dt$$

Change variable from t to $x = \omega t$, in which case the new limits are $x = 0$

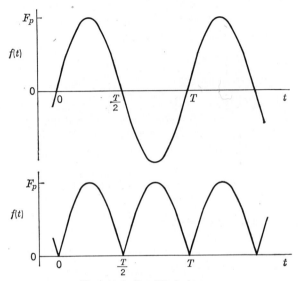

FIG. 11-6. Rectified sine wave.

and $x = \omega T/2 = \pi$. The *integral* then becomes

$$\frac{F_p}{\omega} \int_0^\pi \sin x \, dx = \frac{F_p}{\omega} \Big[- \cos x \Big]_0^\pi = \frac{F_p}{\omega} \Big[-(-1) + 1 \Big] = \frac{2F_p}{\omega}$$

Therefore, the average value of $f(t)$ is

$$F_{av} = \frac{2}{T} \left(\frac{2F_p}{\omega} \right) = \frac{2F_p}{\pi}$$

and the form factor is

$$\text{Form factor} = \frac{F_p/\sqrt{2}}{2F_p/\pi} = \frac{\pi}{2\sqrt{2}} = 1.11$$

This result will be used in discussing scale characteristics of rectifier instruments.

11-3. Fourier Series. A function $f(t)$ may be expressed over a time interval $T = 2\pi/\omega$ as an infinite series of harmonically related single-frequency terms in the form

$$f(t) = \frac{a_0}{2} + a_1 \cos \omega t + a_2 \cos 2\omega t + a_3 \cos 3\omega t + \cdots$$
$$+ b_1 \sin \omega t + b_2 \sin 2\omega t + b_3 \sin 3\omega t + \cdots \quad (11\text{-}7)$$

If $f(t)$ is a periodic function of period T, then this series gives $f(t)$ for all t. The infinite series may be written completely in summation notation as

$$f(t) = \frac{a_0}{2} + \sum_{n=1}^{\infty} (a_n \cos n\omega t + b_n \sin n\omega t)$$

Each pair of terms of like frequency may also be combined, since

$$a_n \cos n\omega t + b_n \sin n\omega t = \sqrt{a_n^2 + b_n^2} \sin \left(n\omega t + \tan^{-1} \frac{a_n}{b_n} \right)$$

Define $c_n = \sqrt{a_n^2 + b_n^2}$ and $\tan \phi_n = a_n/b_n$. Then the Fourier series may be written

$$f(t) = \frac{a_0}{2} + \sum_{n=1}^{\infty} c_n \sin (n\omega t + \phi_n) \quad (11\text{-}8)$$

Certain mathematical restrictions on $f(t)$ must be satisfied if the series representation is to be valid. For instance, the function must be single valued and cannot have an infinite number of discontinuities or an infinite number of maxima or minima over the interval T. Most physical time functions satisfy requirements for expansion in a Fourier series.

The Fourier series has many uses, both practical and conceptual. One of its primary implications is that, in linear systems, it is possible to analyze nonsinusoidal periodic waveforms by use of single-frequency theory. Each component of $f(t)$ may be treated separately to obtain the single-frequency effects and then, by linear superposition, all the separate effects may be added algebraically to obtain the nonsinusoidal result. This procedure will be demonstrated in studying the response of a d'Arsonval galvanometer to nonsinusoidal signals.

It is necessary to know the constants a_n and b_n (or c_n and ϕ_n), which depend upon $f(t)$, in order to apply the series. Many different ways have been devised to obtain them. If $f(t)$ is a current or voltage waveform available in the laboratory, then a harmonic wave analyzer or a spectrum analyzer may be used to determine the unknown constants experimentally. If $f(t)$ is specified in graphical form, but its equation is not obtainable, there are numerous graphical computation methods available for determining the constant coefficients. Finally, if $f(t)$ is known as an explicit function of t, the constants a_n and b_n may be determined from the integrals

$$a_n = \frac{2}{T} \int_0^T f(t) \cos n\omega t \, dt \qquad b_n = \frac{2}{T} \int_0^T f(t) \sin n\omega t \, dt \qquad (11\text{-}9)$$

The correctness of Eq. (11-9) may be shown in a straightforward manner. Multiply $f(t)$ in Eq. (11-7) by $\cos n\omega t \, dt$ and integrate from 0 to T.

$$\int_0^T f(t) \cos n\omega t \, dt =$$

$$\int_0^T \left(\frac{a_0}{2} \cos n\omega t + a_1 \cos \omega t \cos n\omega t + a_2 \cos 2\omega t \cos n\omega t + \cdots \right.$$

$$\left. + b_1 \sin \omega t \cos n\omega t + b_2 \sin 2\omega t \cos n\omega t + \cdots \right) dt \qquad (11\text{-}10)$$

It may be established readily that for any integers, k and r, including zero,

$$\int_0^T \sin k\omega t \cos r\omega t \, dt = 0$$

$$(11\text{-}11)$$

$$\int_0^T \cos k\omega t \cos r\omega t \, dt = 0 \qquad k \neq r$$

Accordingly, all integrals on the right of Eq. (11-10) are zero except one, which is

$$\int_0^T a_n \cos^2 n\omega t \, dt = \frac{a_n T}{2}$$

and this establishes the a_n given by Eq. (11-9).

In exactly similar fashion, the correctness of the b_n formula in Eq. (11-9) may be verified by multiplying $f(t)$ in Eq. (11-7) by $\sin n\omega t \, dt$ and integrating from 0 to T. The additional relation

$$\int_0^T \sin k\omega t \sin r\omega t \, dt = 0 \qquad k \neq r \qquad (11\text{-}12)$$

comes into play, and the only nonzero integral is

$$\int_0^T b_n \sin^2 n\omega t \, dt = \frac{b_n T}{2}$$

which agrees with b_n in Eq. (11-9).

The average value of $f(t)$ is equal to $a_0/2$, which is obvious by inspection of Eq. (11-7). Also, in Eq. (11-9), with $n = 0$, it is seen that a_0 is twice the *definition* of F_{av}.

The rms value of $f(t)$ is equal to the square root of the sum of the squares of the rms values of each of the individual components of $f(t)$. This is demonstrated by inserting the series expansion of $f(t)$, Eq. (11-8), into the defining equation for F_{rms}.

$$F_{\text{rms}}^2 = \frac{1}{T} \int_0^T \left[\frac{a_0}{2} + c_1 \sin(\omega t + \phi_1) + c_2 \sin(2\omega t + \phi_2) + \cdots \right]^2 dt$$

When $f(t)$ is squared, all terms except $(a_0/2)^2$ and $c_n^2 \sin^2 n\omega t$ become zero upon integration, in view of the relation given in Eq. (11-12). Then, after integration,

$$F_{\text{rms}}^2 = \frac{1}{T} \left[\left(\frac{a_0}{2} \right)^2 T + c_1^2 \frac{T}{2} + \cdots + c_k^2 \frac{T}{2} + \cdots \right]$$

Therefore, $$F_{\text{rms}}^2 = \frac{a_0^2}{4} + \sum_{k=1}^{\infty} \frac{c_k^2}{2} = \sum_{k=0}^{\infty} F_{k\,\text{rms}}^2 \qquad (11\text{-}13)$$

where $k = 0$ corresponds to the d-c term in $f(t)$.

As a simple application of this result, consider the waveform shown in Fig. 11-7. A single-frequency current of peak value I_p is superimposed upon a direct current, I_{dc}. The rms value of the total current may be obtained immediately from the result in Eq. (11-13).

$$I_{\text{rms}}^2 = I_{dc}^2 + \frac{1}{2} I_p^2 \qquad (11\text{-}14)$$

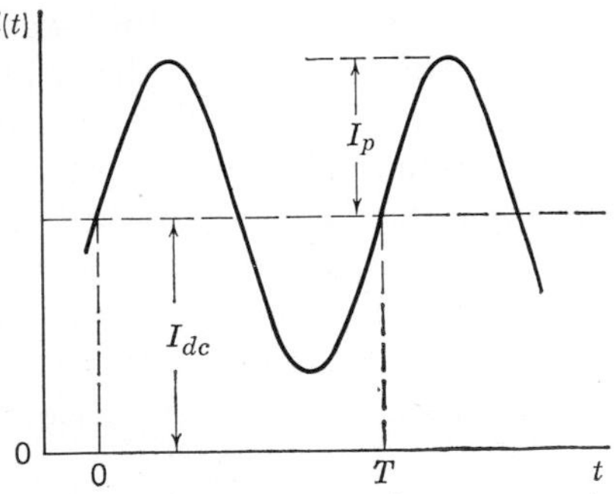

FIG. 11-7. Sine wave plus d-c component.

An alternative to using Eq. (11-13) is to insert the instantaneous current

$$i(t) = I_{dc} + I_p \sin(\omega t + \beta)$$

into the defining equation for rms value, Eq. (11-5).

$$I_{\text{rms}}^2 = \frac{1}{T} \int_0^T [I_{dc} + I_p \sin(\omega t + \beta)]^2 dt$$

Squaring and integrating the three resulting terms leads to Eq. (11-14); the cross-product term yields zero, upon integration, and the term $I_p^2/2$ arises from integrating the square of the sinusoidal term.

11-4. Galvanometer Response to Nonsinusoidal Input. The steady-state response of a d'Arsonval galvanometer to a single-frequency applied voltage, $E_p \sin \omega t$, was discussed in Chap. 4. It is expressed by Eqs. (4-53) and (4-54), repeated below.

$$\theta = \frac{I_p}{K} \frac{Q}{\frac{\omega}{\omega_0} \sqrt{1 + Q^2 \left(\frac{\omega}{\omega_0} - \frac{\omega_0}{\omega} \right)^2}} \sin \left[\omega t - \tan^{-1} \frac{1}{Q \left(\frac{\omega_0}{\omega} - \frac{\omega}{\omega_0} \right)} \right] \qquad (11\text{-}15)$$

where $I_p = E_p/(R + R_m)$ is the peak value of the current applied to the resistive circuit.   The average value of θ is seen to be zero when $\omega \neq 0$. Moreover, as the applied angular frequency increases beyond ω_0, the peak value of θ approaches zero rather rapidly.

$$\theta_p = \frac{I_p}{K} \left(\frac{\omega_0}{\omega}\right)^2 \qquad \omega \gg \omega_0 \qquad (11\text{-}16)$$

Hence, unless auxiliary circuits and rectifiers are employed, the d'Arsonval movement is not useful as an *indicating meter* for the measurement of a-c currents and voltages.   This movement may be used for the *recording* of nonsinusoidal signals, however, in applications of the kind described in Sec. 4-11.   Its use is restricted to low-frequency signals because of the limited response characteristics shown in Fig. 4-8.

An ideal recording instrument produces at its output an exact replica (except for size) of the input waveform.   From the Fourier-series point of view, this means that the relative amplitude response of the recorder must be the same at all frequencies of the input signal.   Also, the phase shift introduced by the recorder must be either zero at all frequencies of the input signal or a constant times the frequency, so that equal time delay is introduced for all frequencies.   The galvanometer is imperfect in both these respects, unless all angular frequencies of the input signal are much less than ω_0.   If all frequencies of the applied signal satisfy $\omega \ll \omega_0$, then θ is given from Eq. (11-15) by

$$\theta = \frac{I_p}{K} \sin \omega t \qquad \omega \ll \omega_0 \qquad (11\text{-}17)$$

This shows that all applied frequencies produce the same relative amplitudes of θ and that the phase shift is essentially zero at all frequencies. No distortion is introduced.

Amplitude distortion occurs when the peak amplitudes, c_n, of the harmonics of the input time function do not bear the same relative relationship in the output.   *Phase distortion* (or time-delay distortion) occurs when the phase angles, ϕ_n, of the harmonics of the input do not bear the same relative relationships in the output.   Since the peak value of θ is a function of frequency, and the phase angle of θ is not a constant times the frequency, the galvanometer may be expected under some circumstances to introduce considerable distortion of both types.

A specific example of steady-state distortion effects will be given in terms of an applied nonsinusoidal signal containing only two frequencies. Let the applied nonsinusoidal voltage be

$$e(t) = E_p(\sin \omega t + \sin 3\omega t) \qquad (11\text{-}18)$$

The third harmonic amplitude is equal to that of the fundamental and bears the phase relation indicated. One cycle of this symmetrical non-sinusoidal waveform is shown in Fig. 11-8. Assume that the voltage $e(t)$ has been applied for a sufficiently long time for the transient to die out and that the galvanometer operates over the linear region of its working range. The instantaneous angular deflection, θ, may be found from Eq. (11-15) for each of the two frequencies of $e(t)$. The two results may then be superimposed to obtain the complete response.

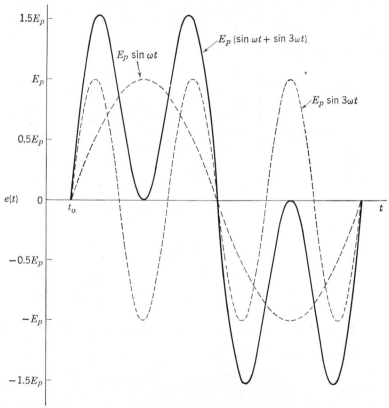

Fig. 11-8. Periodic signal with third harmonic.

The parameter Q is an important factor in determining the faithfulness of the output relative to the input, unless all angular frequencies of the applied signal are much less than ω_0. It was shown in Chap. 4 that $Q = 1/\sqrt{2}$ represents the largest value of Q which avoids a resonant peak. This value of Q corresponds to a slightly underdamped mode of transient operation, with relative damping factor $k = 0.707$. An examination of the curves of Fig. 4-9 also indicates that the phase shift is more nearly proportional to frequency with $Q = 1/\sqrt{2}$ than for other values of Q given. A more detailed analysis indicates that, for least distortion, a Q only slightly larger than $Q = 0.707$ is the optimum choice. There-fore, $Q = 1/\sqrt{2}$ will be assumed in this example. The amplitude and phase characteristics for this value of Q are reproduced from Figs. 4-8 and 4-9 in Fig. 11-9.

Suppose the fundamental frequency of $e(t)$ is $\omega = \omega_0/2$. The galva-nometer response, θ_1, at this frequency may be calculated from Eq. (11-15), or estimated from the curves of Fig. 11-9.

$$\theta_1 = \frac{0.97 I_p}{K} \sin{(\omega t - 43.3°)} \qquad\qquad \omega = \frac{\omega_0}{2}$$

The steady-state response to the third harmonic of $e(t)$, of frequency

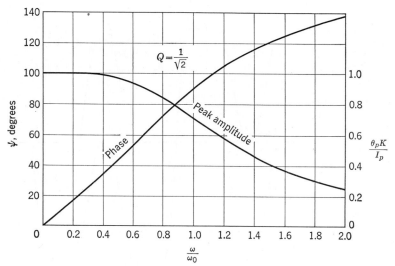

FIG. 11-9. Galvanometer steady-state response characteristics.

$3\omega_0/2$, is found in similar fashion.

$$\theta_3 = \frac{0.406 I_p}{K} \sin{(3\omega t - 120.6°)} \qquad\qquad 3\omega = \frac{3\omega_0}{2}$$

The *relative* amplitude of the third harmonic output is $0.406/0.97 = 0.419$ times the fundamental output, while in $e(t)$ the third harmonic amplitude was equal to that of the fundamental. Moreover, the phase angle of the third harmonic output has shifted relative to that of the fundamental output. The fundamental output is shifted by $43.3°$, and the third harmonic output would have to be shifted by $3(43.3°) = 129.9°$ to avoid phase dis-tortion. These two output components of θ are shown in Fig. 11-10 along with their sum, which represents the total response.

$$\theta = \frac{0.97 I_p}{K} \left[\sin{(\omega t - 43.3°)} + 0.419 \sin{3(\omega t - 40.2°)} \right] \qquad \omega = \frac{\omega_0}{2}$$

The most pronounced distortion in this example is the reduction in relative amplitude of the third harmonic, which produces a major shape change of the output waveform in comparison with that of $e(t)$. Loss of symmetry in the waveform is also incurred, resulting from unequal time delay of the two frequencies. The fundamental phase lag of 43.3°, which is 0.74 radian, corresponds to a delay time of $0.74/\omega$ sec. (For example, with $\omega = 740$ radians per sec, the time delay of the fundamental is 1 msec.) The third harmonic delay time is obtained by converting 40.2°

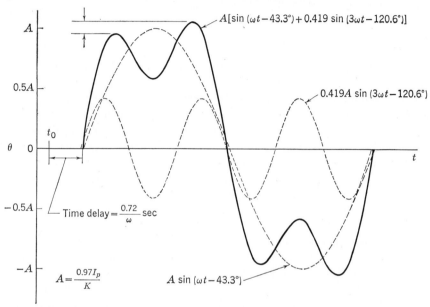

FIG. 11-10. Galvanometer response to signal of Fig. 11-8 ($\omega = \omega_0/2$).

to 0.70 radian. This time delay is $0.70/\omega$ sec; less than that of the fundamental in this case. Thus, the third harmonic output leads the fundamental by about 3.1°, in terms of the phase of the fundamental. The total output waveform is delayed by approximately $0.72/\omega$ sec, as indicated in Fig. 11-10.

It should be emphasized that the galvanometer output given in Fig. 11-10 is one cycle of the steady-state response to $e(t)$. It does not contain the transient resulting from the initial application of $e(t)$ to the galvanometer. The difference in waveshape between θ and $e(t)$ is very noticeable in this example and would constitute an intolerable degree of distortion in most applications.

A considerable improvement results if the fundamental frequency of $e(t)$ is reduced. Let the input signal have the same waveshape, but a fundamental angular frequency $\omega = 0.1\omega_0$. When this signal is applied to the same galvanometer, with $Q = 1/\sqrt{2}$, the fundamental output will be, from Eq. (11-15)

$$\theta_1 = \frac{0.9999 I_p}{K} \sin (\omega t - 8.1°) \qquad\qquad \omega = 0.1\omega_0$$

The third harmonic, at an angular frequency $3\omega = 0.3\omega_0$, produces a steady-state deflection

$$\theta_3 = \frac{0.996 I_p}{K} \sin (3\omega t - 25°) \qquad\qquad 3\omega = 0.3\omega_0$$

The total response of the linear galvanometer is obtained by superimposing the two separate results.

$$\theta = \frac{I_p}{K}\left[\sin (\omega t - 8.1°) + 0.996 \sin 3(\omega t - 8\tfrac{1}{3}°) \right] \qquad \omega = 0.1\omega_0$$

The galvanometer output follows $e(t)$ rather faithfully in this case. The relative amplitudes of the two output frequencies differ by only 0.4 per cent; the third harmonic has not been appreciably shifted in phase relative to the fundamental output. Three times the phase shift of the fundamental is 24.3° which is very nearly equal to the actual phase shift of 25° of the third harmonic output. Thus, both frequencies experience essentially the same time delay, equal to $0.14/\omega$ sec.

These examples provide a tangible idea of the important role played by Fourier series in waveform analysis. The same principles may be applied when $e(t)$ contains any number of different frequencies and relative phase angles. The galvanometer response may be computed for each component of $e(t)$, as in these examples, and then recombined to synthesize the total response to the applied $e(t)$. The significance of the amplitude and phase characteristics of any device that transmits a nonsinusoidal signal is also apparent from these examples.

A more complete analysis than presented here is required to deduce the optimum conditions for the most faithful galvanometer response. It is clear that a compromise is required between amplitude and phase distortion. For instance, if a value of Q larger than $1/\sqrt{2}$ is employed, a more uniform amplitude response extending to higher frequencies without displaying too large a resonant peak may be achieved, as indicated in the curves of Fig. 4-8. This leads to some reduction in amplitude distortion. However, the departure of the phase angle from a constant times the frequency becomes greater as Q is increased, and more phase distortion is introduced. One over-all conclusion from such considerations is that a significant amount of distortion is inevitable for signals containing frequencies in excess of about $0.4\omega_0$. Good quality mechanical oscillographs employ d'Arsonval galvanometers with ω_0 of about 15,000 radians per sec ($f_0 = 2,500$ cps). Hence, faithful response to signals with 60 cps fundamental frequency and as many as 16 harmonics may be expected. For viewing and recording frequencies close to and higher than the ω_0 attainable in galvanometers, the cathode-ray oscillograph, which combines very wide frequency response with high input impedance, is the most commonly used instrument.

11-5. Galvanometer Square-wave Response (Time-domain Analysis). A "square" wave (really a rectangular wave) consists of a periodic train of precisely rectangular pulses. A square-wave voltage is shown in Fig. 11-11. The peak value, E, is attained instantaneously at $t = 0$, and $e(t)$ remains constant at this value for half the period. Then, at $t = T/2$, the voltage drops to zero instantaneously and remains at zero for the duration of the period. In effect, E is switched on and off periodically for equal time intervals. The response of a system to square waves of various periods provides a quick, visual measure of its capability of handling nonsinusoidal signals. The interpretation of the response may be made either on the

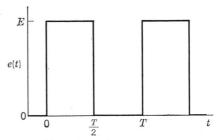

FIG. 11-11. Square wave.

basis of transient or steady-state analysis of the system. Square waves generated by electronic means may have rise times, and fall times, that are very short compared with T. Hence, it is possible to approximate the ideal waveform of Fig. 11-11 very closely.

The response of a d'Arsonval galvanometer to an applied square-wave voltage may be found from the transient analysis of Chap. 4. It is also possible to obtain the result from the steady-state analysis by expressing $e(t)$ in a Fourier series. Both approaches will be illustrated here to demonstrate the correspondence between frequency and time-domain analysis.

From the transient point of view, start with an initially inert galvanometer at the instant $e(t)$ is applied in series with resistance R. The behavior of θ vs. t during the interval $0 < t < T/2$ is given by Eq. (4-37), in the oscillatory case. It will be noted that ω and T in Eq. (4-37) do not represent the same quantities as the ω and T used in the Fourier series, or in Fig. 11-11. To avoid confusion of notation, Eq. (4-37) may be expressed entirely in terms of $\omega_0 t$ and the relative damping coefficient, k, by use of Eqs. (4-34) and (4-35). Then, Eq. (4-37) becomes

$$\theta = \frac{I}{K} - \frac{I\epsilon^{-k\omega_0 t}}{K\sqrt{1-k^2}} \sin\left(\omega_0 t \sqrt{1-k^2} + \tan^{-1}\frac{\sqrt{1-k^2}}{k}\right)$$

$$0 < t < \frac{T}{2} \qquad (11\text{-}19)$$

Recall that $\omega_0 = \sqrt{S/J}$, used in the transient analysis, is exactly the same as ω_0 in the steady-state analysis, and that Q and k are related by

$2k = 1/Q$. Also, $\theta_s = I/K$, where $I = E/(R + R_m)$, and K is the instrument constant.

A reasonably fast response occurs when $k = 1/\sqrt{2}$, and this corresponds to the same value of Q that was used in the preceding section. With $k = 1/\sqrt{2}$, Eq. (11-19) becomes

$$\theta = \frac{I}{K} - \frac{\sqrt{2}\,I}{K}\,\epsilon^{-\frac{\omega_0 t}{\sqrt{2}}}\sin\left(\frac{\omega_0 t}{\sqrt{2}} + \frac{\pi}{4}\right) \qquad 0 < t < \frac{T}{2} \qquad (11\text{-}20)$$

For simplicity, assume the half period, $T/2$, is long enough for the transient term to become negligible compared with I/K. The required value

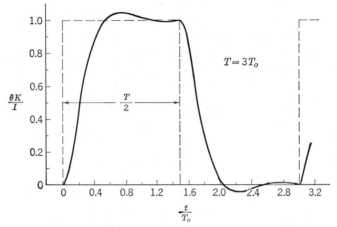

Fig. 11-12. Galvanometer square-wave response.

of $T/2$ may be estimated from Fig. 4-5, with $k = 1/\sqrt{2}$, to be at least $1.3T_0$. Detailed computation using Eq. (11-20) shows that θ remains within less than 0.2 per cent of I/K for t equal to or greater than $1.5T_0$. Therefore, at $T/2 = 1.5T_0$, θ will have essentially reached its steady-state value, I/K, to within a fraction of a per cent. A plot of Eq. (11-20) is given in Fig. 11-12 for $T/2 = 1.5T_0$.

The behavior of θ during the interval $T/2$ to T is formulated using the boundary condition ideas of Sec. 4-5. The steady-state term for θ during the second half period is zero, since $e(t)$ is zero. Hence, the transient term will be the same as that of Eq. (11-20) except for sign. Because of the simplifying condition that θ reaches the steady-state value I/K at $t = T/2$, the equation for θ during the second half period follows immediately from Eq. (11-20).

$$\theta = \frac{\sqrt{2}\,I}{K}\,\epsilon^{-\frac{\omega_0}{\sqrt{2}}\left(t - \frac{T}{2}\right)}\sin\left[\frac{\omega_0}{\sqrt{2}}\left(t - \frac{T}{2}\right) + \frac{\pi}{4}\right] \qquad \frac{T}{2} < t < T \qquad (11\text{-}21)$$

At $t = T$, θ will have returned essentially to zero because T has been deliberately chosen to be large enough to allow the transient to become negligible.   The return to zero is shown in Fig. 11-12.   As $e(t)$ goes through its periodic changes, θ will behave in accordance with Eqs. (11-20) and (11-21) over each cycle because the transient term becomes negligible at the end of each half cycle.   Therefore, these two equations, and the corresponding curves in Fig. 11-12, represent the *steady-state* response of the galvanometer to the square-wave input.

The galvanometer output is not a very faithful replica of the input for this square wave.   If the period of the square wave were increased, the solution which has been developed indicates that θ would become more "square" as a time function.   The build up from zero to I/K and the decay from I/K to zero are not affected by an increase in T.   However, a longer square-wave period permits the galvanometer deflection to remain essentially constant at I/K, or at zero, for a longer time interval than in the case of Fig. 11-12.   An example of the response when T is

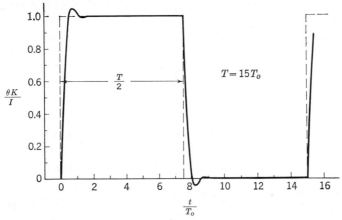

Fig. 11-13. Galvanometer square-wave response.

increased by a factor of 5 is given in Fig. 11-13.   The galvanometer output in this case resembles the input waveshape more closely.   An additional increase in T would improve further the agreement between input and output waveforms.

11-6. Galvanometer Square-wave Response (Frequency-domain Analysis).   The galvanometer response to a square-wave input may also be determined on the basis of a steady-state analysis, using Eq. (11-15) for each frequency contained in the Fourier series of $e(t)$.   First, it is necessary to find the Fourier-series representation of the square wave.   The mathematical expression for $e(t)$ with the arbitrary choice of $t = 0$ as shown in Fig. 11-11 is

$$e(t) = E \qquad\qquad 0 < t < \frac{T}{2}$$

$$e(t) = 0 \qquad\qquad \frac{T}{2} < t < T \tag{11-22}$$

The coefficients a_n and b_n in the Fourier series of Eq. (11-7) may be obtained from the integrals of Eq. (11-9). Since $e(t)$ is zero over the second half period, these integrals become

$$a_n = \frac{2}{T} \int_0^{T/2} E \cos n\omega t\, dt \qquad b_n = \frac{2}{T} \int_0^{T/2} E \sin n\omega t\, dt$$

and are easily integrated for so simple a time function. For the a_n,

$$a_n = \frac{2E}{\omega T} \int_0^{\omega T/2} \cos n\omega t\, d(\omega t) = \frac{2E}{2\pi n} \left[\sin n\omega t \right]_0^{\omega t = \pi}$$

Hence,
$$a_n = \frac{E \sin n\pi}{n\pi} \tag{11-23}$$

Therefore, for all $n \neq 0$, $a_n = 0$. For $n = 0$, $a_0 = E$. The result for a_0 may also be obtained by inspection of $e(t)$, since a_0 is twice the average value of $e(t)$, which on an area basis is, obviously, $E/2$ for the square wave in Fig. 11-11.

The coefficients b_n are evaluated by the same procedure.

$$b_n = \frac{2E}{\omega T} \int_0^{\omega T/2} \sin n\omega t\, d(\omega t) = \frac{2E}{2\pi n} \left[-\cos n\omega t \right]_0^{\omega t = \pi}$$

Hence,
$$b_n = \frac{E(-\cos n\pi + 1)}{n\pi} \tag{11-24}$$

Therefore, $b_1 = 2E/\pi$, $b_2 = 0$, $b_3 = 2E/3\pi$, $b_4 = 0$, and so forth. The pattern is evidently $b_n = 0$ for n even, and $b_n = 2E/n\pi$ for n odd.

The complete Fourier series of the square wave is thus

$$e(t) = \frac{E}{2} + \frac{2E}{\pi} \left(\sin \omega t + \frac{1}{3} \sin 3\omega t + \frac{1}{5} \sin 5\omega t + \cdots \right) \tag{11-25}$$

The *amplitude spectrum* of the square wave is given in Fig. 11-14.

Each frequency component of the galvanometer response may be obtained from Eq. (11-15) for the corresponding component of $e(t)$. The results may then be superimposed, as was done in Sec. 11-4. The response to the d-c component of $e(t)$ may be obtained by allowing ω to approach zero in Eq. (11-15), while fixing the product ωt at the value $\pi/2$. The result is independent of Q and is given by

$$\theta_{dc} = \frac{I}{2K} = \frac{E}{2(R + R_m)K}$$

since the d-c component of $e(t)$ is $E/2$.

The fundamental frequency of $e(t)$ corresponding to the previous choice of $T/2 = 1.5T_0$ is

$$\omega = \frac{2\pi}{T} = \frac{2\pi}{3T_0} = \frac{\omega_0}{3}$$

Hence, the galvanometer response to the fundamental component of $e(t)$, which has a peak value $2E/\pi$, is obtained from Eq. (11-15) with $Q = 1/\sqrt{2}$ and $\omega = \omega_0/3$.

$$\theta_1 = \frac{0.633I}{K} \sin(\omega t - 27.9°) \qquad\qquad \omega = \frac{\omega_0}{3}$$

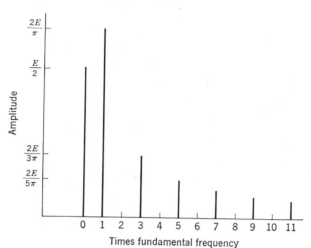

Fig. 11-14. Amplitude spectrum of square wave.

Similarly, the response to the third harmonic of $e(t)$, which has a peak value $2E/3\pi$, is found from Eq. (11-15) to be

$$\theta_3 = \frac{0.150I}{K} \sin(3\omega t - 90°) \qquad\qquad 3\omega = \omega_0$$

The fifth harmonic output is

$$\theta_5 = \frac{0.043I}{K} \sin(5\omega t - 127°) \qquad\qquad 5\omega = \frac{5\omega_0}{3}$$

All the individual components of θ may be obtained in this manner. Both the amplitude spectrum of $e(t)$ and the amplitude response of the galvanometer drop off as ω increases, so it is not necessary to extend the series very far before satisfactory accuracy is achieved. For example, the points shown in Fig. 11-15 were computed by dropping all terms beyond the fifth harmonic of $e(t)$. This provides convincing evidence that the steady-state analysis agrees with the transient analysis. The small discrepancies between steady-state calculations and the transient result, shown by the curve in Fig. 11-15, are within the errors expected from neglect of the seventh and higher harmonics (the peak value of the seventh harmonic is $0.016\ I/K$).

While this has been an elementary example, it illustrates the correla-

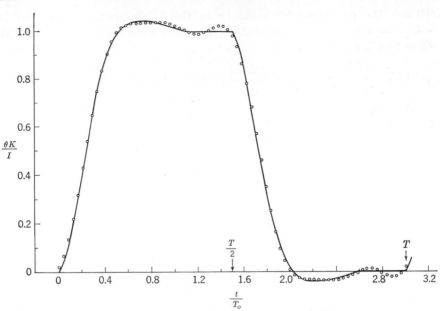

FIG. 11-15. Illustrating results of steady-state computations.

tion between frequency and time-domain analysis. Defects in the galvanometer response may be looked upon from either of two equivalent points of view. From the standpoint of transient analysis, the galvanometer is unable to follow the abrupt changes in $e(t)$ because of its finite speed of response. From the standpoint of steady-state analysis, failure to reproduce a square wave is attributed to amplitude and phase distortion. Either point of view leads to precisely the same results. It is remarkable that two such seemingly different sets of characteristics are so intimately related that they give exactly the same quantitative results.

11-7. Rectifier Instruments. The d'Arsonval movement is not directly useful as an indicating meter for alternating current because the average deflection is zero when a single-frequency signal is impressed on the movement. Moreover, if the angular frequency of the impressed signal is much greater than $\omega_0 = \sqrt{S/J}$, Eq. (11-16) indicates that even the instantaneous deflection approaches zero. Consequently, when an a-c signal is applied, the d'Arsonval pointer will either vibrate about zero or remain at rest at a zero reading.

Because the d'Arsonval meter is too valuable to discard for a-c applications, various circuits have been developed that enable this movement to produce a steady, readable indication of an applied a-c signal. The general scheme is to modify the waveform to be measured so that a different waveform with a nonzero average value is produced, as indicated by the block diagram of Fig. 11-16. The altered waveform (which bears a known relationship to the applied a-c signal) is then impressed on the d'Arsonval movement, which responds to the average (or d-c) value of the altered waveform. There are many different types of waveform operators, and they often include electronic amplifiers to increase the over-all sensitivity of the instrument. Switchable attenuators of various types may be incorporated to achieve sensitivity control. The input impedance to the waveform operator may also be designed over a wide range to provide very low impedance for ammeter applications and very high impedance for voltmeter applications. Also, the over-all system may be capable of operating on direct current as well as on alternating current, thus giving a double-purpose instrument. In the midst of these complexities, one must not lose sight of the fact that the vital operation is the production of a d-c component from an input signal whose average value is zero.

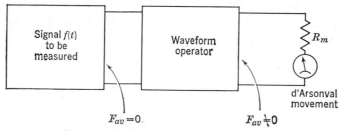

FIG. 11-16. General scheme for a-c meter.

The large amount of flexibility possible in the design of waveform operators has led to many different versions of such instruments. They are generally classed as electronic instruments, including such devices as vacuum-tube voltmeters and amplifier-detectors. Rectifiers are simple elements that may be used to provide the necessary conversion of the a-c waveform to one containing a d-c component. Rectifiers were described in Sec. 9-3, and it is suggested that the reader review the brief description presented there. When rectifiers alone are used in the waveform operator, the device is called a rectifier instrument. Several basic forms of such instruments are discussed in the following sections. For reasons to be described, the usual rectifier instrument incorporates a bridge arrangement of four rectifiers and is used with a d'Arsonval movement as a sensitive ammeter or voltmeter.

11-8. Single- and Double-element Rectifier Instruments. A simple rectifier voltmeter may be constructed by connecting a single rectifier in series with a d'Arsonval movement and external resistance, R_1, as indicated in Fig. 11-17. Suppose a sinusoidal voltage $e(t) = E_p \sin \omega t$ is applied to the terminals of this instrument. When $e(t)$ is a voltage rise in the direction of its arrow in Fig. 11-17, the rectifier experiences a forward voltage and its resistance is low. This permits a substantial current, $i(t)$, to pass through the movement during the positive half cycle of $e(t)$. For an ideal rectifier, the forward resistance is zero and $i(t)$ is proportional to the voltage applied to the instrument terminals in the interval $0 < t < T/2$. However, the forward resistance of an actual rectifier is a function of current, generally decreasing as $i(t)$ increases. Therefore, the meter current is not necessarily a sine loop. This distortion is overcome if the external series resistance, R_1, is much greater than

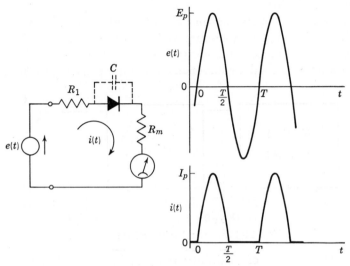

FIG. 11-17. Single-element rectifier voltmeter.

the forward resistance of the rectifier. If R_1 is also much larger than the internal impedance of $e(t)$ at all frequencies of the nonsinusoidal $i(t)$, then $i(t)$ is given approximately by

$$i(t) = \frac{E_p}{R} \sin \omega t \qquad 0 < t < \frac{T}{2} \qquad (11\text{-}26)$$

where $R = R_1 + R_m$. The forward voltage across the rectifier under these circumstances is only a small fraction of $e(t)$, with most of the drop occuring across R. In practice, the value of R_1 required to "swamp" the rectifier forward resistance might well be larger than R_m, so the movement resistance might also be negligible in Eq. (11-26).

When $e(t)$ swings into its negative half cycle, during the interval $T/2 < t < T$, the rectifier experiences a reverse voltage and displays high resistance. Then, the meter current becomes very small (zero for an ideal rectifier with infinite reverse resistance) and remains essentially zero during the negative half cycle of $e(t)$. Thus, the current waveform through the meter resembles closely the sine loop shown in Fig. 11-17. The essential accomplishment has been the conversion of the sinusoidal $e(t)$ into a nonsinusoidal current waveform. The average or d-c value of the sine loop is obviously one-half the average value of the rectified sine wave of Fig. 11-6, which was found by integration to be $F_{av} = 2F_p/\pi$. The deflection, θ, of the meter will depend only upon the d-c component of the sine loops, if $\omega \gg \omega_0$. Therefore, the deflection is given by

$$\theta = \frac{I_p}{\pi K} = \frac{E_p}{\pi K R} \qquad\qquad R \text{ large} \qquad (11\text{-}27)$$

and is proportional to the peak value of the applied voltage.

The principal difficulty with this voltmeter occurs during the negative half cycles of $e(t)$. The reverse voltage appearing across the rectifier is approximately equal to $e(t)$, since the current is essentially zero. Some rectifiers cannot tolerate appreciable reverse voltage. For instance, a copper-oxide rectifier, often used in rectifier instruments, may be permanently damaged by reverse voltages exceeding several volts. Hence, the rectifier of Fig. 11-17 might well be destroyed on the negative half cycles of $e(t)$. A diode rectifier is capable of withstanding larger inverse voltages and might be used in place of the semiconductor type in the single-rectifier instrument.

A further difficulty is traceable to the capacitance, C, inherently associated with the rectifier. As the frequency of $e(t)$ increases, the reactance of C becomes small compared with the reverse resistance of the rectifier. Then, on negative half cycles of $e(t)$, this permits current to pass through the meter during the interval for which zero current is desired. Thus, the presence of C tends to negate the rectifier action at high frequencies. Indeed, if $1/\omega C$ is much less than R_1, the inverse current through the meter will be nearly the same as that in the forward direction. Rectifier capacitance places an upper useful limit on frequencies that may be handled with this type of instrument. Practical rectifier instruments are useful over the audio range of frequencies, and in some cases might be capable of acceptable accuracy to frequencies as high as 100 kc per sec.

The objectional reverse voltage across the rectifier may be virtually eliminated by adding a second rectifier in shunt with the meter and its series rectifier, as shown in Fig. 11-18. With the polarity indicated by the arrow symbol, it is seen that the shunt rectifier does not appreciably affect the circuit during positive half cycles of $e(t)$, since it experiences a reverse voltage and offers high resistance. This reverse voltage is not excessive, being equal to the meter-plus-series rectifier drop, which is a small percentage of the applied voltage with R_1 large. On negative half cycles of $e(t)$, the shunt rectifier experiences a forward voltage that produces low resistance.   The low resistance effectively bypasses the meter movement and carries essentially all the current on negative half cycles. This is a positive action insuring a small meter current.   Meanwhile, the inverse voltage applied to the series rectifier is held within safe limits because most of the voltage drop now occurs across R_1 on negative half cycles of $e(t)$.   In effect, the two rectifiers protect each other from excessive inverse voltage, and, at the same time, produce unidirectional current through the meter movement.   The rectifiers may be regarded as voltage-sensitive switches.   Synchronism of their operation automatically follows the dictates of the voltage appearing across their terminals. Inclusion of the shunt rectifier does not, of course, circumvent the inherent capacitance limitations mentioned previously.

The circuit of Fig. 11-18 may also be used as an a-c ammeter, with $R_1 = 0$ in order to achieve minimum ammeter resistance.   The input resistance of such an ammeter depends markedly on current, and R_m is

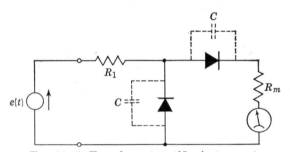

FIG. 11-18. Two-element rectifier instrument.

not always small compared with the forward resistance of the rectifiers. Hence, if the ammeter is placed in a low-impedance circuit, its time-varying resistance will distort the current waveform.

The circuit of Fig. 11-17 would not be useful as an ammeter because the instrument's resistance becomes very large on negative half cycles, and a large reverse voltage appears across the rectifier.   This would represent an extreme case of molesting the current in the act of measuring it since, in effect, an alternating switch is placed in the current lead.   The operation of the entire circuit would be seriously disrupted, assuming that the rectifier did not break down under the reverse voltage.

11-9. Bridge-rectifier Instruments.   Negative half cycles of the applied voltage do not contribute to the deflection of the rectifier instruments of Figs. 11-17 or 11-18.   If anything, the reverse current diminishes the average value of the meter current.   The sensitivity of the instrument may be doubled if negative half cycles are converted into useful output.   An arrangement of four rectifiers in a bridge configuration, as shown in Fig. 11-19, accomplishes full-wave rectification.   This is the

usual circuit found in commercial instruments. Four copper-oxide rectifiers may be stacked compactly in a small unit mounted within the case
of the d'Arsonval meter. This bridge arrangement is not employed to
achieve a null, but to produce meter current during the half cycles that
were discarded in the sine-loop case.

The sequence of events for an applied voltage $e(t) = E_p \sin \omega t$ is indicated in Fig. 11-19. When $e(t)$ is a voltage rise in the direction of its
arrow, rectifiers A and C experience forward voltage, while rectifiers B
and D are subjected to reverse voltage. Hence, the low-resistance path
is through rectifiers A and C during the positive half cycle of $e(t)$, assuming that capacitances C_B and C_D are negligible. Current passes through

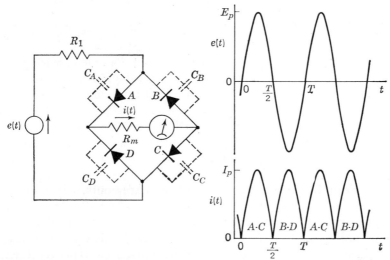

FIG. 11-19. Bridge-rectifier instrument.

the meter movement from left to right. On negative half cycles of $e(t)$,
rectifiers B and D experience forward voltage while A and C incur reverse
voltage. The low-resistance path is now through rectifiers B and D, neglecting the effects of C_A and C_C. Although the current drawn from $e(t)$
reverses, the direction of the current, $i(t)$, through the meter remains
from left to right. Thus, pairs of rectifiers in opposite bridge arms conduct on alternate half cycles to maintain unidirectional meter current.
Note also that rectifier pairs A-B and C-D protect one another from
excessive reverse voltages in a manner similar to that in the double-rec-
tifier case of Fig. 11-18.

If R_1 is much larger than the sum of the forward resistance of the two
rectifiers in series, the resistance of the over-all instrument will be constant and essentially equal to $R = R_1 + R_m$. If, in addition, R is also
large compared with the internal impedance of $e(t)$ at all frequencies of

the nonsinusoidal $i(t)$, then the meter current is given approximately by

$$i(t) = \frac{E_p}{R} |\sin \omega t| \tag{11-28}$$

where the two bars signify absolute magnitude. The fundamental angular frequency of the rectified sine wave is 2ω. Hence, if $\omega \gg \omega_0/2$, the deflection of the meter will depend only upon the d-c component of $i(t)$. The average value of a rectified sine wave of peak value F_p was found to be $F_{\text{av}} = 2F_p/\pi$. Therefore, the deflection of the bridge-rectifier instrument is

$$\theta = \frac{2I_p}{\pi K} = \frac{2E_p}{\pi KR} \qquad R \text{ large} \tag{11-29}$$

This is twice the deflection obtained in the sine-loop case, Eq. (11-27), for the same applied voltage.

The bridge arrangement is also used as an a-c ammeter with $R_1 = 0$. In this case, as before, the input resistance to the meter is a function of the current, and the current waveform is not a rectified sine wave when the meter is inserted in a low-impedance circuit. Since the forward resistance of the rectifiers decreases with an increase in current, the current waveform in a low-impedance circuit that was originally sinusoidal will display sharper peaks than a sine wave, owing to insertion of the meter.

11-10. Scale Characteristics of Rectifier Instruments. Scales of rectifier instruments are usually marked directly in rms values, based on the assumption that the meter current waveform will be a rectified sine wave. In other words, the form factor for a sine wave, which was shown to be 1.11, is incorporated into the actual scale markings. This represents a pitfall in the use of such instruments because the pointer of the d'Arsonval movement actually responds to the average value of the meter current. Consequently, the reading will not represent the rms value of nonsinusoidal input voltages or currents.

In order to express the problem quantitatively, scale markings may be related to angular deflection of the movement. For example, in the case of a bridge-rectifier voltmeter with a large series R, the voltmeter reading, V, is given by

$$V = 1.11KR\theta \tag{11-30}$$

The factor by which θ is multiplied is called the "scale factor," and it includes the 1.11 form factor. The scale factor is constant if R is large. If the applied voltage, $e(t)$, is a sinusoid of peak value E_p, the angular deflection is given by Eq. (11-29). The reading, V, then follows from Eq. (11-30).

$$V = 1.11KR \frac{2E_p}{\pi KR} = 0.707E_p$$

In this case the reading is equal to the rms value of $e(t)$, which is no surprise because that is the deliberate intent of the design.

If $e(t)$ is a nonsinusoidal voltage, the reading may be either higher or lower than the rms value of $e(t)$, depending upon its waveform. For example, a direct voltage $e(t) = E$ (which is, of course, a nonsinusoidal waveform), or a square-wave voltage of peak-to-peak amplitude $2E$ (which has a d-c component E) both produce the same deflection, $\theta = E/KR$. Hence, the reading, obtained from Eq. (11-30), is $V = 1.11E$. This is 11 per cent *higher* than the rms value of the direct voltage and about 22 per cent *lower* than the rms value of the square wave. For another example, consider the triangular wave of Fig. 11-3. Its average value was found to be one-half the peak value, and its rms value is $1/\sqrt{3}$ times the peak value. If a voltage with this waveform, and of peak value E_p, is applied to the bridge-rectifier voltmeter, the deflection will be $\theta = E_p/2KR$. The voltmeter reading, obtained from Eq. (11-30), is $V = 0.555E_p$. This is about 4 per cent lower than the actual rms value of the equilateral-triangle waveform.

Once the idea of this built-in scale factor is understood, it is unnecessary to compute θ. The principles outlined indicate that the factor by which the meter reading must be multiplied to obtain the rms value of any waveform is 0.9 times the form factor of the waveform. Thus, the greater the deviation of the form factor from 1.11, the greater the departure of the reading from the actual rms value.

The scale of the bridge-rectifier voltmeter with a large R is essentially uniform because θ is a constant times the peak value of the applied voltage. However, low-range voltmeters often have nonuniform scales because the low values of R_1 required are not large enough to swamp the forward resistance of the pair of series rectifiers. At low values of current, the forward resistance of the rectifiers is larger than at high current values. Thus, the scale factor becomes smaller for small currents and corresponding small angular deflections. This leads to crowding of scale divisions toward the zero end of the scale. Consequently, a bridge-rectifier milliammeter with $R_1 = 0$ displays a very compressed scale over the low-current portions, when used with a uniform-radial-field d'Arsonval movement. Moreover, the ratio of forward to reverse resistance is a function of current and contributes an additional factor to scale nonuniformity.

Rectifier instruments are subject to a considerable number of errors and are not capable of high accuracy. Some of the errors mentioned include waveform errors, scale readability errors, and high-frequency errors. In addition, rectifiers may undergo change with age, and thus alter the instrument calibration. Changes in temperature also affect rectifier performance. Despite all these difficulties, the combination of high sensitivity and low cost makes this type of instrument a popular choice for use in the audio-frequency range.

11-11. Diode-voltmeter Analysis. The rectifier voltmeter circuit of Fig. 11-17 may be modified by interchanging the rectifier and R_1 so that a capacitor, C, may be placed across the series combination of R_1 and the d'Arsonval movement, as shown in Fig. 11-20. A diode is used for the rectifier because it is capable of withstanding the large reverse voltages encountered in this circuit. It also has other advantages over the copper-oxide rectifier such as smaller rectifier capacitance, lower forward resistance, and higher ratio of forward to reverse resistance. This circuit is called a diode voltmeter and is widely used to convert alternating voltage to direct voltage. With proper design, the direct voltage across $R = R_1 + R_m$ may be made equal to the *peak* value of the applied alternating voltage, regardless of its waveform. This type of circuit is found at the input of vacuum-tube voltmeters and is capable of satisfactory performance up to hundreds of megacycles per second. In such applications, electronic amplifiers are used to amplify the voltage across R, thereby increasing the sensitivity of the voltmeter. The d'Arsonval movement is placed at the amplifier output. The circuit is also the same as a half-wave rectifier with capacitor filter, used as a low-current d-c power supply.

Inclusion of the capacitor across R results in a major change in the operation and characteristics of the circuit. For simplicity, assume that the diode is an ideal rectifier (zero forward resistance, infinite reverse resistance), and that its capacitance is negligible. When $e(t) = E_p \cos \omega t$ is a voltage rise in the direction of its arrow, the diode conducts at time $t = t_1 - T$. The capacitor charges from the voltage source, and the current $i(t)$ passes through R. The voltage across R and C follows $e(t)$ when the diode is conducting. When $e(t)$ falls below the voltage across the capacitor at $t = t_2 - T$, the diode experiences a reverse voltage and becomes nonconducting. This occurs shortly after $e(t)$ passes through its peak, if the time constant, RC, is large compared with the period, T. During the subsequent time interval, the capacitor discharges a current through R in the same direction as before. On the next positive half cycle of $e(t)$, the diode conducts again at time $t = t_1$ in Fig. 11-20. The charge lost by the capacitor during the discharge interval is replenished by a surge of diode current. The diode current, i_d, consists of short pulses, and the diode is nonconducting during the major portion of the period, T. Note that the reverse voltage across the diode approaches *twice* the peak value of $e(t)$ and occurs approximately when $e(t)$ is at its maximum negative peak.

It is evident that the capacitor has a profound influence on this circuit. In effect, C serves as a reservoir of charge that maintains $i(t)$ nearly constant during the entire period. The diode operates as a valve permitting a large current surge, once per cycle, to replenish the charge lost by C during the discharge interval.　When $RC \gg T$, the voltage $e(t)$ is almost completely disconnected from the input, except for extremely short diode-conduction intervals.　Hence, the effective input impedance of the peak voltmeter is very high.

An expression for the direct output voltage, E_{dc}, across R enables determination of a suitable value for RC to achieve peak voltmeter action.

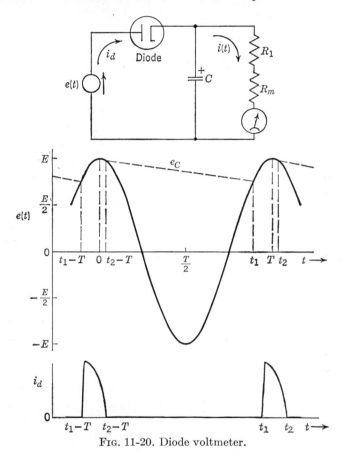

FIG. 11-20. Diode voltmeter.

The analysis is simplified by assuming the diode stops conducting at the peak of $e(t)$, as shown in Fig. 11-21, rather than continuing slightly beyond the peak.　This approximation will not seriously affect the area under the e_R curve of Fig. 11-21, especially when RC is large compared with T, the case of most interest in peak voltmeter design.　The voltage across R or C may be expressed as

$$
\begin{aligned}
e_R = e_C &= E\epsilon^{-t/RC} & 0 &\leq t \leq t_1 \\
e_R = e_C &= E \cos \omega t & t_1 &\leq t \leq T
\end{aligned}
\qquad (11\text{-}31)
$$

At $t = t_1$, which is the diode cut-in time, the two voltages must be equal.

$$E\epsilon^{-t_1/RC} = E \cos \omega t_1 \qquad (11\text{-}32)$$

The average value of e_R is E_{dc} and may be obtained from the area under the curve of Fig. 11-21.

$$
\begin{aligned}
E_{dc} &= \frac{1}{T} \int_0^{t_1} E\epsilon^{-t/RC} \, dt + \frac{1}{T} \int_{t_1}^{T} E \cos \omega t \, dt \\
&= \frac{-RCE}{T} \left[e^{-t/RC} \right]_0^{t_1} + \frac{E}{\omega T} \left[\sin \omega t \right]_{t_1}^{T} \\
&= \frac{-\omega RCE}{\omega T} (\epsilon^{-t_1/RC} - 1) + \frac{E}{2\pi} (0 - \sin \omega t_1) \\
&= \frac{E}{2\pi} \left[\omega RC(1 - \epsilon^{-t_1/RC}) - \sin \omega t_1 \right] \qquad (11\text{-}33)
\end{aligned}
$$

This expresses E_{dc} in terms of the diode cut-in time, t_1.

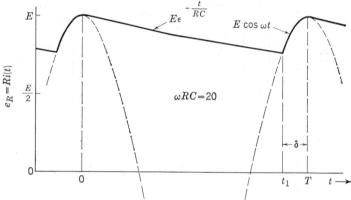

Fig. 11-21. Approximate output waveform of diode voltmeter.

It may be proved that E_{dc} approaches E as $\omega RC \to \infty$. Let $t_1 + \delta = T$, where δ is the diode-conduction interval. Then, as ωRC approaches infinity, δ approaches zero and

$$\epsilon^{-t_1/RC} = 1 - \frac{t_1}{RC} + \cdots \approx 1 - \frac{T - \delta}{RC} \qquad \delta \ll T \qquad (11\text{-}34)$$

$$\sin \omega t_1 = \sin (\omega T - \omega \delta) = -\sin \omega \delta \approx -\omega \delta \qquad \delta \ll T \qquad (11\text{-}35)$$

Insert these approximate relations into Eq. (11-33).

$$E_{dc} \approx \frac{E}{2\pi} \left[\omega RC \left(1 - 1 + \frac{T}{RC} - \frac{\delta}{RC} \right) + \omega \delta \right] = \frac{E}{2\pi} (2\pi - \omega \delta + \omega \delta) = E$$

While this result shows that peak detection is possible, the real question is how large must ωRC be in practice to yield an E_{dc} that is essentially equal to E. The diode cut-in time must be found, and unfortunately Eq. (11-32), which contains this information, is transcendental. However, a curve of ωt_1 vs. ωRC may be developed by solving Eq. (11-32) graphically. The resulting curve is given in Fig. 11-22. With corresponding values of ωRC and ωt_1 established, E_{dc} may be computed from Eq. (11-33) or from

$$E_{dc} = \frac{E}{2\pi}\left[\omega RC(1 - \cos \omega t_1) - \sin \omega t_1\right] \tag{11-36}$$

The curve of E_{dc}/E vs. ωRC, given in Fig. 11-22, shows that E_{dc} is about 5 per cent less than E with $\omega RC = 50$ and is only about 1 per cent less

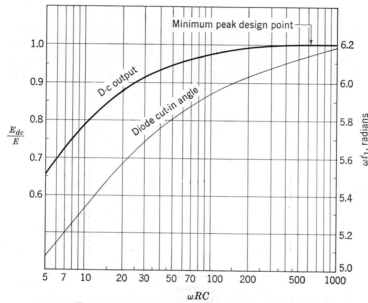

FIG. 11-22. Diode voltmeter characteristics.

than E with $\omega RC = 180$. The design criterion for peak detection is usually stated as

$$f \geqq \frac{100}{RC}$$

where $f = \omega/2\pi$, and this corresponds to $\omega RC \geqq 628$ for which E_{dc} and E are indistinguishable in Fig. 11-22.

A good approximation to these results for large ωRC is obtained by describing the two voltage states across R or C by the two straight lines shown in Fig. 11-23. The capacitor discharge is assumed to be linear, and the small portion of the approach of $e(t)$ to its peak is also approximated by a straight line. Clearly, E_{dc} is the difference between the rectangular area ET and the shaded triangular area, divided by T. The base of the triangle is T and its altitude may be obtained from Eq. (11-34). Hence,

$$E_{dc} \approx \frac{1}{T}\left[ET - \frac{1}{2} T \left(\frac{t_1 E}{RC}\right)\right] = E\left(1 - \frac{\omega t_1}{2\omega RC}\right) \qquad (11\text{-}37)$$

Since ωt_1 is still required, an even cruder approximation may be made by using $t_1 = T$, which gives a somewhat smaller value of E_{dc} by modifying the shaded triangle of Fig. 11-23 to a right triangle of slightly larger area. Then

$$E_{dc} \approx E\left(1 - \frac{\pi}{\omega RC}\right) \qquad (11\text{-}38)$$

These approximate results may be compared with the curve of Fig. 11-22. For example, with $\omega RC = 20$, Eq. (11-38) yields $E_{dc} = 0.84E$, while Eq. (11-37) gives, with $\omega t_1 = 5.57$, the value $E_{dc} = 0.86E$. These are not greatly different from the value $E_{dc}/E = 0.88$ for $\omega RC = 20$ in the curve

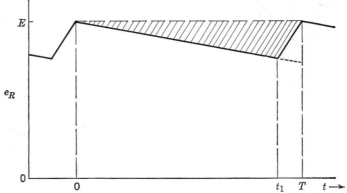

Fig. 11-23. Straight line approximation of output waveform.

of Fig. 11-22. For larger values of ωRC, the approximations improve. For instance, with the usual minimum design value, $\omega RC = 200\pi$, Eq. (11-38) shows that E_{dc} is only 0.5 per cent less than E, which is very nearly an exact result.

It is clear from the operation of this circuit that the diode-voltmeter output will be equal to the peak value of $e(t)$ for any waveform, provided that $\omega RC \geqq 200\pi$. The scale of the d'Arsonval meter of Fig. 11-20 may be marked directly in peak volts. If it is marked in rms volts of a sine wave (as is often the case) by including 0.707 in the scale factor, the scale will be in error if the waveform of $e(t)$ is not sinusoidal. The waveform error is similar to that described in detail for the bridge-rectifier instrument.

11-12. Thermocouple Instruments. The diode voltmeter produces an output equal to the peak value of the applied voltage for any waveform, provided that ωRC is sufficiently large. It is also desirable to have an instrument yielding the rms value of the applied voltage for any waveform. Neither diode voltmeters nor rectifier instruments have this capability. However, there are a number of different types of instruments that do exhibit this desirable characteristic, such as the electrostatic, moving-iron, and electrodynamometer types discussed in the next chapter. Another type is based on the emf produced by a thermocouple and is often used to measure current at high frequencies.

The hot junction of the thermocouple is attached to a *heater element* of resistance R that carries the current, i, to be measured (see Fig. 11-24). The temperature of the heater element depends upon the current through it, since the instantaneous power dissipated in the form of heat is $i^2 R$.

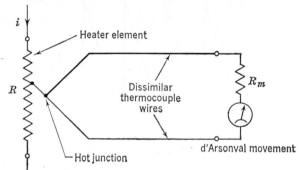

FIG. 11-24. Thermocouple instrument.

A sensitive d'Arsonval movement is placed across the thermocouple and constitutes the cold junction. The thermal emf drives current through the meter movement, which may be calibrated directly in rms value of the current, i, through the heater. This calibration will hold regardless of the waveform of the current because the *average* power dissipated in the heater element is equal to the square of the rms value of the current times R.

The range of frequencies over which this type of meter is responsive may be extended to hundreds of megacycles, where scale corrections may become necessary. The meter scale is not uniform, since the thermocouple emf depends upon the square of the heater current. Scale marks are not exactly in a square-law pattern because of a number of secondary effects on the scale factor such as change in heater-element resistance with temperature. Even though this meter is subject to a number of errors, such as variation in ambient (cold-junction) temperature, instruments with accuracies in the range $\frac{1}{2}$ to 2 per cent are commercially available and are indispensable for high-frequency current measurements.

It is interesting to note that, once again, the wedding of auxiliary elements to the d'Arsonval movement has enhanced its over-all utility and importance as an indicating instrument.

PROBLEMS

11-1 (§1). In the slide-back–voltmeter circuit of Fig. 9-6, $e = E_p \sin \omega t$ and has negligible internal impedance, $R = 6,800$ ohms, the resistance of the ammeter is negligible, $E = 45$ volts, and $r \ll R$. Assume that the rectifier has infinite reverse resistance and constant forward resistance equal to 100 ohms. (a) For $k \geqq 0.8$, the meter reads zero, but for $k < 0.8$ there are nonzero readings. Compute E_p. (b) Compute the meter reading for a control setting $k = 0.5$.

11-2 (§2). Find the form factor of the sawtooth waveform of Fig. 11-25.

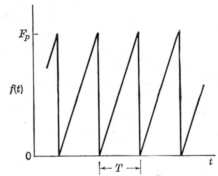

FIG. 11-25. Sawtooth waveform.

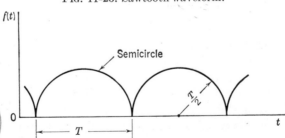

FIG. 11-26. Periodic train of semicircles.

11-3 (§2). Find the form factor of a waveform consisting of a periodic succession of semicircles of radius $T/2$, as shown in Fig. 11-26.

11-4 (§3). Find an expression for the rms value of the current waveform in Fig. 11-7 by direct integration, using the definition in Eq. (11-5).

11-5 (§3). Show by detailed series summation that the square root of the sum of the squares of the rms values of the individual Fourier components of a square wave is equal to the rms value of the square wave.

11-6 (§3). Determine the Fourier series of the sawtooth waveform of Fig. 11-25.

11-7 (§4). Consider the nonsinusoidal galvanometer input of Sec. 11-4 for the case of $\omega = 0.1 \ \omega_0$. If $\omega_0 = 1,000$ radians per sec, compute the difference in time delay between the two components of the galvanometer output.

11-8 (§5). Show that Eq. (11-19) is obtained from Eq. (4-37).

11-9 (§6). Find the peak value and phase angle of the seventh harmonic galvanometer output resulting from the square-wave input of period $T = 3T_0$ of Sec. 11-6.

11-10 (§6). Determine the Fourier series for the square wave of Fig. 11-11 when $t = 0$ is selected at the middle of the positive rectangular pulse.

11-11 (§8). A test was performed on 5,000 rectifiers using the circuit of Fig. 11-27. The meter, M, is a 0 to 5-ma d-c milliammeter of negligible resistance compared with 5,000 ohms. The reverse resistances of the rectifiers were all essentially infinite, but the forward resistances were variable and not zero. The mean of the 5,000 milliammeter readings was 4.85 ma. Readings of less than 4.80 ma were obtained for

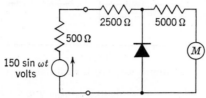

FIG. 11-27. Rectifier test circuit.

1,000 rectifiers. Assume that the forward resistance follows a normal distribution. (a) Compute the mean and standard deviation of the forward resistance of the rectifiers. (b) Estimate the number of cases in which the milliammeter reading was off scale in the above test.

11-12 (§9). An exponential current of period T is given by

$$i = I_p \epsilon^{-5t/T} \qquad\qquad 0 < t < T$$

This current is applied to a bridge-rectifier milliammeter (calibrated to read rms of a sinusoid). Compute the factor by which the meter reading should be multiplied to yield the rms value of the current.

11-13 (§9). The total resistance, R_a, of the bridge-rectifier ammeter in Fig. 11-19, with $R_1 = 0$, is given by

$$R_a = 10(1 - 0.1|e|)\text{ohms} \qquad\qquad 0 < |e| < 5 \text{ volts}$$

where e is the instantaneous voltage across the ammeter. The meter is connected to an a-c generator of emf $= 10 \sin \omega t$ volts, and of internal resistance equal to 20 ohms. Compute the peak value of the current through the meter movement.

11-14 (§11). For the diode voltmeter of Sec. 11-11, determine the approximate value of ωRC required for E_{dc} to be within 0.1 per cent of E.

11-15 (§11). A direct voltage is applied to a peak diode voltmeter whose scale is calibrated to read rms volts of a sine wave. The meter reading is 36 volts, rms. What is the value of the applied direct voltage?

11-16 (§11). A triangular voltage waveform of the shape given in Fig. 11-3 is applied to a peak diode voltmeter whose scale is calibrated in rms volts of a sine wave. If the meter reading is used for the rms value of this wave, determine the per cent error of this mistake.

11-17 (§12). A thermocouple-type a-c voltmeter is connected in series with one ideal rectifier. A sinusoidal voltage of 50 volts rms is applied across the series combination. What is the reading on the meter?

11-18 (§12). A d'Arsonval d-c milliammeter, a thermocouple milliammeter, and a bridge-rectifier milliammeter are connected in series. A unidirectional periodic current shown in Fig. 11-28 is passed through the series combination.   This waveform is a clipped saw tooth superimposed upon a direct current of 1 ma.   What are the meter readings?

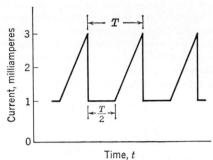

FIG. 11-28. Clipped saw tooth with d-c component.

11-19 (§12). Repeat Prob. 11-18 for a current waveform consisting of the saw-tooth waveform of Fig. 11-25, of peak-to-peak value 1 ma, superimposed on a direct current of 1.5 ma. (The peak value of the total waveform is 2.5 ma).

11-20 (§12). In Fig. 11-29, an ideal rectifier is connected in series with a meter, M, and energized by a sinusoidal generator $e = 10 \sin \omega t$ volts in series with a reversible

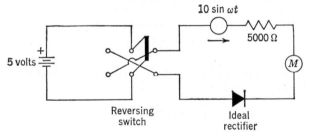

FIG. 11-29. Clipping circuit.

5-volt battery. The 5,000-ohm resistance represents the equivalent resistance of the two generators and the meter.   Determine the readings on M for each position of the reversing switch when (a) M is a d'Arsonval d-c milliammeter, (b) M is a thermocouple milliammeter, (c) M is a bridge-rectifier milliammeter, with scale calibrated in rms milliamperes of a sine wave.

CHAPTER 12

SQUARE-LAW METER MOVEMENTS

Three different types of meter movements whose average deflection is proportional to the square of the rms value of applied voltage or current are discussed in this chapter. These movements are especially valuable since they are relatively free of waveform errors. Because of the complexity of the physical system comprising these movements, it is not possible to develop torque expressions for their operation by direct application of the basic force law. However, the fundamental principles of an energy method of determining forces in these cases are presented and illustrated with examples. Application of the energy method leads to laws of deflection from which some of the factors influencing the design, use, and limitations of these instruments may be appreciated. The electro-dynamometer movement is distinguished from the others by virtue of two independent inputs to the movement. It receives most attention because of its many interesting possible uses, as well as its importance as a transfer instrument and as a wattmeter.

12-1. Law of Average Deflection. The moving element of most meters may be considered to be a rigid body so constrained that it has only one degree of freedom—pure rotation about a fixed axis. Currents or voltages applied to the instrument create forces on the moving element that produce a resultant instantaneous torque about its axis of rotation. The torque may be a complicated function of the applied currents or voltages. Whatever its form, it is opposed by a restraining torque, usually provided by a spring or springs attached to the moving element. Moreover, the moment of inertia of the moving element must be overcome, and other torques, such as those attributable to damping, are always present. The damping torques are usually designed to give rapid settling time so that steady-state conditions are attained quickly. If the system is linear, the general form of the differential equation of motion is essentially the same as that of the d'Arsonval movement.

$$K_1 \frac{d^2\theta}{dt^2} + K_2 \frac{d\theta}{dt} + S\theta = T_\theta \qquad (12\text{-}1)$$

where K_1 is the moment of inertia of the moving system, K_2 is the damping coefficient, and S is the spring constant. T_θ is the component of the

319

applied torque in the θ direction, resulting from the application of currents or voltages to the instrument. The coefficients K_1, K_2, and S are substantially constant in most instruments.

The general solution of Eq. (12-1) consists of a steady-state term plus a transient term, as was indicated in Chap. 4.

$$\theta = \theta_s + \theta_t$$

In a-c meters, the reading is observed after the pointer has settled to a steady indication and represents the useful information provided by the meter. This implies that the transient term, θ_t, of the general solution has become negligible compared with the steady-state term, θ_s.

The steady-state term may be a very complicated function of time, depending upon the driving torque, T_θ. For instance, if currents or voltages applied to the instrument are nonsinusoidal, the instantaneous torque and, consequently, θ_s are nonsinusoidal. However, if the applied currents or voltages are periodic, then the steady-state term will also be periodic, and θ_s may be represented by a Fourier series [see Eq. (11-8)].

$$\theta_s = \frac{a_0}{2} + \sum_{n=1}^{\infty} c_n \sin (n\omega t + \phi_n) \tag{12-2}$$

This form of the steady-state solution may be inserted into Eq. (12-1) to explore the general relationship between the instantaneous torque and the instantaneous steady-state deflection. But this is not a particularly fruitful approach since the unknown Fourier coefficients depend upon the function T_θ.

Motion of the system is, fortunately, not this complicated because the rotatable element is usually incapable of following the instantaneous variations of the applied torque. Instead, the reading observed is the average value of the steady-state solution.

$$\theta_{\mathrm{av}} = \frac{1}{T} \int_0^T \theta_s \, dt = \frac{a_0}{2} \tag{12-3}$$

where T is the period. It is possible to observe pointer vibration about the average value when the frequency applied to the meter is sufficiently low. But, in the usual case, the movement is designed so that the angular frequency $\omega_0 = \sqrt{S/K_1}$ is much less than the lowest frequencies ever measured.

The average deflection may be related to the instantaneous torque by multiplying Eq. (12-1) by dt/T and integrating from 0 to T. Assuming that K_1, K_2, and S are not functions of time, Eq. (12-1) then becomes

$$\frac{K_1}{T} \int_0^T \frac{d^2\theta_s}{dt^2} \, dt + \frac{K_2}{T} \int_0^T \frac{d\theta_s}{dt} \, dt + \frac{S}{T} \int_0^T \theta_s \, dt = \frac{1}{T} \int_0^T T_\theta \, dt$$

The first two integrals are zero, as may be seen by differentiating Eq. (12-2). For example, the second integral may be evaluated by finding $d\theta_s/dt$ from Eq. (12-2), which is

$$\frac{d\theta_s}{dt} = \omega \sum_{n=1}^{\infty} nc_n \cos{(n\omega t + \phi_n)}$$

The integral from 0 to T of $d\theta_s/dt$ is zero, because every integrand in the sum contains an equal number of symmetrical positive and negative half cycles during the interval T.

The third integral is, by definition, the average value of θ_s, which is also the average value of θ when θ_t has become negligible. Therefore,

$$\frac{S}{T}\int_0^T \theta_s\, dt = S\theta_{av} = \frac{1}{T}\int_0^T T_\theta\, dt = T_{av}$$

or
$$\theta_{av} = \frac{1}{S}\frac{1}{T}\int_0^T T_\theta\, dt = \frac{T_{av}}{S} \tag{12-4}$$

The conclusion that the average deflection is proportional to the average torque does not seem especially profound. However, the steps outlined are valuable in acquiring a basic understanding of the assumptions underlying this conclusion and give insight into the a-c behavior of meter movements.

The law of average deflection given in Eq. (12-4) is really not restricted to a-c meters. For example, in the case of the d'Arsonval movement, the d-c torque was found to be $T = nBAI$, for a direct current I. It follows that the instantaneous torque for an alternating current is $T_\theta = nBAi$, and this form was used in Chap. 4. With this torque, assuming that nBA is not a function of time, the law of average deflection becomes

$$\theta_{av} = \frac{nBA}{ST}\int_0^T i\, dt = \frac{I_{av}}{K}$$

where K is the instrument constant, and I_{av} is the average value of the current applied to the movable coil. If i is a direct current, then $I_{av} = I_{dc}$ and this becomes the same law of deflection used in Chap. 3. If i is a sinusoidal current, its average value is zero so the average deflection of the instrument is zero. Finally, if i is a rectified sine wave, as in the case of the bridge-rectifier instrument, then I_{av} is $2/\pi$ times the peak value of i, and there will be a nonzero average deflection.

Once an expression for the instantaneous torque is found, the law of average deflection in Eq. (12-4) may be integrated, and the characteristics of the meter may be studied. It is first necessary to find T_θ. An energy method for doing this is described in the following section.

12-2. Force and Energy. The basic force law in Eq. (3-1) gives the instantaneous force exerted on a charge, q, moving with velocity $\mathbf{v}$ in an electric and magnetic field. In principle, this force law may be used to determine electrostatic forces on charged conductors, magnetic forces on current-carrying conductors, or to determine forces in cases where combined effects of both fields are present. A simple magnetic example was presented in the case of the d'Arsonval galvanometer. However, there are few physical systems in which it is practical to obtain a result by this direct approach. The chief difficulty is the problem of integrating the infinitesimal force contributions over all the charges and currents that comprise the aggregate system. Fortunately, there is an alternative and powerful method for the determination of forces that uses the simpler process of differentiation, rather than integration. It is based on the change in energy stored in the electromagnetic field of an assemblage of charged, current-carrying conductors that results when one of the conductors undergoes a displacement. The energy method is indispensable for determining forces, and corresponding torques, on the movable element of the three types of meters to be discussed in this chapter.

The over-all principles of the energy method of determining forces in the case of combined electric and magnetic fields will be presented. This indicates the generality of the method, but applications in the simpler cases of either primarily electric or primarily magnetic fields are of immediate concern. Therefore, illustrations for special cases are given in Sec. 12-3 to provide a more tangible idea of the method.

Consider a system of fixed, rigid conductors that bear different electric charges and carry different electric currents. Both electric and magnetic fields are associated with such a system. For example, two fixed current-carrying loops of wire with a potential difference between the loops are surrounded by both electric and magnetic fields. There will be a certain total energy, W, stored in the electric and magnetic fields. The field energy concept is based on the existence of forces, of the kind given by Eq. (3-1), that act on a small test charge at any point in the electromagnetic field. Forces are also exerted by the fields on all of the fixed conductors.

Allow one of the fixed conductors to undergo an arbitrary infinitesimal displacement, $d\mathbf{s}$. Let $\mathbf{f}$ be the net force exerted by the field on the conductor. Then the work involved in this displacement is $\mathbf{f} \cdot d\mathbf{s}$. If no other energy is supplied to the system during the displacement, the energy stored in the field changes because energy must be conserved. The work is equal to the change in stored energy of the electromagnetic field.

$$dW = -\mathbf{f} \cdot d\mathbf{s} = -f_s\, ds \qquad (12\text{-}5)$$

where dW is the *increase* in the stored energy, and f_s is the component

of **f** in the direction of the displacement, $d\mathbf{s}$.   The algebraic sign of Eq.
(12-5) may be seen to be correct from the following reasoning.   If $d\mathbf{s}$ is
selected to coincide with the net force, **f**, exerted by the field on the conductor, then the field does work on the conductor and the stored energy
must decrease.   Hence, for this particular $d\mathbf{s}$, the work, $f_s\,ds$, is positive
and the *increase* in stored energy is negative.   Thus, the component of
the force in the direction $d\mathbf{s}$ exerted by the field on the conductor is
given by

$$f_s = -\frac{dW}{ds} \tag{12-6}$$

The direction of the displacement is arbitrary, so there is no loss in
generality when considering only a single component of **f**.   If the three-
dimensional vector force, **f**, is desired, each of its components may be
obtained by finding the partial derivative of the stored energy with
respect to each of three orthogonal coordinates.   This may be shown
formally by examining the total differential of W in a specific coordinate
system.   For instance, in rectangular coordinates,

$$dW = \frac{\partial W}{\partial x}\,dx + \frac{\partial W}{\partial y}\,dy + \frac{\partial W}{\partial z}\,dz$$

But
$$\mathbf{f}\cdot d\mathbf{s} = f_x\,dx + f_y\,dy + f_z\,dz$$

Therefore, the orthogonal components of the force are given by

$$f_x = -\frac{\partial W}{\partial x} \qquad f_y = -\frac{\partial W}{\partial y} \qquad f_z = -\frac{\partial W}{\partial z} \tag{12-7}$$

The relationships may be generalized for any coordinate system by

$$\mathbf{f} = -\mathbf{\nabla} W \tag{12-8}$$

where $\mathbf{\nabla} W$ is the gradient of W.

Equations (12-6) or (12-8) form the underlying basis for the energy
method of determining forces.   They require that an expression for W
be known as a function of the coordinates.

There are several points of technique that must be recognized for most
effective use of the energy method.   The stipulation that no other energy
is supplied when the body is allowed to undergo a displacement deserves
scrutiny.   It means, in the electrostatic case, that all charges must be
maintained constant when the conductor is displaced.   In the magnetic
case, all flux linkages must be maintained constant when the conductor
is displaced.   However, dW/ds is often obtained with less mathematical
complexity under conditions of constant potential of all conductors, in
the electrostatic case, and under conditions of constant current, in the
magnetic case.   These quantities may be maintained constant by pro-

viding external sources of energy; for example, batteries to maintain constant potentials. But the use of such external sources of energy upsets Eq. (12-6), which is based on the premise that all the work done by the field on the displaced body is derived from the energy stored in the field. In the case of constant potentials and constant currents, the increase in stored energy for the same displacement is no longer dW, but is given by

$$dW' = -f_s \, ds + dW_1 \qquad (12\text{-}9)$$

This states that the increase in stored energy in the field, dW', is equal to the energy expended in the displacement plus the energy supplied from the external sources, dW_1, used to maintain constant potentials and constant currents. The component of the force in the direction $d\mathbf{s}$ is, of course, the same as before.

Introduction of the term dW_1 does not produce serious complications. It may be shown, in general, that dW_1 is exactly twice the change in the stored energy (an electrostatic example is presented in the following section).

$$dW_1 = 2 \, dW'$$

With f_s the same as in the previous case, it follows that

$$f_s = +\frac{dW'}{ds} = -\frac{dW}{ds} \qquad (12\text{-}10)$$

This result states that when work is done on the conductor by the fields, with potentials and currents constant, there is an *increase* in stored energy in the field by an amount equal to dW'. The explanation is that the external source not only supplies the energy necessary to do the work, but in addition increases the stored energy by an equal amount.

Since dW and dW' only differ in algebraic sign, one might regard this as trivial, especially because other factors in the system may be used to determine whether the force exerted on the conductor is one of attraction or repulsion. Then, only the magnitude of f_s is needed and may be obtained from either approach. But the influence on the total energy exchange in the system is brought out by exploring these matters with the hope of dispelling the mystery surrounding conditions that are held constant. If close attention is paid to algebraic signs, exactly the same force result is obtained with the relations that have been presented whether all charges and flux linkages are held constant, or whether all potentials and currents are held constant.

The moving element of most meters undergoes pure rotation. Hence, it is useful to formulate an expression for torque in terms of stored energy in the fields. This is accomplished with reference to Fig. 12-1. The distance between axis of rotation of the body and point of application of the net force exerted by the field on the rotatable body is signified by r. For a displacement, dx, that is perpendicular to r, $dx = r\, d\theta$. Then Eq. (12-7) becomes

$$f_x = -\frac{\partial W}{\partial x} = -\frac{1}{r}\frac{\partial W}{\partial \theta}$$

But rf_x is the component of torque in the θ direction, about the axis of rotation. Hence,

$$T_\theta = \pm \frac{\partial W}{\partial \theta} \tag{12-11}$$

Thus, the torque about a specified axis may be obtained directly from the change in stored energy of the system when the moving element is allowed to undergo a small angular displacement, $d\theta$. If all charges and flux linkages are maintained constant, no external energy is supplied, and the minus sign of Eq. (12-11) pertains. If all potentials and currents are maintained constant, the plus sign of Eq. (12-11) is required. In either case, the same result is obtained for the torque.

The force results are obtained for fixed values of charge and flux linkages, or fixed potentials and currents. These results are applicable to time-varying quantities, provided that the frequency is low enough to permit neglect of retardation-time effects. This is called the *quasi-stationary* state. One may envision the time-varying charges, flux linkages, currents, and voltages

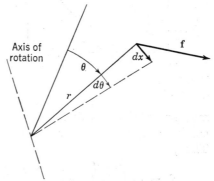

Fig. 12-1. Force and torque relations.

to be fixed temporarily while the analysis procedure of displacing the conductor is carried out. After the force or torque relationship is obtained, the time-varying quantities may be permitted to vary slowly and the mathematical form of the force result is unchanged.

12-3. Examples of Force and Energy. Consider the two fixed conductors, A and B, of Fig. 12-2. If all charges are zero when the switch is open, there is no field and no stored energy. After the switch is closed, the conductors become charged to a potential difference

$$V = E = V_B - V_A$$

When the switch is closed, a charging current, i, is drawn from the battery and Kirchhoff's voltage law yields

$$E = iR + \frac{q}{C} \tag{12-12}$$

where R is the resistance of the battery circuit, C is the capacitance between conductors, and it is assumed that the medium surrounding the conductors is perfectly insulating. (Note that one of the conductors is grounded so that C is the only capacitance required to describe the relationship among the charges.) Multiply both sides of Eq. (12-12) by $dq = i\,dt$ and integrate from zero to time t, at which time the charge, q, has attained the steady-state value, $Q = CV$.

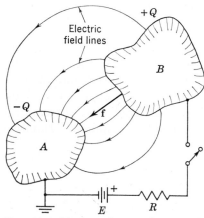

FIG. 12-2. Two-conductor electrostatic system.

$$\int_0^t Ei\,dt = \int_0^t i^2 R\,dt + \int_0^Q \frac{q\,dq}{C}$$

The integral on the left is the total energy supplied by the battery. The $i^2 R$ integral is energy dissipated as heat in R, and the remaining integral is the energy stored, W, in the electrostatic field.

$$W = \int_0^Q \frac{q\,dq}{C} = \frac{1}{2}\frac{Q^2}{C}$$

$$= \frac{1}{2}CV^2 = \frac{1}{2}QV \quad (12\text{-}13)$$

The component of the net force, $\mathbf{f}$, on conductor B in a direction x may be obtained, with Q constant, by opening the switch and allowing conductor B to undergo a small displacement in the positive x direction. Then,

$$f_x = -\left(\frac{\partial W}{\partial x}\right)_Q = -\frac{\partial}{\partial x}\left(\frac{1}{2}\frac{Q^2}{C}\right) = -\frac{1}{2}Q^2\frac{\partial}{\partial x}\left(\frac{1}{C}\right) = \frac{1}{2}\frac{Q^2}{C^2}\frac{\partial C}{\partial x}$$

Exactly the same result is obtained for f_x when the potential difference, V, is maintained constant. This is accomplished by keeping the switch closed during the displacement, dx, and carrying out the displacement so slowly that there is negligible drop across R produced by charge drawn from the battery. Then,

$$f_x = +\left(\frac{\partial W}{\partial x}\right)_V = \frac{\partial}{\partial x}\left(\frac{1}{2}CV^2\right) = \frac{1}{2}V^2\frac{\partial C}{\partial x} = \frac{1}{2}\frac{Q^2}{C^2}\frac{\partial C}{\partial x}$$

This agrees with the result obtained with Q constant.

If the x axis is directed from conductor A toward conductor B, then a positive displacement, dx, represents an increase in distance between conductors, and a decrease in capacitance. Hence, $\partial C/\partial x$ is negative, and f_x is directed opposite to the x axis, from conductor B toward A. Alternatively, if the x axis is directed from conductor B toward A, then a positive displacement, dx, represents a decrease in distance between conductors, and an increase in capacitance. Hence, $\partial C/\partial x$ is positive, and f_x is directed along the x axis, again from conductor B toward A. Thus, the force result is the same even though the direction of the coordinate axis is reversed.

If C is known as a function of the coordinates, then the detailed expression for f_x, as well as for any other component of $\mathbf{f}$, may be found. However, the result obtained has value even in its present form because it indicates that f_x depends upon the square of the potential difference between conductors. (It is known that C is a function of the geometry and the medium only.) If the potential difference is a slowly varying function of time, then the instantaneous force is given by the same form deduced for the electrostatic case.

The energy relations under these two conditions may be explored to show that the energy supplied by the battery in the case of constant potential is equal to twice the change in the field energy. Let dC represent the change in capacitance that results from the displacement, dx. Then, in the case of constant charge, the potential difference between conductors after the displacement is

$$V' = \frac{Q}{C + dC} = \frac{Q}{C}\left(1 + \frac{dC}{C}\right)^{-1} = V\left(1 - \frac{dC}{C}\right)$$

The *increase* in stored energy in the electric field, with Q constant, is

$$dW = \frac{1}{2}Q(V' - V) = -\frac{1}{2}\frac{QV}{C}dC = -\frac{1}{2}V^2\,dC \qquad (12\text{-}14)$$

If the displacement, dx, produces an increase in C, then dC is positive, $V' < V$, and the stored energy decreases. If C decreases as a result of the displacement, then dC is negative, $V' > V$, and the stored energy increases.

In the case of constant potential, the charge after the displacement is different from the initial charge and is given by

$$Q' = (C + dC)V = Q + V\,dC$$

The energy supplied by the battery, beyond the resistance R, with constant voltage, V, maintained between conductors, is

$$dW_1 = V(Q' - Q) = V^2\,dC \qquad (12\text{-}15)$$

The *increase* in stored energy in the electric field is

$$dW' = \tfrac{1}{2}V(Q' - Q) = \tfrac{1}{2}V^2\,dC \qquad (12\text{-}16)$$

Thus, it has been shown that $dW_1 = 2\,dW'$, and also that $dW' = -dW$.

For a magnetic field example, consider the two coils in Fig. 12-3 of self-inductance L_1 and L_2, and mutual inductance M. It is assumed that the net charge on each circuit is zero. Before the switches are closed, there is no field and hence no stored energy. After both switches are closed, steady currents I_1 and I_2 become established in coils 1 and 2, respectively. If both switches are closed at $t = 0$, Kirchhoff's voltage law yields the equations

$$E_1 = i_1 R_1 + L_1 \frac{di_1}{dt} + M \frac{di_2}{dt}$$

$$E_2 = i_2 R_2 + L_2 \frac{di_2}{dt} + M \frac{di_1}{dt}$$

$$(12\text{-}17)$$

The sign of M depends upon the details of the windings of the two coils as well as their relative orientation, and may be positive or negative.

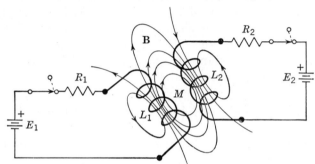

Fig. 12-3. Two coupled coils.

Multiply the first equation by $i_1\,dt$ and the second equation by $i_2\,dt$, add the two equations, and then integrate from zero to time t, at which time the currents i_1 and i_2 have attained their steady-state values I_1 and I_2. The total energy supplied will be represented by the integrals containing E_1 and E_2, while the energy dissipated will be given by the terms involving R_1 and R_2. The remaining integrals represent energy stored in the magnetic field and are given by

$$W = \int_0^{I_1} L_1 i_1\,di_1 + \int_0^{I_2} L_2 i_2\,di_2 + \int_0^{I_1, I_2} M\,d(i_1 i_2)$$

Integrate and obtain

$$W = \tfrac{1}{2}L_1 I_1{}^2 + \tfrac{1}{2}L_2 I_2{}^2 + M I_1 I_2 \qquad (12\text{-}18)$$

The first two terms may be interpreted as energy stored in the self-inductances, for if either I_1 or I_2 is zero, the remaining stored energy is that in the field of a single inductance.

A component of the force acting on one of the coils may be obtained from the energy expression in Eq. (12-18) by displacing the coil in some direction x. The simplest procedure is to maintain currents constant (rather than flux linkages). If the magnetic permeability of the medium stays constant, which is not necessarily true in the case of ferromagnetic media, then L_1 and L_2, as well as I_1 and I_2, are constant. The only quantity that changes as a result of the displacement, dx, is the mutual inductance, M. Therefore,

$$f_x = + \frac{\partial W}{\partial x} = I_1 I_2 \frac{\partial M}{\partial x} \qquad (12\text{-}19)$$

The ease with which this result is obtained should make the entire study of energy exchange worthwhile, since it is far more complicated to obtain the result with flux linkages held constant. The correct result is obtained for f_x even though energy is supplied to the system from external sources that maintain the currents constant when the coil is displaced.

If the complete expression for the force is desired, it is necessary to know the mutual inductance between the two coils as a function of the coordinates. However, even without this knowledge, Eq. (12-19) is valuable. It shows that the force is proportional to the product of coil currents, since it is known that M depends only upon the geometry of the coils and the medium characteristics. If the currents are slowly varying functions of time, then the instantaneous component of the force in the x direction will also be a function of time and may be obtained by replacing the direct currents in Eq. (12-19) by time-varying currents.

12-4. Electrostatic Voltmeter. The torque produced in electrostatic instruments arises from forces exerted by an electric field on charged conductors. There are several different types of electrostatic instruments including electroscopes, string and quadrant electrometers, and electrostatic voltmeters. Analysis of the electrostatic voltmeter will illustrate the principles governing this class of instruments.

The electrostatic voltmeter contains a variable air capacitor with one set of plates pivoted in jeweled bearings and the other set of plates fixed. The arrangement is indicated schematically in Fig. 12-4. A pointer attached to the rotatable plates enables direct scale indication of the angular location. The restoring torque may be provided by a pair of spiral springs, and damping may be incorporated by attaching vanes to the moving system (air damping). When an alternating voltage, e, is applied between the plates, charges flow onto and off the plates. The forces among these charges produce a torque about the axis of rotation, acting in the same direction regardless of the polarity of e. Hence, the average torque is not zero. The forces tend to rotate the plates so that C is increased. It is primarily the fringing field of the capacitor that provides the torque. Despite its misleading name containing the term " . . . static," the instrument is useful as a d-c or a-c voltmeter.

Determination of an expression for the torque would be difficult indeed were it not for the powerful energy method. By analysis of the energy stored in the electric field between the capacitor plates, it is possible to determine some of the important factors upon which the torque depends and to hold the detailed geometry of the system at bay. The instantaneous voltage across the capacitor is $e = q/C$, if the leakage resistance of the capacitor is neglected. This is an excellent assumption for air capacitors, provided corona or high-voltage arcing does not occur.

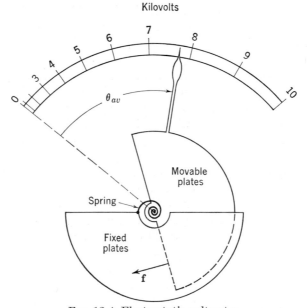

FIG. 12-4. Electrostatic voltmeter.

Accordingly, the instantaneous energy stored in the electric field is, from Eq. (12-13),

$$W = \frac{1}{2}\frac{q^2}{C} = \frac{1}{2}Ce^2 \qquad (12\text{-}20)$$

The instantaneous torque may be obtained by maintaining either q constant, or e constant, and permitting the movable plates to undergo a small angular displacement, $d\theta$. Application of Eq. (12-11) for the case of constant e calls for use of the plus sign.

$$T_\theta = +\left(\frac{\partial W}{\partial \theta}\right)_e = \frac{\partial}{\partial \theta}\left(\frac{1}{2}Ce^2\right) = \frac{1}{2}e^2\frac{\partial C}{\partial \theta} \qquad (12\text{-}21)$$

The same result may be obtained with q held constant, in which case the minus sign of Eq. (12-11) must be used.

The instantaneous torque depends upon the square of the instantaneous value of the applied voltage and upon the manner in which C changes with θ.   The average torque over a complete period, T, of the alternating voltage is

$$T_{av} = \frac{1}{T} \int_0^T T_\theta \, dt = \frac{1}{2} \frac{\partial C}{\partial \theta} \frac{1}{T} \int_0^T e^2 \, dt = \frac{1}{2} \frac{\partial C}{\partial \theta} E_{rms}^2 \qquad (12\text{-}22)$$

Note that the indicated integration is, by *definition*, the square of the rms value of the alternating voltage, e.   This means that the average torque depends upon the rms value of the voltage applied to the capacitor plates regardless of its waveform.   Thus, this instrument may be calibrated directly in rms volts, and there will be no waveform error of the kind encountered in rectifier and peak voltmeter instruments.

The law of deflection is obtained by inserting the average torque into Eq. (12-4).

$$\theta_{av} = \frac{T_{av}}{S} = \frac{1}{2S} \frac{\partial C}{\partial \theta} E_{rms}^2 = \frac{1}{K} E_{rms}^2 \qquad (12\text{-}23)$$

where K is the instrument "constant" which is generally a function of θ. This is called a square-law instrument because θ_{av} is proportional to the square of the quantity being measured.   But θ_{av} may also depend upon other variables, such as θ when K is not constant.

The scale characteristics depend upon K, which may be controlled within limits by suitable shaping of the capacitor plates.   For example, it is rather easy to make C equal to a constant times θ.   In this case, K is a constant, assuming S does not vary with θ, which is almost invariably true.   This is not a particularly desirable design, because it yields a square-law voltage scale, shown in Fig. 12-4, which is very compressed at the zero end of the scale.   Its readability is severely limited for small voltages.   In some designs an attempt is made to make $\partial C/\partial \theta$ inversely proportional to E_{rms}, with the intent of achieving a uniform scale.   This may be done with fair success over the upper 50 to 60 per cent of the scale.   The lower portion of the scale inevitably remains compressed since an extremely large change in capacitance (approaching infinity) for small angular deflections is required for small voltages.

Several aspects of electrostatic voltmeters may be appreciated from the foregoing analysis.   It is apparent that this voltmeter may be used for either direct or alternating voltages and that the range of frequencies over which it will operate may be very large.   Thus, the instrument may be calibrated at d-c, and the same calibration holds at a-c since the deflection is independent of the waveform of e.   The input impedance of the voltmeter in d-c applications is extremely high, after the initial charging current has subsided.   However, the a-c input impedance, which is equal to the reactance of C, leaves something to be desired. To achieve a high a-c input impedance, C must be kept small. This has the accompanying advantage of reducing the weight of the moving element. But the average torque is reduced when C, and its derivative, is reduced, and this aggravates a torque limitation inherent in this instrument. The torque-to-weight ratio is far less than in the d'Arsonval movement. The torque may be increased for a given weight of the movable plates by employing closer spacing between plates, but there is a limit beyond which this approach may not be used. Close mechanical tolerances become more difficult and more expensive to achieve, and voltage breakdown between plates is invited when the plate separation is too small.

It may be seen that there are several conflicting factors to be considered in the design of this instrument. Satisfactory compromises have been worked out in commercial instruments that range from the hundred-volt region into the kilovolt range, for both d-c and high-frequency applications.

12-5. Moving-iron Instruments. The torque produced in a moving-iron instrument arises from magnetic forces exerted on a movable iron element located in the field produced by a fixed coil. When current is passed through the coil, a force is produced on the movable iron element. The self-inductance of the coil, and hence its stored energy, is changed as a result of movement of the element.

There are several types of moving-iron instruments in common use, such as moving-vane, inclined-coil, and repulsion types (employing two iron elements, one of which is fixed). All these instruments are based on the same principles. A simple plunger-type moving-iron instrument, shown in Fig. 12-5, will be used as a specific example, even though modern types have been found to be superior in accuracy, sensitivity, and scale characteristics. The iron plunger is free to rotate on an axis and is restrained by a spiral spring. The alternating current, i, in the fixed coil produces a force, **f**, on the plunger that tends to pull it into the coil regardless of the polarity of i. A pointer attached to the plunger indicates its angular location directly on a scale, when equilibrium has been reached between the average applied torque and the restoring torque produced by the spring.

An expression for the instantaneous torque may be obtained by application of the energy principles outlined previously. If stray capacitance is neglected, which may not be justified at high frequencies, this is equivalent to neglecting the energy stored in the electric field. The instantaneous stored energy in the magnetic field may be seen from Eq. (12-18) to be

$$W = \tfrac{1}{2}Li^2 \qquad\qquad (12\text{-}24)$$

where L is the self-inductance of the coil into which the plunger moves.

The instantaneous torque is readily obtained from this energy expression by maintaining i constant and allowing the plunger to undergo a small angular displacement, $d\theta$. Equation (12-11) may be applied, using the plus sign.

$$T_\theta = + \left(\frac{\partial W}{\partial \theta}\right)_i = \frac{\partial}{\partial \theta}\left(\frac{1}{2}Li^2\right) = \frac{1}{2}i^2\frac{\partial L}{\partial \theta} \tag{12-25}$$

The instantaneous torque is a function of the square of the instantaneous current and will, therefore, have a nonzero average value. In practice, the torque is a more complicated function of the current than would

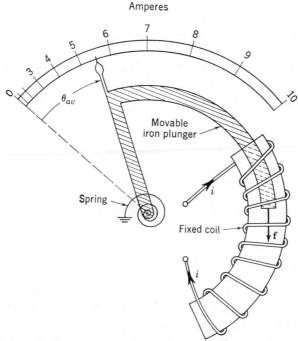

Amperes

FIG. 12-5. Moving-iron instrument.

appear from Eq. (12-25). The self-inductance, L, not only depends upon θ but also upon the current, because of the presence of ferromagnetic material. Moreover, eddy-current losses in the iron plunger introduce additional frequency-dependent factors that limit the versatility of the instrument.

The average torque is

$$T_{av} = \frac{1}{T}\int_0^T T_\theta\, dt = \frac{1}{2}\frac{\partial L}{\partial \theta}\frac{1}{T}\int_0^T i^2\, dt = \frac{1}{2}\frac{\partial L}{\partial \theta}I_{rms}^2 \tag{12-26}$$

Note that the indicated integration represents, by *definition*, the square

of the rms value of the coil current.   Therefore, within the errors of neglecting the dependence of L on the current, the average torque depends
upon the rms value of the coil current for any waveform of current.
However, there are waveform errors in this instrument owing to the non-
linearity of the iron.   Also, hysteresis effects become bothersome in
d-c applications.   Consequently, it may be expected that a d-c calibration of this instrument will not hold precisely for alternating current.
Discrepancies of a few per cent might be encountered in the typical
instrument.

The law of deflection is obtained by inserting the average torque into
Eq. (12-4).

$$\theta_{av} = \frac{T_{av}}{S} = \frac{1}{2S}\frac{\partial L}{\partial \theta} I_{rms}^2 = \frac{1}{K} I_{rms}^2 \qquad (12\text{-}27)$$

where K, the instrument "constant," is a complicated function of θ and
somewhat dependent upon the current through L and its frequency.
While θ_{av} is proportional to I_{rms}^2, the scale characteristics are not necessarily square-law since they also depend upon K.   If L is a constant
times θ, then K is approximately constant, and a square-law scale results.
This is a rather limited type of scale, as may be seen in Fig. 12-5.   By
suitable design of iron vanes, a more uniform scale may be achieved,
especially over the upper portions of the scale, by attempting to make
$\partial L/\partial \theta$ an inverse function of I_{rms}.   Compression toward the zero end of
the scale is unavoidable because $\partial L/\partial \theta$ cannot be made infinite as I_{rms}
approaches zero.

Moving-iron instruments are inexpensive, rugged, and capable of accuracies to better than 1 per cent in the power frequency range.   Although
they are subject to small waveform errors and susceptible to stray external magnetic fields, they are widely used in a-c power applications.   Voltmeters may be constructed by inclusion of a series resistor.   However,
since L is large, the increase in coil reactance with frequency produces a
significant frequency error.   This may be partially overcome, and the
range extended up to two or three thousand cycles per second, by shunting a portion of the series resistor with a capacitor, C.   As the frequency
increases, the increase in inductive reactance of L is offset by the decrease
in capacitive reactance of C.   This tends to maintain the total series
impedance nearly constant over a limited frequency range.   A similar
frequency compensation circuit is discussed quantitatively in Sec. 12-11
for a more exacting case where the phase angle of the impedance must
be minimized.

12-6. Electrodynamometer Movement.   The electrodynamometer
movement is particularly interesting because it has two independent circuits that permit its use in numerous applications such as ammeters,

voltmeters, wattmeters, and varmeters. The torque produced in this
movement arises from magnetic forces exerted between current-carrying
coils, one of which is rotatable. (Some movements possess two rotatable coils.) The operation may be thought of, qualitatively, in terms of
a d'Arsonval movement whose permanent magnet is replaced by an elec-
tromagnet. A fixed coil, split into two portions, produces the field in
the volume occupied by the moving coil.

A schematic representation of the arrangement is given in Fig. 12-6.
A more realistic idea of the coils and mechanical features may be seen in
Fig. 12-7. The fixed coil, C, consists of two windings that produce a
moderately uniform magnetic field in the environment of the movable

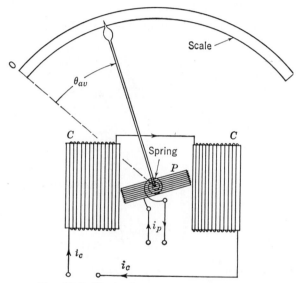

FIG. 12-6. Electrodynamometer movement.

coil, P. Symbols C, for the fixed coil, and P, for the movable coil, are
used because in wattmeter applications the fixed coil is called the *current*
coil, and the movable coil is called the *potential* coil. Interaction of the
field produced by the fixed coil, C, with the current through coil P,
results in a torque, as in the d'Arsonval movement. The torque is
opposed by spiral springs that also serve as current leads to the movable
coil. A pointer, attached rigidly to the rotatable coil, indicates its angular location directly on a scale that may be calibrated in volts, amperes,
watts, or other quantities, depending upon the way in which the independent coils are energized.

It may be seen, qualitatively, that the movement is capable of producing a nonzero average torque when used with alternating current, despite
its similarities with the d'Arsonval movement. For example, if the fixed

and movable coils are connected in series, the field produced by the fixed coil reverses at the same time that the current in coil P reverses; hence, the instantaneous torque remains unidirectional.

An expression for the instantaneous torque may be determined by the energy method in terms of the mutual inductance between the fixed and movable coils. The electric field between the coils may be neglected, although this may cause some error if there is an appreciable potential difference between the coils. Then, the stored energy residing in the magnetic field is given by Eq. (12-18).

$$W = \tfrac{1}{2}L_c i_c{}^2 + \tfrac{1}{2}L_p i_p{}^2 + M i_c i_p \qquad (12\text{-}28)$$

where L_c and L_p are the self-inductances of coils C and P, respectively, and M is the mutual inductance between them. The instantaneous

FIG. 12-7. Electrodynamometer instrument.   (*Courtesy of General Electric Company.*)

torque is readily obtained by maintaining i_c and i_p constant while allowing coil P to undergo an infinitesimal angular displacement, $d\theta$. Then, using Eq. (12-11), the instantaneous torque becomes

$$T_\theta = +\,\frac{\partial W}{\partial \theta} = i_c i_p\,\frac{\partial M}{\partial \theta} \qquad (12\text{-}29)$$

The instantaneous torque is proportional to the product of the two coil currents. If the coils are connected in series, the instantaneous torque is proportional to the square of the meter current. This and other special cases will be treated later.

The average torque, in terms of i_c and i_p, is

$$T_{\mathrm{av}} = \frac{1}{T}\int_0^T T_\theta\,dt = \frac{\partial M}{\partial \theta}\,\frac{1}{T}\int_0^T i_c i_p\,dt \qquad (12\text{-}30)$$

and the law of average deflection is

$$\theta_{\text{av}} = \frac{T_{\text{av}}}{S} = \frac{1}{S} \frac{\partial M}{\partial \theta} \frac{1}{T} \int_0^T i_c i_p \, dt = \frac{1}{KT} \int_0^T i_c i_p \, dt \qquad (12\text{-}31)$$

The instrument "constant," K, is a function of $\partial M / \partial \theta$. Hence, the coil design, which determines the M vs. θ characteristic, is an important factor in determining the scale characteristics.

Since no external current is required in the d'Arsonval movement to produce the field in the region of the movable coil, it is obvious that the electrodynamometer movement requires more power for its operation. Moreover, the magnetic flux density produced by the fixed coil is far less than is attained with permanent magnets, so the sensitivity is less. These are considerable disadvantages of the movement. Further, the instrument is rather expensive because the coils must be designed and manufactured carefully to achieve prescribed scale characteristics. In other words, M as a function of θ must be controlled accurately.

Nevertheless, there are many important applications of the electrodynamometer movement, the best known of which is the wattmeter. Of equal importance from a measurements standpoint is its use as a *transfer* instrument, as described in the following section. The movement is confined primarily to low-frequency applications, and its useful frequency range may be extended up to several thousand cycles per second with careful design. The principal high-frequency limitations are imposed by stray coil capacitance, a portion of which varies with angular location of the movable coil. In addition, eddy currents produced in nearby metallic objects become increasingly bothersome at high frequencies. The movement is susceptible to stray external magnetic fields because the fixed field is not very intense; hence, it is usually housed inside a laminated magnetic shield.

12-7. Electrodynamometer Ammeters and Voltmeters. The electrodynamometer movement may be used as an ammeter by connecting the fixed and movable coils in series, as indicated in Fig. 12-8. A fixed series resistor may be added to convert this ammeter to a voltmeter. When the instantaneous coil currents are equal, $i_c = i_p = i$, the law of average deflection in Eq. (12-31) becomes

$$\theta_{\text{av}} = \frac{1}{S} \frac{\partial M}{\partial \theta} \frac{1}{T} \int_0^T i^2 \, dt = \frac{1}{K} I_{\text{rms}}^2 \qquad (12\text{-}32)$$

The average deflection is proportional to the square of the rms value of the alternating current, i, regardless of its waveform.

Operation with alternating current at power frequencies is disturbed very little by stray capacitance and eddy-current effects in a well-designed instrument. Hence, the instrument constant, K, is practically the same for both direct current and alternating current.   Consequently, the electrodynamometer ammeter may be used as a transfer instrument to calibrate a-c meters in terms of d-c standards, using the electrodynamometer instrument as a steppingstone.   This is its most important application. The scale of the electrodynamometer ammeter may be calibrated at direct current by direct comparison with accurate d-c instruments.   This calibration holds with good accuracy at power frequencies.   Thus, d-c accuracy is readily transferrable to alternating current via the electrodynamometer ammeter, which may be compared directly with a-c instruments.

A square-law scale has limited use at small deflections, so the coils of the electrodynamometer ammeter and voltmeter are designed for as uniform a scale as possible.   An M vs. θ characteristic yielding a fair degree of uniformity over the upper portions of the scale is realizable.   An inevitable compression at low scale readings remains because $\partial M/\partial\theta$ cannot be made infinite as θ approaches zero.

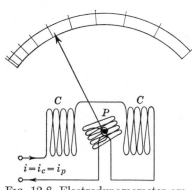

$i=i_c=i_p$

Fig. 12-8. Electrodynamometer ammeter.

Since current is delivered to the movable coil through its restoring springs, there is an upper limit (about 0.2 amp) beyond which the simple series connection of Fig. 12-8 becomes impractical. High-current ammeters may be constructed by use of suitable shunt arrangements.   These shunts are complicated by the requirement that currents in both fixed and movable coils must be maintained precisely in phase at all frequencies for which the instrument is used.   The shunts must be designed to achieve equal phase shift in both coils.   In voltmeter applications, the series resistor must be large compared with the total impedance of the series-connected coils, since their reactance is a function of frequency.   This is especially important because the equivalent self-inductance of the series-connected coils is also a function of M, and hence of θ.

12-8. Electrodynamometer Wattmeter Principles.   One of the most common uses of the electrodynamometer movement is in the measurement of power.   Although subject to systematic errors, it may be used to indicate both d-c and a-c power for any waveform of current and voltage and is not restricted to sinusoidal applications.

Suppose the current in the fixed coil is made equal to the current, i, through a load impedance whose power is to be measured.   Further, suppose the current through the movable coil is made proportional to the load voltage, e.   This may be accomplished by connecting a fixed resistor, R_p, in series with the movable coil and placing the series combination across the load. Then the current through the movable coil is $i_p = e/R_p$. Both of these current conditions cannot be realized simultaneously. *If they were,* the average law of deflection would become

$$\theta_{av} = \frac{1}{S} \frac{\partial M}{\partial \theta} \frac{1}{T} \int_0^T i_c i_p \, dt = \frac{1}{SR_p} \frac{\partial M}{\partial \theta} \frac{1}{T} \int_0^T ie \, dt = \frac{1}{KR_p} P_{av} \quad (12\text{-}33)$$

Thus, it is seen that if $i_c = i$, and if i_p is proportional to e, the average deflection is proportional to the average power in the load for any waveform. Recall from Chap. 2 that the *definition* of average power is

$$P_{av} = \frac{1}{T} \int_0^T p \, dt = \frac{1}{T} \int_0^T ei \, dt$$

Note also that the instrument constant, K, is the same for any waveform. Therefore, the scale of the wattmeter may be calibrated directly in watts in the d-c case, and the same calibration will hold for any other waveform, within the frequency limitations of the instrument.

The scale characteristics, in terms of watts, may be made rather uniform because the requirement is that $\partial M/\partial \theta$ be essentially constant to achieve a uniform scale, rather than inversely proportional to the quantity being measured, as was true in the ammeter and voltmeter cases. When the movable coil axis is oriented at 90° with respect to the axis of the fixed coil, the mutual inductance is zero. This orientation may be made to coincide with mid-scale deflection of the wattmeter. With suitable coil design, the mutual inductance may be made to vary linearly with θ for angular deflections on either side of the $M = 0$ point, over a considerable range, as indicated in Fig. 12-9. As a consequence, the scale of the wattmeter is quite uniform over a substantial portion of its range about mid-scale. A typical scale is shown in Fig. 12-9. As the movable-coil axis approaches the axis of the fixed coil, the change in M for a given change in θ diminishes, and this accounts for slight crowding of the scale marks at both the low and the high extremes. By shifting the initial orientation of the movable coil, scale crowding at either the low or the high end may be eliminated at the expense of increased nonuniformity at the other end of the scale. The design of the coils and resulting scale represents an engineering compromise between the total angular excursion of the pointer and the extent to which readability is sacrificed. In any event, the scale characteristics of a wattmeter may be made superior to those of an electrodynamometer ammeter or voltmeter.

The wattmeter deflection may be expressed in terms of its scale reading. Let P_r represent the actual reading of the wattmeter in watts. Then P_r is given in integral form in terms of the coil currents from Eq. (12-33).

$$P_r = KR_p\theta_{av} = \frac{R_p}{T} \int_0^T i_c i_p \, dt \quad (12\text{-}34)$$

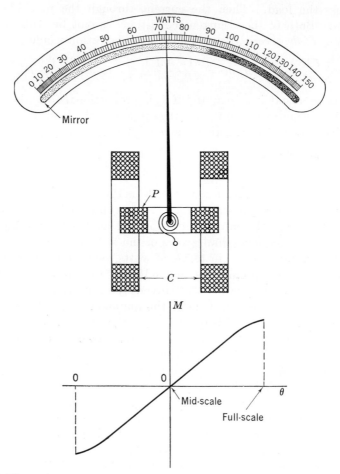

FIG. 12-9. Electrodynamometer wattmeter and scale.   (*Scale, courtesy of General Electric Company.*)

where KR_p is the scale factor.   This formulation is exactly the same, in principle, as that used for scale readings in the case of rectifier instruments in Sec. 11-10.

12-9. Inherent Wattmeter-connection Errors.   Difficulties in attempting to achieve the proper coil currents in the wattmeter to make its indication proportional to the average load power, P_{av}, are illustrated in Fig. 12-10 for the simple case of a resistive load, R.   With connection A, the current in the movable coil, P, is proportional to the load voltage, e, as desired.   However, the current in the fixed coil, C, includes both the load current, i, and the current through R_p, and hence is too large.   With connection B, the fixed-coil current is equal to the load current, as desired.

But the current through the movable coil is too large because the voltage across the series combination exceeds e, by an amount equal to the voltage drop across the fixed coil. These inherent connection difficulties will be recognized as essentially the same as those in the voltmeter-ammeter method of Sec. 5-6.

The two connections may be analyzed easily if the reactance of the wattmeter coils is neglected. Let R_c designate the resistance of the fixed

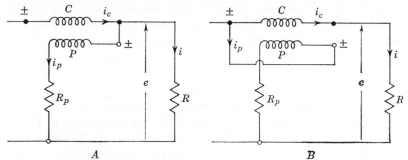

FIG. 12-10. Two wattmeter connections.

coil, and assume that R_p includes the resistance of the movable coil. Then, with connection A, the currents and voltages are related by

$$e = iR = i_p R_p \qquad i_c = i + i_p = i\left(1 + \frac{R}{R_p}\right)$$

The wattmeter reading is obtained by application of Eq. (12-34).

$$P_r = \frac{R_p}{T} \int_0^T i\left(1 + \frac{R}{R_p}\right)\frac{e}{R_p}\, dt = \frac{1}{T}\int_0^T ie\, dt + \frac{R_p}{T}\int_0^T i_p{}^2\, dt$$

Therefore, $$P_r = RI_{\text{rms}}^2 + R_p I_{p_{\text{rms}}}^2 = P_{\text{av}} + P_p \qquad (12\text{-}35)$$

where P_p is the average power dissipated in the movable coil circuit. Thus, the wattmeter reading exceeds the load power by an amount equal to P_p.

With connection B, the following relations may be seen from Fig. 12-10:

$$e = iR \qquad i_c = i \qquad i_p = \frac{e + iR_c}{R_p} = \frac{i}{R_p}(R + R_c)$$

In this case the wattmeter reading is given by

$$P_r = \frac{R_p}{T}\int_0^T \frac{i^2}{R_p}(R + R_c)\, dt = \frac{R + R_c}{T}\int_0^T i^2\, dt$$

Therefore, $$P_r = RI_{\text{rms}}^2 + R_c I_{\text{rms}}^2 = P_{\text{av}} + P_c \qquad (12\text{-}36)$$

where P_c is the average power dissipated in the fixed coil. The wattmeter reading is again higher than the load power, in this case by an amount equal to P_c.

The conclusions in Eqs. (12-35) and (12-36) are exactly the same for reactive loads (see Prob. 12-13).

A natural question is, of course, which connection should be used. Although P_p is usually greater than P_c in a commercial instrument, connection A is preferred when the input impedance of the power source is small compared with the load impedance. There are several sound reasons for this choice. For one, with small R_c, and an essentially constant impressed voltage, the power loss in R_p is substantially constant under variable load conditions. Hence, a *constant* correction is applicable to different readings that result from varying the load impedance. The correction may be computed from a knowledge of R_p (usually supplied with the instrument) and a knowledge of the load voltage. The correction may also be established by temporarily disconnecting the load and observing the wattmeter reading, which is approximately equal to P_p. This reading will not correspond exactly to the power loss in R_p under load conditions because of the change in voltage across R_c under load, as well as the change in load voltage resulting from the voltage drop across the internal impedance of the source. However, the no-load reading is often an acceptable approximation in practice, especially if the correction is small.

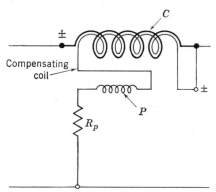

FIG. 12-11. Compensated wattmeter.

With connection B, the correction P_c is usually smaller than with connection A. Hence, this connection might be preferred if no corrections are to be made, and if measurements are being conducted under variable voltage conditions. It is bothersome to apply corrections in the case of connection B because P_c is a function of the load current. Moreover, even though R_c is small, it may vary appreciably owing to heating of the fixed coil (which may carry sizable currents), and this complicates the computation of accurate corrections. Finally, under the usual constant-voltage conditions, there is no handy means for measuring P_c directly in terms of the wattmeter reading.

A *compensated* wattmeter employs an auxiliary coil to obviate the need for correcting the readings when connection A is used. The compensating coil, illustrated schematically in Fig. 12-11, is connected in series with coil P, but is wound in physical intimacy with the fixed coil. The field produced by the compensating coil opposes that produced by coil C, to an extent just necessary to reduce the reading by an amount P_p. Thus, a compensated wattmeter is capable of indicating the actual load power, without correction. The compensating coil may be checked by disconnecting the load. If the compensation is correct, the wattmeter indication will be zero, rather than P_p as in the uncompensated case.

The fixed coil of the wattmeter is also referred to as the *current* coil, or the *series* coil, because of its manner of connection with respect to the load. Similarly, the movable coil is referred to as the *potential* coil, or the *shunt* coil. The movable coil receives its current via the restoring springs, and this places an upper practical limit on the amount of current that is safe to pass through this coil. For this reason, it is used as the shunt coil, and R_p serves to limit the current to safe values for the particular operating voltage of the instrument. The fixed coil is capable of carrying much larger currents and is, accordingly, used to bear the load current. Ordinarily, the current-coil terminals in an actual instrument are physically larger than the terminals of the potential-coil circuit. They are designated by large solid circles in the wattmeter figures. Since both coils may be damaged by excessive currents, it is customary to specify current ratings on the current coil and voltage ratings on the potential circuit. These must not be exceeded without risking permanent damage to the instrument and should be checked carefully. It is entirely possible for the wattmeter reading to fall within the range of the instrument even though coil ratings are exceeded.

The bulk of the voltage drop across the potential circuit of the wattmeter occurs across R_p. Hence, if R_p were connected directly to the current-coil terminal, there would be a sizable voltage between the coils. This voltage is accompanied by an intense electric field between the coils, because of their close physical proximity. The associated forces might affect the instrument calibration. To avoid this source of error, the potential coil should always be connected directly to one of the current-coil terminals, as in Fig. 12-10. The potential-circuit terminal that is connected directly to coil P, inside the instrument, is designated with the symbol $\pm$, by manufacturer's convention. Also, the internal connection of the current coil is made so that an upscale reading is obtained in single-phase measurements when the current-coil terminal designated $\pm$ is connected to the line end, as shown in Fig. 12-10.

12-10. Wattmeter Analysis for Sinusoidal Operation. An expression for the wattmeter reading in the particular case of sinusoidal voltage applied to a passive load impedance is worth obtaining because these are the conditions under which the wattmeter is often used. Assume that the currents in the wattmeter coils are sinusoidal and are given by the expressions

$$i_c = \text{Re}\,\{\mathbf{I}_c \epsilon^{j\omega t}\} = \text{Re}\,\{I_c \epsilon^{j\phi_c}\epsilon^{j\omega t}\} = I_c \cos\,(\omega t + \phi_c)$$
$$i_p = \text{Re}\,\{\mathbf{I}_p \epsilon^{j\omega t}\} = \text{Re}\,\{I_p \epsilon^{j\phi_p}\epsilon^{j\omega t}\} = I_p \cos\,(\omega t + \phi_p)$$

where I_c and I_p are the peak values of the currents, and the phase angles ϕ_c and ϕ_p are arbitrary. The average value of the product of these two currents has, in effect, been derived in Sec. 2-8, with different symbols.

$$\frac{1}{T} \int_0^T i_c i_p \, dt = \frac{1}{2} I_c I_p \cos (\phi_c - \phi_p) = \frac{1}{2} \text{Re } \{\mathbf{I}_c \mathbf{I}_p^*\}$$

Substitute into Eq. (12-34) to obtain the expression for the wattmeter reading

$$P_r = \frac{1}{2} R_p I_c I_p \cos (\phi_c - \phi_p) = \frac{1}{2} R_p \text{ Re } \{\mathbf{I}_c \mathbf{I}_p^*\} \qquad (12\text{-}37)$$

In the first form, the factor of 2 may be broken into the product of two $\sqrt{2}$ factors. Then, in words, the wattmeter reading is given by R_p times the product of the rms values of the coil currents multiplied by the cosine of the angle between coil currents. The second form, in terms of complex currents, is most useful for the analysis of various wattmeter connections.

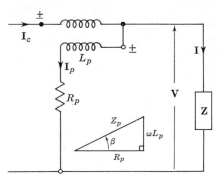

FIG. 12-12. Single-phase sinusoidal watt-meter application.

The wattmeter shown in Fig. 12-12 is connected for power measurements to a load of complex impedance $\mathbf{Z}$, using the conventional connection in which the power in R_p is included in the reading. The reactance of the potential coil, ωL_p, is often negligible, but will be included here for completeness. The various currents, voltages, and impedances may be designated by complex quantities. The entire analysis may be carried out algebraically, instead of using the crutch of phasor diagrams.

The complex load voltage, $\mathbf{V}$, of arbitrary phase angle, ψ, is

$$\mathbf{V} = V \epsilon^{j\psi} = \mathbf{IZ} = IZ \epsilon^{j\alpha} = \mathbf{I}_p \mathbf{Z}_p = I_p Z_p \epsilon^{j\beta}$$

where α is the phase angle of the load impedance, and β is the phase angle of the potential circuit.

$$\tan \beta = \frac{\omega L_p}{R_p}$$

The current in the fixed coil is $\mathbf{I}_c = \mathbf{I} + \mathbf{I}_p$. The wattmeter reading is obtained from Eq. (12-37).

$$\begin{aligned} P_r &= \tfrac{1}{2} R_p \text{ Re } \{\mathbf{I}_c \mathbf{I}_p^*\} = \tfrac{1}{2} R_p \text{ Re } \{\mathbf{I} \mathbf{I}_p^* + \mathbf{I}_p \mathbf{I}_p^*\} \\ &= \tfrac{1}{2} R_p I_p{}^2 + \tfrac{1}{2} R_p \text{ Re } \{\mathbf{I} \mathbf{I}_p^*\} = P_p + \tfrac{1}{2} R_p \text{ Re } \{\mathbf{I} \mathbf{I}_p^*\} \quad (12\text{-}38) \end{aligned}$$

As expected, a portion of the reading is traceable to the power, P_p, dissipated in R_p.

The second term of Eq. (12-38) may be evaluated by using

$$\mathbf{I} = \frac{\mathbf{V}}{\mathbf{Z}} = \frac{V\epsilon^{j\psi}}{Z\epsilon^{j\alpha}} = \frac{V}{Z}\,\epsilon^{j(\psi-\alpha)} \qquad \mathbf{I}_p^* = \frac{\mathbf{V}^*}{\mathbf{Z}_p^*} = \frac{V\epsilon^{-j\psi}}{Z_p\epsilon^{-j\beta}} = \frac{V}{Z_p}\,\epsilon^{j(\beta-\psi)}$$

It then becomes

$$\frac{1}{2}\,R_p\,\mathrm{Re}\left\{\frac{V^2}{ZZ_p}\,\epsilon^{j(\beta-\alpha)}\right\} = \frac{1}{2}\,R_p\,\frac{V^2}{ZZ_p}\cos{(\beta-\alpha)} = \frac{1}{2}\,VI\,\frac{R_p}{Z_p}\cos{(\alpha-\beta)}$$

Note that the phase angle of $\mathbf{V}$ has dropped out. Thus, Eq. (12-38) becomes

$$P_r = P_p + \frac{1}{2}\,VI\,\frac{R_p}{Z_p}\cos{(\alpha-\beta)} \qquad\qquad (12\text{-}39)$$

If the reactance of the potential circuit is neglected, $\omega L_p = 0$, then $\mathbf{Z}_p = R_p$ and $\beta = 0$. Equation (12-39) then becomes

$$P_r = P_p + \tfrac{1}{2}VI\cos\alpha = P_p + P_Z \qquad \omega L_p = 0 \qquad (12\text{-}40)$$

The reading is equal to the load power, P_Z, plus the power dissipated in the potential circuit, P_p, in this special case.

If ωL_p is not negligible, this introduces an error in the reading over and above the P_p term. The second term in Eq. (12-39) becomes

$$\frac{1}{2}\,VI\,\frac{R_p}{Z_p}\,(\cos\alpha\cos\beta + \sin\alpha\sin\beta) = \frac{1}{2}\,\frac{VIR_p}{Z_p^2}\,(R_p\cos\alpha + \omega L_p\sin\alpha)$$

using $\cos\beta = R_p/Z_p$ and $\sin\beta = \omega L_p/Z_p$. With $Z_p^2 = R_p^2 + (\omega L_p)^2$, this may also be written

$$\frac{1}{2}\,VI\left[\frac{R_p^2\cos\alpha}{R_p^2 + (\omega L_p)^2} + \frac{R_p\omega L_p\sin\alpha}{R_p^2 + (\omega L_p)^2}\right] \qquad (12\text{-}41)$$

In practically all cases of interest, ωL_p is sufficiently small compared with R_p to permit $(\omega L_p)^2$ to be neglected with respect to R_p^2 in the denominator of Eq. (12-41). Applying this approximation, and adding the P_p term, the final result for the wattmeter reading becomes

$$P_r \approx P_p + P_Z + \tfrac{1}{2}VI\,\frac{\omega L_p}{R_p}\sin\alpha \qquad (\omega L_p)^2 \ll R_p^2 \qquad (12\text{-}42)$$

The additional error term, containing $\omega L_p/R_p = \tan\beta$, depends not only upon the phase angle of the potential circuit, but also upon the phase angle, α, of the load impedance. If $\mathbf{Z}$ is an inductive load, α lies in the first quadrant and the error term is positive; that is, the reading is higher than in the case of $\omega L_p = 0$. If the load is capacitive, then α

lies in the fourth quadrant and the error term is negative; that is, the reading is less than in the case of $\omega L_p = 0$. For a resistive load, the error term is zero, but the exact result in Eq. (12-41) is still slightly dependent upon ωL_p as may be seen from

$$P_r = P_p + \frac{P_z}{1 + \tan^2 \beta} = P_p + P_z \cos^2 \beta \qquad \alpha = 0 \qquad (12\text{-}43)$$

The additional error depends sensitively upon the load and may amount to a significant portion of the reading for highly reactive loads. As the phase angle of the load approaches 90°, P_z tends toward zero while the additional error term stays finite. To illustrate, suppose the following conditions pertain in a given measurement:

$$V = 140 \text{ peak volts} \qquad \tan \beta = 0.02$$
$$I = 5 \text{ peak amperes} \qquad R_p = 1{,}000 \text{ ohms}$$
$$\alpha = 78°$$

Since the phase angle of the potential circuit is small, then $\omega L_p \approx 0.02 R_p$, and

$$Z_p = R_p \sqrt{1 + \left(\frac{\omega L_p}{R_p}\right)^2} \approx R_p$$

Hence, the power loss in R_p is

$$P_p \approx \frac{1}{2} \frac{V^2}{R_p} = \frac{19{,}600}{2{,}000} = 9.8 \text{ watts}$$

The load power is

$$P_z = \frac{1}{2} V I \cos \alpha = \frac{1}{2}(140)(5)(0.208) = 72.8 \text{ watts}$$

The additional error owing to reactance of the potential circuit is

$$\frac{1}{2} V I \tan \beta \sin \alpha = \frac{1}{2}(140)(5)(0.02)(0.978) = 6.8 \text{ watts}$$

Therefore, the wattmeter reading is

$$P_r = 9.8 + 72.8 + 6.8 = 89.4 \text{ watts}$$

12-11. Compensation for Potential-coil Reactance. Many wattmeters are compensated for the error resulting from the reactance, ωL_p, of the potential coil. One type of compensation circuit is shown in Fig. 12-13. The resistance kR, where k is a constant, includes the resistance of coil P. As the frequency is increased, the shunting effect of capacitor C becomes more pronounced, and this tends to offset the increase in ωL_p with frequency. The objective is to select suitable values of the design parameters C, R, and k so as to extend the range of frequencies over which the equivalent impedance is maintained essentially resistive.

The circuit is basically a low Q resonant circuit. Its possibilities in this application are disclosed by examining the impedance expression.

$$\mathbf{Z}_p = kR + j\omega L_p + \frac{R}{1 + j\omega RC}$$

$$= kR + \frac{R}{1 + (\omega RC)^2} + j\omega \left[L_p - \frac{R^2 C}{1 + (\omega RC)^2} \right] \quad (12\text{-}44)$$

If the product RC is selected such that $(\omega RC)^2 \ll 1$ at the highest frequency of interest, then for all lower frequencies the impedance is approximately

$$\mathbf{Z}_p \approx R(k + 1) + j\omega(L_p - R^2 C) \qquad (\omega RC)^2 \ll 1$$

If, in addition, $R^2 C$ is made equal to L_p, then the impedance is maintained essentially resistive and equal to $R(k + 1)$, so long as the frequency is low enough to permit neglect of $(\omega RC)^2$ compared with 1. With such design, the resistance R_p, used in previous discussions, would be made equal to $R(k + 1)$.

The phase angle of $\mathbf{Z}_p$ is the critical factor in producing the wattmeter error, as indicated by Eq. (12-42). Without compensation ($C = 0$), this phase angle is given by

$$\tan \beta = \frac{\omega L_p}{R(k + 1)} = \frac{\omega L_p}{R_p}$$

With compensation, the phase angle, β', is obtained from Eq. (12-44).

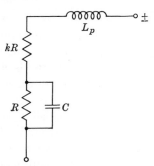

FIG. 12-13. Compensation for potential-coil reactance.

$$\tan \beta' = \frac{\omega L_p + \omega L_p(\omega RC)^2 - \omega R^2 C}{R(k + 1) + kR(\omega RC)^2} \qquad (12\text{-}45)$$

If the circuit is designed so that $R^2 C = L_p$, this becomes

$$\tan \beta' = \frac{\omega L_p(\omega RC)^2}{R(k + 1) + kR(\omega RC)^2}$$

Therefore,

$$\frac{\tan \beta'}{\tan \beta} = \frac{(\omega RC)^2}{1 + (\omega RC)^2 k/(k + 1)} \qquad (12\text{-}46)$$

For $(\omega RC)^2 \ll 1$, it is apparent that a very considerable reduction in phase angle results. For example, with $\omega RC = 0.1$, $\tan \beta'$ is only about 1 per cent of $\tan \beta$. Thus, in the numerical example of the preceding section, a compensation circuit with $R(k + 1) = 1,000$ ohms would reduce the additional error of 6.8 watts to a negligible level of about 0.07 watt, with $\omega RC = 0.1$.

The reduction in phase angle of $\mathbf{Z}_p$ is not critically dependent upon k for small ωRC. Values of k considerably larger than 1 are used in practice, primarily to protect coil P in the event capacitance C develops a short circuit. (See also Prob. 12-17.)

12-12. Special Applications of Electrodynamometer Movement. There is nothing peculiar about the electrodynamometer movement that restricts its applications to wattmeters. Indeed, it has been shown that there may be some difficulty in making the reading correspond faithfully to the power dissipated in the load to which the wattmeter is connected. Several ideas for uses of this movement other than as an ammeter, voltmeter, or wattmeter are described below.

If the coil currents are both sinusoidal and have the same frequency, the average deflection, using Eqs. (12-37) and (12-34), is given by

$$\theta_{\mathrm{av}} = \frac{1}{2K} I_c I_p \cos \left(\phi_c - \phi_p \right) = \frac{1}{2K} \operatorname{Re} \left\{ \mathbf{I}_c \mathbf{I}_p^* \right\} \qquad (12\text{-}47)$$

Since average deflection depends upon phase difference between coil currents, one might consider the possibility of using this movement as a phase-angle meter. Suppose a sinusoidal voltage, represented by the complex quantity $\mathbf{E}$, is applied to a linear network, as shown in Fig. 12-14a. The phase angle between $\mathbf{E}$ and the output current of the network is to be measured. Designate the network output current by $\mathbf{I}_p$ and apply it to coil P of an electrodynamometer movement. Supply coil C with a current $\mathbf{I}_c$, directly from $\mathbf{E}$. This current will be in phase with $\mathbf{E}$ if R is large compared with both ωL_c and the internal reactance of $\mathbf{E}$. The deflection of the movement is then proportional to the cosine of the desired phase difference. The deflection will also depend upon the magnitude of the currents, and this poses difficulties in calibrating the scale directly in phase difference. However, adjustable attenuators could be used to maintain the currents at standardized values, indicated by two ammeters, for which the phase-angle calibration would hold. This arrangement is shown in Fig. 12-14b.

An alternative, and more satisfactory arrangement, would be to apply the current $\mathbf{I}_c$ through a phase-shifting network of known and adjustable phase shift, as shown in Fig. 12-14c. When the phase-shifting network is adjusted for maximum deflection of the movement, the phase difference between $\mathbf{E}$ and $\mathbf{I}_p$ may be read directly from the phase-shifter setting. This method is obviously independent of the calibration of the electrodynamometer. It only requires that the currents be large enough to give adequate sensitivity for the phase adjustment. The maximum of the cosine function in Eq. (12-47) is rather broad, so the sharpness of the adjustment is poor. To overcome this obstacle, the phase shifter could be adjusted to produce a zero reading, where the slope of the θ_{av} vs. phase angle is steepest. This would define the phase-shifter setting more precisely, and the null adjustment would correspond to coil currents that were 90° out of phase.

Another possibility is to use the electrodynamometer as a portion of a frequency meter. Suppose a sinusoidal voltage, $e(t)$, whose frequency is

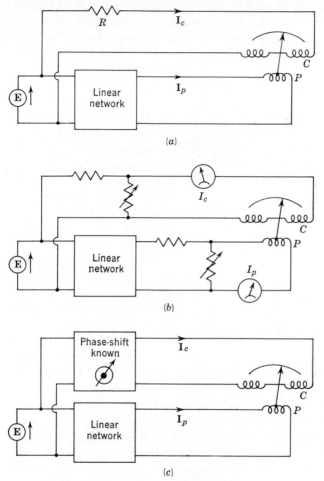

FIG. 12-14. Phase-shift measurements.

to be determined, is applied to coil P, as shown in Fig. 12-15. A sinusoidal oscillator of variable and known frequency is connected to coil C. For any given angular frequency, ω, of the oscillator, the average deflection over a time interval $t_2 - t_1$ is given by

$$\theta_{\mathrm{av}} = \frac{1}{K(t_2 - t_1)} \int_{t_1}^{t_2} I_c \cos(\omega t + \phi_c) I_p \cos(\omega_1 t + \phi_p)\, dt \quad (12\text{-}48)$$

where ω_1 is the unknown angular frequency of $e(t)$.   It can be shown that θ_{av} is zero for all $\omega \neq \omega_1$, provided that the interval $t_2 - t_1$ is properly chosen.   A rigorous demonstration is beyond the scope of this text, but the following qualitative reasoning should be helpful.   Obviously, if $\omega = \omega_1$, then θ_{av} is given by Eq. (12-47) and is nonzero, provided that $\phi_c - \phi_p$ is not an odd multiple of $\pi/2$.   Further, it is known from Chap. 11 that θ_{av} is zero if ω and ω_1 are harmonically related, where it is understood that $t_2 - t_1$ is the period of the lower frequency.   Let ω deviate slightly from ω_1 and envision what will happen to the deflection that was steady at $\omega = \omega_1$.   The deflection will vary slowly and periodically from a maximum, through zero, to a minimum negative reading, and so forth.   In fact, the low-frequency oscillation of the pointer will be equal to the difference between ω and ω_1.   The average value of θ will be zero if $t_2 - t_1$ is an interval equal to the period of this difference frequency.   By this reasoning, it becomes apparent that the only possible condition under which θ_{av} is not zero is $\omega = \omega_1$.

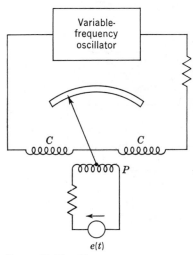

FIG. 12-15. Frequency measurements.

The oscillator frequency may be adjusted until a steady nonzero reading is obtained.   Then $\omega = \omega_1$, and the result is independent of the calibration of the electrodynamometer and is as trustworthy as the accuracy with which the oscillator frequency is known.   There are an infinite number of different values of θ_{av} for the condition $\omega = \omega_1$, depending upon the phase difference between coil currents.   If ω is changed slightly and then shifted back to its former value, the new steady deflection will generally differ from the former value.   Thus, in tuning ω to ω_1, the oscillator may be adjusted until θ_{av} is not only steady but also displays maximum deflection.

The foregoing discussion suggests that the electrodynamometer movement may be used as a harmonic wave analyzer.   To illustrate, suppose $e(t)$ is the square wave shown in Fig. 12-16 and is applied to coil P of Fig. 12-15.   The Fourier series of this wave was developed in Eq. (11-25). When the frequency of the oscillator approaches one of the harmonics of $e(t)$, the electrodynamometer pointer will start to oscillate with small amplitude and high frequency.   (Larger frequency differences lie entirely outside the range of response of the movement, owing to its damping and large moment of inertia.)   As a particular harmonic of $e(t)$ is approached more and more closely, the frequency of oscillation of the pointer will decrease while its peak amplitude will increase. Finally, when the pointer comes to rest at a steady deflection, this signifies that the oscillator frequency is equal to the particular harmonic of $e(t)$ that was approached. By suitable adjustment of the oscillator frequency, the maximum possible value of θ_{av} may be obtained. This corresponds to

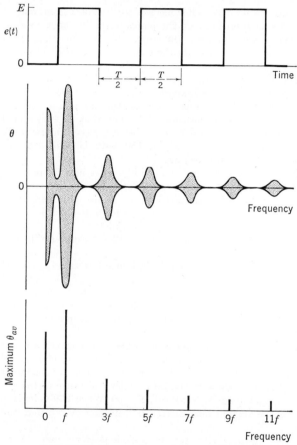

FIG. 12-16. Harmonic analyzer application.

in-phase coil currents, so $\cos (\phi_c - \phi_p) = 1$. This maximum value of θ_{av} is proportional to the amplitude of the particular harmonic of $e(t)$, assuming that the circuits are nonreactive at all frequencies of operation. By this procedure, it is evident that the relative amplitude spectrum of $e(t)$ could be determined, as indicated in Fig. 12-16. The relative phase of the harmonics is not disclosed, as is true in most harmonic wave analyzers.

There are other interesting uses that may be envisioned for this fascinating movement.   The student is urged to criticize the practical difficulties that might be encountered in the arrangements suggested here and to explore additional possibilities of his own.

PROBLEMS

12-1 (§3). A parallel-plate capacitor has a plate area of 2 sq in. and a plate separation of 5 mm.   The medium between the plates has a dielectric constant of 4.   The potential difference between plates is 100 volts.   Neglect the fringing field and determine (a) the charge on each plate, (b) the energy stored in the electric field, and (c) the force of attraction between the plates.

12-2 (§3). Two circular one-turn coils of radii r_1 and r_2, carrying currents i_1 and i_2, respectively, are placed a distance D apart in air.   The axes of the coils are coincident (that is, the planes of the coils are parallel, and the line joining the circle centers is perpendicular to the planes of the coils).   Assume that $D \gg r_2$ and determine an approximate expression for the total force produced between the two coils.

12-3 (§4). A voltage $e = 100 + 100 \sin 150t$ volts is applied to an electrostatic voltmeter.   Compute the meter reading.

12-4 (§4). The electrostatic voltmeter of Fig. 12-4 has six parallel fixed plates equispaced at 4-mm intervals, and 5 interleaved semicircular movable plates that move in planes midway between the fixed plates, in air.   The radius of the movable plates is 4 cm.   Neglect fringing, edge effects, and plate thickness.   (a) Determine the equation for the law of deflection of this voltmeter.   (b) Full-scale deflection of 10 kv rms occurs at $\theta = 100°$, as shown in Fig. 12-4.   Compute the numerical value of the spring constant, S.

12-5 (§5). The law of deflection of a moving-iron ammeter is $I_{rms} = 4\theta_{av}^{n}$ amp, where θ is in radians and n is a constant.   When the meter current is zero, the self-inductance is 10 mh.   The spring constant is $S = 0.16$ newton-meter (per radian).   (a) Determine an expression for the self-inductance of the meter as a function of θ and n.   (b) With $n = \frac{3}{4}$, find the meter current and scale deflection, in degrees, that correspond to a self-inductance of 60 mh.

12-6 (§5). The moving-iron ammeter of Fig. 12-5 is converted to a 0 to 500-volt 60-cps voltmeter by adding a resistor in series with the coil, which has a self-inductance $L = (0.01 + 0.2\theta)/4\pi$ henry, where θ is in radians.   The total angular span of the meter scale is 100°.   (a) Compute the total series resistance of the voltmeter.   (b) Compute the value of the spring constant, S.   (c) When 250 volts is applied to the voltmeter, what is the angular deflection?   Is it greater or less than the 5-amp scale mark?

12-7 (§5). A moving-iron voltmeter and a diode peak voltmeter (calibrated in rms volts of a sinusoid) are connected in parallel.   A voltage $E(\sin \omega t + 0.5 \sin 2\omega t)$ volts is applied.   The diode voltmeter reads 100 volts rms.   What does the moving-iron voltmeter indicate?

12-8 (§8). The current coil of an electrodynamometer wattmeter is connected to a 24-volt d-c emf in series with a 6-ohm resistor.   The potential circuit is connected through an ideal rectifier to a 60-cps sinusoidal emf of zero internal impedance and peak voltage of 100 volts.   Neglect the reactance of the wattmeter coils. $R_p = 1,000$ ohms.   Compute the wattmeter reading.

12-9 (§8). An uncompensated electrodynamometer wattmeter reads 250 watts when direct currents of 1.0 amp and 0.05 amp exist in its current coil and potential coil, respectively. (*a*) What will this wattmeter read when a current

$$10 \sin (377t + 15°) + 5 \sin 1131t \qquad \text{amp}$$

is applied to its current coil, and a voltage

$$500 \cos (377t - 30°) + 800 \sin (754t + 45°) \qquad \text{volts}$$

is applied to its potential circuit? The potential-circuit inductance is negligible.
(*b*) What is the resistance of the potential-coil circuit?

12-10 (§8). The square-wave voltage of Fig. 12-16 has a peak value $E = 100$ volts
and a period $T = 0.01$ sec. It is applied to the potential coil of an electrodynamometer wattmeter. A current $10 \sin 628t$ amp is passed through the current coil.
What does the wattmeter read?

12-11 (§9). The square-wave voltage of Fig. 12-16 has a peak value $E = 50$ volts.
It is applied to the circuit of Fig. 12-10, connection A, where $R = 500$ ohms and $R_p =$
4,000 ohms. Assume that the reactance of the wattmeter is negligible. Compute
the wattmeter reading.

12-12 (§9). A *zero-center-scale* compensated wattmeter is to be connected between
a 100-volt (rms) line and a 100-ohm resistive load. The wattmeter has negligible
current-coil impedance, negligible potential-circuit reactance, and has provisions for
switching the compensation off or on. Determine the wattmeter reading, in watts, for
each of the eight conditions indicated in the table. $R_p = 2,000$ ohms.

Compensation winding	± Terminal connection	
	Current coil	Potential circuit
(*a*) Off		
	Line	Line
(*b*) On		
(*c*) Off		
	Line	Load
(*d*) On		
(*e*) Off		
	Load	Line
(*f*) On		
(*g*) Off		
	Load	Load
(*h*) On		

In all cases the unmarked potential-circuit terminal is connected correctly to the side
of the line that does not contain the current coil. The unmarked current-coil terminal
is connected so as to permit power to be delivered to the load in each case.

12-13 (§10). The load, R, in the circuits of Fig. 12-10 is replaced by an arbitrary
impedance, $\mathbf{Z}$, and e is a sinusoidal voltage. Neglect the reactance of the wattmeter
coils. Show that with connection A, the wattmeter reads high by an amount equal
to the dissipation in the potential circuit; and that with connection B, the wattmeter
reads high by an amount equal to the dissipation in coil C.

12-14 (§10). The wattmeter in Fig. 12-12 has negligible current-coil impedance, $R_p = 5,000$ ohms and $\omega L_p = 100$ ohms. What will it read in a 110-volt single-phase line delivering power to a load $Z = 100 - j173$ ohms?

12-15 (§10). In the circuit of Fig. 12-12, $R_p = 5,000$ ohms, $\omega L_p = 40$ ohms, $V = 100$ volts, rms, and $I = 10$ amp, rms. The load impedance is highly capacitive. The wattmeter reads 30 watts. Compute the phase angle of the load impedance.

12-16 (§10). Connection B of Fig. 12-10 is used to measure the power delivered from a sinusoidal source of peak voltage, V, to a load impedance, Z. Determine an approximate expression for the wattmeter reading, with $(\omega L_p)^2 \ll R_p{}^2$, and compare the additional error term with that of Eq. (12-42). Do not neglect R_c, L_c, R_p, or L_p.

12-17 (§11). The frequency compensation circuit of Fig. 12-13 is designed using $L_p = R^2C$ and $k = 2$. (a) What is the phase angle of Z_p when $\omega RC = 0.1$? (b) If the circuit is redesigned using $k = 9$, but maintaining $R_p = R(k + 1)$ constant, what is the phase angle of Z_p at the same frequency of part (a)?

12-18 (§11). The compensating circuit of Fig. 12-13 has been designed with $L_p = R^2C$ and $k = 10$. Compute the deviation of the magnitude of the impedance, Z_p, from its low-frequency value, $11R$, when the compensated phase angle of the potential circuit, β', is $3°26'$.

ALTERNATING-CURRENT BRIDGE ANALYSIS

Alternating-current bridges were introduced in Chap. 9, where balance equations, bridge classifications, and several examples of bridges used to measure electrical parameters were presented. Because the a-c bridge is so versatile and so widely used, as described in Sec. 9-13, it is desirable to explore analysis methods that are flexible and generally applicable to the bridge configuration.

An exact solution for the unbalanced bridge is obtained from the direct-current bridge analysis of Chap. 10. The compensation theorem is applied to the slightly unbalanced bridge. Circle loci are presented, and this leads to an understanding of balance convergence. Voltage sensitivity of the a-c bridge is defined and studied in several examples. Voltage transfer functions under variable-frequency conditions are discussed and illustrated for the resonance and Wien bridges.

13-1. Unbalanced A-C Bridge. The notation to be used for a-c bridges was defined in Fig. 9-17 and is repeated in Fig. 13-1. All analyses are confined to the steady sinusoidal state. Balance conditions for the bridge are found by equating products of impedances in opposite bridge arms. Thus,

$$\mathbf{Z}_1\mathbf{Z}_0 = \mathbf{Z}_4\mathbf{Z}_2 \qquad (13\text{-}1)$$

where $\mathbf{Z}_3 = \mathbf{Z}_0$ represents the value of $\mathbf{Z}_3$, considered to be variable and required for balance. When Eq. (13-1) is satisfied, the detector current (and voltage) is zero.

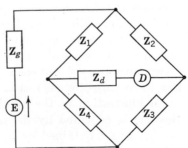

FIG. 13-1. Four-arm a-c bridge.

A general expression for the detector current in the unbalanced bridge may be obtained by exactly the same methods used for d-c bridges in Chap. 10. In the exact solution of the Wheatstone bridge, Eq. (10-6), it is only necessary to replace the d-c quantities by corresponding a-c quantities. Suppose that the bridge is unbalanced by changing $\mathbf{Z}_3$ by an amount $\mathbf{Z}$ from its balance value, $\mathbf{Z}_0$. To obtain $\mathbf{I}_d$, the complex detector current, from Eq. (10-6) replace E by $\mathbf{E}$, B by $\mathbf{Z}_g$, M by $\mathbf{Z}_1$, P by $\mathbf{Z}_2$,

X_0 by $\mathbf{Z}_0$, R by $\mathbf{Z}$, N by $\mathbf{Z}_4$, G by $\mathbf{Z}_d$, and, of course, I_g by $\mathbf{I}_d$ (see Fig. 10-1). Then Eq. (10-6) becomes

$$\mathbf{I}_d = \frac{E}{(\mathbf{Z}_g + \mathbf{Z}_2 + \mathbf{Z}_0 + \mathbf{Z}_g\mathbf{Z}_2/\mathbf{Z}_1)(\mathbf{Z}_d + \mathbf{Z}_4 + \mathbf{Z}_0 + \mathbf{Z}_d\mathbf{Z}_4/\mathbf{Z}_1)} \left[\frac{\mathbf{Z}}{1 + \mathbf{kZ}} \right]$$

(13-2)

$$\text{where} \quad \mathbf{k} = \frac{\mathbf{Z}_1(\mathbf{Z}_2 + \mathbf{Z}_d) + (\mathbf{Z}_g + \mathbf{Z}_4)(\mathbf{Z}_1 + \mathbf{Z}_2 + \mathbf{Z}_d)}{\mathbf{Z}_1(\mathbf{Z}_g + \mathbf{Z}_2 + \mathbf{Z}_0 + \mathbf{Z}_g\mathbf{Z}_2/\mathbf{Z}_1)(\mathbf{Z}_d + \mathbf{Z}_4 + \mathbf{Z}_0 + \mathbf{Z}_d\mathbf{Z}_4/\mathbf{Z}_1)}$$

In similar fashion, other equations of Chap. 10 may be converted to corresponding complex equations and applied to a-c bridges. If that were all there was to the matter, there would be no need to go further. However, there are important differences between the d-c and a-c cases, even though the form of the equations is preserved. The complex quantities are functions of frequency, and this represents an additional variable as compared with the d-c case. Also, there are two distinct and independent balance conditions implied in Eq. (13-1), and phase angles are important quantities. Moreover, the change, $\mathbf{Z}$, consists of two independent parts, the real and imaginary components of $\mathbf{Z}$. These items, and their consequences, will receive major attention in this chapter.

13-2. Application of Compensation Theorem. In most a-c bridge applications, extreme bridge unbalance is of minor interest. The slightly unbalanced bridge receives most study, as was also true in the d-c case. Bridge sensitivity, bridge accuracy, behavior of balance adjustments, and other pertinent factors may be appraised in terms of slight deviations from balance. In consequence, the approximate compensation theorem becomes a preferred analysis method. It may be applied directly in each specific case, with no need to resort to formulas, and the problem is reduced to a series of minor calculations. While results may also be obtained from general formulas, such as Eq. (13-2), it is usually more satisfactory to work out each bridge individually for the particular quantity to be varied in each case.

An illustration of the application of the approximate compensation theorem is provided by the inductance bridge of Fig. 13-2a. Balance conditions are obtained by equating products of impedances in opposite bridge arms.

$$R_1(R_3 + j\omega L_3) = R_4(R_2 + j\omega L_2)$$

The real and imaginary parts of this equation must be separately equal. Hence, the two independent balance conditions that must be satisfied to attain zero detector output are

$$R_1R_3 = R_4R_2 \qquad R_1L_3 = R_4L_2 \tag{13-3}$$

where the angular frequency, ω, has been canceled. This signifies that bridge balance is independent of frequency so long as the bridge arms may be represented by the circuit elements designated in Fig. 13-2a. The resistive balance is the same as that required in a Wheatstone bridge if L_2 and L_3 were zero. The reactive balance implies that the phase angles, α_2 and α_3, of the two inductive arms are equal. This may be seen by rearranging Eq. (13-3).

$$\frac{R_1}{R_4} = \frac{R_2}{R_3} = \frac{L_2}{L_3} = \frac{\omega L_2}{\omega L_3}$$

Therefore,

$$\tan \alpha_3 = \frac{\omega L_3}{R_3} = \tan \alpha_2 = \frac{\omega L_2}{R_2} \tag{13-4}$$

The detector current may be obtained for a small change in any bridge element from the balance value required in Eq. (13-3) by application of

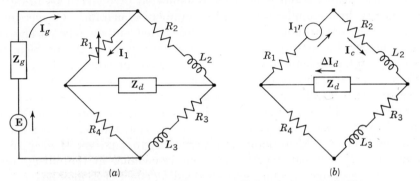

FIG. 13-2. Compensation theorem applied to inductance bridge.

the compensation theorem. For example, let R_1 change from its balance value by a small amount, r. First, it is necessary to obtain the current through R_1 at balance, and this is found from the generator current.

$$I_g = \frac{E}{Z_g + \dfrac{[R_2 + R_3 + j\omega(L_2 + L_3)](R_1 + R_4)}{R_1 + R_2 + R_3 + R_4 + j\omega(L_2 + L_3)}}$$

By use of the current-splitting rule, the current, I_1, through R_1 follows directly.

$$I_1 = \frac{R_2 + R_3 + j\omega(L_2 + L_3)}{R_1 + R_2 + R_3 + R_4 + j\omega(L_2 + L_3)} I_g$$

The change in currents throughout the bridge circuit resulting from the change, r, in R_1 is given by a "compensation" generator, $I_1 r$, acting in series with R_1 as shown in Fig. 13-2b. In this circuit, r has been neglected compared with R_1, and this permits the generator impedance to be removed with small error, as was shown in Sec. 10-4. The total current delivered by the compensation generator is

$$\mathbf{I}_c = \frac{\mathbf{I}_1 r}{R_1 + R_2 + j\omega L_2 + \dfrac{(R_3 + R_4 + j\omega L_3)\mathbf{Z}_d}{R_3 + R_4 + j\omega L_3 + \mathbf{Z}_d}}$$

The current-splitting rule gives the change in detector current from its balance value of zero.

$$\Delta \mathbf{I}_d = \frac{R_3 + R_4 + j\omega L_3}{R_3 + R_4 + j\omega L_3 + \mathbf{Z}_d} \mathbf{I}_c$$

The fractional error in this result is, at most, equal to r/R_1.

Numerical calculations may become somewhat involved in a-c bridges, and facility in manipulating complex numbers is helpful. Conversions from rectangular to polar form may be carried out quickly on special slide rules. The compensation theorem always reduces the problem to a series of minor calculations, no matter how complicated the bridge circuit, as illustrated by this example. The computational problem is eased to some extent if full advantage is taken of impedance levels encountered in practical bridges. In many cases, the generator impedance, $\mathbf{Z}_g$, is much less than the impedance of the bridge arms and may be neglected with small error. Also, many practical detectors possess a very high impedance, $\mathbf{Z}_d$, compared with the input impedance at the output terminals of the bridge, in which case the loading effect of $\mathbf{Z}_d$ may be ignored with good approximation.

13-3. Detector-voltage Circle Loci. Graphical methods are used frequently in engineering analysis, and a-c bridges are not exceptions. *Phasor diagrams* representing complex quantities are sometimes useful in steady-state circuit analysis and may also be constructed for bridge circuits. This technique permits graphical visualization of bridge behavior under variable off-balance conditions. Examination of the complex detector voltage in terms of loci in the complex plane is particularly revealing.

To simplify the discussion without losing the characteristic features of bridge behavior, assume that the generator impedance is zero and that the detector impedance is infinite in the four-arm bridge of Fig. 13-1. These assumptions are not unrealistic in certain practical bridge circuits. Then the complex detector voltage, $\mathbf{E}_d$, is obtained directly from the voltage-divider rule.

$$\mathbf{E}_d = \left(\frac{\mathbf{Z}_1}{\mathbf{Z}_1 + \mathbf{Z}_4} - \frac{\mathbf{Z}_2}{\mathbf{Z}_2 + \mathbf{Z}_3} \right) \mathbf{E}$$

and is a voltage rise from the junction of Z_1 and Z_4 to that of Z_2 and Z_3. Cross-multiply and cancel the numerator terms, $\pm Z_1 Z_2$.

$$\frac{E_d}{E} = \frac{Z_1 Z_3 - Z_2 Z_4}{(Z_1 + Z_4)(Z_2 + Z_3)} \qquad (13\text{-}5)$$

Clearly, the detector voltage is zero when $Z_1 Z_3 = Z_2 Z_4$, which is the familiar balance equation.

Designate one circuit element in the bridge with the symbol s and consider it to be a real variable. If all other parameters are constant, Eq. (13-5) may be placed in the form

$$\frac{E_d}{E} = \frac{As + B}{Cs + D} \qquad (13\text{-}6)$$

where A, B, C, and D are complex constants. For example, if the four bridge-arm impedances are expressed in rectangular form, $Z_k = R_k + jX_k$, where $k = 1, 2, 3, 4$, and the single variable circuit element is $R_1 = s$, then

$$A = R_3 + jX_3$$
$$B = jX_1(R_3 + jX_3) - (R_2 + jX_2)(R_4 + jX_4)$$
$$C = R_2 + R_3 + j(X_2 + X_3)$$
$$D = [R_4 + j(X_1 + X_4)][R_2 + R_3 + j(X_2 + X_3)]$$

The form of Eq. (13-6) indicates that the locus of E_d/E in the complex plane is a circle as s is varied. Undoubtedly the student has already encountered this form in connection with circle loci for networks, but perhaps he has been unaware of the general circle equation. It is easy to prove that Eq. (13-6) represents a circle in the complex plane, but the algebra is rather unwieldy. A proof is outlined below, and the student is urged to fill in the algebraic details.

Express the four complex constants in rectangular form, and let u and v represent the real and imaginary components of E_d/E, respectively. Then Eq. (13-6) becomes

$$\frac{E_d}{E} = u + jv = \frac{(a + jb)s + (c + jd)}{(e + jf)s + (g + jh)} \qquad (13\text{-}7)$$

where a, b, c, d, e, f, g, h are real constants representing the real and imaginary parts of A, B, C, D, as is evident on comparison with Eq. (13-6). This complex equation relating the real variables u, v, and s implies two real equations. The proof consists of eliminating s from these two equations and showing that the resulting equation in u and v is that of a circle.

Cross-multiply Eq. (13-7), collect all terms in s, and equate real and imaginary parts. The equation of the reals and imaginaries, in that order, is

$$(a - ue + vf)s = ug - vh - c$$

$$(b - ve - uf)s = vg + uh - d$$

Divide the first equation by the second, as suggested by the horizontal ruling, and s is eliminated. The proof is seen to be complete upon cross

Curve number	a	b	c	d	e	f	g	h
1	a	0	c	d	0	0	1	0
2	0	b	c	d	0	0	-1	0
3	a	b	0	0	0	0	1	0
4	0	$-fg$	gk	0	0	f	g	0
5	0	0	$2gk$	0	0	f	g	0
6	0	$2k_2e$	0	$-2k_1h$	e	0	0	h

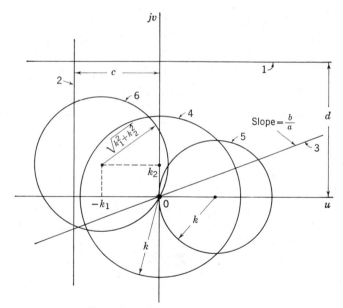

Fig. 13-3. Examples of circle loci.

multiplication, because all terms in uv cancel. [The uv terms that cancel upon cross multiplication are $(fh - eg)uv$.] Terms only in u^2, u, v^2, v, and constants remain. This means that the equation involving u and v is that of a circle.

Although the proof is complete, the circle equation may be manipulated, if desired, to determine explicit formulas for the coordinates of the center of the circle, and its radius. When all terms in u^2, u, v^2, and v are collected, and the squares completed, the following equation results:

$$(u - u_0)^2 + (v - v_0)^2 = \rho^2 \tag{13-8}$$

This is the equation of a circle with center at $u = u_0$, $v = v_0$, and ρ^2 is the square of the circle radius.

$$u_0 = \frac{bg + cf - ah - de}{2(fg - eh)} \qquad v_0 = \frac{ce + df - ag - bh}{2(fg - eh)}$$

$$\rho^2 = u_0{}^2 + v_0{}^2 + \frac{ad - bc}{fg - eh} \tag{13-9}$$

These results show that the circle degenerates into a straight line if $fg = eh$, for then the coordinates of the circle center, as well as its radius, become infinite.

Several examples of circles in the complex plane (uv plane) are given in Fig. 13-3 for special values of the constants. These suggest that circles with any radius and center, or any straight line, may be obtained by suitable choice of constants. Thus, it has been shown that Eq. (13-6) represents a circle in the complex plane, including a straight line as a degenerate form. Any complex equation in this form is that of a circle, even if the variable, s, corresponds to the frequency, as is sometimes the case.

13-4. Resonance-bridge Loci. The resonance bridge of Fig. 13-4 provides an example of detector-voltage loci. The subscripts in arm 3 have been dropped for convenience. The open-circuit output voltage of the resonance bridge is

$$\mathbf{E}_d = \left(\frac{R_1}{R_1 + R_4} - \frac{R_2}{R_2 + R + jX} \right) \mathbf{E}$$

where $X = \omega L - 1/\omega C$ is the equivalent reactance of the resonant circuit in arm 3, and it is assumed that the impedance of $\mathbf{E}$ is zero. Cross-multiply and cancel the $\pm R_1 R_2$ terms.

$$\frac{\mathbf{E}_d}{\mathbf{E}} = \frac{R_1 R + jR_1 X - R_2 R_4}{(R_1 + R_4)(R_2 + R + jX)} \tag{13-10}$$

The output voltage is zero when *both* $X = 0$ and $R_1 R = R_2 R_4$ are satisfied, the latter being the Wheatstone-bridge balance equation.

Suppose $R_1 = s$ is variable. Then Eq. (13-10) is in the circle form of Eq. (13-6).

$$\frac{\mathbf{E}_d}{\mathbf{E}} = \frac{(R + jX)s - R_2 R_4}{(R_2 + R + jX)s + R_4(R_2 + R + jX)} \qquad R_1 = s \tag{13-11}$$

If the general results of the preceding section are applied to this equation, it is found that in the denominator

$$e = R_2 + R \qquad f = X \qquad g = R_4(R_2 + R) \qquad h = R_4 X$$

Therefore, $fg - eh = 0$, and the locus is a straight line in the complex plane.

The equation of the line may be found in the uv plane, but it is easier to consider the phasor diagram in terms of a coordinate system with

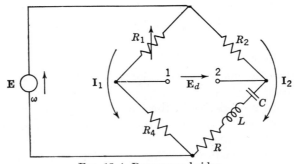

FIG. 13-4. Resonance bridge.

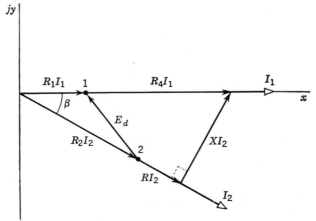

FIG. 13-5. Phasor diagram for resonance bridge; R_1 variable.

shifted origin. The complex xy plane, indicated in Fig. 13-5, leads to a rapid graphical solution. The x axis is selected to coincide with the current I_1. For definiteness in drawing the phasor diagram in Fig. 13-5, it is assumed that the reactance is positive; that is, the current I_2 lags behind I_1 by an angle β. The complex detector voltage, E_d, is directed from point 2 to point 1 in this diagram. As R_1 is varied, point 2 remains fixed and point 1 moves along the x axis from $x = 0$ (where $R_1 = 0$) to $x = E$ (where $R_1 \gg R_4$). Thus, the output-voltage locus with R_1 variable is immediately seen to be a straight line, with a minimum of computation. The equation of the line in the uv plane may be obtained with $\mathbf{E}_d/\mathbf{E} = u + jv$ in Eq. (13-11), by eliminating s.

$$v = \frac{R_2 X}{(R + R_2)^2 + X^2}$$

The origin of the uv plane is at point 2 of Fig. 13-5, and the uv axes are parallel to the xy axes.

As another illustration, suppose the reactance, X, is varied. This may be accomplished readily by varying the frequency of $\mathbf{E}$. Again a circle

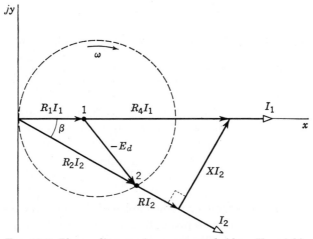

FIG. 13-6. Phasor diagram for resonance bridge; X variable.

locus results, for with $X = s$, Eq. (13-10) is in the circle form of Eq. (13-6).

$$\frac{\mathbf{E}_d}{\mathbf{E}} = \frac{(jR_1)s + R_1R - R_2R_4}{j(R_1 + R_4)s + (R_1 + R_4)(R_2 + R)} \qquad X = s \qquad (13\text{-}12)$$

In this case, using the notation of Sec. 13-3, $e = 0$, $h = 0$, and

$$fg - eh = (R_1 + R_4)^2(R_2 + R)$$

so the result is a circle.

The circle locus is again readily obtained from the phasor diagram to avoid the shifted uv axes. When X is varied, point 1 on the phasor diagram of Fig. 13-6 remains fixed, while point 2 follows the dashed circular locus. The circle is traversed in a clockwise direction as X varies from $-\infty$ to $+\infty$, which corresponds to varying the frequency from zero to infinity. Since X tends toward infinity at these two extremes, this means that $\mathbf{I}_2$, and hence $\mathbf{I}_2R_2$, go to zero. Thus, the locus is a closed circle. The y coordinate of the circle is easily seen by inspection to be

$y_0 = 0$. The x coordinate is given by $x_0 = I_{20}R_2/2$, where I_{20} is the value of I_2 when $X = 0$.

$$I_{20} = \frac{E}{R + R_2} \qquad x_0 = \frac{R_2 E}{2(R + R_2)}$$

The circle radius is equal to x_0.

If not satisfied with this graphical procedure, the formal equation of the circle in xy coordinates is readily obtained from the phasor diagram of Fig. 13-6.

$$x = R_2 I_2 \cos \beta \qquad y = R_2 I_2 \sin \beta \qquad \tan \beta = \frac{X}{R_2 + R} = \frac{y}{x}$$

Eliminate X, I_2, and β from these equations, complete the square, and obtain

$$\left[x - \frac{R_2 E}{2(R + R_2)} \right]^2 + y^2 = \left[\frac{R_2 E}{2(R + R_2)} \right]^2$$

The general circle form in Eq. (13-6) is useful for recognizing that the locus is a circle but, as shown by these examples, it is easier to analyze the bridge in a shifted coordinate system. The loci of $\mathbf{E}_d$ are valuable in studying the approach to balance when different bridge parameters are varied. This interesting aspect of bridge behavior is discussed in the next section.

13-5. Balance Convergence. The choice of circuit elements for bridge-balance adjustment usually represents a compromise among several factors. Ratio and product-arm bridges, described in Chap. 9, contain two adjustable elements, each of which may be used to independently satisfy one of the two balance equations. This is desirable to avoid interaction between the two adjustments and to permit rapid approach to bridge balance. However, accuracy requirements might prohibit this type of arrangement because continuously variable elements are usually not as accurate as step-adjusted elements. The available step adjustments might not permit fine enough control as balance is approached. Another consideration is the ease and speed with which the null is attained. The number of successive adjustments required to achieve a null might be an important factor in practice. Obviously, the greater the number of adjustments, the more time consuming becomes attainment of the null. Other factors, such as change in stray capacitance when an element is varied, also play a role in the final choice.

A study of the approach to balance resulting from successive adjustments of variable bridge elements reveals information that may serve as a guide in deciding which elements should be adjustable, and which elements fixed. The convergence to balance is readily appreciated in terms

of detector-voltage loci. For example, consider the resonance
which R_1 and ω are adjustable. If R_1 is adjusted first so that a min.
detector output is obtained, the point 1 in Fig. 13-7 moves along a straight
line to the vicinity of point 3, where the magnitude of $\mathbf{E}_d$ is a minimum
with respect to R_1 as a variable. The detector responds only to the magnitude of $\mathbf{E}_d$, and not its phase, so this is a rather broad minimum when
the bridge is as far off balance as indicated in Fig. 13-7. The uncertainty
in the location of point 3 has a corresponding range of possible locations
of $\mathbf{E}_d$, indicated by the sector emanating from point 2. If the angular
frequency, ω, is then varied (which means X is varied), point 3 remains

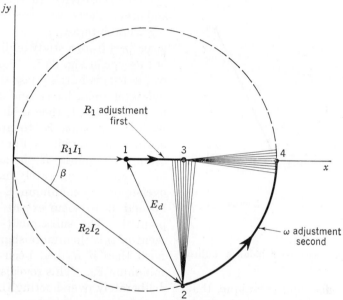

FIG. 13-7. Initial balance adjustments in resonance bridge.

fixed and point 2 follows the circular arc indicated in Fig. 13-7, until
point 4 is reached. Here, $\mathbf{E}_d$, extending from point 4 to point 3, is a
minimum with respect to ω as the variable. The minimum is again not
sharply defined, since the bridge is far from balance. The range of possible locations of $\mathbf{E}_d$, associated with the uncertainty in location of point
4, is indicated by the sector emanating from point 3. All the changes
in the magnitude of $\mathbf{E}_d$ have been relatively slight thus far. However,
when R_1 is adjusted for a second time, the point 3 will move along a
straight line toward point 4, and $\mathbf{E}_d$ will dip very sharply. Successive
and alternate adjustments of ω and R_1 will make $\mathbf{E}_d$ progressively smaller.
    The scale of Fig. 13-7 has to be enlarged considerably to follow the
detailed behavior of $\mathbf{E}_d$ with successive adjustments. A hypothetical

example is given in Fig. 13-8, where it has been assumed that the first frequency adjustment is slightly smaller than required to achieve $X = 0$ (point 4).   When R_1 is adjusted for the second time, point 3 moves to the right.   Suppose the adjustment leaves R_1 at point 5, slightly short of the exact value required for balance.   Then ω is increased until point 6 is reached.   (Note that as balance is approached more and more closely, the circular-arc segments are so small that they are essentially straight-line segments.)   Readjustment of R_1 might next produce point 7.   This process may be continued until a satisfactorily small value of $\mathbf{E}_d$ results. In practice, $\mathbf{E}_d$ is never exactly zero, since drift of circuit elements, limited detector sensitivity, thermal noise, and other effects are always present.

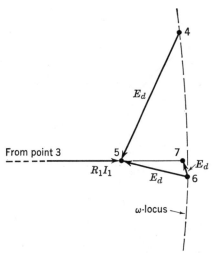

FIG. 13-8. Successive balance adjustments in resonance bridge.

Several interesting effects may be visualized from a study of diagrams of the type in Fig. 13-7.   For example, if $R_1\mathbf{I}_1$ is initially less than the radius of the ω-locus, and ω is the first adjustment, then ω should be set for *maximum* $\mathbf{E}_d$ to approach balance most rapidly.   For another example, suppose R_1 is adjusted first and is deliberately made to overshoot the minimum $\mathbf{E}_d$, going beyond it to some extent toward point 4.   The subsequent adjustment of ω is then more sharply defined than if R_1 had been set for minimum $\mathbf{E}_d$.   This reveals an important balancing technique, that of deliberately overshooting the minimum point to hasten attainment of a satisfactory null.

Analysis of balance convergence is simplified when the bridge is close to balance.   The denominator of Eq. (13-5) may be assumed to be constant for small changes in bridge-arm impedances in the vicinity of balance.   The detector voltage is then essentially proportional to the numerator of Eq. (13-5).

$$\frac{\mathbf{E}_d}{\mathbf{E}} = (\mathbf{Z}_1\mathbf{Z}_3 - \mathbf{Z}_2\mathbf{Z}_4)K\epsilon^{j\alpha} \qquad (13\text{-}13)$$

where $K\epsilon^{j\alpha}$ represents the reciprocal of the denominator, assumed to be constant.   When a single element is varied, this equation is in the form of Eq. (13-6) with $C = 0 = e + jf$.   Hence, both e and f are zero, which means that $fg - eh = 0$.   Thus, Eq. (13-13) represents a straight line in the complex plane.

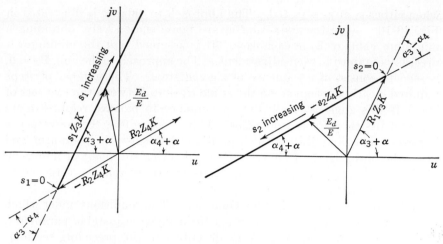

Fig. 13-9. Adjustment loci.

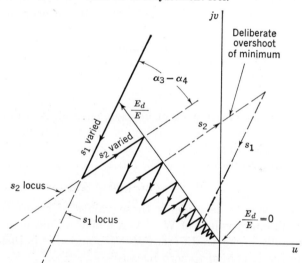

Fig. 13-10. Balance convergence near balance.

To illustrate, let $\mathbf{Z}_1 = R_1 = s_1$ and $\mathbf{Z}_2 = R_2 = s_2$ be two variable resistances in resistive bridge arms 1 and 2, respectively. Then, expressing the remaining impedances in polar form, Eq. (13-13) becomes

$$\frac{\mathbf{E}_d}{\mathbf{E}} = (Z_3\epsilon^{j\alpha_3}s_1 - R_2Z_4\epsilon^{j\alpha_4})K\epsilon^{j\alpha} \qquad R_1 = s_1, X_1 = 0$$

$$\frac{\mathbf{E}_d}{\mathbf{E}} = (-Z_4\epsilon^{j\alpha_4}s_2 + R_1Z_3\epsilon^{j\alpha_3})K\epsilon^{j\alpha} \qquad R_2 = s_2, X_2 = 0$$

The loci of $\mathbf{E}_d/\mathbf{E}$ in the uv plane are shown in general terms in Fig. 13-9 when either s_1 or s_2 is varied.   The approach to balance is illustrated in Fig. 13-10.   Adjustments s_1 and s_2 are made successively, obtaining a minimum value of $\mathbf{E}_d$ in each case.   It is assumed that the minimum is precisely obtained in each adjustment.   The approach to the null, $\mathbf{E}_d = 0$, is seen to consist of a sequence of zig-zag steps.   The number of steps required clearly depends upon the angle $\alpha_3 - \alpha_4$ between the two sets of loci.   If this angle is small, the convergence to balance requires more adjustments than for larger angles.   If $\alpha_3 - \alpha_4 = 90°$, the convergence is most rapid, and this is the condition that exists in ratio-arm and product-arm bridges.   Deliberately overshooting the point of minimum $\mathbf{E}_d$, in the correct direction, again leads to more rapid convergence to balance in this example.

13-6. Derivative of a Complex Quantity.   The conditions under which minimum output voltage is obtained for a given adjustable parameter, s, may be obtained graphically as described in the preceding sections. However, an analytical solution is often desired.   It may be obtained by setting the derivative of the *magnitude* of $\mathbf{E}_d$ with respect to s equal to zero.

Consider the complex variable, $\mathbf{W}$, which has real and imaginary parts, u and v, respectively, each of which is a function of the single real parameter s.

$$\mathbf{W} = u(s) + jv(s) \tag{13-14}$$

The complex quantity may represent voltage, current, impedance, admittance, or others.   The precise meaning of the maximum or minimum value of $\mathbf{W}$ is that its magnitude is a maximum or minimum.   Thus, the quantity to be differentiated is not $\mathbf{W}$, but is its magnitude.

$$W = \sqrt{u^2 + v^2} \tag{13-15}$$

Setting dW/ds equal to zero yields those values of s corresponding to maximum or minimum values of $\mathbf{W}$.   As a matter of mathematical technique, it is usually easier to differentiate W^2, and this is justified when setting the derivative equal to zero because

$$\frac{d(W^2)}{ds} = 2W\frac{dW}{ds} = 0 \qquad \text{when} \qquad \frac{dW}{ds} = 0$$

Therefore, from Eq. (13-15), differentiating the square of the magnitude yields

$$\frac{d(W^2)}{ds} = 2u\frac{du}{ds} + 2v\frac{dv}{ds} = 0$$

and
$$\frac{u}{v} = -\frac{\dfrac{dv}{ds}}{\dfrac{du}{ds}} \tag{13-16}$$

This represents the general condition that must be satisfied among u, v, and s for a maximum or minimum value of $\mathbf{W}$.

A common error in investigating maximum or minimum values of complex quantities is to set the derivative of the complex quantity itself equal to zero. This is a meaningless procedure, as may be seen from examination of the complex plane. When s is varied, a locus of $\mathbf{W}$ in the complex uv plane is traversed, as indicated in general in Fig. 13-11. For any value of s, the change in the complex quantity, $\mathbf{W}$, owing to an infinitesimal change in s is

$$d\mathbf{W} = \left(\frac{du}{ds} + j\frac{dv}{ds}\right)ds \qquad (13\text{-}17)$$

Note that $d\mathbf{W}$ generally has both a real and imaginary part. Examination of Fig. 13-11 reveals that the condition for maximum or minimum magnitude of $\mathbf{W}$ corresponds to points on the locus, such as a and b, where $d\mathbf{W}$ is perpendicular to $\mathbf{W}$. It does not correspond to the condition $d\mathbf{W}/ds = 0$, which specifies a stagnation point; that is, a point where $\mathbf{W}$ does not change at all when s changes.

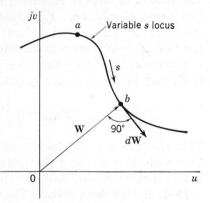

FIG. 13-11. Illustrating derivative of complex variable.

At any point on the locus, the line coinciding with $\mathbf{W}$ has a slope given by the tangent of the phase angle of $\mathbf{W}$, which is v/u. Similarly, the slope of the line coinciding with $d\mathbf{W}$ may be obtained from Eq. (13-17). This slope is $(dv/ds)/(du/ds)$. Two lines are perpendicular when their slopes are negative reciprocals. Thus, when imposing the requirement that $\mathbf{W}$ and $d\mathbf{W}$ be perpendicular, the condition for maximum or minimum $\mathbf{W}$, one obtains

$$\frac{\dfrac{dv}{ds}}{\dfrac{du}{ds}} = -\frac{1}{\dfrac{v}{u}} = -\frac{u}{v} \qquad (13\text{-}18)$$

This agrees with Eq. (13-16), obtained by setting the derivative of the magnitude of $\mathbf{W}$ equal to zero. It should be reiterated that setting $d\mathbf{W}/ds$ equal to zero has no bearing on finding the conditions for maximum and minimum values of $\mathbf{W}$.

For an illustration, return to Eq. (13-12) which specifies the output voltage of the resonance bridge of Fig. 13-4 when the reactance, $X = s$, is variable. The graphical solution in Fig. 13-6 for minimum $\mathbf{E}_d$ gives $X = 0$, provided $R_1 I_1 > R_2 I_2/2$ (otherwise $X = 0$ corresponds to a maximum). The same result is obtained analytically from $dE_d/dX = 0$, where E_d is the magnitude of $\mathbf{E}_d$. From Eq. (13-12), the square of the magnitude of $\mathbf{E}_d$ is

$$E_d{}^2 = \frac{[R_1{}^2 X^2 + (R_1 R - R_2 R_4)^2]E^2}{(R_1 + R_4)^2 X^2 + [(R_1 + R_4)(R_2 + R)]^2} = \frac{k_1{}^2 X^2 + k_2{}^2}{k_3{}^2 X^2 + k_4{}^2} \quad (13\text{-}19)$$

where $k_1 = R_1 E$, $\quad k_2 = (R_1 R - R_2 R_4)E$, $\quad k_3 = (R_1 + R_4)$, and $k_4 = (R_1 + R_4)(R_2 + R)$. Then,

$$\frac{d(E_d{}^2)}{dX} = 0 = \frac{(k_3{}^2 X^2 + k_4{}^2)2k_1{}^2 X - (k_1{}^2 X^2 + k_2{}^2)2k_3{}^2 X}{(k_3{}^2 X^2 + k_4{}^2)^2}$$

The root of interest in balancing the bridge is $X = 0$, in agreement with the graphical solution. (The root $X \to \infty$ is of no interest in balancing the bridge.) The second derivative, evaluated at $X = 0$, indicates that the root $X = 0$ gives a maximum value of $\mathbf{E}_d$ if $R_1 I_1 < R_2 I_2/2$, and a minimum value of $\mathbf{E}_d$ if this inequality is reversed. The minimum value of $\mathbf{E}_d$ may be found from Eq. (13-19) with $X = 0$.

$$E_{d_{\min}} = \frac{|R_1 R - R_2 R_4|E}{(R_1 + R_4)(R_2 + R)}$$

This result is also obtainable directly from the circuit diagram of Fig. 13-4 with $X = 0$, using the voltage-divider rule. The minimum value is zero if the Wheatstone-bridge balance equation is satisfied.

13-7. Bridge Sensitivity. The voltage sensitivity of an a-c bridge with respect to a variable parameter, s, is defined as the change in magnitude of detector voltage, from its balance value of zero, divided by the infinitesimal change in the parameter s that produced the unbalance. The parameter s may represent any quantity upon which $\mathbf{E}_d$ depends, such as circuit elements in the bridge arms or frequency (if bridge balance depends upon frequency). This definition is the same, in principle, as the definition of voltage sensitivity used for d-c bridges. In the a-c case, however, it is necessary to specify the bridge output more carefully, because it is characterized by both magnitude and phase. The magnitude of $\mathbf{E}_d$ is selected in the definition since the usual bridge detector is not responsive to the phase angle of the voltage applied to its terminals. In cases where a phase-sensitive detector is used, bridge sensitivity may be defined in terms of the change in phase angle of $\mathbf{E}_d$, rather than the change in its magnitude.

For purposes of discussion, the complex detector voltage may be represented in the rectangular form of Eq. (13-14).

$$\mathbf{E}_d = u(s) + jv(s) \quad (13\text{-}20)$$

where the real and imaginary parts of $\mathbf{E}_d$ are functions of the variable s. The locus of $\mathbf{E}_d$, for variable s, may be represented in the complex plane as in Fig. 13-12a. Note that $\mathbf{E}_d$ experiences a 180° phase reversal when s is varied through its balance value, s_0. This phase reversal will always occur when the locus is a smooth curve passing through the point $\mathbf{E}_d = 0$.

The magnitude of $\mathbf{E}_d$, given by $\sqrt{u^2 + v^2}$, may be plotted vs. the variable parameter s, as shown in Fig. 13-12b. The 180° phase reversal is suppressed in this curve; instead, there is a cusp at the point $s = s_0$ where $E_d = 0$. However, the phase reversal may be indicated by one of

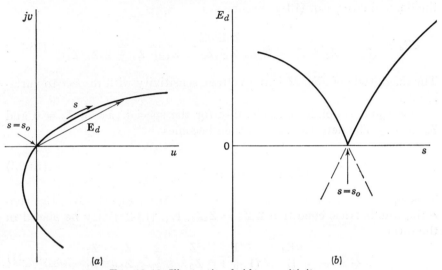

(a)   (b)

FIG. 13-12. Illustrating bridge sensitivity.

the dashed curves, if desired, and this also conveys the idea that the derivative has the same *magnitude* at the point $s = s_0$, whether approached from values of s greater or less than s_0. The discontinuity in the derivative, indicated by the cusp, is more apparent than real and does not cause any mathematical complications. This becomes obvious upon examination of the derivative of Eq. (13-20).

$$\frac{d\mathbf{E}_d}{ds} = \frac{du}{ds} + j\frac{dv}{ds}$$

The magnitude of $d\mathbf{E}_d/ds$ is

$$\frac{dE_d}{ds} = \sqrt{\left(\frac{du}{ds}\right)^2 + \left(\frac{dv}{ds}\right)^2} \tag{13-21}$$

For a smooth locus, du/ds and dv/ds are well-behaved functions of s at all points on the locus, including the point $s = s_0$. Hence, the *magnitude* of $d\mathbf{E}_d/ds$ is independent of the algebraic sign of ds at all points on the curve of Fig. 13-12b, including the point $s = s_0$.

The voltage sensitivity is given by Eq. (13-21) when the magnitude of the derivative is evaluated at $s = s_0$. It may be interpreted graphically as the magnitude of the slope of the curve of Fig. 13-12b at the point $s = s_0$, where it is understood that the curve continues along one of the dashed extensions.

A formula for voltage sensitivity may be developed from Eq. (13-2), using $\mathbf{E}_d = \mathbf{I}_d\mathbf{Z}_d$, when the variable element is contained in $\mathbf{Z}_3$. Recall that $\mathbf{I}_d$, and hence $\mathbf{E}_d$, is zero when $\mathbf{Z}_3 = \mathbf{Z}_0$. Let $\mathbf{Z}_3$ change by an infinitesimal amount to $\mathbf{Z}_0 + d\mathbf{Z}$. Then, neglecting $\mathbf{k}\,d\mathbf{Z}$ compared with 1 in the denominator, Eq. (13-2) becomes

$$d\mathbf{E}_d = \frac{\mathbf{Z}_d\mathbf{E}\,d\mathbf{Z}}{(\mathbf{Z}_g + \mathbf{Z}_2 + \mathbf{Z}_0 + \mathbf{Z}_g\mathbf{Z}_2/\mathbf{Z}_1)(\mathbf{Z}_d + \mathbf{Z}_4 + \mathbf{Z}_0 + \mathbf{Z}_d\mathbf{Z}_4/\mathbf{Z}_1)} \qquad (13\text{-}22)$$

The magnitude of $d\mathbf{E}_d/d\mathbf{Z}$ is the voltage sensitivity with respect to variable $\mathbf{Z}_3$.

This result simplifies considerably for the special case of $\mathbf{Z}_g = 0$ and $\mathbf{Z}_d \rightarrow \infty$. The detector voltage then becomes

$$d\mathbf{E}_d = \frac{\mathbf{Z}_1\mathbf{E}\,d\mathbf{Z}}{(\mathbf{Z}_2 + \mathbf{Z}_0)(\mathbf{Z}_1 + \mathbf{Z}_4)} \qquad \mathbf{Z}_g = 0 = \mathbf{Y}_d \qquad (13\text{-}23)$$

This equation may also be obtained directly from Eq. (13-5). Incorporating the balance condition $\mathbf{Z}_1\mathbf{Z}_0 = \mathbf{Z}_2\mathbf{Z}_4$, Eq. (13-23) may be placed in the form

$$\frac{d\mathbf{E}_d}{\mathbf{E}} = \frac{\mathbf{F}}{(1 + \mathbf{F})^2}\frac{d\mathbf{Z}}{\mathbf{Z}_0} \qquad \mathbf{F} = \frac{\mathbf{Z}_0}{\mathbf{Z}_2} = \frac{\mathbf{Z}_4}{\mathbf{Z}_1} \qquad (13\text{-}24)$$

The *bridge factor*, $\mathbf{F}/(1 + \mathbf{F})^2$, is seen to be an important measure of the sensitivity. The change in detector voltage expressed as a fraction of the voltage applied to the bridge is equal to the bridge factor times the fractional change in the bridge arm impedance.

Several special cases are of interest. When the pair of bridge arms that are series-connected across $\mathbf{E}$ each have the same phase angle, then $\mathbf{F}$ is real and positive. In this case, the value of F required to maximize the bridge factor, and hence the voltage sensitivity, is given by

$$\frac{d}{dF}\left[\frac{F}{(1 + F)^2}\right] = \frac{(1 + F)^2 - 2F(1 + F)}{(1 + F)^4} = 0$$

This yields $F = 1$, and the maximum value of the bridge factor is, accordingly, $\frac{1}{4}$.

When the pair of bridge arms that are series-connected across $\mathbf{E}$ bear relative phase angles of 90°, then $\mathbf{F}$ is imaginary. In this case, with $\mathbf{F} = \pm jG$, the *magnitude* of the bridge factor is $G/(1 + G^2)$. The value of G required to maximize the bridge factor is given by

$$\frac{d}{dG}\left[\frac{G}{1+G^2}\right] = \frac{(1+G^2) - G(2G)}{(1+G^2)^2} = 0$$

This yields $G = 1$ and a corresponding maximum value of $\frac{1}{2}$ for the magnitude of the bridge factor.

Although the bridge factor is less than unity in both of these cases, it may exceed unity when the magnitude of $(1 + \mathbf{F})$ is less than unity. This requires that the phase angle of $\mathbf{F}$ be greater than 90° and may be achieved when the arms that are series-connected across $\mathbf{E}$ have a difference in phase angle that exceeds 90°. This may be accomplished with an inductive arm series-connected with a capacitive arm. With lossless elements, which implies an infinite Q of the resonant arms, the bridge factor is theoretically infinite, since $\mathbf{F} = -1$. However, in practice, such a result is prohibited by resistance that is inevitably associated with elements in the bridge arms.

13-8. Displacement Measurements by Change of Capacitance. A tangible example of the significance of the bridge sensitivity ideas in the preceding section is provided by a specific engineering problem of measuring small mechanical displacements. In this section, a simple bridge will be analyzed and designed for use with a variable capacitor whose capacitance depends upon the mechanical displacement of one of its plates. This is one illustration of the many ways in which bridges may be used to provide a sensitive measure of a small change in an electrical quantity.

A variable capacitor of special design is shown schematically in Fig. 13-13. A small mechanical displacement, Δ, caused by a force acting on the deformable plate, produces an increase in capacitance. Suppose this capacitor is placed in arm 3 of a DeSauty bridge, which may be balanced initially by adjusting C_4 (see Fig. 13-14). When the spring plate

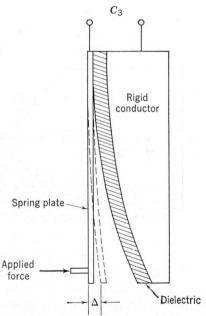

FIG. 13-13. Displacement-dependent capacitor.

is displaced, the increase in capacitance of C_3 results in a change in detector voltage. The change in detector voltage may be used as a measure of the displacement, and the detector may be calibrated to read displacement directly. When extremely small displacements are of interest, it is obviously desirable to have as large a change in $\mathbf{E}_d$ as possible for a given change in capacitance.

Assume that a low-impedance generator and a high-impedance detector will be used in the design of the bridge. The detector voltage is then given by the voltage-divider rule.

$$\mathbf{E}_d = \left[\frac{R_1}{R_1 + 1/j\omega C_4} - \frac{R_2}{R_2 + 1/j\omega C_3} \right] \mathbf{E} = \frac{j\omega(R_1 C_4 - R_2 C_3)\mathbf{E}}{(1 + j\omega R_1 C_4)(1 + j\omega R_2 C_3)}$$
$$(13\text{-}25)$$

Clearly, the bridge is balanced when $R_1 C_4 = R_2 C_3$. The initial adjustment of C_4 produces bridge balance for the value of C_3 that corresponds to a zero reference value of displacement of its deformable plate. Then, when C_3 changes by a small amount, dC, owing to a small displacement, Δ, the magnitude of the change in $\mathbf{E}_d$ from zero is, from Eq. (13-25)

$$dE_d = \frac{E\omega R_2\, dC}{\sqrt{1 + (\omega R_1 C_4)^2}\,\sqrt{1 + (\omega R_2 C_3)^2}} \tag{13-26}$$

where dC has been ignored in comparison with C_3 in the denominator.

The bridge sensitivity with respect to the change in C_3 is dE_d/dC. It is a function of frequency, even though the balance condition is independent of frequency. For very low frequencies, where $(\omega R_1 C_4)^2 \ll 1$ and $(\omega R_2 C_3)^2 \ll 1$, the voltage sensitivity is proportional to frequency. However, at very high frequencies, where the inequalities are reversed, the sensitivity becomes

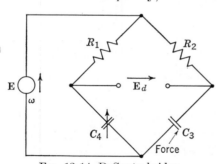

Fig. 13-14. DeSauty bridge.

$$\frac{dE_d}{dC} = \frac{E}{\omega R_1 C_3 C_4} \qquad \omega \to \infty$$

and is seen to decrease with an increase in frequency. Thus, there must be some intermediate frequency at which the voltage sensitivity is a maximum.

To explore the conditions for maximum sensitivity, let $R_1 = R_2 = R$, and this demands that $C_4 = C_3 = C$ to satisfy the balance equation. Then the bridge sensitivity becomes, from Eq. (13-26),

$$\frac{dE_d}{dC} = \frac{E\omega R}{1 + (\omega RC)^2} = \frac{E}{C}\frac{\omega RC}{1 + (\omega RC)^2} \tag{13-27}$$

This expression could have been obtained directly from Eq. (13-24) with $d\mathbf{Z}/\mathbf{Z}_0 = dC/C$, $\mathbf{F} = 1/j\omega RC$ (or $G = 1/\omega RC$). A plot of the bridge sensitivity vs. the dimensionless frequency variable, ωRC, is given in Fig. 13-15. As expected from the development of the preceding section, the maximum sensitivity occurs at $\omega RC = 1$. This corresponds to a value $G = 1$ and a maximum bridge factor of $\frac{1}{2}$. Hence, the maximum voltage sensitivity is given by $E/2C$, as shown in Fig. 13-15. The larger the value of E, the greater the sensitivity. It may also be seen from the preceding section that the assumption of equal resistances has not impaired the maximum sensitivity, for with $G = 1/\omega R_1 C_4 = 1/\omega R_2 C_3$, the same maximum value is obtained. The maximum is seen to be rather broad, so the frequency is not a critical design matter, and the final calibration will be relatively insensitive to small changes in frequency.

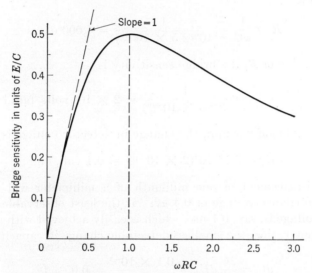

Fig. 13-15. Dependence of bridge sensitivity on frequency.

It is interesting to note that if generator and detector are interchanged in the circuit of Fig. 13-14, then the detector voltage is given by

$$\mathbf{E}_d = \left[\frac{R_1}{R_1 + R_2} - \frac{1/j\omega C_4}{1/j\omega C_4 + 1/j\omega C_3} \right]\mathbf{E} = \frac{(R_1 C_4 - R_2 C_3)\mathbf{E}}{(R_1 + R_2)(C_3 + C_4)} \quad (13\text{-}28)$$

The same balance condition pertains, of course, but the bridge sensitivity no longer depends on frequency. In this case, the voltage sensitivity with respect to a small change, dC, in C_3 is

$$\frac{dE_d}{dC} = \frac{R_2 E}{(R_1 + R_2)(C_3 + C_4)} = \frac{E}{C_3} \frac{F}{(1 + F)^2} \quad (13\text{-}29)$$

where $F = R_1/R_2 = C_3/C_4$. While the sensitivity is independent of frequency, its maximum value, occurring with $F = 1$ ($R_1 = R_2 = R$), is only one-half that attainable with the former arrangement of detector and generator.

For a specific design example, suppose that the displacement-sensitive capacitor has an initial value $C_3 = 250$ $\mu\mu$f when $\Delta = 0$ and that there is a linear change in capacitance, for small displacements, equal to 20 $\mu\mu$f per 0.1 mm. A low-impedance oscillator producing an output voltage $E = 1$ volt at an angular frequency $\omega = 10^6$ radians per sec will be assumed. (Use of higher voltage would increase the sensitivity.) The equations necessary to design the bridge, and to calculate its sensitivity, have been developed. Using an equal resistive arm design, which does not compromise the sensitivity, the value of R required for maximum sensitivity is

$$R = \frac{1}{\omega C} = \frac{1}{10^6(2.5 \times 10^{-10})} = 4{,}000 \text{ ohms}$$

With this value of R, the bridge sensitivity is

$$\frac{dE_d}{dC} = \frac{E}{2C} = \frac{1}{2(2.5 \times 10^{-10})} = 2 \times 10^9 \text{ volts/farad}$$

With $dC = 200$ $\mu\mu$f per mm, the change in detector voltage is

$$dE_d = 2 \times 10^9 (2 \times 10^{-10}) = 0.4 \text{ volt/mm}$$

Thus, a displacement of one millionth of a millimeter will produce a detector unbalance voltage of 0.4 μv. If the least observable change in detector voltage is, say, 0.1 mv, which is easily achieved with a vacuum-tube voltmeter, then the smallest detectable change in capacitance is

$$dC = \frac{2C}{E} dE_d = \frac{0.1 \times 10^{-3}}{2 \times 10^9} = 0.05 \text{ } \mu\mu\text{f}$$

This corresponds to a mechanical displacement of 250 millionths of a millimeter.

13-9. Voltage-transfer Functions. Bridges are sometimes used as selective networks in filter and feedback applications. Both the amplitude and the phase characteristics of the detector voltage as a function of frequency may become important in such cases. In these applications, the bridge elements are usually fixed for balance at some specified frequency, and the frequency is the variable that produces detector output. The complex ratio of the input voltage applied to the bridge and the output voltage appearing at the detector terminals is a useful quantity for analysis purposes and is the *voltage-transfer function* of the bridge. Analysis of the voltage-transfer function of a resonance bridge provides an illustration.

A resonance bridge with four equal resistors is shown in Fig. 13-16. Assuming that $\mathbf{Z}_g = 0$ and that $\mathbf{Z}_d \to \infty$, for simplicity, the complex voltage-transfer function of this bridge is

$$\mathbf{K} = K\epsilon^{j\phi} = \frac{\mathbf{E}_d}{\mathbf{E}} = \frac{R}{2R} - \frac{R}{2R + jX} = \frac{jX}{2(2R + jX)} \qquad (13\text{-}30)$$

where $X = \omega L - 1/\omega C$ is the reactance of the tuned circuit. A study

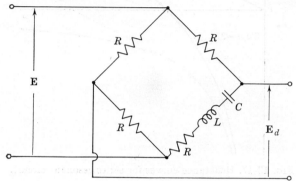

FIG. 13-16. Resonance bridge.

of the behavior of $\mathbf{K}$ as a function of frequency reveals pertinent information about the bridge in filter and feedback applications.

When $X = 0$, Eq. (13-30) indicates that $\mathbf{K} = 0$, since the resistive balance condition is already satisfied by use of four equal resistors. The magnitude and phase angle of $\mathbf{K}$ are

$$K = \frac{1}{2\sqrt{4\left(\dfrac{R}{X}\right)^2 + 1}} \qquad \phi = \tan^{-1}\frac{2R}{X} \qquad (13\text{-}31)$$

The appearance of R/X in both expressions as a single variable makes it tempting to analyze $\mathbf{K}$ as a function of X rather than of ω, despite the fact that X is not proportional to frequency. This may be done to obtain an initial view of the behavior of $\mathbf{K}$. The manner in which X varies with ω is given in Fig. 13-17 and is the familiar reactance curve of a series resonant circuit. The frequency at which X is zero is designated by $\omega_0 = 1/\sqrt{LC}$. The slope to the reactance curve at $\omega = \omega_0$ is of particular interest.

$$\frac{dX}{d\omega} = L + \frac{1}{\omega^2 C} \qquad \left(\frac{dX}{d\omega}\right)_{\omega_0} = L + L = 2L \qquad (13\text{-}32)$$

Because the slope of the capacitive reactance curve at $\omega = \omega_0$ is equal to the slope of the inductive reactance curve, X is approximately equal to $2L(\omega - \omega_0)$ for small deviations of ω from ω_0.

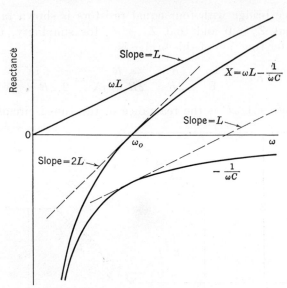

FIG. 13-17. Reactance curves for series resonant circuit.

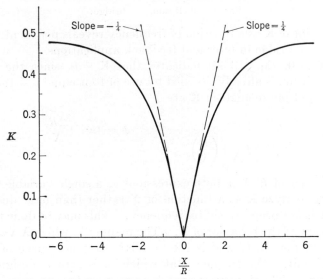

FIG. 13-18. Magnitude of voltage-transfer function of resonance bridge.

A plot of the magnitude of **K** as a function of X/R, based on Eq. (13-31), is given in Fig. 13-18. The magnitude of **K** is zero at $X = 0$. For $(X/R)^2 \gg 4$, K approaches the asymptotic value $\frac{1}{2}$ for both positive and negative values of X. Close to resonance, where $(X/R)^2 \ll 4$, K becomes tangent to a line of slope $+\frac{1}{4}$ or $-\frac{1}{4}$, depending upon whether X is positive or negative, respectively. This means that at bridge balance, $dK/dX = 1/4R$. The magnitude of $dK/d\omega$ at balance is found easily from Eq. (13-32).

$$\frac{dK}{d\omega} = \frac{dK}{dX}\frac{dX}{d\omega} \qquad \left(\frac{dK}{d\omega}\right)_{\omega_0} = \frac{1}{4R}2L = \frac{L}{2R} \tag{13-33}$$

The curve of K vs. X/R is seen to be symmetrical because K is an *even* function of X/R. This implies that K is not a symmetrical function of frequency.

A plot of the phase angle of **K** as a function of X/R is given in Fig. 13-19 and is based on Eq. (13-31). This plot indicates that for $X > 0$, ϕ lies

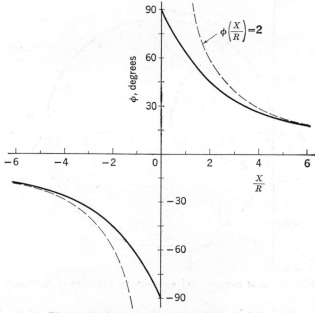

FIG. 13-19. Phase of voltage-transfer function of resonance bridge.

in the first quadrant and approaches zero as $X \to \infty$. For $X < 0$, ϕ lies in the fourth quadrant and approaches zero as $X \to -\infty$. When the magnitude of X/R is large compared with 2, the curve approaches the hyperbola $\phi(X/R) = 2$. At $X = 0$, ϕ experiences a discontinuity of 180° and is not defined. The magnitude of **K** is zero at this value of X, so this does not imply discontinuous behavior of **K**.

The magnitude and phase information may be portrayed together in the complex plane, as shown in Fig. 13-20. The locus of **K** for variable X is seen to be a circle with center at $u = \frac{1}{4}$, $v = 0$ and radius $\frac{1}{4}$. The fact that this is a circle should come as no surprise, since it was shown in Sec. 13-3 that the form of Eq. (13-30) is that of a circle. Moreover, the circle equation may be obtained immediately from Eq. (13-31) by use of the trigonometric identity $\sqrt{1 + \tan^2 \phi} = \sec \phi$. Then, the magnitude of **K** is

$$K = \frac{1}{2\sqrt{\tan^2 \phi + 1}} = \frac{1}{2} \cos \phi \qquad (13\text{-}34)$$

This is the equation of a circle in the polar coordinates K, ϕ.

The principal objection to the foregoing analysis is that it has not revealed explicitly the dependence of **K** on angular frequency. This may

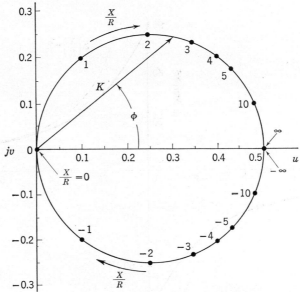

Fig. 13-20. Locus of complex voltage-transfer function of resonance bridge.

be overcome by introducing ω into the equations and plots. A formulation in terms of the resonance frequency and the Q of the resonant bridge arm enables **K** to be expressed in terms of two parameters.

$$\omega_0 = \frac{1}{\sqrt{LC}} \qquad Q = \frac{\omega_0 L}{R} = \frac{1}{\omega_0 RC} = \frac{1}{R}\sqrt{\frac{L}{C}}$$

With these parameters, X/R becomes

$$\frac{X}{R} = \frac{\omega L - 1/\omega C}{R} = Q\left(\frac{\omega}{\omega_0} - \frac{\omega_0}{\omega}\right)$$

Insert this expression for X/R into Eq. (13-31).

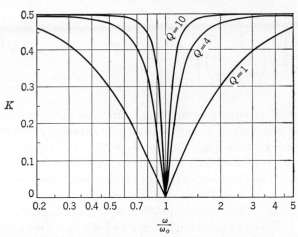

Fig. 13-21. Magnitude of voltage-transfer function as a function of frequency.

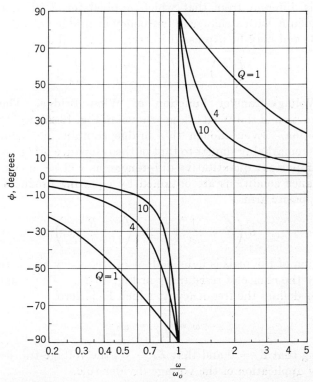

Fig. 13-22. Phase of voltage-transfer function as a function of frequency.

$$K = \frac{1}{2\sqrt{\left[Q\left(\dfrac{\omega}{\omega_0} - \dfrac{\omega_0}{\omega}\right)\right]^2 + 1}} = \frac{1}{2}\cos\phi \qquad \tan\phi = \frac{2}{Q\left(\dfrac{\omega}{\omega_0} - \dfrac{\omega_0}{\omega}\right)}$$

$$(13\text{-}35)$$

As expected, **K** is a more complicated function of ω than of X. Curves showing the behavior of K and ϕ as a function of ω/ω_0 for three different values of Q are given in Figs. 13-21 and 13-22. The normalized frequency variable, ω/ω_0, is plotted on a logarithmic scale, and this leads to symmetrical curves. The symmetrical result comes about because $(\omega/\omega_0 - \omega_0/\omega)$ has the same *magnitude* for $\omega_1 = k\omega_0$ as it does for $\omega_2 = (1/k)\omega_0$, where k is any constant. The logarithmic scale is, of course, characterized by the fact that log k has the same magnitude as log $1/k$. Obviously, the shape of the curves would not be symmetrical on a linear frequency scale.

The locus of **K** in the complex plane is still a circle, as indicated by the cosine function in Eq. (13-35). The frequency scale along the locus, however, is different from that which applied for X/R in Fig. 13-20. The change in K with a change in frequency at bridge balance is given by Eq. (13-33) and may be expressed in terms of Q and ω_0.

$$\left(\frac{dK}{d\omega}\right)_{\omega_0} = \frac{L}{2R} = \frac{\omega_0 L}{\omega_0 2R} = \frac{Q}{2\omega_0} \qquad (13\text{-}36)$$

13-10. Voltage-transfer Function of Wien Bridge. The voltage-transfer function of the Wien bridge, shown in Fig. 13-23, will be analyzed in this section. Even though this bridge contains no inductance, its behavior is remarkably similar to that of the resonance bridge. However, there are important quantitative differences, as will be shown.

The balance conditions are obtained by equating products of impedances in opposite arms.

$$R\left(R + \frac{1}{j\omega C}\right) = 2R\left(\frac{R}{1 + j\omega RC}\right) \qquad (13\text{-}37)$$

The equation of the reals is independent of frequency and is found to be satisfied by the choice of resistances in Fig. 13-23. The equation of the imaginaries defines the frequency at which $\mathbf{E}_d$ is zero.

$$\omega = \frac{1}{RC} = \omega_0$$

Assuming that $\mathbf{Z}_g = 0$ and that $\mathbf{Z}_d \to \infty$, the voltage-transfer function is given by application of the voltage-divider rule.

$$\mathbf{K} = Ke^{j\phi} = \frac{\mathbf{E}_d}{\mathbf{E}} = \frac{R}{3R} - \frac{R/(1 + j\omega RC)}{R/(1 + j\omega RC) + R + 1/j\omega C} \qquad (13\text{-}38)$$

Expressed in terms of $y = \omega RC$, this becomes, after manipulation,

$$\mathbf{K} = \frac{j(y - 1/y)}{3[3 + j(y - 1/y)]} \tag{13-39}$$

It is seen that $\mathbf{K} = 0$ when $y = 1$, which corresponds to $\omega = \omega_0$. This form shows that the quantity $(y - 1/y)$ may be regarded as a single

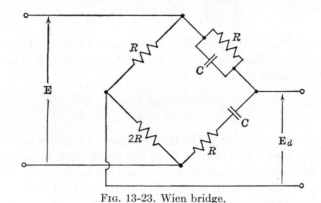

FIG. 13-23. Wien bridge.

variable. It has the same functional dependence on frequency as the reactance, X, in the resonance bridge. In the resonance bridge,

$$\frac{X}{R} = \frac{\omega L}{R} - \frac{1}{\omega RC}$$

and in the Wien bridge,

$$Y = y - \frac{1}{y} = \omega RC - \frac{1}{\omega RC}$$

In fact, when $Q = 1$ in the resonance bridge, then $L/R = RC$, and even the coefficients of X/R agree with those of $Y = y - 1/y$. The magnitude and phase of $\mathbf{K}$ in terms of the new variable Y become, from Eq. (13-39),

$$K = \frac{1}{3\sqrt{9\left(\dfrac{1}{Y}\right)^2 + 1}} = \frac{1}{3}\cos\phi \qquad \phi = \tan^{-1}\frac{3}{Y} \tag{13-40}$$

The similarity between the behavior of $\mathbf{K}$ as a function of Y and the voltage-transfer function of the resonance bridge as a function of X/R is seen clearly on comparison of these results with Eq. (13-31). For $Y^2 \gg 9$, K approaches the asymptotic value $\frac{1}{3}$ for both positive and negative values of Y, rather than the value $\frac{1}{2}$ in the case of the resonance bridge. Close to resonance, where $Y^2 \ll 9$, K becomes tangent to a line of slope $+\frac{1}{9}$ or $-\frac{1}{9}$, rather than the values $\pm\frac{1}{4}$ in the resonance bridge. Since

$$\frac{dY}{d\omega} = RC + \frac{1}{\omega^2 RC} \qquad \left(\frac{dY}{d\omega}\right)_{\omega_0} = 2RC$$

the magnitude of $dK/d\omega$ at $\omega = \omega_0$ is

$$\left(\frac{dK}{d\omega}\right)_{\omega_0} = \frac{1}{9}(2RC) = \frac{2}{9\omega_0} \tag{13-41}$$

rather than $Q/2\omega_0$ in the case of the resonance bridge. Thus, the ratio of the resonance-bridge slope to the Wien-bridge slope, when both bridges are null at the same frequency, is

$$\frac{\text{Resonance-bridge slope}}{\text{Wien-bridge slope}} = \frac{9Q}{4}$$

and this is true even when R in the resonance bridge is not equal to R in the Wien bridge. It is evident from this result that, so long as $Q > \frac{4}{9}$, the resonance-bridge output is more sensitive to frequency changes in the vicinity of balance than is the Wien-bridge output.

The phase characteristics of the Wien bridge are also very similar to those of the resonance bridge. For $Y > 0$, ϕ lies in the first quadrant and approaches zero as $Y \to \infty$. For $Y < 0$, ϕ lies in the fourth quadrant and approaches zero as $Y \to -\infty$. At $Y = 0$, ϕ experiences a discontinuity of $180°$. This over-all behavior is exactly the same as in the case of the resonance bridge. However, in the Wien bridge, for $|Y| \gg 3$, the phase characteristic approaches the hyperbola $\phi Y = 3$, rather than the hyperbola $\phi(X/R) = 2$ as in the resonance bridge.

While the similarities and differences are seen easily in terms of the distorted frequency variable, Y, it is usually desirable to obtain explicit relations for $\mathbf{K}$ in terms of ω. This is accomplished in terms of a single variable, ω/ω_0, since

$$Y = \omega RC - \frac{1}{\omega RC} = \frac{\omega}{\omega_0} - \frac{\omega_0}{\omega}$$

Insert this expression for Y into the amplitude and phase functions of Eq. (13-40).

$$K = \frac{1}{3\sqrt{\left[\dfrac{3}{\dfrac{\omega}{\omega_0} - \dfrac{\omega_0}{\omega}}\right]^2 + 1}} = \frac{1}{3}\cos\phi \qquad \tan\phi = \frac{3}{\dfrac{\omega}{\omega_0} - \dfrac{\omega_0}{\omega}} \tag{13-42}$$

Curves showing the behavior of K and ϕ as a function of ω/ω_0 are given in Fig. 13-24. Again, a logarithmic frequency scale has been used to obtain symmetrical curves. The circular locus in the complex plane is given in Fig. 13-25. The similarity between these results and those of the resonance bridge is evident, especially for low Q. The two bridges behave almost identically for $Q = \frac{2}{3}$, the only difference being that the asymptotic value of K for extreme unbalance in the resonance bridge is $\frac{1}{2}$ rather than $\frac{1}{3}$ as in the Wien bridge.

One application of a-c bridges is the selective suppression of one frequency of a nonsinusoidal signal, without affecting the relative relation-

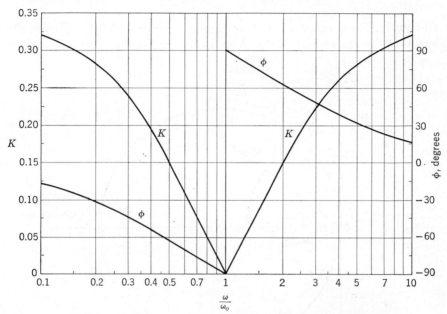

FIG. 13-24. Voltage-transfer characteristics of Wien bridge.

ships among the other frequencies. Suppose it is desired to eliminate the fundamental of a nonsinusoidal signal applied to the bridge, so that the harmonics may be examined separately. The resonance bridge is superior to the Wien bridge in this application, where minimum distortion of the harmonics is required. Both bridges may be balanced at the fundamental frequency of the applied voltage, and excellent rejection may be achieved with either bridge.

To prevent relative distortion of the harmonics in the output of the resonance bridge, the requirement is that at $\omega = 2\omega_0$ and higher, the term

$$\frac{2}{Q\left(\dfrac{\omega}{\omega_0} - \dfrac{\omega_0}{\omega}\right)} = \frac{4}{3Q} \quad \text{at} \quad \omega = 2\omega_0$$

shall be negligible compared with 1 to avoid phase distortion. This will ensure zero phase shift for all harmonics. The requirement for preventing distortion of the relative amplitudes of the harmonics is less stringent; $(4/3Q)^2$ must be negligible compared with 2. These inequalities may be satisfied in the resonance bridge by use of a high Q.

The corresponding term in the Wien-bridge analysis is

$$\frac{3}{\dfrac{\omega}{\omega_0} - \dfrac{\omega_0}{\omega}} = 2 \quad \text{at} \quad \omega = 2\omega_0$$

Obviously, the number 2 is not negligible compared with 1. Hence, the harmonics in the output of the Wien bridge will suffer substantial phase

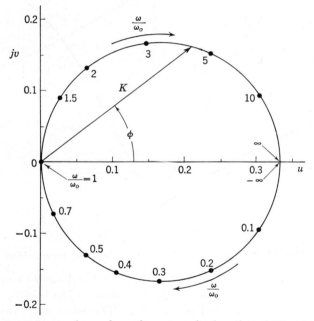

Fig. 13-25. Locus of complex voltage-transfer function of Wien bridge.

and amplitude distortion. In effect, the Wien-bridge performance in this application is the same as that obtained in the resonance bridge with $Q = \frac{2}{3}$, which is clearly too low a Q to avoid distortion of the harmonic output of the bridge.

13-11. Narrow-band Approximation. The behavior of the voltage-transfer function in the near vicinity of balance is often of particular interest. When ω is nearly equal to ω_0, computation of the difference between two nearly equal numbers is required for the two bridges that have been analyzed. Therefore, it is advantageous to define a fractional deviation of ω from ω_0 by

$$\delta = \frac{\omega}{\omega_0} - 1 \tag{13-43}$$

The same thing was done in Chap. 4 when a similar mathematical situation was encountered with the vibration galvanometer. This type of approximation is used frequently, since the term $(\omega/\omega_0 - \omega_0/\omega)$ often arises in the analysis of resonant systems. It was shown in Sec. 4-14 that, by use of the binomial expansion, the difference term becomes

$$\frac{\omega}{\omega_0} - \frac{\omega_0}{\omega} \approx 2\delta \qquad\qquad \delta \ll 1 \tag{13-44}$$

to a good approximation if $\delta \ll 1$. This restricts the application of the narrow-band approximation to angular frequencies that are very close to ω_0.

When Eq. (13-44) is introduced into Eq. (13-35), the magnitude and phase of the voltage-transfer function of the resonance bridge become,

$$K_r \approx \frac{1}{2\sqrt{\left(\frac{1}{Q\delta}\right)^2 + 1}} \qquad\qquad \tan\phi_r \approx \frac{1}{Q\delta}$$

The Wien-bridge voltage-transfer function becomes, from Eq. (13-42),

$$K_w \approx \frac{1}{3\sqrt{\left(\frac{3}{2\delta}\right)^2 + 1}} = \frac{2\delta}{9} \qquad \tan\phi_w \approx \frac{3}{2\delta}$$

Note that in K_w a further simplification results immediately because $\delta \ll 1$, and $(3/2\delta)^2$ will always be large compared with 1, if the approximation in Eq. (13-44) is not abused. However, the same simplification is not necessarily applicable in K_r. For high Q, it does not invariably follow that $(1/Q\delta)^2$ is large compared with 1, even though $\delta \ll 1$. For example, with $Q = 100$ and $\delta = 0.05$, $(1/Q\delta)^2 = 0.04$ and is *small* compared with 1. However, as $\delta \to 0$, K_r does approach $Q\delta/2$ in the limit for any finite Q.

A plot of the magnitude of the voltage-transfer function is given in Fig. 13-26. This is a universal curve for the resonance bridge, since Q is contained in the frequency-deviation scale. The magnitude of the slope of the K_r vs. $Q\delta$ curve is $\frac{1}{2}$ at $\delta = 0$, and K_r approaches the value 0.5 for $|Q\delta| \gg 1$. The identical curve may be used for the Wien bridge, with $Q = \frac{2}{3}$, provided the amplitude scale is multiplied by $\frac{2}{3}$. The magnitude of the slope of K vs. δ in the vicinity of $\delta = 0$ is essentially constant for both bridges.

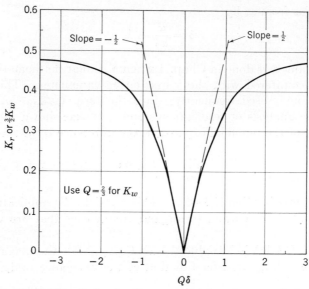

FIG. 13-26. Magnitude of voltage-transfer functions near balance.

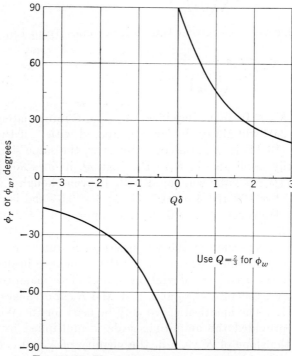

FIG. 13-27. Phase of voltage-transfer functions.

$$\left(\frac{dK_r}{d\delta}\right)_{\delta=0} = \frac{Q}{2} \qquad \left(\frac{dK_w}{d\delta}\right)_{\delta=0} = \frac{2}{9}$$

The ratio of these slopes, $9Q/4$, agrees with the former results because the error of the narrow-band approximation vanishes at $\delta = 0$, and also $d\delta$ is proportional to $d\omega$ [the constant of proportionality, from Eq. (13-43), is $1/\omega_0$].

The phase-angle behavior in the vicinity of resonance may also be displayed by a single curve for both bridges, as shown in Fig. 13-27. With $Q = \frac{2}{3}$, the resonance and Wien bridges have identical phase characteristics, even when the narrow-band approximation is not used.

Advantages resulting from application of the narrow-band approximation should be evident from the relations that have been developed. Simplification results in computations as well as in complexity of equations. For these reasons, the narrow-band approximation is often used for frequencies very close to bridge balance.

PROBLEMS

13-1 (§2). In the inductance bridge of Fig. 13-2a, R_3 and L_3 are the unknowns, $L_2 = 0.1$ henry, $R_4 = 400$ ohms, and R_1 and R_2 are adjustable. Bridge balance is achieved with $R_1 = 200$ ohms and $R_2 = 100$ ohms. (a) Compute R_3 and L_3. (b) Are the balance adjustments independent? (c) With $E = 2$ volts rms, $\mathbf{Z}_g = 50$ ohms, $\mathbf{Z}_d = 500$ ohms, and $\omega = 1,000$ radians per sec, let R_1 change by 2 per cent and compute the change in magnitude and phase angle of the detector voltage.

13-2 (§2). In the Maxwell bridge of Fig. 9-21, R_1 and C_1 are variable, $R_2 = R_4 = R = 1,000$ ohms, and the unknowns, R_x and L_x, are approximately 200 ohms and 0.2 henry, respectively. A sinusoidal voltage of negligible impedance and 10 volts rms output at an angular frequency of 5,000 radians per sec is applied between the junction of R_1, R_2 and R_4, L_x. The minimum perceptible detector voltage is approximately 0.01 volt rms, because of noise and stray pickup in the detector. The detector admittance is negligible. (a) Approximately what size variables, C_1 and R_1, are needed to balance the bridge? (b) If R and R_1 are known to 0.1 per cent (limit of error), and C_1 is known to 0.5 per cent (limit of error), what are the limits of error in the measured values of R_x and L_x, ignoring the uncertainty owing to minimum perceptible detector voltage. (c) Determine the uncertainties in R_x and L_x traceable only to the minimum perceptible detector voltage.

13-3 (§3). Show that Eq. (13-6) may be placed in the form

$$\frac{\mathbf{E}_d}{\mathbf{E}} = \frac{\mathbf{A}}{\mathbf{C}} + \left(\mathbf{B} - \frac{\mathbf{DA}}{\mathbf{C}}\right) \frac{1}{\mathbf{C}s + \mathbf{D}}$$

(a) Prove that the locus of $1/(\mathbf{C}s + \mathbf{D})$, with s variable, is a circle in the complex plane. (b) What are the geometric interpretations of $\mathbf{A}/\mathbf{C}$ and $(\mathbf{B} - \mathbf{DA}/\mathbf{C})$ in the above equation?

13-4 (§4). Derive the xy plane circle equation, given at the end of Sec. 13-4, for the resonance bridge with X variable.

13-5 (§4). With R_1 variable in the resonance bridge of Fig. 13-4, prove that the locus of $\mathbf{E}_d/\mathbf{E}$ in the uv plane is the straight line $v = R_2 X/[(R + R_2)^2 + X^2]$.

13-6 (§4). In the resonance bridge of Fig. 13-4, R and L are the unknowns and the variables are R_4 and ω. The magnitude of the generator voltage remains constant, the internal impedance of the generator is negligible, and the admittance of the detector is negligible. Initially, $R_1 = R_2 = 1,000$ ohms, $C = 0.10$ μf, and $\omega = 2 \times 10^4$ radians per sec. When R_4 is varied, a minimum (not a null) detector indication is observed with $R_4 = 3,000$ ohms. With R_4 set at 3,000 ohms, the frequency is varied, and a minimum (not a null) detector indication is observed at $\omega = 10^4$ radians per sec. Compute the values of R and L.

13-7 (§5). The a-c bridge in Fig. 13-28 is balanced for the parameters shown at an angular frequency $\omega = 10^4$ radians per sec. The two 100 $\mu\mu$f capacitors represent stray capacitance to ground. (a) Calculate (numerically) *two* equivalent but different representations of the unknown arm, $\mathbf{Z}$. (b) Which parameters of the bridge would you make variable, and why? (c) If E is 1 volt rms, what is the detector voltage if the unknown $\mathbf{Z}$ is removed completely? Assume zero generator impedance and zero detector admittance.

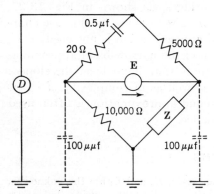

FIG. 13-28. Bridge with stray capacitance.

13-8 (§6). Show that the second derivative with respect to X of Eq. (13-19), evaluated at $X = 0$, is positive if $R_1 I_1 > R_2 I_2/2$, and negative if this inequality is reversed.

13-9 (§7). With $\mathbf{F} = F\epsilon^{j\alpha}$, for what value of F is the magnitude of the bridge factor in Eq. (13-24) a maximum, and what is the expression for the maximum magnitude?

13-10 (§8). In the displacement-measurement bridge of Sec. 13-8, in which equal resistive arms are used, a small bridge unbalance has resulted from a change, dC, in C_3. Compute the error in dE_d if ω has drifted by 10 per cent from its nominal design value, $\omega = 1/RC$.

13-11 (§8). The bridge circuit of Fig. 13-14 is used as a thickness gage to indicate the uniformity of paint sprayed on sheet metal. One plate of capacitor C_3 is a metal disk of area 1 sq in., held against the painted surface. The dielectric constant of the paint is 5. The other plate of C_3 is the metal sheet. Assume $R_1 = R_2 = 1,000$ ohms, $f = 1,000$ cps, zero generator impedance, zero detector admittance, and negligible fringing and flat contact in the disk capacitor. (a) If zero detector reading is required for a nominal paint thickness of 0.002 in., what value of C_4 is required? (b) The smallest readable deflection (from zero) of the detector is 0.1 mv rms. With an applied voltage of 1 volt rms, determine the smallest detectable change in paint thickness from its nominal value. (c) For what value of $R_1 = R_2$ will the bridge sensitivity be a maximum, and what is the corresponding minimum detectable change in paint thickness?

13-12 (§9). In the reactance curves of Fig. 13-17, the slope of the capacitive reactance curve is k times the slope of the inductive reactance curve at $\omega = \omega_1 < \omega_0$, where k is a constant. (a) For what value of ω, in terms of ω_1, is the slope of the capacitive reactance curve equal to $1/k$ times the slope of the inductive reactance curve? (b) Determine an expression for the ratio of the total reactances at these two frequencies.

13-13 (§10). Show that Eq. (13-39) follows from Eq. (13-38).

13-14 (§10). The square wave of Fig. 11-11 is applied to the resonance bridge of Fig. 13-16. The fundamental angular frequency of the square wave is equal to $\omega_0 =$

10,000 radians per sec $= 1/\sqrt{LC}$. With $Q = 2$, compute the relative amplitudes of the third and fifth harmonics in the detector output and their relative time delay.

13-15 (§10). The lossless lattice circuit shown in Fig. 13-29 may be redrawn as a bridge. E is a variable-frequency sinusoidal source. (a) Determine the angular frequency at which the detector voltage is zero. (b) Derive an expression for the voltage-transfer function, assuming zero generator impedance and zero detector admittance. (c) What relation between L_1 and L_2 must be satisfied if the frequency found in part (a) is to be real?

13-16 (§10). Determine an expression for the magnitude of $dK/d\omega$ at $\omega = \omega_0$ for the Wien bridge of Fig. 13-23 with generator and detector interchanged. Compare with Eq. (13-41).

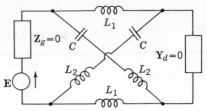

FIG. 13-29. Lossless lattice circuit.

13-17 (§10). The Hay bridge of Fig. 9-20 is used with an infinite-impedance detector and a zero-impedance generator. Consider the generator voltage as a rise toward the junction of R_1 and R_2, and the detector voltage as a rise toward the junction of R_2 and R_3. Assume that $R_1 = R_2 = R_3 = R$, $R_4 = 2R$, $C_1 = C$, and $L_3 = L$. (a) Determine an expression for the voltage-transfer function, $\mathbf{K}$. (b) Under what conditions is $\mathbf{K} = 0$? (c) Determine an expression for the magnitude of $dK/d\omega$ evaluated at bridge balance. (d) Show that the result in part (c) is unaffected by an interchange of generator and detector.

13-18 (§11). In the resonance bridge of Fig. 13-16, E_d/E is to be within 1 per cent of 0.5 when the frequency of E deviates by 5 per cent from the frequency at which $E_d = 0$. (a) How large a Q is required? (b) What error results in the computation if the narrow-band approximation is used? (c) What is the phase shift of $\mathbf{E}_d$ with respect to $\mathbf{E}$ for a 5 per cent frequency deviation, using the value of Q in part (a).

CHAPTER 14

TREATMENT OF DATA

The treatment of experimental data, once obtained, is a matter for thoughtful concern. Not only are accuracy and efficient use of time desirable in processing the data, but proper display and presentation of results may be of critical importance. When plans for treatment of data are made in advance, the required quantity and range of experimental data are often well defined. Moreover, certain experimental techniques may be suggested by preliminary planning for treatment of data.

Accepted conventions for conveying the uncertainty of results in terms of significant figures are discussed first. The brief summary should help to clarify this often-abused matter. Several techniques are outlined for improving the precision of certain types of slide-rule calculations. These, combined with properties of the binomial expansion, extend the possibilities for accurate computations before having to resort to longhand methods or to the desk calculator. An important aspect of presenting experimental results is the graph, and certain rules and accepted practices are summarized. A graph is a good deal more than simply a plot of experimental points. It is an effective analysis tool, and linearization of graphs is emphasized as an important data-processing technique. Representation of experimental results by an equation is frequently desirable, and a number of techniques are given for both rational and empirical cases. Detailed examples are presented from the field of electrical measurements.

14-1. Significant Figures. A numerical statement pertaining to a measured quantity possesses at least three distinct features. Expressed diagrammatically, they are:

$$\begin{pmatrix} \text{Significant} \\ \text{figures} \end{pmatrix} \begin{pmatrix} \text{Location of} \\ \text{decimal point} \end{pmatrix} \begin{pmatrix} \text{Units or} \\ \text{dimensions} \end{pmatrix}$$

Significant figures are digits that convey meaningful information regarding the size of the quantity and must be distinguished clearly from decimal point information.

Because of the interrelationship among the three items, there exists the possibility of ambiguity and confusion. For example, if a resistance has been determined to three significant figures, the result might be stated in several ways:

804×10^2 ohms	80,400 ohms
80.4 kilohms	80.40 kilohms
0.0804 megohm	0.08 megohm

However, only the three statements on the left convey a clear idea of the number of significant figures, in accordance with accepted conventions and practices. These conventions are:

1. The last digit stated represents the point of uncertainty.

2. It is understood (unless specified otherwise) that there is a *total* uncertainty of one unit in the last digit. For instance, the third digit in the resistance is closer to 4 than it is to either 3 or 5. Thus, the resistance lies between 80.35 and 80.45 kilohms.

3. To avoid the appearance of zeros beyond the uncertain digit, an appropriate power of 10 should be used, if necessary.

4. The uncertain digit may be printed in smaller size and may be inferior to the other digits. For example, 0.080_4 megohm.

When rounding off to a specified number of significant figures, the following rules may be followed:

1. If the first digit to be discarded is less than 5, the preceding digit is left unaltered.

2. If the first digit to be discarded is greater than 5, the preceding digit is increased by 1.

3. If the first digit to be discarded is equal to 5 and is followed by digits greater than zero, the digit preceding the 5 is increased by 1.

4. If the first digit to be discarded is equal to 5 and is followed either by zeros or no further digits, the digit preceding the 5 is rounded to its nearest even value. (Choice of *even* rather than *odd* is arbitrary. The idea is that a consistent convention will produce a balancing effect over a large number of cases.)

Thus, when rounding to three significant figures, 52.449 becomes 52.4, 52.46 becomes 52.5, 52.4501 becomes 52.5, 52.45 becomes 52.4, and 52.35 becomes 52.4.

In addition, subtraction, multiplication, and division, it is good practice to carry more digits than are ultimately used. Superfluous digits are then dropped in the final result. In addition or subtraction of two numbers, no digit should be retained, even if it is a significant digit, that is more than one place beyond the last significant digit of the other number. For instance, the numbers 62.1 and 0.533 are added as $62.1 + 0.53 = 62.63$, and then the 3 is dropped. The numbers 62.1 and 0.553 are added as $62.1 + 0.55 = 62.65$, and this is rounded to the nearest even value by dropping the 5. Rounding the precise sum, 62.653, to 62.7 is not meaningful since 0.003 is completely swamped by the total uncertainty of 0.1 in the larger number.

In multiplication or division of two numbers, the per cent uncertainties in each number must be considered. The larger per cent uncertainty is dominant in the result, as shown by Eqs. (7-21) and (7-22). Hence, the number with the smaller per cent uncertainty may be rounded to the per cent uncertainty of the other number before performing the multiplication or division. For example, the uncertainty of 0.47 is about ± 1 per cent, and the uncertainty of 10.23 is about ± 0.05 per cent. Thus, their product may be obtained from $0.47 \times 10.2 = 4.7_{94}$ and rounded to 4.8, which reflects an uncertainty of about ± 1 per cent.

In statistical computations, the number of significant figures retained in the mean is usually one more than in the raw data. This is justified because the standard deviation of the mean is $1/\sqrt{n}$ times that of a single variate. Measures of uncertainty, such as standard deviation and limit of error, are usually stated to one significant figure and need not include more than two significant figures.

14-2. Slide-rule Techniques. If care is exercised, two numbers may be multiplied or divided on a good quality 10-in. slide rule to a precision of a fraction of one per cent. The precision of the result may be improved by use of certain auxiliary techniques. Several examples, based on simple algebraic relations, will illustrate some of the possibilities.

a. Products. The product ab may always be expressed as

$$ab = a(c + d) = ac + ad \tag{14-1}$$

where $b = c + d$. If c is selected to be a power of 10, ac is determined by inspection. Then $d = b - c$ may be multiplied by a, using the slide rule, and the resulting product added to ac. The end result may be more precise than direct slide-rule evaluation of ab, particularly when $|d| \ll c$. For example, if $a = 1.835$ and $b = 11.67$, the direct slide-rule product is 21.4_0. With $c = 10$, $ac = 18.35$, and $d = 1.67$. The slide rule yields $ad = 3.06_2$. Add this to ac and obtain the more precise result $ab = 21.41_2$.

b. Quotients. The quotient a/b may be expressed as

$$\frac{a}{b} = \frac{b + d}{b} = 1 + \frac{d}{b} \tag{14-2}$$

where $d = a - b$. The difference, d, may be positive or negative and is computed by longhand. Then the quotient d/b may be obtained with the slide rule. The result may be more precise than direct slide-rule evaluation of a/b, especially if $|d| \ll b$. For example, with $a = 76.85$ and $b = 66.42$, the direct slide-rule quotient is 1.15_8. Using $d = 10.43$, the more precise indirect result is 1.157_4.

Using the rule of addition of proportions, the quotient a/b may also be expressed as

$$\frac{a}{b} = \frac{a + ca/b}{b + c} \tag{14-3}$$

where c is arbitrary. If c is selected so that the denominator, $b + c$, is a power of 10, then ca/b may be obtained with the slide rule. When a is added to this result, the decimal point is established from $b + c$. The end result may be more precise than direct slide-rule evaluation of a/b, particularly if $|c| \ll b$. For example, if $a = 27.64$ and $b = 12.32$, the direct slide-rule quotient is 2.24_1. With $c = -2.32$, then $b + c = 10$, and the slide-rule result for ca/b is -5.20. Hence, the numerator is $27.64 - 5.20 = 22.44$. The end result for a/b by this indirect method is more precise, 2.244.

c. *Difference between Fractions.* The difference between two fractions a/b and c/d is

$$\frac{a}{b} - \frac{c}{d} = \frac{ad - bc}{bd} \tag{14-4}$$

When the two fractions are nearly equal, small slide-rule errors become highly magnified when the fractions are evaluated directly and then subtracted. Instead, the products ad and bc should be obtained with care, by longhand if necessary, and their difference determined. This difference may then be divided by bd using the slide rule. For example, with $a = 11$, $b = 120$, $c = 60$, and $d = 665$, the slide rule yields $a/b = 0.091_7$ and $c/d = 0.090_2$. The difference is rather vague, 0.001_5. Alternatively, the difference between the products $ad = 7315$ and $bc = 7200$ is 115. Dividing this by the slide-rule product, $bd = 798$, yields a far more precise result, 0.00144_1.

Another technique based on the first procedure described for quotients may be useful if differences between a, b and c, d are small compared with a and c, respectively. With $B = a - b$ and $D = c - d$, then

$$\frac{a}{b} - \frac{c}{d} = 1 + \frac{B}{b} - 1 - \frac{D}{d} = \frac{B}{b} - \frac{D}{d} \tag{14-5}$$

To illustrate, suppose $a = 34.2$, $b = 31.0$, $c = 11.1$, and $d = 10.2$. Then $B = 3.2$ and $D = 0.9$. Divide these differences by b and d, respectively, using the slide rule. Then $0.103_2 - 0.088_2 = 0.015$. In this example, the result contains one more significant figure than is obtained by separate evaluation of a/b and c/d with the slide rule.

14-3. Computations Based on Binomial Expansion. For the binomial expansion

$$(a + b)^n = \frac{a^n}{0!} + \frac{na^{n-1}b}{1!} + \frac{n(n - 1)a^{n-1}b^2}{2!} + \cdots$$

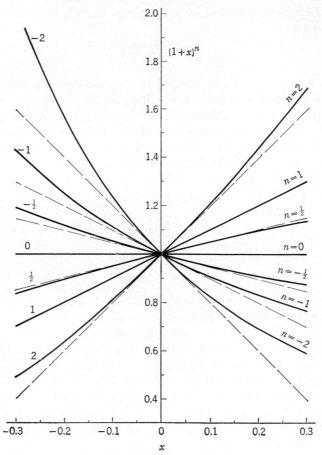

Fig. 14-1. $(1 + x)^n$ for various n.

the term a^n may be factored. Then, with $x = b/a$, the series that is multiplied by a^n becomes

$$(1 + x)^n = 1 + nx + \frac{n(n - 1)x^2}{2} + \cdots \tag{14-6}$$

If $|x| \ll 1$, the x^2 term is very small compared with 1, and the first two terms may be used for approximate computations.

The series is particularly useful for numerical evaluation of square roots of numbers that are close to unity. With $n = \pm\frac{1}{2}$,

$$(1 + x)^{\pm\frac{1}{2}} = 1 \pm \frac{x}{2} + \cdots \tag{14-7}$$

For example,

$$\sqrt{1.01} \approx 1.005 \qquad\qquad \sqrt{0.99} = \sqrt{1 - 0.01} \approx 0.995$$

$$\frac{1}{\sqrt{1.02}} \approx 1 - 0.01 = 0.99 \qquad \frac{1}{\sqrt{0.98}} \approx 1 + 0.01 = 1.01$$

Another special case, often arising, is that of $n = -1$. Then Eq. (14-6) becomes

$$\frac{1}{1 + x} = 1 - x + \cdots \qquad\qquad (14\text{-}8)$$

For example, $1/1.01 \approx 0.99$, and $1/0.98 \approx 1.02$.

Other values of n frequently encountered include ± 2 and $\pm \frac{3}{2}$. The binomial expansion is useful in these and other cases. The acceptability of the approximation may, in all cases, be investigated by evaluating the x^2 term in the series. Graphs of several of these special cases are given in Fig. 14-1 for values of x near zero. A pictorial idea of the error entailed in the linear approximation may be obtained from these curves.

14-4. Graphical Presentation of Data. A graph is a quantitative tool that possesses many desirable advantages. It enables the over-all behavior of quantities to be easily grasped. Such features as maxima, minima, slopes, and points of inflection are revealed at a glance. The graph may be used to determine areas and derivatives. It permits comparison of two or more curves and is especially valuable when used to compare experimental results with theory. These advantages may be fully exploited only if graphs are prepared thoughtfully. Attention must be paid to every feature requiring human judgment, among which are selection of suitable paper, choice of scales, representation of experimental points, and drawing of curves. Labeling of scales and titling of the graph are required for clarity and utility. Other information should be included so that the entire graph represents a complete and self-explanatory summary.

Choice of suitable graph paper may be made from many different commercially available types. The four most common ones are uniform rectangular-coordinate paper, polar-coordinate paper, semi-log paper, and log-log paper. There are also many other special types of graph paper. Once the type of paper has been selected, there remain such matters as size, color, quality of paper, and spacing of adjacent coordinate lines. These must be evaluated, consciously or otherwise, in the course of reaching the most suitable decision.

Choice of coordinate scales is facilitated by following certain rules. First, the scale of the independent variable, by established custom, should always be the abscissa of the graph. Second, the numerical scales should be selected so that the coordinates of any point on the resulting curve

may be read easily and quickly.   This means that rapid visual interpolation should be possible without the need of auxiliary computation.
Third, the scales should be selected so that the smallest division corresponds approximately to the uncertainty of the data.   The scales need
not start from zero, unless the origin has particular significance.   Other
factors arise, depending upon the nature of the data.   If variables are
selected so that the resulting curve is approximately a straight line, then
the scale should be selected to give a slope in the vicinity of unity.   Use
of normalized variables may improve the utility of the graph.   These
matters must be decided upon individually for each case and require
thought and judgment.

Experimental points may be represented in several ways.   They should
always be designated clearly, and every point should be shown, if practical.   Crosses or circles are the most common designations.   A variety
of other symbols are used, such as triangles and squares, especially when
it is necessary to distinguish among different sets of data plotted on the
same paper.   Even if curves pass through all experimental points, the
point symbols should be shown clearly.   This identifies the curve as an
experimental result.   Some individuals favor use of rectangles, rather
than point symbols, where the sides of each rectangle are equal to the
uncertainty of the corresponding variable.   When one of the variables is
much more precise than the other, usually the independent variable, the
rectangle becomes essentially a line segment and gives an immediate
graphic representation of the uncertainty of a given "point."

Drawing the best curve through all points is not always a simple matter.
It often demands a compromise between smoothness of curve and closeness of fit to the experimental points.   The curve usually should not
contain cusps, discontinuities, or other peculiarities—particularly if there
are theoretical reasons for expecting a smooth result.   It is not necessary
for the curve to pass through all experimental points, but there should be
an equal number of points falling on both sides of the curve.   Broken
line graphs, such as the calibration curve of Fig. 5-6, are exceptions.

Finally, it is essential to include labels, titles, and other details so that
complete and accurate information is conveyed.   The coordinate scales
should be marked at major intervals and numbered.   It is not necessary
to number every interval.   The name of the quantity represented by the
scale should be designated along with its units.   The title for the graph
should be brief, yet descriptive.   Other information, such as a legend to
define different sets of symbols used for experimental points, should be
included.   The entire graph, if done well, represents a clear and complete
presentation of experimental results and is worth many words.

14-5. Linear Graphs.   Whenever practicable, graph paper and coordinate variables should be selected to yield a plot that is as close to a straight

line as possible. Aside from the obvious fact that a straight line is the simplest curve, this technique has so many valuable features that it should be given every consideration. It may help disclose experimental errors with a minimum of computation. It reduces the graphical complications of plotting and drawing a smooth curve. If planned in advance, the variables used to linearize the graph may serve as a guide to experimental procedures, by establishing the range and spacing of experimental points to be secured. Finally, a linear graph may lead to a compact formulation of the entire results in terms of a single equation with all constants evaluated numerically.

Linearization of the graph usually requires individual study and treatment for each functional form. This calls upon the ingenuity of the analyst, because there are few standard rules to follow. The technique may be described in terms of examples. Several functions occuring fairly often in electrical measurements may be easily linearized. Detailed applications are given in the sections that follow.

The function

$$y = \frac{ax}{b + cx} \tag{14-9}$$

where a, b, and c are constants, appears frequently in circuits where a variable element is used. The determination of the internal resistance of a battery, as described in detail in Sec. 8-11, is a simple example. In that case, the dependent variable was the voltmeter reading, $V = y$, and the independent variable was the loading rheostat, $R_L = x$.

$$V = \frac{ER_L}{R + R_L}$$

The procedure for linearizing the graph in Sec. 8-11 is generally applicable whenever the form in Eq. (14-9) is encountered. New variables, $1/y$ and $1/x$, are introduced. Then, Eq. (14-9) becomes, in terms of the new variables,

$$\frac{1}{y} = \frac{b + cx}{ax} = \frac{b}{a}\left(\frac{1}{x}\right) + \frac{c}{a} \tag{14-10}$$

A plot of $1/y$ vs. $1/x$ on uniform rectangular-coordinate paper yields a straight line of slope b/a and intercept c/a.

Another form that occurs often is

$$y = cx^n \tag{14-11}$$

where c and n are constants. The case of $n = 1$ is trivial, since Eq. (14-11) is then already in linear form. Cases of $n \neq 1$ arise in many electrical situations. An illustration, outlined in detail in Sec. 14-6, is the power vs. current relationship for a fixed passive load. Another example is the angular deflection of a square-law meter movement vs. current or voltage applied to the movement, when the instrument "constant" is essentially constant. Hysteresis or eddy-current losses as a function of magnetic flux density or frequency fall into this form. The law of current vs. voltage for a diode rectifier approximates very closely the form of Eq. (14-11). There are many other occurrences of this form.

It may be possible to linearize the graph in two ways for the functional form in Eq. (14-11). If n is known from theory, as is often the case, then y may be plotted vs. x^n. The resulting curve will be a straight line of slope c, passing through the origin, assuming the theoretical equation agrees with experiment. Alternatively, y may be plotted vs. x on log-log paper, and neither n nor c need be known in advance. If Eq. (14-11) is an accurate representation of the data, a smooth curve through the experimental points will be a straight line. This is evident upon taking the logarithm of both sides of Eq. (14-11).

$$\log y = \log cx^n = \log c + n \log x \qquad (14\text{-}12)$$

The geometric slope of this line is n, and the intercept, $\log c$, occurs at $y = c$ where $x = 1$. This plot has the advantage that n and c need not be known in advance. Moreover, it possesses scales from which x and y may be read directly.

The exponential function

$$y = c\epsilon^{ax} \qquad (14\text{-}13)$$

where c and a are constants, also turns up frequently in electrical phenomena. Examples of its occurrence have appeared in this text in connection with transient behavior of galvanometers and electric circuits. Many other physical transients follow this exponential form. One method for linearizing a graph that follows Eq. (14-13) is, of course, to plot y vs. ϵ^{ax}, using uniform rectangular-coordinate paper. This may be done if a is known, but the exponential computations and resulting scale are inconvenient. A more satisfactory procedure is to use semi-log paper. A straight line results, as may be seen by taking logarithms of both sides of Eq. (14-13).

$$\log y = \log c + (a \log \epsilon)x \qquad \log \epsilon = 0.4343 \qquad (14\text{-}14)$$

When plotted on semi-log paper, using the linear scale for x, the straight line has a slope $a \log \epsilon$ and intercept $y = c$ for $x = 0$. Values of x and y may be read directly from the scales, and the constants a and c need not be known in advance. This semi-log plot is often used to determine the constant a by indirect measurement of x and y. It is also used to determine c by extrapolation, if the value of y for $x = 0$ is not available from experiment.

These examples do not exhaust the possibilities by any means. For instance, the function

$$y = \frac{a}{\sqrt{b^2 + x^2}} \qquad (14\text{-}15)$$

is linearized in Sec. 14-8. There are many other functional forms that yield to this treatment. It should be emphasized that this is more than simply a matter of obtaining a straight-line graph. As shown by the examples that follow, it may provide a means for graphical determination of unknown quantities and for detecting systematic departures from theoretical expectations. Moreover, it may have an impact on the plan of experimental procedures, such as indicating regions over which experimental data are most useful for subsequent analysis.

14-6. Linear Graph for Power Measurements. Power measurements, using the circuit of Fig. 14-2, may be used to illustrate some of the techniques and advantages of linear graphs. The average power, P_{av}, deliv-

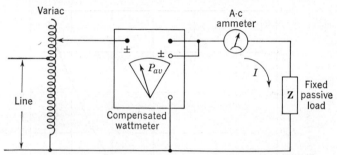

FIG. 14-2. Power measurements with passive load.

ered to a passive load, $\mathbf{Z}$, is measured by means of a compensated watt-meter for a range of measured load currents, I. The resistance of the ammeter is negligible. A variac is used to control the voltage applied to the circuit. The objective is to determine the resistive component, R, of the fixed load impedance. The theoretical equation that pertains to the measurements is, from Sec. 2-8,

$$P_{av} = \tfrac{1}{2}I^2 \operatorname{Re} \{\mathbf{Z}\} = \tfrac{1}{2}RI^2 \qquad (14\text{-}16)$$

This equation is in the form of Eq. (14-11), where n is known from theory to be 2.

The raw data are presented in Table 14-1. A graph of P_{av} vs. I may be plotted from the raw data, as shown in Fig. 14-3. Such a graph is useful for checking the smoothness of the data, but does not possess other features that might be desirable. For instance, the value of the load resistance is not immediately apparent from this graph. Moreover, this plot does not reveal whether there are deviations of the data from the expected theoretical behavior.

TABLE 14-1. POWER AND CURRENT MEASUREMENTS

I peak amp	P_{av} watts
0	0
1.0	20
2.0	80
3.0	180
4.0	325
4.5	415
5.0	530
5.5	655

An improvement results if P_{av} is plotted vs. I^2, as in Fig. 14-4. Theoretically, a straight line would be expected from such a plot. While the experimental points do lie along a straight line for low values of current,

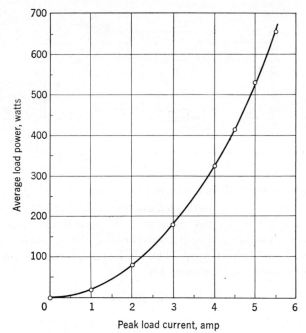

FIG. 14-3. Load power versus current.

they deviate systematically from the dashed theoretical curve at larger values of I. A possible explanation is that the resistance of the load increases owing to the temperature rise produced by increased dissipation. The slope of the theoretical curve yields half the value of R in ohms. This slope may be obtained by selecting any point on the theoretical curve, comfortably distant from the origin.   For example,

$$\frac{R}{2} = \text{slope} = \frac{400 \text{ watts}}{20 \text{ amp}^2} = 20 \text{ ohms}$$

Hence, the value of R for peak currents less than about 4 amp is 40 ohms. The value of R increases for larger values of current.

The advantages of this plot are self-evident.   It permits rapid determination of a weighted value of resistance, based on several points.

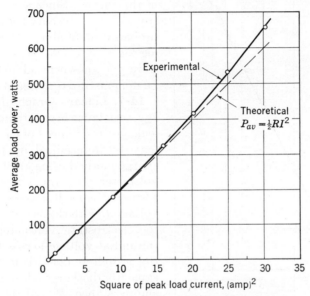

Fig. 14-4. Linear graph for power measurements.

More important, it discloses a systematic deviation from theoretical expectations, which was not apparent from the plot of P_{av} vs. I.   Of course, a plot of a theoretical curve may be superimposed on that of Fig. 14-3, but this would require use of some definite value of R.   It would not necessarily be correct to use a value of R based on the average resistance computed from each point, as is revealed by the plot in Fig. 14-4.

A third possibility for treatment of the data is the log-log plot, indicated in Fig. 14-5.   Here both P_{av} and I may be read directly from the scales, and the raw data are plotted directly without computation.   The linear theoretical result is indicated by the dashed curve.   The intercept of both curves at $I = 1$ amp gives the low-current value $R/2 = 20$ ohms directly from the power scale.   The geometric slope of the theoretical curve yields the exponent $n = 2$, as expected in this case.   This slope may be determined by selecting any pair of well-separated points, as indicated, and measuring the two sides of the right triangle with a ruler, in the same dimensions.   Then

$$n = \tan \phi = \frac{18 \text{ units}}{9.0 \text{ units}} = 2$$

The log-log plot may be seen to have a slight disadvantage in comparison with the plot of Fig. 14-4 because the scales are crowded at the upper end of the curve.   Since $n = 2$ is known from theory, the curve of Fig. 14-4 is probably preferable.   However, the log-log plot would be superior if n were not known in advance, as will be demonstrated in Sec. 14-11.

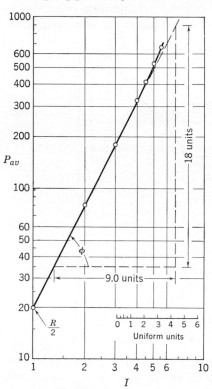

FIG.   14-5. Linear   graph   for   power measurements using log-log plot.

14-7. Linear Graph for Leakage-resistance Measurements. The leakage resistance of a capacitor may be determined by the loss of charge method using an electrostatic voltmeter.   In the circuit of Fig. 14-6, the capacitor is charged to a voltage E with the switch closed, and the electrostatic voltmeter indicates the initial voltage across C.   When the switch is opened at $t = 0$, the capacitor discharges through its leakage resistance, R, and the voltmeter reading follows the capacitor voltage faithfully if the decay is not too rapid.   The capacitance, C_v, of the electrostatic voltmeter is a function of the voltage applied to the movement, and this may introduce complications.   However, if $C_v \ll C$, the voltage across C is given theoretically by

$$V = E\epsilon^{-t/RC} \qquad\qquad t \geqq 0 \qquad (14\text{-}17)$$

The electrostatic voltmeter indicates V directly.   The readings may be observed at measured times, starting at $t = 0$.   Then V may be plotted vs. t, and R is deduced if C is known.

As a specific example, a capacitor with $C = 1.0$ μf and leakage resistance, R, to be determined, is energized from a voltage source $E = 100$ volts.   The maximum capacitance of the electrostatic voltmeter used for the measurement of V is $C_v = 50$ $\mu\mu$f.   This is only 0.005 per cent of C

and is entirely negligible in view of the readability and calibration errors of the voltmeter. The data given in Table 14-2 represent average results of several trials repeated under identical conditions.

A plot of the raw data in Fig. 14-7 indicates that a smooth curve may be passed through all experimental points. Since $\epsilon^{-1} = 0.368$, the time constant is easily determined from this graph to be $RC = 48$ sec at the point $V = 36.8$ volts. With $C = 1.0$ μf, it follows that the leakage resistance, R, is 48 megohms.

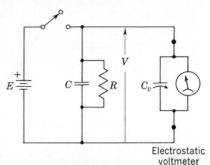

The fact that the experimental points lie along a smooth curve does not necessarily ensure that the decay of voltage is mathematically exponential. (In capacitors with solid dielectrics, a phenomenon called "absorption" often produces departures from a simple exponential decay.) The validity of applying Eq. (14-17) in analysis of the results must be investigated. One method is to compute V from Eq. (14-17) using $E = 100$ volts and $RC = 48$ sec for a number of different times, t. The theoretical curve may be plotted in Fig. 14-7 to see how closely it fits with the experi-

Fig. 14-6. Leakage resistance measurements by loss of charge.

TABLE 14-2. CAPACITOR VOLTAGE-DECAY MEASUREMENTS

V	t
volts	sec
100	0
81	10
57	27
39	45
29	60
21	75

mental curve. When this is done, the data are found to be consistent with Eq. (14-17) in this case. This validation procedure involves theoretical calculations in which experimental values (E and RC) are required for each point. The two curves are fitted at $t = 0$ and $t = 48$ sec. Should the theoretical curve, developed in this manner, deviate from the experimental curve, there might be reasons other than purely theoretical ones for the disagreement. Moreover, this method requires that a smooth curve be drawn through the theoretical points, which takes care and time.

A more satisfactory procedure that entails less labor is possible. Since Eq. (14-17) is in the form of Eq. (14-13), it may be linearized using semi-

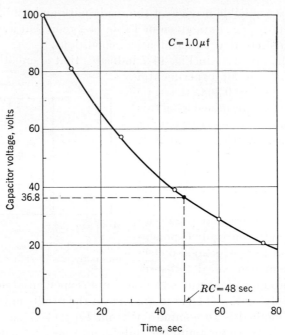

FIG. 14-7. Capacitor voltage decay.

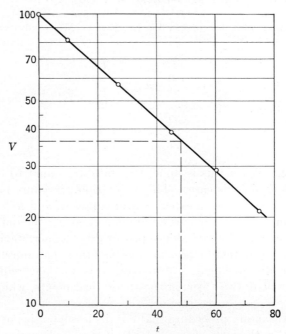

FIG. 14-8. Linear graph for voltage decay.

log paper.   The raw data are plotted directly on semi-log paper as indicated in Fig. 14-8.   No computation is required, and no reliance is placed on the value of RC.   A ruler may be used very easily to establish the extent to which the experimental points lie on a straight line.   If they do, as is the case in Fig. 14-8, the behavior of V in accordance with Eq. (14-17) is verified.   Then it is fully justified to evaluate RC based on Eq. (14-17).   The slope of the line in Fig. 14-8 may be used to determine RC if desired.   However, the experimental points fit the straight line so well that it is preferable to read out the value of RC corresponding to $V = 36.8$ volts.

14-8. Linear Graph for Inductor Measurements.   Another illustration of the linearization procedure is provided by the data of Table 14-3,

TABLE 14-3. INDUCTOR MEASUREMENTS

f (freq) cps	V (volts) rms	I (amp) rms
20	100	0.324
40	100	0.259
60	100	0.207
80	100	0.166
100	100	0.138
120	100	0.118
140	100	0.102

obtained using the circuit of Fig. 14-9.   The frequency of the sinusoidal generator is varied over the range 20 to 140 cps while maintaining the

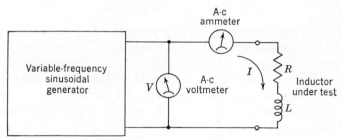

FIG. 14-9. Inductor measurements.

output voltage constant.   The alternating current drawn from this generator by the inductor under test is measured with an ammeter of negligible impedance.   The objective is to determine the resistance, R, and self-inductance, L, of the inductor.   The theoretical equation governing the readings V and I is

$$V = I \sqrt{R^2 + (\omega L)^2} \tag{14-18}$$

where $\omega = 2\pi f$.

A plot of the raw data, I vs. f, shown in Fig. 14-10 displays a smooth behavior.   The current decreases as ωL increases with frequency.   One possible approach to determining R and L is to plot V/I vs. f, as in Fig. 14-10.   If this curve is extrapolated to $f = 0$, which involves guesswork,

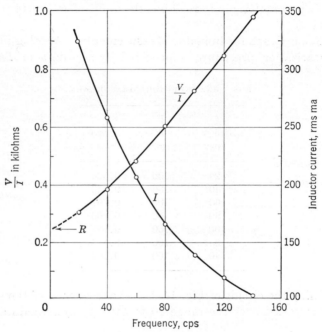

Fig. 14-10. Plot of inductor data.

the value of R may be read directly from the V/I scale at $f = 0$.   A resistance of approximately 250 ohms might be estimated.   (It would be preferable to measure the d-c resistance of the inductor directly, but presumably this information is unavailable.)   Using this value of R, the quantity $(V/I)^2 - R^2$ may be computed, and its square root plotted vs. f.   This will be a straight line of slope $2\pi L$ passing through the origin, provided that the data follow Eq. (14-18).

$$\sqrt{\left(\frac{V}{I}\right)^2 - R^2} = 2\pi L f$$

This method is really unsatisfactory because it depends upon the estimate for R, which is subject to uncertainty by the extrapolation of the V/I curve.

An improved procedure is to linearize the data in terms of new variables $(V/I)^2$ and f^2. Theoretically, this should yield a straight line, since the square of Eq. (14-18) is

$$\left(\frac{V}{I}\right)^2 = R^2 + (2\pi L)^2 f^2$$

When the data are plotted with these new variables in Fig. 14-11, a reasonably straight line results. The slope of the line leads to a deter-

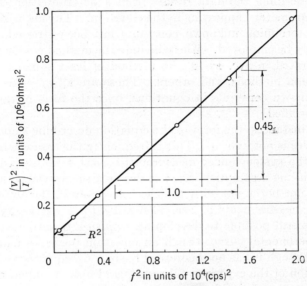

Fig. 14-11. Linear graph for inductor measurements.

mination of L and may be evaluated by selecting any two well-spaced points.

$$(2\pi L)^2 = \text{slope} = \frac{45 \times 10^4 \text{ ohms}^2}{10^4 \text{ sec}^{-2}} = 45 \text{ (ohm-sec)}^2$$

It follows that $L = 1.07$ henrys.

Extrapolation of the straight line to $f = 0$ is now more definite and may be used to determine R^2. The scale has rather limited readability at $f = 0$. If desired, R^2 may be computed from the known slope and one selected point on the straight line. For example, at $f^2 = 1.6 \times 10^4$ cps^2, the curve indicates $(V/I)^2 = 0.8 \times 10^6$ ohms^2. Therefore,

$$R^2 = [80 - 45(1.6)] \times 10^4 = 8 \times 10^4 \text{ ohms}^2$$

Hence, $R = 0.28$ kilohm.

The linearization procedure has not only given values of L and R in essentially one analysis operation, but also provides evidence that the measurements are consistent with theoretical expectations based on Eq. (14-18). While other methods may also be used to obtain L and R from these data, the linearization procedure is probably the shortest and most satisfactory approach.

14-9. Empirical Equations. It is obvious from the preceding sections that an equation may be found to describe experimental data, when a smooth curve results from graphing the measured quantities. When the form of the equation is known from theoretical analysis, a numerical equation describing the data results from a determination of the constants, or parameters, appearing in the equation. The linearization technique of determining unknown constants has been stressed, but other methods may be employed. These include the method of selected points, to be illustrated in Sec. 14-10, the method of least squares, successive approximation methods, and others. These are all methods for determining unknown constants in equations, once the form of the equation has been specified.

In many instances, the form of the equation describing smooth experimental curves is not known. This is frequently the case when nonlinear aspects of the system under measurement exert a noticeable effect, or when simplifying assumptions used to derive a theoretical equation for a system are not borne out with sufficient accuracy in the actual system. The power measurements of Sec. 14-6 fall into this category. Nevertheless, it is still possible to develop an *empirical* equation that fits the smooth experimental curve. Such an equation possesses many advantages even though it has no theoretical basis. An equation is a compact representation of the experimental results and may be superior to a presentation in terms of a table or graph. Moreover, a mathematical interrelationship of the measured quantities is revealed. The equation may be useful in calculations requiring interpolation between experimental points. It also may be differentiated and integrated, thus avoiding tedious and time-consuming graphical or numerical analysis.

The principal difficulty with empirical equations is the determination of the simplest form that fits the experimental curve with the required accuracy. Once a form is established, the constants appearing in the equation may be evaluated by the same methods used for theoretical equations. A straightforward approach that will always work for a smooth curve is to express the unknown function as a Fourier series. The Fourier coefficients may be evaluated by use of many different graphical methods. However, a closed form for the equation is usually desired. Moreover, the equation should represent a good compromise between complexity of its form and closeness of its fit to the experimental curve. Unfortunately, there is no direct means available for determining the optimum form. The procedure is one of trial. A general knowledge of the behavior of functions is used to guess at a form that might be suitable. Once a guess is made, it may be tested by linearizing the equation, if possible, or by other methods such as successive numerical differences. If the form is not satisfactory, another guess is made. The work of evaluating constants should be avoided until the *form* of the equation has been tested.

14-10. Empirical Equation for Variable Capacitor. To illustrate the determination of an empirical equation, the variable capacitor data of Table 14-4 will be analyzed by two methods. The capacitor consists of

TABLE 14-4. VARIABLE CAPACITOR MEASUREMENTS

β deg	C $\mu\mu f$
25	11
50	29
75	50
100	80
125	118
150	163

a set of fixed and rotatable plates. The angle, β, is read directly from a pointer and dial assembly, with pointer attached to the rotatable shaft of the capacitor. Six values of C, determined by bridge measurements, are given with corresponding angular settings of the rotatable plates. The objective is to find a numerical equation for C as a function of β that is a reasonably accurate representation of these data.

The first step is to plot C vs. β and to draw a smooth curve through the experimental points. At the same time, it is desirable to convert β from degrees to radians to facilitate numerical calculations. The six experimental points are shown by open circles in Fig. 14-12 along with a smooth curve that passes through all points except the lower two, which are straddled. (The triangles and solid circles represent calculated values to be discussed later.)

The next step is to guess at a suitable form of an equation to represent the smooth curve of Fig. 14-12. A parabola appears to be worthy of test. Note that the dotted extension of the curve to $\beta = 0$, despite uncertainty in how to draw it, does not display zero slope at $\beta = 0$. This means that C must contain a term involving the first power of β, to ensure that $dC/d\beta$ will not be zero at $\beta = 0$. Try the parabolic form

$$C = k + a\beta + b\beta^2 \tag{14-19}$$

The ultimate suitability of this function may be tested after the unknown constants, k, a, and b, are determined, by plotting C vs. β and comparing with the curve in Fig. 14-12.

Before too much labor is invested, however, it is well to test the suitability of this functional form, based on the somewhat uncertain extension of the plot in Fig. 14-12 to $\beta = 0$. The dashed extension indicates that $C = 4 \ \mu\mu f$ is a reasonable estimate for C at $\beta = 0$. Hence, a tenta-

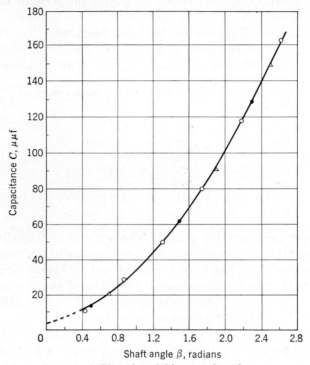

FIG. 14-12. Plot of variable capacitor data.

tive value of k is 4. With this value, Eq. (14-19) may be linearized by forming $C' = C - k$ and dividing by β.

$$\frac{C'}{\beta} = \frac{C - k}{\beta} = a + b\beta \qquad (14\text{-}20)$$

A plot of C'/β vs. β may be made using selected points from the smooth curve of Fig. 14-12, five of which are given in Table 14-5. This plot is shown in Fig. 14-13. The points lie very nearly on a straight line, indicating that the selected parabolic form will probably serve as an adequate description of the curve. At the same time, the constants may be evaluated readily. The intercept of the best straight line through the points of Fig. 14-13 yields a value $a = 10$, and the slope of the line gives $b = 19.2$. However, these values may be somewhat unreliable because an uncertain extrapolation was made to determine the value of k. A tentative equation for C is

$$C = 4 + 10\beta + 19.2\beta^2 \tag{14-21}$$

The accuracy with which this equation agrees with the curve of Fig. 14-12 may be checked by computing and plotting several points. The

TABLE 14-5. SMOOTHED DATA AND LINEARIZED VARIABLE

β rad	Smoothed C $\mu\mu$f	$C' = C - 4$ $\mu\mu$f	C'/β $\mu\mu$f/rad
0.6	17	13	21.7
1.0	33	29	29.0
1.6	69	65	40.7
2.0	101	97	48.5
2.4	139	135	56.3

three points indicated by triangles were calculated from Eq. (14-21). The point at $\beta = 0$ is not shown, but of course it agrees with the dashed extension of the curve at $\beta = 0$.

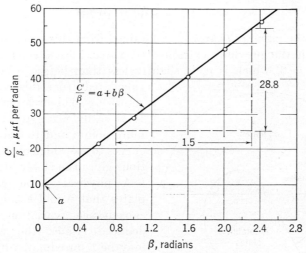

FIG. 14-13. Linear graph for variable capacitor.

The result in Eq. (14-21) might be entirely satisfactory, depending upon the required accuracy. However, a procedure that avoids the need for projecting the curve beyond the range of experimental points, which is generally poor practice, leads to a more satisfactory result. The method of selected points may be used. Three well-spaced points selected from the smooth curve may be used to set up three simultaneous equations in the three unknowns, k, a, and b. With the first, middle, and last points from Table 14-5, the simultaneous equations to be solved for k, a, and b are

$$17 = k + 0.6a + 0.36b$$
$$69 = k + 1.6a + 2.56b$$
$$139 = k + 2.4a + 5.76b$$

The determinant of this set of equations is

$$\Delta = \begin{vmatrix} 1 & 0.6 & 0.36 \\ 1 & 1.6 & 2.56 \\ 1 & 2.4 & 5.76 \end{vmatrix} = 1.44$$

The unknowns are determined by Cramer's rule. For example

$$a = \frac{\begin{vmatrix} 1 & 17 & 0.36 \\ 1 & 69 & 2.56 \\ 1 & 139 & 5.76 \end{vmatrix}}{\Delta} = 8.6$$

Similarly, b and k are determined to be $b = 19.7$ and $k = 4.7$. Hence, the equation for C determined by this method is

$$C = 4.7 + 8.6\beta + 19.7\beta^2 \tag{14-22}$$

Note that the value of C at $\beta = 0$ obtained from this equation is a little higher than the previous extrapolated value. As a consequence, the slope at $\beta = 0$, which is a, is slightly less than before. Three points calculated from this equation are shown by solid circles in Fig. 14-12. It is really necessary to compute more points and to draw complete curves to see which of the two equations gives the closer fit.

A physical shape of capacitor plates that would account for this capacitance variation may be deduced. Since the capacitance may be approximated by an equation in the form of Eq. (14-19), it follows that

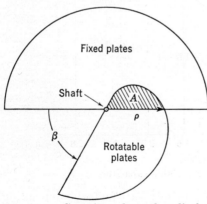

FIG. 14-14. Capacitor plates that display parabolic variation.

$$dC = (a + 2b\beta)\, d\beta$$

For a parallel-plate air capacitor, C is a constant times the plate area, $C = KA$, where K contains the spacing between plates, the dielectric constant, and the number of plates. Hence, $dC = K\, dA$. For the capacitor shown in Fig. 14-14, an area element, dA, corresponding to an increment $d\beta$ in β is

$$dA = \frac{1}{2} \rho^2 \, d\beta$$

Therefore, $\qquad dC = K \, dA = \frac{K}{2} \rho^2 \, d\beta = (a + 2b\beta) \, d\beta$

The shape of the rotatable plates is given in polar coordinates (ρ, β) by canceling $d\beta$ and solving for ρ.

$$\rho = \sqrt{\frac{2}{K}} \, \sqrt{a + 2b\beta} \qquad\qquad (14\text{-}23)$$

The plate shape in Fig. 14-14 is drawn to conform with the size of a and b determined for the curve in Fig. 14-12.

14-11. Empirical Equation for Law of Deflection. A final illustration of techniques for determining empirical equations is afforded by the nonuniform scale characteristics of a moving-iron ammeter. In Sec. 12-5 it was shown that the law of deflection of such an instrument is given by

$$\theta_{\text{av}} = \frac{1}{2S} \frac{\partial L}{\partial \theta} I^2_{\text{rms}} \qquad\qquad (14\text{-}24)$$

If $\partial L / \partial \theta$ is a constant, then θ_{av} is proportional to the square of the rms current. The resulting scale is crowded at low values of current, as indi-

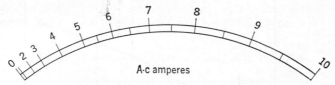

FIG. 14-15. Moving-iron ammeter scale.

cated in the scale shown in Fig. 14-15. Detailed analysis of the scale geometry leads to an equation for I_{rms} in terms of the angular deflection, θ_{av}, which will be designated simply as θ. If $\theta / I^2_{\text{rms}}$ is integrable, then an equation for L as a function of θ may be obtained.

As a first step, the angles of various scale marks may be measured as accurately as possible with a protractor. These angles are given in Table 14-6 and represent the raw data from which an empirical equation may be derived. After converting θ to radians, these points are plotted, as in Fig. 14-16. A smooth curve is then drawn through the points. The curve is then studied with a view in mind of guessing a suitable function that might represent it.

The general appearance of this curve, as well as the actual meter scale, suggest a square-law behavior. Therefore, the next logical step is to attempt to linearize the graph by plotting the square of the current vs. θ,

with the hope that a straight line will result.   Such a graph is shown in
Fig. 14-17, using the same points as are given in Table 14-6 because the

TABLE 14-6. SCALE DIVISION ANGLES
(Raw Data)

I_{rms} amp	θ deg
0	0
2	3
3	6
4	11
5	17
6	24
7	33
8	44
8.5	51
9	58
9.5	66
10	75

data are so smooth.   The value of I_{rms}^2 is seen to droop away from a
linear curve above currents of approximately 7 amp (50 amps²).   This
shows that I_{rms}^2 is more complicated than simply some constant times θ.
If I_{rms}^2 were a constant times θ, then Eq. (14-24) shows that $\partial L/\partial \theta$ would

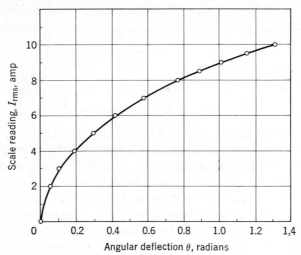

FIG. 14-16. Ammeter scale characteristics.

be a constant, from which it follows that L would be proportional to θ.

The deviation from a linear relationship in Fig. 14-17 may be studied
more closely by examining the difference between the actual curve and
the fairly well-defined dashed line drawn tangent to the actual curve at
low values of current.   In other words, the square of the current may be

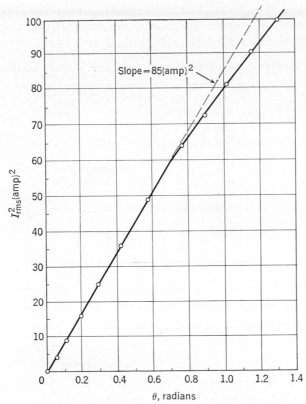

Fig. 14-17. Linear graph for scale characteristics.

expressed as

$$I_{rms}^2 = k\theta - f(\theta) \qquad (14\text{-}25)$$

where $f(\theta)$ represents the deviation of I_{rms}^2 from a linear relation. The constant, k, may be determined from the slope of the dashed line in Fig. 14-17. It is equal to 85 amp².

Possible mathematical forms for $f(\theta)$ may be explored by first developing a curve. Differences between $k\theta$ and I_{rms}^2 for a number of points selected from the smooth curve of Fig. 14-17 may be calculated. Table 14-7 shows some selected points, along with calculated values of $f(\theta)$. A plot of $f(\theta)$ is given in Fig. 14-18. A smooth curve drawn among the points suggests that $f(\theta)$ may be proportional to some power of θ. The following functional form deserves test.

$$f(\theta) = c\theta^n \qquad (14\text{-}26)$$

where c and n are to be determined. This is the same form as Eq. (14-11) and may be linearized by use of a log-log plot. This permits the form of the function to be tested, and if the resulting points fall along a straight line, the values of c and n are readily determined from the same plot. Accordingly, the data for $f(\theta)$ in Table 14-7 are plotted on log-log paper

TABLE 14-7. SELECTED POINTS AND DIFFERENCE VARIABLE

θ rad	I^2_{rms} amp^2	$f(\theta) = 85\theta - I^2_{rms}$ amp^2
0	0	0
0.2	17	0
0.4	34	0
0.6	50	1
0.8	66	2
1.0	80	5
1.1	87	6
1.2	93	9
1.3	99	11

in Fig. 14-19. It is seen that a straight line is not too unreasonable a fit, and this indicates that the form of $f(\theta)$ in Eq. (14-26) may be satisfactory.

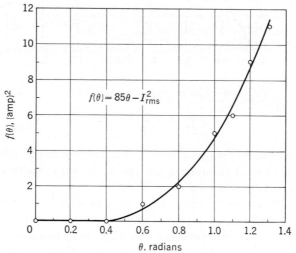

FIG. 14-18. Power-law behavior of correction function.

The constants, c and n, are determined directly from the log-log plot. In drawing the straight line, note that larger differences are favored since the smaller differences are inherently subject to greater uncertainty. The value of $c = f(1)$ is determined at $\theta = 1$, where $\log \theta = 0$. The result is $c = 5$ amp^2. The geometric slope of the line, measured in units of a linear scale, is equal to the exponent of θ.

$$n = \text{slope} = \frac{8.2 \text{ units}}{2.6 \text{ units}} \approx 3$$

Hence, $f(\theta)$ is determined.

$$f(\theta) = 5\theta^3 \tag{14-27}$$

Therefore, the complete equation derived for I_{rms}^2 is, using Eq. (14-25),

$$I_{rms}^2 = 85\theta - 5\theta^3 = 5\theta(17 - \theta^2) \tag{14-28}$$

The equation representing the original curve in Fig. 14-16 is the square root of this result.

$$I_{rms} = \sqrt{5\theta} \sqrt{17 - \theta^2} \tag{14-29}$$

As a final check, I_{rms} should be calculated from Eq. (14-29) for various values of θ and the results plotted on Fig. 14-16. This permits evaluation of the over-all fit of Eq. (14-29) to the raw data.

With an empirical equation determined for the scale characteristics, one may return to Eq. (14-24) to solve for the inductance, L, as a function of θ. Insert the expression for I_{rms}^2 from Eq. (14-28), solve for $\partial L/\partial\theta$, and integrate.

$$L = \int \frac{2S\theta \, d\theta}{5\theta(17 - \theta^2)} = \frac{2S}{5} \int \frac{d\theta}{17 - \theta^2}$$

A table of integrals gives

$$\int \frac{dx}{c^2 - x^2} = \frac{1}{2c} \ln \frac{c + x}{c - x}$$

Therefore, with $c^2 = 17$, L becomes

$$L = \frac{S}{5\sqrt{17}} \ln \frac{\sqrt{17} + \theta}{\sqrt{17} - \theta} + L_0 \tag{14-30}$$

where L_0 is the constant of integration and is the zero-current value of L occurring at $\theta = 0$.

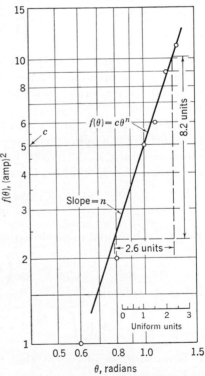

FIG. 14-19. Linear graph for correction function.

Though it is not immediately apparent from this result, L is essentially a constant times θ for $\theta \leqq 0.6$ radian. For larger values of θ, L increases with θ at a more rapid rate. This may be seen from plotting Eq. (14-30), but a more elegant approach is to expand L by use of the convergent series

$$\ln{(1 + x)} = x - \frac{x^2}{2} + \frac{x^3}{3} - \cdots \qquad -1 < x < +1$$

Consider the two logarithmic terms

$$\ln{(\sqrt{17} \pm \theta)} = \ln{\sqrt{17}} + \ln{\left(1 \pm \frac{\theta}{\sqrt{17}}\right)}$$

The difference between the term with the plus sign and the one with the minus sign, upon applying the series expansion, becomes

$$\ln{\frac{\sqrt{17} + \theta}{\sqrt{17} - \theta}} = \frac{2\theta}{\sqrt{17}} + \frac{2\theta^3}{51\sqrt{17}} + \cdots \qquad \frac{\theta}{\sqrt{17}} < 1$$

Therefore, the convergent series representing L is, from Eq. (14-30),

$$L = \frac{2S\theta}{85}\left(1 + \frac{\theta^2}{51} + \cdots\right) + L_0 \qquad (14\text{-}31)$$

For $\theta = 0.6$, the θ^2 term is only 0.007. This shows that the departure from a linear function of θ is only 0.7 per cent at $\theta = 0.6$. Thus, L is essentially a constant times θ for $\theta \leq 0.6$, and this agrees with previous conclusions.

The series result in Eq. (14-31) suggests that L could have been obtained from a series expansion of $\partial L/\partial\theta$. Indeed, this would have been necessary if the result had not been integrable. To illustrate, reexamine $\partial L/\partial\theta$, obtained from I^2_{rms}.

$$\frac{\partial L}{\partial\theta} = \frac{2S\theta}{5\theta(17 - \theta^2)} = \frac{2S}{85}\left(1 - \frac{\theta^2}{17}\right)^{-1}$$

Using the binomial expansion, this becomes

$$\frac{\partial L}{\partial\theta} = \frac{2S}{85}\left(1 + \frac{\theta^2}{17} + \cdots\right)$$

Integrate termwise.

$$L = \frac{2S}{85}\left[\int d\theta + \int \frac{\theta^2\,d\theta}{17} + \cdots\right] = \frac{2S\theta}{85}\left(1 + \frac{\theta^2}{51} + \cdots\right) + L_0$$

It is no surprise, of course, that this result agrees with the series for L in Eq. (14-31).

TEXTBOOK REFERENCES

Beers, Yardley: "Introduction to the Theory of Error," Addison-Wesley Publishing Company, Cambridge, Mass., 1953.

Buckingham, H., and E. M. Price: "Principles of Electrical Measurements," Philosophical Library, Inc., New York, 1957.

Canfield, Donald T.: "The Measurement of Alternating-current Energy," McGraw-Hill Book Company, Inc., New York, 1940.

Carhart, Henry S., and George W. Patterson, Jr.: "Electrical Measurements," Allyn and Bacon, Inc., New York, 1895.

Curtis, Harvey L.: "Electrical Measurements," McGraw-Hill Book Company, Inc., New York, 1937.

Drysdale, C. V., and A. C. Jolley: "Electrical Measuring Instruments, Part One: Commercial and Indicating Instruments; Part Two: Induction Instruments, Supply Meters and Auxiliary Apparatus," Ernest Benn Ltd., London, 1924.

Edgcumbe, Kenelm, and F. E. J. Ockenden: "Industrial Electrical Measuring Instruments," Sir Isaac Pitman & Sons, Ltd., London, 1933.

Fry, Thornton C.: "Probability and Its Engineering Uses," D. Van Nostrand Company, Inc., Princeton, N.J., 1928.

Ginzton, Edward L.: "Microwave Measurements," McGraw-Hill Book Company, Inc., New York, 1957.

Golding, E. W.: "Electrical Measurements and Measuring Instruments," 3d ed., Sir Isaac Pitman and Sons, Ltd., London, 1942.

Goodwin, H. M.: "Precision of Measurements and Graphical Methods," McGraw-Hill Book Company, Inc., New York, 1919.

Gray, Andrew: "Absolute Measurements in Electricity and Magnetism," Macmillan and Company, London, vol. I, 1888; vol. II, 1893.

Greenwood, Ivan A., Jr., J. Vance Holdam, Jr., and Duncan Macrae, Jr.: "Electronic Instruments," Radiation Laboratory Series, vol. 21, McGraw-Hill Book Company, Inc., New York, 1948.

Hague, B.: "Alternating Current Bridge Methods," 5th ed., Sir Isaac Pitman and Sons, Ltd., London, 1946.

Harris, Forest K.: "Electrical Measurements," John Wiley & Sons, Inc., New York, 1952.

Hartshorn, L.: "Radio-frequency Measurements by Bridge and Resonance Methods," Chapman and Hall, Ltd., London, 1940.

Hund, August: "High-frequency Measurements," 2d ed., McGraw-Hill Book Company, Inc., New York, 1951.

Karapetoff, V.: "Experimental Electrical Engineering," vol. 1, 2d ed., John Wiley & Sons, Inc., New York, 1915.

Kinnard, Isaac F.: "Applied Electrical Measurements," John Wiley & Sons, Inc., New York, 1956.

421

Knowlton, Archer E.: "Electric Power Metering," McGraw-Hill Book Company, Inc., New York, 1934.

Laws, Frank A.: "Electrical Measurements," 2d ed., McGraw-Hill Book Company, Inc., New York, 1938.

Michels, Walter C.: "Advanced Electrical Measurements," 2d ed., D. Van Nostrand Company, Inc., Princeton, N.J., 1941.

————: "Electrical Measurements and Their Applications," D. Van Nostrand Company, Inc., Princeton, N.J., 1957.

Northrup, Edwin F.: "Methods of Measuring Electrical Resistance," McGraw-Hill Book Company, Inc., New York, 1912.

Owen, David: "Alternating Current Measurements," 3d ed., Methuen and Company, Ltd., London, 1950.

Palmer, A. de Forest: "The Theory of Measurements," McGraw-Hill Book Company, Inc., New York, 1912.

Partridge, Gordon R.: "Principles of Electronic Instruments," Prentice-Hall, Inc., Englewood Cliffs, N.J., 1958.

Skroder, Carl E., and M. Stanley Helm: "Circuit Analysis by Laboratory Methods," Prentice-Hall, Inc., Englewood Cliffs, N.J., 1946.

Smith, Arthur Whitmore: "Electrical Measurements in Theory and Application," 5th ed., McGraw-Hill Book Company, Inc., New York, 1959.

Stout, Melville B.: "Basic Electrical Measurements," Prentice-Hall, Inc., Englewood Cliffs, N.J., 1950.

Terman, Frederick Emmons: "Measurements in Radio Engineering," McGraw-Hill Book Company, Inc., New York, 1935.

———— and Joseph Mayo Pettit: "Electronic Measurements," 2d ed., McGraw-Hill Book Company, Inc., New York, 1952.

Vigoureaux, P., and C. E. Webb: "Principles of Electric and Magnetic Measurements," Prentice-Hall, Inc., Englewood Cliffs, N.J., 1936.

Waugh, Albert E.: "Elements of Statistical Method," 3d ed., McGraw-Hill Book Company, Inc., New York, 1952.

Worthing, Archie G., and Joseph Geffner: "Treatment of Experimental Data," John Wiley & Sons, Inc., New York, 1943.

ANSWERS TO PROBLEMS

Chapter 2

2-1. (a) $a + 13b/3$, $(a^2 + 26ab/3 + 121b^2/5)^{1/2}$; (b) $2/\pi$, $1/\sqrt{2}$; (c) $0.6479, 0.7173$

2-3. $i = \dfrac{\omega CE}{\sqrt{1 + (\omega RC)^2}} \cos(\omega t + \phi - \tan^{-1}\omega RC)$

2-4. See Eq. (4-51) with $\theta = y$ and $SI_p/K = A$

2-9. $\mathbf{I}_3 = \dfrac{\mathbf{Z}_1\mathbf{I}_a + \mathbf{Z}_2\mathbf{I}_b}{\mathbf{Z}_1 + \mathbf{Z}_2 + \mathbf{Z}_3}$

2-10. $\mathbf{V}_1 = \dfrac{\mathbf{Z}_3(\mathbf{Z}_1\mathbf{E}_b + \mathbf{Z}_2\mathbf{E}_a)}{\mathbf{Z}_1\mathbf{Z}_2 + \mathbf{Z}_1\mathbf{Z}_3 + \mathbf{Z}_2\mathbf{Z}_3}$

2-11. (a) $\mathbf{Z}_1 + \dfrac{\mathbf{Z}_2\mathbf{Z}_3}{\mathbf{Z}_2 + \mathbf{Z}_3}$; (b) $\mathbf{Z}_3 + \dfrac{\mathbf{Z}_1\mathbf{Z}_2}{\mathbf{Z}_1 + \mathbf{Z}_2}$; (c) $\mathbf{Z}_1 + \mathbf{Z}_2 + \dfrac{\mathbf{Z}_1\mathbf{Z}_3}{\mathbf{Z}_2}$

2-12. $\mathbf{Y}_a\mathbf{Y}_b + \mathbf{Y}_a\mathbf{Y}_c + \mathbf{Y}_b\mathbf{Y}_c = \dfrac{\mathbf{Y}_c}{\mathbf{Z}_1} = \dfrac{\mathbf{Y}_a}{\mathbf{Z}_2} = \dfrac{\mathbf{Y}_b}{\mathbf{Z}_3}$

2-13. $\mathbf{I}_{23} = \dfrac{-\mathbf{E}}{R_1 + R_2 + 2j\omega(L + M - 1/2\omega^2 C)}$

2-15. $\mathbf{I}_2 = \dfrac{\mathbf{E}_a\mathbf{Z}_2 + \mathbf{E}_b\mathbf{Z}_1}{\mathbf{Z}_1\mathbf{Z}_2 + \mathbf{Z}_1\mathbf{Z}_3 + \mathbf{Z}_2\mathbf{Z}_3}$

2-16. $\mathbf{I}_L = \dfrac{\mathbf{E}\mathbf{Y}\mathbf{Y}_b\mathbf{Y}_L}{(\mathbf{Y} + \mathbf{Y}_a)(\mathbf{Y}_b + \mathbf{Y}_c + \mathbf{Y}_L) + \mathbf{Y}_b(\mathbf{Y}_c + \mathbf{Y}_L)}$

2-17. (a) $-\frac{1}{27}$ amp; (b) $-\frac{1}{24}$ amp, using approximate theorem

Chapter 3

3-1. 3.42×10^{-4} newton, mutually perpendicular to $d\mathbf{s}$ and $\mathbf{B}$

3-2. $T = nBiA$, $A = \pi R^2$

3-3. $42°21'$

3-5. $19.9°$

3-6. $B = \dfrac{k\theta}{\tan 2\theta}$

3-7. 0.3 mm per μa, 0.6 mm per μa; 0.003 mm per μvolt, 0.006 mm per μvolt; 0.6 megohm

3-8. (a) No effect; (b) increase; (c) decrease; (d) increase; (e) no effect

3-9. (a) 400 megohms; (b) 0.006 radian

3-10. 49 ohms, 0.008 μa per mm

3-11. Galvanometer B

3-12. $R_s = 100, 11.1, 1.01$ ohms

3-13. Protects galvanometer from large currents that it might receive with no shunt

3-14. (a) 0.02 μa per division; (b) 0.03 μa per division; (c) 100 ohms

3-15. $R_{12} = 450$ ohms, $R_{23} = 45$ ohms, $R_3 = 5$ ohms; 0.05 mm
3-16. $I_1/I_2 = 9.36$, $I_1/I_3 = 86.6$
3-17. With circuit of Fig. 3-19b, $R_4 = 272$ ohms, $R_3 = 40$ ohms
3-19. $A = 0.38$
3-20. 5 db
3-21. $R_1 = 87$ ohms, $R_2 = 2,860$ ohms; 3.46 db
3-22. $+9$ per cent, $\frac{5}{9}$ ohm
3-23. 40.2 amp
3-24. $R_1 = 60$ ohms (6 mw), $R_2 = 600$ ohms (60 mw), $R_3 = \frac{2}{3}$ ohm (67 watts)
3-25. (a) -0.03, -0.6, -3, -6 per cent; (b) 0.156 ohm; (c) 1.67 ohms
3-26. 0.011 ohm
3-27. 133 volts
3-28. (a) 200 ohms per volt; (b) 4 ma; (c) 150 volts; (d) $V_A = 40$ volts, $V_B = 50$ volts, $V_C = 30$ volts
3-29. 95 volts
3-30. (a) 0.05, 0.2, 1, 5, 20, 100 megohms; (b) 50
3-31. 25 volts, 30 volts no load
3-32. 8.8 ma
3-33. 0.074 watt
3-34. (a) 180 volts; (b) 360 volts

Chapter 4

4-1. $JL_m \dfrac{d^3\theta}{dt^3} + \dfrac{d^2\theta}{dt^2}[D_aL_m + (R + R_m)J] + \dfrac{d\theta}{dt}\left[SL_m + \left(\dfrac{S}{K}\right)^2 + D_a(R + R_m) \right]$
$$+ \theta S(R + R_m) = \dfrac{SE}{K}$$

4-2. Add term $S\theta_0$ to right side of Eq. (4-14).

4-3. $\theta = \theta_s + \left(\theta_s - \theta_0 + \dfrac{A_0}{p_2} \right)\left[\dfrac{p_2\epsilon^{p_1t}}{p_1 - p_2} + \dfrac{p_1\epsilon^{p_2t}}{p_2 - p_1} \right] + \dfrac{A_0}{p_2}\, \epsilon^{p_2t}$

4-6. $50\sqrt{3}$ ohms
4-7. 5.75 sec
4-8. (a) 0.4017 radian; (b) 80 ohms
4-9. (a) 0.1081 radian; (b) 43.8 ohms
4-10. (a) $\theta = 0.500 - 0.559\epsilon^{-t} \sin (2t + 63.5°)$; ($b$) 1.2×10^{-9} newton-meter-sec per radian
4-11. $1.06T_0$
4-12. $t_m - t_s = \dfrac{T}{2\pi} \sin^{-1} \dfrac{T_0}{T}$
4-13. 18.4 sec
4-14. (a) 2,000 mm; (b) 15 mm; (c) 540×10^{-12} newton-meter
4-15. $\theta_m = 0.263$ radian, $\lambda = \pi/2$
4-16. (a) 5.33 μa; (b) 0.693
4-17. 0.1155, $T = 6\frac{2}{3}$ sec
4-18. 93.2 mm
4-25. $1.283\omega_0$
4-26. 2.1° at $\omega/\omega_0 = 0.36$
4-27. 0.53
4-28. 5 per cent
4-29. 49.5 db

Chapter 5

5-1. 1.2 amp

5-2. 4.42 amp

5-3. 12 volts

5-4. (a) $\dfrac{V_1}{I_1} = \dfrac{XR_v(R + R_a + X)}{R(X + R_v) + XR_v}$; (b) No. $\dfrac{V_1}{I_1} = R_a + X$

5-6. $\dfrac{50(R_aX + R_aR_v - X^2)}{X(X + R_v)}$; $X = \dfrac{R_a}{2} + \sqrt{\left(\dfrac{R_a}{2}\right)^2 + R_aR_v}$

5-7. Starting with voltmeter reading 9.7 volts, corrections are 0.31, 0.51, 0.11, −0.19, 0.21.

5-8. Starting with voltmeter reading 8 volts, per cent corrections are −6.9, −4.5, −4.3, −4.6, −3.2, −1.5, 0.3, 1.8, 1.2, 1.5, 0.6, −0.4, −1.0.

5-9. (a) $I_{20}/I = 1.042$; (b) 1.047

5-10. 42°21′

5-11. $\dfrac{\Delta R_0}{R_0[1 + (R_0 + \Delta R_0)/(R_1 + R_2)]}$. R_0 is more sensitive if $R_0 < (R_1 + R_2)$; otherwise R_2 is more sensitive.

Chapter 6

6-2. (a) 5; (c) 60; (d) 69

6-4. 1.4816 volts ± 0.18 per cent

6-5. $\bar{v} = 104.4$, $A = 1.52$, $\sigma = 1.85$

6-6. (a) Median = 999 ohms, mode = 999 ohms; mean = 998.97 ohms; (b) 2.1 ohms; (c) 97 per cent

6-7. (b) $P = 0.693/k$; (c) probably not because of sharp peak at $x = 0$

6-12. 866, if 0.1 ohm is standard deviation; 688, if 0.1 ohm is probable error.

6-13. 16

6-14. 22,937, assuming mean is 0.400 in.

6-15. 10

6-16. (a) 917, assuming mean resistance is 10,000 ohms; (b) 54,500

6-17. 8,280, assuming mean diameter is 0.1000 in.

6-18. Three points on curve are $n = 100$, $t = 2.81$; $n = 20$, $t = 2.24$; $n = 10$, $t = 1.96$.

6-19. (a) $\sigma = 1.33$ amp; (b) 683, 997; (c) 0.495

6-20. (b) 2.16 ± 0.58 megawatt; (c) 2.8 megawatts

Chapter 7

7-2. (a) σ; (b) $\sqrt{2}$; (c) $\sqrt{2}\,\sigma$

7-3. 0.5

7-4. 0.0013

7-5. 240 ± 19.3 ohms

7-6. 0.17 per cent

7-7. 0.707 per cent

7-8. $\sigma_w = k\sigma_u/u$

7-9. $\dfrac{L_w}{w} = a\left(\dfrac{L_u}{u}\right) + b\left(\dfrac{L_v}{v}\right) + c\left(\dfrac{L_x}{x}\right)$

7-10. (a) 5,000 ± 707 watts. (b) Each contributes equally.

7-11. Connection C, $\sqrt{5}/2$ ohms

7-12. 0.98 ohm

7-13. 0.71 per cent

7-14. $T = 6 \pm 0.26$ sec, $D/J = 0.7 \pm 0.16$ sec^{-1}

7-15. $2{,}100^{+133}_{-149}$ ohms, approximate limits ± 141 ohms

7-16. $2{,}500^{+16}_{-34}$ ohms, approximate limits ± 25 ohms

Chapter 8

8-1. (a) 139 ohms; (b) 150 ohms; (c) with $X/R_s = \rho = \epsilon^{\ln \rho}$, points at ordinates $\rho = A$ and $\rho = 1/A$ are seen to be equidistant from ordinate $\rho = 1$ on a log scale. Then show that $\frac{1}{2} - F$ at $\rho = A$ is equal to $F - \frac{1}{2}$ at $\rho = 1/A$.

8-2. $41\frac{1}{4}$ kilohm

8-3. 2,000 ohms

8-4. 26.8 kilohms

8-5. $0.13R_s \leqq X \leqq 7.87R_s$

8-6. (a) $F_0 = 1$, $F_\infty = (R + R_m)/(R + R_m + R_1)$;
(b) $X = R_1(R + R_m)/(R_1 - R - R_m)$

8-7. Adjustable $R_1 = 600$ ohms in series with battery; 26.1 ohms in shunt with 100-ohm movement

8-8. (a) 4,500 ohms; (b) 4,046 ohms

8-9. On "high," scale runs from 475 ohms to ∞, with 1,975 ohms at mid-scale. On "low," scale runs from 0 to 52.6 ohms, with 12.65 ohms at mid-scale.

8-10. (a) 50.3 ohms, 108.7 ohms; (b) 7,990 ohms

8-11. $\dfrac{dS}{S} = \dfrac{S + R_m}{(R + R_1)R_m}\left[dR - \left(\dfrac{R_m S}{R_m + S} + R + R_1 \right) \dfrac{dE}{E} \right]$

8-13. $S = 0$ to 4 ohms, $S_1 = 0.048$ ohm, $S_2 = 8.0$ ohms, $R_1 = 1{,}000$ ohms, $R_2 = 99$ kilohms

8-14. If $\dfrac{V_1}{I_1} + \dfrac{V_2}{I_2} > 2\dfrac{V_1}{I_2}$, V_1/I_1 is the better approximation; if the inequality is reversed, V_2/I_2 is better.

8-15. 55.8 megohms ± 1.5 per cent

8-17. $I = \dfrac{I_1 I_2 R_a}{R(I_1 - I_2)}$

8-19. $E_0 = \dfrac{R_v V_1 V_2}{R(V_2 - V_1) + R_v V_2}$

8-20. (a) $R_a = \dfrac{RR_1(I_1 - I_2)}{I_2(R + R_1) - R_1 I_1}$; (b) $R \gg R_1$, $R \gg R_a$

8-21. 0.127 ohm

8-22. Additional term appears, $R/R_v E$. Shifts line directly upward in linear graph by a fixed amount $R/R_v E$.

8-24. $\delta \approx (R_2 - R_1)/R_v$

8-25. Ratio $= (dS/S)/(dI/I)$

8-26. Theoretically zero

8-27. Exact deflection $= 16.38$ mm (16.52 mm, 20.0 mm)

Chapter 9

9-1. $I_m = \dfrac{E_2(r_1 + R) - E_1 kR}{(r_1 + R)(r_2 + R_m) + kR(r_1 + R - kR)}$

9-2. $R_i = 250$ kilohms

9-3. 2.514 amp $\pm$ 0.11 per cent

9-4. $E_x = 1.0200$ volts, $R_x \approx 24$ ohms [assuming $(B + N) \gg 51$ ohms].

9-6. $\dfrac{dE_x}{E_x} = \dfrac{B\, dR}{(M + N)(B + M + N)}$

9-7. (a) $dI_m = \dfrac{E_1 dR_b}{R_m(R_a + R_b) + R_a R_b}$; (b) $\dfrac{dR_b}{R_b} = \dfrac{-dE_1}{E_1}$

9-8. (a) 0.20 volt; (b) 1.1 per cent

9-9. (a) Not achieved; (b) Move slider to 0.222 volt and see if galvanometer deflection is observable.

9-10. (a) $(9.1 \times 10^{-6} + 4.5 \times 10^{-8} R_x + 10^{-10} R_x{}^2)^{1/2}$; (b) 0.75 kilohm

9-11. $A = 47.3$ ohms, $C = 127$ ohm per amp

9-12. $k > \frac{1}{4}$

9-13. (a) $R_x = R_2 R_4/R_1 + C_1 R_4/C_2$, $L_x = R_2 R_4 C_1 - R_4/\omega^2 R_1 C_2$; (b) 2.55×10^4 ohms, 58.3 mh

9-14. (a) $C_x = R_1 C_4/R_2$; (b) theoretically one, with lossless capacitors

9-15. $R_x = R_2 R_4/R_1$, $L_x = 1/\omega^2 C_3$

9-16. $R_x = R_2 R_4/R_1$, $L_x = R_2 R_4 C_1$

9-17. (a) $R_1 C_2 = R_4 C_3(1 - \omega^2 L_2 C_2)$, $R_1 R_3 = R_2 R_4$; (b) $\omega > 1/\sqrt{L_2 C_2}$; (c) no

9-18. (a) $\omega_0{}^2 = 1/R_x C_x R_4 C_4$; (b) $\omega_0/\omega_1 = \sqrt{1 - R_1 C_2/R_4 C_x} \approx 1 - R_1 C_2/2 R_4 C_x$; (c) 1 per cent, $R_x = \infty$.

9-19. (a) $\omega = 1/RC$; (b) all frequencies; (c) no frequencies

9-20. $L_4 = R_4 C_1(R_1 + R_2)$, $M_x = R_2 R_4 C_1$

9-21. (a) $R_x = R_2 R_4/R_a$, $L_x = CR_2(R_4 + R_b + R_4 R_b/R_a)$; (b) R_x, R_b; (c) yes

9-23. (a) 1,500 ohms; (b) 0.1

Chapter 10

10-1. (a) 3.03 miles; (b) ± 113 ft

10-3. $dI_g = \dfrac{E\, dM}{[B(1 + M/P) + M + N][G(1 + M/N) + M + P]}$

10-4. 18.5 mm

10-5. 0.31 per cent

10-6. (a) 500 ohms; (b) 0.56 per cent; (c) 0.80 per cent; (d) 36.5 mw before interchange, 1.38 mw after interchange.

10-7. (a) galvanometer; (b) 1.36 per cent

10-8. (a) $\dfrac{\Delta X}{X_0} = \dfrac{dI_g}{MNE}\left[\dfrac{BNK'}{X_0} + BNM + C'K' + MC'X_0\right]$ where $C' = B + M + N$ and $K' = GM + GN + MN$; (b) $X_0 = \sqrt{BNK'/MC'}$; (c) Because $I_x \to \infty$ as $X_0 \to 0$ with $B = 0$.

10-10. No, 1.4

10-11. (a) 100 ohms; (b) circuit of Fig. 10-1

10-12. (a) -0.4 mm; (b) ± 0.2 mm; (c) 730

10-13. 1. (a) 0.032 per cent; (b) 952 ohms; (c) 56.7 μa per division; (d) 0.625 watts; (e) 0.124 per cent.   2. (a) 312.52 ohms; (b) 0.0037 per cent; (c) 2.27 μamp per division.   3. 0.0035 per cent

10-14. ± 0.08 per cent

10-15. ± 0.125 per cent

10-16. 0.0213 amp

10-17. (a) 210 ohms; (b) 0.2 ma

10-18. (a) 20 amp; (b) 0.067 μa

Chapter 11

11-1. (a) 36 volts; (b) 0.72 ma

11-2. 1.15

11-3. 1.04

11-4. See Eq. (11-14).

11-5. $E_{\text{rms}} = E/\sqrt{2}$; use $\displaystyle\sum_0^\infty \frac{1}{(2k+1)^2} = \frac{\pi^2}{8}$

11-6. $f(t) = \dfrac{F_p}{2} + \dfrac{F_p}{\pi} \displaystyle\sum_{k=1}^\infty \frac{(-1)^{k+1} \sin k\omega t}{k}$

11-7. 41 μsec

11-9. $\theta_7 = \dfrac{0.0164I}{K} \sin (7\omega t - 143.4°)$

11-10. $e(t) = \dfrac{E}{2} + \dfrac{2E}{\pi} \displaystyle\sum_{k=1}^\infty \frac{(-1)^{k+1} \cos (2k+1)\omega t}{2k+1}$

11-11. (a) 427 ± 27 ohms; (b) 7

11-12. 1.43

11-13. 0.366 amp

11-14. 1,000π

11-15. 51 volts

11-16. 23 per cent high

11-17. 35.4 volts

11-18. d'Arsonval, 1.50 ma; thermocouple, 1.63 ma; bridge rectifier, 1.67 ma

11-19. d'Arsonval, 2.0 ma; thermocouple, 2.02 ma; bridge rectifier, 2.22 ma

11-20. (a) 0.218 ma, 1.217 ma; (b) 0.416 ma, 1.68 ma; (c) 0.242 ma, 1.35 ma

Chapter 12

12-1. (a) 9.13×10^{-12} coulomb; (b) 456×10^{-10} joule; (c) 913×10^{-8} newton

12-2. $\dfrac{6\pi^2 i_1 i_2 r_1{}^2 r_2{}^2 D \times 10^{-7}}{(r_2{}^2 + D^2)^{5/2}}$

12-3. 122 volts

12-4. (a) $\theta_{\text{av}} = 10^{-9} E_{\text{rms}}^2/18\pi S$; (b) $0.01/\pi^2$ newton-meter

12-5. (a) $L = 0.01[1 + \theta^{2(1-n)}/(1-n)]$ henry; (b) 5.59 amp, 89.5°

12-6. (a) 48.8 ohms; (b) 0.456 newton-meter; (c) 26.2°, 1.2° upscale from 5-amp mark

12-7. 86 volts rms

12-8. 127.3 watts

12-9. (a) 1,768 watts; (b) 5,000 ohms

12-10. 318.3 watts

12-11. 2.81 watts

12-12. (a) 100; (b) 95; (c) 105; (d) 100; (e) −100; (f) −105; (g) −105; (h) −110

12-14. 31.6 watts

12-15. −87°56′

12-16. Result is the same as in Eq. (12-42) with $P_p = 0$, P_Z = load power plus current-coil power, I = load current, α = phase angle of series combination of Z and $R_c + j\omega L_c$.

12-17. (a) 0.019°; (b) 0.193°

12-18. −0.54R

Chapter 13

13-1. (a) 200 ohms, 0.2 henry; (b) no; (c) 5.4 mv, $-1.4°$

13-2. (a) 0.2 μf, 5,000 ohms; (b) ± 0.3 per cent in R_x, ± 0.7 per cent in L_x; (c) ± 1.22 per cent in R_x, ± 0.244 per cent in L_x

13-3. (b) **A/C** shifts circle center; **B** $-$ **DA/C** changes magnitude of circle radius and rotates circle about its center.

13-6. 2,323 ohms, 0.1 henry

13-7. (a) 2.27 megohms in shunt with 20 henry, 17.4 kilohms in series with 19.84 henry; (b) R_1 and C_1; (c) 0.047 volt rms

13-8. Second derivative is positive if $R_1(R_2 + 2R) > R_2R_4$.

13-9. $F = 1$; $1/2(1 + \cos \alpha)$

13-10. 0.46 per cent for increase in ω; 0.56 per cent for decrease in ω

13-11. (a) 560 $\mu\mu$f; (b) 0.057×10^{-3} in.; (c) 284 kilohms, 0.4×10^{-6} in.

13-12. (a) $k\omega_1$; (b) -1

13-14. $E_{d_3}/E_{d_5} = 1.59$; 7.8 μsec

13-15. (a) $\omega = 1/C \sqrt{L_2 - L_1}$; (b) $\dfrac{\mathbf{E}_d}{\mathbf{E}} = \dfrac{1 + \omega^2 C(L_1 - L_2)}{1 + \omega^2 C(L_1 + L_2)}$; (c) $L_2 \geqq L_1$

13-16. $\sqrt{2}\ RC/5$, which is 1.27 times that in Eq. (13-41)

13-17. (a) $\mathbf{K} = \dfrac{R(1 - \omega^2 LC) + j\omega(L - R^2C)}{2R - 3\omega^2 LCR + j\omega(6R^2C + L)}$; (b) $\omega^2 LC = 1$, $L = R^2C$; (c) $\sqrt{2LC/25}$

13-18. (a) 144; (b) 2.8 per cent; (c) $+8.1°$, $-7.7°$

INDEX

Certain problems (with their answers on pages 423–429) provide additional general information not found within the text, and are included among the index entries.

431